FRONT PAGE

World War II

HISTORY IN THE HEADLINES 1939-1945

FRONT PAGE

World War II

HISTORY IN THE HEADLINES 1939-1945

JOHN DAVISON

BROWN REFERENCE GROUP

ISBN: 978-1-8404-4279-3

The Brown Reference Group Ltd
First Floor
9-17 St. Albans Place
London N1 ONX
www.brownreference.com

Editor: Peter Darman
Designer: Dave Allen
Picture Researcher: Sophie Mortimer
Index: Indexing Specialists
Managing Editor: Tim Cooke
Production Director: Alastair Gourlay
Editorial Director: Lindsey Lowe

Printed and bound in Singapore

1 3 5 7 9 10 8 6 4 2

Picture credits
All newspaper front pages: John Frost Newspapers except the following:
Topfoto: 201
Additional photographs: Robert Hunt Library

Special thanks to John Frost Newspapers for supplying all the newspaper front pages

Front cover: New York's *The Sun* announces the end of the war in Europe
Background images: Robert Hunt Library

Back cover image: The outbreak of World War II, as reported in London's *The Star*

CONTENTS

Introduction

TODAY IT IS DIFFICULT TO SEE WORLD WAR II WITHOUT THE BENEFIT OF HINDSIGHT. THE TURNING POINTS—OPERATION BARBAROSSA, PEARL HARBOR, THE BATTLE OF MIDWAY, D-Day—seem obvious. The outcome seems inevitable. This book presents the conflict not as history but as it was experienced by the people who lived through it: as a jumble of events whose eventual outcome and ultimate significance did not become apparent for months or even years. It reproduces facsimile front pages from newspapers printed around the world to replicate how contemporaries learned about the progress of the conflict. At the time, newspapers were tremendously important: they were still how most people received their news. In Britain, for example, the major papers had a combined circulation of over 23 million by 1948 and a far greater secondary readership—the majority of the population.

The front pages offer a new view of the war as it unfolded. As well as highlighting all the major events of the conflict, they also reveal other sides of wartime life: advertisements, sports reports, weather forecasts, and domestic news that had little if any connection with the conflict. Stories of heroism rub shoulders with petty crime, movie releases, and electioneering. Events overseas jostle for space with the home front: air raids, blackouts, the destruction of property, evacuation, rationing, and conscription.

▲ WRITERS SUCH AS ERNEST Hemingway (left) reported on the war for the benefit of domestic audiences. On the right stands Robert Capa, one of the most famous photographers of World War II.

THE WARTIME PRESS

The status of newspapers in the 1940s was reflected by the quality of the reporters and photographers who worked as war correspondents. Some reporters such as Ernie Pyle became public figures for their candid reports on the fighting men; others, like Ernest Hemingway, were major writers before the war began. Such high-profile personalities were recruited by daily and Sunday newspapers, as well as by the news magazines, which usually published weekly and featured extended photographic essays. Although such publications tended to be limited in size and print-run as the war went on, because of the shortage of newsprint, they lost none of their appeal.

Even where there was little direct censorship, most reporters and editors considered themselves part of the war effort rather than as independent observers. As such, they tended to put a positive gloss on events. In 1940, for example, British newspapers hailed the "miracle of Dunkirk," in which a defeat was turned into a victory in the eyes of the press. Likewise, at the end of 1941 the U.S. press swung 100 percent behind the war effort after the "treacherous" Japanese attack on Pearl Harbor. Now that the Soviet Union was an ally, U.S. papers gleefully reported Red Army victories over the Nazis, even if they did refer to their Russian allies as "Reds."

THE PRESS AND CENSORSHIP

Within the Soviet Union a central censorship office, known as Glavlit, had been established by the Bolsheviks in 1922. It had absolute authority to subject the performing arts and all publications to preventive censorship, and suppress political dissent by shutting down "hostile" newspapers. This strict censorship through World War II and into the 1980s).

In Nazi Germany all newspapers were controlled by the authorities. On coming to power in 1933, Hitler began to use the press for propaganda, suppressing opposition newspapers and purging newspapers of Jewish or liberal journalists. From the Propaganda Ministry, Joseph Goebbels supervised more than 3,600 newspapers and hundreds of magazines. Each morning he received the editors of the Berlin daily newspapers, and correspondents from the news services for other cities and towns, and gave them precise directives on what was to be featured in the news that day. He expected them to praise Hitler and to show a sympathetic attitude toward members of the party.

CENSORSHIP AND THE ALLIES

The Western Allies also exercised press censorship to a greater or lesser degree. In Australia, strict censorship was imposed to prevent valuable information getting into enemy hands. Many articles consequently appeared that referred to unidentified troops from unnamed units being positioned at unidentified locations—and many reporters criticized the censors for being too excessive.

In the United States, Byron Price's Office of Censorshop controlled the press from December 19, 1941, until August 15, 1945. It could censor communications at its "absolute discretion." More than 10,000 censors examined mail, cables, newspapers, magazines, films, and radio broadcasts in the most extensive government censorship of the media in U.S. history. In fact, voluntary self-censorship worked just as well. Newspapers did not publish photographs of dead U.S. troops until 1944, for example. Reporters knew the war's biggest story—the development of the atom bomb—two years in advance, and kept the secret. They knew the war's longest story, too—President Roosevelt's failing health—and kept that secret as well. But there were inevitable slips. In August 1942, for example, a newspaper columnist received a "very stern letter" from the U.S. government because she had described the weather during a trip with her husband—First Lady Eleanor Roosevelt promised not to make the same mistake again.

▶ THE DEATH OF HITLER as reported by the U.S. service publication *Stars and Stripes*. Unique among the many military publications, *Stars and Stripes* operated (and still does) as a First Amendment newspaper, free of control and censorship. It was published continuously in Europe from 1942, and from 1945 in the Pacific theater.

1939

DURING THE FIRST HALF OF 1939, EUROPE MOVED INEXORABLY TO WAR. THE GERMAN ARMY INVADED POLAND ON SEPTEMBER 1, FRANCE AND BRITAIN DECLARED WAR ON GERMANY TWO DAYS LATER, AND THE WORLD'S BIGGEST EVER CONFLICT HAD BEGUN.

FOR MANY WESTERN EUROPEANS, THE MOMENT WHEN THEY KNEW WAR WAS INEVITABLE CAME IN MARCH 1939. ADOLF HITLER HAD ALREADY EXPANDED THE FRONTIERS OF GERMANY. IN 1938 HE had annexed Austria and united the two countries. Then he had made threatening gestures to his southeastern neighbor, Czechoslovakia. Face with Hitler's threats, the prime ministers of the United Kingdom and France agreed to the break-up of Czechoslovakia at the Munich talks of September 1938—a conference to which the Czechs were not invited. There were strong antiwar sentiments throughout western Europe, and the Munich Agreement was greeted with enthusiasm by many.

ANNEXATION

In March 1939, however, Hitler simply gobbled up the rest of Czechoslovakia, annexing some regions, allowing Hungary to take a share, and creating a puppet state in Slovakia. It became suddenly clear to western Europeans that Hitler was still bent on expansion and that he had to be stopped. It was also clear where his next victim lay, and so Britain and France both gave guarantees to protect Poland.

Tension mounted during spring and summer 1939. In August 1939, the world was shocked to learn of a nonaggression pact between the Soviet Union and Germany. Hitler wanted a free hand in Poland, and Stalin wanted some security, having lost faith in France and Britain as possible allies against Hitler. The pact sealed Poland's fate. Hitler invaded on September 1, and Soviet forces then moved in from the east on September 17.

▲ THE GERMAN ARMY ROLLS into Bohemia in March 1939. It and Moravia were designated German "protectorates" by Hitler. German troops also occupied Slovakia, the rest of the Czech state.

Britain and France could do little. A small offensive against Germany soon petered out, and the war in the west settled down to what was called the "phoney war" for the remainder of 1939. The main action was at sea, where German U-boats began raiding Allied shipping.

In eastern Europe, Stalin used the freedom of action he gained from the Nazi–Soviet pact to invade Finland. The year ended with stalemate in the west and many questions unanswered.

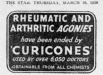

THE STAR, THURSDAY, MARCH 16, 1939

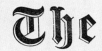

The Star

LATE NIGHT

THE LONDONER'S EVENING PAPER
No. 15,839. ONE PENNY. THURSDAY, MARCH 16, 1939. RADIO: Page Two. WEATHER : Page Three.

HITLER TAKES OVER SLOVAKIA

Ruthenia, Annexed by Hungary, Offers Herself to Rumania

HITLER DEFINES CZECHS' STATUS

German Protectorate And Puppet Government

Climax to a week of coup and counter-stroke in what was once Czecho-Slovakia came to-day. These things happened within a few hours:

Germany declared (through Goering) that she had "no designs" on Slovakia.

Hitler took the Slovak State under his protection. Now it will share the fate of Bohemia and Moravia.

Hungary completed her conquest of Ruthenia, eastern end of the old Czecho-Slovakia, and, announcing the victory, offered her victim "extensive autonomy."

Ruthenia, already occupied by Hungarian troops, countered this move by belatedly offering herself as a going concern to Rumania, nervously watching developments from the frontier.

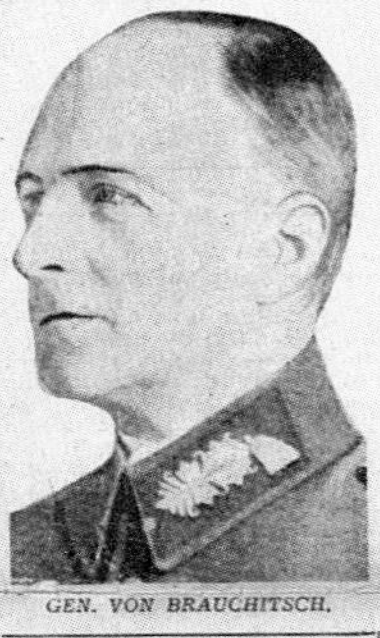

GEN. VON BRAUCHITSCH.

While Ruthenia's fate lay in the balance, Hitler was proclaiming, through his Foreign Minister, Von Ribbentrop, the new status for the Czechs.

PUPPET GOVERNMENT

They are to become citizens of a German protectorate with a Government of their own, subject to veto by a Reich Director. All Czech territory occupied by German troops will be incorporated in Greater Germany, and a Customs Union between Germany and the Czechs will be set up.

German nationals living in the Protectorate will become German citizens, to whom the German anti-Jewish laws will apply.

Before the proclamation was read, Hitler appeared on the castle balcony and was cheered by thousands of German residents in Prague.

The rest of the proclamation dealt with the past, going over the familiar lines that for a thousand years Bohemia and Moravia had been part of the German people's "living space," and that a centre of unrest had been created by the "artificial formation of Czecho-Slovakia."

5,000 Arrests In Prague

THE announcement that Hitler was taking over Slovakia came as a surprise even to Berlin.

The stroke followed the usual technique—an appeal for help.

Dr. Tiso, Slovak Premier, sent Hitler a telegram placing the State under his protection and asking him to take over.

Occupation of Slovakia by German troops has now begun.

Hitler left Prague this afternoon by car for an unrevealed destination. Bratislava was suggested.

Only a few hours earlier Slovakia's independence had been guaranteed. Field Marshal Goering had issued a communication saying Germany had no designs on, and was about to withdraw her troops from, Slovakia. He even mentioned 48 hours as the time within which the soldiers would be withdrawn.

Slovak's new constitution, it is expected, will be along the lines of those for the Czech remnant announced to-day.

RUTHENIA'S FATE

While Slovakia was being absorbed "by request," Ruthenia was trying to give herself away, but not to her conqueror.

Hungarian troops, marching right through from south to north, had established complete control and linked up with the Poles on the northern frontier.

Count Teleki, the Hungarian Prime Minister, announcing the triumph to the Hungarian Parliament in Budapest, said Ruthenia had twice asked Hungary for help.

Now, the Count declared, Hungary would restore her old frontiers on the Carpathian mountains. Local self-government for the Ruthenians was promised.

CHEERS AND TEARS

The Hungarian M.P.s cheered, some wept with emotion.

But while they were doing so, Father Voloshin, Ruthenian Premier, had fled, with his Ministers, from his country to Rumania, and invited the Rumanians to accept his country as a gift.

How Rumania was to accept the offer, with Hungary in possession, was not explained.

Following the Ruthenian Premier over the frontier went three battalions of infantry, artillery, armoured cars and warplanes.

One further touch of paradox: While Voloshin was offering his country to Rumania, his delegates were actually on their way to Budapest to negotiate with Hungary.

PRAGUE SUICIDES

No time has been lost by Germany in taking severe repressive measures in the newly occupied Czech State. Secret police under Herr Himmler are at work "tapping" telephone conversations, and 5,000 "suspects" were rounded up, and despatched to concentration camps.

Herr Wilhelm von Neumark, honorary British Vice-Consul at Brunn, is reported to have committed suicide because of the German invasion. Another reported suicide, one of many, is that of M. Melnik, head of the Prague broadcasting station.

General von Brauchitsch, Commander-in-Chief of the German Army, who arrived in Prague last night, has issued a proclamation ordering that all public services must be carried on, and that stoppage of work will be treated as sabotage.

All privately-owned radio sets must be surrendered.

The round-up of "unreliable" subjects was aided by the curfew, which keeps Prague citizens at home in the evening. Sudeten German informers helped the secret police by bringing information.

Passports of Jews in Czech provincial cities have been called in—whether for cancellation or for stamping with the red "J" used for Jews in Germany, is not known. All Jewish-owned factories were taken over by commissars.

Dr. Hacha is to stay in office, for the time at least, as President of the Czech provinces. He saw Hitler this afternoon.

—*Reuter, British United Press, and Exchange.*

∴ Hitler's proclamation Page Seven.

London's Refugee Scenes

By A "Star" Reporter

LONDON had refugee scenes to-day—at the Czech Legation in Grosvenor-place, S.W., now without a nation to represent.

Hundreds of Czechs and Germans from Cecho-Slovakia called to learn their fate.

Harassed, weary officials could hardly cope with the rush.

Men and women came to have their passports visa-ed and to inquire about their money.

"WE ARE FINISHED"

Tired-eyed Novotny, the porter, who fought in the British Army during the War, directed callers upstairs to inquire about money, downstairs to join the queue outside the passport office.

I asked to see the Press Attache. "There is no one you can see," said a little Czech official, flinging up his arms and shaking his head. "We are finished. There is nothing more. It's all in the papers."

Downstairs the passageway was thronged with men and women of every type.

MEN WITH A DISPATCH BOX

During the afternoon a uniformed messenger and a young man in a lounge suit and felt hat left the Legation.

The messenger carried a black metal dispatch box. Both he and the young man had under their arms large sealed brown paper parcels.

Nine of the eleven Czech mystery men who flew to Croydon by special plane from Prague, were among the visitors.

They arrived so early that they had to wait on the steps until a girl secretary rang the bell.

When the door was opened for her by an official, the nine men, all holding bulging brief cases, filed in and were told to wait in the marble-pillared hall.

While each man was being interviewed, the rest stood in groups, whispering.

Frequently they mentioned the name of Gen. Sirovy, former Czech Defence Minister. An official gave an assurance that the general was not at the Legation, but was still in Prague.

GESTAPO TERROR

A Czech made an impassioned "man-to-man" appeal to photographers not to take pictures of people visiting the Legation.

"Such pictures," he said, "will go straight back to the Gestapo. To the man you photograph it is a matter of life and death.

"A photograph going back to the Gestapo may well mean that the subject can never return for fear of the concentration camp."

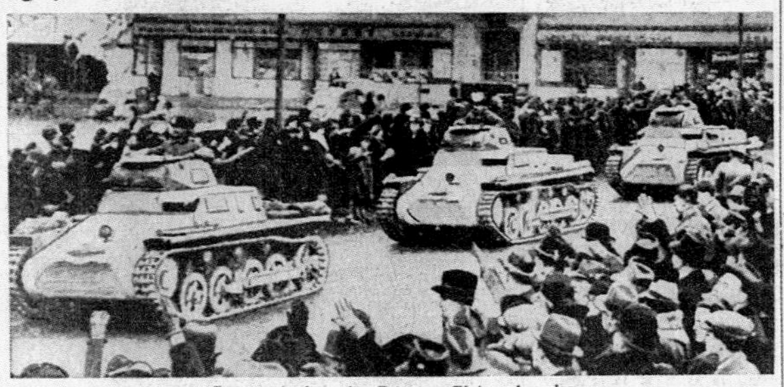

German tanks enter Brunn. Picture by wire.

DALADIER MAY COME TO LONDON

From Our Own Correspondent
PARIS, Thursday.

BRITAIN and France are planning a conference at which they will prepare to face the next Hitler or Mussolini move.

France fears that, as a reward for the blessing Mussolini gave (reluctantly, it may be) to his Czecho-Slovak coup, Hitler is likely to give Germany's full support to Mussolini's claims on France.

Messages have been exchanged between Mr. Chamberlain and M. Daladier.

WAR CHIEFS AT CONFERENCE

Mr. Chamberlain, I understand, suggested that M. Daladier and M. Bonnet should accompany the French President to London next week, and that the conference should take place during the Presidential visit.

The chief of the British Navy, Army and Air Force, as well as General Gamelin, head of the French General Staff, General Georges, his right-hand man, Admiral Darlan, Chief of the Naval Staff, and the head of the Air Staff, would attend.

DUCHESS AT SPEEDWAY

The Duchess of Kent is to attend a special speedway charity meeting at West Ham Stadium, on June 6, it was stated in London to-day by Major Vernon Brook, chairman of the Speedway Control Board.

THE TRUE TEST OF A LONDONER

BY THE MAN IN THE STREET

PAGE THREE

* * *

REST OF THE NEWS

On their way to visit the market in New Cut and Lower Marsh, Lambeth, on Tuesday, Queen Mary and the Princess Royal will stop outside the Old Vic to receive bouquets.—**Page 2.**

Viscountess Helen Adare was fined £50 for offering a bribe so that her "L." driver-maid should pass her driving-test.—**Page 3.**

Dr. Elizabeth Sym Cook, a Glasgow woman medical practitioner, was killed when she was struck by the [illegible] was ticking over on the ground and was to have been piloted by Mrs. Margaret Fairweather, daughter of Lord Runciman.—**Page 5.**

Details of Britain's colossal naval building program of 200 warships were given in the House of Commons this afternoon when measures taken to guard against submarines and air attack were described.—**Page 6.**

Hitler's Proclamation, and other news affecting Czechs and Slovaks.—**Page 7.**

Sir John Anderson announced in the House of Commons this afternoon that a new Government Bill would provide for an Exchequer grant towards reasonable capital expenditure by employers in providing shelters for workshops and establishments in vulnerable areas.—**Page 10.**

EDEN PLANS COUNCIL OF STATE

By Our Political Correspondent

THERE was considerable discussion at Westminster to-day over Mr. Eden's plea for unity of effort and a truly National Government in his Commons speech last night.

Reconstruction of the Cabinet to include members of all parties is impossible, for the Opposition would not co-operate in any Government under the present leadership.

Mr. Eden has, however, an alternative suggestion to put before the Government and the country. He wants to have established a Council of State on which all parties would be represented.

Its function would be to consult with the Government on foreign affairs and [illegible] policy of this country.

In some ways, it would be like the Foreign Affairs Committees in America and France.

The appointment of such a body, he argues, would place foreign policy above party and would regain that continuity which was the practice before the war.

Membership of the Council would include all Privy Councillors, who are either in the House of Commons or the House of Lords.

By this means Mr. Eden believes this country would show the world that it was united on foreign affairs.

Mr. Eden is expected to develop this idea in a speech to be made in London to-night.

GIRL WINS OLDEST RACE

Miss Jean Farrow, 19-year-old daughter if a Hull ship owner, to-day won the Kiplingcotes East Yorkshire Horse Race, the oldest horse race in the country.

BERLIN ENVOY MAY RETURN TO REPORT

THE Prime Minister said in the Commons this afternoon that the question of whether the British Ambassador in Berlin should return to London to report was now under consideration.

Asked whether the British Government contemplated protesting to Germany against the invasion of Czecho-Slovakia, Mr. Chamberlain replied that he would require notice of the question.

Sir John Simon, Chancellor of the Exchequer, said that no request had been made for the transfer of any gold reserve held by the Czecho-Slovak Bank up to the present, and the Government had asked the Bank of England not to make any exceptional transfer of gold or balances without reference to the Government.

'Remove This Peril,' Cries Churchill

Mr. Winston Churchill, presiding at the annual meeting of the Early Closing Association in London to-day, referred to "the shadow over the world of arbitrary, aggressive power, manifested in a form which fills us with the deepest sorrow."

He added: "If the shadow were lifted an expansion of life would be offered immediately to hundreds of millions of people in every land.

"But across it all falls this shadow, and we must concentrate our attention upon relieving the world from this great danger and peril, and guard against hideous oppression from without."

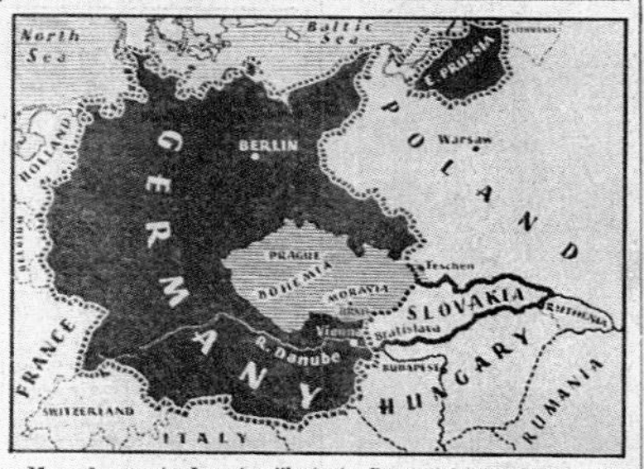
North Sea
Baltic Sea
E. PRUSSIA
BERLIN
GERMANY
POLAND
Warsaw
HOLLAND
PRAGUE
BOHEMIA
MORAVIA
Teschen
SLOVAKIA
RUTHENIA
Vienna
Bratislava
R. Danube
BUDAPEST
HUNGARY
RUMANIA
FRANCE
SWITZERLAND
ITALY

Map drawn to-day to illustrate Germany's new frontier is already out of date. Slovakia now comes under Hitler's "protection," as well as Bohemia and Moravia.

Queen In Tears As She Watches Blind Children

In tears the Queen watched four blind children at play at the headquarters of the National Institute for the Blind this afternoon.

She and the King made a tour of the headquarters, which celebrates its jubilee this year.

A loyal address in Braile was presented to them. When the Queen admired some blue beads with which the children were playing one of them asked a lady-in-waiting to give them to her. This was done.

Picture on Page Six.

Heaviest Harvey Ever

Len Harvey, British heavyweight boxing champion, weighed in at 13st. 2lb. this afternoon for his British Empire title fight with Larry Gains at Harringay to-night.

This is the heaviest he has ever been.

True Count sums up the chances on page 10.

▲ THE STAR, LONDON, THURSDAY MARCH 16, 1939

Events in Europe brought home to Londoners, whose evening paper captures the confusion of Czech and German refugees as news comes through of the takeover of Slovakia. *The Star* struggles to keep up with the speed of events: the map it has commissioned was already out-of-date by the time the edition went to print. A light-hearted movie advertisement is a reminder that war still remained some way off.

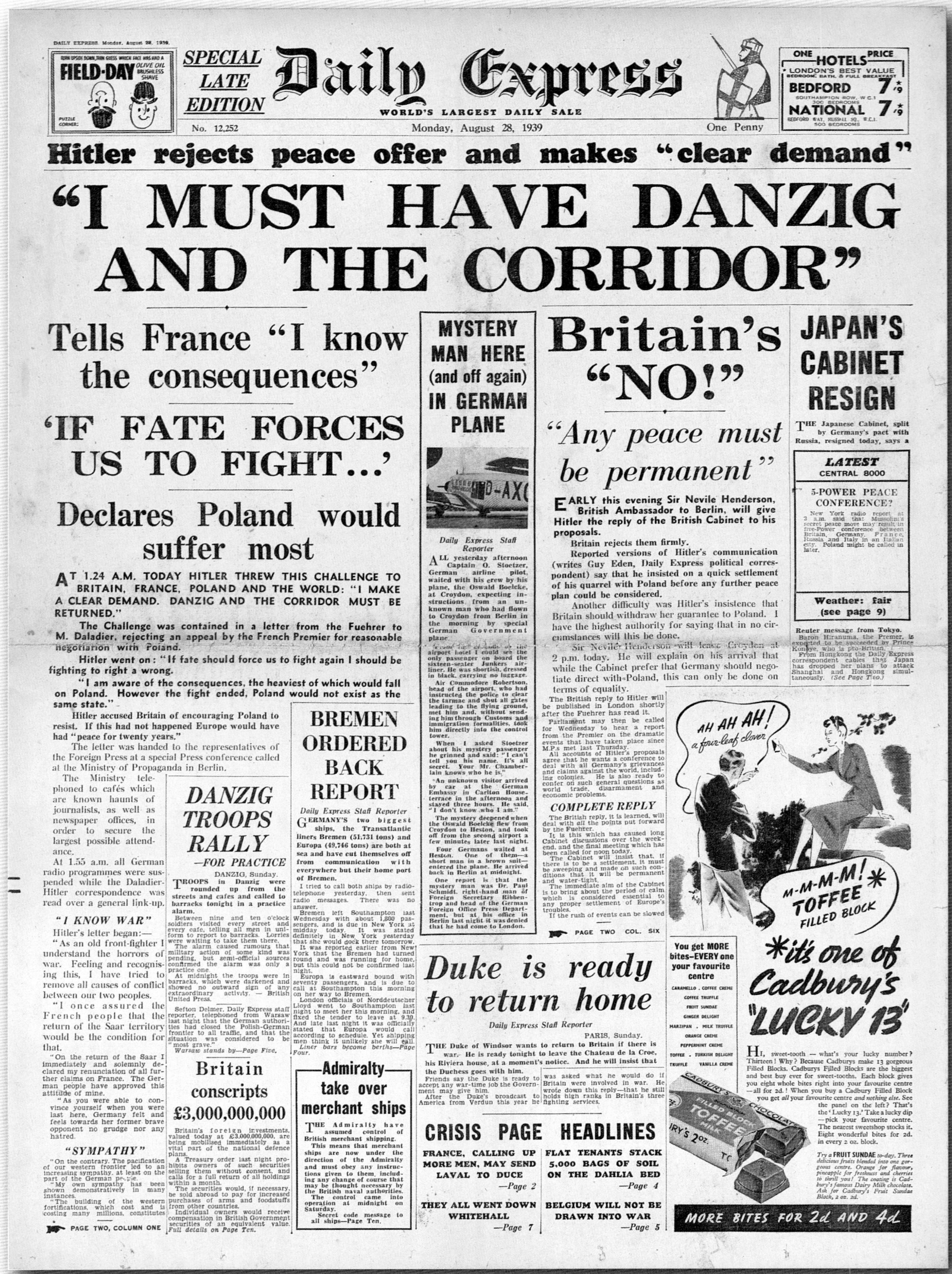

DAILY EXPRESS. Monday, August 28, 1939.

TURN UPSIDE DOWN, THEN GUESS WHICH FACE HAS HAD A FIELD-DAY OLIVE OIL BRUSHLESS SHAVE
PUZZLE CORNER:

SPECIAL LATE EDITION

Daily Express

WORLD'S LARGEST DAILY SALE
No. 12,252 Monday, August 28, 1939 One Penny

ONE PRICE HOTELS
LONDON'S BEST VALUE
BEDROOM, BATH, & FULL BREAKFAST
BEDFORD 7/9
SOUTHAMPTON ROW, W.C.1
300 BEDROOMS
NATIONAL 7/9
BEDFORD WAY, RUSSELL SQ., W.C.1
500 BEDROOMS

Hitler rejects peace offer and makes "clear demand"

"I MUST HAVE DANZIG AND THE CORRIDOR"

Tells France "I know the consequences"

'IF FATE FORCES US TO FIGHT...'

Declares Poland would suffer most

AT 1.24 A.M. TODAY HITLER THREW THIS CHALLENGE TO BRITAIN, FRANCE, POLAND AND THE WORLD: "I MAKE A CLEAR DEMAND. DANZIG AND THE CORRIDOR MUST BE RETURNED."

The Challenge was contained in a letter from the Fuehrer to M. Daladier, rejecting an appeal by the French Premier for reasonable negotiation with Poland.

Hitler went on: "If fate should force us to fight again I should be fighting to right a wrong.

"I am aware of the consequences, the heaviest of which would fall on Poland. However the fight ended, Poland would not exist as the same state."

Hitler accused Britain of encouraging Poland to resist. If this had not happened Europe would have had "peace for twenty years."

The letter was handed to the representatives of the Foreign Press at a special Press conference called at the Ministry of Propaganda in Berlin.

The Ministry telephoned to cafés which are known haunts of journalists, as well as newspaper offices, in order to secure the largest possible attendance.

At 1.55 a.m. all German radio programmes were suspended while the Daladier-Hitler correspondence was read over a general link-up.

"I KNOW WAR"

Hitler's letter began:—

"As an old front-fighter I understand the horrors of war. Feeling and recognising this, I have tried to remove all causes of conflict between our two peoples.

"I once assured the French people that the return of the Saar territory would be the condition for that.

"On the return of the Saar I immediately and solemnly declared my renunciation of all further claims on France. The German people have approved this attitude of mine.

"As you were able to convince yourself when you were last here, Germany felt and feels towards her former brave opponent no grudge nor any hatred.

"SYMPATHY"

"On the contrary. The pacification of our western frontier led to an increasing sympathy, at least on the part of the German people.

"My own sympathy has been shown demonstratively in many instances.

"The building of the western fortifications, which cost and is costing many millions, constitutes

PAGE TWO, COLUMN ONE

DANZIG TROOPS RALLY

—FOR PRACTICE

DANZIG, Sunday.

TROOPS in Danzig were rounded up from the streets and cafes and called to barracks tonight in a practice alarm.

Between nine and ten o'clock soldiers visited every street and every cafe, telling all men in uniform to report to barracks. Lorries were waiting to take them there.

The alarm caused rumours that military action of some kind was pending, but semi-official sources confirmed the alarm was only a practice one.

At midnight the troops were in barracks, which were darkened and showed no outward sign of any extraordinary activity. — British United Press.

Sefton Delmer, Daily Express staff reporter, telephoned from Warsaw last night that the German authorities had closed the Polish-German frontier to all traffic, and that the situation was considered to be "most grave."

Warsaw stands by—Page Five.

Britain conscripts £3,000,000,000

Britain's foreign investments, valued today at £3,000,000,000, are being mobilised immediately as a vital part of the national defence plans.

A Treasury order last night prohibits owners of such securities selling them without consent, and calls for a full return of all holdings within a month.

The securities would, if necessary, be sold abroad to pay for increased purchases of arms and foodstuffs from other countries.

Individual owners would receive compensation in British Government securities of an equivalent value.

Full details on Page Ten.

BREMEN ORDERED BACK REPORT

Daily Express Staff Reporter

GERMANY'S two biggest ships, the Transatlantic liners Bremen (51,731 tons) and Europa (49,746 tons) are both at sea and have cut themselves off from communication with everywhere but their home port of Bremen.

I tried to call both ships by radio-telephone yesterday, then sent radio messages. There was no answer.

Bremen left Southampton last Wednesday with about 1,800 passengers, and is due in New York at midday today. It was stated definitely in New York yesterday that she would dock there tomorrow.

It was reported earlier from New York that the Bremen had turned round and was running for home, but this could not be confirmed last night.

Europa is eastward bound with seventy passengers, and is due to call at Southampton this morning on her way to Bremen.

London officials of Norddeutscher Lloyd went to Southampton last night to meet her this morning, and fixed the tender to leave at 9.30. And late last night it was officially stated that Europa would call according to schedule. Yet shipping men think it unlikely she will call.

Liner bars become berths—Page Four.

Admiralty take over merchant ships

THE Admiralty have assumed control of British merchant shipping.

This means that merchant ships are now under the direction of the Admiralty and must obey any instructions given to them, including any change of course that may be thought necessary by the British naval authorities.

The control came into operation at midnight on Saturday.

Secret code message to all ships—Page Ten.

MYSTERY MAN HERE (and off again) IN GERMAN PLANE

Daily Express Staff Reporter

ALL yesterday afternoon Captain O. Stoetzer, German airline pilot, waited with his crew by his plane, the Oswald Boelcke, at Croydon, expecting instructions from an unknown man who had flown to Croydon from Berlin in the morning by special German Government plane.

From the grounds of the airport hotel I could see the only passenger on board the sixteen-seater Junkers air-liner. He was shortish, dressed in black, carrying no luggage.

Air Commodore Robertson, head of the airport, who had instructed the police to clear the tarmac and shut all gates leading to the flying ground, met him and, without sending him through Customs and immigration formalities, took him directly into the control tower.

When I asked Stoetzer about his mystery passenger he grinned and said: "I can't tell you his name. It's all secret. Your Mr. Chamberlain knows who he is."

An unknown visitor arrived by car at the German Embassy in Carlton House-terrace in the afternoon and stayed three hours. He said, "I don't know who I am."

The mystery deepened when the Oswald Boelcke flew from Croydon to Heston, and took off from the second airport a few minutes later last night.

Four Germans waited at Heston. One of them—a short man in a brown suit—entered the plane. He arrived back in Berlin at midnight.

One report is that the mystery man was Dr. Paul Schmidt, right-hand man of Foreign Secretary Ribbentrop and head of the German Foreign Office Press Department, but at his office in Berlin last night it was denied that he had come to London.

Britain's "NO!"

"Any peace must be permanent"

EARLY this evening Sir Nevile Henderson, British Ambassador to Berlin, will give Hitler the reply of the British Cabinet to his proposals.

Britain rejects them firmly.

Reported versions of Hitler's communication (writes Guy Eden, Daily Express political correspondent) say that he insisted on a quick settlement of his quarrel with Poland before any further peace plan could be considered.

Another difficulty was Hitler's insistence that Britain should withdraw her guarantee to Poland. I have the highest authority for saying that in no circumstances will this be done.

Sir Nevile Henderson will leave Croydon at 2 p.m. today. He will explain on his arrival that while the Cabinet prefer that Germany should negotiate direct with Poland, this can only be done on terms of equality.

The British reply to Hitler will be published in London shortly after the Fuehrer has read it.

Parliament may then be called for Wednesday to hear a report from the Premier on the dramatic events that have taken place since M.P.s met last Thursday.

All accounts of Hitler's proposals agree that he wants a conference to deal with all Germany's grievances and claims against the world, including colonies. He is also ready to confer on such general questions as world trade, disarmament and economic problems.

COMPLETE REPLY

The British reply, it is learned, will deal with *all* the points put forward by the Fuehrer.

It is this which has caused long Cabinet discussions over the week-end, and the final meeting which has been called for noon today.

The Cabinet will insist that, if there is to be a settlement, it must be sweeping and made on such conditions that it will be permanent and water-tight.

The immediate aim of the Cabinet is to bring about the period of calm which is considered essential to any proper settlement of Europe's troubles.

If the rush of events can be slowed

PAGE TWO COL. SIX

JAPAN'S CABINET RESIGN

THE Japanese Cabinet, split by Germany's pact with Russia, resigned today, says a Reuter message from Tokyo.

Baron Hiranuma, the Premier, is expected to be succeeded by Prince Konoye, who is pro-British.

From Hongkong the Daily Express correspondent cables that Japan has dropped her plans to attack Shanghai and Hongkong simultaneously. *(See Page Two.)*

LATEST

CENTRAL 8000

5-POWER PEACE CONFERENCE?

New York radio report at 3 a.m. said that Mussolini's secret peace move may result in five-Power conference between Britain, Germany, France, Russia and Italy in an Italian city. Poland might be called in later.

Weather: fair (see page 9)

Duke is ready to return home

Daily Express Staff Reporter

PARIS, Sunday.

THE Duke of Windsor wants to return to Britain if there is war. He is ready tonight to leave the Chateau de la Croe, his Riviera house, at a moment's notice. And he will insist that the Duchess goes with him.

Friends say the Duke is ready to accept any war-time job the Government may give him.

After the Duke's broadcast to America from Verdun this year he was asked what he would do if Britain were involved in war. He wrote down this reply—that he still holds high ranks in Britain's three fighting services.

CRISIS PAGE HEADLINES

FRANCE, CALLING UP MORE MEN, MAY SEND LAVAL TO DUCE —Page 2
FLAT TENANTS STACK 5,000 BAGS OF SOIL ON THE DAHLIA BED —Page 4
THEY ALL WENT DOWN WHITEHALL —Page 7
BELGIUM WILL NOT BE DRAWN INTO WAR —Page 5

AH AH AH! a four-leaf clover
M-M-M-M! TOFFEE FILLED BLOCK
*it's one of Cadbury's "LUCKY 13"
You get MORE bites–EVERY one your favourite centre
CARAMELLO . COFFEE CREME
COFFEE TRUFFLE
FRUIT SUNDAE
GINGER DELIGHT
MARZIPAN . MILK TRUFFLE
ORANGE CREME
PEPPERMINT CREME
TOFFEE . TURKISH DELIGHT
TRUFFLE VANILLA CREME
HI, sweet-tooth — what's your lucky number? Thirteen! Why? Because Cadburys make 13 gorgeous Filled Blocks. Cadburys Filled Blocks are the biggest and best buy ever for sweet-tooths. Each block gives you eight whole bites right into your favourite centre —all for 2d.! When you buy a Cadbury Filled Block you get *all* your favourite centre *and nothing else*. See the panel on the left? That's the 'Lucky 13.' Take a lucky dip —pick your favourite centre. The nearest sweetshop stocks it. Eight wonderful bites for 2d. in every 2 oz. block.
Try a FRUIT SUNDAE *to-day. Three delicious fruits blended into one gorgeous centre. Orange for flavour, pineapple for freshness and cherries to thrill you! The coating is Cadbury's famous Dairy Milk chocolate. Ask for Cadbury's Fruit Sundae Block, 2 oz. 2d.*
MORE BITES FOR 2d AND 4d

▲ DAILY EXPRESS, LONDON, MONDAY AUGUST 28, 1939

The *Express* reports plenty of evidence that the British government is taking the mounting crisis in Poland seriously, freezing overseas investment and taking control of merchant shipping. For all his defiance, Hitler probably still thought that the British and French would not stand by Poland: Four days later, Europe was at war.

Danzig
AUGUST 1939

I N SPRING 1939, HITLER BEGAN TO MAKE DE-MANDS ABOUT THE PORT OF DANZIG AND THE POLISH CORRIDOR. UNDER THE TREATY OF VERSAILLES, DANZIG HAD BEEN MADE A FREE CITY (DEMILITARIZED AND ADMINISTERED by the League of Nations). A corridor of land giving Poland an outlet to the sea cut East Prussia off from the rest of Germany.

Hitler demanded the incorporation of Danzig into Germany and a German-controlled corridor to East Prussia. To apply pressure, in April 1939 he repudiated a nonaggression pact he had signed with Poland five years earlier.

For the press in Britain the world situation looked bleak. In April, Hitler's Italian ally Mussolini invaded Albania while a tide of refugees fled to France from Spain to escape the victorious fascists there. In East Asia Japanese forces were trying to conquer China, and Japan's civilian cabinet was forced to resign in the summer.

Referring to Danzig and the corridor, Hitler boasted that he was not afraid of war, but he hoped (and may have expected) that Britain and France would back down without helping Poland, as they had over his demands against Czechoslovakia the year before. But the public mood in these two countries had now changed utterly, and war was seen as inevitable.

▲ THE CITY OF DANZIG IN 1939. The city, which had been German territory before 1919, was designated a "free city" by the League of Nations, but Hitler demanded that it be returned to Germany.

Invasion of Poland

SEPTEMBER 1939

THE SIGNING OF A NONAGGRESSION PACT WITH THE SOVIET UNION ON AUGUST 23, 1939, GAVE HITLER THE SECURITY HE NEEDED TO INVADE POLAND. HIS ARMED FORCES HAD been preparing the invasion for some months. A trumped up incident was used as the immediate pretext. German special forces faked a raid on a German radio station at Gleiwitz: the massive German invasion of Poland that followed was officially described as a reaction to this provocation.

and proceeded to execute what became known as "blitzkrieg" (lightning war).

Neither the German nor the Allied press reported the outbreak of war in a particularly triumphalist fashion. There was none of the optimism and enthusiasm that had accompanied the outbreak of war in 1914, for example. Certainly in Britain and France, there was a grim fatalism that the war had to be fought, and that there was no other way of stopping Hitler.

VULNERABLE BORDER

Poland shared a border of 3,000 miles (4,800 km) with Germany, and, because of the German occupation of large areas of Czechoslovakia in March 1939, western Poland was particularly vulnerable to the German forces. The Polish high command had made the decision to defend the west of the country, which was where the main industrial centers were situated. However, the decision was to prove strategically disastrous. More than a million and a half German troops, supported by 2,500 tanks and almost 2,000 aircraft, smashed through the thin border defenses

▲ POLISH CAVALRY HEADS TOWARD the front. Luftwaffe air supremacy made ground movements by any Polish forces during daylight hours extremely hazardous.

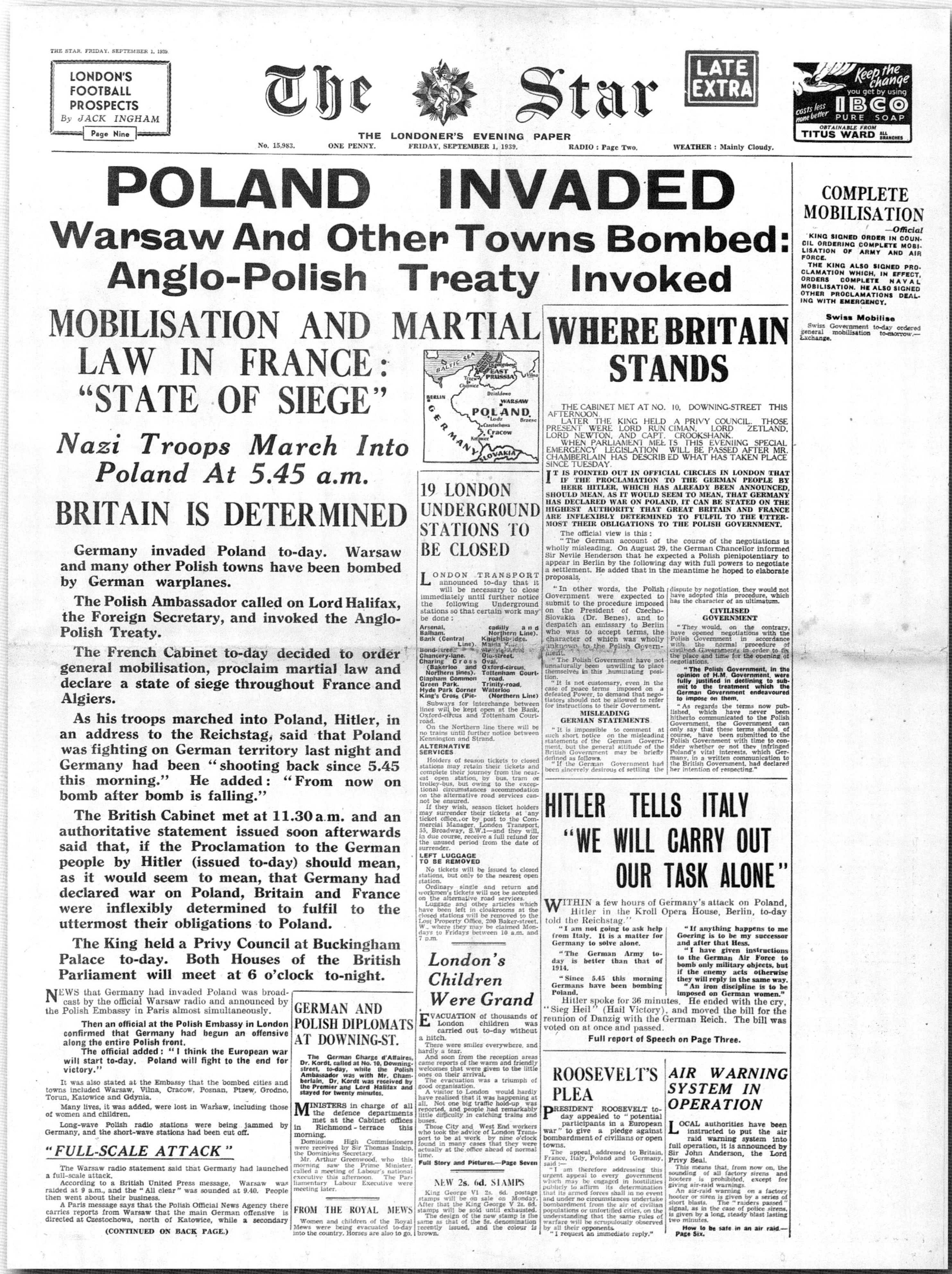

THE STAR. FRIDAY, SEPTEMBER 1, 1939.

LONDON'S FOOTBALL PROSPECTS
By JACK INGHAM
Page Nine

The Star

LATE EXTRA

THE LONDONER'S EVENING PAPER

No. 15,983. ONE PENNY. FRIDAY, SEPTEMBER 1, 1939. RADIO : Page Two. WEATHER : Mainly Cloudy.

POLAND INVADED

Warsaw And Other Towns Bombed: Anglo-Polish Treaty Invoked

MOBILISATION AND MARTIAL LAW IN FRANCE: "STATE OF SIEGE"

Nazi Troops March Into Poland At 5.45 a.m.

BRITAIN IS DETERMINED

Germany invaded Poland to-day. Warsaw and many other Polish towns have been bombed by German warplanes.

The Polish Ambassador called on Lord Halifax, the Foreign Secretary, and invoked the Anglo-Polish Treaty.

The French Cabinet to-day decided to order general mobilisation, proclaim martial law and declare a state of siege throughout France and Algiers.

As his troops marched into Poland, Hitler, in an address to the Reichstag, said that Poland was fighting on German territory last night and Germany had been "shooting back since 5.45 this morning." He added: "From now on bomb after bomb is falling."

The British Cabinet met at 11.30 a.m. and an authoritative statement issued soon afterwards said that, if the Proclamation to the German people by Hitler (issued to-day) should mean, as it would seem to mean, that Germany had declared war on Poland, Britain and France were inflexibly determined to fulfil to the uttermost their obligations to Poland.

The King held a Privy Council at Buckingham Palace to-day. Both Houses of the British Parliament will meet at 6 o'clock to-night.

NEWS that Germany had invaded Poland was broadcast by the official Warsaw radio and announced by the Polish Embassy in Paris almost simultaneously.

Then an official at the Polish Embassy in London confirmed that Germany had begun an offensive along the entire Polish front.

The official added: "I think the European war will start to-day. Poland will fight to the end for victory."

It was also stated at the Embassy that the bombed cities and towns included Warsaw, Vilna, Cracow, Posnan, Ptzew, Grodno, Torun, Katowice and Gdynia.

Many lives, it was added, were lost in Warsaw, including those of women and children.

Long-wave Polish radio stations were being jammed by Germany, and the short-wave stations had been cut off.

"FULL-SCALE ATTACK"

The Warsaw radio statement said that Germany had launched a full-scale attack.

According to a British United Press message, Warsaw was raided at 9 a.m., and the "All clear" was sounded at 9.40. People then went about their business.

A Paris message says that the Polish Official News Agency there carries reports from Warsaw that the main German offensive is directed at Czestochowa, north of Katowice, while a secondary

(CONTINUED ON BACK PAGE.)

GERMAN AND POLISH DIPLOMATS AT DOWNING-ST.

The German Charge d'Affaires, Dr. Kordt, called at No. 10, Downing-street, to-day, while the Polish Ambassador was with Mr. Chamberlain. Dr. Kordt was received by the Premier and Lord Halifax and stayed for twenty minutes.

MINISTERS in charge of all the defence departments met at the Cabinet offices in Richmond-terrace this morning.

Dominions High Commissioners were received by Sir Thomas Inskip, the Dominions Secretary.

Mr. Arthur Greenwood, who this morning saw the Prime Minister, called a meeting of Labour's national executive this afternoon. The Parliamentary Labour Executive were meeting later.

FROM THE ROYAL MEWS

Women and children of the Royal Mews were being evacuated to-day into the country. Horses are also to go.

BALTIC SEA
EAST PRUSSIA
Konigsberg
Vilno
Trzew
Chojnice
Dzialdowo
BERLIN
WARSAW
POLAND
Lodz
Brzesc
Czestochowa
Cracow
Katowice
GERMANY
SLOVAKIA

19 LONDON UNDERGROUND STATIONS TO BE CLOSED

LONDON TRANSPORT announced to-day that it will be necessary to close immediately until further notice the following Underground stations so that certain work may be done:

Arsenal.
Balham.
Bank (Central Line).
Bond-street.
Chancery-lane.
Charing Cross (Bakerloo and Northern lines).
Clapham Common
Green Park.
Hyde Park Corner
King's Cross (Piccadilly and Northern Line).
Knightsbridge.
Maida Vale.
[illegible]
Old-street.
Oval.
Oxford-circus.
Tottenham Court-road.
Trinity-road.
Waterloo (Northern Line)

Subways for interchange between lines will be kept open at the Bank, Oxford-circus and Tottenham Court-road.

On the Northern line there will be no trains until further notice between Kennington and Strand.

ALTERNATIVE SERVICES

Holders of season tickets to closed stations may retain their tickets and complete their journey from the nearest open station, by bus, tram or trolley-bus, but owing to the exceptional circumstances accommodation on the alternative road services cannot be ensured.

If they wish, season ticket holders may surrender their tickets at any ticket office, or by post to the Commercial Manager, London Transport, 55, Broadway, S.W.1—and they will, in due course, receive a full refund for the unused period from the date of surrender.

LEFT LUGGAGE TO BE REMOVED

No tickets will be issued to closed stations, but only to the nearest open station.

Ordinary single and return and workmen's tickets will not be accepted on the alternative road services.

Luggage and other articles which have been left in cloakrooms at the closed stations will be removed to the Lost Property Office, 200 Baker-street, W., where they may be claimed Mondays to Fridays between 10 a.m. and 7 p.m.

London's Children Were Grand

EVACUATION of thousands of London children was carried out to-day without a hitch.

There were smiles everywhere, and hardly a tear.

And soon from the reception areas came reports of the warm and friendly welcomes that were given to the little ones on their arrival.

The evacuation was a triumph of good organisation.

A visitor to London would hardly have realised that it was happening at all. Not one big traffic hold-up was reported, and people had remarkably little difficulty in catching trains and buses.

Those City and West End workers who took the advice of London Transport to be at work by nine o'clock found in many cases that they were actually at the office ahead of normal time.

Full Story and Pictures.—Page Seven

NEW 2s. 6d. STAMPS

King George VI 2s. 6d. postage stamps will be on sale on Monday. After that the King George V 2s. 6d. stamps will be sold until exhausted.

The design of the new stamp is the same as that of the 5s. denomination recently issued, and the colour is brown.

WHERE BRITAIN STANDS

THE CABINET MET AT NO. 10, DOWNING-STREET THIS AFTERNOON.

LATER THE KING HELD A PRIVY COUNCIL. THOSE PRESENT WERE LORD RUNCIMAN, LORD ZETLAND, LORD NEWTON, AND CAPT. CROOKSHANK.

WHEN PARLIAMENT MEETS THIS EVENING SPECIAL EMERGENCY LEGISLATION WILL BE PASSED AFTER MR. CHAMBERLAIN HAS DESCRIBED WHAT HAS TAKEN PLACE SINCE TUESDAY.

IT IS POINTED OUT IN OFFICIAL CIRCLES IN LONDON THAT IF THE PROCLAMATION TO THE GERMAN PEOPLE BY HERR HITLER, WHICH HAS ALREADY BEEN ANNOUNCED, SHOULD MEAN, AS IT WOULD SEEM TO MEAN, THAT GERMANY HAS DECLARED WAR ON POLAND, IT CAN BE STATED ON THE HIGHEST AUTHORITY THAT GREAT BRITAIN AND FRANCE ARE INFLEXIBLY DETERMINED TO FULFIL TO THE UTTERMOST THEIR OBLIGATIONS TO THE POLISH GOVERNMENT.

The official view is this:

"The German account of the course of the negotiations is wholly misleading. On August 29, the German Chancellor informed Sir Nevile Henderson that he expected a Polish plenipotentiary to appear in Berlin by the following day with full powers to negotiate a settlement. He added that in the meantime he hoped to elaborate proposals.

"In other words, the Polish Government were expected to submit to the procedure imposed on the President of Czecho-Slovakia (Dr. Benes), and to despatch an emissary to Berlin who was to accept terms, the character of which was wholly unknown to the Polish Government.

"The Polish Government have not unnaturally been unwilling to place themselves in this humiliating position.

"It is not customary, even in the case of peace terms imposed on a defeated Power, to demand that negotiators should not be allowed to refer for instructions to their Government.

MISLEADING GERMAN STATEMENTS

"It is impossible to comment at such short notice on the misleading statements of the German Government, but the general attitude of the British Government may be briefly defined as follows.

"If the German Government had been sincerely desirous of settling the dispute by negotiation, they would not have adopted this procedure, which has the character of an ultimatum.

CIVILISED GOVERNMENT

"They would, on the contrary, have opened negotiations with the Polish Government in accordance with the normal procedure of civilised Governments in order to fix the place and time for the opening of negotiations.

"The Polish Government, in the opinion of H.M. Government, were fully justified in declining to submit to the treatment which the German Government endeavoured to impose on them.

"As regards the terms now published, which have never been hitherto communicated to the Polish Government, the Government can only say that these terms should, of course, have been submitted to the Polish Government with time to consider whether or not they infringed Poland's vital interests, which Germany, in a written communication to the British Government, had declared her intention of respecting."

HITLER TELLS ITALY "WE WILL CARRY OUT OUR TASK ALONE"

WITHIN a few hours of Germany's attack on Poland, Hitler in the Kroll Opera House, Berlin, to-day told the Reichstag."

"I am not going to ask help from Italy. It is a matter for Germany to solve alone.

"The German Army to-day is better than that of 1914.

"Since 5.45 this morning Germans have been bombing Poland.

"If anything happens to me Goering is to be my successor and after that Hess.

"I have given instructions to the German Air Force to bomb only military objects, but if the enemy acts otherwise they will reply in the same way.

"An iron discipline is to be imposed on German women."

Hitler spoke for 36 minutes. He ended with the cry, "Sieg Heil" (Hail Victory), and moved the bill for the reunion of Danzig with the German Reich. The bill was voted on at once and passed.

Full report of Speech on Page Three.

ROOSEVELT'S PLEA

PRESIDENT ROOSEVELT to-day appealed to "potential participants in a European war" to give a pledge against bombardment of civilians or open towns.

The appeal, addressed to Britain, France, Italy, Poland and Germany, said:—

"I am therefore addressing this urgent appeal to every government which may be engaged in hostilities publicly to affirm its determination that its armed forces shall in no event and under no circumstances undertake bombardment from the air of civilian populations or unfortified cities, on the understanding that the same rules of warfare will be scrupulously observed by all their opponents.

"I request an immediate reply."

AIR WARNING SYSTEM IN OPERATION

LOCAL authorities have been instructed to put the air raid warning system into full operation, it is announced by Sir John Anderson, the Lord Privy Seal.

This means that, from now on, the sounding of all factory sirens and hooters is prohibited, except for giving air-raid warnings.

An air-raid warning on a factory hooter or siren is given by a series of short blasts. The "raiders passed" signal, as in the case of police sirens, is given by a long, steady blast lasting two minutes.

How to be safe in an air raid.—Page Six.

COMPLETE MOBILISATION

—Official

KING SIGNED ORDER IN COUNCIL ORDERING COMPLETE MOBILISATION OF ARMY AND AIR FORCE.

THE KING ALSO SIGNED PROCLAMATION WHICH, IN EFFECT, ORDERS COMPLETE NAVAL MOBILISATION. HE ALSO SIGNED OTHER PROCLAMATIONS DEALING WITH EMERGENCY.

Swiss Mobilise

Swiss Government to-day ordered general mobilisation to-morrow.—Exchange.

▲ THE STAR, LONDON, FRIDAY SEPTEMBER 1, 1939

Although Britain and France were not yet at war with Germany (Paris and London would declare war on September 3), conflict is now inevitable. In London, the evacuation of schoolchildren has begun and subway stations are closed for "certain work"—preparation for use as bomb shelters. *The Star* has left a whole column empty for late news, and been rewarded with the announcement of mobilization by George VI.

Die Glocke

Wiedenbrücker Zeitung

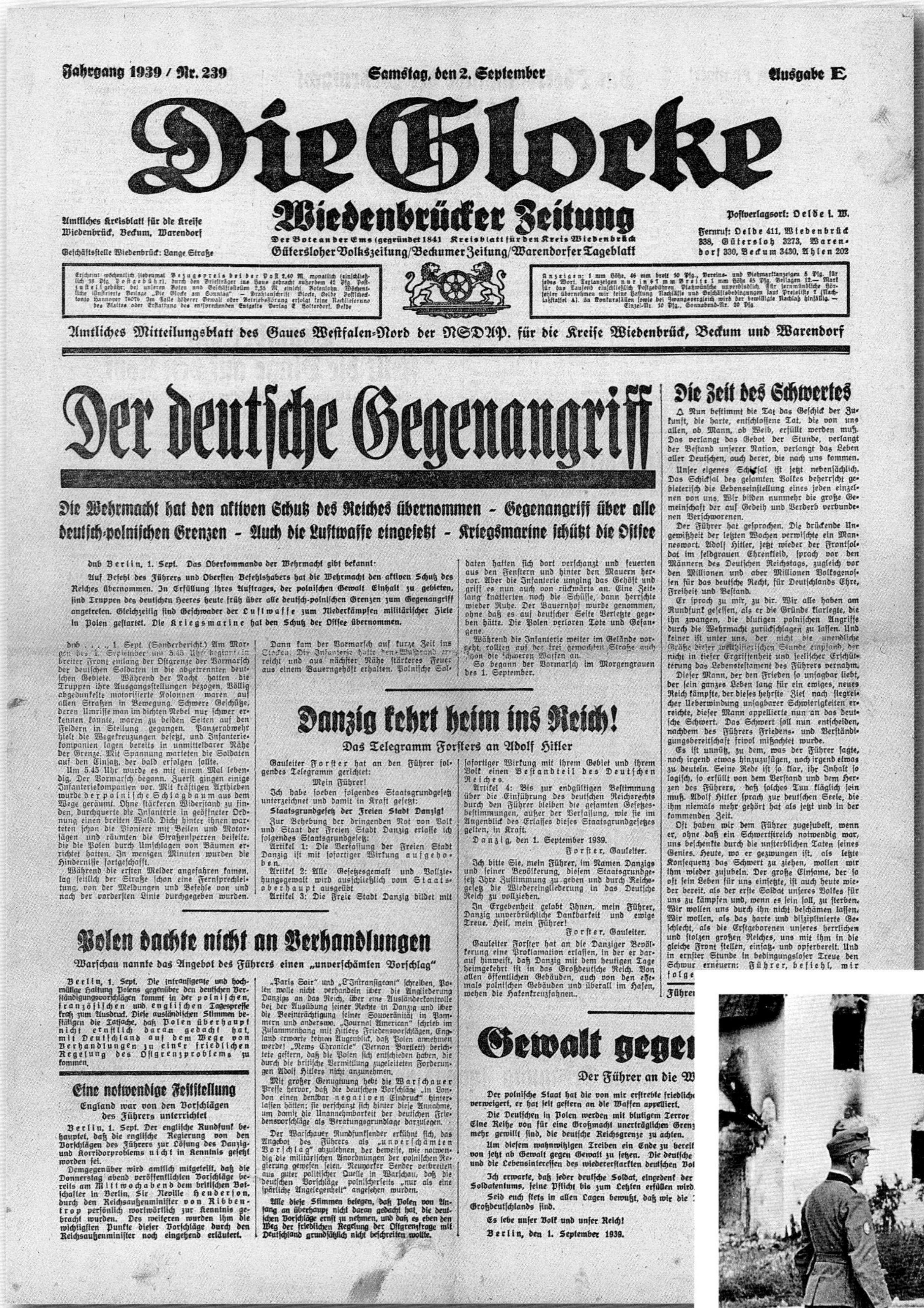

Jahrgang 1939 / Nr. 239 — Samstag, den 2. September — Ausgabe E

Amtliches Kreisblatt für die Kreise Wiedenbrück, Beckum, Warendorf

Der Bote an der Ems (gegründet 1841) · Kreisblatt für den Kreis Wiedenbrück

Gütersloher Volkszeitung / Beckumer Zeitung / Warendorfer Tageblatt

Amtliches Mitteilungsblatt des Gaues Westfalen-Nord der NSDAP. für die Kreise Wiedenbrück, Beckum und Warendorf

Der deutsche Gegenangriff

Die Wehrmacht hat den aktiven Schutz des Reiches übernommen - Gegenangriff über alle deutsch-polnischen Grenzen - Auch die Luftwaffe eingesetzt - Kriegsmarine schützt die Ostsee

Die Zeit des Schwertes

Danzig kehrt heim ins Reich!

Das Telegramm Forsters an Adolf Hitler

Polen dachte nicht an Verhandlungen

Warschau nannte das Angebot des Führers einen „unverschämten Vorschlag"

Eine notwendige Feststellung

England war von den Vorschlägen des Führers unterrichtet

Gewalt gegen...

Der Führer an die W...

◀ DIE GLOCKE (THE BELL), NORTH RHINE–WESTPHALIA, SATURDAY SEPTEMBER 2, 1939

A local newspaper from western Germany reports the official account of the invasion of Poland as a necessary defense against Polish incursions on German soil. The headlines read "German counteroffensive. The Wehrmacht has taken on the active defense of the Reich—Counter-attack launched the length of the German–Polish border—Luftwaffe also called in—Kriegsmarine defending the Baltic. DNB [official news agency]. 1st September. Reported by the Wehrmacht High Command: On the orders of the Führer and Supreme Commander, the Wehrmacht has taken on active defense of the Reich. German troops, ordered to curb the Polish aggression, crossed the German–Polish border this morning, launching a counter-attack. At the same time Luftwaffe squadrons took off to destroy military targets. The Kriegsmarine has taken on protection of the Baltic."

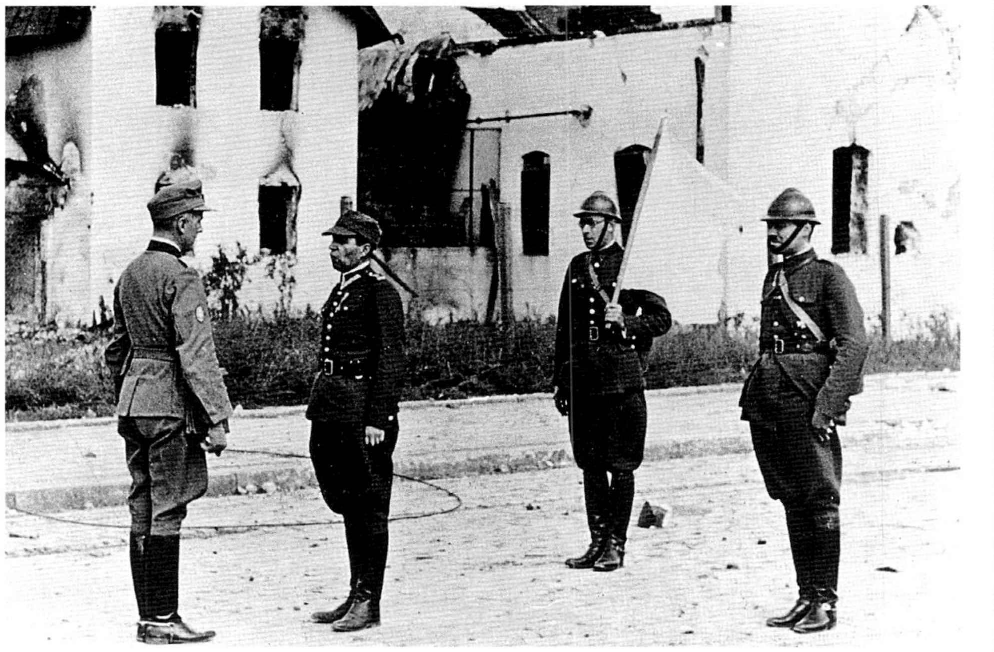

▲ POLISH TROOPS SURRENDER to a German officer in September 1939. Following their military victory, the Germans began their campaign to reduce the Poles to slave status and annihilate Polish Jewry. As part of their new racial order in eastern Europe, the Nazi *Herrenvolk* (master race) intended to ruthlessly exploit the "inferior" Poles.

L'ŒUVRE

FONDATEUR : GUSTAVE TERY
9, RUE LOUIS-LE-GRAND (2e arr)
Adresse Télégraphique : ŒUVRE - PARIS

QUATRIEME EDITION DE PARIS — 0 fr. 50

N° 8.735. — Samedi 2 septembre 1939.

TÉL. : OPERA 65-00 et la suite
CHÈQUE POSTAL N° 1046

Le pacte germano-soviétique?
On vous a expliqué que c'était
un "facteur de paix".
Comme vous pouvez voir.

HITLER A ATTAQUÉ

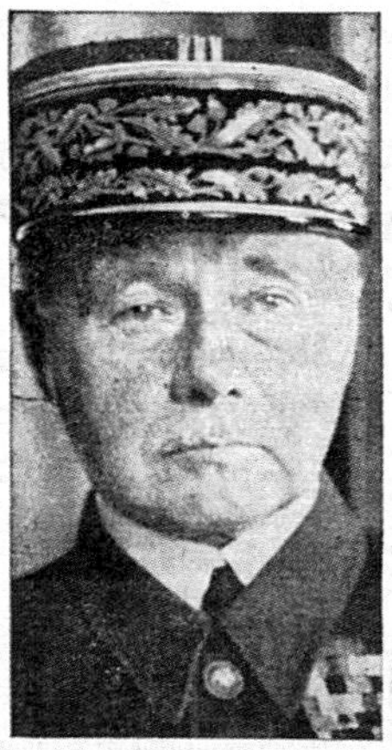

Le général Gamelin, commandant en chef de l'armée française

MOBILISATION GENERALE aujourd'hui en France et en Angleterre

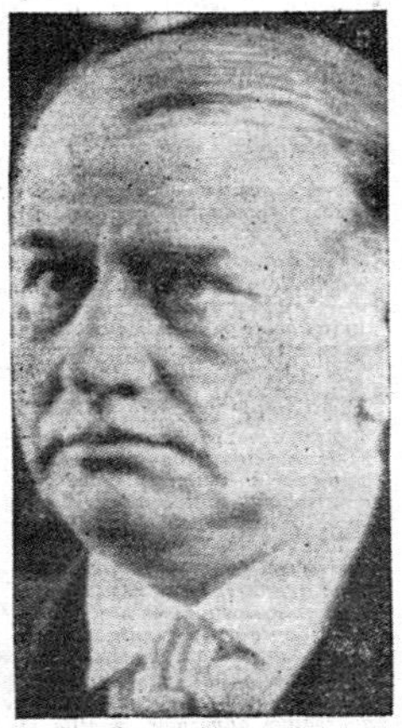

M. Edouard Daladier, Président du Conseil

Sur quatre points, les troupes allemandes ont violé la frontière polonaise

Bombardements par avions de Varsovie, Cracovie, Gdynia et de plusieurs autres villes

---

L'ETAT DE SIEGE est proclamé dans la métropole et l'empire

Chambre et Sénat se réunissent cet après-midi à 15 h.

Et maintenant discipline !

« — La logique voudrait que tout se réglât pacifiquement.
« — Malheureusement, le monde n'est pas mené par la seule logique. »
Ce que disait notre manchette de mercredi, Hitler s'est chargé de nous le démontrer hier.
Après avoir fait lancer par la « radio » un long et confus « papier », d'où on ne savait fait très bien s'il ressortait qu'il avait fait à la Pologne des propositions qui n'avaient pas été examinées, ou s'il maintenait ces mêmes propositions en les rendant publiques, il a déclenché au petit jour l'action militaire.
Les destins de l'Europe et du monde se sont ainsi noués à l'aube du 1er septembre.
Et quand on lit l'effarant discours par lequel le président-chancelier a justifié devant le Reichstag sa décision fatale, on reste confondu devant la disproportion de la cause invoquée et de ses effroyables effets possibles.
Paris et la France se sont donc trouvés hier matin réveillés par le fameux « éclair dans la nuit », annoncé depuis quelque temps déjà par le Reichskanzeler.

Seulement, l'éclair n'a pas produit ce qu'en attendait le Zeus allemand.
Les Français ont dit :
— Alors, bon ! voilà les folies qui recommencent !
Et les derniers mobilisables sont rentrés chez eux préparer leur départ.
Quant à nous, il ne nous reste plus qu'à faire ce que nous avons toujours fait en pareille circonstance :
Nous avons pu critiquer la politique d'un gouvernement, la discuter — comme au temps de la Ruhr. A partir du moment où le choix est fait, par les hommes ou par les événements, et où le pays tout entier est engagé, nous ne chicanons plus.
Nous disons à M. Daladier ce que nous aurions dit aussi bien à M. Léon Blum ou à M. Louis Marin, président du Conseil en pareille occurrence :
— Vous êtes le responsable des destinées du pays. Agissez au mieux. Sauvez la paix « s'il est encore possible de la faire. « Tenez le coup » s'il faut la tenir. Nous sommes tous derrière vous.

Double démarche à Berlin des ambassadeurs de Paris et de Londres

DERNIERE HEURE

Le gouvernement français a été saisi hier, ainsi que plusieurs gouvernements, d'une initiative italienne tendant à assurer le règlement des difficultés européennes.
Après en avoir délibéré, le gouvernement a donné une réponse positive.

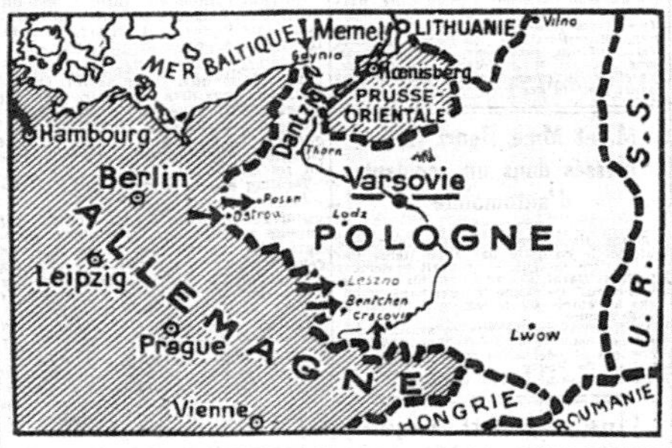

Carte de la Pologne (les flèches indiquent les principaux points d'attaque des troupes allemandes)

LA SUISSE MOBILISE

M. Daladier a conféré longuement avec les chefs de l'armée

Energique déclaration de M. Chamberlain aux Communes :

"Le moment est venu où l'action plutôt que les discours est nécessaire"

"La responsabilité incombe à un seul homme"

Précision historique

Mise au point du gouvernement français

On a communiqué, hier après-midi, dans les couloirs du Palais-Bourbon, le texte d'une note qui avait été lue à la radio-diffusion française, et qui émanait des services de la présidence du Conseil. Voici ce document :

1) Ce matin, sans déclaration de guerre, l'Allemagne a attaqué la Pologne. Dès 6 heures, et sans avertissement préalable, Cracovie a été bombardée.

2) Ces faits donnent sa signification véritable au communiqué lu dans la nuit par la Radio allemande et indiquant a extremis un plan de paix germano-polonaise.

3) On ne peut voir là qu'un grossier simulacre de la dernière heure, destiné à rejeter sur la Pologne la responsabilité de l'agression, méthodiquement préparée par l'Allemagne et sur le point de se déclencher.

3) Les propositions allemandes n'avaient jamais été présentées officiellement, ou même valablement à la Pologne, ni directement, ni par l'intermédiaire de l'Angleterre. Le gouvernement allemand les a fait connaître au public comme pratiquement repoussées avant même que la Pologne en ait eu connaissance et ait pu s'exprimer à leur égard.

4) L'Allemagne a invoqué, dans son communiqué, le fait qu'un plénipotentiaire polonais aurait dû se présenter avant le 30 août, date limite. Or, jamais cette date n'avait été indiquée comme devant avoir ce caractère.

5) C'est au moment même où le contact venait d'être pris entre les deux pays par l'intermédiaire de M. Lipski et de M. von Ribbentrop, que l'Allemagne a fait savoir que la négociation — qui n'avait pas encore été nouée — devait être considérée comme rompue et les propositions allemandes comme abandonnées.

▲ L'ŒUVRE, PARIS, SATURDAY SEPTEMBER 2, 1939

France and its empire are in a state of siege, announces the liberal Paris daily *L'Œuvre*, calling on its readers to keep their discipline. At the top, the paper's famous manchette, or "cuff" declares "The German Soviet Pact? You were told it would help peace. As you can see."

Britain at war

SEPTEMBER 1939

IT IS DIFFICULT FROM A MODERN PERSPECTIVE, KNOWING WHAT WE DO ABOUT THE HUGE GLOBAL CONFLICT THAT WORLD WAR II BECAME, TO UNDERSTAND WHAT PEOPLE FELT IN THE FIRST FEW MONTHS OF HOSTILITIES.

In Britain, for example, there was enormous fear of bombing raids, and some two million women and children were evacuated from cities in a carefully planned operation. One of those encouraging the children to leave for safer areas was the young Princess Elizabeth, later to become Queen Elizabeth II. She broadcast on the BBC radio program *Children's Hour*.

A particular fear was that poison gas would be used against populated areas, and so gas masks were issued to everyone. However, when the air raids had not materialized by the end of 1939, people began to move back to their original homes.

Politics changed as men like Winston Churchill in Britain, firm opponents of the previous government policy of appeasement, were brought into the

government. Although Britain was at war with Germany, there were many who felt that Stalin's Soviet Union represented just as great a threat. He had, after all, invaded Poland along with Hitler and taken over large areas of that country. In November he invaded Finland, which prompted calls in some quarters of Britain and France for a declaration of war. Politicians resisted, preferring to focus on the threat from Germany.

RESTRICTED THEATER OF WAR

During the first months of the war in 1939, many countries remained neutral, including Italy and Japan, even though they were close supporters of Nazi Germany. Belgium and Holland were also neutral, and so active hostilities were confined to the short Franco–German border.

▲ YOUNG BRITISH CHILDREN ARE evacuated from the city of London in September 1939. Operation Pied Piper planned to move 3.5 million children in three days.

In the stalemate in the west, the war at sea took on an important role. Britain was not self sufficient in food, and German raiders, both U-boats and surface vessels, were determined to attack its sea lanes. German U-boats attacked Royal Navy bases, and in one raid sank a battleship, HMS *Royal Oak*, to the shock of the British public.

DAILY TELEGRAPH & MORNING POST, SEPTEMBER 4

Imperial
FOR BETTER LETTERS

IMPERIAL TYPEWRITER COMPANY LTD, LEICESTER
London Office: 81 Kingsway, W.C.2 (Phone HOL 2696)

USE A TYPEWRITER MADE IN ENGLAND

LATE LONDON EDITION

The Daily Telegraph
and Morning Post

for the cleanest shave
ROLLS RAZOR
21/- 27/6

NO. 26,288   LONDON, MONDAY, SEPTEMBER 4, 1939   BROADCASTING—Page Six   ONE PENNY

GREAT BRITAIN AT WAR

THE KING'S MESSAGE TO THE EMPIRE

MR. CHURCHILL FIRST LORD: POST FOR MR. EDEN

PREMIER SETS UP WAR CABINET

VISCOUNT GORT TO COMMAND FIELD FORCE

The Prime Minister announced yesterday in a message broadcast to the Empire, that as from 11 o'clock in the morning, Great Britain was at war with Germany.

The Commonwealth of Australia proclaimed a state of war three hours later, New Zealand followed and France was at war from 5 o'clock in the afternoon. Canada has given an assurance of effective co-operation.

The House of Commons met at noon to hear from Mr. Chamberlain the declaration that Britain was at war.

In the Lords a similar announcement was made by Lord Halifax. M.P.s will meet again to-day at 3 o'clock.

PREMIER SEES THE KING

At 6 o'clock in the evening the King broadcast a rallying call to the Empire. An hour later Mr. Chamberlain had an audience of his Majesty.

It was later announced that the Prime Minister has established a War Cabinet, consisting of eight members in addition to himself.

It includes Mr. Winston Churchill, who has joined the Government as First Lord of the Admiralty, the post he held at the outbreak of war in 1914.

Mr. Eden returns to the Government as Dominions Secretary, without a seat in the War Cabinet, to which he will have special access.

NEW CHIEF OF STAFF

It was also announced that the King has appointed:

Gen. Viscount Gort, V.C., Chief of the Imperial General Staff, to be Commander-in-Chief of British Field Forces;

Gen. Sir Edmund Ironside to succeed as Chief of the Imperial General Staff; and

Gen. Sir Walter Kirke to be Commander-in-Chief of Home Forces.

FALSE RAID ALARM

Half an hour after Britain entered the war there was an air raid warning. It proved to be a false alarm, but it provided a test for the machinery.

An Order in Council makes to-day a banking holiday and no savings bank business will be transacted.

New regulations for motorists provide that the running boards and bumpers of cars must be painted white. Petrol to be rationed from Sept. 16.

The Admiralty announced that all British merchant ships are liable to be examined by the Navy. The Navy is at its war stations in full strength, supplemented by armed merchant ships as auxiliary cruisers. The naval convoy system has already been reintroduced.

Hitler is to take over supreme command of the German forces on the Eastern front. In a proclamation to the German people he found it necessary to state that whoever offended against national unity "need expect nothing other than annihilation as an enemy of the nation."

PREMIER'S HISTORIC DECLARATION

BY OUR OWN REPRESENTATIVE

WESTMINSTER, Sunday.

"This country is now at war with Germany."

The sentence came from the Prime Minister's lips in tones of sharp precision.

A profound silence fell upon the House, not of surprise or anxiety as the calm, stern faces testified, but of grim satisfaction.

Hundreds of men on the crowded green benches drew a long breath of relief that the issue was declared and joined beyond a peradventure. Conditions, circumstance and chance united to invest the Prime Minister's declaration with arresting dramatic force.

As dusk gathered the night before he had made a provisional, ad interim statement which, the words are not too strong, bewildered and shocked the House by its vagueness.

He told members then that he was waiting for the result of consultations with France, but his promise to

(Continued on Page Nine, Column Four)

WAR CABINET OF NINE

MR. CHURCHILL BACK AT ADMIRALTY

MINISTER OF HOME SECURITY

A War Cabinet of nine has been set up on the lines of that established in December, 1916. It was announced from No. 10, Downing-street last night that the King had approved its constitution as follows:

PRIME MINISTER AND FIRST LORD OF THE TREASURY: Mr. Neville Chamberlain.

CHANCELLOR OF THE EXCHEQUER: Sir John Simon.

SECRETARY OF STATE FOR FOREIGN AFFAIRS: Viscount Halifax.

MINISTER FOR CO-ORDINATION OF DEFENCE: Adml. of the Fleet Lord Chatfield.

FIRST LORD OF THE ADMIRALTY: Mr. Winston Churchill.

SECRETARY OF STATE FOR WAR: Mr. Leslie Hore-Belisha.

SECRETARY OF STATE FOR AIR: Sir Kingsley Wood.

LORD PRIVY SEAL: Sir Samuel Hoare.

MINISTER WITHOUT PORTFOLIO: Lord Hankey.

Mr. Churchill replaces Earl Stanhope as First Lord of the Admiralty and Sir Samuel Hoare replaces Sir John Anderson as Lord Privy Seal.

OUTSIDE THE CABINET

Later it was announced from Downing-street that the King's approval had also been given to the following appointments of Ministers not in the War Cabinet:

LORD PRESIDENT OF THE COUNCIL: Earl Stanhope (formerly First Lord of the Admiralty).

LORD CHANCELLOR: Sir Thomas Inskip (formerly Dominion Secretary).

SECRETARY OF STATE FOR THE HOME DEPARTMENT AND MINISTER OF HOME SECURITY: Sir John Anderson (formerly Lord Privy Seal).

SECRETARY OF STATE FOR DOMINION AFFAIRS: Mr. Anthony Eden.

Mr. Eden is to have special access to the Cabinet in order to be in the best position to maintain contact between it and the Dominions.

Lord Hankey, who is 62, was better known as Sir Maurice Hankey, until he retired from the Secretaryship of the Cabinet last year, after holding that position since 1912. During the last war he was Secretary of the War Cabinet and later of the Imperial War Cabinet.

BRITISH ARMY LEADERS

SIR E. IRONSIDE'S POST

It was announced last night that the King, on the advice of the Government, had approved the following appointments:

Commander-in-Chief, British Field Forces: Gen. VISCOUNT GORT, V.C.

Chief of Imperial General Staff: Gen. SIR EDMUND IRONSIDE.

Commander-in-Chief, Home Forces: Gen. SIR WALTER KIRKE.

Lord Gort, who is 53, a captain in the Grenadier Guards in 1914, won the M.C. in 1915, the D.S.O. to which he added two bars, in 1917 and in 1918 the V.C.—the latter, when commanding his battalion, for forcing the crossing of the Canal du Nord though three times wounded.

He became Commandant, Staff College, Camberley, 1936, Military Secretary, Secretary for War, 1937, and Chief of the Imperial General Staff later in the same year.

Sir Edmund Ironside, who is 59, commanded a brigade in France during the war, was Commander-in-Chief Allied troops, Archangel, Oct., 1918-Oct., 1919, and has since commanded the 2nd Division, Aldershot Bn., Quarter-Master-General in India, and last July was appointed Inspector-General of Overseas Forces.

Sir Walter Kirke, who is 62, was Director-General, Territorial Army, from 1936 till appointed Inspector-General, Home Forces, in July. Formerly he held important commands in India.

JAPAN TO BE NEUTRAL

PLEDGE TO BRITAIN

SHANGHAI, Sunday.

It is reliably learned that the Japanese Government is to remain neutral in the present European war.

Assurances to this effect are stated to have been given to the British Government.—Reuter.

DUKE OF KENT

TAKES UP WAR POST AS REAR ADMIRAL

The Admiralty announces that Rear Admiral the Duke of Kent has taken up his new appointment.

His Royal Highness was to have assumed the position of Governor-General of Australia in the autumn.

BANKS SHUT TO-DAY

Banks, including the Post Office Savings Bank and other savings banks, will be closed to-day. They will reopen to-morrow.

Details—Page 11.

SIR A. W. LAWRENCE DEAD

Sir Alexander W. Lawrence, a grandson of Lawrence of Lucknow, has died in London at the age of 65.

Mr. Tennyson Cole

Mr. P. Tennyson Cole, painter of portraits of King Edward VII. and many famous men, died on Saturday. He was 77.

Obituaries—Page 11

HIS MAJESTY'S BROADCAST

The following message was broadcast by the King from Buckingham Palace throughout the Empire at 6 o'clock last evening:

In this grave hour, perhaps the most fateful in our history, I send to every household of my peoples, both at home and overseas, this message, spoken with the same depth of feeling for each one of you as if I were able to cross your threshold and speak to you myself.

For the second time in the lives of most of us we are at war. Over and over again we have tried to find a peaceful way out of the differences between ourselves and those who are now our enemies. But it has been in vain.

We have been forced into a conflict. For we are called, with our Allies, to meet the challenge of a principle which, if it were to prevail, would be fatal to any civilised order in the world.

It is the principle which permits a State, in the selfish pursuit of power, to disregard its treaties and its solemn pledges; which sanctions the use of force, or threat of force, against the Sovereignty and independence of other States.

Such a principle, stripped of all disguise, is surely the mere primitive doctrine that might is right; and if this principle were established throughout the world, the freedom of our own country and of the whole British Commonwealth of Nations would be in danger.

But far more than this—the peoples of the world would be kept in the bondage of fear, and all hopes of settled peace and of the security of justice and liberty among nations would be ended.

This is the ultimate issue which confronts us. For the sake of all that we ourselves hold dear, and of the world's order and peace, it is unthinkable that we should refuse to meet the challenge.

It is to this high purpose that I now call my people at home and my peoples across the Seas, who will make our cause their own.

I ask them to stand calm, firm and united in this time of trial. The task will be hard. There may be dark days ahead, and war can no longer be confined to the battlefield. But we can only do the right as we see the right, and reverently commit our cause to God.

If one and all we keep resolutely faithful to it, ready for whatever service or sacrifice it may demand, then, with God's help, we shall prevail.

May He bless and keep us all.

BRITISH FLEET BEGINS THE BLOCKADE

Shipping Liable To Examination

CONVOY SYSTEM REINTRODUCED

An Admiralty announcement last night, that all British merchant vessels are liable to examination by the British Naval Contraband Control Service, indicated that the blockade of Germany had begun.

Ships will not normally be detained on interception longer than is necessary to establish their identity if they are:

Ships on Government charter.

Ships bound direct for British or allied ports and which will discharge all their cargo and passengers in such ports.

Ships whose last port of call was British or allied and which have a special war clearance therefrom.

THREE CONTROL BASES

Other British ships may on interception on certain routes be required to put into a contraband control base for more detailed examination. They are, therefore, advised to call at contraband control bases as follows:

Ships proceeding eastward through the English Channel with the intention of passing the Downs, if not calling at any other Channel port, should call at Weymouth for contraband control examination.

Ships bound for European ports on routes to the North of Scotland should call at Kirkwall.

Ships bound eastward through the Straits of Gibraltar should call at Gibraltar.

The Royal Navy is fully mobilised and at its war stations in full strength, supplemented by a number of fully commissioned armed merchant ships as auxiliary cruisers.

The Admiralty, profiting by past experience, has already taken certain measures which were developed slowly during the last war. Among these is the reintroduction of the convoy system for merchant shipping to assist the Merchant Navy in its vital duty of ensuring the overseas traffic of the British Commonwealth and its Allies.

HITLER GOES TO POLISH FRONT

TO COMMAND ARMIES

BERLIN, Sunday.

Hitler left the Chancellery in Berlin this evening for the eastern front, where he is to assume command of the German Armies. Four bodyguards were on the running-board of his car.

Earlier in the day he had announced his intention to go east in a message to the German Army on the western front, which, with others, was broadcast.

To the German people he declared:

"If the soldier is fighting at the front no one shall profit by the war. If the soldier fails at the front no one at home shall evade his duty.

"It was the lack of unity in 1918 that led to collapse. Whoever offends against this unity need expect nothing else than annihilation as an enemy of the nation."—British United Press and Reuter.

Hitler's message and German reply to British ultimatum—Page 7.

600 GERMANS ARRESTED

BOMBAY, Sunday.

More than 600 Germans have been arrested throughout India since the British declaration of war. They will be interned.—B.U.P.

DOMINIONS AT WAR

AUSTRALIA AND NEW ZEALAND

Australia and New Zealand yesterday declared war on Germany in support of the action of Great Britain.

The Canadian Cabinet met for two hours and it was stated afterwards that an official statement would be issued later. In a message to Mr. Chamberlain on Saturday, the Canadian Premier, Mr. Mackenzie King, said that the Dominion would stand by the side of Britain.

The Australian Prime Minister, Mr. Menzies, in a broadcast last night, stated:

"It is my melancholy duty to inform you that, in consequence of Germany's persistence in her invasion of Poland, Great Britain has declared war, and Australia is also at war.

"No harder task could fall to the lot of a democratic leader than to make such an announcement.

"The great family of British nations is now involved in a struggle which we must, at all costs, win. We believe in our hearts that we shall win."

"BRUTALLY PLAIN"

After reviewing the events of the past week and the Franco-British peace efforts, Mr. Menzies continued:

"It is brutally plain that it was Hitler's ambition to bring under Germany as many European nations as he could. The unchecked pursuance of this policy would have made the whole of Europe insecure, but a halt has been called to this resort to force.

"There was never a doubt where Britain stood—there stand the people of the British world.

"We do not know what lies ahead or the length of the journey, but I urge calmness, confidence and resolution. I know that you will show that Australia is ready—with defence forces, foodstuffs and money—and God grant that the world will soon be delivered from this agony."

Fuller Reports—Page 10

MAP OF WAR AREA

A map of particular value in following the war communiqués from Poland is reproduced on Page 12. It shows the chief towns of western and central Poland and the frontiers near the area affected.

FIERCE FIGHTING ON TWO POLISH SECTORS

MANY WEEK-END RAIDS BY GERMAN WARPLANES

THRUST INTO EAST PRUSSIA CLAIMED IN WARSAW

Fighting on a more extensive scale is developing on both the main fronts in Poland.

The German attempt to cut the Corridor between Chojnice and Graudenz was reported in Warsaw last night to have failed. At the same time it was stated that the Poles had recovered certain of their towns in this zone and had penetrated across the border into East Prussia.

Further air raids were made on Polish towns over the week-end. A Polish Foreign Office statement estimates that 1,500, including women and children, have been killed and wounded by bombing since Friday.

Below are messages from our special correspondents in Warsaw and Katowice.

POLES CHEER DECLARATIONS

FROM OUR SPECIAL CORRESPONDENT

WARSAW, Sunday.

The Germans occupied Rybnik, Teschen, Frystal, and have reached the suburbs of Katowice. They are pouring in by the Moravian Gate to cut communications between Katowice and Cracow.

Constant raids occurred at Crakow to-day.

The civilian population has evacuated Katowice. From Crakow heavy rifle and artillery fire is heard from all along the frontier.

The German minority indulged in sabotage and espionage in this area and cut all telephone lines from Katowice at noon to-day.

Next day they took refuge in the coal mines at Siemianowice. They surrendered when the machine-gun fire, but surrendered when heavy artillery was called in.

CZECH LEGION

Preparations are far advanced for the formation of an independent Czech Legion on Polish soil to fight for Czech freedom.

The Czechs are greatly encouraged by the declaration of solidarity with Poland issued by the Slovak Minister in Warsaw.

A Polish company is defending the munitions depot at Westerplatte, Danzig, against a German division. They are offering desperate resistance in the face of bombardment by heavy artillery and the guns of the warship Schleswig Holstein.

The total German losses are now given as 37 planes.

News of the British war declaration caused a tremendous outburst of joy in Warsaw. A crowd, numbering tens of thousands, marched to the British Embassy in Nowy Swiat-street, shouting, "Long live King George" and "Long live England."

Colonel Beck appeared on the balcony of the Embassy with the Ambassador, Sir Howard Kennard.

AT FRENCH EMBASSY

Raising a hand to hush the cheering, Col. Beck said, "We never doubted that England would fight with Poland."

Still cheering, the crowds surged on to the French Embassy, stopping on the way to raise cries of "Long live Jugoslavia" at the Jugoslav Legation. There were moving scenes outside the French Embassy. The crowd sang the patriotic song "Never shall the German foe tread our soil," with two fingers of the right hand solemnly raised. A French military attaché

CITY IN DARKNESS

Warsaw is now settling down to wartime conditions. All windows are criss-crossed with strips of paper. At night there is complete darkness.

Trams and buses, showing blue lights, rattle along at little more than a walking pace through the black streets. Night life is dead, cabarets are deserted.

The present half-hearted German raids on Warsaw have given the population a chance to grow accustomed to the A.R.P. instructions.

Admirable discipline is shown and no panic.

A communiqué issued on Saturday night states that the German Government proposed on Friday to Poland, through the Dutch Legation in Warsaw, that bombing be confined to military objectives. The Polish Government accepted.

It is alleged that Germany bombed 20 open cities on Saturday, several, including Torun, Radom, Bydgoszcz, Grudziadz and Mielec, more than once. At Torun children's grounds were bombed.

The communiqué adds that elsewhere villages, farms, even individuals and farm carts were bombed. The total casualties in the first two days' war are estimated to be 1,500 killed and wounded, including many women and children.

THE BOMBING OF KATOWICE

STREAM OF REFUGEES

From Our Special Correspondent

KATOWICE, Sunday.

At 8.45 this morning I was awakened by the sound of gun-fire and I saw 40 German bombers dropping incendiary bombs. The Poles brought their anti-aircraft batteries into action, but none was shot down.

Some time later there was an outburst of firing from the centre. Eight miles away. The population had been warned by radio to expect an A.R.P. practice, so were undisturbed.

The Polish anti-aircraft guns were shooting wildly and between the raids I saw the Polish second-line defence, and saw the unmasking of the heavy artillery behind it.

Continued on Page Nine, Column Three

News Summary: Other Pages

HOME

Prime Minister's broadcast announcement that Britain was at war with Germany. (P. 9.)

Official declaration of war in "London Gazette" (P. 11.)

Socialists and Liberals refused to be represented in War Cabinet; will give aid from outside. (P. 10.)

Anglo-French declaration that civilian populations will be spared in conduct of hostilities. (P. 10.)

Recruiting offices besieged. (P. 10.)

London crowds' calmness when air-raid warning sounded. (P. 9.)

Theatres and cinemas closed. (P. 6.)

Scheme for rationing certain foods may be introduced within next fortnight. (P. 10.)

Gold coin or bullion or foreign exchange to be offered for sale to Treasury. (P. 4.)

Board of Trade to insure cargoes and commodities against war risks from this morning. (P. 4.)

Government plans for growing more food at home. (P. 5.)

Consumption of coal, gas and electricity to be reduced 25 per cent. to conserve fuel supplies. (P. 6.)

Doctors and nurses in emergency hospital services called out for immediate duty. (P. 11.)

Traders warned of penalties for doing business with the enemy. (P. 4.)

Provisions of National Service (Armed Forces) Act. (P. 6.)

PARLIAMENT

Two days' debates in both Houses of Parliament. (Pp. 5 and 6.)

EMPIRE

Manifestations of loyalty to Britain by Dominions and Colonies. (P. 10.)

FOREIGN

M. Daladier's broadcast: "We are fighting for liberty." (P. 10.)

French envoy's last words with our cabinet. (P. 9.)

Proclamation invoking Neutrality Act to be made in U.S.: Roosevelt calls Cabinet. (P. 10.)

Franco broadcasts appeal to Governments and nations to localise the war. (P. 7.)

Text of German reply to British ultimatum. (P. 7.)

Unrest among Germans. (P. 9.)

FINANCE

Problems of financing in war. (P. 13.)

Many advances in heavy dealing on Wall Street. (P. 3.)

SPORT

Doncaster Race Committee abandons four-day meeting. (P. 8.)

Sports gathering prohibited. (P. 10.)

Page		Page
CITY	3 & 4	OBITUARY 11
CROSSWORD	8	PICTURES 8
LAW NOTICES	11	PROPERTY MKT. 4
LATEST WILLS	11	SPORT 8
LETTERS	7 & 8	WOMEN 3

LATE NEWS

News received after this edition had gone to press will be found in the stop press column on Page 10.

Privy Council Office, 3rd September, 1939.

IT IS NOTIFIED THAT A STATE OF WAR BETWEEN HIS MAJESTY AND GERMANY AS FROM 11 O'CLOCK A.M. TO-DAY, THE 3RD SEPTEMBER, 1939.

A facsimile of the opening paragraph of the "London Gazette."

be definite to-day did not allay the anxieties in which they went home.

Definite he was this Sunday-morning. The tragic irony that a proclamation of war which will convulse the world and determine its destinies should be made in the sunshine of a Sunday struck home to every heart.

It happened that the first alarm of war had thrilled through the House even before he spoke.

The sirens of air-raid warning wailed over Westminster while members were assembling, and they

▲ LE SOIR (THE EVENING), BRUSSELS, MONDAY SEPTEMBER 4, 1939

The francophone Belgian daily reports Germany's failure to respond to a British and French ultimatum to leave Poland, and Neville Chamberlain's assertion that "Hitler can only be stopped by force." Sandwiched between France and Germany, the Belgians watched the onset of war nervously: as in World War I, they would clearly be rapidly dragged into the conflict.

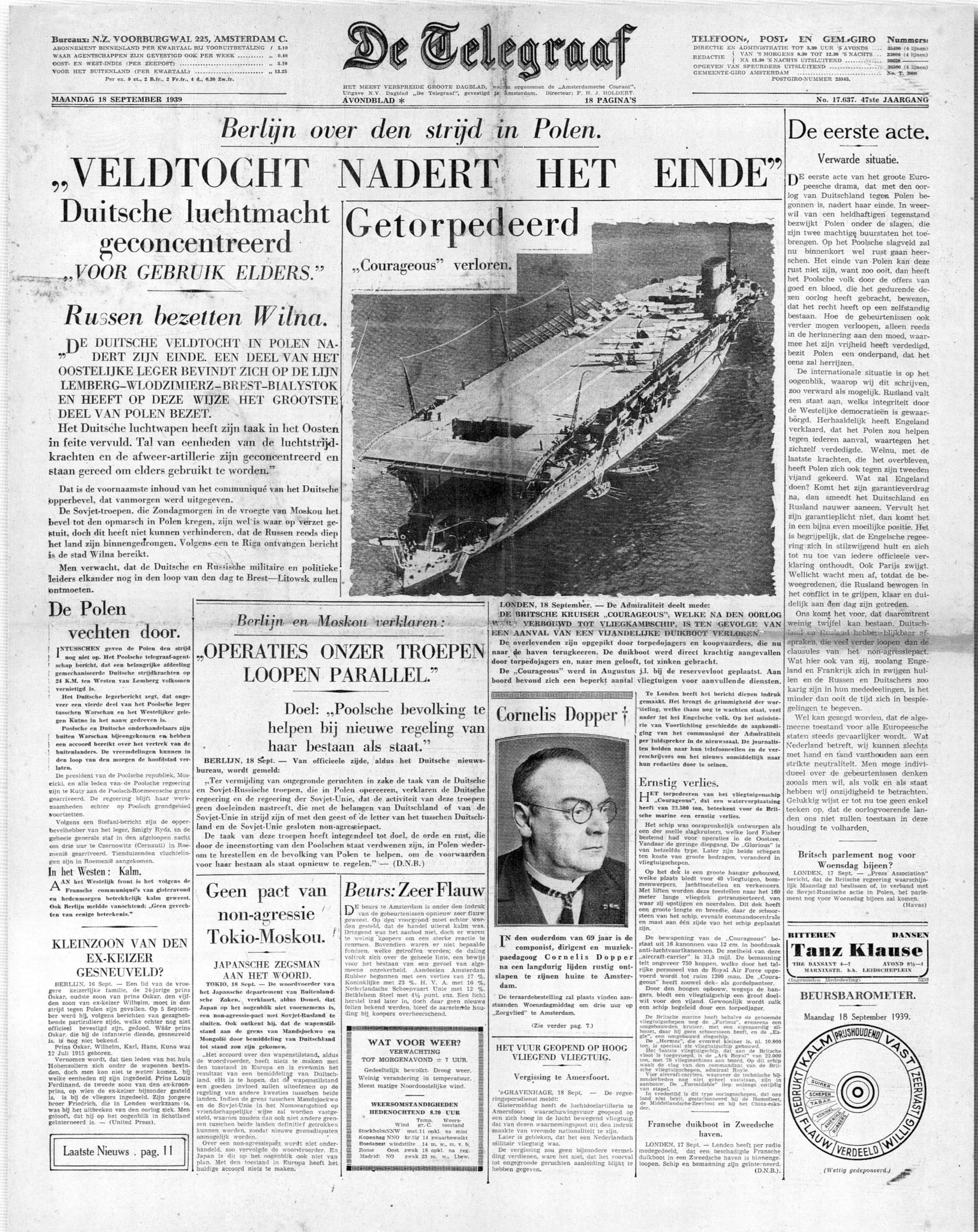

Bureaux: N.Z. VOORBURGWAL 225, AMSTERDAM C.
ABONNEMENT BINNENLAND PER KWARTAAL BIJ VOORUITBETALING ƒ 3.10
WAAR AGENTSCHAPPEN ZIJN GEVESTIGD OOK PER WEEK .... „ 0.40
OOST- EN WEST-INDIE (PER ZEEPOST) .... „ 3.10
VOOR HET BUITENLAND (PER KWARTAAL) .... „ 13.25
Per ex. 9 ct., 2 B.fr., 2 Fr.fr., 4 d., 0.30 Zw.fr.

MAANDAG 18 SEPTEMBER 1939

De Telegraaf

HET MEEST VERSPREIDE GROOTE DAGBLAD, waarin opgenomen de „Amsterdamsche Courant". Uitgave N.V. Dagblad „De Telegraaf", gevestigd te Amsterdam. Directeur: F. H. J. HOLDERT.
AVONDBLAD * 18 PAGINA'S

TELEFOON-, POST- EN GEM.-GIRO Nummers:
DIRECTIE EN ADMINISTRATIE TOT 5.30 UUR 'S AVONDS .... 35400 (4 lijnen)
REDACTIE { VAN 'S MORGENS 8.30 TOT 12.30 'S NACHTS .. 33800 (4 lijnen)
NA 12.30 'S NACHTS UITSLUITEND 36628
OPGEVEN VAN SPEURDERS UITSLUITEND .... 36500 (4 lijnen)
GEMEENTE-GIRO AMSTERDAM .... No. T. 3000
POSTGIRO-NUMMER 23345.

No. 17.637. 47ste JAARGANG

Berlijn over den strijd in Polen.

„VELDTOCHT NADERT HET EINDE"

Duitsche luchtmacht geconcentreerd

„VOOR GEBRUIK ELDERS."

Russen bezetten Wilna.

„DE DUITSCHE VELDTOCHT IN POLEN NADERT ZIJN EINDE. EEN DEEL VAN HET OOSTELIJKE LEGER BEVINDT ZICH OP DE LIJN LEMBERG–WLODZIMIERZ–BREST–BIALYSTOK EN HEEFT OP DEZE WIJZE HET GROOTSTE DEEL VAN POLEN BEZET.

Het Duitsche luchtwapen heeft zijn taak in het Oosten in feite vervuld. Tal van eenheden van de luchtstrijdkrachten en de afweer-artillerie zijn geconcentreerd en staan gereed om elders gebruikt te worden."

Dat is de voornaamste inhoud van het communiqué van het Duitsche opperbevel, dat vanmorgen werd uitgegeven.

De Sovjet-troepen, die Zondagmorgen in de vroegte van Moskou het bevel tot den opmarsch in Polen kregen, zijn wel is waar op verzet gestuit, doch dit heeft niet kunnen verhinderen, dat de Russen reeds diep het land zijn binnengedrongen. Volgens een te Riga ontvangen bericht is de stad Wilna bereikt.

Men verwacht, dat de Duitsche en Russische militaire en politieke leiders elkander nog in den loop van den dag te Brest—Litowsk zullen ontmoeten.

Getorpedeerd

„Courageous" verloren.

LONDEN, 18 September. — De Admiraliteit deelt mede:
DE BRITSCHE KRUISER „COURAGEOUS", WELKE NA DEN OORLOG WERD VERBOUWD TOT VLIEGKAMPSCHIP, IS TEN GEVOLGE VAN EEN AANVAL VAN EEN VIJANDELIJKE DUIKBOOT VERLOREN.

De overlevenden zijn opgepikt door torpedojagers en koopvaarders, die nu naar de haven terugkeeren. De duikboot werd direct krachtig aangevallen door torpedojagers en, naar men gelooft, tot zinken gebracht.

De „Courageous" werd in Augustus j.l. bij de reservevloot geplaatst. Aan boord bevond zich een beperkt aantal vliegtuigen voor aanvullende diensten.

Te Londen heeft het bericht diepen indruk gemaakt. Het brengt de grimmigheid der worsteling, welke thans nog te wachten staat, veel nader tot het Engelsche volk. Op het ministerie van Voorlichting geschiedde de aankondiging van het communiqué der Admiraliteit per luidspreker in de nieuwszaal. De journalisten holden naar hun telefooncellen en de verschrijvers om het nieuws onmiddellijk naar hun redacties door te seinen.

Ernstig verlies.

HET torpedeeren van het vliegtuigenschip „Courageous", dat een waterverplaatsing heeft van 22.500 ton, beteekent voor de Britsche marine een ernstig verlies.

Het schip was oorspronkelijk ontworpen als een der snelle slagkruisers, welke lord Fisher bestemd had voor operaties in de Oostzee. Vandaar de geringe diepgang. De „Glorious" is van hetzelfde type. Later zijn beide schepen ten koste van groote bedragen, veranderd in vliegtuigschepen.

Op het dek is een groote hangar gebouwd, welke plaats biedt voor 48 vliegtuigen, bommenwerpers, jachttoestellen en verkenners. Met liften worden deze toestellen naar het 160 meter lange vliegdek getransporteerd, van waar zij opstijgen en neerdalen. Dit dek heeft een groote lengte en breedte, daar de schoorsteen van het schip, evenals commandocentrale en mast aan één zijde van het schip geplaatst zijn.

De bewapening van de „Courageous" bestaat uit 16 kanonnen van 12 cm. in hoofdzaak anti-luchtvaartkanonnen. De snelheid van deze „aircraft-carrier" is 31,5 mijl. De bemanning telt ongeveer 750 koppen, welke door het talrijke personeel van de Royal Air Force opgevoerd wordt tot ruim 1200 man. De „Courageous" heeft zoowel dek- als gordelpantser.

Door den hoogen opbouw, wegens de hangars, biedt een vliegtuigschip een groot doelwit voor den vijand. Gewoonlijk wordt zulk een schip begeleid door een torpedjager.

De Britsche marine heeft behalve de genoemde vliegtuigschepen nog de „Furious", eveneens een omgebouwden kruiser, met een eigenaardig silhouet, daar hij geen schoorsteen heeft, en de „Eagle", een omgebouwd slagschip.

De „Hermes", die evenwel kleiner is, nl. 10.800 ton, is speciaal als vliegtuigschip gebouwd.

Het laatste vliegtuigschip, dat aan de Britsche vloot is toegevoegd, is de „Ark Royal" van 22.000 ton, met 70 vliegmachines aan boord. Op dit schip waait de vlag van den commandant van de Britsche vliegtuigschepen, admiraal Royle.

Vier aircraft-carriers, waarover de technische bijzonderheden nog niet geheel vaststaan, zijn in aanbouw. De „Formidable" liep onlangs ontijdig van stapel.

In vredestijd is dit type oorlogsschepen, dat ons land niet bezit, gestationneerd bij de Homefleet, de Middellandsche-Zeevloot en bij het China-eskader.

Fransche duikboot in Zweedsche haven.

LONDEN, 17 Sept. — Londen heeft per radio medegedeeld, dat een beschadigde Fransche duikboot in een Zweedsche haven is binnengeloopen. Schip en bemanning zijn geïnterneerd. (D.N.B.).

De Polen vechten door.

INTUSSCHEN geven de Polen den strijd nog niet op. Het Poolsche telegraaf-agentschap bericht, dat een belangrijke afdeeling gemechaniseerde Duitsche strijdkrachten op 24 K.M. ten Westen van Lemberg volkomen vernietigd is.

Het Duitsche legerbericht zegt, dat ongeveer een vierde deel van het Poolsche leger tusschen Warschau en het Westelijker gelegen Kutno in het nauw gedreven is.

Poolsche en Duitsche onderhandelaars zijn buiten Warschau bijeengekomen en hebben een accoord bereikt over het vertrek van de buitenlanders. De vreemdelingen kunnen in den loop van den morgen de hoofdstad verlaten.

De president van de Poolsche republiek, Moscicki, en alle leden van de Poolsche regeering zijn te Kuty aan de Poolsch-Roemeensche grens gearriveerd. De regeering blijft haar werkzaamheden echter op Poolsch grondgebied voortzetten.

Volgens een Stefani-bericht zijn de opperbevelhebber van het leger, Smigly Rydz, en de geheele generale staf in den afgeloopen nacht om drie uur te Czernowitz (Cernauti) in Roemenië gearriveerd. Tienduizenden vluchtelingen zijn in Roemenië aangekomen.

In het Westen: Kalm.

AAN het Westelijk front is het volgens de Fransche communiqué's van gisteravond en hedenmorgen betrekkelijk kalm geweest. Ook Berlijn meldde vanochtend: „Geen gevechten van eenige beteekenis."

KLEINZOON VAN DEN EX-KEIZER GESNEUVELD?

BERLIJN, 16 Sept. — Een lid van de vroegere keizerlijke familie, de 24-jarige prins Oskar, oudste zoon van prins Oskar, den vijfden zoon van ex-keizer Wilhelm, moet in den strijd tegen Polen zijn gevallen. Op 5 September werd hij, volgens berichten van gezaghebbende particuliere zijde, welke echter nog niet officieel bevestigd zijn, gedood. Wáár prins Oskar, die bij de infanterie diende, gesneuveld is, is nog niet bekend.

Prins Oskar, Wilhelm, Karl, Hans, Kuno was 12 Juli 1915 geboren.

Vernomen wordt, dat tien leden van het huis Hohenzollern zich onder de wapenen bevinden, doch men kon niet te weten komen, bij welke eenheden zij zijn ingedeeld. Prins Louis Ferdinand, de tweede zoon van den ex-kroonprins, op wien de ex-keizer bijzonder gesteld is, is bij de vliegers ingedeeld. Zijn jongere broer Friedrich, die in Londen werkzaam is, was bij het uitbreken van den oorlog ziek. Men gelooft, dat hij op het oogenblik in Schotland geïnterneerd is. — (United Press).

Laatste Nieuws . pag. 11

Berlijn en Moskou verklaren:

„OPERATIES ONZER TROEPEN LOOPEN PARALLEL."

Doel: „Poolsche bevolking te helpen bij nieuwe regeling van haar bestaan als staat."

BERLIJN, 18 Sept. — Van officieele zijde, aldus het Duitsche nieuwsbureau, wordt gemeld:

„Ter vermijding van ongegronde geruchten in zake de taak van de Duitsche en Sovjet-Russische troepen, die in Polen opereeren, verklaren de Duitsche regeering en de regeering der Sovjet-Unie, dat de activiteit van deze troepen geen doeleinden nastreeft, die met de belangen van Duitschland of van de Sovjet-Unie in strijd zijn of met den geest of de letter van het tusschen Duitschland en de Sovjet-Unie gesloten non-agressiepact.

De taak van deze troepen heeft integendeel tot doel, de orde en rust, die door de ineenstorting van den Poolschen staat verdwenen zijn, in Polen wederom te hrestellen en de bevolking van Polen te helpen, om de voorwaarden voor haar bestaan als staat opnieuw te regelen." — (D.N.B.)

Geen pact van non-agressie Tokio-Moskou.

JAPANSCHE ZEGSMAN AAN HET WOORD.

TOKIO, 18 Sept. — De woordvoerder van het Japansche departement van Buitenlandsche Zaken, verklaart, aldus Domei, dat Japan op het oogenblik niet voornemens is, een non-agressie-pact met Sovjet-Rusland te sluiten. Ook ontkent hij, dat de wapenstilstand aan de grens van Mandsjoekwo en Mongolië door bemiddeling van Duitschland tot stand zou zijn gekomen.

„Het accoord over den wapenstilstand, aldus de woordvoerder, heeft niets te maken met den toastand in Europa en is evenmin het resultaat van een bemiddeling van Duitschland. eHt is te hopen, dat de wapenstilstand een goeden invloed zullen uitoefenen op de regeling van andere kwesties tusschen beide landen. Indien de grens tusschen Mandsjoekwo en de Sovjet-Unie in het Nomoeangebied op vriendschappelijke wijze zal worden vastgesteld, waarom zouden dan ook niet andere grenzen tusschen beide landen definitief getrokken kunnen worden, zoodat nieuwe grensdisputen onmogelijk worden.

Over een non-agressiepact wordt niet onderhandeld, zoo vervolgde de woordvoerder. En Japan is dit op het oogenblik ook niet van plan. Met den toestand in Europa heeft het huidige accoord niets te maken.

Beurs: Zeer Flauw

DE beurs te Amsterdam is onder den indruk van de gebeurtenissen opnieuw zeer flauw geweest. Op den voorgrond moet echter worden gesteld, dat de handel uiterst kalm was. Dringend was het aanbod niet, doch er waren te weinig koopers om een sterke reactie te remmen. Bovendien waren er niet bepaalde fondsen, welke getroffen werden; de daling voltrok zich over de geheele linie, een bewijs voor het bestaan van een gevoel van algemeene onzekerheid. Aandeelen Amsterdam Rubber begonnen met een verlies van 17 %, Koninklijke met 23 %, H. V. A. met 16 %, Nederlandsche Scheepvaart Unie met 12 %, Bethlehem Steel met 4½ punt, enz. Een licht herstel trad later in, doch daar geen nieuwe feiten bekend werden, bleef de aarzelende houding bij koopers overheerschend.

WAT VOOR WEER?
VERWACHTING TOT MORGENAVOND ± 7 UUR.
Gedeeltelijk bewolkt. Droog weer. Weinig verandering in temperatuur. Meest matige Noordoostelijke wind.

WEERSOMSTANDIGHEDEN HEDENOCHTEND 8.20 UUR

	Wind	Temp. gr. C.	Weerstoestand
Stockholm	NNW mat.	11	opkl. na mist
Kopenhag	NNO kr.tig	14	zwaarbewolkt
Boedapest	windstilte	14	m. w., m. v. b.
Rome	Oost zwak	18	opkl. na reg.
Madrid:	NO zwak	23	m. w., l.bew.

Cornelis Dopper †

IN den ouderdom van 69 jaar is de componist, dirigent en muziekpaedagoog Cornelis Dopper na een langdurig lijden rustig ontslapen te zijnen huize te Amsterdam.

De teraardebestelling zal plaats vinden aanstaanden Woensdagmiddag om drie uur op „Zorgvlied" te Amsterdam.

(Zie verder pag. 7.)

HET VUUR GEOPEND OP HOOG VLIEGEND VLIEGTUIG.

Vergissing te Amersfoort.

's-GRAVENHAGE, 18 Sept. — De regeeringspersdienst meldt:

Gistermiddag heeft de luchtdoelartillerie te Amersfoort waarschuwingsvuur geopend op een zich hoog in de lucht bewegend vliegtuig, dat van dezen waarnemingspost uit den indruk maakte van vreemde nationaliteit te zijn.

Later is gebleken, dat het een Nederlandsch militair vliegtuig was.

De vergissing zou geen bijzondere vermelding verdienen, ware het niet, dat het voorval tot ongegronde geruchten aanleiding blijkt te hebben gegeven.

De eerste acte.

Verwarde situatie.

DE eerste acte van het groote Europeesche drama, dat met den oorlog van Duitschland tegen Polen begonnen is, nadert haar einde. In weerwil van een heldhaftigen tegenstand bezwijkt Polen onder de slagen, die zijn twee machtige buurstaten het toebrengen. Op het Poolsche slagveld zal nu binnenkort wel rust gaan heerschen. Het einde van Polen kan deze rust niet zijn, want zoo ooit, dan heeft het Poolsche volk door de offers van goed en bloed, die het gedurende dezen oorlog heeft gebracht, bewezen, dat het recht heeft op een zelfstandig bestaan. Hoe de gebeurtenissen ook verder mogen verloopen, alleen reeds in de herinnering aan den moed, waarmee het zijn vrijheid heeft verdedigd, bezit Polen een onderpand, dat het eens zal herrijzen.

De internationale situatie is op het oogenblik, waarop wij dit schrijven, zoo verward als mogelijk. Rusland valt een staat aan, welks integriteit door de Westelijke democratieën is gewaarborgd. Herhaaldelijk heeft Engeland verklaard, dat het Polen zou helpen tegen iederen aanval, waartegen het zichzelf verdedigde. Welnu, met de laatste krachten, die het overbleven, heeft Polen zich ook tegen zijn tweeden vijand gekeerd. Wat zal Engeland doen? Komt het zijn garantieverdrag na, dan smeedt het Duitschland en Rusland nauwer aaneen. Vervult het zijn garantieplicht niet, dan komt het in een bijna even moeilijke positie. Het is begrijpelijk, dat de Engelsche regeering zich in stilzwijgend hult en zich tot nu toe van iedere officieele verklaring onthoudt. Ook Parijs zwijgt. Wellicht wacht men af, totdat de beweegredenen, die Rusland bewogen in het conflict in te grijpen, klaar en duidelijk aan den dag zijn getreden.

Ons komt het voor, dat daaromtrent weinig twijfel kan bestaan. Duitschland en Rusland hebben blijkbaar afspraken, die veel verder loopen dan de clausules van het non-agressiepact. Wat hier ook van zij, zoolang Engeland en Frankrijk zich in zwijgen hullen en de Russen en Duitschers zoo karig zijn in hun mededeelingen, is het minder dan ooit de tijd zich in bespiegelingen te begeven.

Wel kan gezegd worden, dat de algemeene toestand voor alle Europeesche staten steeds gevaarlijker wordt. Wat Nederland betreft, wij kunnen slechts met hand en tand vasthouden aan een strikte neutraliteit. Men moge individueel over de gebeurtenissen denken zooals men wil, als volk en als staat hebben wij onzijdigheid te betrachten. Gelukkig wijst er tot nu toe geen enkel teeken op, dat de oorlogvoerende landen ons niet zullen toestaan in deze houding te volharden.

Britsch parlement nog voor Woensdag bijeen?

LONDEN, 17 Sept. — „Press Association" bericht, dat de Britsche regeering waarschijnlijk Maandag zal beslissen of, in verband met de Sovjet-Russische actie in Polen, het parlement nog voor Woensdag bijeen zal komen. (Havas)

BEURSBAROMETER.

Maandag 18 September 1939.

KALM PRIJSHOUDEND VAST ZEERVAST WILLIG VERDEELD FLAUW GEDRUKT

(Wettig gedeponeerd.)

▲ DE TELEGRAAF (THE TELEGRAPH), AMSTERDAM, MONDAY SEPTEMBER 18, 1939

The Dutch morning paper declares: "Berlin reports on the fighting in Poland. Campaign drawing to a close." It also reports the sinking of the British aircraft carrier *Courageous* by a U-boat. For many Dutch people, *The Telegraaf* relied too much on reports from Berlin. After the war it was banned from publishing for 30 years for its pro-German coverage, although the ban was lifted after only a few years and the newspaper went on to become one of the most popular in the Netherlands.

News Chronicle

FRANKLYN'S MILD TOBACCO 9½ OZ

No. 29,139 — ONE PENNY — SATURDAY, SEPTEMBER 23, 1939

BARGAINS BY POST — See Page Two

Russia To Control Half Poland

NEW FRONTIER PASSES THROUGH WARSAW

Stalin Gets The Oil, Hitler, Steel Areas

RUSSIA WILL GAIN MORE THAN HALF THE AREA OF POLAND AND APPROXIMATELY HALF THE POPULATION BY HER AGREEMENT WITH GERMANY, IT WAS ANNOUNCED YESTERDAY IN BERLIN.

The line of demarcation, between the zones to be occupied by the two armies, follows the rivers Pissa, Narew, Vistula and San and gives to Russia 96,467 square miles of territory and to Germany 52,584 square miles. The population in both areas is approximately 16,000,000.

The Soviet frontiers now advance west to Modlin, the famous fortress at the junction of the Narew and Vistula, 15 miles north-west of Warsaw, and pass through Warsaw itself to the confluence of the Vistula and the San.

The line then follows the course of the San through Przemysl to Sanok and the Hungarian frontier near Lupkow.

Rumanian Border Covered

Russia, therefore, occupies not only the whole length of the Polish-Rumanian frontier, but also the whole length of the frontier with Sub-Carpathian Ukraine.

The partition of Warsaw, through which the Vistula flows, gives to Germany the west bank, on which is the main city. Russia gets the east bank, where lies the suburb of Praga, about half the size of Warsaw proper.

To the south the Russian frontier starts on the Polish-East Prussian border, about 20 miles north of Novogrod.

Industrial Gains

In the industrial partition the Soviet has gained:

OILFIELDS: These are all in Galicia, in the Drohobycz area. In 1938 Poland had 27 refineries employing 3,200 workers. Total crude oil production was 502,000 tons. Refined products included: Petrol, 141,000 tons; oil, 141,000 tons; gas oil and fuel oil, 91,000 tons.

TIMBER: Poland's timber exports in 1938 were 1,680,422 tons.

AGRICULTURE: The fields of Poland in 1937-38 yielded 2,171,000 tons of wheat, 7,000,000 tons of rye, 1,300,000 tons of barley, 34,000,000 tons of potatoes.

Coal and Iron

Germany obtains all Poland's coal mines, all the heavy industrial area, including most of the newly-developed "industrial" triangle of Sandomierz, in which, during the past two years, Poland has invested large sums, and most of the textile regions. This is what these acquisitions mean to Hitler:

HEAVY INDUSTRIES.—Principal coal mines are in Silesia and Kielce; main metallurgical centres are Warsaw, Lodz, Bydgoszcz and Poznan; armament centres are Sandomierz and Radom. Iron and steel production in 1937 (metric tons) was: Pig iron, 724,000 tons; 1,148,000; rolled iron and welded, 1,047,000.

TEXTILES: In this Russia, which takes over Bialystok as a share. Main centres now German are Lodz and Bielsko. In 1936 Poland had 1,875,623 spindles and 61,331 looms in the cotton industry and 791,453 spindles and 13,520 looms in the woollen trade.

How Towns Went

The principal towns falling to the partitioning Powers are:
To Russia:

BIALYSTOK: Population 60,000; second only to Lodz as textile centre; specialised in imitation "Harris Tweed."

VILNA: Capital of medieval Lithuania. Ceded to Lithuania after the war, but seized by Poles. Population 200,000. Extensive industries and large timber and grain exports.

LUBLIN: Population 70,000. Armaments-making town. Other industries include textiles, soap, tobacco and sugar.

LWOW: Austrian from 1712 to the end of the Great War. Manu-

TURN TO PAGE EIGHT, Col. THREE

TWO UNKNOWN SUBMARINES IN AMERICAN WATERS

—Roosevelt Statement
From Our Own Correspondent
WASHINGTON, Friday.

PRESIDENT ROOSEVELT startled his Press conference at the White House today by announcing that two submarines, "nationality unknown," had been sighted near the coasts of the United States.

One was seen in the Pacific, off the point where Alaska meets the Canadian border. The other was in the Atlantic, off Boston.

"THEY MIGHT BE SWISS!"

There were quick questions.

Were the submarines within the orbit of the newly-instituted navy patrols now ranging the United States coasts? The President said the patrols were operating along the coastline from its most northern point on the Atlantic side, right down to the Carribean Sea, but there was no patrol at present on the Pacific Coast.

We tried to get more specific information on the probable identity of the submarines.

"Might they be Canadian?" somebody asked. Mr. Roosevelt brought this line of questioning to an abrupt close by saying "They *might* be Swiss."

Allied War Council In England

THE Supreme War Council of the Allies met in England yesterday.

They were in complete agreement on action to meet war developments since they last met and the course to be followed to give effect to the Allied plans.

Britain's representatives were: The Prime Minister, Lord Halifax (the Foreign Secretary) and Lord Chatfield (Minister for Co-ordination of Defence).

France was represented by M. Daladier (the Premier), M. Dautry (Minister of Armaments), General Gamelin (Commander-in-Chief of the French Armed Forces) and Admiral Darlan (Chief of Naval Staff).

TWO SITTINGS

France's delegates flew to a South Coast aerodrome, and the meeting was held in a Sussex committee room.

There were sittings in the morning and the afternoon, and developments which have taken place since they last met in France on September 14, were reviewed and their effect on the future course of events.

The question of munitions and supplies was considered and agreement was reached on procedure for co-ordinating and perfecting arrangements to be made by both Governments.

Butter Controlled

BUTTER supplies are to be requisitioned and the distribution controlled as from today.

This is to facilitate equitable distribution pending the introduction of rationing, announces the Ministry of Information.

An order has been made requisitioning all butter in registered cold stores in Britain, and all butter manufactured in Britain after last night.

Gasbags For Cars Here Soon

LONDON gas companies are preparing for the supply of gas in bags for commercial vehicles and private cars.

Arrangements will be made for fitting the bags at the works and depots of the companies and at many garages and service stations through whom it is expected the bulk of the fuel will be supplied.

It is also hoped to make early arrangements with automobile engineers for the fitting of gas carburettors alongside the existing petrol ones.

Manufacture and fitting of the bags will be undertaken by firms with the necessary facilities, and it is hoped that the gas will be retailed at a price comparing favourably on a mileage basis with that of petrol.

Technical provisions to be settled before supplies are available are being discussed, and a notice calling attention to them will be made soon.

At a London garage last night I was shown a rough quotation of £15 for altering a medium-powered car to burn gas (twixt the Motoring Correspondent). For the use of compressed gas, a cylinder can be fitted to the car and the necessary alterations made to the engine for about £50.

BLACK-OUT TIME
TONIGHT IS 6.57
TOMORROW 6.54

LATE NEWS

71,900 Czech Arrests

The secret German "Freedom Station" declared in a broadcast last night that Dr. Goebbels had lied when he said only a few arrests had taken place in Bohemia and Moravia. The announcer said he knew of a report which had been submitted to Herr Hitler saying that up to last Sunday the number of arrests made in the Czech provinces was 71,976.—B.U.P.

Quiet Day On Western Front

PARIS, Friday.—The French official communiqué issued to-night states: "It has been quiet all day along the entire front. Our naval forces are continuing to ensure effectively the protection of our convoys and to beat off enemy submarines."—Exchange.

Dr. Benes and His Generals

Balloon on the roof of a gas-fuelled motor-van in Leeds this week

Dr. Benes in London yesterday with three chiefs of the new Czecho-Slovak Legion now being formed in Britain. Left to right: Colonel Moravec, General Serge Ingr, Dr. Benes and General Rudolf Viest.

RUMANIAN PREMIER'S MURDER
SECOND DOLLFUSS CRIME

From WILLIAM FORREST
News Chronicle War Correspondent
BUCHAREST, Friday.

M. ARMAND CALINESCU, the murdered Premier of Rumania, was a little man like Dollfuss and, like Dollfuss, he personified his country's resistance to Nazi domination.

In circumstances which, down to the seizure of the radio station, present a striking parallel with the Vienna 1934 coup, he died like Dollfuss. The analogy is too close to escape notice and the indignation among the people of Bucharest last night was all the greater on that account.

M. Calinescu, sworn enemy of the Iron Guards, was assassinated in Bucharest while driving home from the War Ministry. Accomplices of the assassins seized the Bucharest radio station and broadcast the announcement that the Premier had been killed by Iron Guards.

Behind the Iron Guards the people of Rumania have always seen the hand of Germany.

WHAT NEXT?

At a time when the Germans are represented by an economic mission in Bucharest which is exerting the utmost pressure to obtain a supply of Rumanian oil and wheat, Rumania's strong man, who was credited in the public mind with pro-Allies sympathies, has been eliminated.

"What next?" For the present all is quiet in the country. Fears which were felt when the radio announcement was made that M. Calinescu's death might be the signal for an Iron Guard rebellion, have not materialised.

Justice of the grimmest kind was meted out to the assassins of M. Calinescu. They were taken out to the scene of the crime and executed by a firing squad in full view of the assembled public. One was still alive after the volley, and he was dispatched by shots from an officer's revolver.

Two of the assassins arrived near the scene of the shooting—one a tall youth of 19—burst out laughing when the police began questioning them.

The arrested men announced that the leader of the conspiracy was a lawyer named Dumitrescu.

Dumitrescu said that the assassination was an act of revenge for the murder of the Iron Guard leader Codreanu, who was shot last year while trying to escape from the police.

[A Reuter message from Bucharest states that according to semi-official sources an inquiry into the murder of M. Calinescu has established that the crime had no foreign or international significance.]

Priestley's Wartime Journey, Page 3; Robert Lynd on Chivalry, Page 4; Gardening, Radio, £100 Crossword, Page 6; Today's Football Fixtures and Buchan's Diary, Page 7

It accounts for the extra wear, the deeper satisfaction you feel in your Lotus or Delta shoes, that they began well. They had the birth and breeding of leather and workmanship. Experience of over a century of shoemaking goes to the perfection of every pair that bears the Lotus or Delta mark. Yet they are priced at from as little as 17/11 per pair, or in better qualities up to two guineas.

◄ NEWS CHRONICLE, LONDON, SATURDAY SEPTEMBER 23, 1939
"Quiet Day on the Western Front" reads the late news: the conflict remained largely a phoney war for the western Allies, although a submarine scare is an indication of growing wariness in the United States. The news from the east was more grim, with a crackdown on Czech opponents of the Nazis and the murder of the Romanian prime minister. Worse for the Allies was the revelation of the secret clauses of the Nazi–Soviet Nonaggression Pact, under which the Red Army invaded eastern Poland. Britain and France, having declared war on Germany for violating Polish territorial integrity, were in no position to sanction their potential Soviet allies.

► ON SEPTEMBER 28, AT BREST-LITOVSK, Red Army and German Army commanders held a joint victory parade before German forces withdrew west behind the new demarcation line in divided Poland. The vehicles in the photograph are Russian OT-26 flamethrower tanks.

The New York Times.

LATE CITY EDITION
Fair and slightly colder today. To-morrow fair, slowly rising temperatures.
Temperature Yesterday—Max., 59; Min., 50

Section 1

VOL. LXXXIX....No. 29,849

Entered as Second-Class Matter, Postoffice, New York, N. Y.

NEW YORK, SUNDAY, OCTOBER 15, 1939

PPP

Including Rotogravure Picture, Magazine and Book Review.

TEN CENTS

TWELVE CENTS Beyond 200 Miles Except West of Pa.—South of Va.

Copyright, 1939, by the New York Times Company.

CITY'S OWN AIRPORT IN USE AS TERMINUS IN WORLD AVIATION

6 Canadian Officials Land at North Beach in Preliminary to Dedication Today

GREETED BY MAYOR'S AIDE

Three Great Transport Lines Await Approval of Shift to $40,000,000 Field

---

Democratic Convention Is Invited to Rose Bowl

Special to The New York Times.

PASADENA, Calif., Oct. 14—Bidding for the Democratic National Convention for 1940, a tentative option on Pasadena's Rose Bowl has been taken by local party members, H. W. Nichols, Park Superintendent of Pasadena, announced today.

BIG NAVY SHAKE-UP FOLLOWS DISCOVERY OF FAULTS IN SHIPS

Bureaus of Construction and Repairs and Engineering Unified by President's Order

THREE ADMIRALS SHIFTED

Weight Added to 12 New Destroyers After Original Design Affects Their Stability

By HANSON W. BALDWIN
Special to The New York Times.

U-BOAT SINKS BRITISH BATTLESHIP; 396 OF 1,200 ON ROYAL OAK RESCUED; SOVIET-FINNISH ACCORD HELD NEAR

Nazis Held Ready to Lose 200 Planes to Sink a Ship

By Telephone to The New York Times.

ROME, Oct. 14—The German Air Force has plans to blast the British Fleet off the seas by allotting 200 planes for the bombing of each warship, according to the Vie Dell'Aria, the official newspaper of the Italian Air Force.

PARLEY IS HALTED

Agreement in Principle Hinted as Paasikivi Leaves Moscow

ALANDS THREAT DOUBTED

Russia Believed Ready to Back Status Quo of Islands if Others Are Granted

By The United Press.

MOSCOW, Sunday, Oct. 15.

The International Situation

LINDBERGH SPEECH ASSAILED IN SENATE

Lundeen Stirs Storm by Proposing That We Seize British Islands in Caribbean

By CHARLES W. HURD
Special to The New York Times.

WASHINGTON, Oct. 14

NAVY LOSS IS HEAVY

Admiralty Believes 804 Missing Are All Dead —Captain Saved

SOME SURVIVORS INJURED

29,150-Ton Vessel Went Down So Rapidly More Than One Hit Is Suspected

By RAYMOND DANIELL
Special Cable to The New York Times.

LONDON, Oct. 14—A torpedo from a German submarine sent the battleship Royal Oak to the bottom of the sea today and struck grief into more than 800 British homes.

BERLIN GUNS ROAR TO FIGHT OFF PLANE

Unidentified Craft Arrives at High Altitude—Explosion to Northwest Is Heard

Wireless to The New York Times.

BERLIN, Sunday, Oct. 15.

BLOCKADE DOOMED, ELATED NAZIS SAY

Sinking of Royal Oak Proves Futility of British Navy's Efforts, Berlin Hears

Wireless to The New York Times.

BERLIN, Oct. 14

REGISTRATION SETS OFF-YEAR RECORD

Rush in Final Hours Brings the City Total to 2,067,751— Council to Be Smaller

Major Sports Yesterday

FOOTBALL

HORSE RACING

Dispatches from Europe and the Far East are subject to censorship.

▲ THE NEW YORK TIMES, SUNDAY OCTOBER 15, 1939

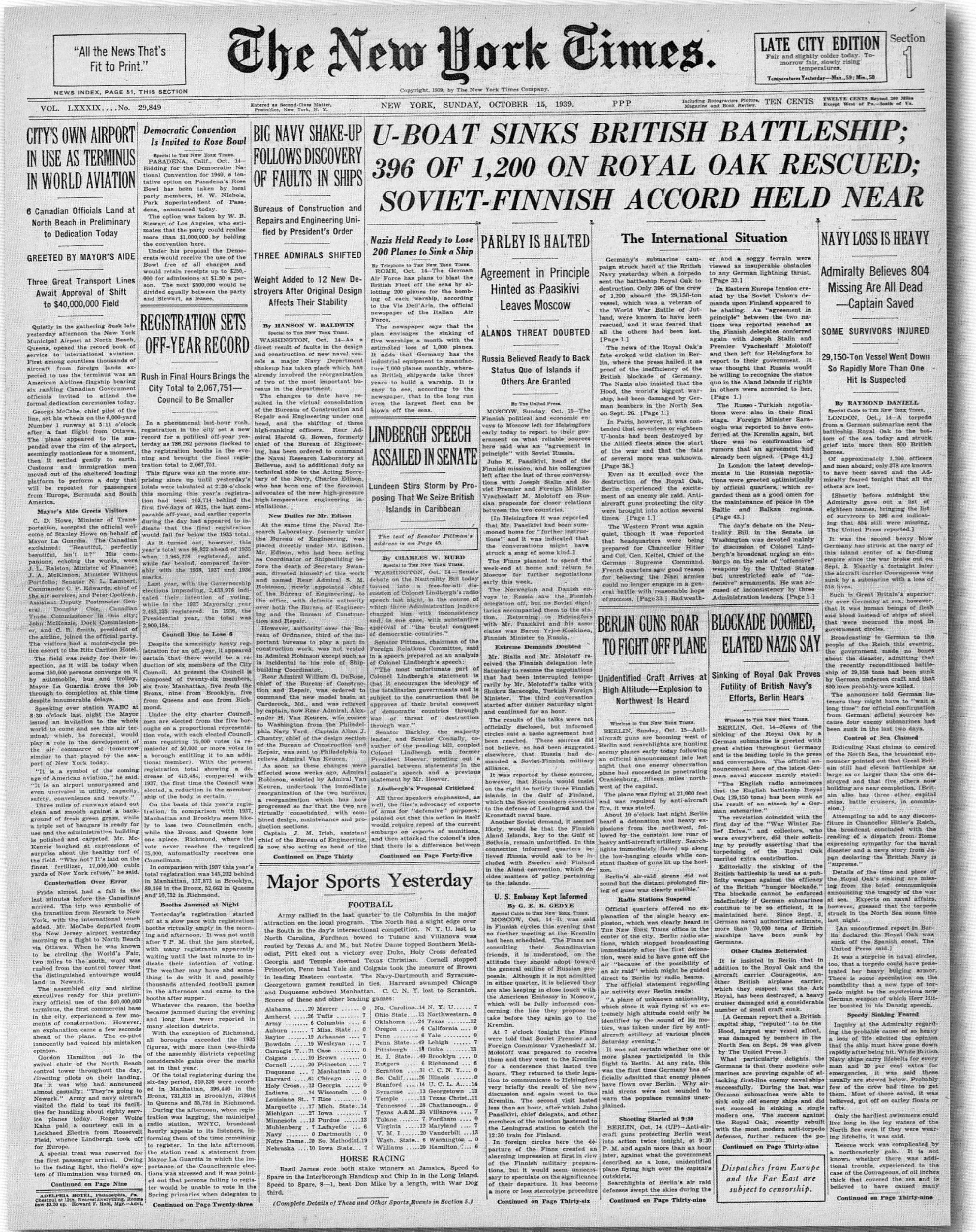

"All the news that's fit to print" is the *Times*' proud boast, and a packed front page does it justice. New Yorkers learn of the loss of a British battleship in a daring raid on the Royal Navy base at Scapa Flow, Scotland, and of Germany's determination to attack Britain's fleet at nearly any cost. A digest of international news directs readers to fuller stories inside. Among home news is a report of a hostile reaction toward aviator and national hero Charles Lindbergh, for his apparent sympathies with the Nazis. But the front page still has room for many readers' priority: the sports results.

▶ DAILY EXPRESS, LONDON, THURSDAY NOVEMBER 9, 1939
Throughout the war, newspapers on all sides seized on any evidence that the enemy's leaders lacked public support. As the *Express* points out, had Hitler followed his usual timetable, he may well have been killed by the bomb planted by George Elser in the beer cellar where once a year Hitler met with his old Nazi comrades. Elser, a communist with profound Protestant sympathies, believed that killing Hitler would stop the war and prevent further bloodshed. Along with a photograph highlighting the absurdity of bureaucracy—half a street in blackout, the other half still lit up—the Express has room to celebrate its own success: such is the general appetite for news on the 68th day of the war that it is selling 2 million copies a day. The advertisement at lower right encourages housewives to enjoy a midmorning break with a glass of sweet white wine, which might be an acknowledgment of the national nervousness as Britons waited for the war to begin in earnest.

Daily Express

WORLD'S LARGEST DAILY SALE

No. 12,315 — Thursday, November 9, 1939 — One Penny

4 a.m. EDITION — A defiant shriek "I'm ready for a five-year war!" then—

HITLER ESCAPES EXPLOSION IN A BEER CELLAR

ROYAL OAK SCANDAL

Who was to blame? SEE OPINION, PAGE SIX

6 dead, 60 hurt: Reported attempt with time-bomb

27 MINUTES AFTER HIS SPEECH

TWENTY-SEVEN MINUTES AFTER HITLER ENDED A HYSTERICAL SPEECH IN THE BUERGERBRAU BEER CELLAR AT MUNICH LAST NIGHT—A SPEECH IN WHICH HE CRIED THAT HE WAS READY FOR A FIVE-YEARS' WAR WITH BRITAIN—THE BUILDING WAS SHAKEN BY AN EXPLOSION WHICH KILLED SIX MEMBERS OF THE "OLD GUARD" OF THE NAZI PARTY, AND INJURED SIXTY OTHER PEOPLE.

HITLER HAD ALREADY LEFT AND WAS NOT HURT. HE LEFT EARLIER THAN HE ORIGINALLY INTENDED AS HE WAS SUMMONED BACK TO BERLIN BY IMPORTANT STATE BUSINESS.

The identities of the dead and injured are unknown, it is officially stated, says the British United Press from Berlin this morning.

Police admitted that the explosion was due to an "explosive body"—not to a defective boiler, as was suggested at first. The official statement says that the outrage was inspired by foreign agents, and a reward has been offered for the discovery of the perpetrators.

Munich-Berlin phone cut

New York radio stations go so far as to report that the explosion was caused by a time-bomb, placed in position by some one posing as a Nazi Storm-trooper.

Neither Goering nor Ribbentrop attended the meeting, but Hitler's deputy, Rudolf Hess, Dr. Goebbels and the Nazi Labour Front leader, Dr. Ley, were all there.

After the explosion, reports from Berlin said that telephone communications with Munich had been "interrupted by a disturbance." The Havas Amsterdam correspondent says they were cut.

The official statement issued by the German Ministry of Propaganda in Berlin this morning says:—

"The Fuehrer arrived in Munich yesterday in connection with the anniversary of the Old Guard for a short visit. Instead of Hess, the Fuehrer himself made a speech in the Buergerbrauhaus.

"Since affairs of state compelled the Fuehrer to return in the course of the night, he left the Buergerbrau sooner than was expected, and entered the train which was held in readiness.

"Shortly afterwards an explosion took place in the Buergerbrau cellar, killing six Old Guards and injuring more than sixty others.

"The attempt seems traceable to foreign instigation, and has aroused fanatical indignation in Munich.

"To ascertain the perpetrators a reward of £25,000 is offered."

Hitler has been a target for assassins ever since his rise to power six years ago.

In March 1933 twenty people were arrested and charged with plotting his death. Churches were occupied by police. Sewers were searched.

In June 1934 Hitler, alleging that he had discovered a conspiracy among his own Nazi Party, destroyed seventy-seven of its leaders in the famous "blood purge."

Since then many similar attempts have been reported, and there was a mass trial in which several hundred plotters were concerned.

■ BACK PAGE, COLUMN FOUR

FOREIGN PAGE DOG COMES TO THE FRONT PAGE

"Vot, mein Fuehrer has to fine years' hard labour himself sentenced ! . . ."

'We will never capitulate'

THEY'RE STILL AT SIXES AND SEVENS

The thin dotted line between Black-out and Light on Kilburn High-road last night at six. Shops on the West Hampstead side are open now until seven o'clock. Those across the road, in Willesden, are "curfewed" at six. " It's like having one blind eye, walking down that way," says Hilde Marchant on Page Seven.

BRUSSELS: Report from Henry Fast, Daily Express Correspondent

Holland fears attack is now imminent

HOLLAND is in imminent danger. Pressing demands have been made at The Hague by Germany. An attack on Holland was planned for today ; it has now been put off, but only, perhaps, for a few days.

The Dutch answer has been morally the new peace appeal : materially, the opening on a large scale of the sluices which flooded some of the frontier regions.

There was little doubt yesterday that the peace appeal of King Leopold and Queen Wilhelmina was largely a diplomatic move to strengthen the international position of Holland and Belgium.

Such a move meets Germany's desire for peace, and the hope expressed by Hitler that neutral countries should offer to evolve a peace plan.

According to one of my informants Germany has asked Holland not only for military air bases, but also for the control of the port of Flushing.

These demands have been daily refused by the Dutch, who have also told Germany they will resist.

3 Kings join plea

KING CHRISTIAN OF DENMARK, King Haakon of Norway, King Gustav of Sweden, and President Kallio of Finland, sent telegrams to Queen Wilhelmina and King Leopold yesterday contradicting them on their peace plan and wishing it success.

R.A.F. BAG TWO NAZI PLANES

TWO R.A.F. pilots of the Coastal Command, patrolling over the North Sea yesterday, won a fight with three Nazi planes.

PILOT No. 1 reported by radio. "I have made contact with the enemy." One minute later his radio flashed : "I have destroyed one enemy seaplane."

Back at his base, he said : "The fight took place 100 feet above the sea. A Heinkel seaplane came out of the clouds above and behind me. "He tried to get on my tail. I did a steep turn, and my air gunner and I got in bursts at close range. The enemy plane dived into the sea and sank."

PILOT No. 2 sighted a German flying boat at 100 feet and dived five times to attack. Several bursts of fire entered the flying boat's engines, and the rear gunner's cockpit was seen to be empty after the second dive.

After the fifth dive the flying boat went down, partly out of control. The British rear gunner reported the sighting of a second Nazi flying boat during the fight. The pilot waited till he had settled the first machine, then he turned on the second and silenced its front guns. He made three close circuits while his rear gunner shattered the enemy's wings and engines. Then, without a bullet left, he turned for home.

Daily Express WARTIME NET SALE

THE restriction in the return of unsold copies which was imposed by all newspapers in October has had its effect on net sales.

Some newspapers have suffered more than others.

THE DAILY EXPRESS SOLD 2,523,861 COPIES EVERY DAY THROUGHOUT OCTOBER.

The Daily Express, therefore, not only continues to have the world's largest daily net sale, but is now the only daily newspaper in Great Britain with a net sale in excess of 2,000,000 copies a day.

Auditors' Certificate

We have examined the books and accounts of the London Express Newspaper, Limited, and certify that the average net daily sale of the Daily Express at the recognised trade terms or published prices (as defined by and arriving at in accordance with the instructions of the Audit Bureau of Circulations Limited) during the month of October 1939 was 2,523,861 copies.

Deloitte, Plender, Griffith & Co., Chartered Accountants. November 6, 1939.

City of Flint to sail

NEW YORK, Wednesday.—United States Lines tonight radioed Captain Joseph Gainard, master of the City of Flint, now in Bergen, Norway, to sail back to New York with her holds empty.

It is presumed that her cargo, which includes tractors and leather, will be sold in Norway.

U.S. guns

...nesday. — The ... have placed an ...rth of machine ... Ordnance Cor-

—British United

BOSS IS ANGRY WITH E DAILY EXPRESS
—See Page Twelve

Planes over Belgium were not British

BRUSSELS, Wednesday. The Belgian Defence Ministry to-... of Belgian ... ad been proved ... hat the planes ... nor French. ... anes flew over ... it was added. ... photographs...

Nazis send Rumania oil shares soaring

BUCHAREST, Wednesday. — Oil shares in the Bucharest Stock Market opened 16 per cent. above yesterday's prices, after having doubled in price in the last fortnight—because of attempts by Germans to corner crude oil supplies.—British United Press.

Britain fixes trade pact with Bulgars

A trade payments agreement between Britain and Bulgaria was announced by the Foreign Office last night. The terms are set out in a series of Notes exchanged by Lord Halifax, Foreign Secretary, and the Bulgarian Minister in London, M. Momtchiloff.

Dominion celebrates 100 years as nation

WELLINGTON, Wednesday.—Lord Galway, Governor-General, today opened New Zealand's Centennial Exhibition at Wellington, celebrating the Dominion's first hundred years as a nation.—Reuter.

This is the POINT when I pause!

Modern wives who work with zest, during their mid-morning rest

— make a POINT of it

These are times when we all have to 'keep going.' A glass of White Point Wine gives a new start to the day just at those between times when breakfast seems a long way off and lunch isn't yet in sight.

2/6 A BOTTLE

White POINT

White Sweet Wine

WHY DO POINT BRAND WINES — COST ONLY 2/6 A BOTTLE?

PRODUCED AND BOTTLED BY VINE PRODUCTS LTD., KINGSTON, SURREY

◀ HITLER GIVES HIS SPEECH at the Bürgerbräukeller on November 8. While he was speaking the would-be assassin, Georg Elser, was arrested at the Swiss border by two German customs officials (he had tried to cross the border illegally). He was eventually interrogated and tortured by the Gestapo in Berlin, where he admitted to planting the bomb. He ended up in Dachau concentration camp, where he was shot on April 9, 1945.

◄ NEW YORK HERALD TRIBUNE, PARIS, MONDAY NOVEMBER 27, 1939

Published in Europe as well as in New York, the *Herald Tribune* was one of the leading international English language papers. As befits its reputation for authoritative reporting—some of its correspondents were highly esteemed—the *Tribune*'s front page carries thousands of words with no space wasted and no room for any kind of image. Among news of ships sunk and airplanes destroyed in Europe, two articles might have been particularly interesting to Americans overseas: the prediction of bumper Christmas shopping, and the news of a hike in income tax. The top tax rate rose to 75 percent later in the year; the cost of the war later drove it as high as 94 percent.

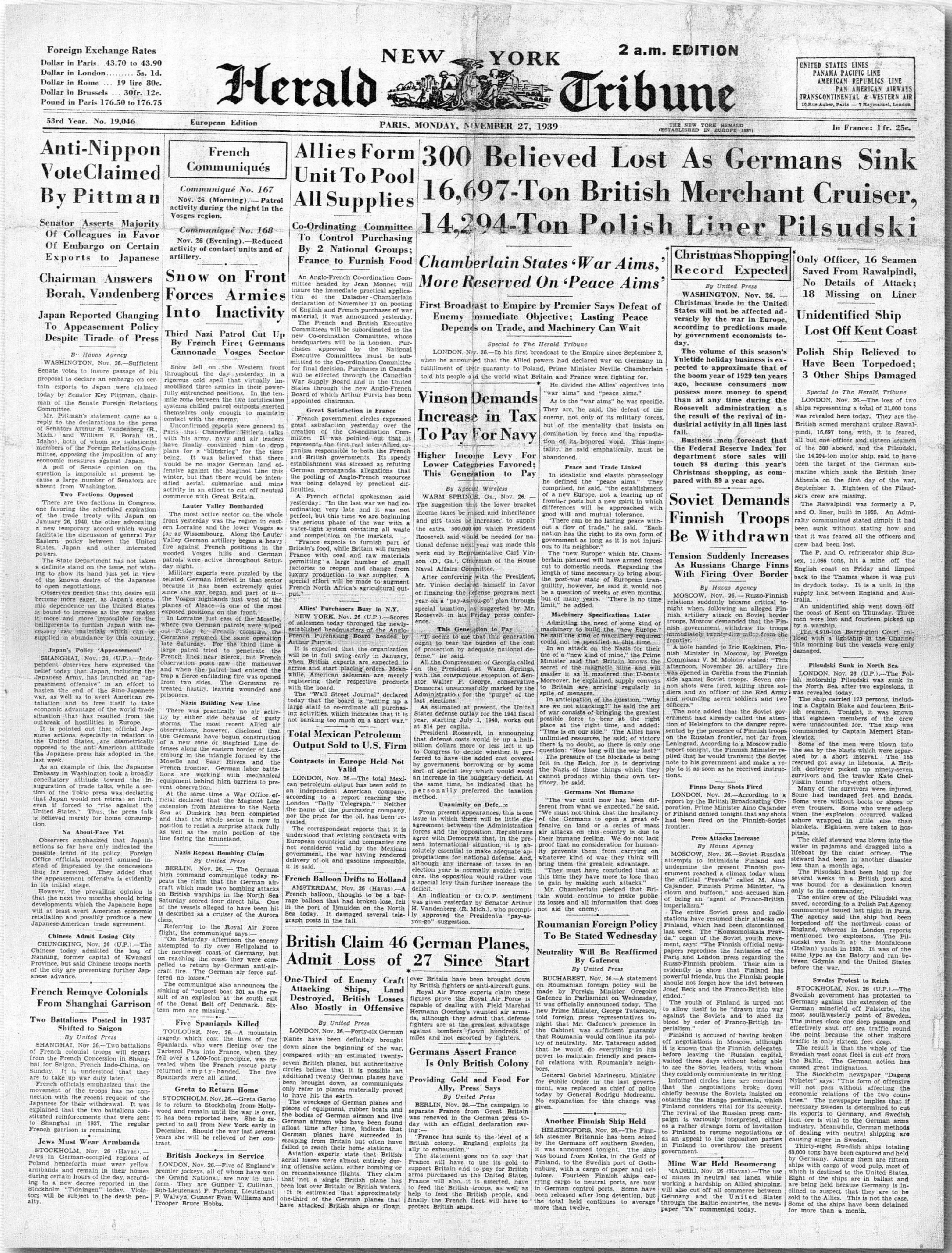

Foreign Exchange Rates

Dollar in Paris.. 43.70 to 43.90
Dollar in London........ 5s. 1d.
Dollar in Rome ... 19 lire 80c.
Dollar in Brussels ... 30fr. 12c.
Pound in Paris 176.50 to 176.75

NEW YORK
Herald Tribune

2 a.m. EDITION

UNITED STATES LINES
PANAMA PACIFIC LINE
AMERICAN REPUBLICS LINE
PAN AMERICAN AIRWAYS
TRANSCONTINENTAL & WESTERN AIR
10 Rue Auber, Paris — 7 Haymarket, London

53rd Year. No. 19,046   European Edition   PARIS, MONDAY, NOVEMBER 27, 1939   THE NEW YORK HERALD (ESTABLISHED IN EUROPE 1887)   In France: 1 fr. 25c.

Anti-Nippon Vote Claimed By Pittman

Senator Asserts Majority Of Colleagues in Favor Of Embargo on Certain Exports to Japanese

Chairman Answers Borah, Vandenberg

Japan Reported Changing To Appeasement Policy Despite Tirade of Press

By Havas Agency

WASHINGTON, Nov. 26.—Sufficient Senate votes to insure passage of his proposal to declare an embargo on certain exports to Japan were claimed today by Senator Key Pittman, chairman of the Senate Foreign Relations Committee.

Mr. Pittman's statement came as a reply to the opposition expressed as a reply to the contention of the press of Senators Arthur H. Vandenberg (R., Mich.) and William E. Borah (R., Idaho), both of whom are isolationist members of the Foreign Relations Committee, opposing the imposition of any economic measures against Japan.

A poll of Senate opinion on the question is impossible at present because a large number of Senators are absent from Washington.

Two Factions Opposed

There are two factions in Congress, one favoring the scheduled expiration of the trade treaty with Japan on January 26, 1940, the other advocating a new temporary accord which would facilitate the discussion of general Far Eastern policy between the United States, Japan and other interested powers.

The State Department has not taken a definite stand on the issue, not wishing to show its hand just yet in view of the known desire of Japan to open negotiations.

Observers predict that this desire will become more eager, as Japan's economic dependence on the United States is bound to increase as the war makes it more and more impossible for the belligerents to furnish Japan with the necessary raw materials which can be supplied in abundance in this country.

Japan's Policy 'Appeasement'

SHANGHAI, Nov. 26. (U.P.)—Independent observers here expressed the belief today that Japan, including the Japanese Army, has launched an "appeasement offensive" in an effort to hasten the end of the Sino-Japanese war, as well as to avert American retaliation and to free itself to take economic advantage of the world trade situation that has resulted from the outbreak of hostilities in Europe.

It is pointed out that Japanese actions, especially in relation to the United States, are diametrically opposed to the anti-American attitude the Japanese press has adopted in the last week.

As an example of this, the Japanese Embassy in Washington took a broadly conciliatory attitude toward the inauguration of trade talks, which is in action of the Tokio press was specifically that Japan would not retreat an inch, even if forced to "rise against the United States." Thus, the press talk is believed merely for home consumption.

No Change Yet

Observers emphasized that Japan's actions so far have only indicated the possible trend of its policy. Foreign Office officials appeared amused instead of impressed by the concessions thus far received. They added that the appeasement offensive is evidently in its initial stage.

However, the prevailing opinion is that the next two months should bring developments which the Japanese hope will at least avert American economic retaliation and possibly produce a new Japanese-American trade agreement.

Chinese Admit Losing City

CHUNGKING, Nov. 26 (U.P.)—The Chinese today admitted the loss of Nanning, former capital of Kwangsi Province, but said Chinese troops north of the city are preventing further Japanese advance.

French Remove Colonials From Shanghai Garrison

Two Battalions Posted in 1937 Shifted to Saigon

By United Press

SHANGHAI, Nov. 26.—Two battalions of French colonial troops will depart from the French Concession in Shanghai for Saigon, French Indo-China, on Sunday. It is understood that they are to take up war duty later.

French officials emphasized that the movement of the troops has no connection with the recent request of the Japanese for their withdrawal. It was explained that the two battalions constituted reinforcements that were sent to Shanghai in 1937. The regular French garrison is remaining.

Jews Must Wear Armbands

STOCKHOLM, Nov. 26 (Havas).—Jews in German-occupied regions of Poland henceforth must wear yellow armbands and remain in their homes during certain hours of the day, according to a new decree reported in the Stockholm "Tidningen" today. Violators will be subject to the death penalty.

French Communiqués

Communiqué No. 167
Nov. 26 (Morning).—Patrol activity during the night in the Vosges region.

Communiqué No. 168
Nov. 26 (Evening).—Reduced activity of contact units and of artillery.

Snow on Front Forces Armies Into Inactivity

Third Nazi Patrol Cut Up By French Fire; Germans Cannonade Vosges Sector

Snow fell on the Western front throughout the day yesterday in a rigorous cold spell that virtually immobilized three armies in their powerfully entrenched positions. In the jumble zone between the two fortification systems chilled patrol outposts exerted themselves only enough to maintain contact with the enemy.

Unconfirmed reports were general in Paris that Chancellor Hitler's talks with his army, navy and air leaders have finally convinced him—to drop plans for a "blitzkrieg" for the time being. It was believed that there would be no major German land offensive against the Maginot Line this winter, but that there would be intensified aerial, submarine and mine activity in an effort to cut off neutral commerce with Great Britain.

Lauter Valley Bombarded

The most active sector on the whole front yesterday was the French in eastern Lorraine and the lower Vosges as far as Wissembourg. Along the Lauter Valley German artillery began a heavy fire against French positions in the wooded Vosges hills and German patrols were active throughout Saturday night.

Military experts were puzzled by the belated German interest in this sector because it has been extremely quiet since the war began and part of it—the Vosges highlands just west of the plains of Alsace—is one of the most exposed positions on the front.

In Lorraine just east of the Moselle, where two German patrols were wiped out Friday by French cannonade, the Germans resumed the same operation last night. The bridge over the front is a large patrol tried to penetrate the French lines near Sierck, but French observation posts saw the manœuver and when the patrol had entered the trap a fierce enfilading fire was opened from two sides. The Germans retreated hastily, leaving wounded and prisoners.

Nazis Building New Line

There was practically no air activity by either side because of gusty storms. The most recent Allied air observations, however, disclosed that the Germans have begun construction of a new zone of Siegfried Line defenses along the eastern border of Luxembourg in the triangle formed by the Moselle and Saar Rivers and the French frontier. German labor battalions are working with mechanical equipment behind high barriers to prevent observation.

At the same time a War Office official declared that the Maginot Line extension from Mézières to the North Sea at Dunkirk has been completed and that the whole sector is now in position to resist a surprise attack fully as well as the main portion of the line facing the Rhineland.

Nazis Repeat Bombing Claim

By United Press

BERLIN, Nov. 26.—The German high command communiqué today repeats the claim that the German aircraft which made two bombing attacks on British warships in the North Sea Saturday scored four direct hits. One of the vessels alleged to have been hit is described as a cruiser of the Aurora class.

Referring to the Royal Air Force flight, the communiqué says:

"On Saturday afternoon the enemy attempted to fly over Heligoland to the northwest coast of Germany, but in reaching the coast they were compelled to return by German anti-aircraft fire. The German air force suffered no losses."

The communiqué also announces the sinking of "outpost boat 301 as the result of an explosion at the south exit of the Great Belt off Denmark. Sixteen men are missing."

French Balloon Drifts to Holland

AMSTERDAM, Nov. 26 (Havas).—A French balloon, thought to be a barrage balloon that had broken loose, fell in the port of IJmuiden on the North Sea today. It damaged several telegraph posts in the fall.

British Claim 46 German Planes, Admit Loss of 27 Since Start

One-Third of Enemy Craft Attacking Ships, Land Destroyed, British Losses Also Mostly in Offensive

By United Press

LONDON, Nov. 26.—Forty-six German planes have been definitely brought down since the beginning of the war, compared with an estimated twenty-seven British planes, but authoritative circles believe that it is possible an additional twenty German planes have been brought down, as communiqués only refer to planes materially proved to have hit—the early.

The wreckage of German planes and pieces of equipment, rubber boats and the bodies of German airmen and live German airmen who have been rescued afloat time after time, indicate that German planes have succeeded in escaping from British but often have failed to reach their home stations.

Aviation experts state that British aerial losses were almost entirely through offensive action, either bombing or reconnaissance flights. They claim that not a single British plane has been lost over Britain or by British raids. It is estimated that approximately one-third of the German planes that have attacked British ships or flown over Britain have been brought down by British fighters or anti-aircraft guns.

Royal Air Force experts claim these figures prove the Royal Air Force is more capable of dealing with Field Marshal Hermann Goering's vaunted air armada, although they admit that German fighters are at the greatest advantage against bombers flown hundreds of miles and not escorted by fighters.

Germans Assert France Is Only British Colony

Providing Gold and Food For Ally, Press Says

By United Press

BERLIN, Nov. 26.—The campaign to separate France from Great Britain was renewed in the German press today with an official declaration saying:—

"France has sunk to the level of a British colony. England exploits its ally to exhaustion."

The statement goes on to say that France will have to use its gold to support Britain and to pay for British arms purchased in the United States. France will also, it is asserted, have to feed the British troops, as well as help to feed the British people, and finally the French fleet will have to protect British ships.

Another Finnish Ship Held

HELSINGFORS, Nov. 26.—The Finnish steamer Britannic has been seized by the Germans off southern Sweden, it was announced tonight. The ship was bound from Kotka, in the Gulf of Finland, to the Swedish port of Gothenburg, with a cargo of wood cellulose. Fourteen Finnish ships carrying cargo to neutral ports, now in German control ports, have been released after long detention, but the total held continues to average more than twelve.

Allies Form Unit To Pool All Supplies

Co-Ordinating Committee To Control Purchasing By 2 National Groups; France to Furnish Food

An Anglo-French Co-ordination Committee was established today—application of the Daladier-Chamberlain declaration of November 17 on pooling of English and French purchases of war material, it was announced yesterday.

The French and British Executive Committees will be subordinated to the new Co-ordination Committee, whose headquarters will be in London. Purchases approved by the National Committee must be submitted to the Co-ordination Committee for final decision. Purchases in Canada will be effected through the Canadian War Supply Board and in the United States through the new Anglo-French Board of which Arthur Purvis has been appointed chairman.

Great Satisfaction in France

French government circles expressed great satisfaction yesterday over the creation of the Co-ordination Committee. It was pointed out that it represents the first real inter-Allied co-ordination... beginning...

A French official spokesman said yesterday: "In the last war we had no co-ordination very late and it was not perfect, but this time we are beginning the serious phase of the war with a water-tight system obviating all waste and competition on the markets.

"France expects to furnish part of Britain's food, while Britain will furnish France with coal and raw materials permitting a large number of small factories to reopen and change from luxury production to war supplies. A special effort will be made to augment French North Africa's agricultural output."

This Generation to Pay

"It seems to me that this generation ought to bear the burden of the cost of protection by adequate national defense," he said.

Total Mexican Petroleum Output Sold to U.S. Firm

Contracts in Europe Held Not Valid

LONDON, Nov. 26.—The total Mexican petroleum output has been sold to an independent American company, according to a report reaching the London "Daily Telegraph." Neither the name of the purchasing company, nor the price for the oil, has been revealed.

The correspondent reports that it is understood that existing contracts with European countries and companies are not considered valid by the Mexican government, the war having rendered delivery of oil and gasoline impossible, it is said.

Five Spaniards Killed

TOULOUSE, Nov. 26.—A mountain tragedy which cost the lives of five Spaniards, who were fleeing over the Tartérol Pass into France, when they fell over a 1,500-foot precipice, was revealed when the French rescue party returned empty-handed. The five Spaniards were all killed.

Greta to Return Home

STOCKHOLM, Nov. 26.—Greta Garbo is to return to Stockholm from Hollywood and remain until the war is over, it has been reported here. She is expected to sail from New York early in December. Should she sail last several years she will be relieved of her contract.

British Jockeys in Service

LONDON, Nov. 26.—Four of England's premier jockeys, all of whom have won the Grand National, are now in uniform. They are Gunner T. Cullinan, Sub-Lieutenant F. Furlong, Lieutenant F. Walwyn, Gunner Evan Williams and Trooper Bruce Hobbs.

---

300 Believed Lost As Germans Sink 16,697-Ton British Merchant Cruiser, 14,294-Ton Polish Liner Pilsudski

Chamberlain States 'War Aims,' More Reserved On 'Peace Aims'

First Broadcast to Empire by Premier Says Defeat of Enemy Immediate Objective; Lasting Peace Depends on Trade, and Machinery Can Wait

Special to The Herald Tribune

LONDON, Nov. 26.—In his first broadcast to the Empire since September 3, when he announced that the Allied powers had declared war on Germany in fulfillment of their guaranty to Poland, Prime Minister Neville Chamberlain told his people and the world what Britain and France were fighting for.

He divided the Allies' objectives into "war aims" and "peace aims."

As to the "war aims" he was specific. They are, he said, the defeat of the enemy, not only of its military forces, but of the mentality that insists on domination by force and the repudiation of its honored word. This mentality, he said emphatically, must be abandoned.

Peace and Trade Linked

In idealistic and elastic phraseology he defined the "peace aims." They comprised, he said, "the establishment of a new Europe, not a tearing up of frontier posts but a new spirit in which differences will be approached with good will and mutual tolerance.

"There can be no lasting peace without a flow of trade," he said. "Each nation has the right to its own form of government as long as it is not injurious to its neighbor."

"The 'new Europe' which Mr. Chamberlain pictured will have armed forces cut to domestic needs. Regarding the length of time necessary to bring about the post-war state of European tranquility, however, he said it would not be a question of weeks or even months, but of many years. 'There is no time limit,' he added.

Machinery Specifications Later

Admitting the need of some kind of machinery to build the 'new Europe,' he said the kind of machinery required could not be specified at this time.

Vinson Demands Increase in Tax To Pay For Navy

Higher Income Levy For Lower Categories Favored; This Generation to Pay

By Special Wireless

WARM SPRINGS, Ga., Nov. 26.—The suggestion that the lower bracket income taxes be raised and inheritance and gift taxes be increased to supply the $800,000,000 which President Roosevelt said would be needed for national defense next year was made this week and by Representative Carl Vinson (D., Ga.), Chairman of the House Naval Affairs Committee.

After conferring with the President, Mr. Vinson declared himself in favor of financing the defense program next year on a "pay-as-you-go" plan through special taxation, as suggested by Mr. Roosevelt in his Friday press conference.

President Roosevelt, in announcing that defense costs would be up a half-billion dollars more or less left it up to Congress to decide whether it preferred to have the added cost covered by government borrowing or by some sort of special levy which would avoid an increase in the budgetary deficit. At the same time, he indicated that he personally preferred the taxation method.

Unanimity on Defense

From present appearances, this is one issue in which there will be little disagreement between the Administration forces and the opposition, Republicans agree with Democrats that, in the present international situation, it is absolutely essential to have America carrying on whatever kind of war they think will bring them the greatest advantage.

"They must have concluded that at this time they have more to lose than to gain by making such attacks."

Mr. Chamberlain pledged that Britain would continue to make public its losses and all information that does not aid the enemy.

Christmas Shopping Record Expected

By United Press

WASHINGTON, Nov. 26.—Christmas trade in the United States will not be affected adversely by the war in Europe, according to predictions made by government economists today.

The volume of this season's Yuletide holiday business is expected to approximate that of the boom year of 1929 ten years ago, because consumers now possess more money to spend than at any time during the Roosevelt administration as a result of the revival of industrial activity in all lines last fall.

Business men forecast that the Federal Reserve Index for department store sales will touch 98 during this year's Christmas shopping, as compared with 89 a year ago.

Soviet Demands Finnish Troops Be Withdrawn

Tension Suddenly Increases As Russians Charge Finns With Firing Over Border

By Havas Agency

MOSCOW, Nov. 26.—Russo-Finnish relations suddenly became critical tonight when, following an alleged Finnish artillery attack on Soviet border troops, Moscow demanded that the Finnish government withdraw its troops immediately twenty-five miles from the frontier.

A note handed to Iric Koskinen, Finnish Minister in Moscow, by Foreign Commissar V. M. Molotov stated: "This afternoon, November 26, artillery fire was opened in Carelia from the Finnish side against Soviet troops. Seven cannon shots were fired, killing three soldiers and an officer of the Red Army and wounding seven soldiers and two officers."

The note added that the Soviet government had already called the attention of Helsingfors to the danger represented by the presence of Finnish troops on the Russian frontier, not far from Leningrad. According to a Moscow radio report tonight, the Finnish Minister replied that he would transmit the Soviet note to his government and make a reply to it as soon as he received instructions.

Finns Deny Shots Fired

LONDON, Nov. 26.—According to a report by the British Broadcasting Corporation, Prime Minister Aimo Cajander of Finland denied tonight that any shots had been fired on the Finnish-Soviet frontier.

Press Attacks Increase

By Havas Agency

MOSCOW, Nov. 26.—Soviet Russia's attempts to intimidate Finland and undermine the present Finnish government reached a climax today when the official "Pravda" called M. Aino Cajander, Finnish Prime Minister, "a clown and buffoon," and accused him of being an "agent of Franco-British imperialism."

The entire Soviet press and radio stations have resumed their attacks on Finland, which had been discontinued last week. The "Komsomolskaia Pravda," organ of the Soviet youth movement, says: "The Finnish official newspapers reproduce the fantasies of the Paris and London press regarding the Russo-Finnish problem. Their aim is evidently to show that Finland has powerful friends, but the Finnish people should not forget how the idyll between Josef Beck and the Franco-British bloc ended."

Roumanian Foreign Policy To Be Stated Wednesday

Neutrality Will Be Reaffirmed

By Gafencu

BUCHAREST, Nov. 26.—A statement on Roumanian foreign policy will be made by Foreign Minister Gregoire Gafencu in Parliament on Wednesday, it was officially announced today. The new Prime Minister, George Tatarescu, told foreign press representatives tonight that Mr. Gafencu's presence in the Cabinet was sufficient guaranty that Roumania would continue its policy of neutrality. Mr. Tatarescu added that he would do everything in his power to maintain friendly and peaceful relations with Roumania's neighbors.

General Gabriel Marinescu, Minister for Public Order in the last government, was replaced as chief of police today by General Rodrigu Modreanu. No explanation for this change was given.

Mine War Held Boomerang

MADRID, Nov. 26 (Havas).—The use of mines in neutral sea lanes, while working a hardship on Allied shipping, will also cut off all commerce between Germany and the United States through the Baltic countries, the newspaper "Ya" commented today.

Only Officer, 16 Seamen Saved From Rawalpindi, No Details of Attack; 18 Missing on Liner

Unidentified Ship Lost Off Kent Coast

Polish Ship Believed to Have Been Torpedoed; 3 Other Ships Damaged

Special to The Herald Tribune

LONDON, Nov. 26.—The loss of two ships representing a total of 31,000 tons was revealed here today. They are the British armed merchant cruiser Rawalpindi, 16,697 tons, with it is feared, all but one officer and sixteen seamen of the 300 aboard, and the Pilsudski, the 14,294-ton motor ship, said to have been the target of the German submarine which sank the British liner Athenia on the first day of the war, September 3. Eighteen of the Pilsudski's crew are missing.

The Rawalpindi was formerly a P. and O. liner, built in 1925. An Admiralty communiqué stated simply it had been sunk without stating how and that it was feared all the officers and crew had been lost.

The P. and O. refrigerator ship Sussex, 11,066 tons, hit a mine off the English coast on Friday and limped back to the Thames where it was put in drydock today. It is a unit in the supply link between England and Australia.

An unidentified ship went down off the coast of Kent on Thursday. Three men were lost and fourteen picked up by a warship.

The 4,919-ton Barrington Court collided with a lightship in the Channel this morning but the vessels were only slightly damaged.

Pilsudski Sunk in North Sea

LONDON, Nov. 26.—The Polish motorship Pilsudski was sunk in the North Sea after two explosions, it was revealed today.

The ship carried 173 persons, including a Captain Blake and fourteen British seamen. Tonight, it was known that eighteen members of the crew were unaccounted for. The ship was commanded by Captain Memert Stankiewicz.

Some of the men were blown into the sea by the blasts which were separated by a short interval. The 165 rescued got away in lifeboats. A British destroyer picked up ninety-seven survivors and the trawler Kate Chelyukin found fifty-eight others.

Many of the survivors were injured. Some had bandaged feet and hands. Some were without boots or shoes or even trousers. Some who were asleep when the explosion occurred walked ashore wrapped in little else than blankets. Eighteen were taken to hospitals.

The chief steward was blown into the water in pajamas and dragged into a lifeboat by the chief officer. The steward had been in another disaster less than a month ago.

The Pilsudski had been laid up for several weeks in a British port and was bound for a destination known only to its commander.

The entire crew of the Pilsudski was saved, according to a Polish Pat Agency communiqué issued last night in Paris. The agency said the ship had been torpedoed off the northwest coast of England, whereas in London reports mentioned two explosions. The Pilsudski was built at the Monfalcone (Italian) yards in 1935. It was of the same type as the Batory and ran between Gdynia and the United States before the war.

Swedes Protest to Reich

STOCKHOLM, Nov. 26 (U.P.)—The Swedish government has protested to Germany against the extension of the German minefield off Falsterbo, the most southwesterly point of Sweden. The mines close one deep passage and effectively shut off sea traffic round the point because the other inshore traffic is only sixteen feet deep.

The result is that the whole of the Swedish west coast is cut off from the Baltic. The German action has caused great indignation.

The Stockholm newspaper "Dagens Nyheter" says: "This form of offensive will not pass without affecting the economic relations of the two countries." The newspaper implies that if necessary Sweden is determined to cut its exports to Germany, and Swedish iron ore is vital to the German arms industry. Meanwhile, German methods of dealing with neutral shipping are causing anger in Sweden.

Thirty-eight Swedish ships totaling 65,000 tons have been captured and held by Germany. Among them are fifteen ships with cargo of wood pulp, most of which is destined to the United States. Eight of the ships are in ballast and are being held because Germany is inclined to suspect that they are to be sold to the Allies. This is not the case. Some of the ships have been detained for more than a month.

◄ FINNISH SOLDIERS EXAMINE SOVIET DEAD during the Winter War between Russia and Finland. Under the terms of the Nazi–Soviet Nonaggression Treaty Finland was designated a Soviet sphere of influence. Russian dictator Stalin demanded Finnish islands in the Gulf of Finland be ceded to the USSR. The Finns refused, so Stalin launched an offensive with 600,000 troops. The small, though well-trained, Finnish Army resisted fiercely and halted the Red Army.

◄ MANCHESTER EVENING NEWS, THURSDAY NOVEMBER 30, 1939

One of Britain's leading provincial newspapers makes clear where its sympathies lie in regard to the Soviet invasion of Finland, as it contrasts the 30,000 defenders with Russia's potential 15 million invaders. Even though the Soviets remained potential allies in the struggle against Hitler, the British public was squarely on the Finns' side. The papers presented each Finnish victory as a cause for celebration. Elsewhere, the paper turns its attention to the Japanese and to the conviction of American Nazi leader Fritz Kuhn for embezzlement at the instigation of New York mayor, Fiorello de la Guardia. Kuhn was later imprisoned as an enemy agent. In pride of place at the center of the page is an intensely personal story about one family's sacrifice for the country, guaranteed to bring a lump to the throat of *Evening News* readers.

FINN ATTACKS SURPRISE FOE

Vol. 19. No. 34   New York, Sunday. December 3, 1939★   108 Main+4 Manhattan+16 Comic+32 Coloroto Pages

Story on Page 3

(NEWS foto)

Finn Barricade ↑

Behind splintered wood. thrown up for defense, Finnish riflemen await Soviet troops. Finns, showing surprising strength, reported victories over Russians yesterday.
—*Story on page 3; other pictures on page 54.*

← Death Tightrope

Howard Meyers, 19, stands on 33,000-volt line in Laurelton, Queens. where he crawled, crying that he would jump if police didn't let him alone. Alongside is Patrolman John Albert, who is trying to cajole would-be suicide back. Finally, when told how good a cigaret would taste, youth relaxed momentarily—and Albert grabbed him. Power was turned off during 2½-hour siege, nets (shown) were set up, trains re-routed and halted.
—*Story page 10; other pictures page 54.*

▲ SUNDAY NEWS, NEW YORK, SUNDAY DECEMBER 3, 1939

Newspapers were transformed by the development of smaller, quicker, and more reliable cameras and improved reproduction techniques that emerged during the 1930s. Publications such as the *Sunday News* exploited the possibilities by pairing dramatic images and headlines, paving the way for the modern tabloid. Here, the Finns' resistance to the Soviets is too important to leave out but it plays second fiddle to a remarkable image that turns a minor local episode into front-page news.

The River Plate

DECEMBER 1939

IN ADDITION TO ITS FLEET OF U-BOATS, GERMANY ALSO POSSESSED A NUMBER OF SURFACE RAIDER VESSELS. THE MOST POTENT WERE THE "POCKET BATTLESHIPS," WHICH WERE FAST AND WELL ARMED SHIPS. There were three such ships: *Admiral Graf Spee*, *Admiral Scheer*, and *Grossdeutschland*. In the fall of 1939, the *Admiral Graf Spee* operated in the South Atlantic and in the period up to November she sank or captured nine British vessels.

THE BATTLE OF THE RIVER PLATE

On December 13, 1939, three British vessels, the heavy cruiser *Exeter* and the light cruisers HMS *Ajax* and HMS *Achilles*, commanded by Commodore Harwood, brought the *Admiral Graf Spee* to battle off the coast of Uruguay, at the mouth of the River Plate. The British ships attacked, but in a little more than an hour the *Admiral Graf Spee* had damaged the *Exeter* (which received the full force of the German ship's two 11-inch turrets) and driven off the other two cruisers. In the encounter the *Graf Spee* was damaged and so withdrew into Montevideo harbor for repairs. Its commander, Captain Hans Langsdorff, obtained permission to stay for four days to repair damage. The British, meanwhile, deceived the Germans into believing a large task force had been assembled off Montevideo. Wrongly believing that a major British force had actually been assembled, Langsdorff scuttled his ship rather than face another battle with the Royal Navy. Three days later Langsdorff shot himself. The Battle of the River Plate greatly boosted British prestige and morale, but at considerable cost: The badly injured *Exeter* was out of the war for 15 months.

▲ THE POCKET BATTLESHIP *ADMIRAL GRAF SPEE* was launched in June 1934. The ship's main armament consisted of six 11-inch guns, eight 9-inch guns, and six 3.5-inch guns.

THE DAILY MAIL, Wednesday, December 20, 1939.

Daily Mail

FOR KING AND EMPIRE

NO. 13,621   ★★   WEDNESDAY, DECEMBER 20, 1939   ONE PENNY

GERMANS SCUTTLE 32,000-TONS LINER

INGLORIOUS END . . . Now Nazi Liner Follows Suit

Excess Arms Profits

TREASURY suspicion that machine - tool makers engaged in the national defence programme were making excessive profits has been met by a blank refusal of firms concerned to submit their books to costing.

This was disclosed last night in a report of evidence given before the Select Committee on Estimates by Sir Alan Barlow, Treasury Under-Secretary.

Asked if the sum involved was large, he replied: "Yes, it is pretty considerable."

Sir Alan named a material of which, is used in very large quantities for the manufacture of aircraft. There are about four firms concerned."

Full story—Page TWO.

LATEST NEWS

British Cruiser Was Waiting

"NO GUNFIRE"

From Daily Mail Correspondent
NEW YORK, Tuesday.

GERMANY'S third largest liner, the Columbus (32,581 tons), to-night followed the example of the pocket battleship Admiral Graf Spee by scuttling herself 300 miles off Cape Henry, Virginia.

British cruisers had pursued her and were closing in for capture, according to Rear-Admiral Joseph Taussig, of the United States cruiser Tuscaloosa, in a radio report to the Neutrality Patrol here.

Though believed to be armed, the Columbus, unlike Britain's Rawalpindi, refused to fight, preferring self-destruction.

Rear-Admiral Taussig reported that he was picking up the crew of the liner and would bring them into port.

The Columbus is believed to have been a supply ship for U-boats and German surface raiders.

She left Vera Cruz, Mexico, last Thursday carrying a cargo of food and oil. She was then reported to be making her way to the Norwegian port of Bergen.

All to-day she had been creeping up the American coast closely pursued by British warships.

The October Revolution.
"Sunk," say the Finns.

"Blow after Blow"

The sinking was announced at the White House by Mr. Stephen Early, President Roosevelt's secretary.

He stressed that apparently no action had been fought, but added that a British warship was nearby when the Tuscaloosa approached to pick up the liner's crew.

The only German liners bigger than the Columbus are the Bremen, which was recently allowed to escape by a British submarine, and the Europa. All three belong to the North German Lloyd Line.

Officials of the line in New York appeared stunned by the news of the scuttling. "O, heavens," exclaimed Mr. John Schroeder, the manager, "it's just one blow after another."

Since the outbreak of war the Germans have scuttled 23 passenger and cargo vessels. Total tonnage lost to the enemy by this method amounts to 139,497.

Nineteen ships totalling 88,218 tons have been captured by the British and French Navies.

Shore Guns Sink Red Battleship

Helsinki, Tuesday.

FINNISH coastal batteries at Koivisto, on the Karelian Isthmus, have sunk the 23,256-tons Russian battleship Oktiabrskaya-Revolutia (October Revolution), according to an unconfirmed report received here to-day.

The report states that the Russians knew the range of the Koivisto batteries to be only three miles.

The Finns, however, brought up much heavier and better artillery, and when the battleship was cruising slightly less than four miles off shore they opened-up with a terrific salvo which found its mark.

The Oktiabrskaya-Revolutia has a complement of 1,125 officers and men, and mounts twelve 12in. guns.

Port on Fire

Big fires are burning to-night in the port of Aabo, on the Gulf of Bothnia, following the first serious air raids on Finnish towns since the early days of the war.

Bombs also fell on Helsinki and Viborg, at the western end of the Mannerheim Line, but caused little damage.

Four times in three hours the raiders appeared over Aabo. At 11.36 a.m. ten 'planes dropped bombs on workers' homes. Four wooden houses were set on fire. The flames rapidly spread.

The next alarm was at 12.42 p.m., but this time bombs did not fall. Less than an hour later a new attack set fire to houses near the hospital.

The last raid, at 2.35 p.m., was the worst. The front of a three-story building was blown out and more fires were started.

One Russian 'plane is reported to have been shot down.

A Town of Wood

Aabo, one of Finland's gateways to Scandinavia, is largely made up of wooden buildings. It has been burned many times during its history, the last occasion being in 1827. Normally there is a population of about 80,000, but most of these have been evacuated.

Only four bombers penetrated the dense curtain of anti-aircraft fire around Helsinki, and their bombs fell harmlessly in the suburbs.

The main streets were crowded with Christmas shoppers when the sirens began to wail. People ran for the public shelters and crowded into the basements of the big stores.

The number of raiders are estimated variously at between eight and 19. Two machines are reported to have been brought down.

Nine bombers raided Viborg, two being shot down.—B.U.P., Reuter, and Exchange.

GUN STILL IN POSITION
COLLAPSING MAST & FUNNEL
GUNS GONE FROM AFT TURRET
STERN UNDER WATER

HISTORY will make use of this vivid picture, which gives so dramatically the last moments of the German pocket battleship Graf Spee of Montevideo. Broken by the explosives that scuttled her and ablaze from stem to stern, she settles down, soon to leave only her top superstructure and a cloud of black smoke to mark her "inglorious end." Inset: The 32,000-tons liner Columbus, scuttled off the Virginia coast last night.

R.A.F. Rout Nazi "Super-planes"

TWENTY-ONE German raiders—that is, nearly half the number taking part—have been destroyed by the R.A.F. in fights over Britain and over British waters during the past two months.

Not a single British fighter has been shot down over Britain since the war began.

The 21 German 'planes were brought down in 51 air battles. Thirteen of them were seen by the defenders to strike the ground or water.

An this is the debit side of the R.A.F.'s balance-sheet : in all these combats only ONE British pilot has been wounded—and that only slightly.

The Air Ministry stated last night that more than 12 Messerschmitts are believed to have been brought down in Monday's great air battle over the Heligoland Bight.

One R.A.F. bomber alone accounted for five of them.

Forty Attacks Claimed

At least six of the German 'planes were of the new M.E. 110 type. These the Nazis call their new "destroyer type," and throughout yesterday they were broadcasting fantastic stories of their success.

They claimed that 36 British bombers were brought down in the battle, in which the German fighters launched about 40 separate attacks.

The Air Ministry's dry comment on the R.A.F.'s "36 losses" is: "The total number of British aircraft did not amount to anything like that figure."

Our losses, as already announced, amounted to seven 'planes.

The M.E.110 was paraded with pride before Hitler just previous to the Munich crisis. It was said to have a speed of 379 m.p.h.

Its development was known to the British authorities. The Nazi claims for it were doubted—and the doubt now seems justified.

"Swarm of Flies"

Details of the battle were given last night by the leader of the British formation.

"I could see them collecting like flies waiting to attack us," he said.

Between Heligoland and Wilhelmshaven 25 Messerschmitts were seen.

The bomber that shot down Nazis was cut off from the others while making for home. It seemed to be easy prey, and the Messerschmitts attacked it in force.

The pilot, in an effort to avoid them,

Turn to BACK Page

MORE FOOD THIS WEEK

EXTRA supplies of butter, bacon, and meat have been released by the Ministry of Food so that the shops will have plenty for Christmas.

"We have a large amount of food stored away in case of accidents," a Ministry official said last night, "and are letting the shops have some of it this week.

"As well as their Christmas supplies people will be able to buy for the two days next week when the shops will be closed."

Part of the extra food is to meet the demand caused by men of the Forces home on leave.

CZECH EX-OFFICERS ARRESTED

Prague, Tuesday.

Fifty Czechs have been arrested during the past few days, it is reported in Prague.

About ten are stated to be former officers of the Czech Army, who are alleged to have been implicated in espionage against Germany.—B.U.P.

ERIC FOGG KILLED BY TRAIN

By Daily Mail Reporter

ERIC FOGG, formerly "Uncle Eric" of the B.B.C.'s Northern Children's Hour, musical director for the five years before war broke out of the B.B.C.'s Empire Service, fell under a Tube train at Waterloo Station and was killed yesterday.

Eric Fogg, composer, conductor, and a man "scared stiff" of the black-out, was 36. He was married to Kathleen Mowhouse, the cellist.

Since war began he had been barred from Manchester conducting B.B.C. concerts, but on Monday he left "trembling with nerves," and travelled to London on his way to Bournemouth.

Miss Elvidge, managers of the Manchester hotel where he had been staying, said to me last night: "He was the loneliest man I've ever known. He had hundreds of friends, but he seemed to be so wrapped up in his troubles.

"Lately he had been terribly depressed—the war, his different job, losing his London friends, and most of all the black-out.

"He would go out at night for a short walk round the block and creep along holding the walls all the way, not daring to cross the road. He would tell me how frightened he was of the dark, and I used to say, 'Don't be such a woman.'

"He was a man who needed somebody to protect him from the war thoughts."

Eric Fogg was a boy chorister at Manchester Cathedral and studied under Sir Granville Bantock.

At 14 he became organist at St. John's Church, Deansgate, Manchester.

He joined the B.B.C. in Manchester in 1924.

Mr. Greenwood in Car Smash

Mr. Arthur Greenwood, deputy-Leader of the Opposition, was in a car crash at Chipping Norton, Oxfordshire, yesterday, but was unhurt.

He was driving with his wife to Wales for a three weeks' rest cure.

Their car cam. into collision with two motor-vans. The car and one van were badly damaged, but no one was seriously hurt.

Last night Mr. Greenwood told a reporter that neither he, his wife, nor the driver of the car felt any ill effects. They will continue their journey today in another car.

Mr. Greenwood, who is 60, led the Labour Party for four months last summer while Mr. Attlee was ill.

Port on Fire

"THE Order of the Silver Scuttle."—see Illingworth cartoon, Page SIX.

THE KING HONOURS 'MINE' MEN

THE King, at Portsmouth yesterday pinned decorations on the tunics of five men who are known in Portsmouth as the "Suicide Squad." They are the members of the anti-mine squad who volunteered to tackle the first stranded German mine. It had been dropped in darkness.

Working in mud the five succeeded in rendering it harmless. With them as they worked was a civilian, Dr. A. B. Wood, mines expert at H.M.S. Vernon, the Portsmouth Torpedo and Mines School.

The awards were :

Distinguished Service Order
Lieut.-Commander J. G. D. Ouvry.
Lieut.-Commander Roger Lewis.

Distinguished Service Cross
Lieut. John Glenay.

Distinguished Service Medal
Chief Petty - Officer Charles Baldwin.
A.B. Archibald Vearncombe.

They are the first naval men to be decorated by the King during the war.

Later in the sheds of H.M.S. Vernon the King, accompanied by Lieut.-Commander Ouvry and Lieut.-Commander Lewis, inspected the mines, asking many questions.

Lieut.-Commander Ouvry was married in 1928 at Melbourne to Miss Lorna Evison, of Coulsdon, Surrey. His home is near Portsmouth.

Film Chief Resigns from M. of I.

Sir Joseph Ball, director of the Conservative research department, has asked to be released from the position of director of the film department at the Ministry of Information on account of the pressure of other work.

Sir Kenneth Clark, director of the National Gallery, has been appointed in his place.

NAZIS MACHINE-GUN MORE SHIPS

NAZI pilots, fearing the R.A.F., are continuing their "hit-and-run" attacks on unarmed ships at sea.

Eight more attacks were reported yesterday. Three more ships have been sunk (one by a mine after an air attack had failed), and six British seamen have lost their lives.

Stories of the attacks show clearly the ruthlessness of the new Nazi tactics.

The **Etruria**, 373-tons Grimsby trawler, reached port yesterday. Three of her crew were killed and one injured in an attack by two Nazi 'planes in the North Sea fishing fleet.

Fifteen bombs were dropped. Most of them missed. Then one smashed through the deck and blew a hole in her side.

Although another vessel later offered to take off the crew, they stayed on the damaged ship and got her to port.

The **Active**, 185-tons Aberdeen

trawler, was fishing about a quarter of a mile away from the Etruria.

Skipper D. Sutherland said yesterday that seven bombs were dropped.

The crew began to take to their boat. It .was then that one of the 'planes fired an aerial torpedo, which exploded under the Active and sank her.

The cook, George Watt, and a deck-hand, who had already got into the boat, were hurled into the sea, and Watt disappeared.

The Active sank in a few minutes. The crew managed to get into the boat, which was still afloat.

Two Grimsby trawlers, the 202-tons **Iranian** and the 211-tons **Virginian**, reported when they returned to port yesterday that three German 'planes had flown low, bombed and machine-gunned them on Monday.

The **City of Koke**, 4,373-tons Eller-

man steamer, of Liverpool, was similarly attacked on Sunday.

Yesterday, while her crew were still congratulating themselves on their escape from injury, she was sunk either by a mine or a torpedo.

Eighteen of her crew of 68 were landed yesterday. They said they believed the rest had been picked up.

The **Astros**, 275-tons trawler, of Granton, was attacked yesterday by Nazi planes.

Then, when the crew tried to launch their lifeboat, they were fired on until they sought safety below.

Eventually they were allowed to launch the boat.

And, when darkness fell, the crew of the Astros rowed back. The ship was not sunk. They boarded her, got her to port—and saved their catch.

The **Zelos**, 224-tons, of Granton.

Turn to BACK Page

▲ DAILY MAIL, LONDON, WEDNESDAY DECEMBER 20, 1939

Somewhat confusingly, the *Mail* prints a photograph of the scuttled *Graf Spee* three days earlier, next to a story about the similar fate of the liner *Columbus*. At home in the United Kingdom, the strain of the war is beginning to tell, despite the announcement of increased rations for Christmas. There are early charges of profiteering, the resignation of a war official, and the poignant story of a radio presenter driven to suicide by fear of the blackout.

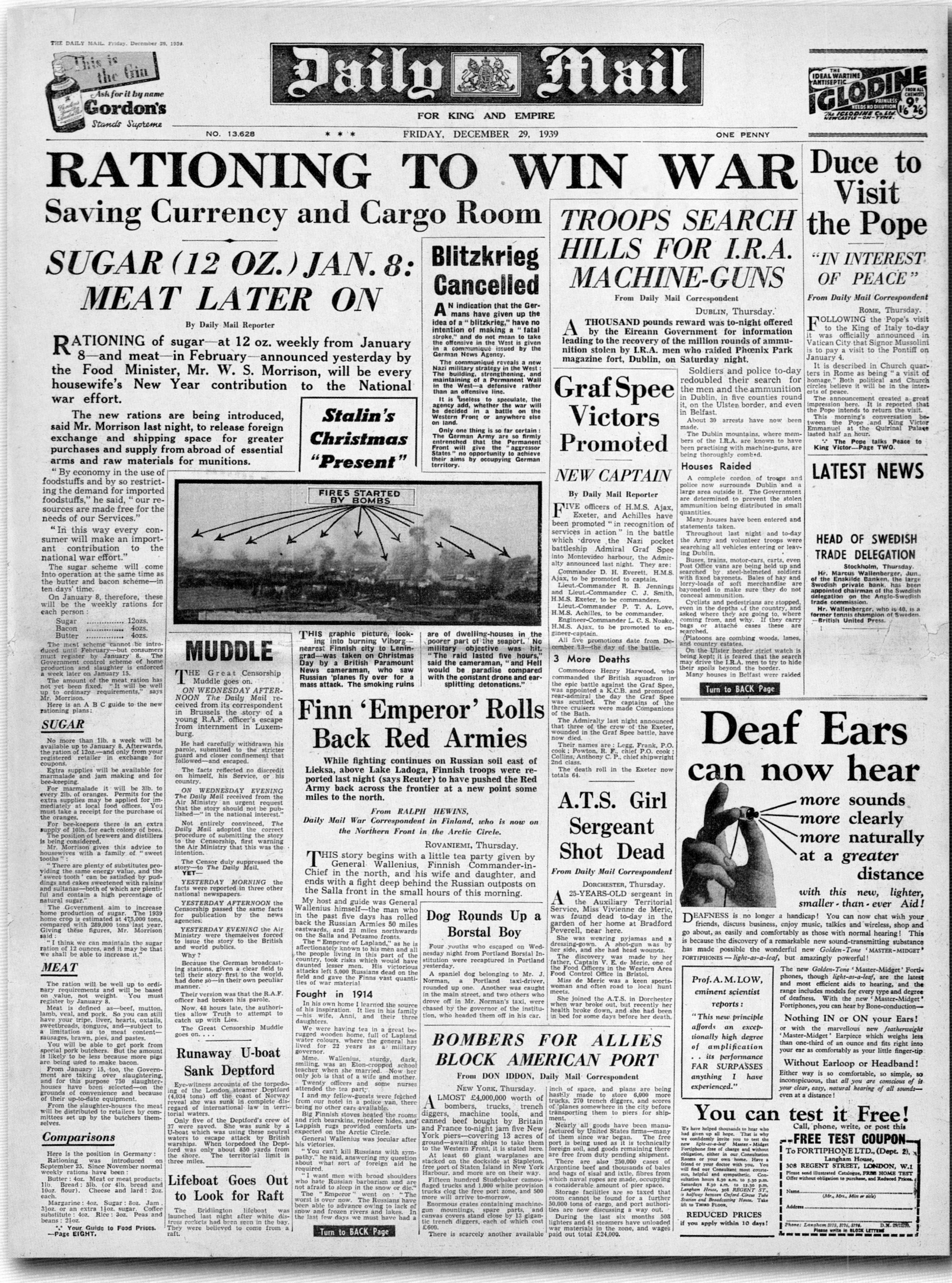

THE DAILY MAIL. Friday, December 29, 1939.

This is the Gin
Ask for it by name
Gordon's
Stands Supreme

Daily Mail

FOR KING AND EMPIRE

THE IDEAL WARTIME ANTISEPTIC
IGLODINE
PAINLESS
NEEDS NO DILUTION
FROM ALL CHEMISTS 9d 1/6 2/6
The IGLODINE Co. Ltd. NEWCASTLE-ON-TYNE.

NO. 13,628 * * * FRIDAY, DECEMBER 29, 1939 ONE PENNY

RATIONING TO WIN WAR

Saving Currency and Cargo Room

SUGAR (12 OZ.) JAN. 8: MEAT LATER ON

By Daily Mail Reporter

RATIONING of sugar—at 12 oz. weekly from January 8—and meat—in February—announced yesterday by the Food Minister, Mr. W. S. Morrison, will be every housewife's New Year contribution to the National war effort.

The new rations are being introduced, said Mr. Morrison last night, to release foreign exchange and shipping space for greater purchases and supply from abroad of essential arms and raw materials for munitions.

"By economy in the use of foodstuffs and by so restricting the demand for imported foodstuffs," he said, "our resources are made free for the needs of our Services."

"In this way every consumer will make an important contribution to the national war effort."

The sugar scheme will come into operation at the same time as the butter and bacon scheme—in ten days' time.

On January 8, therefore, these will be the weekly rations for each person:

Sugar .... 12ozs.
Bacon .... 4ozs.
Butter .... 4ozs.

The meat scheme cannot be introduced until February—but consumers must register by January 8. The Government control scheme of home production and slaughter is enforced a week later on January 15.

The amount of the meat ration has not yet been fixed. "It will be well up to ordinary requirements," says Mr. Morrison.

Here is an A B C guide to the new rationing plans:

SUGAR

No more than 1lb. a week will be available up to January 8. Afterwards, the ration of 12oz.—and only from your registered retailer in exchange for coupons.

Extra supplies will be available for marmalade and jam making and for bee-keeping.

For marmalade it will be 3lb. to every 2lb. of oranges. Permits for the extra supplies may be applied for immediately at local food offices. You must take a receipt for the purchase of the oranges.

For bee-keepers there is an extra supply of 10lb. for each colony of bees.

The position of brewers and distillers is being considered.

Mr. Morrison gives this advice to housewives with a family of "sweet tooths":

"There are plenty of substitutes providing the same energy value, and the 'sweet tooth' can be satisfied by puddings and cakes sweetened with raisins and sultanas—both of which are plentiful and contain a high percentage of natural sugar."

The Government aim to increase home production of sugar. The 1939 home crop is estimated at 475,000 tons, compared with 289,000 tons last year. Giving these figures, Mr. Morrison said:

"I think we can maintain the sugar ration of 12 ounces, and it may be that we shall be able to increase it."

MEAT

The ration will be well up to ordinary requirements and will be based on value, not weight. You must register by January 8.

Meat is defined as—beef, mutton, lamb, veal, and pork. So you can still have your tripe, liver, hearts, oxtails, sweetbreads, tongues, and—subject to a limitation as to meat content—sausages, brawn, pies, and pastes.

You will be able to get pork from special pork butchers. But the amount is likely to be less because more pigs are being used to make bacon.

From January 15, too, the Government are taking over slaughtering, and for this purpose 750 slaughter-houses have been selected—on the grounds of convenience and because of their up-to-date equipment.

From the slaughter-houses the meat will be distributed to retailers by committees set up by the butchers themselves.

Comparisons

Here is the position in Germany:

Rationing was introduced on September 25. Since November normal weekly rations have been:

Butter: 4oz. Meat or meat products: 1lb. Bread: 5lb. (or 4lb. bread and 10oz. flour). Cheese and lard: 2oz. each.

Margarine: 4oz. Sugar: 8oz. Jam: 3½oz. or an extra 1¼oz. sugar. Coffee substitute: 4oz. Rice: 3oz. Peas and beans: 2½oz.

∴ Your Guide to Food Prices.—Page EIGHT.

Blitzkrieg Cancelled

AN indication that the Germans have given up the idea of a "blitzkrieg," have no intention of making a "fatal stroke," and do not mean to take the offensive in the West is given in a communiqué issued by the German News Agency.

The communiqué reveals a new Nazi military strategy in the West: The building, strengthening, and maintaining of a Permanent Wall in the West—a defensive rather than an offensive line.

It is useless to speculate, the agency add, whether the war will be decided in a battle on the Western Front or anywhere else on land.

Only one thing is so far certain: The German Army are so firmly entrenched that the Permanent Front will give the "aggressor States" no opportunity to achieve their aims by occupying German territory.

Stalin's Christmas "Present"

FIRES STARTED BY BOMBS

THIS graphic picture, looking into burning Viborg—nearest Finnish city to Leningrad—was taken on Christmas Day by a British Paramount News cameraman, who saw Russian 'planes fly over for a mass attack. The smoking ruins are of dwelling-houses in the poorer part of the seaport. No military objective was hit. "The raid lasted five hours," said the cameraman, "and Hell would be paradise compared with the constant drone and ear-splitting detonations."

MUDDLE

THE Great Censorship Muddle goes on.

ON WEDNESDAY AFTERNOON The Daily Mail received from its correspondent in Brussels the story of a young R.A.F. officer's escape from internment in Luxemburg.

He had carefully withdrawn his parole, submitted to the stricter guard and closer confinement that followed—and escaped.

The facts reflected no discredit on himself, his Service, or his country.

ON WEDNESDAY EVENING The Daily Mail received from the Air Ministry an urgent request that the story should not be published—"in the national interest."

Not entirely convinced, *The Daily Mail* adopted the correct procedure of submitting the story to the Censorship, first warning the Air Ministry that this was the intention.

The Censor duly suppressed the story—to *The Daily Mail*.

YET—

YESTERDAY MORNING the facts were reported in three other national newspapers.

YESTERDAY AFTERNOON the Censorship passed the same facts for publication by the news agencies.

YESTERDAY EVENING the Air Ministry were themselves forced to issue the story to the British and world publics.

Why?

Because the German broadcasting stations, given a clear field to tell their story first to the world, had done so—in their own peculiar manner.

Their version was that the R.A.F. officer had broken his parole.

Now, 48 hours late, the authorities allow Truth to attempt to catch up with Lies.

The Great Censorship Muddle goes on. . . .

Runaway U-boat Sank Deptford

Eye-witness accounts of the torpedoing of the London steamer Deptford (4,034 tons) off the coast of Norway reveal she was sunk in complete disregard of international law in territorial waters.

Only five of the Deptford's crew of 37 were saved. She was sunk by a U-boat which was using these neutral waters to escape attack by British warships. When torpedoed the Deptford was only about 850 yards from the shore. The territorial limit is three miles.

Lifeboat Goes Out to Look for Raft

The Bridlington lifeboat was launched last night after white distress rockets had been seen in the bay. They were believed to come from a raft.

Finn 'Emperor' Rolls Back Red Armies

While fighting continues on Russian soil east of Lieksa, above Lake Ladoga, Finnish troops were reported last night (says Reuter) to have pushed the Red Army back across the frontier at a new point some miles to the north.

From RALPH HEWINS, Daily Mail War Correspondent in Finland, who is now on the Northern Front in the Arctic Circle.

ROVANIEMI, Thursday.

THIS story begins with a little tea party given by General Wallenius, Finnish Commander-in-Chief in the north, and his wife and daughter, and ends with a fight deep behind the Russian outposts on the Salla front in the small hours of this morning.

My host and guide was General Wallenius himself—the man who in the past five days has rolled back the Russian Armies 50 miles eastwards, and 23 miles northwards on the Salla and Petsamo fronts.

The "Emperor of Lapland," as he is affectionately known to his men and all the people living in this part of the country, took risks which would have daunted lesser men. His victorious attacks left 5,000 Russians dead on the field and gave the Finns vast quantities of war material.

Fought in 1914

In his own home I learned the source of his inspiration. It lies in his family—his wife, Anni, and their three daughters.

We were having tea in a great be-rugged wooden home, full of Lapland water colours, where the general has lived for 22 years as a military governor.

Mme. Wallenius, sturdy, dark, smiling, was an Eton-cropped school teacher when she married. Now her only job is that of a wife and mother.

Twenty officers and some nurses attended the tea party.

I and my fellow-guests were fetched from our hotel in a police van, there being no other cars available.

Big Finnish stoves heated the rooms and rich bearskins, reindeer hides, and Lappish rugs provided comforts unexpected on the Arctic Circle.

General Wallenius was jocular after his victories.

"You can't kill Russians with sympathy," he said, answering my question about what sort of foreign aid he required.

"I want men with broad shoulders who hate Russian barbarism and are not afraid to sleep in the snow or die."

The "Emperor" went on: "The worst is over now. The Russians have been able to advance owing to lack of snow and frozen rivers and lakes. In the last few days we must have had a

Turn to BACK Page

Dog Rounds Up a Borstal Boy

Four youths who escaped on Wednesday night from Portland Borstal Institution were recaptured in Portland yesterday.

A spaniel dog belonging to Mr. J. Norman, a Portland taxi-driver, rounded up one. Another was caught in the main street, and two others who drove off in Mr. Norman's taxi, were chased by the governor of the institution, who headed them off in his car.

BOMBERS FOR ALLIES BLOCK AMERICAN PORT

From DON IDDON, Daily Mail Correspondent

NEW YORK, Thursday.

ALMOST £4,000,000 worth of bombers, trucks, trench diggers, machine tools, and canned beef bought by Britain and France to-night jam five New York piers—covering 13 acres of ground—awaiting ships to take them to the Western Front, it is stated here.

At least 60 giant warplanes are stacked on the dockside at Stapleton, free port of Staten Island in New York Harbour, and more are on their way.

Fifteen hundred Studebaker camouflaged trucks and 1,000 white provision trucks clog the free port zone, and 500 more will arrive to-morrow.

Enormous crates containing machine-gun mountings, spare parts, and canvas covers stand close by 13 gigantic trench diggers, each of which cost £600.

There is scarcely another available inch of space, and plans are being hastily made to store 6,000 more trucks, 270 trench diggers, and scores of 'planes somewhere in the city before transporting them to piers for shipment.

Nearly all goods have been manufactured by United States firms—many of them since war began. The free port is being used as it is technically foreign soil, and goods remaining there are free from duty pending shipment.

There are also 250,000 cases of Argentine beef and thousands of bales and bags of sisal and ixtle, fibres from which naval ropes are made, occupying a considerable amount of pier space.

Storage facilities are so taxed that room cannot be found for a further 50,000 tons of cargo, and port authorities are now discussing a way out.

During the last six months 508 lighters and 61 steamers have unloaded war materials in the zone, and wages paid out total £24,000.

TROOPS SEARCH HILLS FOR I.R.A. MACHINE-GUNS

From Daily Mail Correspondent

DUBLIN, Thursday.

A THOUSAND pounds reward was to-night offered by the Eireann Government for information leading to the recovery of the million rounds of ammunition stolen by I.R.A. men who raided Phœnix Park magazine fort, Dublin, on Saturday night.

Soldiers and police to-day redoubled their search for the men and the ammunition in Dublin, in five counties round it, on the Ulster border, and even in Belfast.

About 30 arrests have now been made.

The Dublin mountains, where members of the I.R.A. are known to have been practising with machine-guns, are being thoroughly combed.

Houses Raided

A complete cordon of troops and police now surrounds Dublin and a large area outside it. The Government are determined to prevent the stolen ammunition being distributed in small quantities.

Many houses have been entered and statements taken.

Throughout last night and to-day the Army and volunteer troops were searching all vehicles entering or leaving Dublin.

Buses, trains, motor-cars, carts, even Post Office vans are being held up and searched by steel-helmeted soldiers with fixed bayonets. Bales of hay and lorry-loads of soft merchandise are bayoneted to make sure they do not conceal ammunition.

Cyclists and pedestrians are stopped, even in the depths of the country, and asked where they are going to, where coming from, and why. If they carry bags or attaché cases these are searched.

Platoons are combing woods, lanes, and country estates.

On the Ulster border strict watch is being kept; it is feared that the search may drive the I.R.A. men to try to hide their spoils beyond the border.

Many houses in Belfast were raided

Turn to BACK Page

Graf Spee Victors Promoted

NEW CAPTAIN

By Daily Mail Reporter

FIVE officers of H.M.S. Ajax, Exeter, and Achilles have been promoted "in recognition of services in action" in the battle which drove the Nazi pocket battleship Admiral Graf Spee into Montevideo harbour, the Admiralty announced last night. They are:

Commander D. H. Everett, H.M.S. Ajax, to be promoted to captain.

Lieut.-Commander R. B. Jennings and Lieut.-Commander C. J. Smith, H.M.S. Exeter, to be commanders.

Lieut.-Commander P. T. A. Love, H.M.S. Achilles, to be commander.

Engineer-Commander L. G. S. Noake, H.M.S. Ajax, to be promoted to engineer-captain.

All five promotions date from December 13—the day of the battle.

3 More Deaths

Commodore Henry Harwood, who commanded the British squadron in the epic battle against the Graf Spee, was appointed a K.C.B. and promoted rear-admiral the day the Graf Spee was scuttled. The captains of the three cruisers were made Companions of the Bath.

The Admiralty last night announced that three of the crew of the Exeter, wounded in the Graf Spee battle, have now died.

Their names are: Legg, Frank, P.O. cook; Powton, R. F., chief P.O. cook; Collins, Anthony C. P., chief shipwright 2nd class.

The death roll in the Exeter now totals 64.

A.T.S. Girl Sergeant Shot Dead

From Daily Mail Correspondent

DORCHESTER, Thursday.

A 25-YEARS-OLD sergeant in the Auxiliary Territorial Service, Miss Vivienne de Meric, was found dead to-day in the garden of her home at Bradford Peverell, near here.

She was wearing pyjamas and a dressing-gown. A shot-gun was by her side, and she had head wounds.

The discovery was made by her father, Captain V. E. de Meric, one of the Food Officers in the Western Area Food Control Office in Bristol.

Miss de Meric was a keen sportswoman and often road to local hunt meets.

She joined the A.T.S. in Dorchester when war broke out, but recently her health broke down, and she had been in bed for some days before her death.

Duce to Visit the Pope

"IN INTEREST OF PEACE"

From Daily Mail Correspondent

ROME, Thursday.

FOLLOWING the Pope's visit to the King of Italy to-day it was officially announced in Vatican City that Signor Mussolini is to pay a visit to the Pontiff on January 4.

It is described in Church quarters in Rome as being "a visit of homage." Both political and Church circles believe it will be in the interests of peace.

The announcement created a great impression here. It is reported that the Pope intends to return the visit.

This morning's conversation between the Pope and King Victor Emmanuel at the Quirinal Palace lasted half an hour.

∴ The Pope talks Peace to King Victor—Page TWO.

LATEST NEWS

HEAD OF SWEDISH TRADE DELEGATION

Stockholm, Thursday.

Hr. Marcus Wallenberger, Jun., of the Enskilde Banken, the large Swedish private bank, has been appointed chairman of the Swedish delegation on the Anglo-Swedish trade commission.

Hr. Wallenberger, who is 40, is a former tennis champion of Sweden.—British United Press.

Deaf Ears can now hear

more sounds
more clearly
more naturally
at a *greater* distance

with this new, lighter, smaller-than-ever Aid!

DEAFNESS is no longer a handicap! You can now chat with your friends, discuss business, enjoy music, talkies and wireless, shop and go about, as easily and comfortably as those with normal hearing! This is because the discovery of a remarkable new sound-transmitting substance has made possible the wonderful new *Golden-Tone* 'MASTER-MIDGET' FORTIPHONES — *light-as-a-leaf*, but amazingly powerful!

Prof. A. M. LOW, eminent scientist reports: "This new principle affords an exceptionally high degree of amplification . . its performance FAR SURPASSES anything I have experienced."

The new *Golden-Tone* 'Master-Midget' Fortiphones, though *light-as-a-leaf*, are the latest and most efficient aids to hearing, and the range includes models for every type and degree of deafness. With the new 'Master-Midget' Fortiphones, you can hear by Bone-conduction—

Nothing IN or ON your Ears!

or with the marvellous new *featherweight* 'Master-Midget' Earpiece which weighs less than one-third of an ounce and fits right into your ear as comfortably as your little finger-tip

Without Earloop or Headband!

Either way is so comfortable, so simple, so inconspicuous, that *all you are conscious of is your clear, easy, natural hearing of all sounds*—even at a distance!

You can test it Free!

We have helped thousands to hear who had given up all hope. That is why we confidently invite you to test the new *light-as-a-leaf* Master-Midget Fortiphone free of charge and without obligation, either in our Consultation Rooms or your own home. Have a friend or your doctor with you. You will find our Consultant most courteous, helpful and sympathetic. Consultation hours 8.30 a.m. to 5.30 p.m. Saturdays 8.30 a.m. to 12.30 p.m. *Langham House, 308 REGENT ST., is halfway between Oxford Circus Tube Station and Broadcasting House.* Take lift to THIRD FLOOR.

REDUCED PRICES if you apply within 10 days!

Call, phone, write, or post this

FREE TEST COUPON

To FORTIPHONE LTD., (Dept. 2), Langham House, 308 REGENT STREET, LONDON, W.1

Please send illustrated Catalogue, FREE HOME TEST Offer without obligation to purchase, and Reduced Prices.

Name.............................. (Mr., Mrs., Miss or title)

Address..............................

Phone: Langham 3173, 3774, 3776. D.M. 29/12/39.

Please write in BLOCK LETTERS

▲ DAILY MAIL, LONDON, FRIDAY DECEMBER 29, 1939

Amid details of the coming rationing and an assurance that New York port is jammed with supplies for the Allies, the *Mail* takes time to complain about the muddled censors—a constant press complaint throughout the war.

Rationing
DECEMBER 1939

FOOD RATIONING IN BRITAIN WAS EXPECTED SOON AFTER THE OUTBREAK OF WAR, BUT WAS DELAYED BY THE GOVERNMENT UNTIL SUCH TIMES THAT IT BECAME ABSOLUTELY NECESSARY. Many people complained that food was being given to "preferential" customers and that rationing should be brought in as a measure of fairness. The government introduced food rationing in January 1940 and most foods were rationed by their weight or by points. Sugar was rationed at 12 ounces per week, but meat was rationed by cost. Therefore each person would be allocated 1 shilling and 10 pence worth of meat per week, 3 pints of milk, 8 ounces of sugar, 4 ounces of butter or fat, 4 ounces of bacon, 2 ounces of tea, 1 ounce of cheese, and 1 egg.

RATIONED FOODSTUFFS

Other foods such as rice, jam, biscuits, tinned food, and dried fruit was rationed by points and not by weight. Each family had to register with a shop or store where the foodstuffs would be purchased and this was the only place where the family could make purchases. Each member of the family had his or her own ration book. Adults had a buff-colored book, children over the age of three had a blue book, and babies had a green book.

SUBSTITUTES AND SHORTAGES

In response to shortages, food substitutes were also seen for the first time. Margarine, for example, was used instead of butter. Many new foods appeared as alternatives to the original products, especially meats. "Spam" was introduced from the United States (during the war Spam actually became a Lend Lease commodity and contributed to the feeding of Allied civilians and service personnel), and could be eaten hot or cold. Corned beef was introduced from New Zealand and Argentina. It was cheap, fatty, and strong tasting. Mention should also be made of egg powder, which could be used for many things. Indeed, the government produced a cook book on how to cook successfully with powdered eggs. As long as British civilian morale held, rationing was tolerated.

▲ THE THREAT OF GAS ATTACK resulted in all British civilians being issued with gas masks.

1940

AS 1940 BEGAN, A WAR LARGELY CONFINED TO NORTHERN EUROPE SHOWED NO SIGNS OF MOVEMENT. BY THE END OF THE YEAR, HOWEVER, GERMANY HAD CONQUERED MOST OF WESTERN EUROPE WHILE FIGHTING RAGED IN NORTH AFRICA.

IN JANUARY 1940 THE WAR BETWEEN THE SOVIET UNION AND FINLAND WAS STILL INTENSE, AND A NEW SOVIET OFFENSIVE STARTING JANUARY 12 EVENTUALLY ALLOWED THE SOVIETS TO DICTATE PEACE terms in March. However, the most important military operations during the year were those in northern and western Europe. Hitler initiated two waves of invasion.

First, in April German forces attacked and swiftly conquered neutral Denmark and Norway. Secondly, and critically, on May 10 they invaded neutral Belgium and Holland in a general offensive against France. Germany's combination of armored thrusts and Luftwaffe air attacks, particularly the daring panzer assault through the supposedly impassable Ardennes region, cut the Allied armies in two. Holland and Belgium fell by the end of May.

Allied troops in northwestern France were forced to retreat in haste to the Channel coast,

▲ FINNISH CIVILIANS PREPARE to leave Vyborg, Finland, rather than live under Soviet rule following the Treaty of Moscow that brought the Winter War to an end.

where some 226,000 British and 110,000 French troops were eventually rescued from the French port of Dunkirk by a makeshift British fleet. The German forces then turned south and swiftly completed the destruction of the French army, forcing France to surrender and imposing a settlement that left northern and western France under direct German control.

BATTLE OF BRITAIN

German forces next prepared for an invasion of Britain, but during the Battle of Britain in late summer 1940 the Luftwaffe was unable to obtain the mastery of the skies that it needed to cover this invasion. Instead, Hitler launched mass bombing raids on British cities (the Blitz) in an attempt to break their citizens' morale.

A crucial side effect of the fall of France was the entry of Italy into the war in June 1940. Italian forces then initiated a series of offensives themselves—in north Africa, in east Africa, and against Greece. The war was spreading its tentacles wider and wider.

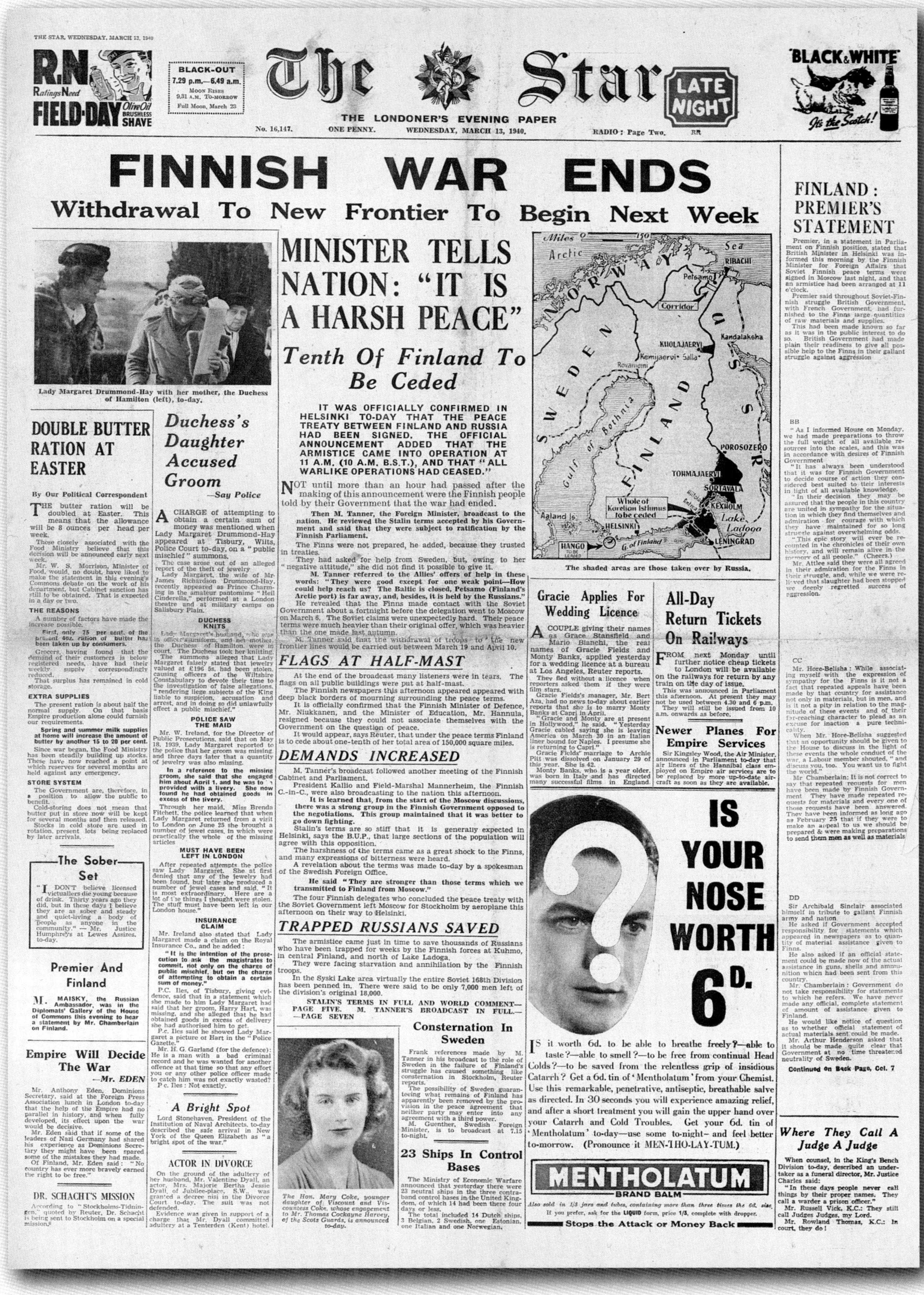

THE STAR, WEDNESDAY, MARCH 13, 1940

R.N. Ratings Need FIELD-DAY Olive Oil Brushless Shave

BLACK-OUT 7.29 p.m.—6.49 a.m. Moon Rises 9.31 A.M. To-morrow. Full Moon, March 23

The Star

LATE NIGHT

THE LONDONER'S EVENING PAPER

No. 16,147. ONE PENNY. WEDNESDAY, MARCH 13, 1940. RADIO: Page Two. RR

"BLACK & WHITE" It's the Scotch!

FINNISH WAR ENDS

Withdrawal To New Frontier To Begin Next Week

Lady Margaret Drummond-Hay with her mother, the Duchess of Hamilton (left), to-day.

MINISTER TELLS NATION: "IT IS A HARSH PEACE"

Tenth Of Finland To Be Ceded

IT WAS OFFICIALLY CONFIRMED IN HELSINKI TO-DAY THAT THE PEACE TREATY BETWEEN FINLAND AND RUSSIA HAD BEEN SIGNED. THE OFFICIAL ANNOUNCEMENT ADDED THAT THE ARMISTICE CAME INTO OPERATION AT 11 A.M. (10 A.M. B.S.T.), AND THAT "ALL WARLIKE OPERATIONS HAD CEASED."

NOT until more than an hour had passed after the making of this announcement were the Finnish people told by their Government that the war had ended.

Then M. Tanner, the Foreign Minister, broadcast to the nation. He reviewed the Stalin terms accepted by his Government and said that they were subject to ratification by the Finnish Parliament.

The Finns were not prepared, he added, because they trusted in treaties.

They had asked for help from Sweden, but, owing to her "negative attitude," she did not find it possible to give it.

M. Tanner referred to the Allies' offers of help in these words: "They were good except for one weak point—How could help reach us? The Baltic is closed, Petsamo (Finland's Arctic port) is far away, and, besides, it is held by the Russians."

He revealed that the Finns made contact with the Soviet Government about a fortnight before the delegation went to Moscow on March 6. The Soviet claims were unexpectedly hard. Their peace terms were much heavier than their original offer, which was heavier than the one made last autumn.

M. Tanner said that the withdrawal of troops to the new frontier lines would be carried out between March 19 and April 10.

FLAGS AT HALF-MAST

At the end of the broadcast many listeners were in tears. The flags on all public buildings were put at half-mast.

The Finnish newspapers this afternoon appeared appeared with deep black borders of mourning surrounding the peace terms.

It is officially confirmed that the Finnish Minister of Defence, Mr. Niukkanen, and the Minister of Education, Mr. Hannula, resigned because they could not associate themselves with the Government on the question of peace.

It would appear, says Reuter, that under the peace terms Finland is to cede about one-tenth of her total area of 150,000 square miles.

DEMANDS INCREASED

M. Tanner's broadcast followed another meeting of the Finnish Cabinet and Parliament.

President Kallio and Field-Marshal Mannerheim, the Finnish C.-in-C., were also broadcasting to the nation this afternoon.

It is learned that, from the start of the Moscow discussions, there was a strong group in the Finnish Government opposed to the negotiations. This group maintained that it was better to go down fighting.

Stalin's terms are so stiff that it is generally expected in Helsinki, says the B.U.P., that large sections of the population will agree with this opposition.

The harshness of the terms came as a great shock to the Finns, and many expressions of bitterness were heard.

A revelation about the terms was made to-day by a spokesman of the Swedish Foreign Office.

He said "They are stronger than those terms which we transmitted to Finland from Moscow."

The four Finnish delegates who concluded the peace treaty with the Soviet Government left Moscow for Stockholm by aeroplane this afternoon on their way to Helsinki.

TRAPPED RUSSIANS SAVED

The armistice came just in time to save thousands of Russians who have been trapped for weeks by the Finnish forces at Kuhmo, in central Finland, and north of Lake Ladoga.

They were facing starvation and annihilation by the Finnish troops.

In the Syski Lake area virtually the entire Soviet 168th Division has been penned in. There were said to be only 7,000 men left of the division's original 18,000.

STALIN'S TERMS IN FULL AND WORLD COMMENT—PAGE FIVE. M. TANNER'S BROADCAST IN FULL.——PAGE SEVEN

The shaded areas are those taken over by Russia.

DOUBLE BUTTER RATION AT EASTER

By Our Political Correspondent

THE butter ration will be doubled at Easter. This means that the allowance will be 8 ounces per head per week.

Those closely associated with the Food Ministry believe that this decision will be announced early next week.

Mr. W. S. Morrison, Minister of Food, would, no doubt, have liked to make the statement in this evening's Commons debate on the work of his department, but Cabinet sanction has still to be obtained. That is expected in a day or two.

THE REASONS

A number of factors have made the increase possible.

First, only 75 per cent. of the present 4oz. ration of butter has been taken up by consumers.

Grocers, having found that the demand of their customers is below registered needs, have had their weekly supply correspondingly reduced.

That surplus has remained in cold storage.

EXTRA SUPPLIES

The present ration is about half the normal supply. On that basis Empire production alone could furnish our requirements.

Spring and summer milk supplies at home will increase the amount of butter by another 15 to 20 per cent.

Since war began, the Food Ministry has been steadily building up stocks. These have now reached a point at which reserves for several months are held against any emergency.

STORE SYSTEM

The Government are, therefore, in a position to allow the public to benefit.

Cold-storing does not mean that butter put in store now will be kept for several months and then released.

Stocks in cold store are used in rotation, present lots being replaced by later arrivals.

The Sober Set

"I DON'T believe licensed victuallers die young because of drink. Thirty years ago they did, but in these days I believe they are as sober and steady and quiet-living a body of people as anyone in the community." — Mr. Justice Humphreys at Lewes Assizes, to-day.

Premier And Finland

M. MAISKY, the Russian Ambassador, was in the Diplomats' Gallery of the House of Commons this evening to hear a statement by Mr. Chamberlain on Finland.

Empire Will Decide The War

—Mr. EDEN

Mr. Anthony Eden, Dominions Secretary, said at the Foreign Press Association lunch in London to-day that the help of the Empire had no parallel in history, and when fully developed, its effect upon the war would be decisive.

Mr. Eden said that if some of the leaders of Nazi Germany had shared his experience as Dominions Secretary they might have been spared some of the mistakes they had made.

Of Finland, Mr. Eden said: "No country has ever more bravely earned the right to be free."

DR. SCHACHT'S MISSION

According to "Stockholms-Tidningen," quoted by Reuter, Dr. Schacht is being sent to Stockholm on a special mission.

Duchess's Daughter Accused Groom

—Say Police

A CHARGE of attempting to obtain a certain sum of money was mentioned when Lady Margaret Drummond-Hay appeared at Tisbury, Wilts, Police Court to-day, on a "public mischief" summons.

The case arose out of an alleged report of the theft of jewelry.

Lady Margaret, the wife of Mr. James Richardson Drummond-Hay, recently appeared as Prince Charming in the amateur pantomime "Heil Cinderella," performed at a London theatre and at military camps on Salisbury Plain.

DUCHESS KNITS

Lady Margaret's husband, who was in officer's uniform, and her mother, the Duchess of Hamilton, were in court. The Duchess took her knitting.

The summons alleged that Lady Margaret falsely stated that jewelry valued at £196 5s. had been stolen, causing officers of the Wiltshire Constabulary to devote their time to the investigation of false allegations, "rendering liege subjects of the King liable to suspicion, accusation and arrest, and in doing so did unlawfully effect a public mischief."

POLICE SAW THE MAID

Mr. W. Ireland, for the Director of Public Prosecutions, said that on May 18, 1939, Lady Margaret reported to the police that her groom was missing, and three days later that a quantity of jewelry was also missing.

In a reference to the missing groom, she said that she engaged him about April 1, and he was to be provided with a livery. She now found he had obtained goods in excess of the livery.

Through her maid, Miss Brenda Fitchett, the police learned that when Lady Margaret returned from a visit to London on June 25 she brought a number of jewel cases, in which were practically the whole of the missing articles.

MUST HAVE BEEN LEFT IN LONDON

After repeated attempts the police saw Lady Margaret. She at first denied that any of the jewelry had been found, but later she produced a number of jewel cases and said, "It is most extraordinary. Here are a lot of the things I thought were stolen. The stuff must have been left in our London house."

INSURANCE CLAIM

Mr. Ireland also stated that Lady Margaret made a claim on the Royal Insurance Co., and he added:

"It is the intention of the prosecution to ask the magistrates to commit, not only on the charge of public mischief, but on the charge of attempting to obtain a certain sum of money."

P.C. Iles, of Tisbury, giving evidence, said that in a statement which she made to him Lady Margaret had said that her groom, Harry Hart, was missing, and she alleged that he had obtained goods in excess of delivery she had authorised him to get.

P.c. Iles said he showed Lady Margaret a picture of Hart in the "Police Gazette."

Mr. H. G. Garland (for the defence): He is a man with a bad criminal record and he was wanted for another offence at that time so that any effort you or any other police officer made to catch him was not exactly wasted?

P.c. Iles: Not exactly.

A Bright Spot

Lord Stonehaven, President of the Institution of Naval Architects, to-day described the safe arrival in New York of the Queen Elizabeth as "a bright spot of the war."

ACTOR IN DIVORCE

On the ground of the adultery of her husband, Mr. Valentine Dyall, an actor, Mrs. Majorie Bertha Jessie Dyall, of Jubilee-place, S.W., was granted a decree nisi in the Divorce Court to-day. The suit was not defended.

Evidence was given in support of a charge that Mr. Dyall committed adultery at a Tenterden (Kent) hotel.

The Hon. Mary Coke, younger daughter of Viscount and Viscountess Coke, whose engagement to Mr. Thomas Cockayne Harvey, of the Scots Guards, is announced to-day.

Consternation In Sweden

Frank references made by M. Tanner in his broadcast to the role of Sweden in the failure of Finland's struggle has caused something like consternation in Stockholm, Reuter reports.

The possibility of Sweden guaranteeing what remains of Finland has apparently been removed by the provision in the peace agreement that neither party may enter into any agreement with a third power.

M. Guenther, Swedish Foreign Minister, is to broadcast at 7.15 to-night.

23 Ships In Control Bases

The Ministry of Economic Warfare announced that yesterday there were 23 neutral ships in the three contraband control bases in the United Kingdom, of which 14 had been there four days or less.

The total included 14 Dutch ships, 3 Belgian, 2 Swedish, one Estonian, one Italian and one Norwegian.

Gracie Applies For Wedding Licence

A COUPLE giving their names as Grace Stansfield and Mario Bianchi, the real names of Gracie Fields and Monty Banks, applied yesterday for a wedding licence at a bureau at Los Angeles, Reuter reports.

They fled without a licence when reporters asked them if they were film stars.

Gracie Fields's manager, Mr. Bert Aza, had no news to-day about earlier reports that she is to marry Monty Banks at Capri in April.

"Gracie and Monty are at present in Hollywood," he said. "Yesterday Gracie cabled saying she is leaving America on March 30 in an Italian liner bound for Naples. I presume she is returning to Capri."

Gracie Fields' marriage to Archie Pitt was dissolved on January 29 of this year. She is 42.

Monty Banks, who is a year older, was born in Italy and has directed many successful films in England.

All-Day Return Tickets On Railways

FROM next Monday until further notice cheap tickets to London will be available on the railways for return by any train on the day of issue.

This was announced in Parliament this afternoon. At present they may not be used between 4.30 and 6 p.m.

They will still be issued from 10 a.m. onwards as before.

Newer Planes For Empire Services

Sir Kingsley Wood, the Air Minister, announced in Parliament to-day that air liners of the Hannibal class employed on Empire air services are to be replaced by more up-to-date aircraft as soon as they are available.

IS YOUR NOSE WORTH 6D.

IS it worth 6d. to be able to breathe freely?—able to taste?—able to smell?—to be free from continual Head Colds?—to be saved from the relentless grip of insidious Catarrh? Get a 6d. tin of 'Mentholatum' from your Chemist. Use this remarkable, penetrative, antiseptic, breathable salve as directed. In 30 seconds you will experience amazing relief, and after a short treatment you will gain the upper hand over your Catarrh and Cold Troubles. Get your 6d. tin of 'Mentholatum' to-day—use some to-night—and feel better to-morrow. (Pronounce it MEN-THO-LAY-TUM.)

MENTHOLATUM BRAND BALM

Also sold in 1/3 jars and tubes, containing more than three times the 6d. size. If you prefer, ask for the LIQUID form, price 1/3, complete with dropper.

Stops the Attack or Money Back

FINLAND: PREMIER'S STATEMENT

Premier, in a statement in Parliament on Finnish position, stated that British Minister in Helsinki was informed this morning by the Finnish Minister for Foreign Affairs that Soviet Finnish peace terms were signed in Moscow last night, and that an armistice had been arranged at 11 o'clock.

Premier said throughout Soviet-Finnish struggle British Government, with French Government, had furnished to the Finns large quantities of raw materials and supplies.

This had been made known so far as it was in the public interest to do so. British Government had made plain their readiness to give all possible help to the Finns in their gallant struggle against aggression

BB

"As I informed House on Monday, we had made preparations to throw the full weight of all available resources into the scales, and this was in accordance with desires of Finnish Government

"It has always been understood that it was for Finnish Government to decide course of action they considered best suited to their interests in light of all available knowledge.

"In their decision they may be assured that the people in this country are united in sympathy for the situation in which they find themselves and admiration for courage with which they have maintained for so long struggle against overwhelming odds.

"This epic story will ever be recounted in the chronicles of their own history, and will remain alive in the memory of all people." (Cheers.)

Mr. Attlee said they were all agreed in their admiration for the Finns in their struggle, and, while we were relieved that slaughter had been stopped we deeply regretted success of aggression.

CC

Mr. Hore-Belisha: While associating myself with the expression of sympathy for the Finns is it not a fact that repeated appeals have been made by that country for assistance not only in materials, but in men, and is it not a pity in relation to the magnitude of these events and of their far-reaching character to plead as an excuse for inaction a pure technicality.

When Mr. Hore-Belisha suggested that an opportunity should be given to the House to discuss in the light of these events the whole conduct of the war, a Labour member shouted, "and discuss you, too. You want us to fight the world."

Mr Chamberlain: It is not correct to say that repeated requests for men have been made by Finnish Government They have made repeated requests for materials and every one of those requests have been answered. They have been informed as long ago as February 25 that if they were to make an appeal to us we should be prepared & were making preparations to send them men as well as materials

DD

Sir Archibald Sinclair associated himself in tribute to gallant Finnish army and nation

He asked if Government accepted responsibility for statements which appeared in newspapers as to quantity of material assistance given to Finns.

He also asked if an official statement could be made now of the actual assistance in guns, shells and ammunition which had been sent from this country.

Mr. Chamberlain: Government do not take responsibility for statements to which he refers. We have never made any official, complete statement of amount of assistance given to Finland.

He would like notice of question as to whether official statement of actual materials sent could be made.

Mr. Arthur Henderson asked that it should be made quite clear that Government at no time threatened neutrality of Sweden.

Continued On Back Page, Col. 7

Where They Call A Judge A Judge

When counsel, in the King's Bench Division to-day, described an undertaker as a funeral director, Mr. Justice Charles said:

"In these days people never call things by their proper names. They call a warder a prison officer."

Mr. Russell Vick, K.C.: They still call Judges Judges, my Lord.

Mr. Rowland Thomas, K.C.: In court, they do!

▲ THE STAR, LONDON, WEDNESDAY MARCH 13, 1940

The London evening paper reports Finland's peace settlement with the Soviet Union, with details of Finland's territorial losses. The right-hand column of the page has been emptied for a transcript of the prime minister's speech to Parliament about Finland. The late news has been inserted so hastily that the paragraphs still begin with the alphabetical codes that tell the typesetter in what order to insert them.

Norway invaded

APRIL 9, 1940

IN EARLY 1940, ALLIED PLANNERS SERIOUSLY CONSIDERED MOVING FORCES INTO NORWAY, A NEUTRAL POWER. THIS STRATEGY WOULD ENABLE THE ALLIES TO SEND HELP TO FINLAND, AND TAKING THE northern Norwegian port of Narvik might affect the German ability to wage war.

TARGET NARVIK

Narvik was important because annually more than 8 million tons (8.1 million tonnes) of iron ore arrived by rail from the nearby Swedish mines and was then taken by coastal steamers to feed Germany's war economy. In 1940, 29 percent of Germany's iron ore came from Sweden through Narvik, and the seizure of this neutral port offered the Allies a potentially cheap means of applying military pressure on Germany. However, the Allies dithered for months, first assembling troops for Narvik, then disembarking them, unsure about violating Norwegian neutrality or provoking

war with the Soviet Union. On April 4, the Allies finally resolved to mine Norwegian coastal waters to interfere with iron ore convoys and to land troops at Narvik and three other Norwegian ports. However, the Allies were too slow.

THE GERMANS STRIKE

Five days later, on April 9, a German invasion force, including 10,000 troops (later rising to 100,000), surface ships, U-boats, and 1,000 aircraft, attacked Denmark and Norway. Denmark was overrun immediately. The first ever airborne assault was made on Oslo and Stavanger airports in Norway, while ships landed troops at six locations. Norway's six divisions had no tanks or effective artillery, while its coastal defenses and navy were generally inferior. However, in Oslo Fjord, shore guns sank the German cruiser *Blücher*, claiming 1,600 lives. The British battlecruiser HMS *Rodney* also engaged the enemy battlecruisers *Scharnhorst* and *Gneisenau*, damaging the latter. By the beginning of May, the Germans controlled most of Norway.

▲ THE GERMAN CRUISER *KÖNIGSBERG* sinks in Bergen harbor after being hit by bombs from British Blackburn Skua dive-bombers.

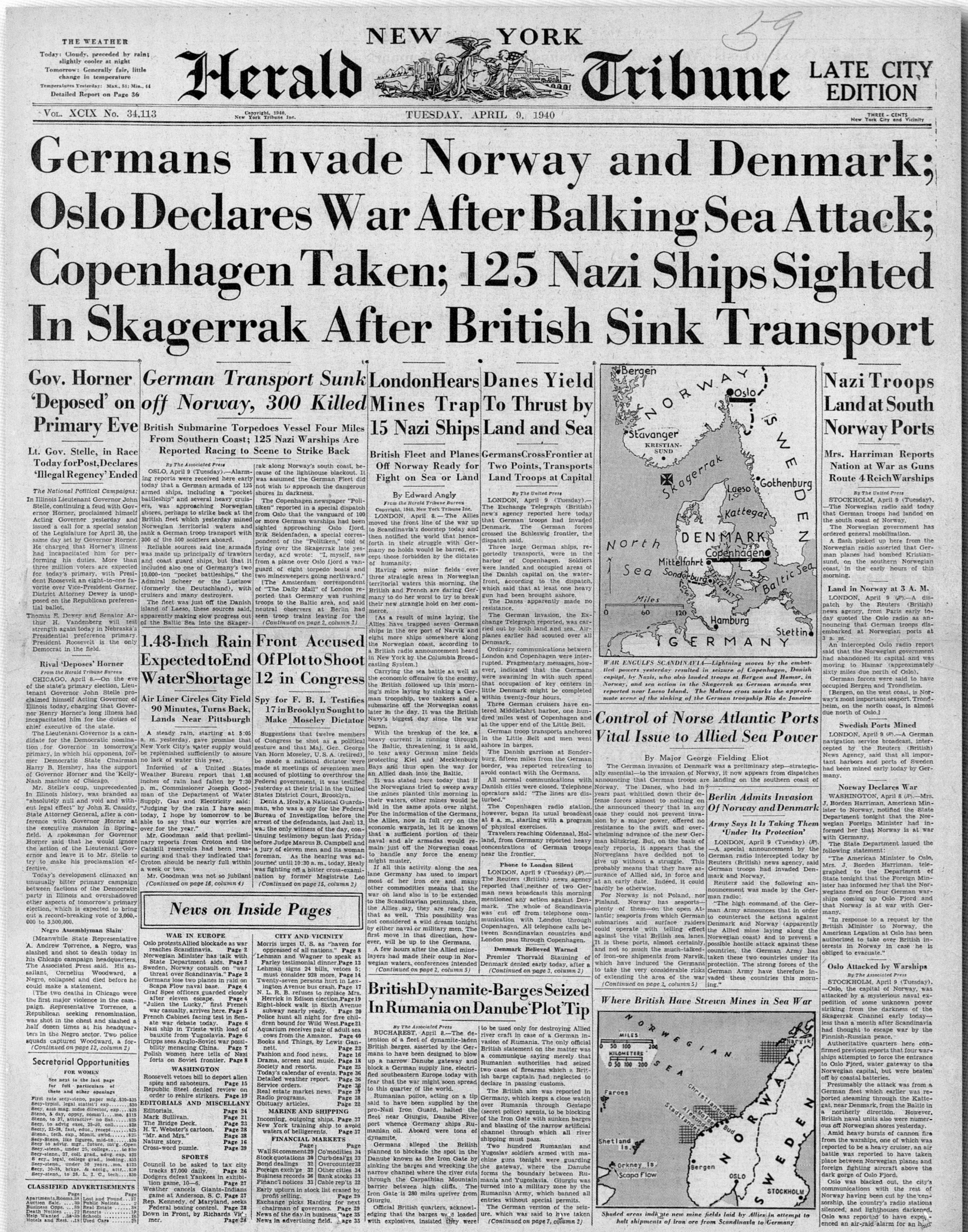

THE WEATHER
Today: Cloudy, preceded by rain; slightly cooler at night
Tomorrow: Generally fair, little change in temperature
Temperatures Yesterday: Max. 51; Min. 44
Detailed Report on Page 36

59

NEW YORK Herald Tribune

LATE CITY EDITION

VOL. XCIX No. 34,113   Copyright, 1940, New York Tribune Inc.   TUESDAY, APRIL 9, 1940   THREE CENTS New York City and Vicinity

Germans Invade Norway and Denmark; Oslo Declares War After Balking Sea Attack; Copenhagen Taken; 125 Nazi Ships Sighted In Skagerrak After British Sink Transport

Gov. Horner 'Deposed' on Primary Eve

Lt. Gov. Stelle, in Race Today for Post, Declares 'Illegal Regency' Ended

The National Political Campaign

In Illinois Lieutenant Governor John Stelle, continuing a feud with Governor Horner, proclaimed himself Acting Governor yesterday and issued a call for a special session of the Legislature for April 30, the same day set by Governor Horner. He charged that Horner's illness had incapacitated him for performing his duties. More than three million voters are expected for today's primary, which President Roosevelt as an expected-to-be-a-favorite over Vice-President Garner. District Attorney Dewey is unopposed on the Republican presidential ballot.

Thomas E. Dewey and Senator Arthur H. Vandenberg will test strength again today in Nebraska's Presidential preference primary. President Roosevelt is the only Democrat in the field.

Rival 'Deposes' Horner

From the Herald Tribune Bureau

CHICAGO, April 8.—On the eve of the state's primary election, Lieutenant Governor John Stelle proclaimed himself Acting Governor of Illinois today, charging that Governor Henry Horner's long illness had incapacitated him for the duties of chief executive of the state.

The Lieutenant Governor is a candidate for the Democratic nomination for Governor in tomorrow's primary, in which his opponent, former Democratic State Chairman Harry B. Hershey, has the support of Governor Horner and the 'Kelly-Nash machine of Chicago.

Mr. Stelle's coup, unprecedented in Illinois history, was branded as "absolutely null and void and without legal effect" by John E. Cassidy, State Attorney General, after a conference with Governor Horner and the executive mansion in Springfield. A spokesman for Governor Horner said that he would ignore the action of the Lieutenant Governor and leave it to Mr. Stelle to try to make his proclamation effective.

Today's development climaxed an unusually bitter primary campaign between factions of the Democratic party in Illinois and overshadowed either aspects of tomorrow's primary election, which is expected to bring out a record-breaking vote of 3,000,000 to 3,500,000.

Negro Assemblyman Slain

(Meanwhile State Representative A. Andrew Torrence, a Negro, was slashed and shot to death today in his Chicago campaign headquarters. The Associated Press said. His assailant, Cornelius Woodward, a Negro, collapsed and died before he could make a statement.

(The two deaths in Chicago were the first major violence in the campaign. Representative Torrence, a Republican seeking renomination, was shot in the chest and slashed a half dozen times at his headquarters in the Negro sector. Two police squads captured Woodward, a Negro.)

(Continued on page 12, column 2)

Secretarial Opportunities

FOR WOMEN

See next to the last page for full particulars of there and other openings

First rate secty-stenos, paper mfg....$30-$35
secy-typist, legal (steno's) age....$30
secy. and mag. staff, diction....$35
Steno. & dep. (appt. comm't).... res. $115
Steno. to 31, attractive- on Dist.....$25
Sec. to adving exec. 28-40. col.....$38
Secty, 25-38, fast, educ, copol.....$25
Steno., tech. exp., Mimel, certd.....$25
Secy.-Steno. like figures, 26-40....$35
Secty to adving man., future, img'l..open
Secy.-steno., under 25, college....to $30
Secy-steno., IT. coll. grad., educ exp. $35
R secy, legal, college grad., looking..$35
Secy.-steno., 25-35, bkps. & secty....$30
Secty. 30-35, bkps. & secty., attr.....$30
Secy-steno., to 28, L. I. Col, tech.....$25

CLASSIFIED ADVERTISEMENTS

Announcements, Rooms, 55 | Lost and Found..22
Auction Sale. ....35 | Public Notices 2
Business Opp...90 | Real Estate
Death Notices...23 | Resorts....25
Help Wanted ..34-35 | Schools.......1
Hotels and Rest..19 | Used Cars

German Transport Sunk off Norway, 300 Killed

British Submarine Torpedoes Vessel Four Miles From Southern Coast; 125 Nazi Warships Are Reported Racing to Scene to Strike Back

By The Associated Press

OSLO, April 9 (Tuesday).—Alarming reports were received here early today that a German armada of 125 armed ships, including a "pocket battleship" and several heavy cruisers, was approaching Norwegian shores, perhaps to strike back at the British fleet which yesterday mined Norwegian territorial waters and sank a German troop transport with 300 of the 500 soldiers aboard.

Reliable sources said the armada was made up principally of travelers and coast guard ships, but that it included also one of Germany's two 10,000-ton "pocket battleships," the Admiral Scheer or the Luetzow (formerly the Deutschland), with cruisers and many destroyers.

The fleet was just off the Danish island of Laeso, these sources said, apparently making slow progress out of the Baltic Sea into the Skagerrak along Norway's south coast, because of the lighthouse blackout. It was assumed the German Fleet did not wish to approach the dangerous shores in darkness.

The Copenhagen newspaper "Politiken" reported in a special dispatch from Oslo that the vanguard of 100 or more German warships had been sighted approaching Oslo Fjord. Erik Seidenfaden, a special correspondent of the "Politiken," told of flying over the Skagerrak late yesterday, and wrote: "I, myself, saw from a plane over Oslo Fjord a vanguard of eight torpedo boats and two minesweepers going northward."

(Continued on page 2, column 1)

1.48-Inch Rain Expected to End Water Shortage

Air Liner Circles City Field 90 Minutes, Turns Back, Lands Near Pittsburgh

A steady rain, starting at 5:05 a. m. yesterday, gave promise that New York City's water supply would be replenished sufficiently to assure a lack of water this year.

Informed of a United States Weather Bureau report that 1.48 inches of rain had fallen by 7:30 p. m., Commissioner Joseph Goodman of the Department of Water Supply, Gas and Electricity said: "Judging by the rain I have seen today, I hope by tomorrow to be able to say that our worries are over for the year."

London Hears Mines Trap 15 Nazi Ships

British Fleet and Planes Off Norway Ready to Fight on Sea or Land

By Edward Angly
From the Herald Tribune Bureau
Copyright, 1940, New York Tribune Inc.

LONDON, April 8.—The Allies moved the front line of the war up to Scandinavia's doorstep today and then notified the world that henceforth in their struggle with Germany no holds would be barred, except those forbidden by the dictates of humanity.

Having sown mine fields over three strategic areas in Norwegian territorial waters this morning, the British and French are daring Germany to do her worst to try to break the naval and air blockade of her commerce.

[As a result of mine laying, the Allies have trapped seven German ships in the ore port of Narvik and eight more ships somewhere along the Norwegian coast, according to British radio announcement heard in New York by the Columbia Broadcasting System.]

Carrying the sea battle as well as the economic offensive to the enemy, the British followed up this morning's mine laying by sinking a German troopship, two tankers and a German ore ship. It was the British Navy's biggest day since the war began.

With the breakup of the ice, a heavy current is running through the Baltic, threatening, it is said, to tear away German mine fields protecting Kiel and Mecklenburg Bays and thus open the way for Allied dash into the Baltic.

(Continued on page 2, column 2)

Danes Yield To Thrust by Land and Sea

Germans Cross Frontier at Two Points, Transports Land Troops at Capital

By The United Press

LONDON, April 9 (Tuesday).—The Exchange Telegraph (British) news's agency reported here today that German troops had invaded Denmark. The German forces crossed the Schleswig frontier, the dispatch said.

Three large German ships, reportedly transports, were in the harbor of Copenhagen. Soldiers were landed and occupied areas of the Danish capital on the waterfront, according to the dispatch, which said that at least one heavy gun had been brought ashore.

The German invasion, the Exchange Telegraph reported, was carried out by both land and sea. Airplanes earlier had scouted over all Denmark.

Ordinary communications between London and Copenhagen were interrupted. Fragmentary messages, however, indicated that the Germans were swarming in with such speed that occupation of key centers in little Denmark might be completed within twenty-four hours.

(Continued on page 7, column 2)

Front Accused Of Plot to Shoot 12 in Congress

Spy for F. B. I. Testifies 17 in Brooklyn Sought to Make Moseley Dictator

Suggestions that twelve members of Congress be shot as a political gesture and that Maj. Gen. George Van Horn Moseley, U. S. A. (retired), be made a national dictator were made at meetings of seventeen men accused of plotting to overthrow the federal government, it was testified yesterday at their trial in the United States District Court, Brooklyn.

Denis A. Healy, a National Guardsman, who was a spy for the Federal Bureau of Investigation before the arrest of the defendants, last Jan. 11, was the only witness of the day, continuing testimony begun last Friday before Judge Marcus B. Campbell and a jury of eleven men and its woman forewoman. As the hearing was adjourned until 10:30 a. m. today, Healy was fighting off a bitter cross-examination by former Magistrate Carl P. Goodwin, and was not so jubilant.

(Continued on page 15, column 2)

WAR ENGULFS SCANDINAVIA—Lightning moves by the embattled powers yesterday resulted in seizure of Copenhagen, Danish capital, by Nazis, who also landed troops at Bergen and Hamar, in Norway, and saw action in the Skagerrak as German armada was reported near Laeso Island. The Maltese cross marks the approximate scene of the sinking of the German troopship Rio de Janeiro.

Control of Norse Atlantic Ports Vital Issue to Allied Sea Power

By Major George Fielding Eliot

The German invasion of Denmark was a preliminary step—strategically essential—to the invasion of Norway, if now appears from dispatches announcing that German troops are landing on the southern coast of Norway. The Danes, who had in years past whittled down their defense forces almost to nothing on the announced theory that in any case they could not prevent invasion by a major power, offered no resistance to the swift and overwhelming advance of the new German blitzkrieg. But, on the basis of early reports, it appears that the Norwegians have decided not to give up without a struggle. This probably means that they have assurance of Allied aid, in force and at an early date. Indeed, it could hardly be otherwise.

For Norway is not Poland, nor Finland. Norway has seaports—plenty of them—on the open Atlantic! reports from which German submarines and surface raiders could operate with telling effect against the vital British sea lanes. It is these ports, almost certainly, and not so much the much-talked-of iron-ore shipments from Narvik, which have induced the Germans to take the very considerable risk of extending the area of the war into Scandinavia.

Berlin Admits Invasion Of Norway and Denmark

Army Says It Is Taking Them 'Under Its Protection'

By The United Press

LONDON, April 9 (Tuesday) (P).—A special announcement by the German radio intercepted today by Reuters (British) news agency, said German troops had invaded Denmark and Norway.

Reuters said the following announcement was made by the German radio:

"The high command of the German Army announces that in order to counteract the actions against Denmark and Norway (apparently the Allied mine laying along the Norwegian coast and to prevent a possible hostile attack against these countries, the German Army has taken these two countries under its protection. The armed forces of the German Army have therefore invaded these countries this morning."

Nazi Troops Land at South Norway Ports

Mrs. Harriman Reports Nation at War as Guns Route 4 Reich Warships

By The United Press

STOCKHOLM, April 9 (Tuesday).—The Norwegian radio said today that German troops had landed on the south coast of Norway.

The Norwegian government has ordered general mobilization.

A flash picked up here from the Norwegian radio asserted that German planes had bombed Kristiansand, on the southern Norwegian coast, in the early hours of this morning.

Land in Norway at 3 A. M.

OSLO, April 9 (P).—A dispatch by the Reuters (British) news agency, from Paris early today quoted the Oslo radio as announcing that German troops disembarked at Norwegian ports at 3 a. m.

An intercepted Oslo radio report said that the Norwegian government had abandoned its capital and was moving to Hamar (approximately sixty miles due north of Oslo).

German forces were said to have occupied Bergen and Trondheim.

(Bergen, on the west coast, is Norway's most important seaport. Trondheim, on the north coast, is almost ninety miles north of Oslo.)

Swedish Ports Mined

LONDON, April 9 (P).—A German navigation service broadcast, intercepted by the Reuters (British) News Agency, said that all important harbors and ports of Sweden had been mined early today by Germany.

Norway Declares War

WASHINGTON, April 8 (P).—Mrs. J. Borden Harriman, American Minister to Norway, notified the State Department tonight that the Norwegian Foreign Minister had informed her that Norway is at war with Germany.

The State Department issued the following statement:

"The American Minister to Oslo, Mrs. J. Borden Harriman, telegraphed to the Department of State tonight that the Foreign Minister has informed her that the Norwegians fired on four German warships coming up Oslo Fjord and that Norway is at war with Germany.

"In response to a request by the British Minister to Norway, the American Legation at Oslo has been authorized to take over British interests in Norway in case he is obliged to evacuate."

Oslo Attacked by Warships

By The Associated Press

STOCKHOLM, April 9 (Tuesday).—Oslo, the capital of Norway, was attacked by a mysterious naval expedition of some unknown power striking from the darkness of the Skagerrak Channel early today—less than a month after Scandinavia had thought to escape war by the Finnish-Russian peace.

Authoritative quarters here confirmed previous reports that four warships attempted to force the entrance to Oslo Fjord, water gateway to the Norwegian capital, but were beaten off by coastal batteries.

Presumably the attack was from a German fleet which earlier was reported steaming through the Kattegat, near Denmark, from the Baltic in a northerly direction. However, British naval units also were numerous off Norwegian shores yesterday.

And heavy bursts of cannon fire from the warships, one of which was reported to be a heavy cruiser, an air battle was reported to have taken place between Norwegian planes and foreign fighting aircraft above the dark gorge of Oslo Fjord.

Oslo was blacked out, the city's communications with the rest of Norway having been cut by the censorship, the country's radio stations silenced, and lighthouses darkened. Oslo was reported to have experienced an air-raid alarm for an hour.

News on Inside Pages

WAR IN EUROPE

Oslo protests Allied blockade as war reaches Scandinavia.   Page 2
Norwegian Minister fears talk with State Department aids.   Page 3
Sweden, Norway consult on 'war' threat over Scandinavia.   Page 2
Germans lose two planes in raid on Scapa Flow naval base.   Page 4
Graf Spee officers guarded closely after eleven escape.   Page 4
"Julien the Lucky," first French war casualty, arrives here. Page 5
French Cabinet facing test in Senate war debate today.   Page 6
Nazi ship in Trieste with load of bauxite from Yugoslavia. Page 6
Cripps sees Anglo-Soviet war possibility menacing China. Page 7
Polish women hire tells of Nazi cruelty on Soviet frontier. Page 8

WASHINGTON

Roosevelt vetoes bill to deport alien spies and saboteurs.   Page 15
Republic Steel denied review on order to rehire strikers. Page 19

CITY AND VICINITY

Morris urges U. S. as a "haven for oppressed of all nations." Page 4
'Lehman and Wagner to speak at Farley testimonial dinner. Page 14
Lehman signs 24 bills, vetoes 5; must consider 208 more. Page 16
Twenty-seven persons hurt in Lexington Avenue bus crash. Page 17
N. L. R. B. refuses to replace Mrs. Herrick in Edison election. Page 19
Eight-block walk in Sixth Avenue subway nearly ready.   Page 24
Police hunt all night for five children bound for Wild West. Page 11
Aquarium receives pair of adult sea cows from the Amazon. Page 16
Books and Things, by Lewis Gannett.   Page 15
Fashion and food news.   Page 16
Drama, screen and music. Page 14
Society and resorts.   Page 23
Today's calendar of events. Page 36
Detailed weather report. Page 36
Service orders.   Page 36
Real estate market news. Page 37
Radio programs.   Page 24
Obituary articles.   Page 23

MARINE AND SHIPPING

Incoming, outgoing ships. Page 37
New York training ship to avoid waters of belligerents.   Page 37

FINANCIAL MARKETS

Wall St. comment. .23 | Co'modities 34
Stock quotations 29 | Curb dealings 33
Bond dealings . 30 | Overcounter29
Foreign exch'ge 32 | Other cities 34
Business records 36 | Bank stocks 33
Finance indexes 31 | Cable rep'ts 32
Dividends .....33 | List erased by

EDITORIALS AND MISCELLANY

Editorials.   Page 21
Mark Sullivan.   Page 21
The Bridge Deck.   Page 23
H. T. Webster's cartoon. Page 24
"Mr. and Mrs."   Page 38
Nature story.   Page 16
Cross-word puzzle.   Page 38

SPORTS

Council to be asked to tax city tracks $7,500 daily.   Page 27
Dodgers defeat Yankees in exhibition game, 10—6.   Page 27
Weather cancels Giants-Indians game at Anderson, S. C. Page 27
Rep. Kennedy, of Maryland, seeks Federal boxing control. Page 28
Down in Front, by Richards Vidmer.   Page 26

British Dynamite-Barges Seized In Rumania on Danube Plot Tip

By The Associated Press

BUCHAREST, April 8.—The detention of a fleet of dynamite-laden British barges, asserted by the Germans to have been designed to blow up a narrow Danube gateway and block a German supply line, electrified southeastern Europe today with fear that the war might soon spread to this quarter of the world.

Rumanian police, acting on a tip said to have been supplied by the pro-Nazi Iron Guard, halted the fleet near Giurgiu, Danube River port whence Germany ships Rumanian oil. Aboard were tons of dynamite.

Germans alleged the British planned to blockade the port in the Danube known as the Iron Gate by asking the barges and wrecking the narrow channel where the river cuts through the Carpathian Mountain barrier between high cliffs. The Iron Gate is 280 miles upriver from Giurgiu.

Official British quarters, acknowledging that the barges were loaded with explosives, insisted they were to be used only for destroying Allied river craft in case of a German invasion of Rumania. The only official British statement on the matter was a communique saying merely that Rumanian authorities had seized six cases of firearms which a British barge captain had neglected to declare in passing customs.

The British aim was reported in Germany, which keeps a close watch over Rumania through Gestapo (secret police) agents, to be blocking of the Iron Gate with sunken barges and blasting of the narrow artificial channel through which all river shipping must pass.

Two hundred Rumanian and Yugoslav soldiers armed with machine guns tonight were guarding the gateway, where the Danube forms the boundary between Rumania and Yugoslavia. Giurgiu was turned into a military zone by the Rumanian Army, which banned all entries without special permits.

The German version of the seizure, which was said to have taken

(Continued on page 7, column 2)

Where British Have Strewn Mines in Sea War

Shaded areas indicate new mine fields laid by Allies in attempt to halt shipments of iron ore from Scandinavia to Germany.

▲ NEW YORK HERALD TRIBUNE, NEW YORK, TUESDAY APRIL 9, 1940

Amid news of the German invasion of Norway and Denmark, New Yorkers read details of a plot to overthrow the federal government by shooting members of Congress and installing a dictator. Unlikely as the plot seems today, it suggests the real fear of subversion that gripped the United States. Real life continues, however: Inside the paper, readers are promised details of the arrival of two sea cows from the Amazon for the city aquarium.

ROOSEVELT HAILS AMERICAN REPUBLICS

NIGHT EDITION
★★★★★
Official Forecast: Occasional light rain; showers tonight; showers tomorrow.
SCHOOL NEWS ON PAGE 26

The Sun

Copyright, 1940, by The New York Sun, Inc.

**LATE NEWS—PICTURES
SCHOOLS—CIVIL SERVICE**
Temperature—Min., 36; Max., 45.
(Detailed weather report on page 20.)
LATE MARKET PRICES

VOL. CVII—NO. 192—DAILY.

NEW YORK, MONDAY, APRIL 15, 1940.

Entered as Second Class Matter Post Office, New York, N. Y.

THREE CENTS.

BRITISH TROOPS GET ASHORE AT VARIOUS NORSE POINTS

NEW WORLD WARNING ISSUED BY PRESIDENT

He Tells Pan American Union Any Challenge Must Be Met by Force—Condemns Europe's Racism and Violence.

WASHINGTON, April 15 (A. P.).—Terming wars abroad "more horrible and destructive than ever," President Roosevelt said today the twenty-one American republics could keep open the way to eventual peace "only if we are prepared to meet force with force if challenge is ever made."

Mr. Roosevelt spoke before the governing board of the Pan American Union on the observance of the organization's fiftieth anniversary and proclaimed a determination of the Western Hemisphere "to live in peace and make this peace worth while."

In words broadcast throughout the nation and transmitted abroad by short wave, the President designated to belligerent by name when he used their words apparently directed at recent European developments.

"We of this hemisphere have no need to seek a new international order, we already have found it. This was not won by hysterical oratories or violent movements of troops.

"We did not sharp out nations capture Governments, or uproot innocent people from the homes they had built. We did not travel aboard doctrines of race superiority, or claim dictatorship through an armed revolution.

"The inter-American order was built solidly by hatred and terror. It has been paved by the endless and effective work of men of good will."

President Is Unsmiling.

Introduced by Secretary Hull, the President spoke slowly without a single smile or any of his usual play of humor. Around a big mahogany table were gathered the diplomats of Latin America who comprise the governing board of the Pan American Union.

Seated beyond the table is straight good chairs were the envoys of England, Australia, Finland, China and many another country outside the hemisphere.

Secretary Wallace attended, and

Continued on Page 5.

Stowaway Travels in Style

Arrives With Trunk and Three Suitcases to Receive Telegram at Pier.

One day out of Genoa there emerged from below the decks of the liner Manhattan one William H. Hahnstadt, who had been in Germany. He was a stowaway, of course, but none of your living below decks with the cargo for him. After he had given himself up, he turned up with a trunk, three suitcases and a briefcase which he somehow had spirited aboard and which contained a presentable enough wardrobe.

The final touch of amusing sneak, however, came as the Manhattan finally eased into her berth today.

"Wire for Mr. Hahnstadt!" came the cry of a telegraph messenger.

Hahnstadt said that he was a civil engineer with a family in Rio de Janeiro. Business conditions, he found some time before the war opened, were ideal for him in Germany.

He went there to seek his fortune with an American passport, which is the only reason they'd let him back. A naturalized citizen of German extraction, he is picking up his son here for a short reunion.

After all his traveling around, he

Continued on Page 5.

SAYS FBI BOUGHT AMMUNITION FOR PLOT DEFENDANTS

Healy Admits He Used U.S. Funds to Get Shells for Target Practice.

Ammunition used by the sixteen alleged seditionists on trial in the Federal Court, Brooklyn, for target practice at their camp near Narrowsburg, N. Y., was paid for from funds supplied through the Federal Bureau of Investigation, the prosecution's key witness, Dennis A. Healy, testified today.

The defendants being tried before Judge Marcus Campbell are accused of plotting to overthrow the United States Government and are charged with the theft of ammunition from Government armories at fortheteenth of their plans.

Healy has testified how he gained their confidence and then informed the FBI. The defense contends he was a provocateur employed by the communists to foment trouble.

"You didn't steal that ammunition, did you?" Lawyer Healy demanded.

The witness denied that he did.

Admits Buying Ammunition.

Under the cross-examination of former Magistrate Leo J. Healy, counsel for ten defendants, the witness admitted he had purchased ammunition from a sporting goods store on Warren street to be used by the defendants, and that agents

Desires Stealing Ammunition.

Continued on Page 2.

BRITISH MINE FIELD REPORTED IN BALTIC

Map showing field said by London to have been laid boldly when Germany by British. The only area reported unmined is the Little Belt, the channel along Jutland.

Nazis Said to Burn Records At Embassy in Netherlands

Low Countries Watching Frontiers Anxiously Though Maintaining Outward Calm— Tokio Anxious Over East Indies.

William C. Kerker, NBC correspondent in Berlin, broadcast at 8 A. M., Eastern standard time, today that officials of the German embassy in Amsterdam had started to burn all political documents.

THE HAGUE, April 15—The Low Countries, determined not to be taken unawares by any threatening moves of Europe's warring Powers, maintained an alert watch on their frontiers today, but official circles were outwardly calm and there were signs of public anxiety over the future.

Holland has established a curfew ruling, according to a British Broadcasting Company report today from London, which said the population of the Netherlands has been warned not to leave their homes after 8 o'clock at night.

The report said further that defensive measures along the Dutch-German border had been intensified. Soldiers with fixed bayonets are patrolling the border as well as the streets of the towns situated along the border.

Special defense measures were taken in both the Netherlands and Belgium, but these were closely maintained as military secrets. Theatre and cafe life in all the larger cities did a normal peacetime business.

Government circles expressed indignation over foreign reports that there was imminent possibility of action by either the Germans or the allies which might spread the war to the lowlands. The rumors were termed ill considered and malicious.

Operations Are Combined.

The breaking of silence over the troop movements with the announcement that British forces had landed at several points in Norway shows that it is still possible to

Continued on Page 2.

Tennis Blocks Divorce Plans of Helen Vinson

LOS ANGELES, April 15 (A. P.)— An eastern tennis schedule is interfering with plans of actress Helen Vinson for a quick divorce from Fred Perry, the net star, who wants to fight the action but can't just yet.

Miss Vinson asked that the suit be set for trial next Thursday so she could leave for New York at the week end. The request was refused on pleas of Perry's attorney that his client, now in New York, could not return until May without jeopardizing his standing in forthcoming eastern professional tournaments.

BULLETINS

Nazis Report Arms Plant Seized.

BERLIN, April 15 (A. P.).—The DNB, official German news agency, said today that the Germans had occupied a powder factory at Honefoss and had seized large stores of light and heavy weapons in a munitions factory at Kongsberg. It listed the town of Hvalshon also as occupied.

Murmansk Reported Barred to Nazis.

Premier Molotov of Russia has refused Nazi ships entrance into the Russian port of Murmansk, according to a report broadcast by station VLQ at Sydney, Australia. The report was heard by the National Broadcasting Company short wave listening post in New York at 4:30 A. M., Eastern standard time.

Nazis Claim 300 Prisoners.

BERLIN, April 15 (A. P.).—DNB, official German news agency, reported today that German forces in Norway had captured 300 prisoners, seven cannon and a quantity of small arms and ammunition southeast of Oslo.

German Plane in Forced Landing.

STOCKHOLM, April 15 (A. P.).—A three-motored German Junkers warplane made a forced landing today at Mariestad, ninety miles from the Swedish west coast. It was returning to Germany from dropping leaflets in Norway when it lost its way and exhausted its gasoline. It carried a crew of five. Swedish policy is to intern both the plane and flyers.

Continued on Page 2.

NAVY AND R. A. F. RAID FOE; LANDING IS MADE AT NARVIK

Port Under Control of Naval Guns Which Set Hotel Ablaze—Norsemen Plan Attack in North, but Fall Back in South.

STOCKHOLM, April 15 (A. P.).—British forces were reported today to have landed in Narvik under the protection of naval shellfire which drove the Germans from the northern Norwegian ore port into the mountainous interior.

The British warships which raided Narvik on Saturday, apparently preparatory to a landing by British soldiers or marines, were said to have the city under control of their guns.

They report, from the Norwegian radio at the port of Bodo, south of Narvik, followed a Norwegian army communique reporting that Norwegian troops north and south of Narvik were ready to attack the Germans.

The Norwegian commander said that the German forces had retreated hastily and were believed to be incapable of strong resistance to the Norwegians, who, he said, now were fully mobilized in the north.

"No Heavy Bombardment.

Norwegians said that all German warships in Narvik, hopelessly outweighted by the British naval force, had been sunk while trying to keep the British out of Romhaka Fjord, which controls the port.

According to the Norwegian version, the British battleship Warspite, screened by a division of destroyers, forced the mouth of the fjord. Norwegians considered it improbable that the Germans would be able to land troops in Narvik again.

They said that there had not been any heavy British bombard-

Navajo Nearing Swedish Border.

To southeastern Norway, spuradic fighting between German and Norwegian forces brought the invading Nazis nearer the Swedish border. The Norwegians, meanwhile, were urged to greater efforts by their aging sovereign, King Haakon VII, who had last night broadcast an appeal to his people to fight on for "freedom and independence."

The King, who has been driven from town to town by pursuing German bombers since he abandoned Oslo with his Government last week, spoke from an unidentified station somewhere in the interior.

Despite the heartening effect which the King's appeal was expected to have on Norwegian morale, the country's defenders appeared to be fighting a losing battle on the southern front.

Swedish authorities announced that 2,000 Norwegians, seemingly hard-pressed, had fled across the frontier near Riddu at the southernmost tip of Norway and had been disarmed and interned. The Germans were said to have driven several miles beyond Haldan to Kornsjo, a border station on the

Continued on Page 5.

London Throngs Are Jubilant

'Now We Are Getting Somewhere!' Shout Crowds Cheering Norway Landings.

By GAULT MacGOWAN

*Special Cable Dispatch to The Sun.
Copyright, 1940.*

LONDON, April 15—England is jubilant today. At last, the country feels, it is getting somewhere. The Admiralty's announcement that troops have landed in Norway has been received with tremendous enthusiasm.

In offices and on the streets, comparative strangers are shaking hands, slapping backs and creating a spontaneous "now-we-shan't-be-long" atmosphere. There is a weariness in these last days that has been absent since the outset of hostilities.

Pedestrians surged toward Buckingham Palace and Downing street, the traditional focal points in times of national enthusiasm, in the hope of catching a glimpse of the members of the royal family or leaders in the government, with a consequent opportunity to give vent to their feelings in cheers.

Airmen Set Fire to Large Supply of Gasoline in Stavanger Raid.

NAZIS DENY LOSING ANY PORTS

But Admit Foe May Have Landed in "Non-strategic Nooks"— Lose More Transports.

LONDON, April 15 (A. P.).—Great Britain announced today that she had landed soldiers at several points in Norway to press the war against the German invaders, while her navy and air force hurled new bolts at the Nazis in widespread sectors in and around Scandinavia.

[Berlin denied that British troops had landed at Narvik or any other Norwegian ports occupied by German forces, but admitted that the enemy might have landed somewhere along Norway's jagged coast of nearly 1,000 miles. The coast abounds in little hideouts, but these are strategically unimportant, the Germans said.]

The brief statement in a joint War Office-Admiralty communique was British troops are in Norway and engaged a week and examined with activity.

The British reported in this period:

1. The laying of a huge mine barricade across the entire German Baltic coast from Kiel Bay to Lithuania.

2. The torpedoing of the 10,000-ton German pocket battleship Admiral Scheer by the British submarine Spearfish. The Admiralty did not say whether the Scheer was sunk.

Transports Are Torpedoed.

3. The sinking by British submarines of two German transports, bringing to twelve the total of transport and supply ships reported sunk in recent days. The Admiralty also said that its submarines had scored four hits on a transport convoy in the Skagerrak.

4. Continued British aerial raids on Stavanger and Bergen. A gasoline dump was believed to have been destroyed in a night raid, the fifth since Germany's invasion, at Stavanger and the Admiralty said that one German transport was set afire at Bergen.

5. A British naval squadron led by the battleship Warspite, on Saturday sank seven German destroyers at Narvik, northern Norwegian ore port.

Other Possible Landings.

While official information was lacking regarding the number of

SEESAW FIGHTS ON WEST FRONT

Sallies by Both Sides Net Nothing to Either.

PARIS, April 15 (A. P.).—French and German thrusts into the other's line during the last twenty-four hours ended today with both back in their old positions.

The French said that on the Alsatian sector they succeeded in opening a hole in German entangle-

CRASHES ALARM BO...

Taxi Driver Avoids M... and Disrupts Circuit.

In Belgium, however, an organization of world war veterans suggested creation of a large auxiliary police force recruited from their ranks and designation of concentration camps sites where undesirable foreigners might be detained.

"It is logical to conceive of a surprise attack executed on our railways, our barracks, our public stations, our banks and public installations," the veterans said.

A British reconnaissance plane, attacked by Nazi airmen on the German side of the frontier yesterday, crashed just inside Dutch territory near the village of Bocholtz in the extreme eastern province of Gelderland.

The British plane was believed to have carried a crew of three. Two were found in the wreckage. Thousands witnessed the air battle. British, French and Polish Ministers to Copenhagen arrived in

Continued on Page 2.

In The Sun Today

HERE TO DINE—Hotels & Restaurants.
Starts After Dave Boone Page 15—Adv.

Jersey Liquor Fees Up.

TRENTON, April 15 (A. P.)—An increase of $70,822 in alcoholic beverage tax receipts last month compared to March a year ago was reported today by the State Department. Of the $441,080 collected last month, the largest portion, $454,223, came from the dollar-a-gallon tax on hard liquors. In March a year ago hard liquors produced $371,427.

▶ GERMAN TROOPS LAND SUPPLIES at Narvik in April 1940. Located in the far north of Norway, Narvik was at first beyond the range of German transport aircraft, and with the destruction of their supply ships by the Royal Navy, the German garrison at Narvik was very vulnerable. Indeed, Hitler had already written it off when he heard of its predicament. Narvik finally fell to an Allied assault at the end of May 1940.

◀ THE SUN, NEW YORK, MONDAY APRIL 15, 1940 Readers of the conservative evening daily learn of British troop landings in Norway, but with few details from the British government the report is largely vague. *The Sun* is on safer ground with its own reporter's account of celebrations in London. A crowded front page also has room for President Franklin D. Roosevelt's moves to strengthen unity among all the American countries, a stowaway's escape from Germany to New York, and a celebrity divorce between actress Helen Vinson and tennis star Fred Perry.

Daily Express

DAILY EXPRESS Monday, April 15, 1940.

No. 12,447   Monday, April 15, 1940   One Penny

The Navy has done it again!

Admiralty at midnight said the Nazi cruiser Karlsruhe (pictured here in heavy weather) has been torpedoed and sunk. And....

ADMIRAL SCHEER TORPEDOED

Sister ship to the scuttled Graf Spee

Hit more than once

HITLER'S 10,000-TON POCKET BATTLE-SHIP ADMIRAL SCHEER — SISTER SHIP OF THE INGLORIOUS GRAF SPEE — HAS BEEN TORPEDOED. SHE IS BELIEVED TO BE BADLY DAMAGED. THE 6,000-TON CRUISER KARLSRUHE HAS BEEN TORPEDOED AND SUNK.

The names of these two leading German men-of-war head a long list of Nazi sinkings, cripplings and scuttlings officially announced by the Admiralty at midnight.

Norway's Navy has also had her successes. One German captain scuttled his ship at the very sight of a Norwegian destroyer, while the German tanker Kattegat, the Admiralty declare, has been sunk by the Norwegians in the Skagerrak.

The Admiralty's midnight communiqué was issued within twenty-six hours of the announcement that the Navy had destroyed the German naval forces at Narvik—a victory which was celebrated at Gibraltar yesterday by an order "to fly flags in all his Majesty's warships."

Here is the Admiralty's latest statement in full:—

Some indication of the highly successful work under extremely hazardous conditions of our submarines during the past week can now be given.

DAWN ATTACK

The German pocket battleship Admiral Scheer was successfully attacked by the submarine Spearfish (Lieut.-Commander J. H. Forbes) in the early hours of Thursday morning.

It is probable that the Admiral Scheer was hit by more than one torpedo.

The submarine Truant (Lieut.-Commander C. H. Hutchinson) torpedoed and sank a German cruiser believed to be the Karlsruhe on Tuesday. The sinking of this cruiser has already been announced and admitted by the Germans.

SHIP CAPTURED

Other successes include the sinking of the following German transports and supply ships:—

Tanker Posidonia (3,911 tons), August Leonhardt (2,593 tons), Kreta (2,359 tons), Rio de Janeiro (5,261 tons), Ionia (3,102 tons), Antares (2,593 tons), Moorannd (321 tons), an unknown German ship about 4,000 tons.

On Wednesday two more unknown German ships were sunk and four other ships in convoy were hit by torpedo, the results being unknown.

In addition, the Alster (8,514 tons) has been captured and three trawlers—Friesland, Nordland and Blankenberg—have been brought into a British port.

All these ships are in addition to the six supply ships and the Ravenfeld, which were sunk off Narvik by the Second Destroyer Flotilla on Wednesday, as was announced in the Back Page.

→ BACK PAGE COL. THREE

Nazi Navy cut by a third

HITLER'S Norwegian adventure has cost him—so far —nearly one-third of his surface navy.

According to the best information available early today he has lost—sunk or out of action— fifteen ships (about 100,000 tons).

This week's losses include:—

SCHARNHORST, 26,000 - ton battleship: Heavily damaged.

GNEISENAU, 26,000 tons, her sister ship: Reported by Norwegian authorities sunk.

ADMIRAL SCHEER, 10,000-ton pocket battleship: Torpedoed; fate uncertain, but must be out of action.

BLUECHER, 10,000-ton cruiser: Sunk by shore batteries.

KARLSRUHE, 6,000-ton cruiser: Sunk by British submarine.

TWO LIGHT CRUISERS, 6,000 tons each: Sunk off Bergen.

SEVEN DESTROYERS: Sunk at Narvik by British naval action.

ONE DESTROYER: Sunk by bombing off Trondheim.

The total of merchant ship and transport tonnage sunk or damaged in Norwegian waters is about 90,000.

SWEDISH NAZIS PLANNED COUP

PARIS, Sunday.—Swift action by the Swedish Government thwarted an internal Nazi coup planned for last Thursday night, says a Havas Agency report tonight.

Swedish organisations of Nazi origin had received orders from Berlin to seize strategic points throughout the country, but the Government ordered the arrest of the leaders and put many others under police observation.—Reuter.

3 a.m. MAP

THIS special Daily Express map shows the position on all fronts in Norway at 3 o'clock this morning.

Warburton-Lee of the Hardy killed

Captain B. A. W. Warburton-Lee, commander of the destroyer Hardy, who led his flotilla into Narvik last Wednesday against overwhelming odds, was killed in the action, the Admiralty revealed last night.

The casualty list includes the name of one other officer and fourteen ratings killed, three officers and six ratings seriously injured, and two ratings believed drowned. *The list is on the Back Page.*

THE WHOLE TRUTH ABOUT THE BALKANS

THREE weeks ago Sefton Delmer, chief foreign correspondent of the Daily Express, began a tour of Europe's other danger spot—the Balkans and the Black Sea.

His objects were to investigate conditions there, to discover the extent of the leaks in the Allied blockade, to find out the amount of oil and other commodities passing from the Balkans to Germany.

He was instructed not to begin writing until his investigation was complete in every detail, until he had been able to check and counter-check every fact, so that his report should be the most authoritative possible.

Now the inquiry is complete and Sefton Delmer will set out his discoveries in the first of three remarkable articles in the Daily Express to-morrow.

In this article he will tell of his meetings with Edith von Kohle, fake reporter and cousin of Himmler, of the Nazi money poured into the Balkans, of the swarms of S.S. men who work as civilians in Rumania, of the tremendous Nazi propaganda service all over this part of Europe.

'Bomb King Haakon'
—Nazi order

GERMANY'S air force has taken over from the army the task of "getting" King Haakon.

A report from the Norwegian Government, received by the Foreign Office last night, says that Nazi bombers, "evidently under orders," are attacking each successive place in which he stays.

When the Germans landed in Oslo, King Haakon and the royal family took train to Hamar, eighty miles to the north-east.

SHOCK TROOPS

A flying column of shock troops was ordered by Nazi Commander von Falkenhorst to bring the King back to the capital. The column was beaten off and the King moved to Elverum.

A more powerful detachment, backed by bombers, set out for Elverum. They, too, were foiled. A handful of Norwegians held them up while the King got away. Nazi bombers laid the town in ruins an hour after the royal family had left in a convoy of cars.

The party was machine-gunned by pursuing planes, but arrived safely at Nybergsund, their next headquarters.

This town, too, was practically obliterated by bombers during the week-end, so the royal family moved again.

THIS MORNING IN—

HOLLAND
Troops called out

TROOPS with fixed bayonets and machine-guns are patrolling the streets of Holland's large cities.

Near the frontier there is an 8 p.m. curfew. Roads and bridges are guarded. Batteries along the coast are ready for action.—*See Page Two.*

BELGIUM
Ready for anything

BELGIUM is under emergency measures. She is ready to meet any threat. Soldiers are guarding all public buildings and railway stations.—*See Page Two.*

SWEDEN
Nazi plane shot down

STOCKHOLM issued an official announcement at one o'clock this morning that Swedish anti-aircraft batteries shot down a German plane at Uddevalla, on the west coast yesterday.

Neutrality guards fired warning shots, which it is stated, were ignored. All the crew except one were killed.

Nazi air base is bombed in dawn raid

British planes again bombed the German-occupied airfield at Stavanger, Norway, at dawn yesterday.

A hangar, a runway, and a number of Nazi planes on the airfield were damaged in a low-flying attack.

Anti-aircraft fire was encountered, says the official Air Ministry report, but our planes continued on their way and delivered another attack on the enemy in Hafslord.

Here they machine-gunned seaplanes moored on the water, and silenced an enemy machine-gun post.

£100,000,000 for our war chest

A new list of British-owned American securities to be taken over by the Treasury was announced yesterday.

Bernard Harris says on Page Eight that the securities might yield around £100,000,000 for the war effort.

"B.E.F. NOW LANDING"
—Narvik report

Daily Express Staff Reporter

STOCKHOLM, Monday Morning.

IT was reliably reported in Stockholm last night that British troops had landed south of Narvik and moved into the town. The Germans have retreated to the woods.

The battleship Warspite, in Narvik harbour, is plastering with shells the woods in which the Germans are hiding, Swedish reports state.

Britain's consul in Narvik, Mr. Gibbs, who with his three assistants escaped to Riksgransen on the Swedish frontier, is returning to Narvik. He hopes to arrive there today.

BRILLIANT ACTION

The way for the British disembarkation was cleared by the Navy's brilliant action in sinking seven German destroyers in Narvik Fiord on Saturday.

Here are the other highlights of the situation in the Norwegian theatre of the war against Hitler:

British marines are reported, without confirmation, to have landed at Namsos, the next fiord north of Trondheim, which is in German hands.

The captain of an American freighter telephoned to his Consul-General in Stockholm yesterday that he was putting to sea at once because a naval battle was expected to start round Trondheim at any moment.

The British are said to have brought two battleships, two

■ BACK PAGE, COL. SIX

STOP PRESS

British take over in Narvik

GOTHENBURG, Sunday. — Now definitely confirmed that British are in control in Narvik and that German forces have fled into mountains north east of town.—Exchange.

70,000 Nazis 'on way'

SEVENTY THOUSAND German soldiers, heavily equipped, have passed through Copenhagen, and it is believed they are the vanguard of a Nazi army to attack Sweden.

The first full story of how Copenhagen gave in before it was bombed, of the German planes flew overhead, is told on Page Five.

▲ DAILY EXPRESS, LONDON, MONDAY APRIL 15, 1940

The news from Norway seems positive according to the *Express*, although it turned out that the *Admiral Scheer* had not been sunk but was undergoing a refit. At the foot of the page, the paper flags a series of reports from its correspondent in the Balkans—an example of eyewitness journalism that would become rare later in the war.

Enter Churchill

MAY 10, 1940

WINSTON CHURCHILL HAD BEEN BROUGHT INTO THE BRITISH GOVERNMENT WHEN WAR WAS DECLARED IN SEPTEMBER 1939. AT THAT time, he was made First Lord of the Admiralty—head of the Royal Navy—a crucial appointment. After the German invasion of Norway in April 1939, the position of prime minister Neville Chamberlain had come into question as the British response to the invasion was seen as too tentative.

RESIGNATION

On all sides, from his own Conservative Party and from the socialist Labor Party, there was pressure on Chamberlain to leave office. Winston Churchill stood up in the House of Commons and declared that the German invasion of Norway had been a strategic blunder by Hitler. Few believed him, though in hindsight his analysis was correct. However, most British politicians did believe that Neville Chamberlain's leadership of the country was becoming increasingly inept and was

damaging to the war effort. On May 7, 1940, the House of Commons debated the Norwegian campaign. Leo Amery, a Conservative Member of Parliament, rose to his feet, pointed at Chamberlain, and quoted Oliver Cromwell: "Depart I say and let us have done. In the name of God, go." Realizing that he had lost the support of his own party (of which he was the leader), Chamberlain had no option but to resign, which he did on May 10. A coalition government was formed and Winston Churchill was appointed prime minister. It was not a moment too soon, for on the same day the Germans launched their invasion of France and the Low Countries. Neville Chamberlain was a broken man and would die six months later.

CHURCHILL'S VERDICT

Winston Churchill had this to say about the man he succeeded: "Neville Chamberlain was alert, businesslike, opinionated, and self-confident in a very high degree ... He had formed decided judgements about all the political figures of the day, both at home and abroad. His all pervading hope was to go down in history as the Great Peacemaker."

▲ NEVILLE CHAMBERLAIN (1869–1940), seen here on the left, will forever be associated with the failed policy of appeasement.

Daily Express

No. 12,469   Friday, May 10, 1940   One Penny

CHURCHILL expected to be new Premier

CHAMBERLAIN TO RESIGN

Socialists refuse to join his new Cabinet

BUT THEY MAY BACK WINSTON

Daily Express Political Correspondent GUY EDEN

LATE LAST NIGHT IT WAS BELIEVED CERTAIN THAT TODAY MR. NEVILLE CHAMBERLAIN WILL OFFER HIS RESIGNATION TO THE KING.

It is expected that Mr. Winston Churchill will be sent for and asked to form a new Administration.

There was a possibility yesterday that Mr. Chamberlain would try to reconstruct his Government by dropping many leading Ministers and asking Socialist and Liberal leaders to join, with himself continuing as Premier.

In the evening he saw Mr. Clement Attlee and Mr. Arthur Greenwood, leaders of the Socialist Opposition, and invited them to join the Government. They refused, saying that they could not serve under Mr. Chamberlain.

Mr. Churchill and Lord Halifax were also at the forty-five-minute meeting, which was held in the Cabinet Room at No. 10, Downing-street.

Mr. Chamberlain inquired whether the Socialists would join a Government formed by one of them.

They are believed to have indicated willingness to accept Mr. Churchill's leadership, subject to the endorsement of their action by their party.

Earlier in the day, Conservative M.P.s who had voted against the Government in Wednesday night's Commons division — when the Government's majority fell to eighty-one — had informed Mr. Chamberlain that they would be willing to support any Premier who could form a "truly national Government."

FLAT REFUSAL

They added that, in their view, the Prime Minister should be a Conservative, thus not ruling out Mr. Chamberlain.

The flat refusal of the Socialists to serve under Mr. Chamberlain makes his resignation a virtual certainty, as, without the co-operation of the Socialists, he would also lose the aid of his Conservative critics.

Mr. Chamberlain himself is known to take the view that national unity and the broadest-based Government are essential, in view of existing and expected international developments.

There were meetings all day yesterday, supporters and opponents of the Government holding conferences from early morning until late at night.

STRONG SUPPORT

At first there was strong support among M.P.s for a proposal that Mr. Chamberlain should re-form the Government. Then the attitude of the Socialists ruled this out, and Mr. Churchill's chances of success were canvassed.

It seems beyond question that, he asks for a vote of confidence, Mr. Churchill will get an overwhelming majority in the House of Commons.

Both Houses adjourned yesterday until May 21, but most M.P.s expect that they will be recalled earlier.

Mr. Chamberlain plans to see the King today, and, if he goes from office, Mr. Churchill will begin at once the formation of his new Government. The holders of the chief offices may be known tonight.

Whether Mr. Chamberlain will accept a peerage or remain in the House of Commons would be decided quickly. His own preference is believed to be the Commons.

Lloyd George criticised—Page Six.

CHANGES MUST BE MADE QUICKLY

Daily Express Political Correspondent

"" view is held widely "at there should be no delay in forming a new Government. The posts should not remain vacant as they are virtually at present.

Immense pressure will be put on those concerned to move swiftly to complete the changes by tonight.

13 torpedoes hit Nazi ships

THREE there convoys of Nazi transport and supply ships have been attacked by British submarines, it was revealed last night and thirteen hits were made by torpedoes.

The Admiralty communiqué said: "In an attack on a convoy of ten enemy ships six torpedoes found their marks. Three hits were made on another convoy, and two on a third.

"One ship sailing independently was torpedoed and sunk. Another was driven ashore and destroyed by gunfire and torpedo."

Tommies saved King Haakon

STOCKHOLM, Thursday.—British troops saved King Haakon of Norway from capture during the German advance in the Gudbrands Valley, in Central Norway, says the Oslo correspondent of Aftenhanda.

The Norwegian troops in the valley had exhausted their ammunition. Then British troops came to their aid just in time and held up the Germans long enough for the King to escape in a British warship.—Reuter.

PARIS SEES CHURCHILL AS 'LIVE-WIRE' LEADER

Comment on the British Parliamentary crisis yesterday by the Intransigeant, popular Paris afternoon newspaper :—

THE British people understand circumstances impose a leadership giving rapid action, surer foresight, and a more lively imagination. Mr. Churchill has all three qualities. Do not forget that for years he has foreseen the present events, and that, almost alone at certain periods, he warned his fellow-countrymen. *Tougher Britain: See Page Two.*

Salvo of Nazi bombs crashes close to British aircraft-carrier . .

Great "waterspouts" rise close to the bows of a British aircraft-carrier as an attacking German bomber unloads a salvo. The warship's captain, by brilliant seamanship, manages to keep out of the danger zone.—A Gaumont British News picture.

—And here is a German air attack on a British troopship steaming under naval convoy from Namsos . . . The bombs fall well astern.—British Paramount News picture. Others, Back Page.

War (at the Arsenal) will not take a holiday

Daily Express Industrial Reporter

ABOUT a quarter of the workers in Woolwich Arsenal were told yesterday that they would not, after all, be allowed to start their Whitsun holidays at noon today.

They are to be kept on throughout the holiday period, and in some cases there will be Sunday work as well.

But most of those who have had their holiday cancelled will be employed on maintenance and repairs. There will be very little production work going on at the arsenal, or at any of the other royal ordnance factories throughout the country.

At least three-quarters of the men employed in Government factories will be off at noon today until Tuesday.

By contrast, most privately-owned munition and aircraft plants will not close until tomorrow, and will resume, in most cases, on Tuesday morning.

They hope it rains

Chief of the smaller engineering firms in Bristol are hoping for rain at Whitsun.

They have appealed to their men on grounds of national service to volunteer for work during the holiday at overtime rates, and the response will depend on the weather.

Colonel kept in the Tower

Lieut.-Colonel H. F. L. Williams, accused at a general court-martial in London yesterday of having been "on terms of undue familiarity with a sergeant," said he had been under close arrest for five weeks, nearly all the time in the Tower of London. Story on PAGE THREE.

'MUMMY— I'VE BEEN SHOT'

TWELVE-YEAR-OLD Ivy Kathleen Bartlett went to a window at house in Featherstone-terrace, Southall, Middlesex, yesterday afternoon to look out at her playmates. She pushed the window open, and a moment later ran downstairs crying, "Mummy, I've been shot!"

Her mother laid her on a couch, and the doctor who was called found a bullet in her chest. She was taken to hospital, and the bullet was removed.

Opposite the house where Ivy was staying is a high wall round the car-park of a cinema. In the car-park two men had been shooting.

One of them said last night: "We went into the car-park to have one shot each with a .22 rifle. We aimed at a greenhouse."

"Apparently one of the bullets ricochetted."

'Quake rocks Peru

LIMA (Peru), Thursday.— Strong earthquake tremors shook Lima today. No casualties have yet been reported.—British United Press.

DUTCH STOP RADIO AND CUT PHONES

THE Dutch Government last night closed down radio stations and put new bans on telephone and other communications.

Shortly after eleven o'clock the Amsterdam telephone exchange warned London that no further calls in either direction would be accepted before daylight, at the earliest. Tele-printer services—much used by business firms with connections in Holland — were also suspended.

On Wednesday night ingoing calls were allowed, although the Government reserved the right to take over all lines after 10 p.m.

'WEB OF LIES AND RUMOUR'

Daily Express Staff Reporter

AMSTERDAM, Thursday.

GRAVE reports of a virtual German ultimatum to Holland were denied in Amsterdam tonight. It was also denied that Dutch emissaries had gone to Berlin to negotiate on demands that Dutch ports should be handed over to Germany.

The Dutch Government's spokesman admitted that defensive preparations were being taken. "The Netherlands," he said, "are surrounded by a net of lies and rumours. Our preparedness will not be relaxed."

German troop movements are taking place close to the Dutch frontier, and it is thought that the holiday week-end may be the crucial time.

A Whitsun blitzkrieg is, many Dutchmen believe, a distinct possibility.

Despite reports from Brussels that Belgium will do nothing if Holland alone is attacked, the feeling in Holland—unconfirmed by any official statement—is that Belgium and Holland stand together in all circumstances.

Mackenzie King may reshuffle Cabinet

TORONTO, Thursday.—A Cabinet shuffle will probably be announced by Mr. Mackenzie King before the Canadian Parliament opens next week, it was learned today in Ottawa.

France sent 100 ships

PARIS, Thursday.— More than a hundred French naval units took part in the Norwegian operations, it was announced by the French Admiralty tonight.—British United Press.

Map shows how the Low Countries form hub of nations at war.

▲ DAILY EXPRESS, LONDON, FRIDAY MAY 10, 1940

Given that political correspondent Guy Eden was later a biographer of Churchill, his prediction that Churchill would replace Chamberlain was not surprisingly well informed. The *Express* reports French approval of the new prime minister, but the center of the page reflects a more pressing concern: how to get British workers to give up the traditional Whitsun holiday.

► PARIS-SOIR, PARIS, SATURDAY MAY 11, 1940 The main newspaper in Paris reports the German invasion of the Low Countries and the advance by French and British armies into Belgium. It also details the first direct attacks on France: German bombing of the cities of Nancy, Lille, Colmar, Lyons, Pontoise, and Luxeuil. The front page also carries a grim leader from the newspaper: "France, your most solemn hour is here." It begins, "For eight months, the supreme threat has hung over our borders, our towns, and our countryside" and concludes, "Whatever happens, France will not surrender."

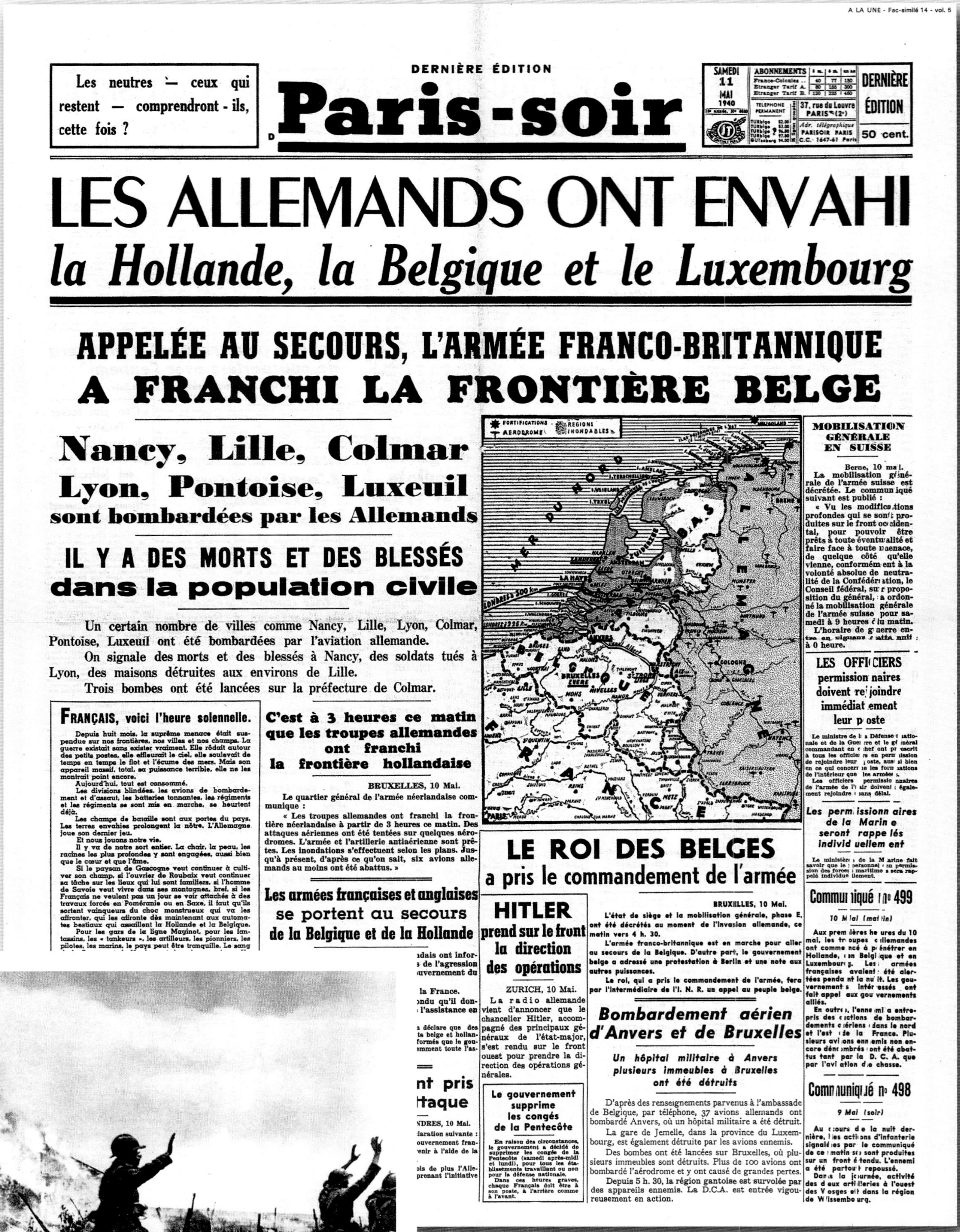

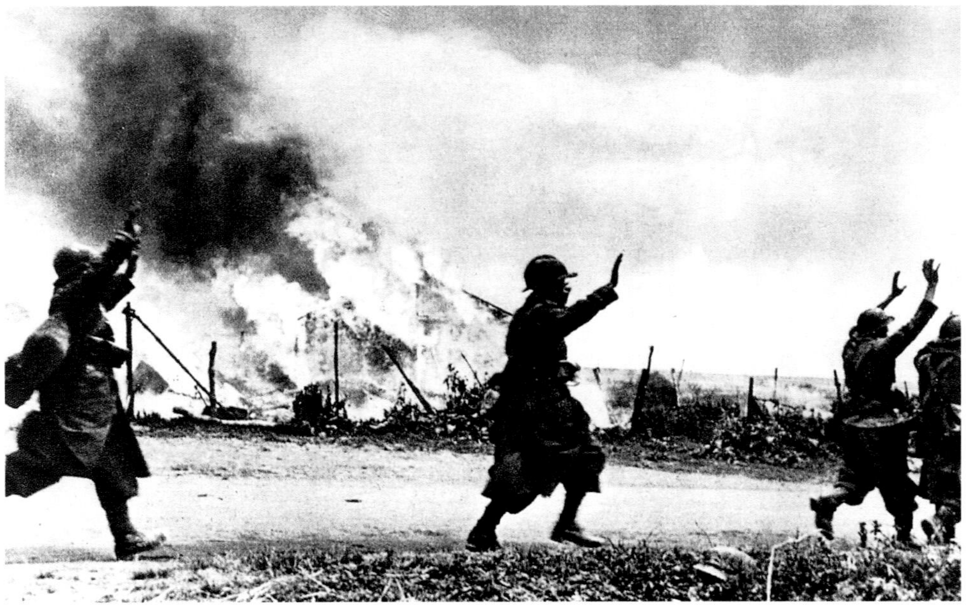

◄ FRENCH TROOPS SURRENDER as German forces smash west toward the English Channel in May 1940. The German breakthrough at Sedan by 1,900 panzers and 175,000 troops decided the campaign.

DERNIÈRE ÉDITION

Les neutres — ceux qui restent — comprendront-ils, cette fois ?

Paris-soir

SAMEDI 11 MAI 1940

DERNIÈRE ÉDITION

50 cent.

LES ALLEMANDS ONT ENVAHI
la Hollande, la Belgique et le Luxembourg

APPELÉE AU SECOURS, L'ARMÉE FRANCO-BRITANNIQUE
A FRANCHI LA FRONTIÈRE BELGE

Nancy, Lille, Colmar Lyon, Pontoise, Luxeuil
sont bombardées par les Allemands

IL Y A DES MORTS ET DES BLESSÉS
dans la population civile

Un certain nombre de villes comme Nancy, Lille, Lyon, Colmar, Pontoise, Luxeuil ont été bombardées par l'aviation allemande.

On signale des morts et des blessés à Nancy, des soldats tués à Lyon, des maisons détruites aux environs de Lille.

Trois bombes ont été lancées sur la préfecture de Colmar.

FRANÇAIS, voici l'heure solennelle.

Depuis huit mois, la suprême menace était suspendue sur nos frontières, nos villes et nos champs. La guerre existait sans exister vraiment. Elle rôdait autour des petits postes, elle effleurait le ciel, elle soulevait de temps en temps le flot et l'écume des mers. Mais son appareil massif, total, sa puissance terrible, elle ne les montrait point encore.

Aujourd'hui, tout est consommé.

Les divisions blindées, les avions de bombardement et d'assaut, les batteries tonnantes, les régiments et les régiments se sont mis en marche, se heurtent déjà.

« Les champs de bataille sont aux portes du pays. Les terres envahies prolongent la nôtre. L'Allemagne joue son dernier jeu.

Et nous jouons notre vie.

Il y va de notre sort entier. La chair, la peau, les racines les plus profondes y sont engagées, aussi bien que le cœur et que l'âme.

Si le paysan de Gascogne veut continuer à cultiver son champ, si l'ouvrier de Roubaix veut continuer sa tâche sur les lieux qui lui sont familiers, si l'homme de Savoie veut vivre dans ses montagnes, bref, si les Français ne veulent pas un jour se voir attachés à la Germanie, forcés en Poméranie, bref, il faut qu'ils sortent vainqueurs du choc monstrueux qui va les affronter, des armées vainqueurs du choc monstrueux qui va les affronter, qui les affronte dès maintenant aux automobiles bestiaux qui assaillent la Hollande et la Belgique.

Pour les gars de la ligne Maginot, pour les fantassins, les « tankistes », les artilleurs, les pionniers, les pilotes, les marins, le pays peut être tranquille. Le sang...

C'est à 3 heures ce matin
que les troupes allemandes
ont franchi
la frontière hollandaise

BRUXELLES, 10 Mai.

Le quartier général de l'armée néerlandaise communique :

« Les troupes allemandes ont franchi la frontière néerlandaise à partir de 3 heures ce matin. Des attaques aériennes ont été tentées sur quelques aérodromes. L'armée et l'artillerie antiaérienne sont prêtes. Les inondations s'effectuent selon les plans. Jusqu'à présent, d'après ce qu'on sait, six avions allemands au moins ont été abattus. »

Les armées françaises et anglaises
se portent au secours
de la Belgique et de la Hollande

...dais ont informé... e du gouvernement... de l'agression... ouvernement du...

la France.

...ndu qu'il don... l'assistance en...

...a déclaré que... la belge et hollan... formés que le gou... mment toute l'as...

...nt pris ...attaque

...NDRES, 10 Mai. ...laration suivante : ...ouvernement fran... ...nir à l'aide du Po... ...ois de plus l'Alle... ...prenant l'initiative

Le gouvernement
supprime
les congés
de la Pentecôte

En raison des circonstances, le gouvernement a décidé de supprimer les congés de la Pentecôte (samedi après-midi et lundi), pour tous les établissements travaillant en vue de la défense nationale.

Dans ces heures graves, chaque Français doit être à son poste, à l'arrière comme à l'avant.

LE ROI DES BELGES
a pris le commandement de l'armée

BRUXELLES, 10 Mai.

L'état de siège et la mobilisation générale, phase E, ont été décrétés au moment de l'invasion allemande, ce matin vers 4 h. 30.

L'armée franco-britannique est en marche pour aller au secours de la Belgique. D'autre part, le gouvernement belge a adressé une protestation à Berlin et une note aux autres puissances.

Le roi, qui a pris le commandement de l'armée, fera par l'intermédiaire de l'I. N. R. un appel au peuple belge.

Bombardement aérien
d'Anvers et de Bruxelles

Un hôpital militaire à Anvers
plusieurs immeubles à Bruxelles
ont été détruits

D'après des renseignements parvenus à l'ambassade de Belgique, par téléphone, 37 avions allemands ont bombardé Anvers, où un hôpital militaire a été détruit.

La gare de Jemelle, dans la province du Luxembourg, est également détruite par les avions ennemis.

Des bombes ont été lancées sur Bruxelles, où plusieurs immeubles sont détruits. Plus de 100 avions ont bombardé l'aérodrome et y ont causé de grandes pertes.

Depuis 5 h. 30, la région gantoise est survolée par des appareils ennemis. La D.C.A. est entrée vigoureusement en action.

HITLER
prend sur le front
la direction
des opérations

ZURICH, 10 Mai.

La radio allemande vient d'annoncer que le chancelier Hitler, accompagné des principaux généraux de l'état-major, s'est rendu sur le front ouest pour prendre la direction des opérations générales.

MOBILISATION GÉNÉRALE EN SUISSE

Berne, 10 mai.

La mobilisation générale de l'armée suisse est décrétée. Le communiqué suivant est publié :

« Vu les modifications profondes qui se sont produites sur le front occidental, pour pouvoir être prêts à toute éventualité et faire face à toute menace, de quelque côté qu'elle vienne, conformément à la volonté absolue de neutralité de la Confédération, le Conseil fédéral, sur proposition du général, a ordonné la mobilisation générale de l'armée suisse pour samedi à 9 heures du matin.

L'horaire de guerre entrera en vigueur ce soir même à 0 heure.

LES OFFICIERS
permissionnaires
doivent rejoindre
immédiatement
leur poste

Le ministre de la Défense nationale et de la Guerre et le général commandant en chef ont prescrit à tous les officiers en congé dans situation où ils se trouvent où qu'ils de rejoindre leur poste, sans aucun délai concernant le form ations de l'Intérieur ont des armées...

Les officiers permissionnaires de l'armée de l'air doivent également rejoindre sans délai.

Les permissionnaires
de la Marine
seront rappelés
individuellement

Le ministre de la Marine fait savoir que le personnel en permission des forces maritimes sera rappelé individuellement.

Communiqué n° 499
10 Mai (matin)

Aux premières heures du 10 mai, les troupes allemandes ont commencé à pénétrer en Hollande, en Belgique et au Luxembourg. Les armées françaises ont alertées pendant la nuit. En Belgique et en Luxembourg... Les armées françaises alertées pendant la nuit. Le gouvernement intéressés ont fait appel aux gouvernements alliés.

En outre, l'ennemi a entrepris des actions de bombardement aériennes dans le nord et l'est de la France. Plusieurs avions ont été mis en cause ont été abattus tant par la D.C.A. que par l'aviation de chasse.

Communiqué n° 498
9 Mai (soir)

Au cours de la nuit dernière, les actions d'infanterie signalée par le communiqué de ce matin se sont produites sur un front étendu. L'ennemi a été partout repoussé.

Dans la journée, activité des deux artilleries à l'ouest des Vosges et dans la région de Wissembourg.

A LA UNE - Fac-similé 14 - vol. 5

A 6

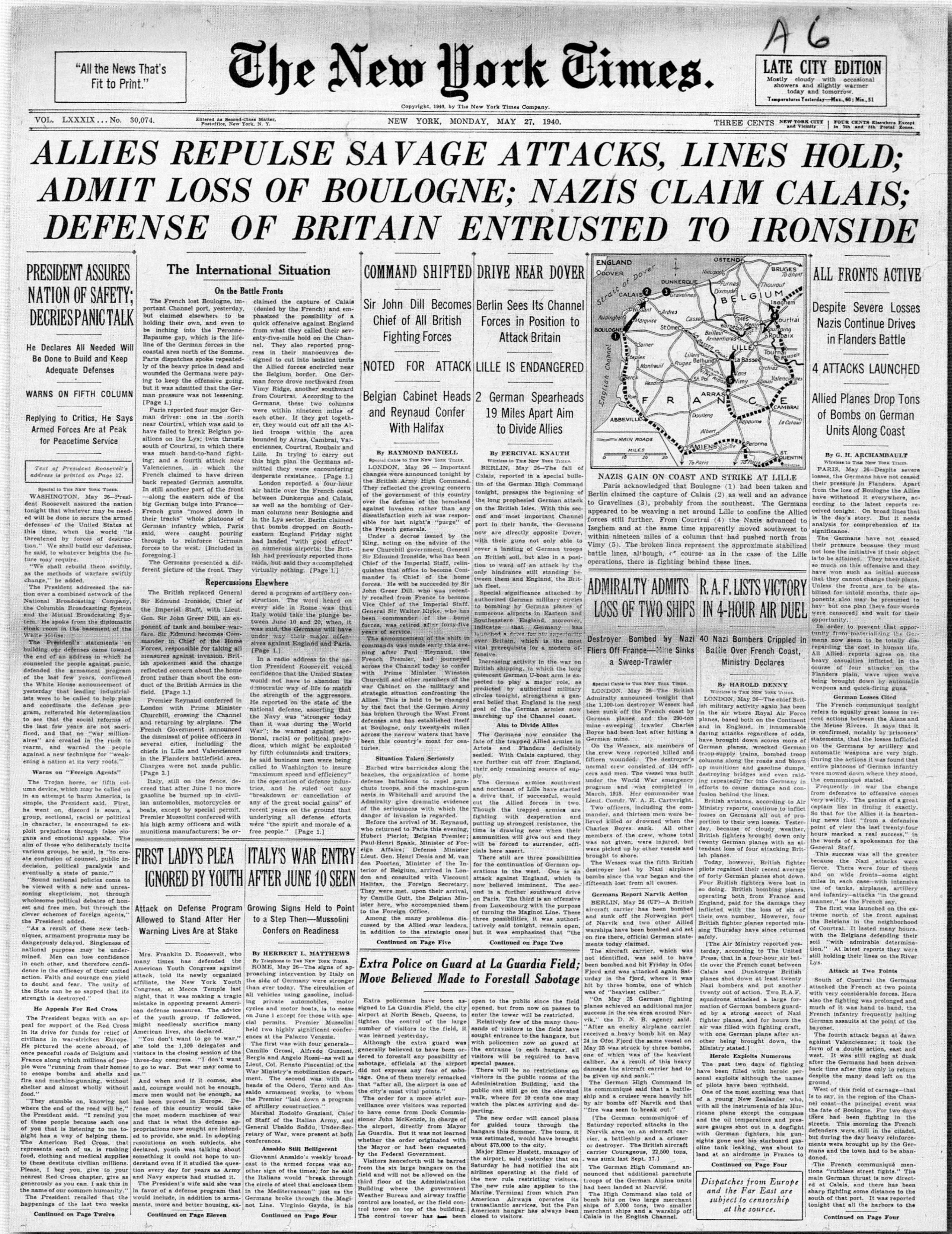

"All the News That's Fit to Print."

The New York Times.

LATE CITY EDITION
Mostly cloudy with occasional showers and slightly warmer today and tomorrow.
Temperature Yesterday—Max., 60; Min., 51

VOL. LXXXIX...No. 30,074.   Entered as Second-Class Matter, Postoffice, New York, N. Y.   NEW YORK, MONDAY, MAY 27, 1940.   THREE CENTS NEW YORK CITY and Vicinity | FOUR CENTS Elsewhere Except in 7th and 8th Postal Zones.

ALLIES REPULSE SAVAGE ATTACKS, LINES HOLD; ADMIT LOSS OF BOULOGNE; NAZIS CLAIM CALAIS; DEFENSE OF BRITAIN ENTRUSTED TO IRONSIDE

PRESIDENT ASSURES NATION OF SAFETY; DECRIES PANIC TALK

He Declares All Needed Will Be Done to Build and Keep Adequate Defenses

WARNS ON FIFTH COLUMN

Replying to Critics, He Says Armed Forces Are at Peak for Peacetime Service

Text of President Roosevelt's address is printed on Page 12.

The International Situation

On the Battle Fronts

Repercussions Elsewhere

FIRST LADY'S PLEA IGNORED BY YOUTH

Attack on Defense Program Allowed to Stand After Her Warning Lives Are at Stake

ITALY'S WAR ENTRY AFTER JUNE 10 SEEN

Growing Signs Held to Point to a Step Then—Mussolini Confers on Readiness

By HERBERT L. MATTHEWS

COMMAND SHIFTED

Sir John Dill Becomes Chief of All British Fighting Forces

NOTED FOR ATTACK

Belgian Cabinet Heads and Reynaud Confer With Halifax

By RAYMOND DANIELL

Extra Police on Guard at La Guardia Field; Move Believed Made to Forestall Sabotage

DRIVE NEAR DOVER

Berlin Sees Its Channel Forces in Position to Attack Britain

LILLE IS ENDANGERED

2 German Spearheads 19 Miles Apart Aim to Divide Allies

By PERCIVAL KNAUTH

NAZIS GAIN ON COAST AND STRIKE AT LILLE

ALL FRONTS ACTIVE

Despite Severe Losses Nazis Continue Drives in Flanders Battle

4 ATTACKS LAUNCHED

Allied Planes Drop Tons of Bombs on German Units Along Coast

By G. H. ARCHAMBAULT

ADMIRALTY ADMITS LOSS OF TWO SHIPS

Destroyer Bombed by Nazi Fliers Off France—Mine Sinks a Sweep-Trawler

R. A. F. LISTS VICTORY IN 4-HOUR AIR DUEL

40 Nazi Bombers Crippled in Battle Over French Coast, Ministry Declares

By HAROLD DENNY

Dispatches from Europe and the Far East are subject to censorship at the source.

Continued on Page Twelve — Continued on Page Eleven — Continued on Page Four — Continued on Page Five — Continued on Page Two — Continued on Page Four

▲ THE NEW YORK TIMES, NEW YORK, MONDAY MAY 27, 1940

The news from Europe is grim as French and British forces are trapped against the coast and Germany plans to invade Britain. The paper reports Roosevelt's promise to build up U.S. defenses alongside his wife's failure to win the support of the American Youth Congress for the president's defense program.

BLACK-OUT 9.37 p.m. to 4.19 a.m.

Sun rises 4.49 a.m.
sets 9.7 p.m.
Moon rises 3.37 a.m.
sets 6.20 p.m.

DAILY SKETCH, MONDAY, JUNE 3, 1940.

BOMBS ON NORFOLK: PAGE THREE

Daily Sketch

BOURNVILLE
COCOA
FOOD AT PRE WAR PRICE
Still 6d PER ¼ LB

BIRD'S
CUSTARD
& JELLIES

No. 9,695 (E**) MONDAY, JUNE 3, 1940 ONE PENNY

DUNKIRK DEFENCE DEFIES 300,000

FOUR-FIFTHS OF B.E.F. SAVED: STORY ON PAGE THREE

'THE NAVY'S HERE'—WITH THE ARMY

◀ DAILY SKETCH, MANCHESTER, MONDAY JUNE 3, 1940
The *Daily Sketch* was one of Britain's most successful populist tabloids from its founding in 1909 until it merged with the *Daily Mail* in the 1970s. Its dramatic front page features an image of British Expeditionary Force (BEF) soldiers landing in Britain after escaping from Dunkirk—and its portrayal of the evacuation as a defiant victory reflects the beginning of a British legend: the Dunkirk spirit.

◀ LONG LINES OF TROOPS wait to be evacuated from the Dunkirk beaches. Over 330,000 British and French troops were saved from German captivity, though for the British Expeditionary Force (BEF) the evacuation meant the loss of all of its vehicles and most of its equipment. BEF morale was at rock bottom, but recovered markedly when the troops returned home to find that they were regarded as a band of heroes. Dunkirk itself fell to the Germans on June 4, along with 40,000 French prisoners.

BLACK-OUT 9.44 p.m. to 4.15 a.m.
Sun rises 4.45 a.m.
sets 9.14 p.m.
Moon rises 10.59 p.m.
sets 12.35 a.m.

DAILY SKETCH, TUESDAY, JUNE 11, 1940.

LONDON ITALIANS ROUND-UP PAGE FIVE

SIMPLE FARE IS SIMPLY FINE WITH H-P SAUCE

Daily Sketch

No. 9,702   (E*)   TUESDAY, JUNE 11, 1940   ONE PENNY

More Please!
BROWN & POLSON *Custard*

ITALY TAKES THE PLUNGE
INTO THE WAR AT MIDNIGHT

ITALY IS TO-DAY AT WAR WITH FRANCE AND BRITAIN, AFTER EIGHT HOURS' NOTICE OF HER DECISION.

HOUR BY HOUR

4 p.m. ITALY DECLARES WAR ON FRANCE AND BRITAIN AS FROM MIDNIGHT.

5.50 Announced Paris placed in state of defence.

6.0 Mussolini to Rome crowd : "The hour of destiny has arrived."

7.0 Ribbentrop gloats: "Victory is guaranteed."

7.5 ANNOUNCED TO-DAY'S SECRET SESSION OF PARLIAMENT POSTPONED.

7.30 Official London statement : "Allies' preparations complete."

7.45 Officials say Turkey resolved to fulfil pact with Allies.
M. REYNAUD TELLS FRANCE : "THE WORLD WILL JUDGE THIS ACT."

8.0 Telephones between Turkey and rest of Europe cut.

9.0 Duff Cooper broadcasts. He says:
"Mussolini will leave nothing behind him but the curses of those he has betrayed.

10.0 French G.H.Q. announce Germans across the Seine west of Paris.

10.30 Bulgaria announced she looks to Russia for protection. Turkish and Greek frontiers guarded.

12.15 a.m. Roosevelt declares : "Full speed ahead to aid Allies."

At 4 p.m. yesterday Count Ciano informed the Allied Ambassadors in Rome that Italy would enter the war on the side of Germany at midnight.

At 6 o'clock Mussolini proclaimed to a war-fevered crowd that Italy had made her "irrevocable" decision.

IT WAS MET BY THE FIRMEST REPLIES BOTH FROM LONDON AND PARIS. IN LONDON IT WAS OFFICIALLY STATED THAT THE ALLIES KNEW HOW TO MEET SWORD WITH SWORD.

PRESIDENT ROOSEVELT, BROADCASTING EARLY TO-DAY, REVEALED THAT MUSSOLINI HAD TURNED DOWN HIS OFFER TO MEDIATE ON ITALY'S CLAIMS, AND SAID THAT HE HAD GIVEN THE ORDER " FULL SPEED AHEAD " FOR ARMAMENTS FOR THE ALLIES.

Violent fighting was continuing last night along the whole Weygand Line, and Paris was placed in a state of defence as the Germans were reported across the Lower Seine at certain points.

—See Pages Two and Three.

New theatres of war are opened up by Italy's entry into the conflict.

▲ DAILY SKETCH, MANCHESTER, TUESDAY JUNE 11, 1940

The long-anticipated entry of Italy into the war on the side of Germany caused little surprise, as Mussolini was Hitler's major ally and was eager for territorial gains now that France had been weakened by German invasion. The *Daily Sketch* still dramatized the announcement by printing whole paragraphs in capitals and introducing a front-page timeline of developments. Inside, it promises to describe the round-up of Italians in London. Virtually all Italian men in Britain were either interned or deported as fascist sympathizers. The advertisement at top left turns rationing into a marketing opportunity by promoting sauce to add taste to even a basic meal.

The fall of France

JUNE 1940

After victories in Holland, Belgium, and northern France in May, the Wehrmacht turned south. Operation "Red" was the code name for this offensive. Although hurriedly organized, it was undertaken by troops whose morale was sky high and who had complete faith in their equipment and the tactics of combining aircraft and tanks that had already proved so devastating. There were two main thrusts: Army Group A to the east of Paris and Army Group B to the west of the capital. General Gerd von Rundstedt's Army Group A, moving toward the Moselle River in front of the Maginot Line, launched an offensive east of Paris. Rundstedt's tanks, reinforced by Army Group B panzers, overcame resistance from the French Fourth Army to break through at Châlons-sur-Marne on June 12.

THE FALL OF PARIS

The French response, the Weygand Line, stretching along the Somme and Aisne rivers, aimed to protect Paris and the interior. Some of France's 65 divisions fought determined actions, but many units lacked manpower and equipment. Air attacks and logistical problems also undermined General Maxime Weygand's vulnerable forces. Paris was declared an "open city" on June 13 to save it from destruction and all French forces withdrew south of the capital, leaving the Maginot Line isolated. German troops entered Paris on June 14 as thousands fled the capital. Germany's Army Group C, deployed from the Maginot Line to the Swiss border, broke through French defenses. German mechanized forces advanced in all directions, crossing the Rhine and Loire rivers. All of the coastal ports between Cherbourg and St. Nazaire were soon captured. On June 15 the evacuation of the remaining Allied troops in northwest France began. Operation Ariel extended this to the Biscay ports from the 16th.

▼ GERMAN TROOPS IN PARIS. For the second time in 20 years France had fought a conflict with Germany, but in 1940 to the misery of war was added national humiliation.

News Chronicle

News Chronicle, Saturday, June 15, 1940.

ROBBIALAC PAINTS — KEEP UPKEEP DOWN — all-ways

No. 29,364 ONE PENNY SATURDAY, JUNE 15, 1940 RADIO, PAGE 7 POSTAGE in U.K. Canada and Newfoundland 1d. Other Places Abroad 1d

BROWN & POLSON CUSTARD — UM-M-M!

PARIS FALLS, BUT THE FRENCH ARMY AND B.E.F. FIGHT ON

In The West

French Report Their Forces Withdraw According To Plan

THE withdrawal of the French troops after yesterday's fall of Paris is going according to plan.

Last night the French issued the following official war communiqué:

"From the sea to the Argonne the battle continues along the whole front, but at certain points with less violence.

"The withdrawal ordered, especially that of the Paris Army announced in this morning's communiqué, has been effected according to our plans.

"Our troops counter-attacked several times. The enemy this morning launched a very violent attack, accompanied by tanks and aircraft, against our positions to the west of the Saar. It was repulsed with heavy losses."

It was as the crisp, clean June sun poured down on Paris that grey-uniformed Germans began their drive into the city.

For the first time since 1871, conquering troops were tramping the boulevards. Tanks rattled in the Champs Elysées.

But the battered French Army steeled itself again, and south, west and east of the city went on fighting furiously.

Firm British Assurance

And Britain, as the news came through, sent France a solemn assurance that she will continue to give her Ally the utmost aid, and a promise that she will continue the struggle at all costs "in France, in this island, upon the oceans, and in the air, wherever it may lead us."

At the same time, battle-weary French soldiers were beginning to hear that, for the past few days, thousands of fresh, fully-equipped British troops — the second B.E.F. — were rushing up to help them and had actually met and fought German troops on the Seine.

In French and British official circles last night the German claim that the whole of the French line from the Channel to the Maginot Line, near Montmédy, had broken down were emphatically denied.

Fighting In The Greatest Order

"Our fighting and our movements are taking place with the greatest order," said the French communiqué.

The Germans claimed that the Seine, outside Paris, was being crossed by German forces on a wide front, that Montmedy at one extreme of the Allied line and Le Havre, at the other, had been captured.

In the Champagne area the French state that the more advanced units of the German Army seem to be aimed at Romilly, on the Seine, about 70 miles south-east of Paris, and St. Dizier, on the Marne, about 120 miles east of Paris.

Last night, for the first time for three days, Tours, the Government's new seat, heard the thunder of anti-aircraft guns and the thud of far-away bombs.

Nazi Radio Plays "March Into Paris"

The German people were told dramatically of the capture of Paris over the radio—they had played to them "The March Into Paris," composed for the occasion—but for the Nazi troops the entry had little enough drama.

The first thing they did was to take over Radio Paris II. station, and soon after listeners heard a German programme.

A few policemen sauntered in the almost deserted streets. In the West End of Paris only one baker's shop was open—a mobile guard, a revolver and a gun slung over his shoulder, guarded the door.

The gay, leafy boulevards were empty, except for a few people who sat staring out of the cafés. Shops were boarded up. Everything had suddenly gone silent.

In the Place de l'Opéra a lonely motor-car stood. On it was a big "For Sale" sign.

The only officials who had stayed

Turn to Back Page, Col. Five

Inside News

Hull is Asked "Will U.S. Declare War?"

From ROBERT WAITHMAN
News Chronicle Correspondent

NEW YORK, Friday.

MR. CORDELL HULL, Secretary of State, was asked at the Press Conference today: "Has the question of a United States declaration of war been projected or discussed?"

His reply was that the American position had been broadcast at home and abroad (or some time as it related to the furnishing of supplies and munitions, and that was all he knew.

This answer startled some of the correspondents at the conference. They expected either an outright or an implied denial that the Government had any such idea under consideration.

NO DENIAL

But there was no denial, and the correspondents were left to draw their own conclusions.

Two hours earlier newspaper men had asked President Roosevelt at the White House conference for comment on an interview with Hitler called to Hearst newspapers here by Karl von Wiegand.

Hitler is reported to have described the idea of a Nazi invasion of American countries as "childish, grotesque, stupid and fantastic." The President said: "That brings up recollections." He added that it was sufficient to observe what has happened to other countries over a period of years.

"ALL WE CAN"

Some newspapers here this afternoon headline the President's comment: "Roosevelt Fears Invasion."

Though again assuring questioners that the United States is doing everything it possibly can to speed help to the Allies, the President said he had not then received the text of M. Reynaud's last appeal (it is known to have arrived in Washington just after Mr. Roosevelt spoke) and could not say anything further.

To another query: "Can we send help in sufficient quantity and with sufficient speed to save the Allies?" the President said it would take him two hours to answer.

BULLITT ARRESTED

There is some excitement here over a report that the United States Ambassador, Mr. William Bullitt, who stayed in Paris to represent the Diplomatic Corps, has been taken into protective custody by the Nazis.

Mr. Hull said that no dispatches had been received from Mr. Bullitt today.

U.S. Aid to France—Page Two

The New B.E.F. is There
By GUY RAMSEY
Page Four

It Mustn't Happen Here

From WILLIAM FORREST,
News Chronicle Special Correspondent

TOURS, Friday.

When the plane in which I travelled from London arrived here this afternoon an airport official climbed aboard and, addressing the passengers, said: "I warn you before you go into Tours you will find no transport there, no accommodation and very little food."

The plane was leaving again in a few minutes to return to London.

*

It might be the last plane out.

With the other passengers—two American ambulance men, a French liaison officer and a Frenchwoman—I decided to take the risk.

*

Now that I've spent four hours in Tours I wonder if I was right. The first thing I wish told on reaching the town was that the Government had left at five this morning for a new seat and many of my colleagues had followed in its wake.

Millions—I do not exaggerate—of refugees were making shift to push on in the same direction. I have seen many an exodus of tortured humanity all over Europe in the past few years, but never anything like this.

The story, however, has been told already; all I can do is to express the fervent hope that every possible measure will be taken in our own land to prevent a repetition of such colossal tragedy when the hour of our supreme trial comes.

Quite half of the German success in this Blitzkrieg has been contributed by these masses of hopeless, homeless wanderers, who have disorganised the front and demoralised the ar[my]

Belgrade Frees Pro-Axis Ex-Premier

BELGRADE, Friday.

IT is learned on high authority that M. Stoyadinovitch, former Yugo-Slav Prime Minister, has been released after being in custody for two months.

Diplomatic quarters say his liberation is a move to improve relations with Italy and Germany.

It is reported that a new Government may be formed which would include M. Stoyadinovitch and would be friendly to the Axis.

It was announced on April 19 that M. Stoyadinovitch was being interned as a result of documents linking him with Nazi activity found when police raided his home.

Later the Government issued a statement saying his internment was "only an internal matter" for the security of the State, and had no foreign political reasons.—Associated Press.

Shots At U-Boat Till Gunners Were In Sea

H.M.S. SCOTSTOUN, 17,046-ton armed merchant cruiser, was torpedoed and sunk by a U-boat on Thursday, and on the same day, in Trondheim Fiord, the 26,000-ton Nazi battleship Scharnhorst was hit by a heavy bomb, and possibly two, by planes of the Fleet Air Arm.

The Scotstoun went down fighting. Her guns thundered to the end as the men loading them stood waist-deep in water passing the shells above their heads to keep them dry.

"I think we got the U-boat," one of them told a News Chronicle correspondent.

All but six of the Scotstoun's complement of 350 were saved. They have been landed at a British port. The crew were making for action stations early on Thursday when the torpedo struck.

The gunners could see only the periscope of the U-boat, which was about 250 yards off.

An SOS was at once put out, but a further explosion carried away the wireless gear.

Eight boats were launched without mishap, but the ninth, a motor launch, overturned and threw its occupants into the sea. All were picked up.

In response to the S.O.S., a re[con]naissance plane located the lifeboats, which were making for the coast.

8 HOURS IN BOATS

After the men had been in the boats about eight hours they were picked up by British naval craft.

An Admiralty communiqué issued in London yesterday stated: "Aircraft of the Fleet Air Arm carried out an attack on German naval units in Trondheim Fiord early yesterday.

"Information has now been received that one hit abaft the funnel was obtained with a heavy bomb on the battleship Scharnhorst.

"It is also reported that possibly a second hit was registered on the same ship."

Hitler May Next Launch Sham Peace Offensive

MR. HAROLD NICOLSON, Parliamentary Secretary, Ministry of Information, said at Leicester last night that while Hitler had fulfilled his prophecy to be in Paris on June 15, he would not fulfil the prophecy that by August 15 he would bring England to her knees.

"When Hitler finds the days are shortening," said Mr. Nicolson, "and the resources of our own industries and those in the United States are building up against him a weight of armaments with which he will be unable to compete, he will realise that victory is no longer possible.

"Then he will turn and twist in the hope of inducing this country and her Allies to make a peace which will be no more a real peace than that he imposed on Czecho-Slovakia.

WILL DEMAND OUR FLEET

"It may be that within the next few days Hitler may launch his peace offensive. He will try to assure the people of France and Britain that he has no desire to subjugate their countries, but that all he desires is their complete disarmament.

"He will say to us that we can keep our Empire except what he wants for himself, but that we must abandon our free democratic institutions and accept a Government nominated from Berlin, and at the same time surrender our fleet to Germany and Italy.

SWOOP ON LONDON

"The moment he obtains our fleet he will swoop upon London and will gradually and thoroughly stamp out the liberties of our country and reduce our people to the level of slaves."

Mr. Nicolson added that the great onrush of German armoured divisions could not continue for ever, and there must come a moment when there would be exhaustion and the French would be able to hold them.

In The East

Fuel Reservoir Near Venice Bombed

IN the other sphere of war—the Mediterranean—action is developing, with the Allies making the pace.

Having won the first land skirmish—on the Libyan border, when they took 62 prisoners—the Allies have since carried out aerial bombing and naval gunfire attacks on numerous objectives, in Italy itself and in her possessions across the Mediterranean.

Last night's French official communiqué stated:

"In the course of the night of June 13-14 a special formation of the Fleet Air Arm, commanded by Captain d'Aillère, bombed and set on fire oil storage tanks in the region of Venice.

"Another formation dropped pamphlets on Rome.

"Our warships shelled, industrial plants and the railway line on the Italian coast."

NO ENEMY SEEN

A naval communiqué issued in Cairo last night stated:

"The Allied Fleet has been at sea since war broke out with Italy.

"Sweeping operations have been carried out in the Mediterranean with the object of protecting shipping and destroying enemy ships.

"No enemy has been sighted so far, although attacks have been made on enemy submarines with successful results."

A Madrid message last night stated that two Italian submarines had taken refuge in Spanish ports during the day.

One entered Algeciras and the other Ceuta, the Spanish Moroccan port of Ceuta.

HEAVY CANNONADES

Both arrived damaged after intense cannonading had been heard off Gibraltar.

Officers said they planned to leave Ceuta to face the enemy after repairs had been effected.

Many Allied warships are stated to be lying in wait in the Straits outside the ports.

Firing was heard in the Straits at 2 o'clock yesterday morning.

The Italian cargo ship Loda (6,107 tons) was forced to beach at Tenerife, Canary Islands, yesterday, after being attacked by a British warship.

The Moscow radio yesterday quoted an announcement by the "Frankfurter Zeitung" that a big Italian offensive is expected to start very soon.

TURIN HAVOC

Italian papers, quoted by the same source, admit the severe effects of the bombardment of Turin by Allied airmen.

The number of killed and wounded is very high, it is stated.

Many factories were destroyed in the first raids.

Germany, a Zurich message says, has been sending dive-bombers and tanks to Italy, in order to strengthen the Italian forces.

This report came in the first place from the Italian frontier.

NEUTRALS SUNK

A naval spokesman in Cairo announced that a Dutch tanker had been sunk in the Mediterranean.

Four lives were lost. The name of the vessel was not given.

A large Greek ship, the name of which is at present unknown, has been sunk by a submarine off Cape Finisterre.

Communiqués on Page Eight describe Allied raids on objectives in Italy's possessions across the Mediterranean.

LATE NEWS

Madrid Celebrates Tangier Move

MADRID, Friday.

MADRID is beflagged today following the Spanish Government's announcement that it is taking over the policing of the Tangier zone of Morocco (opposite Gibraltar).

Falangist (Spanish Fascist Party) bands concentrated in front of the building in the Calle de Alcala, where the party directorate was meeting.

Demonstrators shouted, "France, France" and "Gibraltar is Spanish."—B.U.P.

See Spanish troops move to Tangier—Page Two

Man Shot Dead by Parashot

After passing over a railway bridge at Gwersyllt, near Wrexham, in a motor-car shortly before midnight on Thursday, Walter May (23), was fatally wounded by a parashot.

The bullet from the parashot's Service rifle after piercing the back of the car passed through May's body and emerged through the front of the car.

The driver of the car, Stanley Belfield, said that there was no sandbag control in the vicinity, that he heard no challenge and saw no warning red light. Someone, he said, did call out, but he took it as a request for a lift, which he ignored.

Mobile Nazi Crematoriums

POLISH FRONTIER, Friday.—Responsible people who have just arrived from German-occupied Poland state that Polish hospitals are overflowing with German wounded of all ranks. The wounded men are quoted as saying that the losses in their respective units were enormous.

The great number of dead, it is stated, necessitated wholesale cremations by the wayside in mobile crematoriums, the memory of which was still a nightmare to the wounded troops.—Reuter.

Italian Planes Bomb Orient Express

From Our Own Correspondent
ISTANBUL, Friday.—This morning's Simplon-Orient express—probably the last to run—reports being bombed three times by Italian planes en route. There was no damage.

LONDON BLACK-OUT TIMES
Tonight ...... 9.48 p.m.—4.12 a.m.
Tomorrow .... 9.49 p.m.—4.12 a.m.

Shaded areas show enemy occupied zones

▲ NEWS CHRONICLE, LONDON, SATURDAY JUNE 15, 1940

Not even a story of heroic courage in the face of a U-boat attack can lift the gloom from the *News Chronicle*'s announcement of the defeat of Britain's closest ally. The stark account of conditions in Tours is by William Forrest, an outstanding war correspondent who had barely escaped arrest by the Germans while covering the invasion of Poland—he had to escape via Romania. Forrest had reported on the Russo–Finland War before flying into France; he later covered Allied progress in North Africa, Italy, Normandy, and Germany.

DAILY SKETCH. TUESDAY. JUNE 18. 1940.

CALL-UP OF 3 CLASSES:

BACK PAGE

THE HOUSEWIVES HELP·MEAT·H·P SAUCE

Daily Sketch

No. 9,708   (E*)   TUESDAY, JUNE 18, 1940   ONE PENNY

'I know what I like!'
BROWN & POLSON
CUSTARD POWDER
BROWN & POLSON *Custard*

'We Shall Fight On, Unconquerable'

U.S. Hears Premier's Words

IN a short, historic broadcast last night, relayed to the United States, the Prime Minister, Mr. Churchill, said this concerning Marshal Petain's declaration that the French must cease fighting :

● "The news from France is very bad, and I grieve for the gallant French people who have fallen into this terrible misfortune. Nothing will alter our feelings towards them or our faith that the genius of France will rise again.

● "What has happened in France makes no difference to British faith and purpose. WE HAVE BECOME THE SOLE CHAMPIONS, NOW IN ARMS, TO DEFEND THE WORLD CAUSE.

● "We shall do our best to be worthy of this high honour. We shall defend our island, and, with the British Empire around us, we shall fight on unconquerable until the curse of Hitler is lifted from the brows of men.

● "We are sure that in the end all will be well."

*   *   *

● In Berlin it was stated that pending an armistice, the German advance into France continued in full force.

● Mussolini, accompanied by Count Ciano, left Rome at 8.30 p.m. to meet Hitler about the armistice terms.

*   *   *

● M. Baudouin, new French Foreign Minister, last night said : "We are ready to lay down our arms if we can get an honourable peace, but we are never ready to accept shameful conditions which would mean the end of spiritual freedom for our people."

See also Pages 2 and 3.

EVERY MAN—TO ARMS !

France's decision to "cease the fight" led yesterday to a great rush in London of men and women eager to serve. The new R.A.F. recruiting inquiry bureau (left) was thronged.

*   *

Britain stands fast — resolved to resist any attempt at invasion, by air or sea. Our island home becomes a fortress.

*   *

Standing with us is the Empire and all its vast resources. See middle pages.

▲ DAILY SKETCH, MANCHESTER, TUESDAY JUNE 18, 1940

The *Sketch* greets the grave news from France and the evacuation from Dunkirk with a reassuring image of volunteers for the RAF and with a report of one of Winston Churchill's great war speeches. Churchill's celebrated gift for phrasemaking was perfect for subeditors, producing short, memorable ready-made headlines.

BLACK-OUT 9.48 p.m. to 4.15 a.m.

Sun rises 4.44 a.m.
sets 9.18 p.m.
Moon rises 8.37 p.m.
sets 5.31 a.m.

DAILY SKETCH, WEDNESDAY, JUNE 19, 1940.

IF INVADERS COME: Page Five

Imperial British-made **Typewriters**

For speed, accuracy and dependability

Daily Sketch

No. 9,709 (E*) WEDNESDAY, JUNE 19, 1940 ONE PENNY

"DID YOU SAY ONLY 6D?" "YES—I SAID ONLY 6D"

Erinmore Cigarettes 10 for 6D 5 for 3D

MURRAY, SONS AND CO. LTD., BELFAST

BATTLE OF BRITAIN: R.A.F. ON OFFENSIVE

Dictators Talk Four Hours: French General's Appeal From London

SEE INSIDE PAGES

LET us brace ourselves to our duty and so bear ourselves that if the British Commonwealth and Empire lasts for a thousand years, men will still say: THIS WAS THEIR FINEST HOUR

—The Premier, last night

Let All The Children Go To Safety

THE six-day evacuation from London has ended. These boys and girls have been sent by their parents to the West Country. But about 340,000 children remain in Greater London.

Arrangements should be made at once to remove all children from crowded cities—if necessary to Canada, which has offered to shelter thousands.

France's Foreign Minister has said that his country " has merely asked Germany under what conditions she would consent to stop the slaughter of French children." We shall fight all the better if we know that the children are safe.

▶ RAF PILOTS RACE to their Hurricane fighters in the summer of 1940. On June 30, 1940, Hermann Göring, head of the Luftwaffe, issued a "General Directive for the Operation of the Luftwaffe against England." This included as a priority the destruction of the RAF and its supporting aircraft industry. To achieve this he had at his disposal three air fleets: *Luftflotte* 2, *Luftflotte* 3, and *Luftflotte* 5.

◀ DAILY SKETCH, MANCHESTER, WEDNESDAY JUNE 19, 1940
Churchill's observation only the previous night that "the Battle of Britain is about to begin" has given the *Sketch* its headline and the English language a new phrase. The threat of invasion was closer than ever before or after, and the *Sketch* promises details inside of what to do if it happened. The front page, though, is limited to a ringing appeal from Churchill and a report of the successful evacuation of many of London's children. The report's last line is a subtle endorsement of government propaganda, which discouraged parents from keeping their children in the city with them.

▲ DE TELEGRAAF (THE TELEGRAPH), AMSTERDAM, WEDNESDAY JUNE 26, 1940

The Netherlands was under German control, and only pro-Berlin newspapers like *The Telegraph* were allowed to publish. Dutch readers seeking reasons to be optimistic about their own liberation from occupation would find little to hearten them: "Armistice of Compiègne stipulates: French fleet to be laid up. Armistice applies for entire French Empire."

France divided

JUNE 1940

IN MID-JUNE 1940, FRENCH PRIME MINISTER PAUL REYNAUD RESIGNED AND WORLD WAR I HERO MARSHAL HENRI-PHILIPPE PÉTAIN REPLACED HIM. PÉTAIN REQUESTED GERMAN ARMISTICE TERMS ON JUNE 17. ON THE SAME day the new head of the French government made a broadcast to the French people stating: "With a heavy heart I tell you today that it is necessary to stop the fighting."

The armistice was signed on June 22. By its terms, Germany occupied two-thirds of France. A small state in the southeast continued to be ruled by Pétain's government. It soon became known as Vichy France from the name of its capital, which had been a sleepy spa town famous for its bottled water.

FREE FRENCH

The signature of the armistice had two direct effects on Anglo-French relations. The first direct affect was that certain French forces in Britain, known as the "Fighting French" and later as the "Free French," decided to carry on the struggle. Brigadier General Charles de Gaulle issued an appeal to the French people on June 18 and there was now effectively a rival French government based in Britain.

THE FUTURE OF THE FRENCH FLEET

The second effect concerned the fate of the French fleet. On June 17 Winston Churchill sent a personal message to Petain and Weygand (head of the French armed forces): "I wish to repeat to you my profound conviction that the illustrious Marshal Pétain and the famous General Weygand ... will not injure their ally by delivering over to the enemy the fine French fleet. Such an act would scarify their names for a thousand years of history." President Roosevelt, too, was alarmed and stated that if the Germans were allowed to take over the mighty French fleet "the French government will permanently lose the friendship and goodwill of the government of the United States." But what was to become of it?

▲ FRENCH REPRESENTATIVES SIGN ARTICLES of surrender in the same railroad carriage in which Germany signed the 1918 capitulation.

Britain alone

JULY–AUGUST 1940

FOLLOWING THE FALL OF FRANCE THE BRITISH GOVERNMENT DECIDED TO NEUTRALIZE THE FRENCH FLEET. THE FIRST STEP WAS TO SEIZE FRENCH SHIPS IN BRITISH PORTS. THIS WAS ACHIEVED relatively easily. However, most of the French Fleet was in the African port of Mers-el-Kebir. On July 3, 1940, Winston Churchill gave the order to launch Operation Catapult, the disabling of the French ships at Mers-el-Kebir. When the French refused to surrender, the Royal Navy opened fire, disabling three capital ships and many smaller vessels. The French lost 1,297 killed and 341 wounded in the action. The French Fleet was no longer a threat.

"PROFOUND SADNESS"

On July 4, Churchill expressed his "profound sadness" in the House of Commons over what had taken place, but defended it on the grounds that it was necessary for the survival of Britain. Though Mers-el-Kebir made many French people bitter toward Britain, it was a morale booster for the British themselves. Having

▶ FRENCH WARSHIPS UNDER Royal Navy shell fire at Mers-el-Kebir on July 3, 1940. The attack resulted in the French Navy becoming more hostile to the British than it had been toward the Germans, but the French Fleet had been disabled.

neutralized the threat of French naval vessels being taken over by the Germans, the British still had to withstand enormous threats. In Africa, Italian forces were on the offensive, but the most direct threat came from across the English Channel, where German troops were massing. By July 1940 Britain was truly alone. British convoys were coming under air attack in the Channel, signaling that the Battle of Britain had begun. And German invasion barges were being assembled in French ports. On July 23 Hitler gave the order for the full-scale bombing of Britain and Operation Sealion, the invasion of England.

▲ THE SUN, NEW YORK, WEDNESDAY AUGUST 7, 1940

The Italian invasion of Somaliland did indeed turn out to be a sideshow to an assault on Egypt, as *The Sun* predicts; of more lasting significance to many Americans would be their first glimpse of an obscure senator from Missouri, Harry S. Truman, who would become president just five years later. A legendary British stereotype makes an appearance in the satisfying anecdote about an aristocrat who ordered her chauffeur to arrest a German parachutist.

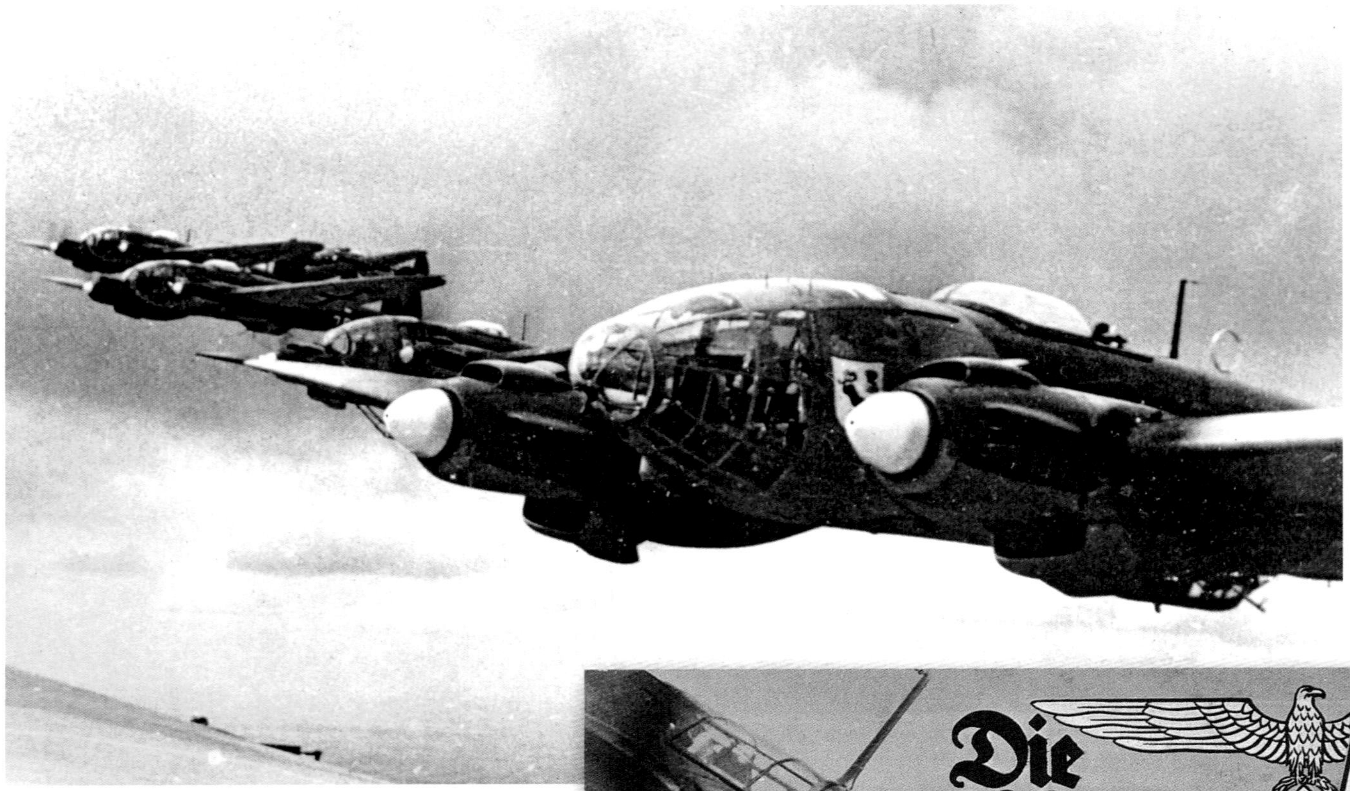

◀ HEINKELS OVER BRITAIN. The He 111 was the mainstay of the German bomber force during the Battle of Britain. In the six weeks from July 1, 1940, the Luftwaffe flew more than 7,000 bomber sorties against Britain and dropped 1,900 tons (1,930 tonnes) of bombs. On August 1 Hitler altered the priorities of the Luftwaffe. It was ordered to attack the RAF. The three Luftwaffe air fleets deployed 3,196 aircraft against the RAF's 570 Spitfires and Hurricanes in southeast England.

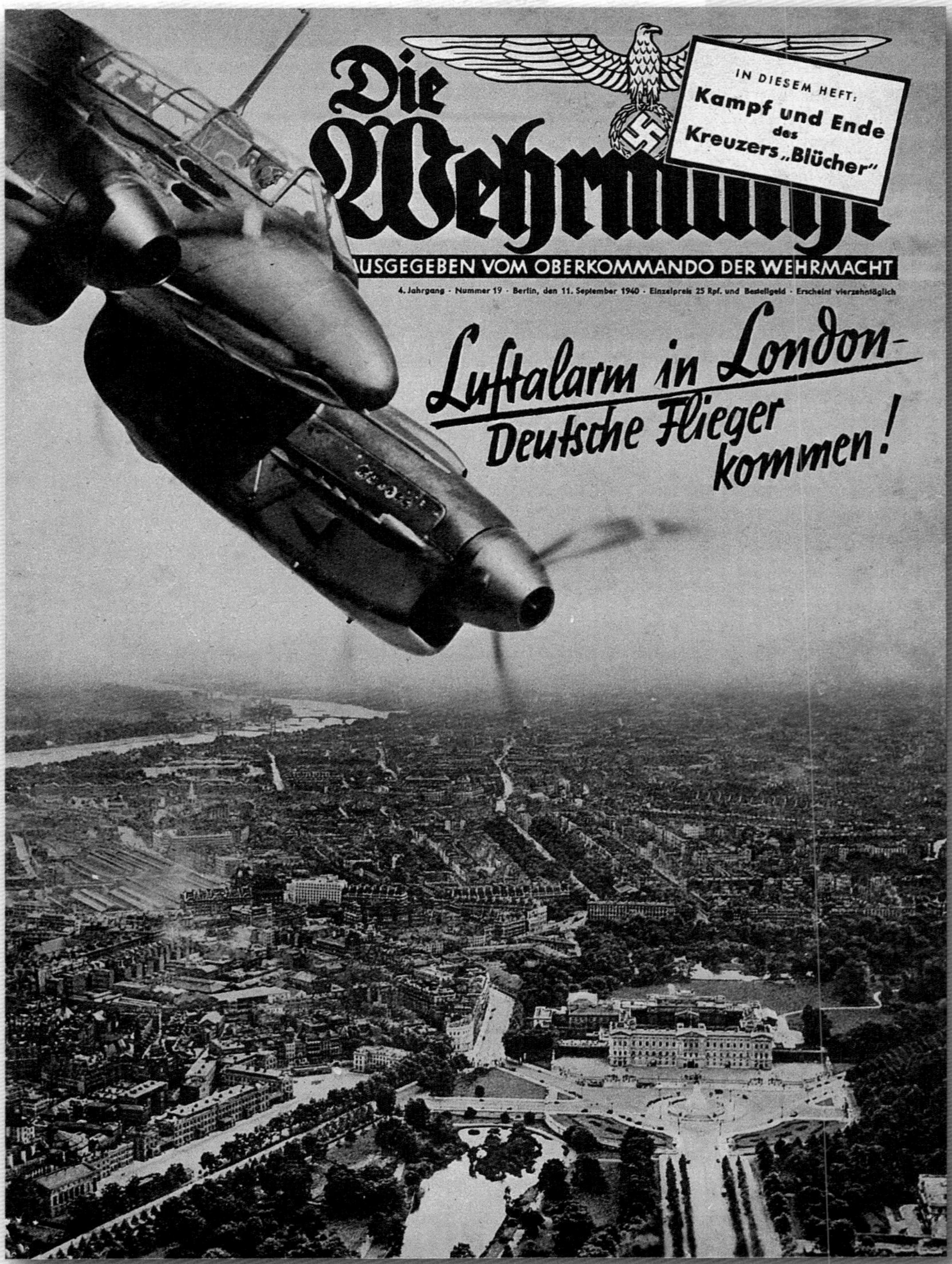

▶ DIE WEHRMACHT, BERLIN, WEDNESDAY SEPTEMBER 11, 1940
Started in 1936 to promote the newly formed Wehrmacht, this illustrated weekly was aimed at young readers with its pocket-money price of 25 Reichspfennig. Edited by the Wehrmacht High Command, this issue uses an expert collage to portray a divebomber approaching Buckingham Palace: "Air-raid alarm in London. The German airmen are coming!" Also promised inside: "The cruiser "Blücher" goes down fighting."

100506

COLEG LLANDRILLO COLLEGE
LIBRARY RESOURCE CENTRE
CANOLFAN ADNODDAU LLYFRGELL

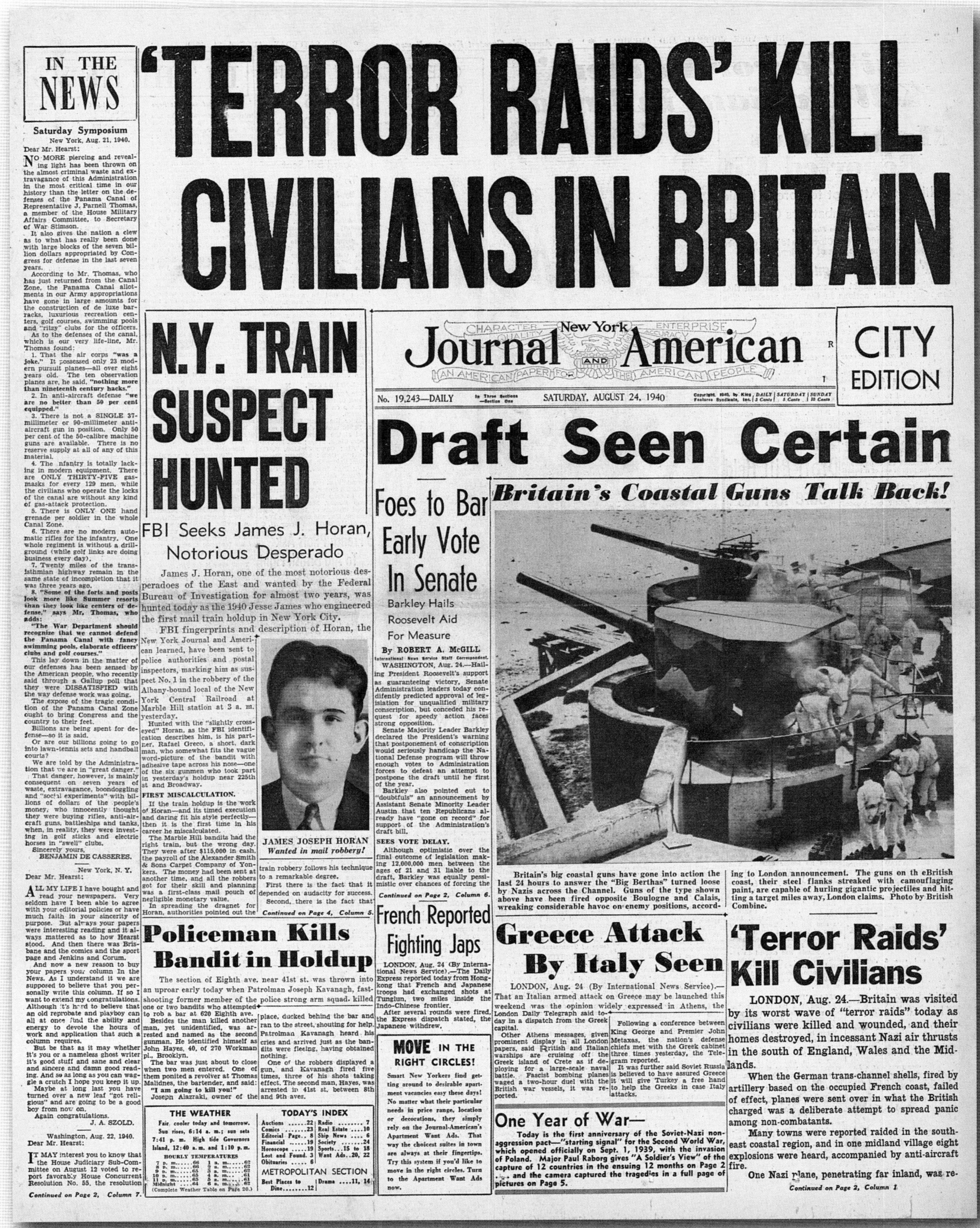

'TERROR RAIDS' KILL CIVILIANS IN BRITAIN

IN THE NEWS

Saturday Symposium

New York, Aug. 21, 1940.

Dear Mr. Hearst:

NO MORE piercing and revealing light has been thrown on the almost criminal waste and extravagance of this Administration in the most critical time in our history than the letter on the defenses of the Panama Canal of Representative J. Parnell Thomas, a member of the House Military Affairs Committee, to Secretary of War Stimson.

It also gives the nation a clew as to what has really been done with large blocks of the seven billion dollars appropriated by Congress for defense in the last seven years.

According to Mr. Thomas, who has just returned from the Canal Zone, the Panama Canal allotments in our Army appropriations have gone in large amounts for the construction of de luxe barracks, luxurious recreation centers, golf courses, swimming pools and "ritzy" clubs for the officers.

As to the defenses of the canal, which is our very life-line, Mr. Thomas found:

1. That the air corps **"was a joke."** It possessed only 23 modern pursuit planes—all over eight years old. The ten observation planes are, he said, **"nothing more than nineteenth century hacks."**

2. In anti-aircraft defense **"we are no better than 50 per cent equipped."**

3. There is not a SINGLE 37-millimeter or 90-millimeter anti-aircraft gun in position. Only 50 per cent of the 50-calibre machine guns are available. There is no reserve supply at all of any of this material.

4. The nfantry is totally lacking in modern equipment. There are ONLY THIRTY-FIVE gas-masks for every 129 men, while the civilians who operate the locks of the canal are without any kind of gas-attack protection.

5. There is ONLY ONE hand grenade per soldier in the whole Canal Zone.

6. There are no modern automatic rifles for the infantry. One whole regiment is without a drill-ground (while golf links are doing business every day).

7. Twenty miles of the trans-isthmian highway remain in the same state of incompletion that it was three years ago.

8. **"Some of the forts and posts look more like Summer resorts than they look like centers of defense," says Mr. Thomas, who adds:**

"The War Department should recognize that we cannot defend the Panama Canal with fancy swimming pools, elaborate officers' clubs and golf courses."

This lay down in the matter of our defenses has been sensed by the American people, who recently said through a Gallup poll that they were DISSATISFIED with the way defense work was going.

The expose of the tragic condition of the Panama Canal Zone ought to bring Congress and the country to their feet.

Billions are being spent for defense—so it is said.

Or are our billions going to go into lawn-tennis sets and handball courts?

We are told by the Administration that we are in "great danger."

That danger, however, is mainly consequent on seven years of waste, extravagance, boondoggling and "social experiments" with billions of dollars of the people's money, who innocently thought they were buying rifles, anti-aircraft guns, battleships and tanks, when, in reality, they were investing in golf sticks and electric horses in "swell" clubs.

Sincerely yours,
BENJAMIN DE CASSERES.

New York, N. Y.

Dear Mr. Hearst:

ALL MY LIFE I have bought and read your newspapers. Very seldom have I been able to agree with your editorial policies or have much faith in your sincerity of purpose. But always your papers were interesting reading and it always mattered as to how Hearst stood. And then there was Brisbane and the comics and the sport page and Jenkins and Corum.

And now a new reason to buy your papers your column In the News. As I understand it we are supposed to believe that you personally write this column. If so I want to extend my congratulations. Although it's hard to believe that an old reprobate and playboy can all at once find the ability and energy to devote the hours of work and application that such a column requires.

But be that as it may whether it's you or a nameless ghost writer it's good stuff and sane and clear and sincere and damn good reading. And so as long as you can waggle a crutch I hope you keep it up.

Maybe at long last you have turned over a new leaf "got religious" and are going to be a good boy from now on.

Again congratulations.

J. A. SZOLD.

Washington, Aug. 22, 1940.

Dear Mr. Hearst:

IT MAY interest you to know that the House Judiciary Sub-Committee on August 12 voted to report favorably House Concurrent Resolution No. 55, the resolution

Continued on Page 2, Column 7.

N.Y. TRAIN SUSPECT HUNTED

FBI Seeks James J. Horan, Notorious Desperado

James J. Horan, one of the most notorious desperadoes of the East and wanted by the Federal Bureau of Investigation for almost two years, was hunted today as the 1940 Jesse James who engineered the first mail train holdup in New York City.

FBI fingerprints and description of Horan, the New York Journal and American learned, have been sent to police authorities and postal inspectors, marking him as suspect No. 1 in the robbery of the Albany-bound local of the New York Central Railroad at Marble Hill station at 3 a. m. yesterday.

Hunted with the "slightly cross-eyed" Horan, as the FBI identification describes him, is his partner, Rafael Greco, a short, dark man, who somewhat fits the vague word-picture of the bandit with adhesive tape across his nose—one of the six gunmen who took part in yesterday's holdup near 225th st and Broadway.

FIRST MISCALCULATION.

If the train holdup is the work of Horan—and its timed execution and daring fit his style perfectly—then it is the first time in his career he miscalculated.

The Marble Hill bandits had the right train, but the wrong day. They were after $115,000 in cash, the payroll of the Alexander Smith & Sons Carpet Company of Yonkers. The money had been sent at another time, and all the robbers got for their skill and planning was a first-class mail pouch of negligible monetary value.

In spreading the dragnet for Horan, authorities pointed out the train robbery follows his technique to a remarkable degree.

First there is the fact that it depended on audacity for success.

Second, there is the fact that

Continued on Page 4, Column 5.

JAMES JOSEPH HORAN
Wanted in mail robbery!

Policeman Kills Bandit in Holdup

The section of Eighth ave. near 41st st. was thrown into an uproar early today when Patrolman Joseph Kavanagh, fast-shooting former member of the police strong arm squad, killed one or two bandits who attempted to rob a bar at 620 Eighth ave.

Besides the man killed another man, yet unidentified, was arrested and named as the second gunman. He identified himself as John Hayes, 40, of 270 Workman pl., Brooklyn.

The bar was just about to close when two men entered. One of them ponited a revolver at Thomas Malidnes, the bartender, and said: **"I am going to kill you!"**

Joseph Alazraki, owner of the place, ducked behind the bar and ran to the street, shouting for help. Patrolman Kavanagh heard his cries and arrived just as the bandits were fleeing, having obtained nothing.

One of the robbers displayed a gun, and Kavanagh fired five times, three of his shots taking effect. The second man, Hayes, was arrested in 41st st. between 8th and 9th aves.

THE WEATHER

Fair, cooler today and tomorrow. Sun rises, 6:14 a. m.; sun sets 7:41 p. m. High tide Governors Island, 12:40 a. m. and 1:10 p. m.

HOURLY TEMPERATURES

7 p. m.	66	1 a. m.	62
8 p. m.	66	2 a. m.	63
9 p. m.	65	3 a. m.	62
10 p. m.	65	4 a. m.	61
11 p. m.	65	5 a. m.	61
Midnight	64	6 a. m.	62

(Complete Weather Table on Page 20.)

TODAY'S INDEX

Auctions	22	Radio	7
Comics	23	Real Estate	10
Editorial Page	8	Ship News	6
Financial	19	Society	24
Horoscope	19	Sports	15 to 18
Lost and Found	3	Want Ads	20, 22
Obituaries	6		

METROPOLITAN SECTION

Best Places to Dine	12	Drama	11, 14

New York Journal and American

CHARACTER QUALITY ENTERPRISE ACCURACY

AN AMERICAN PAPER FOR THE AMERICAN PEOPLE

CITY EDITION

No. 19,243—DAILY In Three Sections—Section One SATURDAY, AUGUST 24, 1940 Copyright, 1940, by King Features Syndicate, Inc. DAILY 3 Cents | SATURDAY 5 Cents | SUNDAY 10 Cents

Draft Seen Certain

Foes to Bar Early Vote In Senate

Barkley Hails Roosevelt Aid For Measure

By ROBERT A. McGILL
International News Service Staff Correspondent.

WASHINGTON, Aug. 24.—Hailing President Roosevelt's support as guaranteeing victory, Senate Administration leaders today condifently predicted approval of legislation for unqualified military conscription, but conceded his request for speedy action faces strong opposition.

Senate Majority Leader Barkley declared the President's warning that postponement of conscription would seriously handicap the National Defense program will throw enough votes to Administration forces to defeat an attempt to postpone the draft until he first of the year.

Barkley also pointed out to "doubtfuls" an announcement by Assistant Senate Minority Leader Austin that ten Republicans already have "gone on record" for support of the Administration's draft bill.

SEES VOTE DELAY.

Although optimistic over the final outcome of legislation making 12,000,000 men between the ages of 21 and 31 liable to the draft, Barkley was equally pessimistic over chances of forcing the

Continued on Page 2, Column 6.

Britain's Coastal Guns Talk Back!

Britain's big coastal guns have gone into action the last 24 hours to answer the "Big Berthas" turned loose by Nazis across the Channel. Guns of the type shown above have been fired opposite Boulogne and Calais, wreaking considerable havoc on enemy positions, according to London announcement. The guns on th eBritish coast, their steel flanks streaked with camouflaging paint, are capable of hurling gigantic projectiles and hitting a target miles away, London claims. Photo by British Combine.

French Reported Fighting Japs

LONDON, Aug. 24 (By International News Service).—The Daily Express reported today from Hongkong that French and Japanese troops had exchanged shots at Tunglun, two miles inside the Indo-Chinese frontier.

After several rounds were fired, the Express dispatch stated, the Japanese withdrew.

MOVE IN THE RIGHT CIRCLES!

Smart New Yorkers find getting around to desirable apartment vacancies easy these days! No matter what their particular needs in price range, location or decorations, they simply rely on the Journal-American's Apartment Want Ads. That way the choicest suites in town are always at their fingertips. Try this system if you'd like to move in the right circles. Turn to the Apartment Want Ads now.

Greece Attack By Italy Seen

LONDON, Aug. 24 (By International News Service).—That an Italian armed attack on Greece may be launched this weekend was the opinion widely expressed in Athens, the London Daily Telegraph said today in a dispatch from the Greek capital.

Other Athens messages, given prominent display in all London papers, said British and Italian warships are cruising off the Greek island of Crete as if deploying for a large-scale naval battle. Fascist bombing planes waged a two-hour duel with the British war vessels, it was reported.

Following a conference between King George and Premier John Metaxas, the nation's defense chiefs met with the Greek cabinet three times yesterday, the Telegram reported.

It was further said Soviet Russia is believed to have assured Greece it will give Turkey a free hand to help the Greeks in case Italy attacks.

One Year of War—

Today is the first anniversary of the Soviet-Nazi non-aggression pact—"starting signal" for the Second World War, which opened officially on Sept. 1, 1939, with the invasion of Poland. Major Paul Raborg gives "A Soldier's View" of the capture of 12 countries in the ensuing 12 months on Page 2 . . . and the camera captured the tragedies in a full page of pictures on Page 5.

'Terror Raids' Kill Civilians

LONDON, Aug. 24.—Britain was visited by its worst wave of "terror raids" today as civilians were killed and wounded, and their homes destroyed, in incessant Nazi air thrusts in the south of England, Wales and the Midlands.

When the German trans-channel shells, fired by artillery based on the occupied French coast, failed of effect, planes were sent over in what the British charged was a deliberate attempt to spread panic among non-combatants.

Many towns were reported raided in the south-east coastal region, and in one midland village eight explosions were heard, accompanied by anti-aircraft fire.

One Nazi plane, penetrating far inland, was re-

Continued on Page 2, Column 1

▲ NEW YORK JOURNAL AND AMERICAN, SATURDAY AUGUST 24, 1940

The battle in Britain's skies was at its height and, despite coastal defenses like the ones pictured, the Blitz was inflicting great damage on industrial towns and cities. With bad news coming from Greece as well as Britain on what the paper prematurely heralds as the war's first anniversary, the U.S. Senate prepares to introduce conscription, supported by President Roosevelt. Local crime stories also get a look-in, and the whole lefthand column is devoted to readers' letters addressed to the paper's legendary proprietor, William Randolph Hearst.

The "Blitz"

SEPTEMBER 1940

IN LATE AUGUST 1940 THE RAF LAUNCHED NIGHT BOMBING RAIDS AGAINST BERLIN, DÜSSELDORF, ESSEN, AND OTHER GERMAN CITIES. THE RAIDS CONTRIBUTED TOWARD A CRITICAL CHANGE IN GERMANY'S STRATEGY, as aircraft were redirected to make retaliatory raids on London. Full-scale bombing raids on London—the "Blitz" —began on September 7 with 500 bombers and 600 fighters.

FATAL ERROR

In late summer 1940, intense air battles took place over the skies of Britain as the Luftwaffe tried to put the RAF out of action. The fighting was inconclusive, but the RAF was finding survival difficult as attacks on airfields stretched its resources. Then, early in September, the Germans began raids on British cities.

Hitler's decision robbed the Luftwaffe of an excellent opportunity, for it was on the verge of achieving air superiority over southern England to make an invasion a real possibility. On

▲ POLICE AND RESCUE workers work frantically to clear debris after a Luftwaffe air raid on London in September 1940.

September 7 London was hit by 1,000 bombers, which did much damage and killed many people. Two days later the Luftwaffe bombed the city again, but RAF Fighter Command was ready and broke up the raid. The bombing reached its greatest intensity on the 15th, with over 1,000 bombers and fighters taking part, but 60 were shot down for the loss of 26 RAF aircraft. The city that suffered the most intense damage was Coventry, which was attacked during the night of November 14. Five hundred civilians died in this one raid.

MORALE MAINTAINED

In spite of Britain's plight, morale was high. The Royal Family remained in London, and there were military successes to report, including a raid against Italian vessels in Taranto harbor and victories against Italian forces in North Africa. The Luftwaffe was now suffering heavy losses, especially during its daylight raids on English cities, which were largely abandoned by the 30th. The failure of the Luftwaffe to achieve air superiority signaled the end of Operation Sealion in 1940.

▲ THE SUN, NEW YORK, FRIDAY SEPTEMBER 13, 1940

The targeting of places familiar to many people who had never visited London, such as Buckingham Palace and Regent's Street, pictured, brings the Blitz home to New Yorkers. In London, the decision by the king and queen to remain in the palace was welcomed as a symbol of their readiness to share the same dangers as everyone else. Wendell Willkie meanwhile campaigns for the presidential elections by promising to keep the country out of the war—in implied contrast to his opponent Roosevelt.

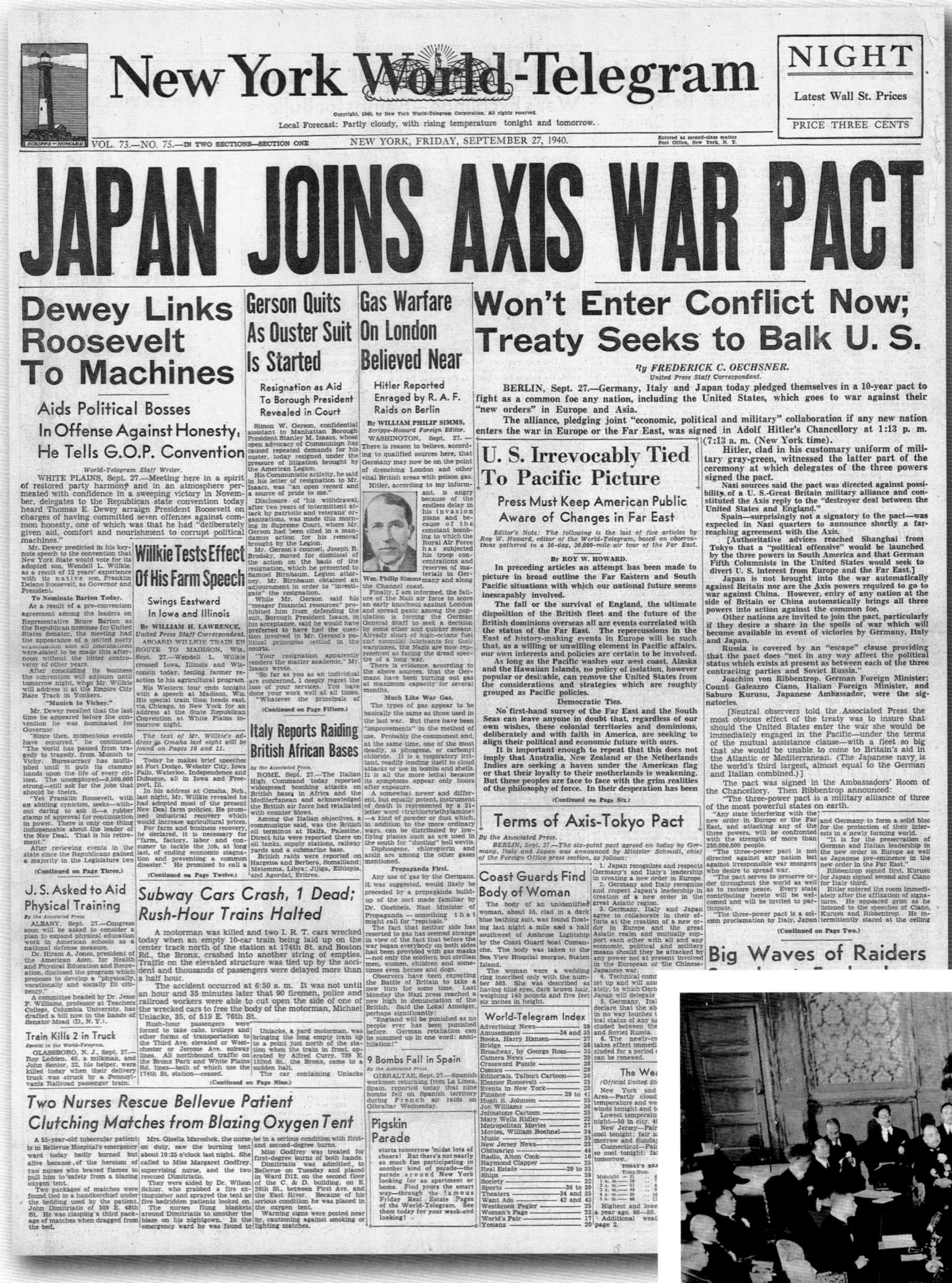

New York World-Telegram

NIGHT
Latest Wall St. Prices

PRICE THREE CENTS

Copyright, 1940, by New York World-Telegram Corporation. All rights reserved.
Local Forecast: Partly cloudy, with rising temperature tonight and tomorrow.

VOL. 73.—NO. 75.—IN TWO SECTIONS—SECTION ONE   NEW YORK, FRIDAY, SEPTEMBER 27, 1940.   Entered as second-class matter Post Office, New York, N. Y.

JAPAN JOINS AXIS WAR PACT

Dewey Links Roosevelt To Machines

Aids Political Bosses In Offense Against Honesty, He Tells G.O.P. Convention

World-Telegram Staff Writer.

WHITE PLAINS, Sept. 27.—Meeting here in a spirit of restored party harmony and in an atmosphere permeated with confidence in a sweeping victory in November, delegates to the Republican state convention today heard Thomas E. Dewey arraign President Roosevelt on charges of having committed seven offenses against common honesty, one of which was that he had "deliberately given aid, comfort and nourishment to corrupt political machines."

Gerson Quits As Ouster Suit Is Started

Resignation as Aid To Borough President Revealed in Court

Simon W. Gerson, confidential assistant to Manhattan Borough President Stanley M. Isaacs, whose open advocacy of Communism has caused repeated demands for his ouster, today resigned under the pressure of litigation brought by the American Legion.

Gas Warfare On London Believed Near

Hitler Reported Enraged by R. A. F. Raids on Berlin

By WILLIAM PHILIP SIMMS, Scripps-Howard Foreign Editor.

WASHINGTON, Sept. 27.—There is reason to believe, according to qualified sources here, that Germany may be on the point of drenching London and other vital British areas with poison gas.

Won't Enter Conflict Now; Treaty Seeks to Balk U. S.

By FREDERICK C. OECHSNER.
United Press Staff Correspondent.

BERLIN, Sept. 27.—Germany, Italy and Japan today pledged themselves in a 10-year pact to fight as a common foe any nation, including the United States, which goes to war against their "new orders" in Europe and Asia.

The alliance, pledging joint "economic, political and military" collaboration if any new nation enters the war in Europe or the Far East, was signed in Adolf Hitler's Chancellory at 1:13 p. m. (7:13 a. m. (New York time).

U. S. Irrevocably Tied To Pacific Picture

Press Must Keep American Public Aware of Changes in Far East

By ROY W. HOWARD.

Willkie Tests Effect Of His Farm Speech

Swings Eastward In Iowa and Illinois

Terms of Axis-Tokyo Pact

By the Associated Press.

Coast Guards Find Body of Woman

Big Waves of Raiders

J. S. Asked to Aid Physical Training

Subway Cars Crash, 1 Dead; Rush-Hour Trains Halted

Two Nurses Rescue Bellevue Patient Clutching Matches from Blazing Oxygen Tent

Italy Reports Raiding British African Bases

9 Bombs Fall in Spain

Pigskin Parade

World-Telegram Index

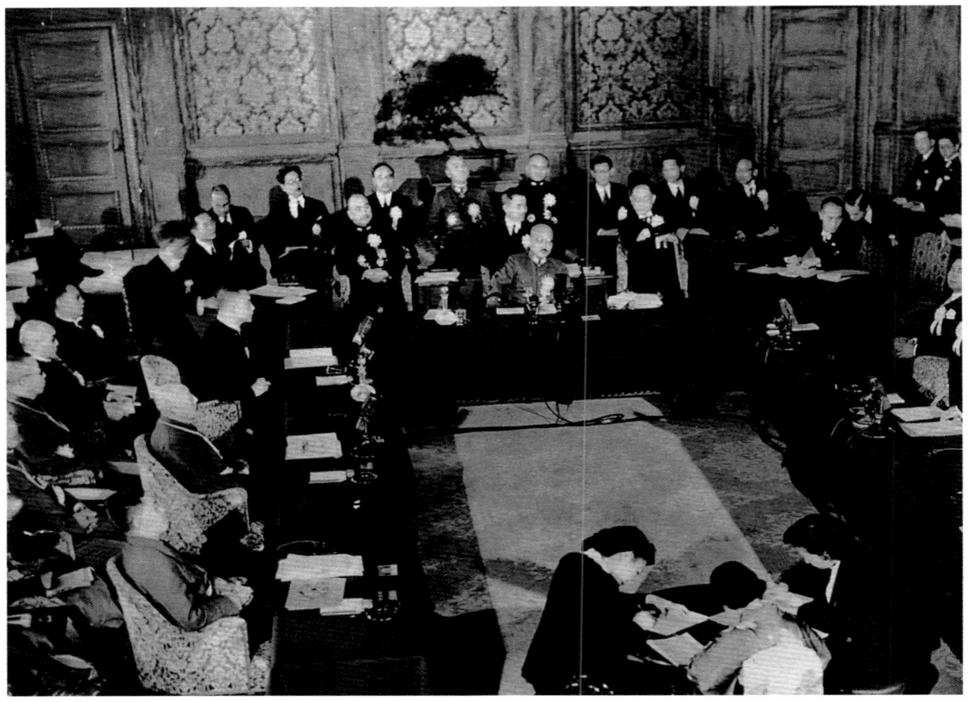

▶ A MEETING OF JAPAN'S Greater East Asia
Co-Prosperity Sphere. Formally announced in August
1940, it was an attempt to create a bloc of Asian
nations free of influence from Western countries.

◀ NEW YORK WORLD-
TELEGRAM, FRIDAY SEPTEMBER
27, 1940

In September 1940 Germany, Italy,
and Japan signed the Tripartite Pact,
pledging mutual support in the event
of attack and promising to establish
the "New Order" in Europe and
"Greater East Asia" in the Far East.
The *World-Telegram* has the benefit of
a report from editor Roy W. Howard,
who has himself just returned from a
month-long trip to East Asia. The
news from London is grim: Hitler's
frustration in the Battle of Britain
leads to rumors that gas attacks on the
capital are imminent. In fact, they
never materialized.

DAILY NEWS

Average net paid circulation
for September exceeded
Daily --- 2,000,000
Sunday - 3,500,000

Copr. 1940 by News Syndicate Co. Inc. **NEW YORK'S** PICTURE NEWSPAPER Trade Mark Reg. U. S. Pat. Off.

FINAL

Vol. 22. No. 86   New York, Thursday, October 3, 1940★   56 Main + 4 Manhattan Pages   2 Cents IN CITY LIMITS | 3 CENTS Elsewhere

PLANE SHORTAGE HINTED BY NAZIS

Fighters Used as Bombers

— Story on Page 3.

Les Miserables. Londoners use the escalator of a subway station for a dormitory. Above them, Nazi bombs are falling. How to get some sleep is the big problem of the Londoner. Despite heavy losses in planes and airmen, the Nazis have shown no letup in their sleep blockade of England. (By Associated Press) —Story on page 16, other pictures on page 29

▲ DAILY NEWS, NEW YORK, THURSDAY OCTOBER 3, 1940

The *Daily News* makes maximum impact with an image that captures the misery of life during the night-time raids of the Blitz: dozens of civilians taking cover in a subway station during an air raid. At the height of the Blitz, some 177,000 Londoners were sleeping in underground stations, despite the objections of the government. The *Daily News'* headline has more than a grain of truth: the Luftwaffe was finding the bombing raids expensive in terms of aircraft and pilots, which is one reason why the Blitz stopped in May 1941.

WEATHER
Cloudy, occasional rains this afternoon. Highest temperature 42 degrees, moderate winds. Cloudy tonight, moderate winds. Cloudy and colder tomorrow.

New York Post

NIGHT EDITION

Founded 1801. Volume 139. No. 293.
Copyright 1940, New York Post, Inc.

NEW YORK MONDAY OCTOBER 28 1940

THREE CENTS

City Roars Greeting to Roosevelt Today

Story in Col. 3

BOMB ATHENS; GREEKS FIGHT

Nation, Invaded by Italy, Asks Turkey's Aid

ENGLISH FLEET RUSHES TO SCENE

President's Day

President Roosevelt's day in the city:

9:15 A. M.—Address at A. Harry Moore School for Crippled Children, Jersey City, broadcast over Station WAAT.

10 A. M.—Welcome by Mayor LaGuardia at Staten Island end of Bayonne Bridge.

11 A. M.—Ground-breaking for Battery-Brooklyn Tunnel at Hamilton Av. and Van Brunt St., Brooklyn, broadcast over WJZ, WABC, WOR and WNYC.

11:30 A. M.—Address with Gov. Lehman at Roosevelt Park, Chrystie and Canal Sts., broadcast over WNYC.

1-2:30 P. M.—Lunch at Hunter College, with broadcast over WNYC at 2 p. m.

2:30 P. M.—Address at E. 38th St. entrance to Midtown Tunnel, broadcast over WNYC.

3:15 P. M.—Inspection of Queensbridge housing project, Queens.

3:45 P. M.—Inspection of LaGuardia Field.

4:20 P. M.—Address at Fordham University.

5-9 P. M.—Dinner and rest in private car at Mott Haven yards.

10:15 P. M.—Address at Madison Square Garden, broadcast over WEAF, WJZ, WHN and WQXR and telecast over W2XBS.

11 P. M.—Departure for Washington from Penn Station.

Roosevelt Landslide Is Believed Likely

Willkie Must Sweep Doubtful and Very Close States For Bare Majority—Polls Give GOP Little Hope

By CHAS. VAN DEVANDER

President Roosevelt's re-election for a third term seems close to a political certainty as the 1940 campaign swings into its final week.

Another New Deal landslide, sweeping 36 to 40 states into the Democratic column, is among the clear possibilities.

Against this prospect supporters of Wendell L. Willkie hope that something approaching a political miracle—a clean sweep of all the doubtful and close states—will give him a bare majority in the electoral college.

The newest Fortune Magazine survey, made public today, cooled off the more ardent Willkieites with a report that 57 per cent of the voters still prefer Mr. Roosevelt.

Gallup Poll

The latest Gallup poll of the nation contributed to the same end by citing a 54.5 per cent popular vote for the President and giving him the lead in 36 states with 410 electoral votes, against

Continued on Page 5, Col. 3

21 to 36

Order numbers for the draft will be published in successive editions of the New York Post tomorrow as rapidly as they are drawn in Washington. Watch the Post for your number.

7th Av. at 24th Becomes a Brook

A passerby seeing Seventh Av. suddenly become a gurgling stream at 24th St., with water bubbling up at almost 50 places, called the Fire Dept. at 3:30 a. m. today.

The Fire Dept., taking a more official view of the matter, called the Water Dept. The leak was shut off at 5:10 a. m., after water had gone down the slight hill at Seventh Ave at that point, flooding a sub-cellar in a loft building at 245 Seventh Ave., and leaking, but not dangerously, into the Seventh Ave. IRT subway station at 23d St.

Traffic on 23d, 24th and 25th Sts. and Seventh Ave. was tied up from 3:30 a. m. to 5:30 a. m. Although the street was considerably damaged on one side, President Roosevelt's scheduled route on Seventh Ave. was not changed.

City Roars Greeting To F. D. R.

Thousands to See Him on Tour of 5 Boroughs—Garden Speech Tonight

New York City, a Democratic and New Deal citadel, was ready with an overwhelming welcome today for President Roosevelt on a whirlwind campaign visit which his supporters hope will assure his victory in the state next Tuesday.

Five or six brief speeches during the day and visits to each of the five boroughs were on the President's schedule, prior to a full-length campaign address tonight in Madison Square Garden over a nation-wide radio hook-up.

Mayor LaGuardia and the city Democratic leaders, putting aside for the moment their local political rivalry, joined in preparations to meet the President and contribute to the success of his campaign visit.

6,000 Police on Route

Virtually the entire police force was on duty, with 6,000 uniformed men stationed along the line of march where hundreds of thousands of New Yorkers will see the President pass during the day.

In his night speech, members of the presidential party said, Mr. Roosevelt will deliver another series of sledge-hammer blows at GOP candidate Wendell L. Willkie in the vein of his Philadelphia attack on "deliberate" and "fantastic misrepresentations" by the Republican nominee and his supporters.

A huge crowd is expected at the Garden, where the President will arrive about 9:45 and speak about 10:15. Doors will be open at 5 p. m. to those holding general admission tickets, and after 7:30 p. m. they will be open to

Continued on Page 3, Col. 4

INDEX

Two Sections 20 Pages

LONDON, Oct. 28 (UP).—**Great Britain will make good its pledge to defend Greek liberty, and the Admiralty already is dealing with the problem of assistance, it was made known today as the war cabinet met to consider a Greek appeal for aid.**

It was believed that British men-of-war already were racing to Greece from Egyptian bases and that Britain's naval and air forces soon would be in the fight.

Britain said that Italian charges of Greek provocations and favoritism toward Britain were "merely part of the familiar Axis routine preceding aggression."

Charalambos Simopoulos, Greek minister, visited the foreign office to discuss defense problems. It was announced authoritatively soon after his visit

52 consecutive days of Nazi bombing have left London battered but unbowed.

that Britain regards Greece as an ally.

Greeks Ask Help

It was revealed that Greece had appealed for "certain" assistance.

Expecting an eventual axis move against Greece, the British press had suggested that the government would at once occupy Crete and other strategically important Greek islands if Italy attacked.

This move should be, on its face, a simple operation, as the British fleet controls the Eastern Mediterranean.

It was not indicated at once whether the British, confronted by greatly superior—numerical-

Continued on Page 2, Col. 4

Girl Tries Death Second Time, Fails

Nancy McQuade, 25, who attempted suicide with another girl on a street corner six years ago, was in critical condition in Bellevue Hospital today following another suicide attempt in the fashionable Southgate Apartments, 400 E. 52d St., where she was living under the name of Jean Edwards.

FOR YOUR GREATER CONVENIENCE

Classified Advertising is now divided into separate classifications, which will appear on different appropriate pages to provide maximum readability and quicker selection.

Late Bulletins

BUDAPEST, Oct. 28 (AP). — Rumors were current in the Balkans today that Russia was preparing to take over the Dardanelles "protectively."

BELGRADE, Yugoslavia, Oct. 28 (AP).—Diplomatic circles heard unconfirmed reports today that Turkey had declared war on Italy.

[The report was denied in Turkey.]

BELGRADE, Oct. 28 (UP).—Official quarters today reported fear that Germany and Italy would demand permission for passage of troops through Yugoslavia if Britain lands troops in Greece, thus threatening to draw all of the Balkans into the conflict.

BELGRADE, Oct. 28 (UP).—A widespread revolt has broken out in Albania, according to reports which seeped over the Jugoslav-Albanian frontier to the town of Pec.

Greeks Battle to Hold Mountain Passes

200,000 Italians Reported Striking Along Albanian Border—Naval Action at Corfu

BELGRADE, Yugoslavia, Oct. 28.—Ten divisions of perhaps 200,000 Italian troops were reported driving into Greece today all along the Albanian frontier in an attack timed with Italian naval blows at the Greek island of Corfu.

Skirted Greek troops battled with the invading motorized forces in the border mountain passes.

Details of the naval action at Corfu, off the Greek-Albanian coast, were not known immediately but observers here wondered whether British naval units, backing up England's guarantee of Greek independence, had reached the scene.

The reported firing, however, might have been between Italian warships and Greek shore bateries on the island, they said.

Corfu Waters Mined

Greek waters off Corfu in the northern Ionian Sea were reported mined last August. The Greek fleet had scheduled "naval maneuvers" there today.

Meanwhile, Yugoslav quarters said the Italian attack on Greece violated the Yugoslav-Italian pact of 1937 because Yugoslavia was not informed in advance of the move.

Official statements, however,

Continued on Page 2, Col. 5

Hitler Meets Mussolini

FLORENCE, Oct. 28 (AP).—Adolf Hitler and Benito Mussolini met here today to discuss new developmentss in the Axis war against Britain as reports arrived that hostilities had broken out between Greece and Italy. Their first talk lasted more than two hours.

The two Axiss leaders began their sessions at 11:30 A. M. and emerged at 1:50 P. M. for luncheon with their foreign ministers and other dignitaries. A second conference was expected to begin about 4 P. M.

[The discussions "resulted in a complete agreement of views," according to a Florence communique broadcast at Berlin.]

The conversations took place in the medieval, battlemented Palazzo Vecchio on the 18th anniversary of the Fascist march on Rome, which put Il Duce in power in Italy.

[Hitler was expected to remain in Italy for an indefinite period to follow military and diplomatic developments, according to a Rome dispatch by United

Continued on Page 8, Col. 7

U. S. May Freeze Greek Credits

NEWARK, Oct. 28 (UP).—President Roosevelt was expected to invoke today the neutrality law and freeze Greek credits in the U. S. as a result of hostilities between Italy and Greece.

BULGARIA REMAINS NEUTRAL

LONDON, Oct. 28 (UP).—Bulgaria will not join Italy in its move against Greece, reliable sources reported today.

LONDON, Oct. 28 (AP).—Air raid precautions were ordered throughout Bulgaria today.

A German radio report today said it had been learned in Berlin that Yugoslavia would remain neutral.

ATHENS, Oct. 28 (AP).—Greece fought with her little army today against invading Italian forces and announced officially that Great Britain was sending her unlimited support.

ATHENS, Oct. 28 (UP).—Fifteen Greek fighting planes and anti-aircraft guns today broke up an Italian aerial attack on principal Green communicatinns centers, including the Athens airport, Eleusis and the Patras harbor.

By PAUL A. TIERNEY
War Editor of The Post

Tenth nation invaded by the Axis since the war began, the Greeks today battled an Italian Army reportedly numbering 200,000 in the mountain passes of the Greco Albantian frontier.

Italian bombs fell on the airports of Athens, the classic capital. With only by a handful of second-class antiaircraft guns and a trifling number of second-class planes the Greeks repelled the first air attack.

Hitler and Mussolini were meeting in Florence.

"Full aid" from England was announced by the Greeks.

Defying an Italian ultimatum demanding military occupation of their country in reprisal for alleged disorders on the Albanian frontier, the Greeks cheered the proclamation of war and gave an ovation to their King as he rode through the streets of Athens.

The British Admiralty took immediate action, and it was reported that the Eastern Mediterranean squadron of the British fleet was already on the way to defend Corfu, the Greek island which the British prevented the Italians from seizing as long ago as 1920.

The Turkish premier issued a statement that "Turkey was stronger than ever," but made no direct announcement of any decision taken by his government. Budapest reported that Russia had decided to occupy the Dardanelles, "protectively." This report was unconfirmed elsewhere.

Sea Battle Believed Imminent

Germany has not yet declared war on Greece. Balkon diplomatic circles expected Germany to remain quiescent for the time being.

The Italian thrust, however, was part of the Axis drive against the British in the Eastern Mediterranean and had for its immediate objectives the seizure of Athens, Corinth

Continued on Page 8, Col. 1

GREECE ON THE FIRING LINE

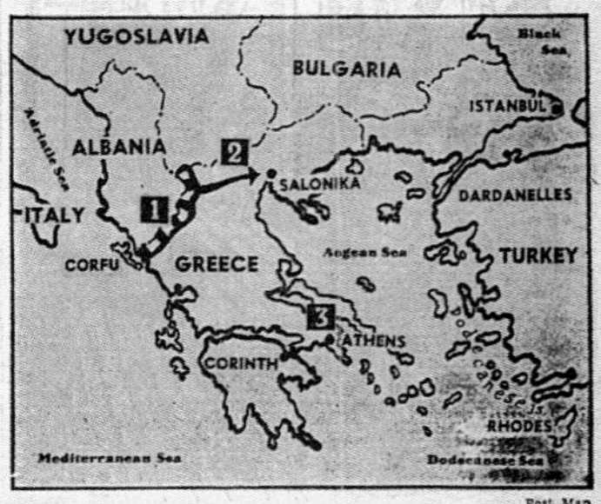

Post Map

ITALIAN TROOPS HAVE INVADED GREECE from the Albanian border (1), and it is expected that one of their principal objectives will be Salonika (2), key to Balkan lines of communication, where they come down to the eastern Mediterranean. A series of air raid alarms was sounded in Athens (3) and the civilian airport 12 miles outside the city was bombed, as was the airport at Corinth.

▲ NEW YORK POST, NEW YORK, MONDAY OCTOBER 28, 1940

Mussolini launched the invasion of Greece from Italian-occupied Albania. Heralded as the beginning of a glorious episode in Italy's history, it was a complete fiasco. During the following months the Italians were unable to defeat the Greeks, and in February 1941 Britain promised to send 100,000 troops to help them. They arrived in early March 1941, forcing Hitler to plan the conquest of Greece to secure his Balkan flank.

THE DAILY MAIL, Thursday, November 14, 1940.

BEAR BRAND STOCKINGS ★FINER—STRONGER★

Daily ✠ Mail

FOR KING AND EMPIRE

LATE WAR NEWS SPECIAL

GOOD WHISKY **JOHNNIE WALKER**

NO. 13,903 ✶ ✶ THURSDAY, NOVEMBER 14, 1940 ONE PENNY

GREATEST BLOW TO DUCE
Taranto Raid Halves Italian Battle Fleet

'ALERT' WAS ON, THE QUEEN USES ARMOURED CAR

ONE STROKE CHANGES POWER BALANCE

Daily Mail Naval Correspondent

ITALY to-day reels under two staggering blows from the British Navy. The magnificent raid by the Fleet Air Arm on Taranto Harbour has cut her proud battle-fleet in half at one blow.

The whole balance of power in the Mediterranean has changed in Britain's favour overnight. The repercussions throughout the wider seas of the world are too great at this moment even to begin to estimate.

The prestige of Italy—as a fighting power in general and a naval power in particular—has suffered such a blow as it will hardly recover from till the war ends.

On top of Mr. Churchill's great news there came last night from the Admiralty evidence that the British Navy has pierced deep into Mussolini's own sea—the Adriatic—to strike at the lines of communication so vital to his hard-pressed armies in Greece.

Cocktails for Molotov

By FROOM TYLER, Daily Mail Foreign Editor

THERE were cocktails for Molotov in Berlin yesterday — but not for Hitler. The teetotal Führer, true to the only pledge he has ever kept, toasted the health of the Soviet Premier in Munich near-beer.

Churchill Tells the Good News

Taranto: How it Was Done

By NOEL MONKS, Daily Mail Air Correspondent

Greeks Joined by Albanians

From CHRONIS PROTOPAPPAS, Daily Mail Reporter

ATHENS, Wednesday.

CONVOY: 6 MORE NAMED

Short Night Raid Again

LOOTING
It's Not, if L.C.C. Give 'Permit'

Navy Hero Wins D.S.O. Again

Bremen Sunk, Say U.S. Reports

Berlin Works Just Vanished

Chief Scout Ill

MORE PRISONERS

TO QUESTION AXIS CONSULS

AID FOR EVACUEES

Engaged!
AND HOW SHE LOVES HER **H. SAMUEL** RING

All Cinemas Say Give Us Sunday

H. SAMUEL
THE EMPIRE'S LARGEST JEWELLER
99 Branches in Gt. Britain

NEW AIR CHIEF FOR FAR EAST

◄ DAILY MAIL, LONDON, THURSDAY NOVEMBER 14, 1940 The *Mail* uses specially drawn maps to celebrate the raid on Taranto Harbor that left three battleships sunk or badly damaged—of Italy's total of six. In the lefthand column is speculation about the possible meaning of the visit to Munich of the Soviet foreign minister Molotov. In the center of the page, the report on the night's bombing has become almost casual with its reference to Londoners' respite "from their usual noisy nights."

◄ WATER COVERS THE DECK of the Italian battleship *Littorio* on the day after the Taranto attack. Repairs to the ship took four months to complete. The torpedoes carried by the British Swordfish had been specially modified to operate in the shallow water of Taranto harbor.

"Daily Herald," Saturday, November 16, 1940.

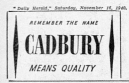

REMEMBER THE NAME
CADBURY
MEANS QUALITY

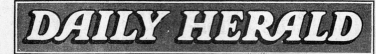

DAILY HERALD

EXTRA LATE EDITION

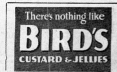

There's nothing like BIRD'S CUSTARD & JELLIES

No. 7725 SATURDAY, NOVEMBER 16, 1940 ONE PENNY

Midlands City Is Now Like A Bombarded French Town

COVENTRY HOMELESS SLEPT BY ROADSIDE THIS MORNING

NOT A MORTAL BLOW —WORK WILL RESTART

By F. G. H. SALUSBURY, "Daily Herald" War Correspondent

COVENTRY, Friday Night

COVENTRY HAS BEEN THE VICTIM OF THE MOST CONCENTRATED, IF NOT THE WORST, RAID SINCE THE WAR BEGAN.

I HAVE JUST COME BACK FROM THE CENTRE OF THE CITY, WHICH NOW LOOKS EXACTLY LIKE ONE OF THOSE FRENCH TOWNS THAT WERE LAID LEVEL DURING THE LAST WAR BY AN INTENSIVE BOMBARDMENT.

The cathedral is in ruins, except for its tower, and over a large area surrounding it there lies the stench of burning houses.

The number of casualties cannot yet be determined, but it is certainly large. (*Preliminary reports, says the Ministry of Home Security, indicate that the number of casualties may number 1,000.*) The damage which has been inflicted on this city must run into millions of pounds.

I was told by one of the inhabitants that the noise of falling bombs was practically continuous, and that after a short time everyone was literally dazed by the noise.

I approached the city from Rugby, and a few miles out of Coventry I encountered the first large body of refugees walking along the roadside exactly as the Belgians and French escaped from the last German invasion.

Children were being carried in their fathers' arms, and pushed along in perambulators. Luggage was piled high in perambulators.

There were suitcases and bundles on people's shoulders; little families trudged along hand in hand with rugs, blankets, and, in fact, anything they could have salved from their ruined homes.

There were also many motor cars parked by the roadside, in which people would pass the night despite the intense cold.

UNDER THE HEDGEROWS

Nevertheless, those with motor cars will be luckier than those without. For despite the hospitality of surrounding towns and villages, it will have been impossible for everyone to get a bed or even shelter.

I saw several people making preparations to lie down under the leeside of buildings or against hedgerows.

Very soon after the raid began the Germans succeeded in starting their first large fire, and from then onwards they had no difficulty in sighting their targets.

Fires in the centre of the city multiplied and spread rapidly despite most magnificent work by the fire brigades' auxiliary fire services and the A.R.P.—indeed, all the services which could be called out to deal with this tragedy.

It was a miracle that the firemen confined the fires as they did. In one place they had to blow up a large building with dynamite to check the path of the flames.

Extra police and A.R.P. also rushed in.

Every conceivable assistance to Coventry has been rendered by her neighbours. But nothing can minimise the appalling extent of the tragedy, which has rendered scores of thousands of people homeless and severely damaged the heart of the city.

On my way to the cathedral I encountered a girl of, perhaps, 12 years of age, and I asked her what she was doing.

The air was thick with smoke and a fire was still blazing in a house not 20 yards away.

"Oh," she said, "I'm just having a look round." I asked her where she was going to sleep that night and she replied, "Why? Here, of course. We were lucky."

"Have you got any water or gas?" I asked. "No," she said, "but we'll do some cooking on an oil stove and the water will turn up from somewhere."

WORKMEN WERE THERE

Then she admitted with a smile that she had been very frightened last night and resumed her tour of inspection.

There was, of course, no work done in Coventry to-day, largely owing to the failure of the power supplies, though I understand there are some factories which manufactured their own electricity.

Nevertheless, the workmen were there, ready to start again if it had been possible.

This is not a mortal blow to our war production by any means, and I should not be surprised if quite soon work is resumed in Coventry to some extent.

The authorities are doing everything possible to get homeless people and refugees out of the city into neighbouring towns and rest centres, but their main difficulty is with transport.

There is nothing like enough transport for the people who wish to be moved, and the result, as I have said, is in these pathetic streams of refugees walking along the roads.

Nevertheless, the spirit of the people, without any exaggeration, is magnificent.

I even saw many smiles.

In every heart there is no fear, only a most passionate hatred of the enemy, and a determination to carry on at all costs.

In fact, the spirit of battered Coventry was very well expressed by a Union Jack which I observed stuck over the shattered doorway of an otherwise completely ruined building.

(Continued on Back Page)

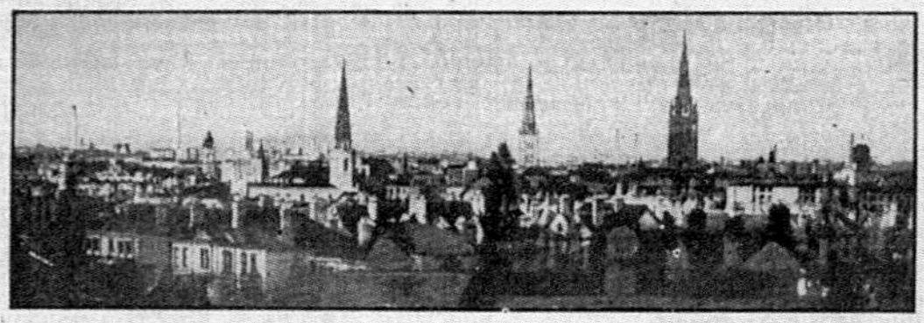

Three famous spires of Coventry—Christ Church, Holy Trinity Church and the Cathedral.

RAF STRIKES AT BERLIN

WHILE the Germans were concentrating their hate on Coventry, R A F bombers were pounding the great Berlin railway stations and goods yards.

Heavy explosive and incendiary bombs caused fires that could be seen for many miles. The damage will increase the transport chaos in Germany already caused by the R A F. (See Page Six.)

Dusk To Dawn Raid

NAZIS SAY 30,000 FIRE BOMBS FELL

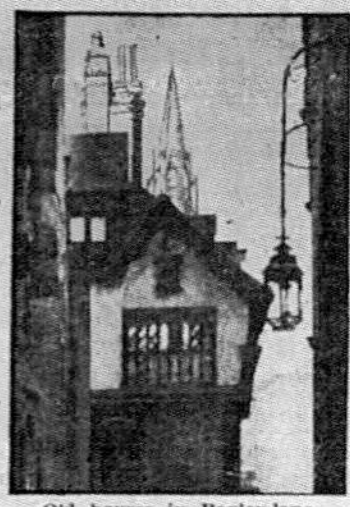

Old houses in Bayley-lane.

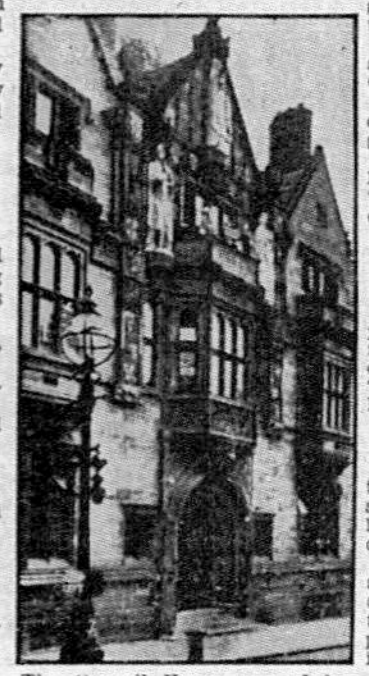

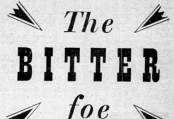

The Council House, opened by the King—then Duke of York—in 1920.

FROM dusk on Thursday to dawn yesterday there was seldom a period of more than two minutes when bombs were not falling on Coventry.

Berlin radio claimed that 500 planes took part in the raid, and that 500 tons of high explosive and 30,000 incendiary bombs were dropped.

"These," said the German High Command, "caused tremendous devastation" and fires that were visible from the Channel coast 125 miles away.

The raid was described by Berlin as a reprisal for the R A F attack on Munich, and was held to be the greatest bombardment in the history of air warfare.

Apparently the Luftwaffe was striving to make Coventry a second Guernica.

At times the attack took the form of dive-bombing and machine-gunning.

"The people of Coventry," the Ministry of Home Security stated, "bore their ordeal with great courage."

To this an official added, "There will be many stories to be told when it is possible to collect them."

Few shops were open in the city yesterday, but in the window of a fruit store, which had been damaged by blast, was the notice, "Business as usual. Nuts to Hitler!"

Died On Duty

Casualties included members of the Civil Defence fire and police services, who are known to have lost their lives while engaged on duty.

Among the places damaged, apart from the 14th century cathedral, was the operating theatre of a hospital, but the hospital—hit three times—was working yesterday as a clearing station.

An isolation hospital was hit, and in one ward some casualties were caused.

Five policemen—three specials and two regulars—were patrolling one street when a bomb was heard falling.

The three specials threw themselves down and the two regulars fell on top of them in an attempt to shield them. The bomb fell almost directly on them and all were killed.

One of the most tragic stories was that of a young Coventry man who had been working in Birmingham and returned to his home town to help with rescue work.

At the very first address to which he was sent he helped to recover the body of his young wife.

The Provost, the very Rev. R. T. Howard, and a party of cathedral watchers attempted to deal with 12 incendiary bombs.

They tackled them with sand and attempted to smother them until a shower of other incendiaries, accompanied this time by high explosives, rendered impossible their efforts to save the cathedral, only the tower and steeple of which remain.

"The cathedral," said the Provost, "will rise again. It will be rebuilt and it will be as great a pride to future generations as it has been to generations in the past."

Two churches, public baths, two clubs, a school, an hotel, four public shelters, five cinemas, a police station, a post office and two first-aid posts were damaged.

Steps were being taken yesterday to shepherd the homeless to emergency feeding centres.

Terrific Din

A policeman suffered injury to his eyes while dealing with one of the many incendiary bombs.

A reporter who watched the raid writes that at times the din was terrific.

The flash and crash of the barrage mingled with the whistle of falling bombs and explosions.

A pall of smoke lay over the town, and the red glare in the sky outdid the full moon in brilliance.

Stabbing through this scene, searchlights endeavoured to catch and hold the raiders in their beams.

(Continued on Back Page)

Egypt's New Premier

Hussein Sirry Pasha has been appointed Prime Minister of Egypt in succession to Hassan Sabry Pasha, who collapsed and died while reading the Speech from the Throne on Thursday.

As Minister of Public Works he came to England in 1938 to study London local government. He has also been Minister of Defence.

November 16, 1940

London Blackout
5.38 p.m.—7.53 a.m.
MOON RISES 6.32 p.m.; SETS 10.11 a.m. To-morrow

21 Down—Three In Last Night's Raid

AFTER a day in which eighteen German bombers and fighters were shot down in raids on Britain—for the loss of one Spitfire and one pilot—London had its worst night blitz for several weeks.

Three more enemy planes were destroyed in the night raids.

London anti-aircraft guns put up the heaviest barrage for weeks when relays of raiders attacked the capital in the early hours this morning.

Raids were widespread over the country. The West Midlands were again bombed, and several towns in the Home Counties.

But London appeared to be the butt of the main attack.

During the first few hours of the the night only single bombers came over, because of bad weather conditions.

80 BOMBERS

They tried without success to ring London with fires.

But when the clouds cleared the raiders came in greater strength and dropped oil bombs and incendiaries, as well as sticks of high explosives.

They repeated their tactics of trying to start a circle of fires.

An A.R.P. worker said, "For the first time the planes came over in formation. Within a few minutes I counted 80 heavy bombers.

"They were flying in close formation from the south due north.

"For numbers it is the worst night of my experience, and hundreds of German planes have been active over the area."

PLANE BLEW UP

A plane was seen to blow up in the sky at Debden, near Saffron Walden, Essex. There was a terrific explosion as parts of it hit the ground.

A second plane was brought down in Essex on Latters Priory Farm, Harlow.

(Continued on Back Page, Col. Six)

STOP PRESS

BERLIN RAIDED AGAIN

NEW YORK, Friday

German broadcast intercepted by National Broadcasting Company said large numbers of British planes attacked Berlin tonight, and six were brought down in Berlin and six near the Channel.

BRITAIN'S OFFER TO RUSSIA

GREAT BRITAIN is still awaiting Moscow's reply to the proposals made to Russia last month.

There were three main items in the proposals it was learned in London last night. They were:

De facto recognition of the incorporation of the Baltic States in the Soviet Union;

A guarantee that Russia would be a participant in any peace settlement after the war; and

An assurance that Britain would not be associated in any attack against Soviet Russia.

The proposals were submitted to M. Vishinsky, the deputy Commissar for Foreign Affairs, on October 22.

AN ITALIAN LIE

The Admiralty states there is no truth in the claim that an Italian submarine has torpedoed a British battleship of the Ramillies class.

Greeks Launch A New Attack

GREEK infantry at dawn yesterday launched a new attack on the Italian positions.

Preceded by a night of careful preparation, it was possibly the most determined attack which the war has seen so far (says a Reuter message from Athens).

The Greeks made the attack with bayonets among the rocky heights north-east of Koritza, the keypoint in Southern Albania.

Their chief objective was the mountain of Ivan, 6,000 feet high, overlooking Koritza.

Bayonet Fighting

Following a further assault with bayonets in the afternoon, the Greeks occupied a great deal of this mountain region.

During the day ten Italian large-calibre guns fell into their hands.

By the occupation of Ivan the Greeks will control still one more important road out of Koritza, making it much more difficult for the Italians to retain the town.

Koritza is not only the largest town of Southern Albania, with a population of 30,000, but it is also a centre of communications.

Its capture would offer the Greeks an entrance to the route leading north to Elbassan, the strategic centre of Albania.

This is where King Zog used to maintain most of his forces before the Italian invasion.

Italy's Offensive

In the Kalamas River sector (wires D. J. Travlos, "Daily Herald" correspondent at Athens) the Greek advance has reached the border line.

In the middle sector, where the Greeks are fighting on Albanian territory, they are reported to be shelling a road running parallel with the frontier.

The cutting of this road would be a serious threat to Italian supplies in this region.

Predictions that an Italian offensive against Greece is imminent were made by some observers on the Jugoslav border yesterday (reports Associated Press).

They based their view on two developments.

There was brisk artillery and air activity on the northern Greek-Albanian border and a change in Italian troop dispositions.

The **BITTER** *foe*

One of the most remorseless enemies we all have to face this winter is—cold. A chilled body means low spirits, discouragement—perhaps illness.

In times of war, it falls to the lot of some great firms to provide the nation with shells, others guns, others 'planes. On us at Wolsey falls another great task. We must ensure the best supply, that war conditions permit, of light perfectly-made wool under and outer wear—so that no man or woman need go cold.

The task is no easy one. We have to make the best possible use of supplies of wool at our command. We have to face mounting costs—yet keep prices at a fair level. We have to guard our vast army of workers—yet ensure maximum production, and an unfailing distribution of our goods up to the limit of war production.

But this is not our first war. Wolsey served England throughout the Crimean War, the Boer War and the war of 1914. You may be sure—with our vast modern organisation—we shall not fail now to provide the same high quality of goods which has stood the test of time.

Don't be indignant if you can't get Wolsey at your usual shop. The amount of Wolsey is limited by decree to-day, and we have tried to distribute stocks fairly; but to-day's shifting populations have in some quarters brought stocks very low. So if you cannot buy Wolsey at your usual shop—look a little further.

Wolsey, Leicester

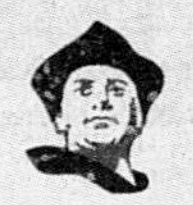

▲ DAILY HERALD, LONDON, SATURDAY NOVEMBER 16, 1940

Established in 1911 as the official newspaper of the British Labor Party, the *Daily Herald* uses library images of Coventry's historic buildings to underline the enormity of the bombing raid on the city on the night of November 14/15. More than 439 German bombers dropped 503 tons (511 tonnes) of high explosives and 30,000 incendiaries on the city of Coventry, in central England. The raid killed 568 people and destroyed or damaged some 60,000 buildings, including the medieval cathedral, which became a symbol of the city's perseverance.

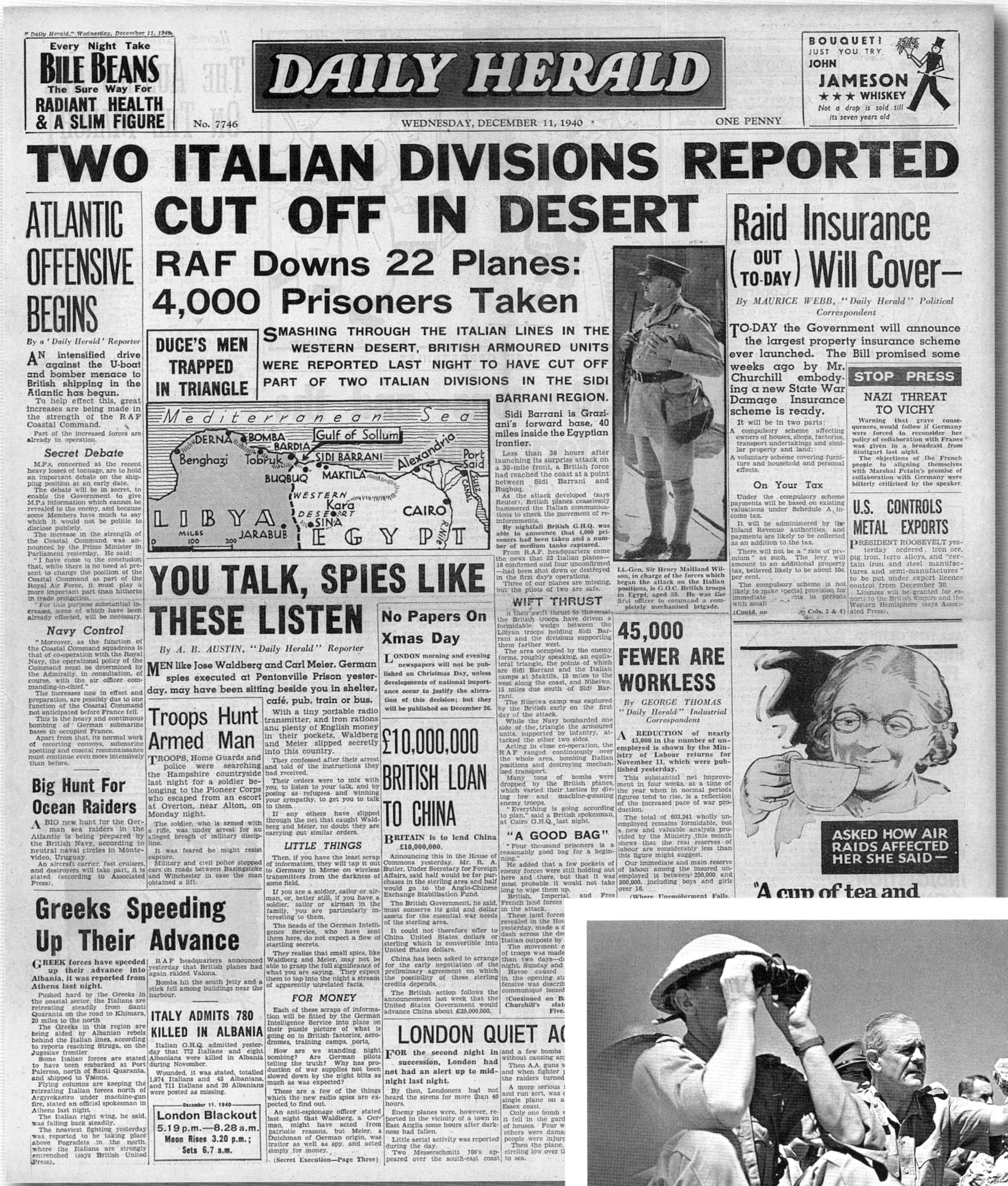

"Daily Herald," Wednesday, December 11, 1940.

Every Night Take
BILE BEANS
The Sure Way For
RADIANT HEALTH
& A SLIM FIGURE

DAILY HERALD

No. 7746 WEDNESDAY, DECEMBER 11, 1940 ONE PENNY

BOUQUET! JUST YOU TRY JOHN JAMESON ★★★ WHISKEY
Not a drop is sold till its seven years old

TWO ITALIAN DIVISIONS REPORTED CUT OFF IN DESERT

RAF Downs 22 Planes: 4,000 Prisoners Taken

DUCE'S MEN TRAPPED IN TRIANGLE

SMASHING THROUGH THE ITALIAN LINES IN THE WESTERN DESERT, BRITISH ARMOURED UNITS WERE REPORTED LAST NIGHT TO HAVE CUT OFF PART OF TWO ITALIAN DIVISIONS IN THE SIDI BARRANI REGION.

Sidi Barrani is Graziani's forward base, 40 miles inside the Egyptian frontier.

Less than 36 hours after launching its surprise attack on a 30-mile front, a British force had reached the coast at a point between Sidi Barrani and Buqbuq.

As the attack developed (says Reuter), British planes ceaselessly hammered the Italian communications to check the movement of reinforcements.

By nightfall British G.H.Q. was able to announce that 4,000 prisoners had been taken and a number of medium tanks captured.

From R.A.F. headquarters came the news that 22 Italian planes—18 confirmed and four unconfirmed—had been shot down or destroyed in the first day's operations.

Three of our planes are missing, but the pilots of two are safe.

WIFT THRUST

n their swift thrust to the coast the British troops have driven a formidable wedge between the Libyan troops holding Sidi Barrani and the divisions supporting them farther west.

The area occupied by the enemy forms, roughly speaking, an equilateral triangle, the points of which are Sidi Barrani and the Italian camps at Maktila, 15 miles to the west along the coast, and Nibeiwa, 15 miles due south of Sidi Barrani.

The Nibeiwa camp was captured by the British early on the first day of the attack.

While the Navy bombarded one side of the triangle the armoured units, supported by infantry, attacked the other two sides.

Acting in close co-operation, the RAF ranged continuously over the whole area, bombing Italian positions and destroying mechanised transport.

Many tons of bombs were dropped by the British planes, which varied their tactics by diving low and machine-gunning enemy troops.

"Everything is going according to plan," said a British spokesman, at Cairo G.H.Q., last night.

"A GOOD BAG"

"Four thousand prisoners is a reasonably good bag for a beginning."

He added that a few pockets of enemy forces were still holding out here and there, but that it was most probable it would not take long to wipe them up.

British, Imperial, and Free French land forces in the attack.

These land forces revealed in the Hou yesterday, made a d dash across the de Italian outposts by

The movement o of troops was made than two days—du night, Sunday and

Havoc caused in the opening st fensive was describ communiqué issued

(Continued on B Churchill's stat Five.

Map: Mediterranean Sea; Gulf of Sollum; DERNA; BOMBA; BARDIA; Benghazi; Tobruk; SIDI BARRANI; Alexandria; Port Said; BUQBUQ; MAKTILA; SUEZ CANAL; WESTERN DESERT; Kara; CAIRO; SINA; R. Nile; LIBYA; EGYPT; JARABUB; MILES 0 100 200

Lt.-Gen. Sir Henry Maitland Wilson, in charge of the forces which began the attack on the Italian positions, is G.O.C. British troops in Egypt, aged 59. He was the first officer to command a completely mechanised brigade.

ATLANTIC OFFENSIVE BEGINS

By a 'Daily Herald' Reporter

AN intensified drive against the U-boat and bomber menace to British shipping in the Atlantic has begun.

To help effect this, great increases are being made in the strength of the RAF Coastal Command.

Part of the increased forces are already in operation.

Secret Debate

M.P.s, concerned at the recent heavy losses of tonnage, are to hold an important debate on the shipping position at an early date.

The debate will be in secret, to enable the Government to give M.P.s information which cannot be revealed to the enemy, and because some Members have much to say which it would not be politic to disclose publicly.

The increase in the strength of the Coastal Command was announced by the Prime Minister in Parliament yesterday. He said:

"I have come to the conclusion that, while there is no need at present to change the position of the Coastal Command as part of the Royal Air Force, it must play a more important part than hitherto in trade protection.

"For this purpose substantial increases, some of which have been already effected, will be necessary.

Navy Control

"Moreover, as the function of the Coastal Command squadrons is that of co-operation with the Royal Navy, the operational policy of the Command must be determined by the Admiralty, in consultation, of course, with the air officer commanding-in-chief."

The increases now in effect and preparation, are possibly due to one function of the Coastal Command not anticipated before France fell.

This is the heavy and continuous bombing of German submarine bases in occupied France.

Apart from that, its normal work of escorting convoys, submarine spotting and coastal reconnaissance must continue even more intensively than before.

Big Hunt For Ocean Raiders

A BIG new hunt for the German sea raiders in the Atlantic is being prepared by the British Navy, according to neutral naval circles in Montevideo, Uruguay.

An aircraft carrier, fast cruisers, and destroyers will take part, it is stated (according to Associated Press).

YOU TALK, SPIES LIKE THESE LISTEN

By A. B. AUSTIN, "Daily Herald" Reporter

MEN like Jose Waldberg and Carl Meier, German spies executed at Pentonville Prison yesterday, may have been sitting beside you in shelter, café, pub, train or bus.

With a tiny portable radio transmitter, and iron rations and plenty of English money in their pockets, Waldberg and Meier slipped secretly into this country.

They confessed after their arrest and told of the instructions they had received.

Their orders were to mix with you, to listen to your talk, and by posing as refugees and winning your sympathy, to get you to talk to them.

If any others have slipped through the net that caught Waldberg and Meier, no doubt they are carrying out similar orders.

LITTLE THINGS

Then, if you have the least scrap of information, they will tap it out to Germany in Morse on wireless transmitters from the darkness of some field.

If you are a soldier, sailor or airman, or, better still, if you have a soldier, sailor or airman in the family, you are particularly interesting to them.

The heads of the German Intelligence Service, who have sent them here, do not expect a flow of startling secrets.

They realise that small spies, like Waldberg and Meier, may not be able to grasp the full significance of what you are saying. They expect them to tap into the night a stream of apparently unrelated facts.

FOR MONEY

Each of these scraps of information will be fitted by the German Intelligence Service into place on their puzzle picture of what is going on in British factories, aerodromes, training camps, ports.

How are we standing night bombing? Are German pilots telling the truth? Why has production of war supplies not been slowed down by the night blitz as much as was expected?

These are a few of the things which the new radio spies are expected to find out.

An anti-espionage officer stated last night that Waldberg, a German, might have acted from patriotic reasons, but Meier, a Dutchman of German origin, was traitor as well as spy, and acted simply for money.

(Secret Execution—Page Three)

Troops Hunt Armed Man

TROOPS, Home Guards and police were searching the Hampshire countryside last night for a soldier belonging to the Pioneer Corps who escaped from an escort at Overton, near Alton, on Monday night.

The soldier, who is armed with a rifle, was under arrest for an alleged breach of military discipline.

It was feared he might resist capture.

Military and civil police stopped cars on roads between Basingstoke and Winchester in case the man obtained a lift.

No Papers On Xmas Day

LONDON morning and evening newspapers will not be published on Christmas Day, unless developments of national importance occur to justify the alteration of this decision; but they will be published on December 26.

£10,000,000 BRITISH LOAN TO CHINA

BRITAIN is to lend China £10,000,000.

Announcing this in the House of Commons yesterday, Mr. R. A. Butler, Under Secretary for Foreign Affairs, said half would be for purchases in the sterling area and half would go to the Anglo-Chinese Exchange Stabilisation Fund.

The British Government, he said, must conserve its gold and dollar assets for the essential war needs of the sterling area.

It could not therefore offer to China United States dollars or sterling which is convertible into United States dollars.

China has been asked to arrange for the early negotiation of the preliminary agreement on which the possibility of these sterling credits depends.

The British action follows the announcement last week that the United States Government would advance China about £25,000,000.

Greeks Speeding Up Their Advance

GREEK forces have speeded up their advance into Albania, it was reported from Athens last night.

Pushed hard by the Greeks in the coastal sector, the Italians are retreating steadily from Santi Quaranta on the road to Khimara, 20 miles to the north

The Greeks in this region are being aided by Albanian rebels behind the Italian lines, according to reports reaching Struga, on the Jugoslav frontier

Some Italian forces are stated to have been embarked at Port Palermo, north of Santi Quaranta, and shipped to Valona.

Flying columns are keeping the retreating Italian forces north of Argyrokastro under machine-gun fire, stated an official spokesman in Athens last night.

The Italian right wing, he said, was falling back steadily.

The heaviest fighting yesterday was reported to be taking place above Pogradets in the north, where the Italians are strongly entrenched (says British United Press).

RAF headquarters announced yesterday that British planes had again raided Valona.

Bombs hit the south jetty and a stick fell among buildings near the harbour.

ITALY ADMITS 780 KILLED IN ALBANIA

Italian G.H.Q. admitted yesterday that 772 Italians and eight Albanians were killed in Albania during November.

Wounded, it was stated, totalled 1,874 Italians and 43 Albanians, and 711 Italians and 20 Albanians were posted as missing.

December 11, 1940
London Blackout
5.19 p.m.—8.28 a.m.
Moon Rises 3.20 p.m.; Sets 6.7 a.m.

LONDON QUIET AG

FOR the second night in succession, London had not had an alert up to midnight last night.

By then, Londoners had not heard the sirens for more than 40 hours.

Enemy planes were, however, reported in the vicinity of a town in East Anglia some hours after darkness had fallen.

Little aerial activity was reported during the day.

Two Messerschmitt 109's appeared over the south-east coast and a few bombs without causing an

Then A.A. guns w and when fighter the raiders turned

A more serious and run sort, was single plane on a Essex coast.

Only one bomb it fell in the gard of houses. Four w others were damag people were injure

Then the plane, circling low over t to sea.

Raid Insurance (OUT TO-DAY) Will Cover—

By MAURICE WEBB, "Daily Herald" Political Correspondent

TO-DAY the Government will announce the largest property insurance scheme ever launched. The Bill promised some weeks ago by Mr. Churchill embodying a new State War Damage Insurance scheme is ready.

It will be in two parts:

A compulsory scheme affecting owners of houses, shops, factories, transport undertakings and similar property and land;

A voluntary scheme covering furniture and household and personal effects.

On Your Tax

Under the compulsory scheme payments will be based on existing valuations under Schedule A income tax.

It will be administered by the Inland Revenue authorities, and payments are likely to be collected as an addition to the tax.

There will not be a "rate of premium" as such. The levy will amount to an additional property tax, believed likely to be about 10s. per cent.

The compulsory scheme is not likely to make special provision for immediate nts to persons with small

(Contd. on Cols. 3 & 4)

STOP PRESS

NAZI THREAT TO VICHY

Warning that grave consequences would follow if Germany were forced to reconsider her policy of collaboration with France was given in a broadcast from Stuttgart last night.

The objections of the French people to aligning themselves with Marshal Petain's promise of collaboration with Germany were bitterly criticised by the speaker.

U.S. CONTROLS METAL EXPORTS

PRESIDENT ROOSEVELT yesterday ordered iron ore, pig iron, ferro alloys, and "certain iron and steel manufactures and semi-manufactures" to be put under export licence control from December 30.

Licences will be granted for exports to the British Empire and the Western Hemisphere (says Associated Press).

45,000 FEWER ARE WORKLESS

By GEORGE THOMAS "Daily Herald" Industrial Correspondent

A REDUCTION of nearly 45,000 in the number of unemployed is shown by the Ministry of Labour returns for November 11, which were published yesterday.

This substantial net improvement in four weeks, at a time of the year when in normal periods figures tend to rise, is a reflection of the increased pace of war production.

The total of 603,241 wholly unemployed remains formidable, but a new and valuable analysis provided by the Ministry this month shows that the real reserves of labour are considerably less than this figure might suggest.

Our immediate and main reserve of labour among the insured unemployed is between 250,000 and 300,000, including boys and girls over 16.

(Where Unemployment Falls,

ASKED HOW AIR RAIDS AFFECTED HER SHE SAID—
"A cup of tea and

◀ DAILY HERALD, LONDON, WEDNESDAY DECEMBER 11, 1940
The news seems positive for British readers: a breakthrough in Egypt, a new offensive in the Atlantic, another quiet night in the Blitz, and falling numbers of unemployed workers. There is even a new insurance plan, underwritten by the government, that will compensate victims of war damage, including those who lose their homes in air raids.

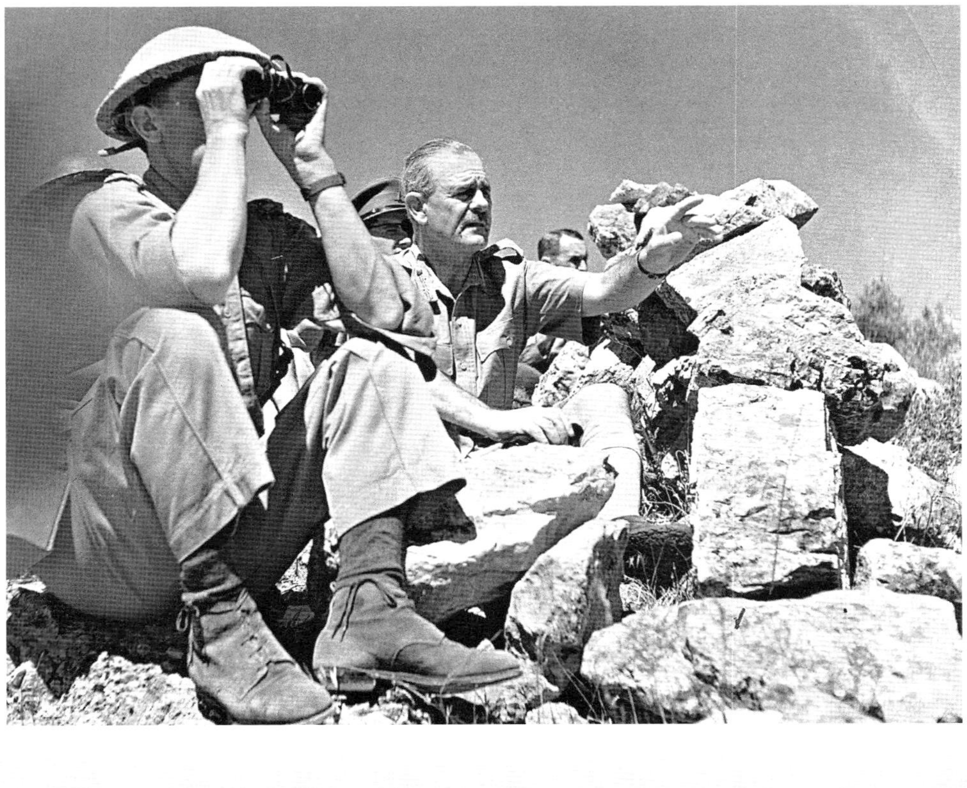

▶ GENERAL SIR ARCHIBALD WAVELL, the British commander-in-chief in North Africa (right, bare headed) inflicted a devastating defeat on Italy's army in North Africa despite being outnumbered over four to one.

▲ DAILY MAIL, LONDON, TUESDAY DECEMBER 31, 1940

St. Paul's Cathedral in London stands defiant during a Luftwaffe bombing raid in one of the iconic images of the war. However, as the reports make clear, many people criticized officials' response to the raid.

Britain defiant

DECEMBER 1940

THE LUFTWAFFE'S NIGHT RAIDS BECAME SO FREQUENT THAT THEY WERE PRACTICALLY CONTINUOUS AS 1940 CAME TO AN END. THE RAF HAD PREVENTED AN INVASION OF BRITAIN but it could not stop the German bombers. Antiaircraft guns on the ground blazed away at the attackers, boosting morale but doing little actual damage to their targets. For civilians, the "Blitz" was emotionally draining more than anything else.

LIVING IN THE "BLITZ"

Men and women hurried home from work to snatch a meal, before heading for shelters when the inevitable air raid sirens screeched their warnings of an impending attack. Once in the shelters, they could do nothing but sit and wait—and hope that a bomb did not score a direct hit. Sleep was all but impossible, and so the next morning the survivors would emerge bleary-eyed to survey the damage that had been done. Many people who were tired of repeatedly interrupting their sleep to go back and forth to the street shelters,

▲ BOMB DAMAGE to London's St. Paul's Cathedral in the aftermath of an air raid.

virtually took up residence in a shelter. The shelters were crowded, invariably stank, and were often damp, but among those who sought refuge in them there arose a new spirit of solidarity and community, a feeling that "Britain can take it" regardless of what the Germans did. Thus the owners of shops that had been reduced to rubble in an air raid put up signs stating "Business as usual," while leaders such as King George VI and his wife and Winston Churchill toured blitzed areas, which boosted public fortitude immensely.

LONDON ABLAZE

London suffered the most. On the night of November 27 the city was set alight and the Guildhall was destroyed. In the same month Joseph Kennedy, American ambassador to Britain, reported to Washington that Britain was beaten. Franklin D. Roosevelt, reelected president for a third time on November 5, 1940, did not believe him. Neither did American journalists who were reporting from Britain. In fact Roosevelt was right and Kennedy was wrong. Britain was battered, but it was far from beaten.

1941

IN JUNE THE GERMANS LAUNCHED THEIR INVASION OF THE SOVIET UNION, WHICH TOOK THEM TO THE GATES OF MOSCOW. IN THE PACIFIC THE JAPANESE ATTACKED THE U.S. FLEET AT PEARL HARBOR. THE CONFLICT HAD BECOME TRULY GLOBAL.

IN 1941 THE WAR BECAME TRULY GLOBAL. THE FIGHTING IN NORTH AFRICA AND THE MEDITERRANEAN INCREASED IN INTENSITY AND MOVED EAST TO SYRIA AND IRAQ; HITLER CONQUERED YUGOSLAVIA AND Greece and then attacked the Soviet Union; while in the Pacific, Japanese forces attacked the U.S. base at Pearl Harbor.

THE WAR IN AFRICA

As the year opened, British forces were winning victories against the Italians in Libya. In February, however, German troops landed in Libya to help their ally. Over the next year, fighting swung back and forth, with neither side able to gain a decisive advantage.

Meanwhile, in Europe Hitler had decided to attack the Soviet Union in the spring. His plans were put back by an anti-German coup in Yugoslavia, and he invaded the Balkans to secure his southern flank in April. On June 22, Hitler launched Operation Barbarossa,

the invasion of the Soviet Union. The Red Army was unprepared, and German forces gained enormous early victories, taking 600,000 prisoners at Kiev. However, the resources of the Soviet Union proved more redoubtable than the German planners had estimated. Slowed by the fall mud, the Wehrmacht's final attempt to take Moscow ground to a halt in the suburbs of the Soviet capital. In the bitter cold the Soviets launched a counterattack that threatened to destroy the German Army.

Meanwhile, the U.S. had been drawn more closely into the war as President Roosevelt gave what aid he could to Britain, most notably under the famous "Lend-Lease" Act of March. As well as aiding Britain, Roosevelt put pressure on Japan, whose ambitions he feared, by imposing an oil embargo in August. This was a key factor in convincing the Japanese (who had little oil of their own) that they should go to war. Roosevelt may have anticipated this, but he had certainly not anticipated that the Japanese would attack directly across the Pacific at Pearl Harbor.

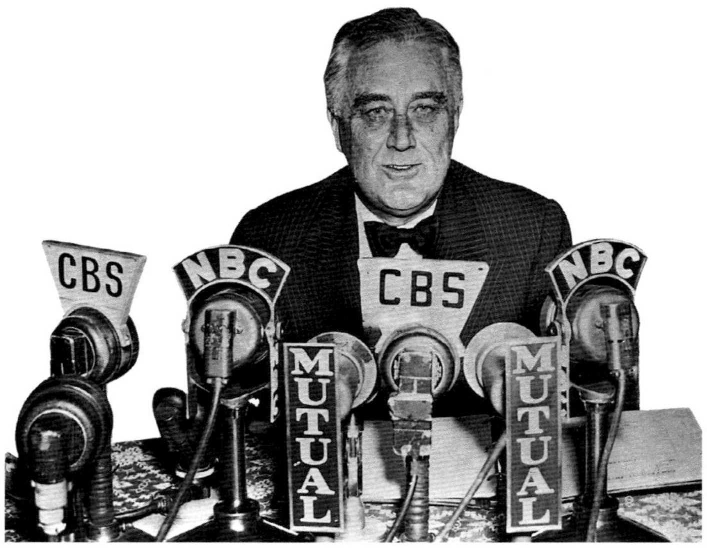

▲ PRESIDENT FRANKLIN D. ROOSEVELT was pro-British and anti-Hitler before the entry of the United States into the war, and was a fervent supporter of Lend-Lease aid to Britain in 1940 and 1941.

▲ NEW YORK WORLD-TELEGRAM, THURSDAY JANUARY 30, 1941

Among local New York news—a crash on 2nd Avenue, the discovery of the body of a missing labor leader—
the *World-Telegram* gives pride of place to Hitler's announcement of unrestrained submarine warfare against
U.S. vessels heading for Britain. The move alienated U.S. public opinion, but reflected the success of
Roosevelt's Lend-Lease program for supplying the Allies with war materials.

THE DAILY MAIL. Saturday, February 8, 1941.

Daily Mail

FOR KING AND EMPIRE

NO. 13,975   **   SATURDAY, FEBRUARY 8, 1941   ONE PENNY

GREATEST BLOW TO HITLER
Weygand Warns the Axis as Benghazi Falls

Shadow Over the Danube

By FROOM TYLER, Daily Mail Foreign Editor

ACROSS the marshlands that lie between Bulgaria and Rumania cracks a queer, tearing sound, seldom heard in early February. It is the Danube ice breaking.

Perhaps the most important item from south-eastern Europe this week has been that the Danube is thawing uncommonly early.

This may possibly be the signal for Hitler's Balkan Blitz.

It is known that Hitler has at least ten divisions in Rumania—about 250,000 men. Obviously these are not needed to police Antonescu's gang.

Little doubt now that they are intended to cross the Danube where it divides Rumania from Bulgaria, surge down the passes of the Rhodope range to the fertile plains of Grecian Thrace.

Their objective: Salonika.

Purposes of the campaign: To rescue Mussolini, now flopping on all fronts, by striking at Greece; to divert British effort in the Middle East; to strike at the flank of Turkey's defences between Adrianople and the Ægean.

Possible opposition: Weather, Bulgaria, Turkey.

★

IN 1940 Hitler waited for the spring. This year he may not do so. Mussolini's need is desperate. The Danube thaws. There have been winter wars in Bulgaria before.

Will Bulgaria fight? Despatches from the Daily Mail man-on-the-spot, Cedric Salter, report a rapid conversion of Bulgarians to a pro-Axis attitude. Goebbels' men have gone on ahead.

Bulgarians are now being persuaded that Turkey is about to attack them.

Will Turkey fight? Turks know that a German thrust through Bulgaria will have as its ultimate objective not Salonika but the Straits. Turkey has made it clear that if her vital interests are threatened she fights.

Bulgaria wishes to be the battleground, for Turkey would not wait until the Germans reached the Turco-Bulgarian frontier.

Bulgaria's King Boris knows that above him is an ever-darkening dilemma. Right and day he is counted by the thought of his country again becoming a battleground.

CEDRIC SALTER cabled last night from Sofia:

Bulgaria is facing her darkest hour since 1918, and Boris alone carries on his shoulders the almost unbearable strain of attempting to save his country's independence.

Boris has so far averted disaster, yet although the sincerest patriots know that the day when German troops march through Bulgaria will be the last day of Bulgaria's independence, there are many who are dazzled by Nazi promises of regaining for them the vital outlet to the Ægean Sea, or who are frightened at the possible consequences of refusal.

There are weakening the King's hand at a moment when unity is most necessary.

★

NO country watches Bulgaria more anxiously than her neighbour Yugoslavia. Hitler could, of course, strike at Greece through that country, but Yugoslavia's fears now are aroused not so much by the prospect of invasion as that of encirclement.

TERENCE ATHERTON, Daily Mail correspondent in Belgrade, summing up the feeling in Yugoslavia last night, cabled:

I believe, on the strength of a wide investigation, that this country will not have to face German invasion. Instead, she will be surrounded and rendered impotent by Bulgaria's occupation and German seizure of Ægean ports, including Salonika.

There are grave fears that in the event of a German invasion of Bulgaria Britain will be too late with her help.

A various change seems to have overtaken official intentions here in the past six weeks. There is an influential current drifting towards acquiescence before "the inevitable."

But the overwhelming majority of the people do not share this fatalism. Neither do the younger Army officers.

CHANNEL FOG

Fog still covered the Strait of Dover last night, and the sea was choppy. The weather was milder, with the wind in the south-west, and the sky was overcast.

'HANDS OFF TUNIS AND BIZERTA!'

ALL Mussolini's colony of Cyrenaica is ours. General Wavell, moving with a speed and secrecy unparalleled in modern warfare, is now in Benghazi, Graziani's G.H.Q. and last stronghold.

What remains of the beaten Italian army is streaming across the bitter desert to Tripoli—little more than a rabble.

The news was given to a staggered world from Cairo G.H.Q. yesterday. Its repercussions were swift and powerful.

General Weygand, at the head of all French North Africa, broadcast to the world that in no circumstances would Hitler be allowed to land men in Tunisia, there to aid his stricken ally. Nor would he be permitted the use of the vital naval bases at Bizerta and Tunis.

Admiral Darlan, according to obviously inspired reports from Vichy, has let it be known that in no circumstances would the French Navy be handed over to Germany.

Should General Wavell decide to push on to Tripoli, he will know that the danger of his armies being outflanked by Germans operating from Tunis is ended.

With the fall of Benghazi the British grip on Mussolini's throat is tightened. The Navy are presented with a finely equipped forward base; the R.A.F. with magnificent new airfields close to the shores of both Sicily and Italy.

Hitler's prospects of lending Mussolini effective aid in the Mediterranean are considerably weakened.

RAF Have Won New Bases for Blows at Italy

By NOEL MONKS, Daily Mail Air Correspondent

AIR Chief Marshal Sir Arthur Longmore, Commander-in-Chief British Air Forces in the Middle East, will benefit most by the fall of Benghazi. At a stroke he is provided with two of the finest air bases in the East.

More important still, Sicily and Italy are brought nearer the strong R.A.F. bomber force in Egypt by several hundred miles.

At Benghazi itself is a magnificent airfield which is only 420 miles from Sicily. Naples is less than 300 miles farther on.

Another airfield, at Benina, is just outside Benghazi.

Air Chief Marshal Longmore will also be able to keep a closer watch on Malta and, if necessary, keep greater and quicker aid to the island in the event of an attempt at invasion.

Seaplanes of the Fleet Air Arm will find a splendid base for their patrolling activities.

The Benghazi bases will neutralise the advantage, Nazi airmen, operating from Sicily, have had in their attacks on British shipping passing through the narrow channel between Sicily and Tunis.

I would say that the occupation of Benghazi at the moment when Hitler has decided on support for the defeated Italian Air Force may cause yet another change in Hitler's plans.

TRIPOLI NEXT?

By Lt.-Col. T. A. LOWE, D.S.O., M.C.
Daily Mail Services Correspondent

WILL General Wavell's next jump be for Tripoli? This would be a brilliant final objective of the campaign in Libya, but whether it could be attempted by land is a matter for conjecture.

A combined landing made from the sea might be easier if the necessary shipping is available.

Tripoli is almost due south of Malta and is only about 190 miles away.

Should General Wavell decide to end his advance at Benghazi, the city would make an excellent British "front line" against any Italian or German-Italian army which the Axis might try to assemble at Tripoli.

Any such army would have to cross 500 miles of desert before it could attack—with the Mediterranean Fleet on its flank.

Prize for Navy

The value of Benghazi from the naval point of view cannot be overestimated.

The harbour is large and sheltered, tideless, and can be entered in any weather—a great asset on this inhospitable coast. It is capable of accommodating the heaviest cruisers.

There are good embarkation facilities, excellent stores accommodation, and machine shops capable of carrying out small repairs.

The harbour has recently been improved at a cost of £500,000. Important sea distances are [cut off]

BACK PAGE, Column FOUR

THE Wavell way in Libya. While the main British forces were pushing on through Derna to Benghazi, a detachment cut right across the desert to the south of Benghazi. Communications with Tripoli were thus destroyed. Arrows show the routes taken by our troops in the cutting-off movement.

TRIPOLI • BENGHAZI • DERNA
BARDIA
Gulf of Sidra
Sirtica Desert
Cyrenaica
LIBYA
0   MILES   100

Benghazi Captured by Master-Stroke

From Daily Mail Correspondent

CAIRO, Friday.

THE master-stroke which brought about the fall of Benghazi—a double drive along the coast and across the desert to cut the Italian communications—was described by a military spokesman here to-night.

Soon after Tobruk had been taken, he said, the British forces divided into two.

One took the coastal road and the other headed through Bomba and El Makili due west towards Benghazi.

The latter force, comprising armoured and mechanised units, was engaged in some fighting with the Italians at El Makili on January 26 and 27.

After overcoming this resistance the British column advanced westwards across 130 miles of waterless desert along a little-used track with a good dry-weather surface.

While their comrades advancing along the coast were engaged through the difficult Jebel Akdar country, they kept south of this range of hills and reached the coast south of Benghazi, cutting the Italians' road communications to Tripoli.

'Wavell the Wizard'

These were the first reactions to the fall of Benghazi in the world's capitals last night:

Vichy: For the first time the French national radio gave a British success first place in its news summary.

New York: All other news was eclipsed in the New York evening papers.

Moscow: Interrupting the news bulletin, the Moscow radio announced: "We have just received news of the capture of Benghazi."

Athens: "Our congratulations to our great Ally; well done," said the official radio.

Cairo: Egyptian quarters commented, "Wavell is a wizard."

'Few Got Away'

Their retreat cut off, the Italian resistance quickly collapsed, enabling Australian troops to enter the town.

It is not believed here that the Italians intended to defend Benghazi.

Their resistance before Derna was probably intended to give them time for the evacuation of the port, but owing to the speed with which the British forces advanced it is not thought that they had time to get many troops or much material away.

Recently two Italian divisions were encamped around the city.

Following is the communiqué:—

Guard for U.S. Rome Embassy

ROME, Friday.—Five hundred Italian troops guarded the United States Embassy in Rome this morning when a number of students paraded through the streets shouting cries against the democracies.

The demonstration was an orderly one, and the students were not allowed to pass the Embassy but were diverted.—B.U.P.

Convoy Raider is Shot Down

A Dornier twin-engined bomber which tried to attack a convoy was shot down by H.M.S. Vanity, a destroyer commanded by Commander H. J. Buchanan, D.S.O., of the Royal Australian Navy, the Admiralty announced last night.

A direct hit was made on the Dornier, which crashed into the sea. There were no survivors.

No damage was done to the convoy or to H.M.S. Vanity, and there were no casualties.

Hitler in Vichy
Duce too, say Rome Reports

From Daily Mail Special Correspondent

NEW YORK, Friday.

HITLER is going to Vichy in an effort to sway Marshal Pétain, according to reports reaching New York to-day. A despatch from Rome states that the Spanish Foreign Minister, Señor Suñer, "has gone to Vichy to join the German Chancellor in bringing pressure on Marshal Pétain."

This was the first indication that Hitler was either in Vichy or on his way there.

According to other Rome reports, Mussolini also is said to be en route to Vichy.

The Rome despatch must have been passed by the censor, so it is presumed that Hitler is definitely going to or is in Vichy.

Great Pressure

The decision of the Spanish Minister to go to Vichy and Hitler's reported presence indicate the tremendous pressure the Nazis are using against Pétain.

There is a hint in the despatches that Suñer may tell Pétain that unless he agrees to Laval's demands Spain will allow the passage of German troops eastward from Spanish Morocco—this at a time when the Italians have turned over Sicily to Hitler, which is only 100 miles or so from Tunisia.

Germany wants the French navy, the armed forces in North Africa, and the naval base at Bizerta.

Axis quarters in Rome, say the messages, are making it plain that Hitler must gain control of French Africa and the French fleet to offset the growing faith of the French in the strength of Britain, backed by the United States.

Darlan Says 'Navy Stays'

ALL radio stations in Unoccupied France last night repeated a denial by General Weygand that France would permit Germany to use the base of Bizerta, in Tunisia, with a view to eventual action in Libya.

General Weygand, who was broadcasting over the Algiers radio in the name of the French Government, also denied that negotiations had taken place with a view to the cession of Bizerta or the landing of German troops at the port.

Messages last night from Vichy dealing with Admiral Darlan's negotiations with M. Laval in Paris were conflicting.

"Reliable quarters" were quoted as stating that Admiral Darlan was making a firm stand.

He was said to have insisted on resigning control of the Navy regarding of any other changes in the Vichy Cabinet and to have refused to surrender the Fleet or France's naval bases to anyone.

He was also credited with the determination to order the Fleet to be scuttled if necessary.

Later it was reported that Laval had insisted on being made Premier with the right to nominate Ministers. It was stated that his return to power was regarded as inevitable.

One report said Admiral Darlan would leave for Vichy late last night. Another denied that any arrangements had been made for him to leave Paris.

Messages from A.P., Reuter, and B.U.P.

FOOD FOR THOUGHT— FOR THE GERMANS

THE official mouthpiece of the German Foreign Office, the Deutsche Diplomatische Korrespondenz—its pronouncements come direct from Hitler and Ribbentrop—gave an example yesterday of how the Germans think.

At the beginning of one column it was highly indignant over the United States decision not to send food to Europe which might fall into German hands.

It quoted "legal facts" to prove that the decision was illegal. It said that food for occupied countries was "a matter of humanity and justice."

BUT—

In the same newspaper in the same column appeared these words:

"Germany herself, according to international law, is under no obligation to supply food to populations in occupied territories and other European countries not involved in the war.

"On the contrary, the German Army of Occupation is justified in demanding provisions and board in proportion to the resources of the country in question."

Cotton Girls to Make Arms

By Daily Mail Reporter

LANCASHIRE'S cotton girls are to quit their looms to start work in arms factories. Within the next few weeks the cotton industry will free 100,000 workers to make munitions.

This big switch-over from making shirts to making shells will follow this blunt warning to the industry by Sir Percy Ashley, Cotton Controller: "Production, especially for the home market, must be drastically cut. We must release workers for armaments."

Employers and workers union leaders have been trying all the week to agree on a scheme which will free the cotton employees from the mills.

They are expected to propose a 50 per cent. cut in the industry's production.

Some of Lancashire's spinning mills and weaving sheds may consequently have to close down.

One estimate yesterday was that 50 spinning mills—with 45,000,000 capital—and 100 weaving mills—capital £2,000,000—may stop.

The cut in production would probably mean ordinarily that 60,000 out of 200,000 women workers and 40,000 out of 150,000 men workers would be discharged.

It is expected that the preliminary scheme will be ready next week.

The Government will have to tackle the question: "How much compensation for the mills that have to close?"

Production for export to the United States and South American countries will not be affected.

But women in Britain will find it easier to get a new spring or summer frock and men will find that they will have to do with fewer new shirts.

It is expected also that many woollen workers will be transferred to arms work.

Plans are already in hand to restrict manufacture of woollen goods. [cut off]

Premier to Broadcast

MR. CHURCHILL will broadcast at 9 o'clock on Sunday night.

The Prime Minister's speech will be heard on the B.B.C.'s Home, Forces, and Overseas services.

FLANDIN URGES 'RESIST'

Vichy, Friday.—Flandin would probably mean ordinarily [cut off] resist.—B.U.P.

Vichy Foreign Minister, is reported to be leading a group urging Pétain to continue to resist Laval's demands.—B.U.P.

JOB FOR ITALIAN PRISONERS

Capetown, Friday.—Four thousand Italian prisoners of war will be employed on the construction of the national road from Capetown to Worcester and through the Montagu pass.—Reuter.

RAF Make Mass Raid on Ports

From Daily Mail Correspondent

DOVER, Friday Night

WAVES of R.A.F. bombers launched another violent assault against Nazis on the invasion coast to-night.

Our bombers seem determined to push the Germans back from the coast by weight of metal.

Doors, windows, and the very earth here shook as their bombs dropped to-night.

The sky over France was lit by a flickering but continuous display of glare from searchlights, A.A. guns—and biggest contributors of all, exploding bombs.

As first the objective appeared to be between Calais and Cap Gris Nez. After half an hour the bombers moved nearer to Boulogne.

Occasionally through the mist a particularly high ... ... from some part ... the echo of a vivid trail of flaming onions" was observed.

'Bulgaria's Fate Rests on Britain'

ISTANBUL, Friday.—A prominent Turkish political figure, speaking to-day on whether Bulgaria would yield to or resist German demands of aggression, said that Britain's military situation might be the deciding factor.

"If Bulgaria could rely on important British land and air forces being rushed to her help in case of an attack by Germany, she would courageously stand up to any Nazi pressure," he said.

Woolton Fixes Bread Price

Lord Woolton has made an Order under which, from Monday, no bread, including fancy bread and rolls, may be sold at prices higher than those on December 2, 1940.

Bread sold at 6d. a quartern, or less, will receive the subsidy of a halfpenny a quartern already announced by the Government.

The new Order does not apply to bread sold as part of a meal or sold to Government departments.

Another Night Raid-Free

Up to midnight last night there were no reports of raiders over any part of Britain.

Eight people were killed when a Nazi bomber dived out of the clouds over an east coast town yesterday and released its cargo of high-explosive bombs. A number of people were injured.

A.A. guns fired on the raider, which had flames shooting from it when it made off.

Bomb Site Workers Get More Pay

Men engaged on clearing bombed sites in the London area are to receive an increase in pay of 3d. an hour to 1s. 6½d. an hour for a total of 47 hours. Building trade workers will get a 3d. per hour increase on a 44-hours week.

"To keep the Blood Pressure normal"

That anxiety, excitement, alarm, and nervous irritation aggravate a susceptibility to abnormal blood pressure, especially in later life, is well-known. That 'Phyllosan' brand tablets, taken regularly three times a day before meals, have a stabilising effect upon blood-pressure has been demonstrated both by clinical tests and by everyday experience over many years.

A doctor writes: "As one of the first prescribers of 'Phyllosan' I should like to add my word of commendation to those which you have no doubt received. I have found it useful in cases of hypertension where there are no signs of organic disease. It seems to keep the blood pressure normal. I cannot speak too highly of 'Phyllosan' in regard to its use in this condition and I shall continue to describe it as before."—M.B.

No less important in this time of stress is the fortifying effect of 'Phyllosan' tablets upon the heart and their revitalising effect upon the whole organism.

A doctor writes: "I am 69 years of age, and recently took up A.R.P. work. My blood pressure was getting very high and I commenced taking 'Phyllosan.' I soon found my condition improving. I don't know of anything to equal 'Phyllosan' for rejuvenating the system."—Mr.)

Just two tiny tablets three times a day before meals! But if you take the tablets regularly, the results will astonish you.

Start taking 'PHYLLOSAN'

to revitalize your Blood, rejuvenate your Arteries, correct your Blood Pressure, fortify your Heart, strengthen your Nerves, and increase your Vital Forces, irrespective of age

Of all chemists: 3/-, 5/3 (double quantity), & 9/-. Including Purchase Tax

Proprietary rights are not claimed apart from the regd. trade mark 'Phyllosan,' the property of Natural Chemicals Ltd.

> "'Phyllosan' is not merely a tonic—it is a creative force in the system"
> (Dr.)
>
> Nothing to equal 'Phyllosan'

General Weygand. He stands firm.

▲ DAILY MAIL, LONDON, SATURDAY FEBRUARY 8, 1941

The Australian capture of Benghazi from the Italians was a bright spot for the Allies after over a year of being on the back foot. With Hitler in command in Europe, North Africa provided the Allies with their first real reasons for optimism.

Desert victory

FEBRUARY 1941

AT THE BEGINNING OF 1941 THE BRITISH ARMY CONTINUED ITS MAJOR OFFENSIVE AGAINST THE ITALIANS IN NORTH AFRICA. IN AUSTRALIA'S FIRST ACTION OF the war, the Australian 6th division led the attack to capture Bardia, just across the Libyan border with Egypt on January 15. Some 70,000 Italian troops, plus large amounts of equipment, were captured. On January 24 the Australians were once again in action when they helped to capture the port of Tobruk. The entire garrison fell into British hands. The campaign was turning into a disaster for the Italians. Their commander, Marshal

Rudolfo Graziani, had begun his offensive with 250,000 troops. By the beginning of February 1941 he was down to 40,000 men as his forces retreated west. The British followed them without respite, taking Derna, in Libya, on January 29

TRIPOLI UNDER THREAT

Between February 3 and 5, the Italians were defeated at the Battle of Beda Fomm. Over the next 10 days the British continued to advance and were poised to take the main Italian-held port of Tripoli. But help was at hand for the Italians: General Erwin Rommel's German units began landing at Tripoli on February 14. They would become the famed Afrika Korps.

▲ ITALIAN TROOPS IN ACTION near Benghazi during the major British offensive in February. Sandstorms were a major problem in the North African theater.

▲ NEW YORK WORLD-TELEGRAM, THURSDAY MARCH 27, 1941

The news from Yugoslavia, and Churchill's reported faith in U.S. support for the revolt, contrasts with the main theme of the *World-Telegram*'s front page: labor unrest. A wave of strikes swept U.S. industry in 1941, inspired in part by left-wing opposition to supporting Europe's war effort and partly by the still depressed state of the economy: more than 10 percent of American workers were unemployed.

Yugoslavia's revolt

MARCH 1941

HAVING MADE HIS MIND UP LATE IN 1940 TO INVADE THE SOVIET UNION, HITLER BEGAN TO PUT PRESSURE ON THE NATIONS OF YUGOSLAVIA, BULGARIA, AND ROMANIA, IN southeastern Europe, to help him. Bulgaria and Romania proved pliable, but in Yugoslavia the army led a coup on March 27 in protest at a government pact with Germany.

BALKAN CAMPAIGN

Adolf Hitler had already decided on an invasion of Greece (through his ally Bulgaria), which was fighting against Italian forces from Albania. Hitler now decided to hit at Yugoslavia as well, and, raging at the Yugoslavs, named the new operation "Punishment". The campaign to secure the Balkans began on April 5 and went well; the final act was the German conquest of the Mediterranean island of Crete, which was achieved after a fierce struggle with British Commonwealth forces.

While the land war in the Balkans was going well for Germany, Britain was still supreme at sea. The Italian fleet in the Mediterranean was defeated at the battle of Cape Matapan, off the Peloponnesian coast of Greece, while the German battleship *Bismarck* was sunk when she tried to enter the Atlantic to attack Allied convoys—although not before she had sunk HMS *Hood*, the Royal Navy's biggest warship.

RUDOLF HESS

This period also saw a strange episode, when Adolf Hitler's deputy Rudolf Hess flew a light aircraft to Scotland, trying to make contact with British antiwar groups. He parachuted into Scotland on May 10 and offered peace with the British Empire if Germany was given a free hand in Europe. Disowned by Hitler, Hess was imprisoned by the British. It is still unclear whether this was a serious attempt at peace or whether Rudolf Hess was mentally disturbed. After the war ended he was transferred to a German prison, where he died in 1987.

▲ ADOLF HITLER WAS INFURIATED when he heard of the coup in Yugoslavia that overthrew the pro-German regime.

BLACK-OUT
ZERO HOUR
TO-NIGHT
UNTIL 6-07 A.M.
MOON RISES 322 MOON SETS (11.9 P.M.)

Daily Express

No. 12,745   Monday, March 31, 1941   One Penny

53

MONDAY MORNING ON THE NEWSFRONTS

MUSSOLINI suffers his worst sea defeat of the war. Score of five—nil, probably increased to six—nil, as Greeks this morning report survivors from a hitherto unclaimed destroyer, bringing Italy's losses to three cruisers and three destroyers. And one of her battleships is damaged, so the disaster may become even greater.

TWO MORE SURPRISES for the Duce.
1 : Diredawa, Abyssinia's third city, is evacuated by Italian troops, who are fleeing towards Addis Ababa.

2 : Roosevelt seizes twenty-nine Italian and Nazi ships.
FRENCH SHORE BATTERIES open fire on British warships trying to intercept a Vichy convoy carrying war material for the Nazis. French bombers, in two waves, follow up the attack.

GERMANS FLEEING BELGRADE

Express Special Correspondent
BELGRADE, Sunday.

WITH Germans scurrying from every Jugo-Slav town and city in a dash for home, Belgrade tonight feels the tension rising.

At the German Legation smoke is pouring from chimneys as the Nazis burn documents.

Today von Heeren, Hitler's Minister, called on Foreign Minister Ninchitch and, it is reported, handed him a virtual ultimatum, demanding Jugo-Slav observance of the Svetkovitch-Markovitch undertakings to the Axis within four days. This would suggest Thursday.

We did not lose one, but these were SUNK, SUNK, SUNK!

The ZARA—completed in 1931. The POLA (right) in 1932. They each carried 705 men. Belonged to Mussolini's fleet of seven 10,000-ton cruisers.

The FIUME, completed in 1931, was another of the Italian heavy cruisers.

Greeks report survivors of third destroyer

Express Naval Reporter BERNARD HALL

SIX Italian warships had been reported sunk up to early today in the greatest naval battle of the war, won in the Mediterranean by Sir Andrew Cunningham without the loss of one British sailor or damage to a single British ship.

After the Admiralty had announced the sinking of five units of the Duce's navy, and implied that there might be more good news to come, Athens reported that survivors of a sixth warship—a large destroyer—had been landed by a Greek destroyer.

This is the Italian casualty list from both sources:—

THREE of the Duce's seven heavy cruisers SUNK.

TWO of his biggest and fastest destroyers SUNK.

ONE fast normal-size destroyer SUNK.

ONE new 35,000-ton battleship of the Littorio class DAMAGED.

The latest Admiralty communiqué, issued last night, states:—

"The Commander-in-Chief Mediterranean reports that no casualties or damage were

SUNK—*Large destroyer VINCENZO GIOBERTI (1936).*
—Jane's Fighting Ships.

sustained by H.M. ships throughout the recent operations. Two of our aircraft are, however, not yet accounted for."

"So far it is confirmed that the following Italian warships have been sunk: The eight-inch gun cruisers Fiume, Pola and Zara, the large destroyer Vincenzo Gioberti, and the destroyer Maestrale."

The Greeks reported that survivors from the Vittorio Alfieri, a sister-ship of the Vincenzo Gioberti, had been put ashore at Piraeus, the port of Athens, with men from the Pola, Fiume and Zara.

SUNK—*The destroyer MAESTRALE (1934).*
—Jane's Fighting Ships.

The three cruisers were up-to-date, 10,000-ton sister ships, carrying 705 men each. They were completed in 1931 and 1932 and had the high speed of 34 knots. Only one ship of this class is now left, the Gorizia, finished in 1930.

The Vincenzo Gioberti and the Vittorio Alfieri were 1,950-ton ships carrying 187 men each. Their speed was 39 knots, each had four 4.7-inch guns and they went into service in 1936. The Maestrale (1,449 tons), also a 4.7-inch gun ship, did 38 knots, and had a crew of 150.

Mussolini, then, has lost the services of 2,579 trained officers and men in this one action.

There may be more losses in men. It may be that two Italian cruisers and a destroyer, reported earlier as severely damaged by British planes between Sicily and Greece, will be added to the casualty list.

The extent of the damage to the 15in.-gun Littorio class battleship is not yet known. It was reported on Saturday, in the first communiqué about the battle.

The fighting began on Friday, when British and Greek ships under Sir Andrew Cunningham sighted Italian battleships, cruisers and destroyers.

The enemy scattered; but the Navy, the Air Force and the Fleet Air Arm went after them.

▶ BACK PAGE, COL. SEVEN

HE PUT OUT HIS TONGUE TOO FAR...

WHY did the Duce dare? Why did he sent his fleet out at last and risk contact with the British?

A clue to his strategy—and our own—may lie in the R.A.F. communiqué on Saturday, which reported that our bombers had attacked Lecce airfield, south of Brindisi, on Friday.

This may indicate that Mussolini had planned to execute an out-and-home dash to lure the British Fleet to within range of German bombers based in Southern Italy.

Our attack on Lecce (a possible Nazi bomber station) before the sea battle may have been an answer to this plan. It was an answer that thwarted it completely.

Or he may have thought he could catch a convoy going into Greece:

Or he may have thought out Eastern Mediterranean Fleet had gone, a report last week said it was "leaving Gibraltar for the Atlantic." But it wasn't.

Roosevelt seizes 31 Axis ships

Express Staff Reporter
NEW YORK, Sunday.

AMERICAN coastguards, armed with Tommy guns, today boarded twenty-eight Italian and two German ships lying in a dozen American ports and seized the vessels in the name of the United States Government.

After a few hours the crews were mustered and marched ashore—nearly 1,500 Italians and 100 Germans—and detained pending charges of mass sabotage or orders for deportation.

The coastguards acted on direct orders from President Roosevelt, following revelations that the crews had been wrecking machinery in the vessels and were preparing to scuttle them.

America's 1917 Espionage Act allows the United States to put guards aboard belligerent vessels to prevent sabotage and to take them over where damage has already been done.

ENGINES DAMAGED

According to the coastguard, most of the ships are freighters of about 4,000 tons, except for the 23,235-ton liner Conte Biancamano, which was laid up at Balboa, Panama Canal Zone.

Reports of the sabotage first reached the authorities from the Conte Biancamano. This vessel's engine cylinders had been put out with oxy-acetylene lamps and piles of tinder had been laid in the holds, ready to fire the vessel.

At least nine of the ships have been seriously damaged.

'Woe woe' pledges African conquest
—in centuries to come

Broadcasting his Sunday pep-talk to Italy's armed forces last night Giovanni (Woe! Woe!) Ansaldo said:—

"This talk must be devoted to the fact that at Keren we have been forced to yield to British pressure. The truth is, our position in the Empire has become more delicate.

"But the Italians, forced to yield in one part of Africa, make it a matter of honour to conquer in another. Never has Italy felt so certain that in centuries to come she will be mistress in Africa."

* Italians flee from Abyssinia key town, Back Page.

Italians quit Diredawa

While reports of a British push towards Diredawa, on the Addis Ababa-Jibuti railway, came from British headquarters in Cairo yesterday, an Italian communiqué made this surprise admission:—

"The Italian troops have evacuated Diredawa and are retreating westwards."

This means that the last line of escape for the Duke of Aosta's army bottled up in the Addis Ababa district has been cut off.

▶ Hope of defending capital vanishes—Back Page.

"800 prisoners for exchange"

The Moscow office of the International Red Cross was quoted yesterday by the German-controlled radio at Hilversum, Holland, for a report that negotiations for the exchange of 800 wounded prisoners between Germany and Britain are nearly concluded.

The report says each country will send its 800 prisoners to Switzerland.

Princess has a chill

Princess Elizabeth has a chill and was unable to go with the King and Queen and Princess Margaret to morning service in Eton College Chapel yesterday. She will, it is expected, be out again in a few days.

FRENCH OPEN FIRE ON OUR NAVY

Convoy had Nazi cargoes

BRITISH warships, attempting to stop a French convoy carrying war material for Germany, were fired on by French shore batteries on the Algerian coast.

They returned the fire, and later were attacked by two waves of French bombers.

The Admiralty revealed this last night in a communiqué which said:—

"Reports had been received that a convoy of four merchant ships, escorted by a French destroyer, was due to pass through the Straits of Gibraltar, and that the convoy carried important war material for Germany.

"Accordingly, orders were given for the interception of the convoy, which, however, passed through the Straits within Spanish territorial waters.

"Our forces caught up with the French ships after they had left Spanish territorial waters and called upon them to stop, so that the normal procedure of visit and search might be carried out.

'In own defence'

"The French shore batteries in the vicinity then opened fire on our ships, notwithstanding that they were merely engaged in the exercise of their legitimate belligerent rights.

"His Majesty's ships were compelled to reply in their own defence, and hits were observed on the shore batteries.

"In view of the action taken by the French batteries our warships would have been fully justified in firing on the French merchant ships and their escort, but in the interests of humanity did not do so, and the merchant ships succeeded in entering the nearby French port of Nemours.

"During the return of our forces to Gibraltar they were twice attacked by French bomber formations, but without suffering damage or casualties."

EXPRESS POLITICAL CORRESPONDENT writes:—

It looks as if the Vichy Government is carrying out Hitler's wishes and trying to pick a quarrel with Britain.

This has been the main objective of German policy since the French capitulation, and first hints of possible success were given when Admiral Darlan announced two weeks ago that unless we permitted French merchant ships to pass through blockade lines with food, they would be escorted by warships.

Big bombs on Calais

WHILE London had its tenth bombless night in succession, R.A.F. planes made a fierce raid on the invasion coast from Calais to Boulogne last night.

Fires blazed up at Calais, and people stood on the Kent coast watching the glare across the sea.

It seemed to the watchers that very heavy bombs were being dropped.

SHIP BOMBED

In daylight yesterday a Coastal Command Blenheim sank a German anti-submarine ship in the Bay of Biscay off the Loire estuary.

Spitfires shot down a Junkers 88 near Middlesbrough, N. Yorks, during the afternoon.

The only bombs dropped on Britain after dark last night fell in East Anglia and south-east Scotland. No one was hurt and there was little damage.

£5,000,000 HEIR DIES FOR R.A.F.

Express Staff Reporter

EX-"PLAYBOY" Robert Loewenstein, who at eighteen inherited £5,000,000, was killed on Saturday in an airfield accident.

He gave up being a "playboy" when war broke out, but been "ferrying" aircraft for the R.A.F.

His father, from whom he inherited his wealth, was Captain Alfred Loewenstein, the Belgian financier.

He, too, was killed in an air accident. It's death caused a sensation, for it was one of the big mysteries of the day—he fell from a plane while crossing the Channel. When war broke out "Bobby" Loewenstein disappeared from the world's playspots and sought to join the air force of his native land, Belgium. He flew home from Nemours, recently he joined the band of men and women who pilot R.A.F. aircraft from station to station—the Air Transport Auxiliary. He flew the fastest fighters as well as heavy bombers, and he flew in all weathers.

"A great scout," his friends said of him yesterday.

Ships "dictator" gives up Sunday
Speedier turn-round

Mr. R. H. Hobhouse, newly appointed north-west regional shipping "dictator," gave up Sunday yesterday to start at once on his new job.

He will have a busy week, because, as a head of Alfred Holland and Co., shipowners, he will also carry on his normal shipping work by agreement with the Ministry of Shipping.

With Mr. Gibson Jarvie, port regional director, he is to see that there is a speedier turn-round of ships from Holyhead to Silloth (Cumberland).

Government want adding machines

The Government want to buy or hire accounting, adding, and calculating machines—urgently required for firms producing aircraft and armaments.

Valuable shipping space will be saved if firms not needing these machines respond to the appeal.

Matsuoka in Rome

BERLIN, Sunday.—Mr. Matsuoka, the Japanese Foreign Minister, left Berlin today for Rome.—Reuter.

3 A.M. LATEST

NAZI ENVOY'S FAMILY LEAVING BELGRADE
BELGRADE, Sunday.—The wife and family of Herr von Heeren, the German Ambassador in Belgrade, are leaving the Jugo-Slav capital tomorrow.—B.U.P.

MALTA: 8 ALERTS
MALTA, Sunday.—Malta has had five night and three day air-raid alarms today. During darkness enemy aircraft dropped some bombs, but there were no casualties and no damage.—Reuter.

as "deadline" for Jugo-Slav capitulation or a Nazi attack.

People fear that under the influence of the smashing blow to his prestige suffered in the Jugo-Slavs' violent repudiation of Svetkovitch and his pro-Nazis, Hitler may embark on retaliation with a direct attack.

Even the Belgrade staff of the German News Agency has received marching orders from the Legation.

Italians, too, are on the run. As a precautionary measure, wives and children of British officials in Belgrade have been faced by the British authorities to leave Jugo-Slavia immediately.

The Jugo-Slav authorities allow no signs of flurry or unease, but reports from the German-Jugo-Slav border tonight

▶ BACK PAGE, COL. ONE

▲ SAN FRANCISCO CHRONICLE, TUESDAY APRIL 15, 1941

The see-saw nature of the war in North Africa is illustrated in this headline. General Erwin Rommel and his Afrika Korps began his first offensive on March 24, 1941. On April 10 his German-Italian army began besieging Tobruk. The garrison was then subjected to a series of ferocious aerial and artillery bombardments.

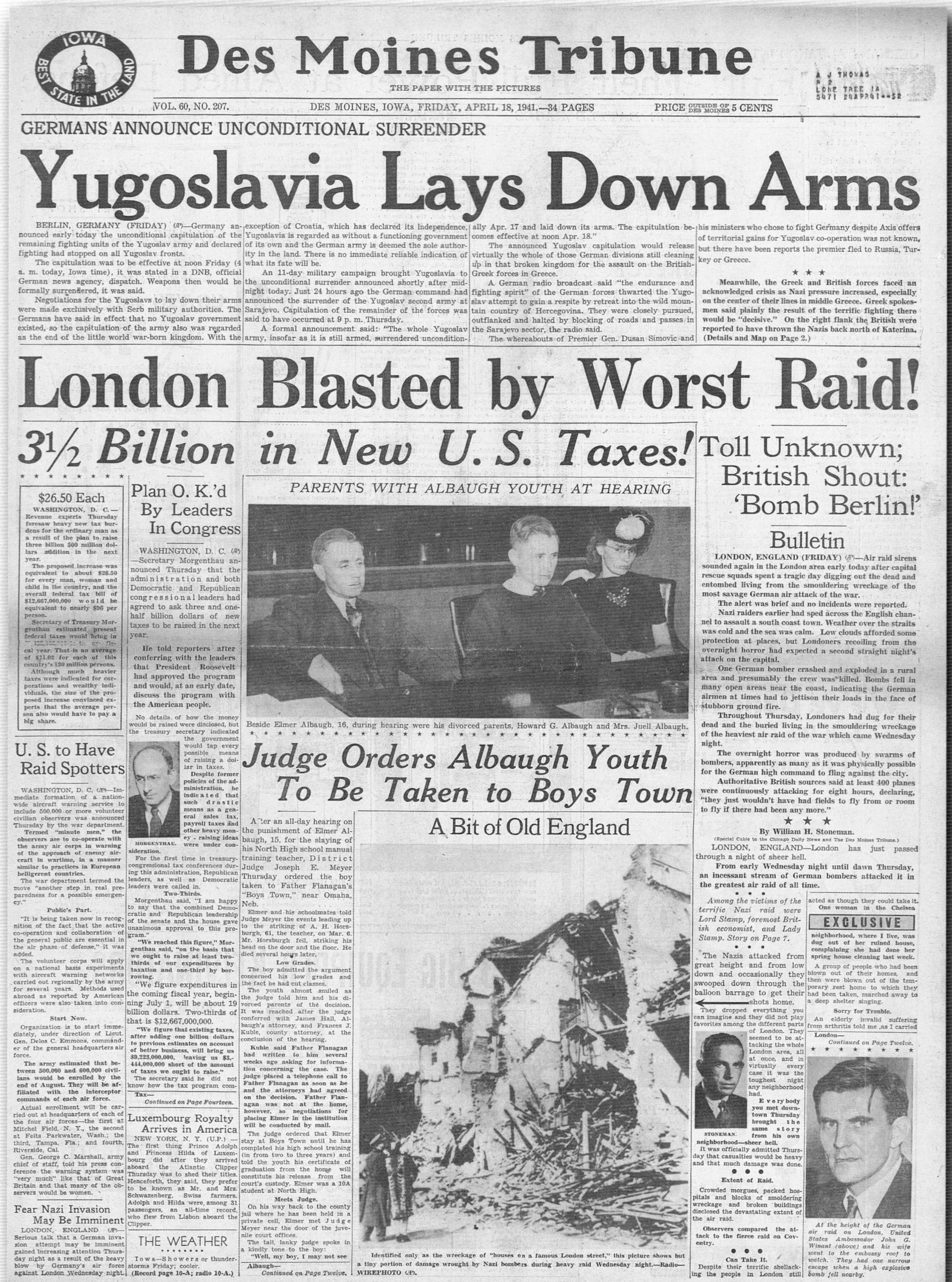

Des Moines Tribune

THE PAPER WITH THE PICTURES

IOWA — BEST STATE IN THE LAND

VOL. 60, NO. 207. DES MOINES, IOWA, FRIDAY, APRIL 18, 1941.—34 PAGES PRICE OUTSIDE OF DES MOINES 5 CENTS

A J THOMAS
R 2
LONE TREE IA
5471 24APR41--52

GERMANS ANNOUNCE UNCONDITIONAL SURRENDER

Yugoslavia Lays Down Arms

BERLIN, GERMANY (FRIDAY) (AP)—Germany announced early today the unconditional capitulation of the remaining fighting units of the Yugoslav army and declared fighting had stopped on all Yugoslav fronts.

The capitulation was to be effective at noon Friday (4 a. m. today, Iowa time), it was stated in a DNB, official German news agency, dispatch. Weapons then would be formally surrendered, it was said.

Negotiations for the Yugoslavs to lay down their arms were made exclusively with Serb military authorities. The Germans have said in effect that no Yugoslav government existed, so the capitulation of the army also was regarded as the end of the little world war-born kingdom. With the exception of Croatia, which has declared its independence, Yugoslavia is regarded as without a functioning government of its own and the German army is deemed the sole authority in the land. There is no immediate reliable indication of what its fate will be.

An 11-day military campaign brought Yugoslavia to the unconditional surrender announced shortly after midnight today. Just 24 hours ago the German command had announced the surrender of the Yugoslav second army at Sarajevo. Capitulation of the remainder of the forces was said to have occurred at 9 p. m. Thursday.

A formal announcement said: "The whole Yugoslav army, insofar as it is still armed, surrendered unconditionally Apr. 17 and laid down its arms. The capitulation becomes effective at noon Apr. 18."

The announced Yugoslav capitulation would release virtually the whole of those German divisions still cleaning up in that broken kingdom for the assault on the British-Greek forces in Greece.

A German radio broadcast said "the endurance and fighting spirit" of the German forces thwarted the Yugoslav attempt to gain a respite by retreat into the wild mountain country of Hercegovina. They were closely pursued, outflanked and halted by blocking of roads and passes in the Sarajevo sector, the radio said.

The whereabouts of Premier Gen. Dusan Simovic and his ministers who chose to fight Germany despite Axis offers of territorial gains for Yugoslav co-operation was not known, but there have been reports the premier fled to Russia, Turkey or Greece.

★ ★ ★

Meanwhile, the Greek and British forces faced an acknowledged crisis as Nazi pressure increased, especially on the center of their lines in middle Greece. Greek spokesmen said plainly the result of the terrific fighting there would be "decisive." On the right flank the British were reported to have thrown the Nazis back north of Katerina. (Details and Map on Page 2.)

London Blasted by Worst Raid!

$3\frac{1}{2}$ Billion in New U. S. Taxes!

$26.50 Each

WASHINGTON, D. C.—Revenue experts Thursday foresaw heavy new tax burdens for the ordinary man as a result of the plan to raise three billion 500 million dollars addition in the next year.

The proposed increase was equivalent to about $26.50 for every man, woman and child in the country, and the overall federal tax bill of $12,667,000,000 would be equivalent to nearly $96 per person.

Secretary of Treasury Morgenthau estimated present federal taxes would bring in [illegible] in the new fiscal year. That is an average of $71.02 for each of this country's 130 million persons.

Although much heavier taxes were indicated for corporations and wealthy individuals, the size of the proposed increase convinced experts that the average person also would have to pay a big share.

Plan O. K.'d By Leaders In Congress

WASHINGTON, D. C. (AP)—Secretary Morgenthau announced Thursday that the administration and both Democratic and Republican congressional leaders had agreed to ask three and one-half billion dollars of new taxes to be raised in the next year.

He told reporters after conferring with the leaders that President Roosevelt had approved the program and would, at an early date, discuss the program with the American people.

No details of how the money would be raised were disclosed, but the treasury secretary indicated the government would tap every possible means of raising a dollar in taxes.

MORGENTHAU.

Despite former policies of the administration, he indicated that such drastic means as a general sales tax, payroll taxes and other heavy money-raising ideas were under consideration.

For the first time in treasury-congressional tax conferences during this administration, Republican leaders, as well as Democratic leaders were called in.

Two-Thirds.

Morgenthau said, "I am happy to say that the combined Democratic and Republican leadership of the senate and the house gave unanimous approval to this program."

"We reached this figure," Morgenthau said, "on the basis that we ought to raise at least two-thirds of our expenditures by taxation and one-third by borrowing.

"We figure expenditures in the coming fiscal year, beginning July 1, will be about 19 billion dollars. Two-thirds of that is $12,667,000,000.

"We figure that existing taxes, after adding one billion dollars to previous estimates on account of better business, will bring us $9,223,000,000, leaving us $3,444,000,000 short of the amount of taxes we ought to raise."

The secretary said he did not know how the tax program com-

Tax—
Continued on Page Fourteen.

U. S. to Have Raid Spotters

WASHINGTON, D. C. (AP)—Immediate formation of a nationwide aircraft warning service to include 500,000 or more volunteer civilian observers was announced Thursday by the war department.

Termed "minute men," the observers are to co-operate with the army air corps in warning of the approach of enemy aircraft in wartime, in a manner similar to practices in European belligerent countries.

The war department termed the move "another step in real preparedness for a possible emergency."

Public's Part.

"It is being taken now in recognition of the fact that the active co-operation and collaboration of the general public are essential in the air phase of defense," it was added.

The volunteer corps will apply on a national basis experiments with aircraft warning networks carried out regionally by the army for several years. Methods used abroad as reported by American officers were also taken into consideration.

Start Now.

Organization is to start immediately, under direction of Lieut. Gen. Delos C. Emmons, commander of the general headquarters air force.

The army estimated that between 500,000 and 600,000 civilians would be enrolled by the end of August. They will be affiliated with the interceptor commands of each air force.

Actual enrollment will be carried out at headquarters of each of the four air forces—the first at Mitchel Field, N. Y., the second at Felts Parkwater, Wash.; the third, Tampa, Fla.; and fourth, Riverside, Cal.

Gen. George C. Marshall, army chief of staff, told his press conference the warning system was "very much" like that of Great Britain and that many of the observers would be women.

Fear Nazi Invasion May Be Imminent

LONDON, ENGLAND (UP)—Serious talk that a German invasion attempt may be imminent gained increasing attention Thursday night as a result of the heavy blow by Germany's air force against London Wednesday night.

Luxembourg Royalty Arrives in America

NEW YORK, N. Y. (U.P.)—The first thing Prince Adolph and Princess Hilda of Luxembourg did after they arrived aboard the Atlantic Clipper Thursday was to shed their titles. Henceforth, they said, they prefer to be known as Mr. and Mrs. Schwazenberg, Swiss farmers. Adolph and Hilda were among 31 passengers, an all-time record, who flew from Lisbon aboard the Clipper.

THE WEATHER

Iowa—Showers or thunderstorms Friday; cooler.
(Record page 10-A; radio 10-A.)

PARENTS WITH ALBAUGH YOUTH AT HEARING

Beside Elmer Albaugh, 16, during hearing were his divorced parents, Howard G. Albaugh and Mrs. Juell Albaugh.

Judge Orders Albaugh Youth To Be Taken to Boys Town

After an all-day hearing on the punishment of Elmer Albaugh, 15, for the slaying of his North High school manual training teacher, District Judge Joseph E. Meyer Thursday ordered the boy taken to Father Flanagan's "Boys Town," near Omaha, Neb.

Elmer and his schoolmates told Judge Meyer the events leading up to the striking of A. H. Horsburgh, 61, the teacher, on Mar. 6. Mr. Horsburgh fell, striking his head on the door and the floor. He died several hours later.

Low Grades.

The boy admitted the argument concerned his low grades and the fact he had cut classes.

The youth almost smiled as the judge told him and his divorced parents of the decision. It was reached after the judge conferred with James Hall, Albaugh's attorney, and Frances J. Kuble, county attorney, at the conclusion of the hearing.

Kuble said Father Flanagan had written to him several weeks ago asking for information concerning the case. The judge placed a telephone call to Father Flanagan as soon as he and the attorneys had agreed on the decision. Father Flanagan was not at the home, however, so negotiations for placing Elmer in the institution will be conducted by mail.

The judge ordered that Elmer stay at Boys Town until he has completed his high school training (in from two to three years) and told the youth his certificate of graduation from the home will constitute his release from the court's custody. Elmer was a 10A student at North High.

Meets Judge.

On his way back to the county jail where he has been held in a private cell, Elmer met Judge Meyer near the door of the juvenile court offices.

The tall, lanky judge spoke in a kindly tone to the boy:

"Well, my boy, I may not see

Albaugh—
Continued on Page Twelve.

A Bit of Old England

Identified only as the wreckage of "houses on a famous London street," this picture shows but a tiny portion of damage wrought by Nazi bombers during heavy raid Wednesday night.—Radio—WIREPHOTO (AP).

Toll Unknown; British Shout: 'Bomb Berlin!'

Bulletin

LONDON, ENGLAND (FRIDAY) (AP)—Air raid sirens sounded again in the London area early today after capital rescue squads spent a tragic day digging out the dead and entombed living from the smouldering wreckage of the most savage German air attack of the war.

The alert was brief and no incidents were reported.

Nazi raiders earlier had sped across the English channel to assault a south coast town. Weather over the straits was cold and the sea was calm. Low clouds afforded some protection at places, but Londoners recoiling from the overnight horror had expected a second straight night's attack on the capital.

One German bomber crashed and exploded in a rural area and presumably the crew was killed. Bombs fell in many open areas near the coast, indicating the German airmen at times had to jettison their loads in the face of stubborn ground fire.

Throughout Thursday, Londoners had dug for their dead and the buried living in the smouldering wreckage of the heaviest air raid of the war which came Wednesday night.

The overnight horror was produced by swarms of bombers, apparently as many as it was physically possible for the German high command to fling against the city.

Authoritative British sources said at least 400 planes were continuously attacking for eight hours, declaring, "they just wouldn't have had fields to fly from or room to fly if there had been any more."

★ ★ ★

By William H. Stoneman.
(Special Cable to the Chicago Daily News and The Des Moines Tribune.)

LONDON, ENGLAND—London has just passed through a night of sheer hell.

From early Wednesday night until dawn Thursday, an incessant stream of German bombers attacked it in the greatest air raid of all time.

• • •

Among the victims of the terrific Nazi raid were Lord Stamp, foremost British economist, and Lady Stamp. Story on Page 7.

• • •

The Nazis attacked from great height and from low down and occasionally they swooped down through the balloon barrage to get their shots home.

They dropped everything you can imagine and they did not play favorites among the different parts of London. They seemed to be attacking the whole London area, all at once, and in virtually every case it was the toughest night any neighborhood had.

STONEMAN.

Everybody you met downtown Thursday brought the same story from his own neighborhood—sheer hell.

It was officially admitted Thursday that casualties would be heavy and that much damage was done.

• • •

Extent of Raid.

Crowded morgues, packed hospitals and blocks of smoldering wreckage and broken buildings disclosed the devastating extent of the air raid.

Observers compared the attack to the fierce raid on Coventry.

• • •

Can Take It.

Despite their terrific shellacking the people in London still acted as though they could take it.

One woman in the Chelsea

EXCLUSIVE

neighborhood, where I live, was dug out of her ruined house, complaining she had done her spring house cleaning last week.

A group of people who had been blown out of their homes, and then were blown out of the temporary rest home to which they had been taken, marched away to a deep shelter singing.

Sorry for Trouble.

An elderly invalid suffering from arthritis told me, as I carried

London—
Continued on Page Twelve.

At the height of the German air raid on London, United States Ambassador John G. Winant (above) and his wife went to the embassy roof to watch. They had one narrow escape when a high explosive bomb fell nearby.

▲ DES MOINES TRIBUNE, IOWA, FRIDAY APRIL 18, 1941

Even in the Midwestern heartland, international headlines top a front page that also includes news of a local trial and of rising U.S. tax demands. The Blitz on London and other British cities fueled U.S. fears of air raids, as reflected in the story of the new raid spotters.

The Daily Telegraph

4 A.M.

and Morning Post

No. 26,798 — LONDON, MONDAY, APRIL 28, 1941 — Printed in LONDON and MANCHESTER — PRICE 1½d.

MR. CHURCHILL : WE CONQUER OR DIE

HITLER CANNOT ESCAPE AVENGING JUSTICE

VICTORY WILL BE WON IN THE WEST

"INDESCRIBABLE RELIEF" AT U.S. AID IN ATLANTIC

Mr. Churchill, in a stirring broadcast to the nation last night, expressed the conviction that the British people meant to "conquer or die" and that it was in the West that victory would be won.

Nothing that was happening now, the Prime Minister said, was comparable in gravity with the dangers through which we had passed; nothing that could happen in the East was comparable with what was happening in the West.

Hitler, he declared, could not find safety from justice in the East, the Middle East or the Far East. To win, he must conquer this island or cut the Atlantic lifeline to the United States.

Against the 70,000,000 malignant Huns, were 200,000,000 people of the British Empire and the United States possessing unchallengeable command of the oceans and with more technical resources than the rest of the world put together.

Other main points from the Prime Minister's speech were:

With this aid from America we could now concentrate our forces on the routes nearer home and take a far heavier toll of the German submarines there.

Mediterranean.—There were signs that the war in the Mediterranean, on the sea, in the desert and in the air would become fierce, varied and widespread. The war might spread to Spain and Morocco, to Turkey and Russia.

Libya.—The forces which cleared the Italians out of Cyrenaica and captured 180,000 prisoners at no time exceeded two divisions, or 30,000 men. He would be surprised to see Gen. Wavell's armies in the position of the German combatants, but we could not expect to purge the province of Germans at once.

Greece.—The Greeks had turned to us for succour. To have refused would have been fatal to the honour of the British Empire. The divisions available for the task were from New Zealand and Australia and only about half the troops engaged came from the Mother Country.

The Battle of the Atlantic had entered a more grim but far more favourable phase.

He had learned with indescribable relief of the decision of the United States to use its Fleet and flying boats to patrol the waters of the Western Hemisphere and to warn ships of U-boats.

Australia refutes Axis lies; Hitler's next problem—Page 5.

DUCE A "WHIPPED JACKAL"

In his broadcast last night the Prime Minister, who spoke for 31 minutes, said:

I was asked last week whether I was aware of some uneasiness which, it was said, existed in the country on account of the gravity as it was described, of the war situation. So I thought it would be a good thing to go and see for myself what this uneasiness amounted to.

And I went to some of our great cities and seaports which had been most heavily bombed, to some of the places where the poorest people have got it worst.

I have come back not only reassured, but refreshed. To leave the offices in Whitehall, with their ceaseless hum of activity and stress, and to go out to the front, by which I mean the streets and wharves of London or Liverpool, Manchester, Cardiff, Swansea or Bristol, is like going out of a hot-house on to the bridge of a fighting ship.

It is a tonic which I should recommend any who are suffering from fretfulness to take in strong doses when they have need of it.

It is quite true that I have seen many painful scenes of havoc and of fine buildings and acres of cottage homes blasted into rubble heaps of ruin, but it is just in those very places where the malice of the savage enemy has done its worst and where the ordeal of the men, women and children has been most severe that I found their morale most high and splendid.

Indeed, I feel comforted by an exaltation of spirit in the people which seemed to lift mankind above the level of material facts into the joyous serenity we think belongs to a better world than this.

"WE SHALL NOT FAIL"

Promise to People

Of their kindness to me I cannot speak, because I have never sought it or dreamed of it and can never deserve it.

I can only assure you that I and my colleagues, or comrades rather, for that is what they are, who deal with every scrap of life and strength, according to the lot granted to us, shall not fail these people or be wholly unworthy of their faithful and generous regard.

The British nation is stirred and moved as it never has been at any time in its long, eventful and famous history, and it is so hardeneyed figure of doom is to the east they that mean to conquer or die.

What a triumph the life of these battered cities is over the worst which fire and bombs can do! What a vindication of the civilised and decent way of living we have been trying to work for and work towards in our island! What a proof of the virtues of free institutions, what a test of the quality of our local authorities and the customs and societies so steadily built!

This ordeal by fire has, in a certain sense, even exhilarated the manhood and womanhood of Britain. The sublime but also terribly sombre experiences and emotions of the battlefield, which for centuries have been reserved for the soldiers and sailors, are now shared for good or ill by the entire population.

All our crowds have been proud of being under fire of the enemy—old men, little children, the crippled, the veterans of former wars, aged women, and the ordinary hard-pressed citizen or subject of the King, as they call him—himself, the sturdy workman who swings a hammer or loads a ship, the skilful craftsman, the members of every kind of A.R.P. service, are proud to feel that they can stand in the line together with our fighting men when one of the greatest causes is being fought out—and fought out it will be, to the end.

This, indeed, is the great heroic period of our history and the light of glory shines on all. You may imagine how deeply I feel my own responsibility to all these millions my responsibility to bear my part of bringing them safely out of this long, stern, scowling valley through which we are marching and not to demand from them their sacrifices and exertions in vain.

The Greek Minister to Egypt, M. Capsalis, stated in Cairo yesterday: "The Greek air force will fight on against the Axis, and the whole of the Greek merchant fleet, running into millions of tons, is at the disposal of the British Government."

(Contd. on Back Page, Col. 3.)

NAZI BLOCKADE OF SPAIN

BAN ON IMPORT OF VITAL GOODS

From Our SPECIAL CORRESPONDENT
MARTIN MOORE
LISBON, Sunday.

Germany in its boycott economic pressure on Spain in an attempt to force her consent to a policy of full co-operation.

The latest move is a refusal to grant a permit for the transport through unoccupied France of an important commercial consignment from a Central European country.

This consignment was already been bought and paid for by the Spanish Government. I am unable to discuss its precise nature, but its delivery is vital to the economic life of Spain.

Though I have direct knowledge only of this one consignment, there can be little doubt that other Continental imports to Spain are also falling under the German ban or will do so unless the Spanish Government yields.

SUÑER'S APPROVAL

Significant of the urgency of Hitler's present demands is that this is the first time he has used the blockade as a weapon.

Hitherto the economic argument used to persuade Spain has been merely the assertion that Germany is able to supply the country with enough food to compensate for what would be lost by breaking with Britain. This argument, however, has not carried much weight.

The present method of economic pressure has certainly been applied by the Germans with the full knowledge, possibly even at the instigation of Señor Suñer, the pro-Nazi Spanish Foreign Minister. His German leanings are so strong that he has been consistently opposed to the acceptance of Anglo-American supplies.

FRANCO RESISTS

I now learn that at a Cabinet meeting, when the latest British credit was discussed, Señor Suñer, in face of all his colleagues, declared his opposition on the ground that it would compromise Spanish foreign policy, which is his own policy of the fullest co-operation with Germany.

He might have carried the day had not Señor Carceller, Minister of Commerce, threatened to resign if the Government refused British help, without which the country would starve.

Gen. Franco, who is determined at all costs to preserve outward unity of government, therefore overruled Suñer.

While the serious nature of the latest German pressure on Spain is undeniable, it shows that the Nazi demands are so far still being resisted by Gen. Franco, his War Minister, Gen. Varella, and other members of the Government, who believe that military co-operation with the Axis would be disastrous.

Taken in conjunction with the Cabinet clash over the British loan, it indicates that Suñer's ascendancy is not yet complete.

2 RAIDERS DOWN LAST NIGHT

SOUTH COAST BOMBS

Two Nazi bombers were reported to have been shot down during raids on this country last night.

Up to early to-day no Alert had been sounded in the London area, but heavy bombs and a large number of incendiaries fell on a south-coast town.

Raiders were also reported off the East Anglian and south-west coasts. At one town in the south-west area bombs were dropped and damage was caused to houses and commercial premises. A very heavy barrage caused the raiders to fly very high. Bombs were also dropped on the north-east Scottish coast. Machine-gun fire from the raider caused no damage.

BRITISH ON BAHREIN

The German radio stated last night that according to reports of eye-witnesses British troops had been landed on Bahrein Island, in the Persian Gulf. The island is governed by a sheikh under British protection.

FIGHTERS GUN MALTA

Fighter aircraft machine-gunned the seaplane base at Malta yesterday. Other planes carried out high-level reconnaissance.

Black-out 8.48 p.m.; 5.7 a.m.
Moon rises 7.30 a.m. to-morrow.

A map showing the south of Greece and towns occupied by German troops. Greek islands in the Ægean and the north coast of Africa can also be seen.

[Map labels: GREECE, TURKEY, Corfu, Corinth, ATHENS, Crete, MEDITERRANEAN SEA, CYPRUS, RHODES, GERMAN OCCUPATION, MALTA 500 MILES, Benghazi, Cyrenaica, Tobruk, Derna, LIBYA, Tripoli, Mersa Matruh, Alexandria, EGYPT, GREEK GOVERNMENT HERE]

GERMAN TROOPS MARCH INTO ATHENS

CAPTURE OF CORINTH CLAIMED

The Germans yesterday announced that their troops had entered Athens and that the swastika was flying over the Acropolis, the historic hill which crowns the Greek capital.

Advanced units of motor-cyclists, it was stated, entered the city at 9.35 a.m. and were followed by heavier mechanised detachments, which had overcome the British rearguard on the road from Thebes.

Greek civilians received the Nazi troops in silence, while the Germans who had remained in Athens gave them a tumultuous welcome.

The Germans also claimed that parachute troops had captured the isthmus of Corinth, which connects the Peloponnesus region with the rest of Greece, and the town of Corinth itself, which is about 35 miles west of Athens.

The Corinth canal, which runs through the isthmus from the Gulf of Corinth to the Gulf of Ægina, it was added, had been secured.

PATRAS CAPTURED

At the western end of the Gulf of Corinth, it was claimed, the "Adolf Hitler Guard" had pushed forward across the Gulf of Patras into the Peloponnesus and, having overcome enemy resistance, had occupied the port of Patras.

In the attack on Corinth, the communiqué stated, a number of British were taken prisoner and the rest "retreated southward."

No other mention was made of British troops being in action. Yesterday's announcement said that German forces at G.H.Q., Cairo, stated: "Our troops are continuing their withdrawal."

According to a message to the New York Times a great part of the British troops and equipment has been safely evacuated from Greece to North Africa.

LAST BRITISH MESSAGE

GREEK CHEERS FOR DEPARTING TROOPS

FROM OUR OWN CORRESPONDENT
ATHENS, Saturday.

This message to-day may be my last from Athens, as the German forces are gradually drawing close, with the British and Greeks fighting rearguard actions. Precise information is unobtainable.

Most of the British soldiers garrisoned around Athens left yesterday amid moving scenes. They were cheered by large crowds bidding them "au revoir."

Yesterday and to-day fewer air-raid warning aircraft guns frequent enemy planes.

In spite of the Athens is crowded from all the over They show a dignified fortitude and perfect vails.

At the top of every A paper to-day is printed:

"Greeks! Be wor history and stand han proud and dignified recognises the bravei of our army nises also our rights. Nazi Pillage Belgrade—

---

3 ENEMY COLUMNS ENTER EGYPT

BRITISH MOBILE FORCES HARASS ADVANCE

From Daily Telegraph Special Correspondent
ARTHUR MERTON
CAIRO, Sunday.

Enemy detachments from Libya crossed the Egyptian frontier at several points yesterday evening, stated to-day's G.H.Q. communiqué. Our light mobile forces remained in contact with them, harassing their advance.

The enemy, apparently mainly Italian troops, moved in three light motorised columns, one by the coastal road, the second on the escarpment near Hellfire Pass, and the third to the south of the pass.

The advance is believed in well-informed circles here to extend no more than 15 to 20 miles inland from the sea, and there is no indication of a sweep to the south. In this advance the Germans and Italians have not at their disposal anything like the men and material that Marshal Graziani had last September when he reached Sidi Barrani and a sweep to the south.

HELP BRITAIN "AT ANY COST"

DECLARATION BY MR. ROCKEFELLER

Mr. John D. Rockefeller, head of the Rockefeller family and one of the world's richest men, has declared his "firm conviction, arrived at in anguish of spirit," that the United States and all the Americas "should stand by the British Empire to the limit and at any cost."

His declaration, made in a letter to the New York Times, calls on the people of America to stand solidly behind President Roosevelt and to see that munitions sufficient to attain victory are "laid down at Britain's door."

"I would rather die fighting the brutal, barbarous, inhuman force represented by Hitlerism," he states, "than live in a world dominated by that force."

Mr. Rockefeller, who says every hour is precious, demands a united determination on the part of labour and capital to keep industry running at top speed and to eliminate "all strikes, lock-outs, labour disputes and stoppages of every character."

FLEET OF 200 MUCH INCREASED NEUTRALITY PATROL

United States destroyers, submarine chasers, minesweepers and other naval craft are being assembled in great numbers along the Atlantic coast for the wide operations of the Neutrality Patrol states A.P.

The patrol, whose area is believed to have been extended to the nearly halfway across the Atlantic, is thought to have been increased from 125 vessels to a fleet of at least 200.

Long-range aeroplanes are now

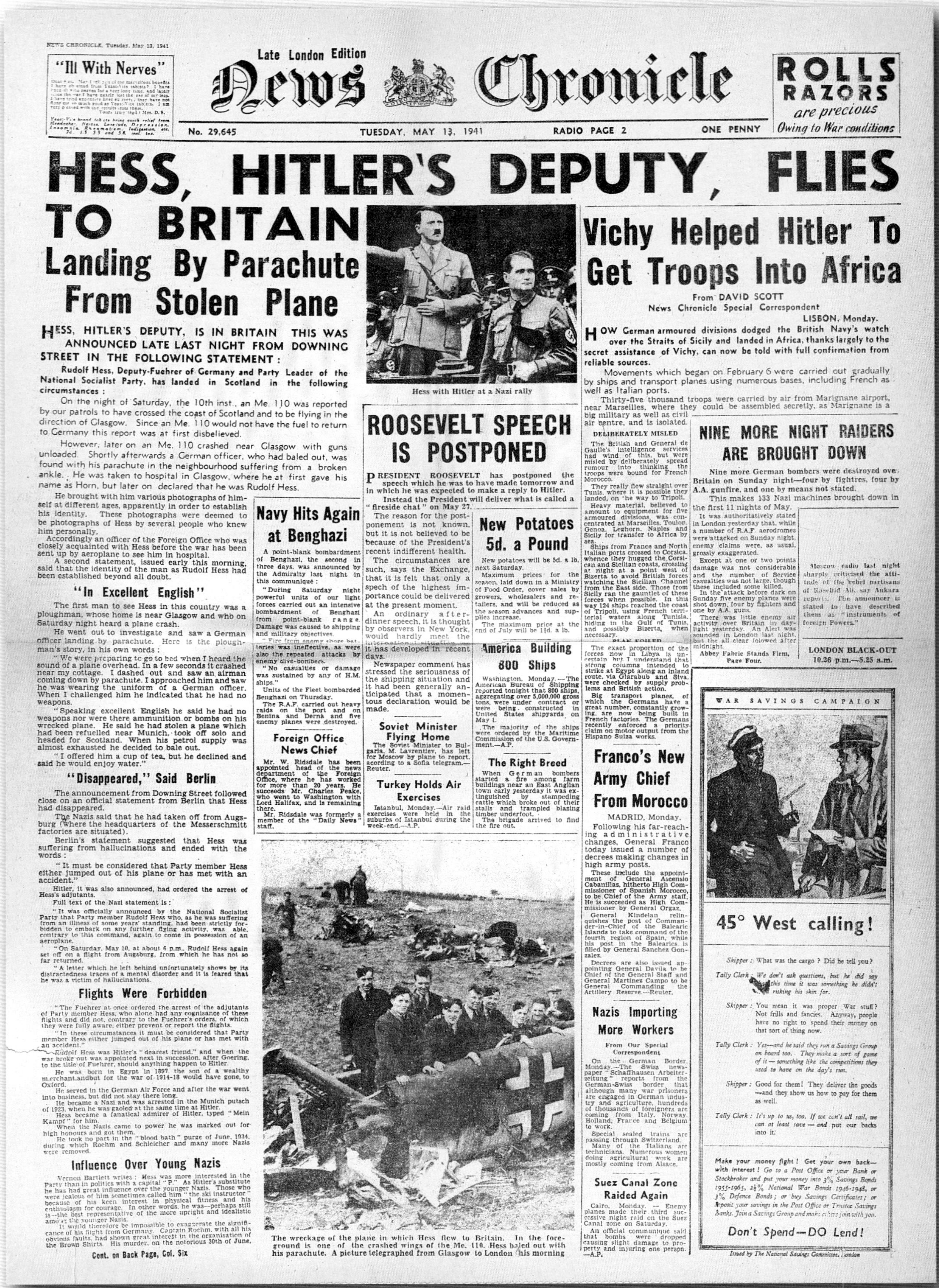

NEWS CHRONICLE, Tuesday, May 13, 1941

"Ill With Nerves"

Dear Sirs. May I tell you of the marvellous benefits I have obtained from Yeast-Vite tablets? I have been ill with nerves for a very long time, and lately since the war I have nearly lost the use of my legs. I have tried expensive liver extracts; they have not done me so much good as Yeast-Vite tablets. I am very pleased with the results from them.

Yours truly (Sgd.) Mrs. D.S.

Yeast-Vite brand tablets bring quick relief from Headaches, Nerves, Lassitude, Depression, Insomnia, Rheumatism, Indigestion, etc. 7d. 1/5 3/3 and 5/8, incl. tax.

Late London Edition

News Chronicle

No. 29,645 TUESDAY, MAY 13, 1941 RADIO PAGE 2 ONE PENNY

ROLLS RAZORS *are precious* *Owing to War conditions*

HESS, HITLER'S DEPUTY, FLIES TO BRITAIN

Landing By Parachute From Stolen Plane

HESS, HITLER'S DEPUTY, IS IN BRITAIN THIS WAS ANNOUNCED LATE LAST NIGHT FROM DOWNING STREET IN THE FOLLOWING STATEMENT:

Rudolf Hess, Deputy-Fuehrer of Germany and Party Leader of the National Socialist Party, has landed in Scotland in the following circumstances:

On the night of Saturday, the 10th inst., an Me. 110 was reported by our patrols to have crossed the coast of Scotland and to be flying in the direction of Glasgow. Since an Me. 110 would not have the fuel to return to Germany this report was at first disbelieved.

However, later on an Me. 110 crashed near Glasgow with guns unloaded. Shortly afterwards a German officer, who had baled out, was found with his parachute in the neighbourhood suffering from a broken ankle. He was taken to hospital in Glasgow, where he at first gave his name as Horn, but later on declared that he was Rudolf Hess.

He brought with him various photographs of himself at different ages, apparently in order to establish his identity. These photographs were deemed to be photographs of Hess by several people who knew him personally.

Accordingly an officer of the Foreign Office who was closely acquainted with Hess before the war has been sent up by aeroplane to see him in hospital.

A second statement, issued early this morning, said that the identity of the man as Rudolf Hess had been established beyond all doubt.

"In Excellent English"

The first man to see Hess in this country was a ploughman, whose home is near Glasgow and who on Saturday night heard a plane crash.

He went out to investigate and saw a German officer landing by parachute. Here is the ploughman's story, in his own words:

"We were preparing to go to bed when I heard the sound of a plane overhead. In a few seconds it crashed near my cottage. I dashed out and saw an airman coming down by parachute. I approached him and saw he was wearing the uniform of a German officer. When I challenged him he indicated that he had no weapons.

"Speaking excellent English he said he had no weapons nor were there ammunition or bombs on his wrecked plane. He said he had stolen a plane which had been refuelled near Munich, took off solo and headed for Scotland. When his petrol supply was almost exhausted he decided to bale out.

"I offered him a cup of tea, but he declined and said he would enjoy water."

"Disappeared," Said Berlin

The announcement from Downing Street followed close on an official statement from Berlin that Hess had disappeared.

The Nazis said that he had taken off from Augsburg (where the headquarters of the Messerschmitt factories are situated).

Berlin's statement suggested that Hess was suffering from hallucinations and ended with the words:

"It must be considered that Party member Hess either jumped out of his plane or has met with an accident."

Hitler, it was also announced, had ordered the arrest of Hess's adjutants.

Full text of the Nazi statement is:

"It was officially announced by the National Socialist Party that Party member Rudolf Hess who, as he was suffering from an illness of some years' standing, had been strictly forbidden to embark on any further flying activity, was able, contrary to this command, again to come in possession of an aeroplane.

"On Saturday, May 10, at about 6 p.m., Rudolf Hess again set off on a flight from Augsburg, from which he has not so far returned.

"A letter which he left behind unfortunately shows by its distractedness traces of a mental disorder and it is feared that he was a victim of hallucinations.

Flights Were Forbidden

"The Fuehrer at once ordered the arrest of the adjutants of Party member Hess, who alone had any cognisance of these flights and did not, contrary to the Fuehrer's orders, of which they were fully aware, either prevent or report the flights.

"In these circumstances it must be considered that Party member Hess either jumped out of his plane or has met with an accident."

Rudolf Hess was Hitler's "dearest friend," and when the war broke out was appointed next in succession, after Goering, to the title of Fuehrer, should anything happen to Hitler.

He was born in Egypt in 1897, the son of a wealthy merchant, and but for the war of 1914-18 would have gone to Oxford.

He served in the German Air Force and after the war went into business, but did not stay there long.

He became a Nazi and was arrested in the Munich putsch of 1923, when he was gaoled at the same time as Hitler.

Hess became a fanatical admirer of Hitler, typed "Mein Kampf" for him.

When the Nazis came to power he was marked out for high honours and got them.

He took no part in the "blood bath" purge of June, 1934, during which Roehm and Schleicher and many more Nazis were removed.

Influence Over Young Nazis

Vernon Bartlett writes: Hess was more interested in the Party than in politics with a capital "P." As Hitler's substitute he has had great influence over the younger Nazis. Those who were jealous of him sometimes called him "the ski instructor" because of his keen interest in physical fitness and his enthusiasm for courage. In other words, he was—perhaps still is—the best representative of the more upright and idealistic among the younger Nazis.

It would therefore be impossible to exaggerate the significance of his flight from Germany. Captain Roehm, with all his obvious faults, had shown great interest in the organisation of the Brown Shirts. His murder, on the notorious 30th of June,

Cont. on Back Page, Col. Six

Hess with Hitler at a Nazi rally

ROOSEVELT SPEECH IS POSTPONED

PRESIDENT ROOSEVELT has postponed the speech which he was to have made tomorrow and in which he was expected to make a reply to Hitler.

Instead the President will deliver what is called a "fireside chat" on May 27.

The reason for the postponement is not known, but it is not believed to be because of the President's recent indifferent health.

The circumstances are such, says the Exchange, that it is felt that only a spech of the highest importance could be delivered at the present moment.

An ordinary after-dinner speech, it is thought by observers in New York, would hardly meet the international situation as it has developed in recent days.

Newspaper comment has stressed the seriousness of the shipping situation and it had been generally anticipated that a momentous declaration would be made.

Navy Hits Again at Benghazi

A point-blank bombardment of Benghazi, the second in three days, was announced by the Admiralty last night in this communiqué:

"During Saturday night powerful units of our light forces carried out an intensive bombardment of Benghazi from point-blank range. Damage was caused to shipping and military objectives.

"Fire from enemy shore batteries was ineffective, as were also the repeated attacks by enemy dive-bombers.

"No casualties or damage was sustained by any of H.M. ships."

Units of the Fleet bombarded Benghazi on Thursday.

The R.A.F. carried out heavy raids on the port and on Benina and Derna and five enemy planes were destroyed.

Foreign Office News Chief

Mr. W. Ridsdale has been appointed head of the news department of the Foreign Office, where he has worked for more than 20 years. He succeeds Mr. Charles Peake, who went to Washington with Lord Halifax, and is remaining there.

Mr. Ridsdale was formerly a member of the "Daily News" staff.

New Potatoes 5d. a Pound

New potatoes will be 5d. a lb. next Saturday.

Maximum prices for the season, laid down in a Ministry of Food Order, cover sales by growers, wholesalers and retailers, and will be reduced as the season advances and supplies increase.

The maximum price at the end of July will be 1½d. a lb.

America Building 800 Ships

Washington, Monday.—The American Bureau of Shipping reported tonight that 800 ships, aggregating over 5,000,000 gross tons, were under contract or were being constructed in United States shipyards on May 1.

The majority of the ships were ordered by the Maritime Commission of the U.S. Government.—A.P.

Soviet Minister Flying Home

The Soviet Minister to Bulgaria, M. Lavrentiev, has left for Moscow by plane to report, acording to a Sofia telegram.—Reuter.

The Right Breed

When German bombers started a fire among farm buildings near an East Anglian town early yesterday it was extinguished by stampeding cattle which broke out of their stalls and trampled blazing timber underfoot.

The brigade arrived to find the fire out.

Turkey Holds Air Exercises

Istanbul, Monday.—Air raid exercises were held in the suburbs of Istanbul during the week-end.—A.P.

The wreckage of the plane in which Hess flew to Britain. In the foreground is one of the crashed wings of the Me. 110. Hess baled out with his parachute. A picture telegraphed from Glasgow to London this morning

Vichy Helped Hitler To Get Troops Into Africa

From DAVID SCOTT

News Chronicle Special Correspondent

LISBON, Monday.

HOW German armoured divisions dodged the British Navy's watch over the Straits of Sicily and landed in Africa, thanks largely to the secret assistance of Vichy, can now be told with full confirmation from reliable sources.

Movements which began on February 6 were carried out gradually by ships and transport planes using numerous bases, including French as well as Italian ports.

Thirty-five thousand troops were carried by air from Marignane airport, near Marseilles, where they could be assembled secretly, as Marignane is a big military as well as civil air centre, and is isolated.

DELIBERATELY MISLED

The British and General de Gaulle's intelligence services had wind of this, but were misled by deliberately spread rumour into thinking the troops were bound for French Morocco.

They really flew straight over Tunis, where it is possible they landed, on the way to Tripoli.

Heavy material, believed to amount to equipment for five armoured divisions, was concentrated at Marseilles, Toulon, Genoa, Leghorn, Naples and Sicily for transfer to Africa by sea.

Ships from France and North Italian ports crossed to Corsica, whence they hugged the Corsican and Sicilian coasts, crossing at night at a point west of Bizerta to avoid British forces watching the Sicilian Channel from the East side. Those from Sicily ran the gauntlet of these forces when possible. In this way 124 ships reached the coast of Tripoli, using French territorial waters along Tunisia, hiding in the Gulf of Tunis, and possibly Bizerta, when necessary.

PLAN FOILED

The exact proportion of the forces now in Libya is uncertain but I understand that strong columns intended to strike at Egypt along an inland route, via Giarabub and Siva, were checked by supply problems and British action.

Big transport planes, of which the Germans have a great number, constantly growing, are now being built in French factories. The Germans recently enforced a priority claim on motor output from the Hispano Suiza works.

NINE MORE NIGHT RAIDERS ARE BROUGHT DOWN

Nine more German bombers were destroyed over Britain on Sunday night—four by fighters, four by A.A. gunfire, and one by means not stated.

This makes 133 Nazi machines brought down in the first 11 nights of May.

It was authoritatively stated in London yesterday that, while a number of R.A.F. aerodromes were attacked on Sunday night, enemy claims were, as usual, grossly exaggerated.

Except at one or two points damage was not considerable and the number of Service casualties was not large, though these included some killed.

In the attack before dark on Sunday five enemy planes were shot down, four by fighters and one by A.A. guns.

There was little enemy air activity over Britain in daylight yesterday. An Alert was sounded in London last night, but the all clear folowed after midnight.

Abbey Fabric Stands Firm, Page Four.

Moscow radio last night sharply criticised the attitude of the rebel partisans of Rashid Ali, say Ankara reports. The announcer is stated to have described them as "instruments of foreign Powers."

LONDON BLACK-OUT 10.26 p.m.—5.25 a.m.

Franco's New Army Chief From Morocco

MADRID, Monday.

Following his far-reaching administrative changes, General Franco today issued a number of decrees making changes in high army posts.

These include the appointment of General Ascensio Cabanillas, hitherto High Commissioner of Spanish Morocco, to be Chief of the Army staff. He is succeeded as High Commissioner by General Orgaz.

General Kindelan relinquishes the post of Commander-in-Chief of the Balearic Islands to take command of the fourth region of Spain, while his post in the Balearics is filled by General Sanchez Gonzalez.

Decrees are also issued appointing General Davila to be Chief of the General Staff and General Martinez Campo to be General Commanding the Artillery Reserve.—Reuter.

Nazis Importing More Workers

From Our Special Correspondent

On the German Border, Monday.—The Swiss newspaper "Schaffhausen Arbeiter-zeitung" reports from the German-Swiss border that although many war prisoners are engaged in German industry and agriculture, hundreds of thousands of foreigners are coming from Italy, Norway, Holland, France and Belgium to work.

Special sealed trains are passing through Switzerland.

Many of the Italians are technicians. Numerous women doing agricultural work are mostly coming from Alsace.

Suez Canal Zone Raided Again

Cairo, Monday. — Enemy planes made their third successive night raid on the Suez Canal zone on Saturday.

An official communiqué said that bombs were dropped causing slight damage to property and injuring one person.—A.P.

WAR SAVINGS CAMPAIGN

45° West calling!

Skipper: What was the cargo? Did he tell you?

Tally Clerk: *We don't ask questions, but he did say that this time it was something he didn't mind risking his skin for.*

Skipper: You mean it was proper War stuff? Not frills and fancies. Anyway, people have no right to spend their money on that sort of thing now.

Tally Clerk: *Yes—and he said they run a Savings Group on board too. They make a sort of game of it—something like the competitions they used to have on the day's run.*

Skipper: Good for them! They deliver the goods—and they show us how to pay for them as well.

Tally Clerk: *It's up to us, too. If we can't all sail, we can at least save*—and put our backs into it.

Make your money fight! Get your own back—with interest! *Go to a Post Office or your Bank or Stockbroker and put your money into 3% Savings Bonds 1955-1965, 2½% National War Bonds 1946-1948, or 3% Defence Bonds; or buy Savings Certificates; or Deposit your savings in the Post Office or Trustee Savings Banks. Join a Savings Group and make others join with you.*

Don't Spend—DO Lend!

Issued by The National Savings Committee, London

▲ NEWS CHRONICLE, LONDON, TUESDAY MAY 13, 1941

The *Chronicle* was gripped by the sudden arrival in Scotland of Nazi deputy leader Rudolf Hess—but its report does not even begin to try to explain his motives. It turned out that Hess had a wild plan to meet King George VI and form an Anglo-German alliance against the Soviet Union. The front page also includes snippets of good news, and an advertisement urging consumers to lend and borrow rather than buy new goods.

◀ THE SUN, SYDNEY, SUNDAY MAY 25, 1941
In Australia, the press focused on the contribution of Australian troops fighting with the Anzacs (Australian and New Zealand Army Corps), who had been deployed in North Africa and, here, in Crete. Despite the optimistic headline, the Anzac campaign in Crete was a disastrous defeat with the loss of many dead and captured. In an echo of former Anzac glories, *The Sun* prints a front-page photograph of a veteran of World War I wearing her medals.

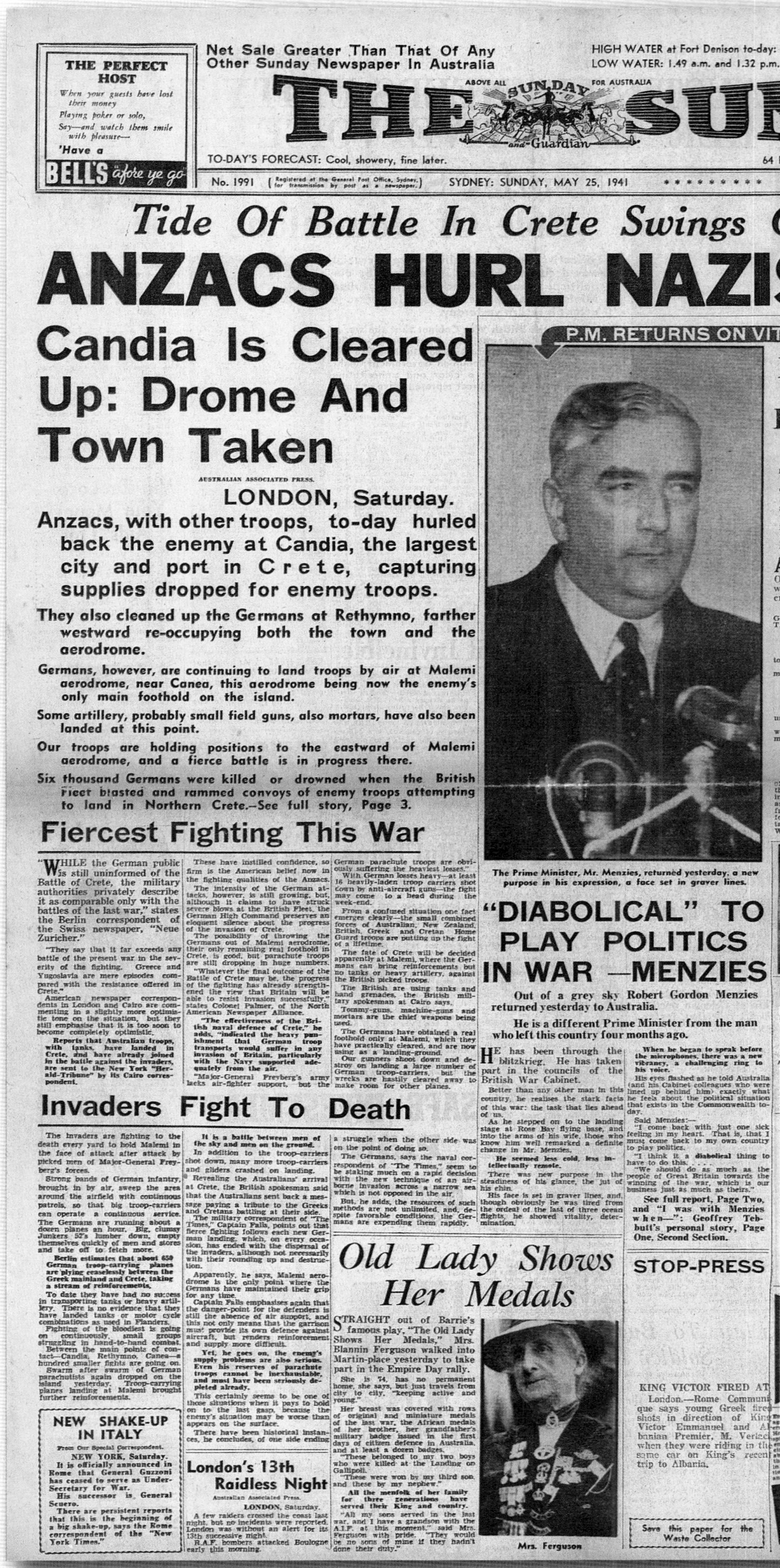

THE PERFECT HOST
When your guests have lost their money
Playing poker or solo,
Say—and watch them smile with pleasure—
'Have a BELL'S afore ye go'

Net Sale Greater Than That Of Any Other Sunday Newspaper In Australia

HIGH WATER at Fort Denison to-day: 7.45 a.m. and 8.4 p.m.
LOW WATER: 1.49 a.m. and 1.32 p.m.

ABOVE ALL — THE SUNDAY SUN and Guardian — FOR AUSTRALIA

TO-DAY'S FORECAST: Cool, showery, fine later. 64 PAGES—THREEPENCE

No. 1991 (Registered at the General Post Office, Sydney, for transmission by post as a newspaper.) SYDNEY: SUNDAY, MAY 25, 1941 Phone: BO333

"PINEAPPLE" PORK SAUSAGES DELICIOUS — Not genuine if loose—Packets only.

Tide Of Battle In Crete Swings Our Way

ANZACS HURL NAZIS BACK

Candia Is Cleared Up: Drome And Town Taken

AUSTRALIAN ASSOCIATED PRESS.

LONDON, Saturday.

Anzacs, with other troops, to-day hurled back the enemy at Candia, the largest city and port in Crete, capturing supplies dropped for enemy troops.

They also cleaned up the Germans at Rethymno, farther westward re-occupying both the town and the aerodrome.

Germans, however, are continuing to land troops by air at Malemi aerodrome, near Canea, this aerodrome being now the enemy's only main foothold on the island.

Some artillery, probably small field guns, also mortars, have also been landed at this point.

Our troops are holding positions to the eastward of Malemi aerodrome, and a fierce battle is in progress there.

Six thousand Germans were killed or drowned when the British Fleet blasted and rammed convoys of enemy troops attempting to land in Northern Crete.—**See full story, Page 3.**

Fiercest Fighting This War

"WHILE the German public is still uninformed of the Battle of Crete, the military authorities privately describe it as comparable only with the battles of the last war," states the Berlin correspondent of the Swiss newspaper, "Neue Zuricher."

"They say that it far exceeds any battle of the present war in the severity of the fighting. Greece and Yugoslavia are mere episodes compared with the resistance offered in Crete."

American newspaper correspondents in London and Cairo are commenting in a slightly more optimistic tone on the situation, but they still emphasise that it is too soon to become completely optimistic.

Reports that Australian troops, with tanks, have landed in Crete, and have already joined in the battle against the invaders, are sent to the New York "Herald-Tribune" by its Cairo correspondent.

These have instilled confidence, so firm is the American belief now in the fighting qualities of the Anzacs.

The intensity of the German attacks, however, is still growing, but, although it claims to have struck severe blows at the British Fleet, the German High Command preserves an eloquent silence about the progress of the invasion of Crete.

The possibility of throwing the Germans out of Malemi aerodrome, their only remaining real foothold in Crete, is good, but parachute troops are still dropping in huge numbers.

"Whatever the final outcome of the Battle of Crete may be, the progress of the fighting has already strengthened the view that Britain will be able to resist invasion successfully," states Colonel Palmer, of the North American Newspaper Alliance.

"The effectiveness of the British naval defence of Crete," he adds, "indicated the heavy punishment that German troop transports would suffer in any invasion of Britain, particularly with the Navy supported adequately from the air.

"Major-General Freyberg's army lacks air-fighter support, but the German parachute troops are obviously suffering the heaviest losses."

With German losses heavy—at least 16 heavily-laden troop carriers shot down by anti-aircraft guns—the fight may come to a head during the week-end.

From a confused situation one fact emerges clearly—the small combined forces of Australian, New Zealand, British, Greek and Cretan Home Guard troops are putting up the fight of a lifetime.

The fate of Crete will be decided apparently at Malemi, where the Germans can bring reinforcements but no tanks or heavy artillery, against the British picked troops.

The British are using tanks and hand grenades, the British military spokesman at Cairo says.

Tommy-guns, machine-guns and mortars are the chief weapons being used.

The Germans have obtained a real foothold only at Malemi, which they have practically cleared, and are now using as a landing-ground.

Our gunners shoot down and destroy on landing a large number of German troop-carriers, but the wrecks are hastily cleared away to make room for other planes.

Invaders Fight To Death

The invaders are fighting to the death every yard to hold Malemi in the face of attack after attack by picked men of Major-General Freyberg's forces.

Strong bands of German infantry, brought in by air, sweep the area around the airfield with continuous patrols, so that big troop-carriers can operate a continuous service. The Germans are running about a dozen planes an hour. Big, clumsy Junkers 52's lumber down, empty themselves quickly of men and stores and take off to fetch more.

Berlin estimates that about 650 German troop-carrying planes are plying ceaselessly between the Greek mainland and Crete, taking a stream of reinforcements.

To date they have had no success in transporting tanks or heavy artillery. There is no evidence that they have landed tanks or motor cycle combinations as used in Flanders.

Fighting of the bloodiest is going on continuously, small groups struggling in hand-to-hand combat.

Between the main points of contact—Candia, Rethymno, Canea—a hundred smaller fights are going on.

Swarm after swarm of German parachutists again dropped on the island yesterday. Troop-carrying planes landing at Malemi brought further reinforcements.

It is a battle between men of the sky and men on the ground.

In addition to the troop-carriers shot down, many more troop-carriers and gliders crashed on landing.

Revealing the Australians' arrival at Crete, the British spokesman said that the Australians sent back a message paying a tribute to the Greeks and Cretans battling at their side.

The military correspondent of "The Times," Captain Falls, points out that fierce fighting follows each new German landing, which, on every occasion, has ended with the dispersal of the invaders, although not necessarily with their rounding up and destruction.

Apparently, he says, Malemi aerodrome is the only point where the Germans have maintained their grip for any time.

Captain Falls emphasises again that the danger-point for the defenders is still the absence of air support, and this not only means that the garrison must provide its own defence against aircraft, but renders reinforcement and supply more difficult.

Yet, he goes on, the enemy's supply problems are also serious. Even his reserves of parachute troops cannot be inexhaustable, and must have been seriously depleted already.

This certainly seems to be one of those situations when it pays to hold on to the last gasp, because the enemy's situation may be worse than appears on the surface.

There have been historical instances, he concludes, of one side ending a struggle when the other side was on the point of doing so.

The Germans, says the naval correspondent of "The Times," seem to be staking much on a rapid decision with the new technique of an air-borne invasion across a narrow sea which is not opposed in the air.

But, he adds, the resources of such methods are not unlimited, and, despite favorable conditions, the Germans are expending them rapidly.

NEW SHAKE-UP IN ITALY

From Our Special Correspondent.

NEW YORK, Saturday.

It is officially announced in Rome that General Guzzoni has ceased to serve as Under-Secretary for War.

His successor is General Scuero.

There are persistent reports that this is the beginning of a big shake-up, says the Rome correspondent of the "New York Times."

London's 13th Raidless Night

Australian Associated Press.

LONDON, Saturday.

A few raiders crossed the coast last night, but no incidents were reported. London was without an alert for its 13th successive night.

R.A.F. bombers attacked Boulogne early this morning.

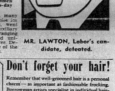

P.M. RETURNS ON VITAL BY-ELECTION DAY

The Prime Minister, Mr. Menzies, returned yesterday, a new purpose in his expression, a face set in graver lines.

"DIABOLICAL" TO PLAY POLITICS IN WAR —MENZIES

Out of a grey sky Robert Gordon Menzies returned yesterday to Australia.

He is a different Prime Minister from the man who left this country four months ago.

HE has been through the blitzkrieg. He has taken part in the councils of the British War Cabinet.

Better than any other man in this country, he realises the stark facts of this war: the task that lies ahead of us.

As he stepped on to the landing stage at Rose Bay flying base, and into the arms of his wife, those who know him well remarked a definite change in Mr. Menzies.

He seemed less cold, less intellectually remote.

There was new purpose in the steadiness of his glance, the jut of his chin.

His face is set in graver lines, and, though obviously he was tired from the ordeal of the last of three ocean flights, he showed vitality, determination.

When he began to speak before the microphones, there was a new vibrancy, a challenging ring to his voice.

His eyes flashed as he told Australia (and his Cabinet colleagues who were lined up behind him) exactly what he feels about the political situation that exists in the Commonwealth to-day.

Said Menzies:—

"I come back with just one sick feeling in my heart. That is, that I must come back to my own country to play politics.

"I think it a **diabolical** thing to have to do this. . . .

"We should do as much as the people of Great Britain towards the winning of the war, which is our business just as much as theirs."

See full report, Page Two, and "I was with Menzies when—": Geoffrey Tebbutt's personal story, Page One, Second Section.

BOOTHBY VOTES FOR GOVT.

From NORMAN STOCKTON

ADELAIDE, Saturday.

In one of the most momentous by-elections since Federation, the electors of Boothby, in South Australia, have decided by an overwhelming majority that there will be no change in the Government of Australia during these fateful hours of our history.

AS progress figures poured into the Central Electoral Office in Adelaide to-night, the will of the people became increasingly clear.

Final figures are:—

GRENFELL PRICE (Govt.)	34,210
T. E. LAWTON (Labor)	26,786
Informal	1,302
Majority for Price	7,424

There are 72,882 voters in the electorate.

National Government became a major issue in the campaign.

Dr. Grenfell Price, his supporters, and the Adelaide Press "plugged" it as the one and only issue.

There were several remarkable features in this remarkable by-election. Chief was the preponderance of women voters, who outnumber the men by 7558.

It is believed that a greater percentage of enrolled women voters went to the polls to-day than enrolled men voters.

Hundreds of young women, many of whom exercised their franchise for the first time in their lives, went into the booths dressed in auxiliary and volunteers' uniforms, ranging from the trim, biscuit-colored uniforms of the Voluntary Services Detachment to the Air Force blue of the Women's Air Auxiliary Corps.

DR. GRENFELL PRICE, winner of the Boothby by-election.

MR. LAWTON, Labor's candidate, defeated.

Old Lady Shows Her Medals

STRAIGHT out of Barrie's famous play, "The Old Lady Shows Her Medals," Mrs. Blannin Ferguson walked into Martin-place yesterday to take part in the Empire Day rally.

She is 74, has no permanent home, she says, but just travels from city to city, "keeping active and young."

Her breast was covered with rows of original and miniature medals of the last war, the African medals of her brother, her grandfather's military badge issued in the first days of citizen defence in Australia, and at least a dozen badges.

"These belonged to my two boys who were killed at the Landing on Gallipoli.

"These were won by my third son, and these by my nephew."

All the menfolk of her family for three generations have served their King and country.

"All my sons served in the last war, and I have a grandson with the A.I.F. at this moment," said Mrs. Ferguson with pride. "They would be no sons of mine if they hadn't done their duty."

Mrs. Ferguson

STOP-PRESS

KING VICTOR FIRED AT

London.—Rome Communique says young Greek fired shots in direction of King Victor Emmanuel and Albanian Premier, M. Verlaci[…] when they were riding in the same car on King's recent trip to Albania.

Save this paper for the Waste Collector

▼ A GERMAN JUNKERS JU 52 transport aircraft in flames over Crete. One in four German paratroopers who took part in the operation were either killed or wounded. There would be no more large-scale German airborne assaults in the war.

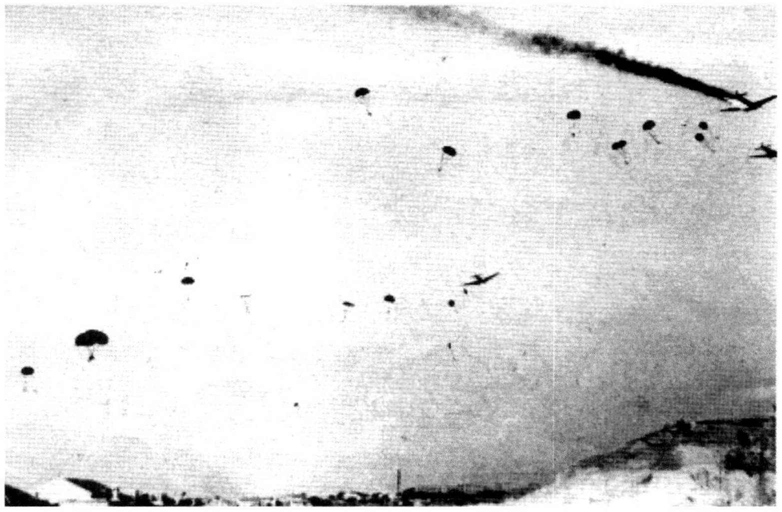

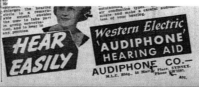

Sunday Dispatch

140th Year. No. 7,282.   2d.   MAY 25, 1941.   Radio Page 7.

H.M.S. HOOD SUNK

"BLOWN UP, FEARED FEW SURVIVORS," STATES ADMIRALTY

World's Largest Warship

THE Admiralty announced last night that the battle cruiser Hood, the world's largest warship, blew up in a fight off the coast of Greenland, when British forces met the Nazi battleship Bismarck.

The Bismarck was damaged, and British ships are carrying on the pursuit.

It is feared there will be few survivors from H.M.S. Hood.

The battle cruiser received an unlucky hit in a magazine, which exploded. She was commanded by Captain R. Kerr, C.B.E., R.N., and was flying the flag of Vice-Admiral L. E. Holland, C.B.

The Hood had a normal complement of 1,341 officers and men.

She was fitted with eight 4.5in. guns, 12 5in. guns, and other armament.

She was begun on September 1, 1916, launched on August 22, 1918, and completed on March 5, 1920.

She had also four 21in. torpedo tubes above water in pairs, and one aircraft.

Fought at Oran

Hood took part in the Battle of Oran. She could travel more than 30 knots.

The Bismarck—a 35,000-ton battleship—was launched in Hitler's presence in 1939. It had an armament of eight 15in. guns, 12 5.9in. guns. It carries four aircraft, and had a speed of 30 knots.

Nazi Claim

First news came in a special announcement by the German High Command broadcast by the German wireless last night. It said:

"A German naval formation operating in the Atlantic under the command of Admiral Luetkens, encountered strong British naval forces in waters off Iceland.

"The German battleship Bismarck destroyed an English battle-cruiser, probably H.M.S. Hood. Another British battleship was forced to turn away. The German naval forces are continuing their operations without having suffered damage worth mentioning."

Briton Who Helped Lepers Killed

Mr. F. E. Bye, a British commercial traveller who gave up his career to work among lepers in Nigeria, was killed by enemy action on the high seas when he was returning to Britain, it was announced yesterday at a meeting of the British Empire Leprosy Relief Association in London, at which he was to have spoken.

Mr. Bye was formerly attached to the American Baptist Mission inter colony at Ogbomosho.

The Troublemakers

"Though we must look for a post-war Europe which includes a German race, I hope we shall take precaution to see that the virus of domination and infection of evil which has for the last 100 years periodically erupted and spread from within Germany will be sterilised," said Capt. Harold Balfour, Under-Secretary for Air, speaking at Broadstairs yesterday.

RAF LONG-RANGE FIGHTERS IN ACTION OVER CRETE: 14 Ju. 52's DESTROYED

NAZI air-borne invaders of Crete clung fiercely throughout yesterday to their hold on Maleme airfield, still the only point on the island where they have managed to establish themselves. Fighting raged all day with British, Imperial, and Greek troops launching attack after attack on the German positions.

British G.H.Q. said last evening: "The Germans have launched their main effort in the Maleme area to extend their original foothold. Intense fighting is continuing.

"Fighting with resolute courage and despite intensive dive-bombing throughout the day, our troops have again inflicted very heavy casualties on the enemy, who has also lost a high proportion of his troop-carrying aircraft. The spirit of our Empire forces remains as high as ever.

"Enemy detachments landed by air yesterday at Heraklion and Rethymo were decisively dealt with. Other parties landed further afield are being mopped up by Empire forces ably assisted by Greek troops."

The British, Imperial, and Greek forces attacking Maleme are operating from positions east of the airfield, between Maleme and Suda Bay. The Nazi operations are harassed continually by shelling from our artillery, which still commands the landing-ground.

British bombers and long-range fighters, operating from Egypt, have gone into action against Maleme. A large number of Ju. 52 troop-carriers on the airfield and neighbouring beach were attacked by our machines on Friday.

The Middle East air communiqué said yesterday: "The enemy aircraft were bombed. Subsequently the enemy were machine-gunned. Preliminary reports say that at least ten enemy aircraft were destroyed. Many others were damaged.

"A reconnaissance carried out later in the day confirmed that many Ju. 52's had been burned out and a large number made completely unserviceable.

"Our long-range fighters also attacked the enemy at Maleme and destroyed at least four large troop-carriers."

The British long-range fighters which are back over Crete are probably Blenheims or the new Beaufighters—well known as night fighters.

It was announced last week that because of the lack of airfields our short-range fighters—including probably Hurricanes—had been withdrawn from Crete, leaving the Germans in command of the air.

Supplies Captured

Small forces of the enemy are believed to be operating still around both Rethymno and Héraklion. In the fierce fighting going on throughout the island with these and other isolated groups, the Greeks and Cretans are said to be fighting "like scalded cats."

German troop-carrying planes operating the "shuttle service" between the Greek mainland and Maleme have succeeded in landing some artillery, probably 75 mm. guns, and mortars, for the invaders.

In other parts of the island where our forces have cleared out the enemy, we have captured supplies dropped for them by their aircraft—probably ammunition, arms, and food.

The task of the Navy in finding and dispersing enemy seaborne convoys attempting to take the supplies and men to Crete is difficult. Many Greek islands are within 60 or 70 miles of Crete, and the Italian Dodecanese are only 50 miles away.

These islands and the narrow waters around them provide the convoys with excellent cover.

In addition, our warships are having to operate under continuous attacks from enemy dive-bombers based on the islands and on the Greek mainland.

No Sea Landing

The success of the Navy, however, is proved by the fact that no enemy landings of any strength have been made from the sea.

Possibly an odd caique, similar to the 40 sunk by the Navy on Wednesday last, have succeeded in reaching the coast. But the value to the invaders of its arrival would be small. The men in it would have to contend with the British and Greek defenders.

Berlin and Rome yesterday continued to put out claims of the big sea and air battle which has been raging in the Aegean since the

airborne invasion of Crete started. The German High Command claimed that their dive-bombers sank three British destroyers off Suda Bay on Friday.

The Rome newspaper Messaggero told its readers that the British Fleet is being "decimated." "During the last five days five cruisers and destroyers have certainly been sunk. Two big battleships, eleven cruisers, and five destroyers have been damaged by hits from torpedoes or heavy bombs," it said.

While these claims should be treated with the greatest reserve —Axis air claims are usually wildly exaggerated—they do at least show that Nazi and Italian bombers are constantly operating against Admiral Cunningham's Fleet.

Berlin Gives Its Version

FIRST reference to the fighting in Crete was contained in a special announcement by the German High Command, broadcast by Berlin Radio yesterday.

It read as follows:

"Since the early hours of the morning of May 20, German parachutists and airborne troops have been in battle on the isle of Crete against parts of the British Army.

"In daring attacks from the air supported by fighters, destroyer groups, bombers, and dive-bombers, these formations conquered strategically important points on the isle.

"After further reinforcement by formations of the German Army, our forces went into attack. The western part of Crete is firmly in German hands."

SHOTS AT ITALIAN KING MAY BE PLOT BY NAZIS

BY A DIPLOMATIC CORRESPONDENT

AN attempt to assassinate King Victor Emmanuel of Italy, kept secret for seven days, but officially announced yesterday, may prove to be part of a German plot to remove an important obstacle to the complete taking over of Italy by Hitler.

No better time from the Nazis' point of view could have been chosen for such an attempt. There has been ever-growing resentment among the Italian people against Mussolini and the Fascist Party for the past few weeks at the failure of the Italian military effort.

The news that the Duke of Aosta, Italian Viceroy of Abyssinia, had been forced to capitulate, finally brought home to them the idleness of Mussolini's boastings.

The natural bent of the people in the circumstances has been to turn to the monarchy for leadership.

Despite the Fascist communiqués on the progress of the war, the people have long realised that without German aid their armies in Albania would have been crushed by the Greeks. They had the bitter memory of hearing of the annihilation of their army in Cyrenaica in the British drive; they heard last week that their East African empire had been finally vanquished.

The Germans are disliked not only by the people who see Nazis in control at many places but by the Fascists themselves.

The Fascists have had to see their Fleet sacrificed at Matapan to enable the Germans to get to Libya; their realise that Hitler has done a deal with Victor over Italian claims against France; they have been refused recognition of Greece as a sphere of Italian influence.

While the Nazis would be glad to see the end of Mussolini and the Fascist Party, it would not suit them to see a restoration to real power of the monarchy.

Without either Mussolini or a king, the complete domination of the country would be an easy matter.

That their instrument of execution on this occasion failed them must be a bitter disappointment.

YOUNG GREEK

The official Rome version of the assassination attempt is that it occurred in Albania on May 17 when King Victor was riding in a car with M. Verlaci, the Quisling Premier, to Tirana's airport after a week's tour of the country.

A young Greek, Milsthios Vasili, "snapped because he had failed to secure a job under the new Albanian Government," fired five shots at the car. All went wide, although one hit one of the back tyres of the car.

"He was saved from being lynched by the crowds lining the route," added the Rome communiqué, "through prompt action in arresting him."

Vasilisci, it is stated, was Albanian national peasant costume in order not to attract attention, a white peasant jacket with a fez, a black Skanderbeg jacket, woollen pompoms, and dark white breeches, with a pair of shoes said to have been made in Greece.

He carried the gun—a small weapon—inside his shirt.

"POETIC MADNESS"

An Italian message from Tirana yesterday said that Vasilisci was affected with poetic madness."

An explanation of the reason for delaying the news was that it had been withheld "while the assassin was questioned."

"His trial is imminent and will occur before a tribunal of the armed forces in Albania."

Another message stated that he was being questioned in an attempt to discover possible accomplices.

This is the third attempt on the life of King Victor Emmanuel. The first was in 1911, and the second at Milan, in April 1928, when terrorists placed explosives made a passage through which one place to explode was exploded, passed.

The King's carriage passed the danger spot only a few minutes before the explosives blew up. Eighteen people were killed and 12 people.

King Victor Emmanuel owes his throne to the assassination of his father, Humbert, who was killed at Monza, near Milan, in 1900.

He has the longest reign of any King in Europe, though Queen Wilhelmina holds the record for the longest reign among Royalty at present.

His consort, Queen Helen, is a Montenegrin, daughter of Nicholas I of Montenegro.

M. Verlaci was pushed into power by the Italians after King Zog fled Albania following the invasion by the Italians in April 1939.

TWO DIVISIONS TRAPPED AS ITALIAN BASE FALLS

SODDU, Italian stronghold in Abyssinia south of Addis Ababa, has been captured by British troops, and has ended the "Battle of the Lakes."

Soddu is 90 miles south-east of Jimma, and is an important centre of communications.

Reporting the news last night, a Nairobi communiqué stated: "By its capture all hopes of escape, except across the country, for the remnants of two Italian divisions vanish.

CAPTURE IS CERTAIN

"Further, other important enemy forces west of the lakes are now separated, and their capture or disintegration is only a matter of time.

"In the sharp engagement preceding the capture of Soddu our West African troops captured several hundred prisoners and a number of guns and tanks, at only slight loss to themselves.

"Farther south, West African troops captured Uando, where 600 Italians, some guns, and four armoured cars were taken."

During the Lake fighting, it is revealed, British forces captured 90 Italians, 1,300 natives, and a large commander at Hula.

In Somaliland a patrol captured 90 prisoners at Tobru.

In Libya a heavy sandstorm in the Tobruk area has held up observation and operations.

In the Sollum area British patrols have continued aggressive tactics.

Our heavy bombers have raided Benghazi Harbour, causing "considerable damage."

LATEST

PETROL COUPONS CAN BE SEIZED

Secretary for Petroleum announces that any person in possession of petrol coupons must carry and produce them on request to any authorised Board of Trade official. Coupons may be impounded if an offence has been committed. Order that coupons can be used only for the vehicle for which they have been issued is reinforced.

NAZIS DENY HITLER MET INONÜ

Berlin official yesterday denied Swiss reports of meeting between Hitler and President İnönü, Turkey, after Greek capitulation.

HITLER GAMBLES ON CRETE VICTORY AS BAIT FOR STALIN

By Sunday Dispatch Diplomatic Correspondent

HITLER'S latest plan is that if he wins the battle for Crete he will meet Stalin and conclude formally the new German-Russian agreement—already in draft form.

If Hitler loses, the meeting will be postponed.

Germany is bringing great pressure to bear upon Russia—using the massing of German troops in Finland, Rumania, and along the German-Russian-Polish frontiers to make Russia agree to her demands.

Under the draft proposals Germany and Russia agree upon a division of interests in the Middle East. Germany to take Irak, and Russia to take Iran (Persia).

Russia agrees to Turkey giving up the British Alliance and Germany plans for a Pan-Arabic Federation under German aegis.

BRIBES, THREATS

Germany, as usual, is coupling bribes with threats. She has suggested that Russia should help herself to the three Turkish provinces of Kars, Artwin, and Ardahan.

These provinces used to be part of Russian Georgia, and they came to Turkey in 1920.

This is a particularly attractive bait to Stalin—as Stalin is a Georgian.

Tnis Turkish-Georgian territory and an outlet on the Persian Gulf would be Russia's "compensation."

Russia, however, in addition to agreeing to strengthen Germany's Middle Eastern plans, would be required to supply Germany with raw material now agreed to be fixed by Germany (in Memorable, Germany, with Russia's approval, is busily engaged bringing direct pressure to bear upon Turkey.

END ALLIANCE

Negotiations are proceeding at the moment both at Ankara and Berlin.

Germany is demanding that the Turks should: (1) Nullify the Anglo-Turkish alliance, and (2) Permit not only the passage of German war material across Turkish territory, to Irak, but, if required, at a later stage, German troops as well.

It is believed that, in the event of the United States declaring a state of non-belligerency, Hitler would try to stage an open German-Russian Alliance.

CONSCRIPTION CAUSES EIRE CRISIS

Ulster Premier Flies To London

AT Mr. de Valera's request, the Eire Speaker has summoned the Dail to meet to-morrow to hear a statement from him on "a matter of urgent public importance."

The following official statement was issued in Dublin yesterday afternoon:

"Following conferences yesterday between members of the Government and of the chief Opposition and Labour parties, the Government has decided to summon the Dail to-morrow to consider the position arising out of the statements made by Mr. Winston Churchill that the question of conscription in Ulster had engaged the attention of the British Government for some time past."

Mr. J. M. Andrews, Northern Ireland Premier, who crossed from Belfast by air, saw Mr. Churchill in London yesterday and discussed the conscription question with him.

Afterwards the following statement was issued by the Northern Ireland Government office in London:

"Mr. Andrews, accompanied by Mr. Gordon and Lord Glentoran, had a discussion to-day with Mr. Churchill and a number of his colleagues on the question of applying conscription to Northern Ireland."

Mr. Churchill informed the Andrews that he welcomed the opportunity of hearing the views of the Government of Northern Ireland on the matter, which would receive the careful consideration of His Majesty's Government."

It is estimated that there are already more than 100,000 men from Northern Ireland either in the Forces or the Merchant Navy.

The application of conscription for men between 18 and 41 would affect about 200,000 men, many of whom are, of course, in reserved occupations.

Another U.S. Strike Threat

ANOTHER strike in an American aircraft factory is threatened. The factory is engaged on British orders.

Members of the United Automobile Workers' Union employed at the North American Aviation Co.'s plant at Inglewood, California, have voted to strike on Wednesday. There are nearly 12,000 men working at the plant who demand a wage increase.

The company are making fighter planes and trainers for Britain and equipment of various kinds for the United States force. Contracts worth about £40,000,000 are in hand.

One Down Over Coast—Destroyed By R.A.F.

AN enemy plane was destroyed off the south coast by R.A.F. fighters yesterday.

Enemy aircraft were reported during the day over N.E., N.W., and S.W. England and South Wales. A single raider circled an N.E. coast town, then dropped one incendiary and land and five H.E. bombs in the sea.

95 Per Cent. Of Food Prosecutions Succeed

During April there were 2,360 prosecutions under the Food Control Orders of which 2,192—more than 95 per cent—were successful. March figures were 2,141 prosecutions, of which 1,934 were successful.

CABINET MEET

Mr. de Valera, accompanied by other members of the Government, held conferences with members of the chief Opposition and Labour parties to consider the position arising out of the statements made by Mr. Winston Churchill that the question of conscription in Ulster had engaged the attention of the British Government for some time.

U.S. "Months Ahead Of Schedule"

AMERICAN industrial machine is producing armaments more quickly than the British Fleet to intervene in the battle of Crete, said yesterday Lieutenant-Commander R. Fletcher, M.P., Parliamentary Private Secretary to the First Lord of the Admiralty, at Ramsgate yesterday:

"The American steel industry," he added, "is producing to all but a fraction of capacity at an annual rate of 90,000,000 tons, and in 12 months' military plane production has risen from 450 to 1,400 a month and is still rising."

More Tourists

The Spanish Government announced yesterday that General Von Massow, Director of the German Air Academy, has arrived in Madrid, with other German officials, who due to take part in the inauguration of the new German Cultural Institute in Madrid on Wednesday.

(Information)

Duff Cooper Has 'Flu

MR. DUFF COOPER, Minister of Information, is in the country, suffering from a mild attack of influenza.

He is expected to be away from work for a few more days.

Guns First

Royal Ordnance factories are the direct of the Ministry of Supply, will all be working on Whit Monday.

▲ SUNDAY DISPATCH, LONDON, SUNDAY MAY 25, 1941

Under the editorship of Charles Eade, the weekly *Dispatch* doubled its circulation during the war to almost 2 million readers. The loss of the battlecruiser HMS *Hood* with only three survivors shocked Britons—it is notable, however, that the *Dispatch* still makes room for the German view of both the sinking of the *Hood* and the fighting on Crete.

The Evening News

No. 18,516   WORLD'S LARGEST EVENING NET SALE   LONDON: TUESDAY, MAY 27, 1941   ONE PENNY

CALOX 1/3 TIN — the economical OXYGEN TOOTH POWDER including Purchase tax

LATE EXTRA

"GOOD TIME COMING" SMITH SECTRIC CLOCKS — plug in to Greenwich time — NO WINDING • NO REGULATING

BLACKOUT 10.46 p.m. to 5.08 a.m.
Moon sets 10.58 p.m.
Rises 7.57 a.m.
CLOSING PRICES PAGE 4

BISMARCK SUNK

Ark Royal Planes Hurl Torpedoes Into Her

MR. CHURCHILL TELLS HOW THE HOOD WAS AVENGED

Torpedo-carrying planes of the Fleet Air Arm.

Navy's American "Spotter" Finds Fleeing Bismarck After Escape In The Mist

H.M.S. Hood is avenged. Bismarck, Germany's "unsinkable" battleship, described by Mr. Churchill as the most powerful warship afloat, has been sunk.

NEWS of this victorious end to one of the most exciting naval chases in history was given to the world to-day in the following Admiralty communique:

"The German battleship Bismarck has been sunk by our naval forces. Details of the operations will be announced as soon as possible."

In the Commons, Mr. Churchill had given an account of Fleet Air Arm attacks on the Bismarck and had sat down. A slip of paper was passed to him. He rose, and amid cheers, announced the sinking. He said she had been destroyed "outside the range of bomber aircraft from France"—which means at least 1,500 miles out in the Atlantic, the commerce raiders being said have a range of more than 3,000 miles.

DAYLIGHT BATTLE

Mr. Churchill revealed that Bismarck was accompanied by the new German heavy cruiser Prince Eugen when she met Hood, with which was our new 35,000-ton battleship Prince of Wales, put into service early on Saturday morning.

Bismarck managed to slip away in poor visibility during Saturday night.

A Catalina scouting plane—one of those sent to us by America—picked her up again at mid-day yesterday.

Fleet Air Arm torpedo-carrying planes from the Ark Royal hit her with two torpedoes: two more "from one of our flotillas" brought her practically to a standstill.

At daylight to-day our battleships attacked; then came the news that Bismarck was sunk. "Measures are being taken in respect of the Prince Eugen," said Mr. Churchill.

Mr. A. V. Alexander, First Lord of the Admiralty, announced at a luncheon in London that the Bismarck was sunk "at eleven o'clock this morning."

"Ark Royal aircraft put two torpedoes into the Bismarck last night," added Mr. Alexander, "and this morning other torpedo bombers from that ship joined officers and men of the Royal Navy in putting the finishing touches to the Bismarck." (Loud cheers.)

Torpedoed Amidships

MAKING his announcement, Mr. Churchill said:

On Wednesday last the new German battleship Bismarck, accompanied by the new 8-inch cruiser Prince Eugen, was discovered by our air reconnaissance at Bergen. On Thursday it was known they had got to sea.

Many arrangements were made to intercept them if they attempted, as seemed probable, to break out into the Atlantic Ocean with a view to striking at our convoys from the U.S.

Meeting at Dawn

During the night of Friday-Saturday our cruisers got into visual contact with them as they were passing through the Denmark Straits between Iceland and Greenland.

At dawn on Saturday morning the Hood and the Prince of Wales intercepted these two enemy vessels. The Hood was struck at about 23,000 yards by a shell which penetrated into one of the magazines and blew up, with only a few survivors.

During the whole of Saturday our ships remained in touch with the Bismarck and arrangements were made for effective battle at dawn yesterday morning.

During the night the weather deteriorated and visibility decreased and the Bismarck, by making a sharp turn, shook off the pursuit.

"WE ARE SATISFIED"
Big Help to Atlantic Hold

A few minutes later Mr. Churchill announced that he had heard the Bismarck was sunk. Continuing his statement, he said:

Great as is our loss of the Hood, the Bismarck must be regarded as the most powerful, as she is the newest battleship in the world.

The striking off the German Navy is a very definite simplification of the task of maintaining the effective mastery of the Northern Seas and the maintenance of the Northern blockade.

I dare say in a few days it will be possible to give a much more detailed account.

Although there is shade as well as light in this picture, I feel we have every reason to be satisfied with the outcome of this fierce and memorable naval encounter.

THE SHIP THAT HITLER LAUNCHED

GERMANY'S greatest battleship, the Bismarck, was claimed to be "unsinkable." She was launched by Hitler himself at Hamburg in February, 1939, before a crowd of 50,000 and was saluted by assembled vessels of the German Navy. She was completed last year.

She had a displacement of 35,000 tons and was 794 feet long with a beam of 118 feet. Her crew was between 1,200 and 1,300.

No battleship of such a size had ever been built in German shipyards before. Her main armament consisted of eight 15-inch and 12 5.9-inch guns.

She was very heavily armoured, had triple propellers and double rudders, and carried four aircraft and secret anti-aircraft armament. At her launching there was a state but ominous hitch. When a bottle of champagne was broken on the bows, the Bismarck did not move. There was an awkward pause of three minutes. When the hull left the slips it went around.

The First Giant

Hitler in his launching speech referred to the sinking of the German Fleet at Scapa Flow and said the Bismarck was the first giant of a new squadron.

It was announced that the Bismarck and her sister ship, Tirpitz, were "in service" last December.

In addition to the Bismarck and Tirpitz, two other 35,000-ton German battleships are completed or about to be completed.

The fact that Admiral Lutjens was transferred to the Bismarck is taken as proof of the Berlin claim that the Scharnhorst and Gneisenau have been put permanently out of action, for he was in command this year of the raid squadron in which these ships were included

PRINCE EUGEN
Of the Hipper Class

The Prince Eugen is one of the five heavy cruisers of the 10,000-ton Hipper class.

She was laid down in 1936 and has only been completed during the last few months. She carries eight 8-inch guns, twelve 4.1-inch A.A. guns, four aircraft, and a complement of 820.

The Bluecher, a sister-ship, was sunk in Oslo fiord by coastal batteries in April, 1940.

OUR NEWEST SHIP
H.M.S. Prince of Wales

The Prince of Wales (35,000 tons) is the sister ship of the King George V, which took Lord Halifax to America. She was launched in May, 1939, and is the fifth battleship to join the Navy.

She is the second of the five battleships of the George V class to be put into service. Three others—Duke of York, Jellicoe and Beatty of the 1937 programme are nearing completion, if not already in service.

She has improved defences against air attack and a special system of under-water protection. Her main armaments are ten 14-inch guns in three turrets and 16 5¼in. guns, with several pompoms. She carries four aircraft, and she has a complement of 1,500.

CATALINA PLANES
"Gift From on High"

The Catalina PBY2B is a 7-seater 13-ton military flying boat, large numbers of which have already flown the Atlantic as part of America's Lease-and-Lend contribution to R.A.F.

When Lord Beaverbrook was Minister of Aircraft Production he

described the Catalina as "a gift from on high ... a crock of gold." Built at San Diego, California, by the Consolidated Aircraft Corporation, the Catalina has a range of 265 m.p.h. and a wing-span of 104ft. Her two engines develop 2,100 h.p.

Bismarck Alone

On this, further rapid dispositions were made by the Admiralty and the Commander-in-Chief, and I may say that at the moment she was known to be at sea, the whole apparatus encounter.

THE BATTLESHIP BISMARCK

The new British battleship Prince of Wales

ARK ROYAL—her planes torpedoed the Bismarck.

SIX DAYS

On Wednesday the Bismarck and Prince Eugen were located by air at Bergen and on Thursday it was known that they had got to sea. On Friday night they were seen by British cruisers between Iceland and Greenland.

On Saturday at dawn they were intercepted by the Prince of Wales and the Hood. The battle cruiser Hood was blown up by a shell at 23,000 yards and the German ships eluded pursuit as the weather became worse at night after being shadowed all day.

Yesterday the Bismarck was sighted by Catalina aircraft at midday making for Brest. In the afternoon planes from the Ark Royal hit her with two torpedoes—one amidships and one astern—rendering her steering ineffective and reducing her speed. Then two more torpedoes from destroyers hit her, bringing her virtually to a standstill.

To-day Bismarck, attacked by British battleships, stood up to gunfire and was sunk—it is believed by further torpedoes.

BISMARCK SUNK THE HOOD FROM 13 MILES' RANGE

From Our Naval Correspondent

Mr. Churchill's disclosure that the shell which blew up the Hood's magazine was fired from 23,000 yards (more than 13 miles) means that the Bismarck's gunners and her shells were first class. It was a lucky shot, but luck and efficiency often go hand in hand. Nothing of the sort at such long range has occurred in naval warfare before.

The extreme range of the Bismarck's guns was 40,000 yards, more than 22 miles.

The Queen Mary and Indefatigable were destroyed in similar fashion at Jutland at ranges of only 18,000 yards. It was believed that the Hood's magazines were safe from such penetration.

"GAS ATTACK"
Streatham's Surprise Test

A surprise "gas attack" is taking place in Streatham this week. The day, time and place are being kept secret.

Similar tests are to be held in Putney, Balham, Tooting, Wandsworth, and Clapham in the next few weeks.

Continued on Back Page, Col. 5

CRICKETER M.P.
P. T. Eckersley's £126,752

Lieutenant P. T. Eckersley, R.N.V.R., M.P. for Manchester Exchange and former Lancashire County cricket captain, who died on War Service in August, aged 36, left £126,752.

FIRESIDE FINANCE
He, She and Their Debts

At Tottenham court to-day:
Magistrate: I take it you and your wife would together over the debts she incurs.
Husband: Oh, no. S
She the debts and I pay them.

EXECUTED
He Fired at King

Rome, Tuesday.—Miha Greek who fired at Kin Emmanuel of Italy Albanian Premier in Al days ago, was shot at T dawn to-day.—A.P. and

MORE ORANG
For the East I

More oranges have ar ondon.
Some of the latest co to reach this country fo button in "blitzed" area be sold in bombed dis London.

It is expected that most going up to the East End.

THE 3s. 8d. LIP
It Cost the Typis

A typist, Mrs. Elfrida aged 36, was at Marlborou day fined £3, with £2 c stealing a lipstick worth from an Oxford-street sho She asked for another li a store to be taken into c audience.

EMPIRE GESTU

Canberra, Tuesday.—"I be a splendid thing Dominions jointly reco of our Parliaments," said Curtin, the Australian leader, to-day.—B.U.P

LAST WORD

I let my wife run my business (said a man at a North London court to-day). When she says "No" to a traveller he knows she means it.

Our Naval Losses Off Crete
2 CRUISERS, 4 DESTROYERS
MORE BRITISH TROOPS ARE LANDED

Mr. Churchill announced in the Commons to-day that we have lost the cruisers Gloucester and Fiji and the destroyers Juno, Greyhound, Kelly and Kashmir in the defence of Crete. The greater part of the crews were saved.

It was stated in Alexandria that all six ships were sunk by air attack.

A "Bad Impression"

Sir Hugh O'Neill (Unionist, Antrim), amid shouts from Members, asked "would it not make a rather bad impression throughout the Empire that once again the Government had buried this issue because of pressure from Southern Ireland?" (Cries of "No.")

Mr. Churchill: I do not think I can put it better than I did than to say he thought it better—(the end of Mr. Churchill's sentence was lost in cheers).

Mr. Churchill, in answer to another question, paid a tribute to Northern Ireland, "for whose loyal aid and continued constant support of our cause no words of praise can be too high."

"Indescribable Fury"

The battle has swayed backwards and forwards with indescribable fury at Canea and also equally furiously though on a

---

BISMARCK FIGHTS TO THE LAST, SAYS BERLIN

Official German News Agency issues this statement:
"The battleship Bismarck, which in her first battle against superior British forces sank Hood and damaged King George, had her whole speed reduced by a hit forward.

"A torpedo-hit in air attack on May 24 (Saturday) again reduced the speed of Bismarck. On May 26 (Monday) four hundred sea miles west of Brest towards 9 a.m. this again hit by two aerial torpedoes, breaking screw and rudder.

"At 11.42 p.m. Admiral Luetjens sent following report to High Command : 'Ship incapable of manoeuvres. Will fight to last shell. Long live Fuehrer. (Signed) Chief of Fleet.'

"Fighting against enemy naval forces which were gradually being reinforced, Bismarck went on fighting until finally on morning of May 27 (to-day) she went down before superior forces."—Reuter.

MR. ALEXANDER ON BISMARCK SINKING

Mr. Alexander in his speech said : As Hitler followed in whole of his ill-gotten career precepts of Bismarck, let us hope destruction of Bismarck, Germany's latest and greatest ship, reduce beginning of end of his reign.

We have suffered severe fighting in Mediterranean in last week. It has been one of greatest and most epic battles of war.

Many editors and men have made greatest sacrifice there. We must put more in all the time if we are to get more out of our victory.

NAVY'S "MAGNIFICENT WORK" OFF CRETE

Stated in Alexandria this afternoon that although British Fleet has undoubtedly suffered some grievous losses off Crete, truly magnificent work which it has carried out under most severe difficulties has ensured that after five days of ceaseless struggle, every attempt by Germans to carry out sea-borne landing is necessary to their success, has so far been completely frustrated, except, possibly, for a few isolated fishing boats.—Reuter.

"OFFENSIVE AGAINST CRETE RESUMED"

Aero-naval offensive against Crete resumed with great fury after 24 hours relative calm, says Rome message to Vichy News Agency.

"Descent of thousands of parachutists continues, for purpose either of reinforcing troops already in the western part of island or to land behind British positions and at various other points.

NO CONSCRIPTION FOR ULSTER

[Mr. Churchill announced in the Commons to-day that conscription would not be applied to Northern Ireland.

He said that the Government had made a number of inquiries in various directions, with the result that they had come to the conclusion that at the present time although there could be no dispute about our rights or the merits, it would be more trouble than it was worth to introduce such a policy.

BERLIN ADMITS IT
Very Reluctantly, Though

When Berlin radio broadcast the official German communique at 8 a.m. to-day it made no mention of the sinking of the Bismarck. The communique should have been broadcast an hour earlier and the announcer apologised for the delay.

But the German news agency this afternoon admitted the sinking.

Earlier in the day a special communique had prepared Germans for the bad news. It said : "The Bismarck has again been engaged in a hard fight with superior enemy forces."

COURT AND STOCK EXCHANGE HELD UP

London greeted news of the sinking of Bismarck with great enthusiasm.

In the Stock Exchange cheering members jumped in the air and waved papers above their heads. At Lloyds the famous Lutine bell was rung.

Judge Sir Gerald Hurst, K.C., interrupted the hearing of a case at Bromley County Court to give the news and there were cheers in court.

At the Plaza, Haymarket, the film was stopped to make the announcement; three or four minutes passed before it could be resumed owing to the loud applause of the audience.

CHANNEL CLOUDY

The Straits of Dover were choppy to-day. The weather was dull and cloudy ; the wind was in the South-West.

[map labels:]
BISM'K SIGHTED FRI:
HOOD SUNK SAT:
GREENLAND
ARCTIC OCEAN
DENMARK STR
BISMARCK LOCATED WED.
BERGEN
ICELAND
Faroes
NORWAY
CANADA
BRITISH ISLES
NEWFOUNDLAND
BREST
ST. NAZAIRE
New York
BISMARCK SUNK TO-DAY

◀ THE EVENING NEWS, LONDON, TUESDAY MAY 27, 1941

The loss of Germany's main battleship *Bismarck*, damaged after its attack on HMS *Hood* and then caught and destroyed by navy airplanes and ships, takes over nearly the whole of *The Evening News* front page. As shocked as the British were by the loss of the *Hood*, they were heartened by the "revenge" sinking of the *Bismarck*. British sea power, it seemed, had been reasserted, despite news of naval losses off Crete.

▼ THE *BISMARCK* IN action in the Atlantic. Following the loss of the *Bismarck*, the German Navy abandoned the use of heavy surface warships for raiding purposes in the Atlantic. From then on the Germans concentrated their efforts in the U-boat war against Allied merchant shipping.

▲ THE SUN, SYDNEY, MONDAY JUNE 9, 1941

Following the fortunes of the Australian troops who took part, *The Sun* reports the Allied
invasion of Syria, controlled by Vichy France. Evidence suggests, however, that censors suppressed
details of the fierceness of the fighting, not least because it was felt that readers would be
dismayed at the strong resistance by Vichy French troops to the very Allies that offered the only
hope of liberating France from German occupation.

Syria
JUNE 1941

ONE OF THE CONSEQUENCES OF THE FALL OF FRANCE WAS THAT THE SMALL RUMP VICHY FRENCH STATE CONTROLLED SEVERAL COLONIES WORLDWIDE. IN SEPTEMBER 1940, Free French forces supported by the Royal Navy had failed to take control of the colony of Dakar in West Africa. In the same month in the Far East, the Japanese took over bases in French Indochina, something the authorities there were unable to resist.

ALLIES MOVE INTO SYRIA

In 1941, the British were extending their control of the Middle East. They had moved into Iraq in April, transporting troops from India, in order to oust the pro-German ruler Rashid Ali. By May, with German forces having overrun Greece and having landed on Crete, Britain had decided to take over Syria, which was ruled from Vichy France. Commonwealth and Free French forces attacked in early June 1941. The Vichy forces under General Henri Dentz resisted fiercely and not until June 21

did the Allied forces occupy the capital, Damascus. Surrender terms were agreed with Dentz on July 14. The conquest of Syria helped secure the eastern Mediterranean and also contributed manpower to the Allied cause. Six thousand of the Vichy French garrison volunteered to serve with the Free French forces. Interestingly, the last charge by British cavalry mounted on horses took place in this campaign.

Later in 1941, British and Soviet forces also moved into Iran, to make sure the oil fields stayed as a stable supply for the Allies, finalizing British control of the region.

▲ A BRITISH TRUCK PULLS an antiaircraft gun during the Allied invasion of Syria in June 1941. The Allied force totaled 20,000 troops.

◀ THE NEW YORK TIMES, SUNDAY JUNE 22, 1941 The start of Operation Barbarossa, Hitler's invasion of the Soviet Union, gets full coverage from the paper that boasts "All the News that's Fit to Print." In this case, that includes an extract from Hitler's proclamation justifying the German invasion as necessary to safeguard "the whole of Europe" from Russia.

The New York Times.

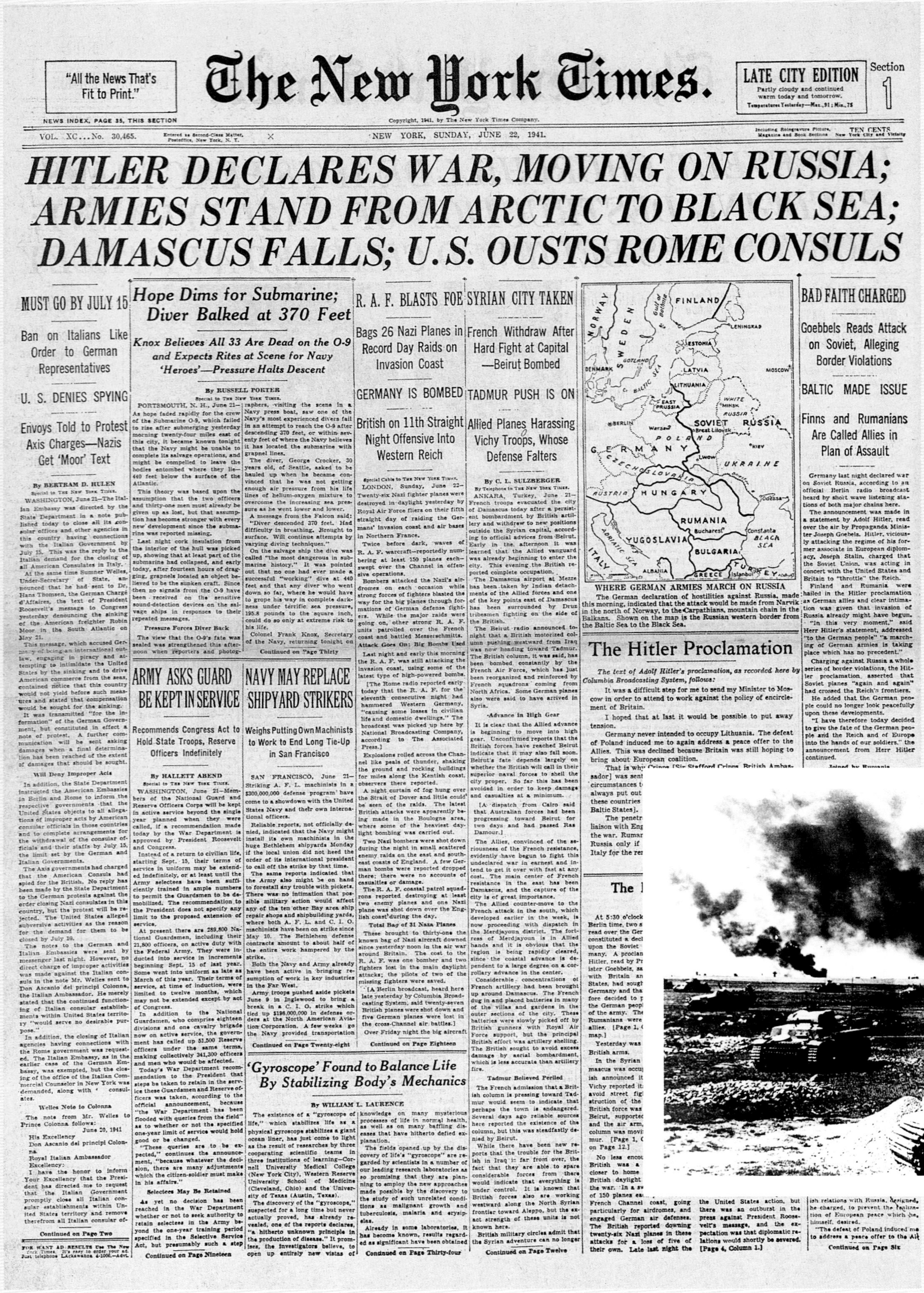

"All the News That's Fit to Print."

LATE CITY EDITION
Partly cloudy and continued warm today and tomorrow.
Temperatures Yesterday—Max.,91 ; Min.,75

Section 1

NEWS INDEX, PAGE 35, THIS SECTION

Copyright, 1941, by The New York Times Company.

VOL. XC...No. 30,465.

NEW YORK, SUNDAY, JUNE 22, 1941.

TEN CENTS

HITLER DECLARES WAR, MOVING ON RUSSIA; ARMIES STAND FROM ARCTIC TO BLACK SEA; DAMASCUS FALLS; U.S. OUSTS ROME CONSULS

MUST GO BY JULY 15

Ban on Italians Like Order to German Representatives

U. S. DENIES SPYING

Envoys Told to Protest Axis Charges—Nazis Get 'Moor' Text

By BERTRAM D. HULEN

Hope Dims for Submarine; Diver Balked at 370 Feet

Knox Believes All 33 Are Dead on the O-9 and Expects Rites at Scene for Navy 'Heroes'—Pressure Halts Descent

By RUSSELL PORTER

R. A. F. BLASTS FOE

Bags 26 Nazi Planes in Record Day Raids on Invasion Coast

GERMANY IS BOMBED

British on 11th Straight Night Offensive Into Western Reich

SYRIAN CITY TAKEN

French Withdraw After Hard Fight at Capital —Beirut Bombed

TADMUR PUSH IS ON

Allied Planes Harassing Vichy Troops, Whose Defense Falters

By C. L. SULZBERGER

WHERE GERMAN ARMIES MARCH ON RUSSIA

BAD FAITH CHARGED

Goebbels Reads Attack on Soviet, Alleging Border Violations

BALTIC MADE ISSUE

Finns and Rumanians Are Called Allies in Plan of Assault

The Hitler Proclamation

The text of Adolf Hitler's proclamation, as recorded here by Columbia Broadcasting System, follows:

ARMY ASKS GUARD BE KEPT IN SERVICE

Recommends Congress Act to Hold State Troops, Reserve Officers Indefinitely

By HALLETT ABEND

NAVY MAY REPLACE SHIPYARD STRIKERS

Weighs Putting Own Machinists to Work to End Long Tie-Up in San Francisco

'Gyroscope' Found to Balance Life By Stabilizing Body's Mechanics

By WILLIAM L. LAURENCE

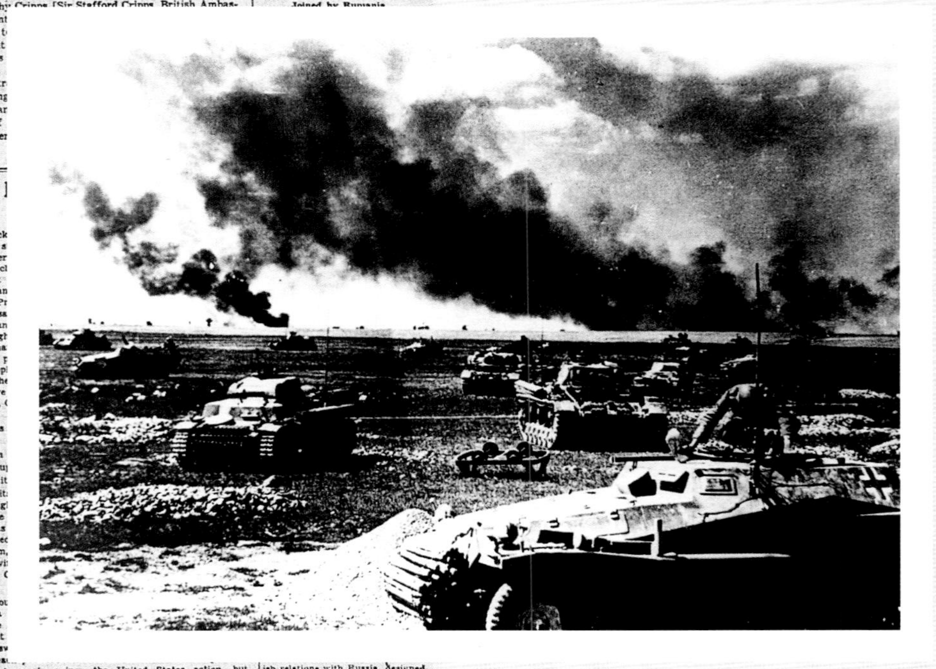

▲ GERMAN PANZERS IN RUSSIA. In the first few days of Barbarossa German armored forces achieved stunning victories. On June 27, for example, the Second and Third Panzer groups linked up and trapped four Soviet armies.

114DE JAARGANG

Nieuwe Amsterdamsche Courant

ALGEMEEN HANDELSBLAD

Maandag 23 Juni 1941

No. 37508 : Twaalf bladzijden
Directeur: Mr. H. M. Planten

AVONDBLAD
ABONNEMENTEN PER KWARTAAL,
PER MAAND EN PER WEEK.
GIRO GEM. AMSTERDAM
H 3000   POSTGIRO 50
TELEFOON 99811 - 99815
INTERLOCAAL R 0423

Uitgave van het „Algemeen Handelsblad" N.V
N.Z. Voorburgwal 234-240, Amsterdam (C)
Hoofdredacteur: D. J. van Balluseck
Amsterdam

Gevechten aan de geheele Russische grens gisteren begonnen

PROCLAMATIE VAN HITLER AAN DUITSCHE VOLK

BERLIJN, 22 Juni. Rijksminister dr. Goebbels heeft hedenochtend te 5.30 uur een oproep van den Führer aan het Duitsche volk voorgelezen.

Hierin stelde de Führer het Duitsche volk op de hoogte van de Sowjet-Russische machinaties tegen het Rijk, in samenwerking met Engeland.

Hij kondigt in zijn oproep aan, dat een front is opgericht van de Noordelijke IJszee tot de Zwarte Zee, samen met het Finsche en Roemeensche leger, ter bescherming van Europa.

Ten slotte deelde dr. Goebbels mede, dat de Führer heeft besloten het lot en de toekomst van het Duitsche Rijk en het Duitsche volk wederom in handen van de soldaten te leggen.

Tekst van den oproep van den Führer

BERLIJN, 22 Juni. (D. N. B.) De Führer heeft den volgenden oproep tot het Duitsche volk gericht.

Duitsch volk, nationaal-socialisten. Door zware zorgen gedrukt, tot maandenlang zwijgen gedoemd, is thans het oogenblik gekomen, waarop ik eindelijk openlijk kan spreken.

Englands omsingelingspolitiek.

Toen het Duitsche rijk op 3 September 1939 de Engelsche oorlogsverklaring ontving, werd de Britsche poging herhaald ieder begin van een consolidatie, en daarmede een opgang, van Europa, door den strijd tegen de sterkste macht van het continent te verijdelen. Zoo heeft Engeland eens in vele oorlogen Spanje te gronde gericht. Zoo voerde het zijn oorlogen tegen Nederland, zoo bestreed het met behulp van geheel Europa later Frankrijk en zoo begon het, omstreeks de eeuwwisseling, met de omsingeling van het Duitsche rijk en begon het in 1914 den wereldoorlog.

...

ZAL OOK BULGARIJE DE BETREKKINGEN MET DE SOWJETS VERBREKEN?

Stefani meldt uit Sofia: elk oogenblik te verwachten.

ROME, 22 Juni. (D. N. B.) Naar Stefani uit Sofia meldt, is het afbreken van de diplomatieke betrekkingen tusschen Bulgarije en Sowjet-Rusland ieder oogenblik te verwachten.

De Bulgaarsche ministerraad, aldus D.N.B. uit Sofia, is Zondagmiddag in buitengewone zitting bijeengekomen.

...

(Men zie verder op bladz. 2.)

ITALIË IN OORLOG MET RUSLAND

Solidair met het Duitsche Rijk.

ROME, 22 Juni. (Stefani.) De Italiaansche regeering heeft den Sowjetambassadeur medegedeeld, dat zij zich van 5.30 uur af in staat van oorlog met de Sowjet-Unie beschouwt.

Uit Berlijn meldt D. N. B.:

De Italiaansche ambassadeur Dino Alfieri heeft vanmorgen den minister van buitenlandsche zaken bezocht en hem in opdracht zijner regeering medegedeeld, dat Italië zich bij de afweer van de bedreiging voor Europa, ontstaan door den opmarsch van het roode leger in het Oosten, algeheel solidair met Duitschland verklaart en zich van hedenochtend half zes af beschouwt als in oorlogstoestand met de Sowjet-Unie.

...

GEHEELE VEESTAPEL IN BESLAG GENOMEN

...

DE DUITSCHE RIJKSMINISTER VAN BUITENLANDSCHE ZAKEN, VON RIBBENTROP, leest voor een groep vertegenwoordigers van de binnen- en buitenlandsche pers de nota voor, welke aan de Sowjet-regeering is gezonden (boven). — Op een front, dat zich uitstrekt van de Noordelijke IJszee tot de Zwarte Zee, zijn gevechten begonnen. Een Duitsche mitrailleur in stelling. (Ass. Press)

DUITSCH WEERMACHTSBERICHT VAN HEDEN

ACTIE IN HET OOSTEN WORDT STELSELMATIG VOORTGEZET

Luchtaanvallen op Odessa, Kiejev, Kaunas en Minsk. — Duitsche motortorpedobooten opereeren in de Oostzee.

Duitsche concentraties bij de Zwarte Zee

Het opperbevel van de Duitsche weermacht maakt bekend:

In het Oosten verloopen de gevechten naar het leger en van het luchtwapen tegen het roode leger stelselmatig en met succes...

Optimistische verwachtingen in Duitsche kringen.

ANKARA, 23 Juni (S. P. T.) Omtrent de oorlogshandelingen aan het Russische front wordt alhier bevestigd, dat Odessa, Kiejev, Sebastopol, Kaunas en Minsk door het Duitsche luchtwapen zijn gebombardeerd.

...

SLOWAKIJE VERBREEKT BETREKKINGEN MET SOWJET-RUSLAND

Dr. Tiso ontvangt den Duitschen gezant.

PRESSBURG, 22 Juni. (D. N. B.) De Slowaaksche regeering heeft vandaag de diplomatieke betrekkingen met de Sowjet Unie verbroken.

...

DE NIEUWE VLEESCHBON

De secretaris-generaal van het departement van Landbouw en Visscherij maakt bekend, dat de volgende bonnen zijn aangewezen voor het koopen de daarbij vermelde rantsoenen:

...

MAISKI CONFEREERT MET EDEN

LONDEN, 22 Juni. (S. P. T.) De Russische ambassadeur in Londen, Maiski, heeft Zondagmorgen een langdurig onderhoud gehad met den Britschen minister van buitenlandsche zaken, Anthony Eden, gevoerd.

GOUVERNEMENT-GENERAAL — SOWJET-UNIE — SLOWAKIJE — HONGARIJE — ZEVENBURGEN — TRANSSYLVANISCHE ALPEN — WALACHIJE — BOEKAREST — JOEGOSLAVIE — BULGARIJE — ZWARTE ZEE

Roemenië eischt thans blijkens den oproep van generaal Antonescu de indertijd aan Sowjet-Rusland afgestane gebiedsdeelen (op onze kaart gearceerd) weer op.
(Archief Hbld. — Eigen teekening.)

VERDUISTER VAN 22.06 TOT 5.18
Zon op 5.18, onder 22.06.
Maan op 4.47, onder 20.34.
Nieuwe maan 24 Juni.

▲ ALGEMEEN HANDELSBLAD (GENERAL COMMERCE PAPER), AMSTERDAM, MONDAY JUNE 23, 1941
Published under German occupation, the esteemed Dutch daily presents Hitler's justification of Operation Barbarossa without criticism. For an alternative view the Dutch turned to the BBC and, when the occupiers banned radios, to flourishing underground newspapers, often run by communist sympathizers.

New York Post

Founded 1801, Volume 140, No. 191. Copyright 1941, New York Post, Inc.

WEATHER
Scattered showers and continued warm tonight and tomorrow, light winds. Lowest temperature tonight about 68 degrees. High tomorrow about 85 degrees.

SPORTS FINAL 7
LATE SPORTS RESULTS ON PAGE 15

NEW YORK   MONDAY   JUNE 30   1941   THREE CENTS

REICH ARMY SPOKESMAN INTIMATES:

HALF WAY TO MOSCOW

Germans Claim Capture of Lwow and Minsk

7 Spies Plead Guilty; FBI Seizes 2 More On Incoming Ships

By JOHNSTON D. KERKHOFF

Seven of 25 persons accused of belonging to a spy ring unexpectedly pleaded guilty when arraigned in Brooklyn today, and the others were held in $25,000 bail each.

While the arraignments were being held before U. S. Commissioner Epstein, FBI agents went down the bay on Coast Guard cutters and seized two stewards from incoming liners.

Those who pleaded guilty included Axel Wheeler-Hill, brother of James Wheeler-Hill, former German-American Bund secretary. It was in Axel Wheeler-Hill's apartment that agents found a short wave radio during the week-end roundup of suspects.

Another who pleaded guilty was a model, Lilly Barbara Carola Stein, who allegedly had moved in society circles extracting information.

The others:

Hartwig Richard Kleiss, seaman; Erwin Wilhelm Siegler, former chief butcher on the S. S. America; Franz Stigler,

LILLY BARBARA Carola Stein, artists' model, was among 29 persons arrested on espionage charges by the FBI.

former chief baker on the America; Leo Waalen, German citizen, and Alfred E. Brokhoff, waterfront mechanic.

Each prisoner was transferred to Brooklyn in an automobile, and with each one rode three to five FBI agents. All were handcuffed.

More Arrests Indicated

The agents activity down the bay indicated that the roundup was not yet over. As one government official said: "I don't want the public to think that these are the only spies in the country."

Eight FBI agents first boarded
Continued on Page 10, Col. 6.

Don't Write To Uncle Sam For a Mate

WASHINGTON, June 30 (AP).—The Census Bureau said today it didn't mind being lonely women where detached males were running loose, but from there on it's up to the girls.

After revealing in a press release last week that men are in the vast majority in several American possessions, the bureau received hundreds of letters from women wanting names and street addresses of likely prospects.

The letters came from nearly every state east of the Mississippi River. They inquired about Guam, Alaska, Puerto Rico and Hawaii, and particularly about the Panama Canal Zone.

The bureau replied: it is against the law to reveal individual names from census records.

Brenda Weds—'Simply'
The Champagne Will Cost Only $750

Brenda Diana Duff Frazier, who has got along pretty well despite the burden of being called Glamour Girl No. 1, becomes Mrs. John Simms (Shipwreck) Kelly today in what the society editors refer to as a simple ceremony.

She wears a $300 wedding gown, there are only 230 guests invited to the reception, and the champagne bill, it is figured, won't be more than $750.

The simplicity extended to Hal Phyfe, family photographer, who said that all other cameramen would be barred. "Anyone who tries to crash will be smashed by 'Shipwreck,'" was Phyfe's zero hour warning.

The wedding is being solemnized at 4:15 p. m. by the Rev. Father Joseph F. Flannelly, of St. Patrick's Cathedral, in the Carlton House living room of Miss Frazier's mother, Mrs. Frederic N. Watriss. There are only 20 guests.

Miss Frazier is being given in marriage by her stepbrother, Frederic Whitney Watriss, Sergeant T. Suffern Tailer is Kelly's best man.

At 5 p. m. there is to be a re-

BRENDA FRAZIER

ception in the Crystal Room of the Ritz-Carlton. Following the reception, the couple will fly to California, and will spend their honeymoon in Honolulu.

In the fall they plan to take an apartment here. Next June when Miss Frazier is 21, she will come into about $4,000,000.

Why It's So Humid

Today's humidity can be blamed on the ocean, according to James H. Kimball, head of the Weather Bureau.

It's so humid because the wind is coming in from the Atlantic, he said.

"I think the high humidity is possibly caused by its accumulation over the last five days when the temperature was above normal," he explained. "The air was dry until yesterday, with a fairly good breeze, and the sudden change has made it so noticeable."

The temperature, which was 77 at midnight, got down to 75 at 3:45 a. m., and then started right back up again, and by 8 a. m. it was 80. Yesterday's temperature at that hour was only 75.

Hourly temperatures today and yesterday were:

Jackson Approved For Court
Senate Committee Acts Unanimously—Rejects Tydings Charge He's 'Unfit'

WASHINGTON, June 30 (AP).—The Senate Judiciary Committee approved unanimously today the nomination of Attorney General Jackson to be an associate Justice of the Supreme Court.

The committee rejected charges by Sen. Tydings (D.-Md.) that Jackson was unfitted for service on the court "by character, philosophy and judicial temperament."

Tydings said that Jackson had rejected his request that Drew Pearson and Robert Allen, columnists be prosecuted for a 1939 "radio broadcast" in which they said Tydings had called on the WPA to build a road and a yacht basin on his estate.

Jackson followed Tydings to the witness stand and said the Justice Dept. had declined to prosecute because it wished to keep the government "out of the numerous fights between newspapers and men in public life."

Calls Tydings Beneficiary

The Attorney General said an investigation by the FBI had shown that WPA improvements ha dnot been made on the Senator's property "but a road was built by the Tydings estate and a yacht harbor adjacent to it."

"The inference is clear that you were a beneficiary," he snapped when Tydings challenged him to prove that WPA work had improved the Senator's property. Tydings said the work, actually decreased the value of the property.

Ten minutes after the committee had acted, Tydings announced in the Senate that he would oppose the nomination when it reached the floor.

FIGHTING ON BORROWED LAND

(war map)

NAZI FORCES HAVE KNIFED THROUGH the outer layer of Soviet defenses, built on territory annexed since 1939, and have captured Minsk (2), in Russia proper, Berlin announces. Advance units have driven on to a point "within sight of Smolensk," 200 miles on the road to Moscow, a spokesman says. A German column advancing on Leningrad has taken Libau, naval base on the Latvian coast; other forces have captured Lwow (3) on the road to Kiev. In the southern sector along the Prut River to the Black Sea (4), the Russians claim complete success in stopping the invasion, and the Nazis make no claims of gains there.

U. S. Nurses on Lost Ship
Marine Believed Killed in Sinking

WASHINGTON, June 30 (AP).—While withholding official confirmation of the sinking, Sumner Welles, Acting Secretary of State, said today American Red Cross nurses were on board a ship reported to have been sunk in the Atlantic with the possible loss of an American marine.

Asked at a press conference about an authoritative report that the ship, carrying 10 U. S. Marines to London, was lost, Welles said he did not believe the Navy was in a position to make an official statement.

Welles added that American nurses were aboard the same vessel with the marines traveling to England to help the ex-panded services of the American Embassy including communications and fire prevention.

Under the Neutrality Act Welles explained, the President had the power to make exceptions to permit Americans in certain instances to travel on belligerent ships.

The marines were on a Dutch vessel, now in British service, which was torpedoed somewhere in the Atlantic, the official said.

Only Saturday the announcement was made here that three officers and 40 enlisted men of the Marine Corps were being sent to London "to facilitate communications between the various U. S. offices located there."

Barrymore Runs Into a Zombie, a Fist and a Bouncer
The Great Profile Slips (While Ducking) After Blonde's Escort Swings

Special to The Post

HOLLYWOOD, June 30.—John Barrymore was struck by a zombie, a young man in a night club and a bouncer early today. He wound up on the sidewalk. The affair took place at Earl Carroll's night club and theatre, where Barrymore had gone to attend the marriage of a pair of jitterbug champions by the Rev. R. Anderson Jardine, who married the Duke and Duchess of Windsor and thereby landed in Hollywood.

As he entered, "Think-a-Drink" Hoffman, who reads your mind and then mixes the drink you are thinking of, was doing his stuff.

"Think Again"

Barrymore thought of a zombie. Hoffman poured the drink, and said, "You could get drunk on what you're thinking of.

That's powerful stuff. You'd better think again."

Barrymore insisted he wanted a zombie, and Hoffman warned him again of the drink's potentialities and said the limit was to one for several years."

He finally got the drink, gulped it down, and weaved his way through the club, stopping to chat with an unidentified blonde. Her escort, Clarence Reed, resented a remark, and warned Barrymore to go away.

"His remark wouldn't bear repeating in nice society," Reed said later.

He "Just Slipped"

Barrymore repeated the remark and Reed let go a haymaker. The Profile ducked, and the blow merely grazed his chin. Barrymore went down, but

ringsiders insisted he had slipped in ducking, and had not been floored by Reed. He was up at the count of one, ready to turn the other profile, when Marcel Lamaze, maitre d'hotel, and a squad of bouncers appeared.

Before you could say, "Elaine Barrie," the Profile was down again, this time on the sidewalk in front of the club.

He missed the wedding.

THE GREAT PROFILE—FLOORED

THE GERMANS ANNOUNCE capture of Minsk, and intimate that Nazi forces are within sight of Smolensk, half way to Moscow. On the road to Leningrad, capture of the Latvian naval base of Libau is announced, and Lwow (Lemberg) on the road to Kiev, has fallen. Further encircling movements, trapping large sections of the Soviet armies, are indicated.

MOSCOW REPORTS annihilation of a German landing party trying to win a foothold at Vilport, on the Gulf of Finland, and claims that the Red Army is standing off Nazi attacks all along the front. It says advance panzer divisions have been trapped.

LONDON ADMITS that the position of Soviet forces is very serious.

THE DECISION hinges on which side can maintain contact with, and reinforce, its advance units which are behind the enemy's lines.

STRIKING AT the German rear, the RAF launched a daylight offensive against Bremen and Oldenburg.

BERLIN, June 30-(AP).—The German advance is half way from Minsk to Moscow, a military spokesman intimated today.

The spokesman claimed that Minsk had fallen and the panzer divisions were racing for Moscow, 450 miles away. He hinted that the vanguard was in sight of Smolensk, only 250 miles from the Soviet capital, and said that encirclement of Soviet troops on the central front was proceeding rapidly.

Announcement of the fall of Minsk followed a communique from Adolf Hitler's field headquarters that Lwow, 50 miles from the German frontier in Sovietized Poland, had fallen at 4:20 a. m., and other claims of Russian defeats.

The German armored divisions admittedly have left many Russians behind them to the west, and it was acknowledged that the country across which they have sped cannot be regarded as German-occupied.

The High Command said that Libau "important Baltic naval base just north of the Lithuanian border, had been seized by Nazi troops. DNB, authoritative news agency, reported isolation of a Red division "somewhere o nthe Baltic coast." The Slovak High Command claimed a break-through of the Soviet front at several points with a continuing advance.

The German radio earlier had claimed capture of Luck, 100 miles northwest of Lwow, but this was not confirmed. The objective in the Nazi drive in the Luck-Lwow sector was believed to be Kiev, 250 miles east of Lwow.

Panzer Force Trapped, Say Russians

MOSCOW, June 30 (AP).—The Red Army still is standing off heavy attacks on the Minsk front in White Russia and far ther south at the Luck-Lwow gateway to the Ukraine, a Soviet communique said today. The repulse of German attempts to land at Vilport also was reported.

Destruction of 53 German warplanes in air battles yesterday and the loss of only 21 Russian craft was announced.

German penetrations in Lithuania to the Dvinsk area—a third of the way to Leningrad—and across Sovietized Poland to the Minsk area—almost a third of the way to Moscow—were acknowledged, but in the Minsk drive German panzer advance communications were trapped, the Red Army declared.

From the Luck-Lwow area to the Black Sea, along the southern flank of the battlefront, a communique said German and Rumanian attempts to smash through into the Ukraine and to cross the Prut River into Bessarabia had been repulsed in fierce fighting.

Describing the German High Command's claims yesterday of vast gains and great destruction as "a manifest lie and boastful humbug," the Moscow communique listed these figures for the two sides:

Tanks destroyed, or captured —2,500 German, up to 900 Russian; planes destroyed—1,500 German, 840 Russian; prisoners —30,000 German, 15,000 Russian.

The German summary of the first week of fighting said the Nazi was machine had destroyed 2,233 Russian tanks, 1,297 armored cars and 4,107 planes, taken 40,000 prisoners, sunk four Soviet destroyers, three submarines and a torpedo boat and seriously damaged the 8,800-ton cruiser Maxim Gorky.]

48,400 Tons of Shipping Claimed by Germans

BERLIN, June 30 (AP).—German bombers and submarines have sunk 48,400 tons since the last report June 22, the High Command announced today.

Pants Ration Cuts Harry To the Quick

LONDON, June 30 (AP).—This is the sad saga of Harry Chambers and his pants.

Six weeks ago Harry sent the pants to the cleaner, who lost them. The cleaner reimbursed him but Harry can't buy a new pair because he lacks the necessary clothing coupons.

So he wrote the proper authorities of his plight and asked for emergency coupons.

He's just heard from them: "Kindly show how many pairs of trousers you still possess on the reverse of the enclosed form."

They'll get this answer: "I am sitting here looking half like a nudist. You know which half. Please hurry with those coupons."

5th Av. Bus Line Gives Jobs to 10 Negro Youths

Ten Negro youths, will be placed as apprentices in the shops of the Fifth Av. Coach Co. called on Mayor LaGuardia at Summer City Hall today with John E. McCarthy, president of the company.

The Mayor wished the youths luck, and commented that their placement was in line with the President's order that there be no racial discrimination in the mechanical defense program.

15 Missing, 18 Burned In Mine Dust Blast

INDIANA, Pa., June 30 (UP).—A dust explosion ripped through an isolated section of the Rochester and Pittsburgh Coal Co.'s McIntyre mine, 12 miles west of here today, severely burning 18 miners and leaving 15 or 16 unaccounted for.

▲ NEW YORK POST, MONDAY JUNE 30, 1941

The *New York Post* echoes the contradictory U.S. response to events in Europe: news from the Eastern Front (in fact, the Germans were more like one-third of the way to Moscow) and the ongoing fear of espionage shares the front page with showbiz gossip, movie news, and weather reports. A cartoon even manages to make light of rationing measures introduced on clothing.

Barbarossa

JUNE–JULY 1941

I IN PLANNING THEIR ATTACK ON THE SOVIET UNION, THE GERMAN HIGH COMMAND BELIEVED HITLER'S OPTIMISTIC CLAIM THAT OPERATION BARBAROSSA WOULD EXPOSE THE HOLLOWNESS OF THE COMMUNIST state, and "bring the whole rotten structure crashing down." They were confident after two years of success.

RAPID ADVANCES

The first few weeks of the invasion seemed to confirm this, as a string of victories, each more staggering than the last, brought the armies closer to Moscow. The German aim was to reach a line east of Moscow, to cut Soviet north–south communications and effectively end the war. The statistics were almost incredible: on the first day, June 22, 1,800 Soviet aircraft were destroyed for the loss of two German aircraft; and by July 27 700,000 Soviet troops were trapped in the Smolensk pocket.

Stalin had not expected the attack and as the three German army groups

▲ TWO SOLDIERS of the German 68th Infantry Division, which was part of Army Group South, on the Eastern Front in the summer of 1941.

moved inexorably eastward, the Soviets seemed to have no adequate response. Even when they tried to hold ground their forces were surrounded and forced to surrender.

One advantage of centralized planning, however, was that the state machine organized a general withdrawal of factories and plant farther to the east, toward the Urals, so that war production could carry on even though most of the western part of the country was in German hands. The Germans themselves made some errors. The decision to move armored units from Army Group Center to assist in the destruction of the Kiev pocket by Army Group South in September meant that the Germans lost momentum. More worryingly for the Germans, by October the rains made rapid movement very difficult.

For most people in western Europe, the whole situation was confusing. They disliked Stalin's communist state, but the Soviet Union was now their ally. If it, and its vast resources, fell to the Germans, could anything stop Hitler?

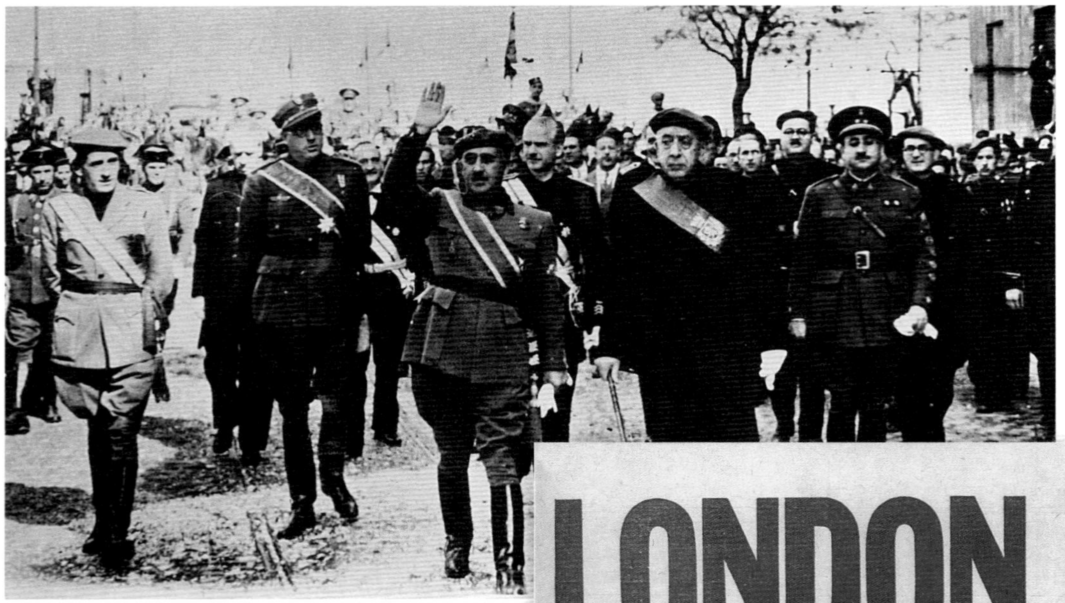

◀ SPANISH DICTATOR FRANCISCO FRANCO (center, arm raised) had no intention of entering the war on the Axis side. He had met with Hitler in October 1940 when the Führer had promised to return Gibraltar to Spain in return for joining the war on Germany's side. The meeting did not go well. Afterward, Hitler said he would rather have some of his teeth removed than meet Franco again.

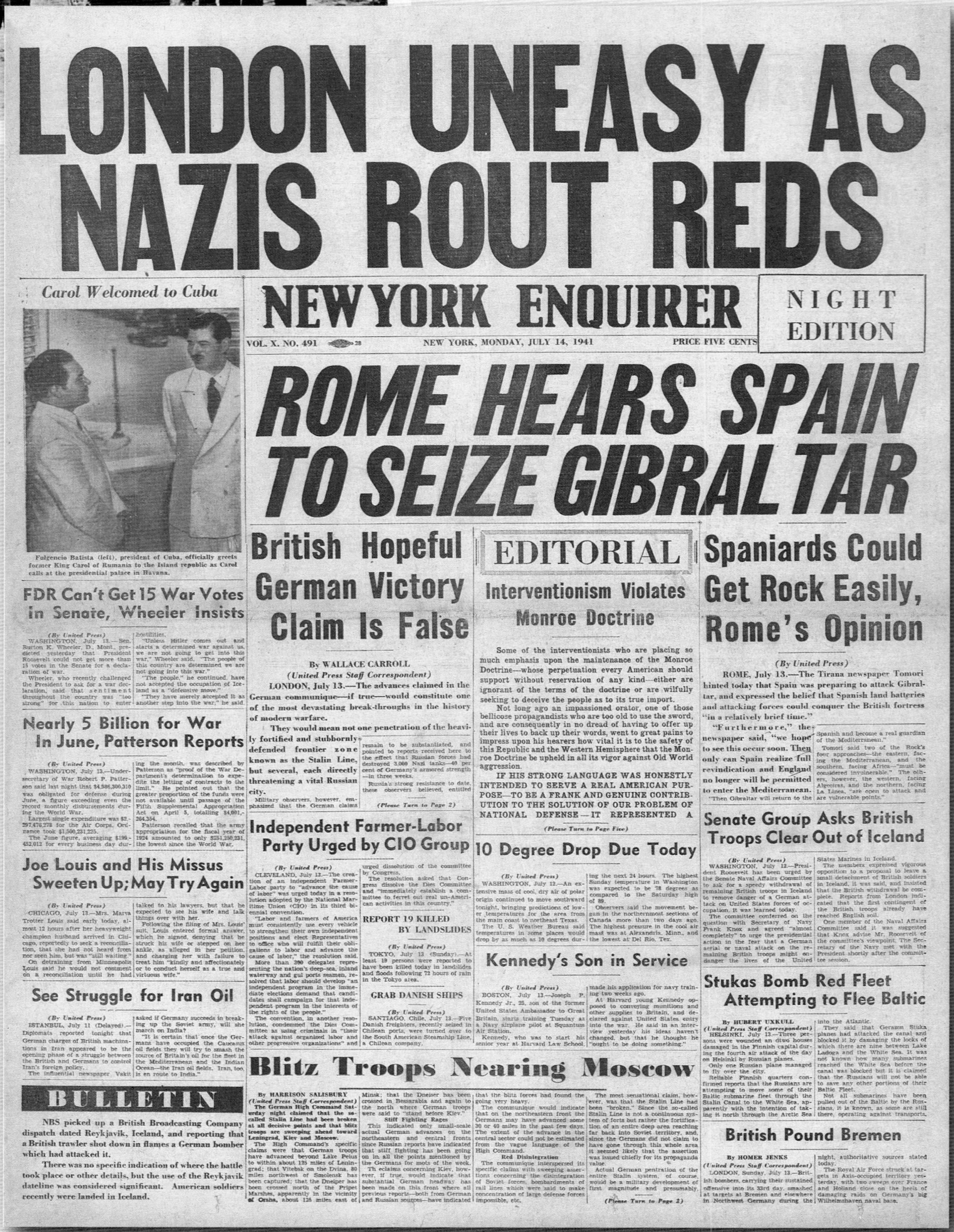

LONDON UNEASY AS NAZIS ROUT REDS

Carol Welcomed to Cuba

Fulgencio Batista (left), president of Cuba, officially greets former King Carol of Rumania to the Island republic as Carol calls at the presidential palace in Havana.

NEW YORK ENQUIRER

NIGHT EDITION

VOL. X. NO. 491 — NEW YORK, MONDAY, JULY 14, 1941 — PRICE FIVE CENTS

ROME HEARS SPAIN TO SEIZE GIBRALTAR

British Hopeful German Victory Claim Is False

By WALLACE CARROLL
(United Press Staff Correspondent)

LONDON, July 13.—The advances claimed in the German communique—if true—would constitute one of the most devastating break-throughs in the history of modern warfare.

They would mean not one penetration of the heavily fortified and stubbornly defended frontier zone known as the Stalin Line, but several, each directly threatening a vital Russian city.

Military observers, however, emphasized that the German claims remain to be substantiated, and pointed to reports received here to the effect that Russian forces had destroyed 3,000 Nazi tanks—40 per cent of Germany's armored strength—in three weeks.

Russia's strong resistance to date, these observers believed, entitled

(Please Turn to Page 2)

EDITORIAL

Interventionism Violates Monroe Doctrine

Some of the interventionists who are placing so much emphasis upon the maintenance of the Monroe Doctrine—whose perpetuation every American should support without reservation of any kind—either are ignorant of the terms of the doctrine or are wilfully seeking to deceive the people as to its true import.

Not long ago an impassioned orator, one of those bellicose propagandists who are too old to use the sword, and are consequently in no dread of having to offer up their lives to back up their words, went to great pains to impress upon his hearers how vital it is to the safety of this Republic and the Western Hemisphere that the Monroe Doctrine be upheld in all its vigor against Old World aggression.

IF HIS STRONG LANGUAGE WAS HONESTLY INTENDED TO SERVE A REAL AMERICAN PURPOSE—TO BE A FRANK AND GENUINE CONTRIBUTION TO THE SOLUTION OF OUR PROBLEM OF NATIONAL DEFENSE—IT REPRESENTED A

(Please Turn to Page Five)

Spaniards Could Get Rock Easily, Rome's Opinion

(By United Press)

ROME, July 13.—The Tirana newspaper Tomori hinted today that Spain was preparing to attack Gibraltar, and expressed the belief that Spanish land batteries and attacking forces could conquer the British fortress "in a relatively brief time."

"Furthermore," the newspaper said, "we hope to see this occur soon. Then only can Spain realize full revindication and England no longer will be permitted to enter the Mediterranean.

"Then Gibraltar will return to the Spanish and become a real guardian of the Mediterranean."

Tomori said two of the Rock's four approaches—the eastern, facing the Mediterranean, and the southern, facing Africa—"must be considered invulnerable." The others, however, the western, facing Algeciras, and the northern, facing La Linea, "are open to attack and are vulnerable points."

FDR Can't Get 15 War Votes in Senate, Wheeler Insists

(By United Press)

WASHINGTON, July 13.—Sen. Burton K. Wheeler, D., Mont., predicted yesterday that President Roosevelt could not get more than 15 votes in the Senate for a declaration of war.

Wheeler, who recently challenged the President to ask for a war declaration, said that sentiment throughout the country was "too strong" for this nation to enter hostilities.

"Unless Hitler comes out and starts a determined war against us, we are not going to get into this war," Wheeler said. "The people of this country are determined we are not going into this war."

"The people," he continued, have not accepted the occupation of Iceland as a "defensive move."

"They have merely accepted it as another step into the war," he said.

Nearly 5 Billion for War In June, Patterson Reports

(By United Press)

WASHINGTON, July 13.—Undersecretary of War Robert P. Patterson said last night that $4,986,300,310 was obligated for defense during June, a figure exceeding even the record monthly disbursements during the World War.

Largest single expenditure was $2,297,476,278 for the Air Corps. Ordnance took $1,500,231,225.

The June figure, averaging $199,452,012 for every business day during the month, was described by Patterson as "proof of the War Department's determination to expedite the letting of contracts to the limit." He pointed out that the greater proportion of the funds were not available until passage of the Fifth Supplemental Appropriation Act on April 5, totalling $4,001,264,354.

Patterson recalled that the army appropriation for the fiscal year of 1924 amounted to only $251,250,231, the lowest since the World War.

Joe Louis and His Missus Sweeten Up; May Try Again

(By United Press)

CHICAGO, July 13.—Mrs. Marva Trotter Louis said early today, almost 12 hours after her heavyweight champion husband arrived in Chicago, reportedly to seek a reconciliation, that she had not heard from nor seen him, but was "still waiting."

On detraining from Minneapolis Louis said he would not comment on a reconciliation until he had talked to his lawyers, but that he expected to see his wife and talk things over with her.

Following the filing of Mrs. Louis' suit, Louis entered formal answer, which he signed, denying that he struck his wife or stepped on her ankle, as alleged in her petition, and charging her with failure to treat him "kindly and affectionately or to conduct herself as a true and virtuous wife."

See Struggle for Iran Oil

(By United Press)

ISTANBUL, July 11 (Delayed).—Diplomats reported tonight that German charges of British machinations in Iran appeared to be the opening phase of a struggle between the British and Germans to control Iran's foreign policy.

The influential newspaper Vakit asked if Germany succeeds in breaking up the Soviet army, will she march on India?

"It is certain that once the Germans have occupied the Caucasus oil fields they will try to smash the source of Britain's oil for the fleet in the Mediterranean and the Indian Ocean—the Iran oil fields. Iran, too, is en route to India."

BULLETIN

NBS picked up a British Broadcasting Company dispatch dated Reykjavik, Iceland, and reporting that a British trawler shot down in flames a German bomber which had attacked it.

There was no specific indication of where the battle took place or other details, but the use of the Reykjavik dateline was considered significant. American soldiers recently were landed in Iceland.

Independent Farmer-Labor Party Urged by CIO Group

(By United Press)

CLEVELAND, July 13.—The creation of an independent Farmer-Labor party to "advance the cause of labor" was urged today in a resolution adopted by the National Maritime Union (CIO) in its third biennial convention.

"Labor and farmers of America must consistently use every vehicle to strengthen their own independent positions and elect Representatives to office who will fulfill their obligations to labor and advance the cause of labor," the resolution said.

More than 300 delegates representing the nation's deep-sea, inland waterway and gul ports seamen, resolved that labor should develop "an independent program in the immediate elections demand that candidates shall campaign for that independent program in the interests of the rights of the people."

The convention, in another resolution, condemned the Dies Committee as using criminals in "their attack against organized labor and other progressive organizations" and urged dissolution of the committee by Congress.

The resolution asked that Congress dissolve the Dies Committee and "immediately establish a committee to ferret out real un-American activities in this country."

REPORT 19 KILLED BY LANDSLIDES

(By United Press)

TOKYO, July 13 (Sunday).—At least 19 persons were reported to have been killed today in landslides and floods following 72 hours of rain in the Tokyo area.

GRAB DANISH SHIPS

(By United Press)

SANTIAGO, Chile, July 13.—Five Danish freighters, recently seized in Chilean ports, were turned over to the South American Steamship Line, a Chilean company.

10 Degree Drop Due Today

(By United Press)

WASHINGTON, July 12.—An extensive mass of cool, dry air of polar origin continued to move southward tonight, bringing predictions of lower temperatures for the area from the main coast to northeast Texas.

The U. S. Weather Bureau said temperatures in some places would drop by as much as 10 degrees during the next 24 hours. The highest Sunday temperature in Washington was expected to be 78 degrees as compared to the Saturday high of 89.

Observers said the movement began in the northernmost sections of Canada more than two days ago. The highest pressure in the cool air mass was at Alexandria, Minn., and the lowest at Del Rio, Tex.

Kennedy's Son in Service

(By United Press)

BOSTON, July 13.—Joseph P. Kennedy Jr., 25, son of the former United States Ambassador to Great Britain, starts training Tuesday as a Navy airplane pilot at Squantum Air Station.

Kennedy, who was to start his senior year at Harvard Law School, made his application for navy training two weeks ago.

At Harvard young Kennedy opposed to convoying munitions and other supplies to Britain, and declared against United States entry into the war. He said in an interview yesterday his ideas haven't changed, but that he thought he "ought to be doing something."

Senate Group Asks British Troops Clear Out of Iceland

(By United Press)

WASHINGTON, July 12.—President Roosevelt has been urged by the Senate Naval Affairs Committee to ask for a speedy withdrawal of remaining British troops in Iceland to remove danger of a German attack on United States forces of occupation, it was learned today.

The committee conferred on the question with Secretary of Navy Frank Knox and agreed "almost completely" to urge the presidential action in the fear that a German aerial or naval attack on the remaining British troops might endanger the lives of the United States Marines in Iceland.

The members expressed vigorous opposition to a proposal to leave a small detachment of British soldiers in Iceland, it was said, and insisted that the British withdrawal be complete. Reports from London indicated that the first contingent of the British troops already have reached English soil.

One member of the Naval Affairs Committee said it was suggested that Knox advise Mr. Roosevelt of the committee's viewpoint. The Secretary of the Navy met with the President shortly after the committee session.

Stukas Bomb Red Fleet Attempting to Flee Baltic

By HUBERT UXKULL
(United Press Staff Correspondent)

HELSINKI, July 13.—Three persons were wounded an dtwo houses damaged in the Finnish capital during the fourth air attack of the day on Helsinki by Russian planes.

Only one Russian plane managed to fly over the city.

Reliable Finnish quarters confirmed reports that the Russians are attempting to move some of their Baltic submarine fleet through the Stalin Canal to the White Sea, apparently with the intention of taking it north through the Arctic Sea into the Atlantic.

They said that Geramn Stuka planes had attacked the canal and blocked it by damaging the locks of which there are nine between Lake Ladoga and the White Sea. It was not known how many submarines reached the White Sea before the canal was blocked but it is claimed that the Russians will not be able to save any other portions of their Baltic Fleet.

Not all submarines have been pulled out of the Baltic by the Russians, it is known, as some are still there, operating against transports.

Blitz Troops Nearing Moscow

By HARRISON SALISBURY
(United Press Staff Correspondent)

The German High Command Saturday night claimed that the so-called Stalin Line had been broken at all decisive points and that blitz troops are sweeping ahead toward Leningrad, Kiev and Moscow.

The High Command's specific claims were that German troops have advanced beyond Lake Peius to within about 125 miles of Leningrad; that Vitebsk on the Dvina, 80 miles northwest of Smolensk has been captured; that the Dneiper has been crossed north of the Pripet Marshes, apparently in the vicinity of Orsha, about 125 miles east of Minsk; that the Dneiser has been crossed in Bessarabia and again to the north where German troops were said to "stand before Kiev."

Stiff Fighting Rages

This indicated only small-scale actual German advances on the northeastern and central fronts since Russian reports have indicated that stiff fighting has been going on in all the points mentioned by the Germans for mots of the week.

Th eclaims concerning Kiev, however, if true, would indicate that substantial German headway has been made on this front where all previous reports—both from German and Russian sources—have indicated that the blitz forces had found the going very heavy.

The communique would indicate that on the northeastern front the Germans may have advanced some 30 or 40 miles in the past few days. The extent of the advance in the central sector could not be estimated from the vague language of the High Command.

Red Disintegration

The communique interspersed its specific claims with sweeping assertions concerning the disintegration of Soviet forces, bombardments of rail lines which were said to make concentration of large defense forces impossible, etc.

The most sensational claim, however, was that the Stalin Line had been "broken." Since the so-called Stalin Line is not a continuous system of forts but rather the fortification of an entire deep area reaching far back into Soviet territory, and, since the Germans did not claim to have gone through this whole area it seemed likely that the assertion was issued chiefly for its propaganda value.

Actual German pentration of the entire Stalin system, of course, would be a military development of first magnitude and presumably,

(Please Turn to Page 2)

British Pound Bremen

By HOMER JENKS
(United Press Staff Correspondent)

LONDON, Sunday, July 13.—British bombers, carrying their sustained offensive into its 33rd day, smashed at targets at Bremen and elsewhere in Northwest Germany during the night, authoritative sources stated today.

The Royal Air Force struck at targets in Axis-occupied terriory yesterday, with two sweeps over France and Holland close on the heels of damaging raids on Germany's big Wilhelmshaven naval base.

▶ NEW YORK ENQUIRER, MONDAY JULY 14, 1941

The *Enquirer* was wrong about Gibraltar—Franco's Spain never tried to seize it—but right about London's unease in the face of news from the Eastern Front. The editorial argues against U.S. involvement in Europe on the grounds of the Monroe Doctrine, which in 1823 laid down the principle that Europe should not interfere in American affairs and vice versa. It is a reminder that even in mid–1941, when the United States was providing essential Allied war materiel under the Lend-Lease scheme, a substantial proportion of Americans were against direct U.S. military involvement in the conflict. A short bulletin notes the enrollment in the Navy of future president John F. Kennedy.

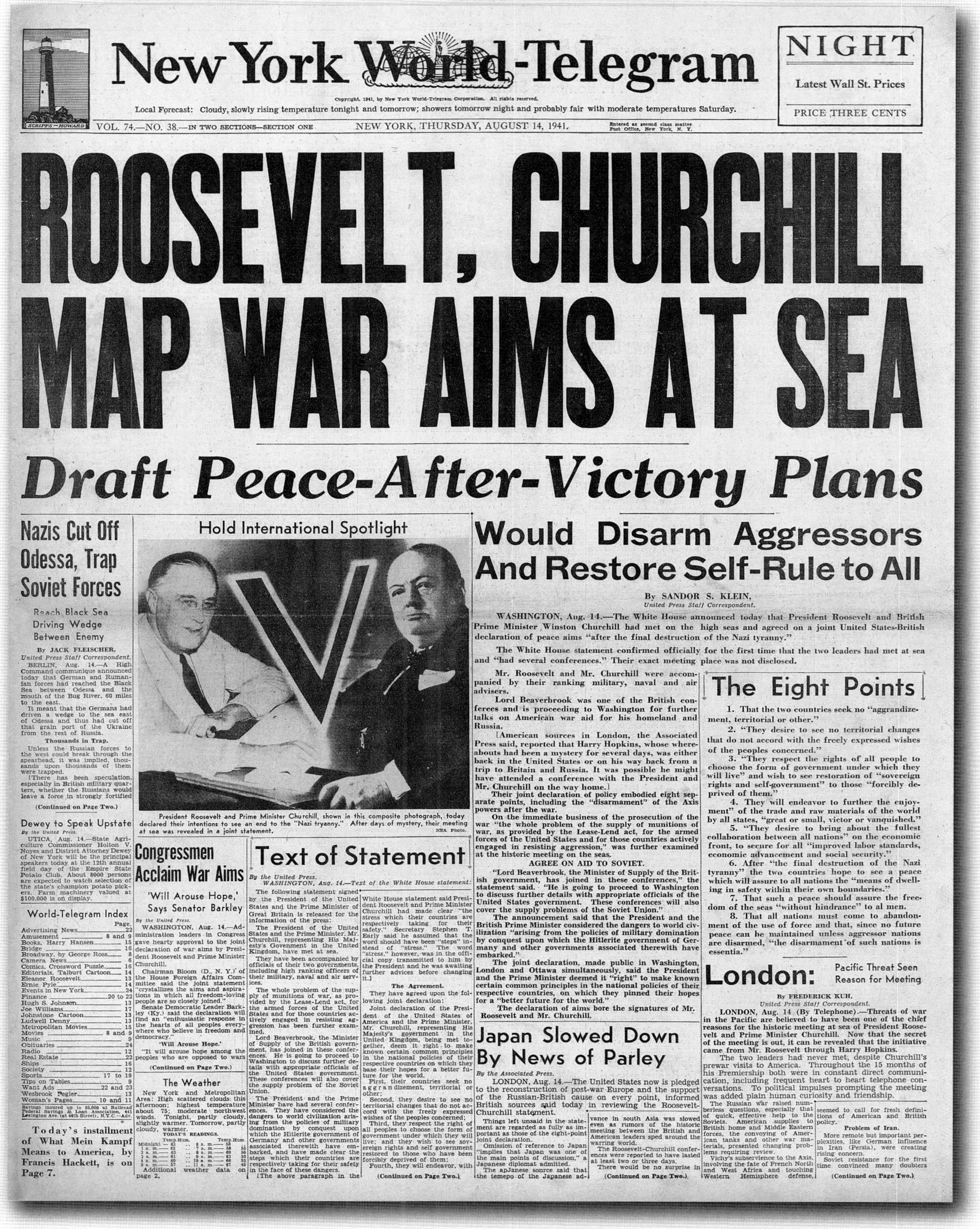

New York World-Telegram

NIGHT

Latest Wall St. Prices

PRICE THREE CENTS

Local Forecast: Cloudy, slowly rising temperature tonight and tomorrow; showers tomorrow night and probably fair with moderate temperatures Saturday.

SCRIPPS—HOWARD

VOL. 74.—NO. 38.—IN TWO SECTIONS—SECTION ONE NEW YORK, THURSDAY, AUGUST 14, 1941. Entered as second class matter Post Office, New York, N. Y.

ROOSEVELT, CHURCHILL MAP WAR AIMS AT SEA

Draft Peace-After-Victory Plans

Nazis Cut Off Odessa, Trap Soviet Forces

Reach Black Sea Driving Wedge Between Enemy

By JACK FLEISCHER,
United Press Staff Correspondent.

BERLIN, Aug. 14.—A High Command communique announced today that German and Rumanian forces had reached the Black Sea between Odessa and the mouth of the Bug River, 60 miles to the east.

It meant that the Germans had driven a wedge to the sea east of Odessa and thus had cut off that grain port of the Ukraine from the rest of Russia.

Thousands in Trap.

Unless the Russian forces to the west could break through the spearhead, it was implied, thousands upon thousands of them were trapped.

[There has been speculation, especially in British military quarters, whether the Russians would leave a force in strongly fortified

(Continued on Page Two.)

Dewey to Speak Upstate

By the United Press.

UTICA, Aug. 14.—State Agriculture Commissioner Holton V. Noyes and District Attorney Dewey of New York will be the principal speakers today at the 12th annual field day of the Empire State Potato Club. About 8000 persons are expected to watch selection of the state's champion potato pickers. Farm machinery valued at $100,000 is on display.

World-Telegram Index

Today's installment of What Mein Kampf Means to America, by Francis Hackett, is on Page 7.

Hold International Spotlight

President Roosevelt and Prime Minister Churchill, shown in this composite photograph, today declared their intentions to see an end to the "Nazi tryanny." After days of mystery, their meeting at sea was revealed in a joint statement. NEA Photo.

Congressmen Acclaim War Aims

'Will Arouse Hope,' Says Senator Barkley

By the United Press.

WASHINGTON, Aug. 14.—Administration leaders in Congress gave hearty approval to the joint declaration of war aims by President Roosevelt and Prime Minister Churchill.

Chairman Bloom (D., N. Y.) of the House Foreign Affairs Committee said the joint statement "crystallizes the aims and aspirations in which all freedom-loving people are so closely joined."

Senate Democratic Leader Barkley (Ky.) said the declaration will find an "enthusiastic response in the hearts of all peoples everywhere who believe in freedom and democracy."

'Will Arouse Hope.'

"It will arouse hope among the peoples who are opposed to wars

(Continued on Page Two.)

The Weather

New York and Metropolitan Area: High scattered clouds this afternoon; highest temperature about 75; moderate northwest winds. Tonight, partly cloudy, slightly warmer. Tomorrow, partly cloudy, warmer.

TODAY'S READINGS.

	Temp.	Hum.		Temp.	Hum.
Midnight	63	..	6 a. m.	58	..
1 a. m.	62	..	7 a. m.	58	55
2 a. m.	62	..	8 a. m.	60	56
3 a. m.	61	..	9 a. m.	63	53
4 a. m.	60	..	10 a. m.	66	53
5 a. m.	57	..	11 a. m.	67	49

Additional weather data on page 2.

Text of Statement

By the United Press.
WASHINGTON, Aug. 14.—Text of the White House statement:

The following statement signed by the President of the United States and the Prime Minister of Great Britain is released for the information of the press:

The President of the United States and the Prime Minister, Mr. Churchill, representing His Majesty's Govenment in the United Kingdom, have met at sea.

They have been accompanied by officials of their two governments, including high ranking officers of their military, naval and air services.

The whole problem of the supply of munitions of war, as provided by the Lease-Lend act, for the armed forces of the United States and for those countries actively engaged in resisting aggression has been further examined.

Lord Beaverbrook, the Minister of Supply of the British government, has joined in these conferences. He is going to proceed to Washington to discuss further details with appropriate officials of the United States government. These conferences will also cover the supply problem of the Soviet Union.

The President and the Prime Minister have had several conferences. They have considered the dangers to world civilization arising from the policies of military domination by conquest upon which the Hitlerite government of Germany and other governments associated therewith have embarked, and have made clear the steps which their countries are respectively taking for their safety in the face of these dangers.

[The above paragraph in the White House statement said President Roosevelt and Prime Minister Churchill had made clear "the stress which their countries are respectively taking for their safety." Secretary Stephen T. Early said he assumed that the word should have been "steps" instead of "stress." The word "stress," however, was in the official copy transmitted to him by the President and he was awaiting further advices before changing it.]

The Agreement.

They have agreed upon the following joint declaration:

Joint declaration of the President of the United States of America and the Prime Minister, Mr. Churchill, representing His Majesty's government in the United Kingdom, being met together, deem it right to make known certain common principles in the national policies of their respective countries on which they base their hopes for a better future for the world.

First, their countries seek no aggrandizement, territorial or other;

Second, they desire to see no territorial changes that do not accord with the freely expressed wishes of the peoples concerned;

Third, they respect the right of all peoples to choose the form of government under which they will live; and they wish to see sovereign rights and self government restored to those who have been forcibly deprived of them;

Fourth, they will endeavor, with

(Continued on Page Two.)

Would Disarm Aggressors And Restore Self-Rule to All

By SANDOR S. KLEIN,
United Press Staff Correspondent.

WASHINGTON, Aug. 14.—The White House announced today that President Roosevelt and British Prime Minister Winston Churchill had met on the high seas and agreed on a joint United States-British declaration of peace aims "after the final destruction of the Nazi tyranny."

The White House statement confirmed officially for the first time that the two leaders had met at sea and "had several conferences." Their exact meeting place was not disclosed.

Mr. Roosevelt and Mr. Churchill were accompanied by their ranking military, naval and air advisers.

Lord Beaverbrook was one of the British conferees and is proceeding to Washington for further talks on American war aid for his homeland and Russia.

[American sources in London, the Associated Press said, reported that Harry Hopkins, whose whereabouts had been a mystery for several days, was either back in the United States or on his way back from a trip to Britain and Russia. It was possible he might have attended a conference with the President and Mr. Churchill on the way home.]

Their joint declaration of policy embodied eight separate points, including the "disarmament" of the Axis powers after the war.

On the immediate business of the prosecution of the war "the whole problem of the supply of munitions of war, as provided by the Lease-Lend act, for the armed forces of the United States and for those countries actively engaged in resisting aggression," was further examined at the historic meeting on the seas.

AGREE ON AID TO SOVIET.

"Lord Beaverbrook, the Minister of Supply of the British government, has joined in these conferences," the statement said. "He is going to proceed to Washington to discuss further details with appropriate officials of the United States government. These conferences will also cover the supply problems of the Soviet Unjon."

The announcement said that the President and the British Prime Minister considered the dangers to world civilization "arising from the policies of military domination by conquest upon which the Hitlerite government of Germany and other governments associated therewith have embarked."

The joint declaration, made public in Washington, London and Ottawa simultaneously, said the President and the Prime Minister deemed it "right" to make known certain common principles in the national policies of their respective countries, on which they pinned their hopes for a "better future for the world."

The declaration of aims bore the signatures of Mr. Roosevelt and Mr. Churchill.

The Eight Points

1. That the two countries seek no "aggrandizement, territorial or other."

2. "They desire to see no territorial changes that do not accord with the freely expressed wishes of the peoples concerned."

3. "They respect the rights of all people to choose the form of government under which they will live" and wish to see restoration of "sovereign rights and self-government" to those "forcibly deprived of them."

4. They will endeavor to further the enjoyment" of the trade and raw materials of the world by all states, "great or small, victor or vanquished."

5. "They desire to bring about the fullest collaboration between all nations" on the economic front, to secure for all "improved labor standards, economic advancement and social security."

6. After "the final destruction of the Nazi tyranny" the two countries hope to see a peace which will assure to all nations the "means of dwelling in safety within their own boundaries."

7. That such a peace should assure the freedom of the seas "without hindrance" to al men.

8. That all nations must come to abandonment of the use of force and that, since no future peace can be maintained unless aggressor nations are disarmed, "the disarmament of such nations is essentia."

Japan Slowed Down By News of Parley

By the Associated Press.

LONDON, Aug. 14.—The United States now is pledged to the reconstruction of post-war Europe and the support of the Russian-British cause on every point, informed British sources said today in reviewing the Roosevelt-Churchill statement.

Things left unsaid in the statement are regarded as fully as important as those of the eight-point joint declaration.

Omission of reference to Japan "implies that Japan was one of the main points of discussion," a Japanese diplomat admitted.

The apJanese sonrce said that the temepo of the Japanese advance in south Asia was slowed even as rumors of the historic meeting between the British and American leaders sped around the warring world.

The Roosevelt-Churchill conferences were reported to have lasted at least two or three days.

There would be no surprise in

(Continued on Page Two.)

London: Pacific Threat Seen Reason for Meeting

By FREDERICK KUH,
United Press Staff Correspondent.

LONDON, Aug. 14 (By Telephone).—Threats of war in the Pacific are believed to have been one of the chief reasons for the historic meeting at sea of President Roosevelt and Prime Minister Churchill. Now that the secret of the meeting is out, it can be revealed that the initiative came from Mr. Roosevelt through Harry Hopkins.

The two leaders had never met, despite Churchill's prewar visits to America. Throughout the 15 months of his Premiership both were in constant direct communication, including frequent heart to heart telephone conversations. To political impulses prompting the meeting was added plain human curiosity and friendship.

The Russian war raised numberless questions, especially that of quick, effective help to the Soviets. American supplies to British home and Middle Eastern forces, the convoying of American tanks and other war materials, presented changing problems requiring review.

Vichy's subservience to the Axis, involving the fate of French North and West Africa and touching Western Hemisphere defense, seemed to call for fresh definitions of American and British policy.

Problem of Iran.

More remote but important perplexities, like German influence in Iran (Persia), were creating rising concern.

Soviet resistance for the first time convinced many doubters

(Continued on Page Two.)

▲ NEW YORK WORLD-TELEGRAM, THURSDAY AUGUST 14, 1941

On a battleship off Newfoundland, Churchill and Roosevelt met to formulate what became known as the Atlantic Charter: eight points that would form the basis of any eventual peace. The *World-Telegram* reports the development in positive terms. At bottom left, a snippet directs readers to a discussion of Hitler's *Mein Kampf*.

Leningrad

SEPTEMBER 1941

ADOLF HITLER SEEMED TO RESERVE A SPECIAL LOATHING FOR THE CITY OF LENINGRAD. PERHAPS IT WAS BECAUSE LENINGRAD WAS THE PLACE WHERE THE REVOLUTION that had brought the communists to power in Russia in 1917 had taken place; perhaps it was because it was named for Vladimir Ilyich Lenin, the first ruler of the communist Soviet Union. Hitler stated in 1942; "St Petersburg (Leningrad's name under the pre-1914 Tsarist regime in Russia) must disappear utterly from the earth's surface."

During the German invasion of the Soviet Union, Leningrad was the target of Army Group North. Within a month of the opening of hostilities, German tanks had cut the main Leningrad-Moscow railroad line, and by the start of September the first German artillery shells began to land on the city. Soviet defense was complicated by the fact that Finnish forces, attempting to retake territory ceded to the Soviet Union after the "Winter War" of 1939–40, moved southward and hampered supply efforts.

BESIEGING THE CITY OF LENINGRAD

Hitler decided against a land attack into the city itself, because he did not want German troops to get held up in hand-to-hand urban warfare. He preferred to starve the city out. The epic siege lasted almost three years. Although all land links were cut, a road across Lake Ladoga functioned when the lake was frozen over during the winter months. Despite this, hundreds of thousands of civilians died in the siege. The heroism of the defenders and the plight of the civilians was significant in creating a more positive view of the Soviet Union in the West.

◄ TROOPS OF THE GERMAN Eighteenth Army march through Narva in August 1941 on their way to Leningrad. The Soviets had pulled back through the town earlier after the Germans had shattered the so-called Luga Line.

ROLLS RAZORS
now unobtainable

Daily Mail

NO. 14,151   ONE PENNY   ✶ ✶   FOR KING AND EMPIRE   WEDNESDAY, SEPTEMBER 3, 1941

LATE WAR NEWS SPECIAL

Sorry to keep you waiting for **Bear Brand** STOCKINGS *But they're worth it!*

THE DAILY MAIL, Wednesday, September 3, 1941.

GERMANS NEARING LENINGRAD

Trenches Dug in the Streets: Vast Battle Raging

From RALPH HEWINS STOCKHOLM, Tuesday.

GERMAN advanced Panzer units in the north are to-night only 20 miles from Leningrad, according to a Berlin spokesman. He declared that these spearheads are standing before Krasnogvardeisk, the railway town immediately south-west of the city.

The Leningrad defences are being subjected to continuous heavy raids by the Luftwaffe as the German Command strive to turn the city into another Warsaw.

Bombing has interrupted the railway link with Moscow, but the Germans, so far, have not reached the railway. The city, therefore, is not yet encircled.

Inside the vast defences, Marshal Voroshilov's forces stand firm. More than 3,500,000 civilians and 1,500,000 soldiers are hourly making the city a still stronger fortress. The defenders are resolved to resist to the last.

FIGHTERS ON PATROL

Parks, gardens, and streets are lined with trenches. Troops and munition lorries are everywhere.

Red Air Force fighters patrol continuously overhead, and the defenders are confident that these fighters and the A.A. defences can save the city from the fate of Warsaw and Rotterdam.

The Germans now are up against Leningrad's main defences. Von Leeb, the German commander, is involved in a perilous race against time.

A gigantic battle is being waged over an immense area. Von Leeb's forces not only stubborn Russian resistance but his forces have to fight their way through boggy forests and sodden fields.

Continuous rain is hampering operations. Roads are almost impassable.

A new German thrust, after a hold-up of nearly two weeks, was obviously expected by Berlin to bring the Battle for Leningrad to a climax.

From Novgorod, at the northern tip of Lake Ilmen, the Germans are striking north in the triangle formed by the Leningrad-Luga and Leningrad-Moscow railways.

Berlin says that this "great operation is proceeding successfully."

South of Lake Ilmen, in their efforts to strike east to cut the Leningrad-Moscow railway the Germans report bitter Russian resistance and "bloody hand-to-hand fighting."

There is no news of fighting on the Finnish Leningrad front, though the Finns claim to have occupied Sakkala, 50 miles south-east of Viborg, and Taipale, just east of Sakkola.

COUNTER-ATTACKS

The Russians, following the evacuation of Viborg are now on their ancient line, behind their 1939 frontier in the Karelian Isthmus.

This runs from Lake Ladoga in the Baltic, 20 miles from Leningrad. M. Lozovsky, the Moscow spokesman, confirmed to-day that the Russians are making local counter-attacks on several sectors of the front.

Counter-attacks on the central front, aimed at cutting off the Gomel "loop," are continuing.

Hundreds of tons of scrap have already been collected from the royal parks and government buildings, and a complete survey of all railings on or around the 18,000 buildings in charge of the Ministry of Works is now in progress.

Radio Death Sentence On Gestapo Man

Daily Mail Radio Station

A GERMAN "Freedom" radio station, operated from a secret spot inside Germany by rebels among Hitler's Brownshirts, last night broadcast a sentence of death on a Gestapo officer.

The announcer called for Karl Buchsenschutz, Gestapo officer, at Frankfort, 23 Grenadierstrasse.

"You have been tried by a secret jury of S.A. officers and found guilty. The sentence is death—and it will be carried out."

The announcer told listeners that Buchsenschutz had murdered three S.A. men, Gerhart Ultrecht, Schwind, and Henschke.

"These three men belonged to a group often called on to execute Hitler's own orders," he said. "They knew too much.

"The Gestapo were ordered to murder them, and they were killed near Kindsvater by Buchsenschutz, who first shot them and then threw hand grenades."

YOUR RAILINGS 'CALLED UP' FOR TANKS

EVERY unnecessary iron gate or railing in Britain will be removed as soon as local authorities have completed a census now being made.

In this way the Ministry of Works expects to collect 500,000 tons of scrap iron which will be forged into tanks and guns for the Army.

Only those gates or railings serving a safety purpose or having an historic or artistic interest will be exempt.

Private owners of railings need not wait to have them listed. If a gate or a railing is easy to dismantle the owners should do the job themselves to save time and labour.

A recent Order in Council absolves tenants from any obligation to landlords for railings in their charge. Receipts will be given and compensation paid in due course.

BANKER OUR U.S. SUPPLY CHIEF

Britain's supply services in the United States have a new chief. Mr. Morris Wilson, 55, deputy-chairman of the British Supply Council in North America, has been appointed chairman in succession to Mr. Arthur Purvis, killed when an Atlantic ferry plane crashed on August 14.

To provide for the heavier duties falling on the council, Mr. E. F. Taylor, representing Canada in Washington on the supply agreement, has been appointed chief executive officer with the title of executive-chairman and president.

Bread—and Jam, says Major Ll. G.

FOODS which "make life more pleasant" were promised by Major Lloyd George, Parliamentary Secretary of the Ministry of Food, when he opened an exhibition at Cardiff yesterday.

There was a time, he said, when drops in imports had caused serious concern—but "that is not so today," he added. "Stocks have greatly improved and we are now doing our best to see that secondary articles of diet from which we have been deprived are increased. Supplies will be small, but they will be fairly and equitably distributed."

Air Ferry Hit Hill in Britain

'Lost' Many Hours: No Survivors

A SENSATION was caused last night when it was announced in Montreal that the missing ocean ferry - plane, which was thought to have been lost in the Atlantic, had crashed on a hillside in Britain. There were no survivors.

Later the Air Ministry in London announced that the wreckage had been found in an isolated and mountainous district on the west coast.

Distinguished scientists and technicians were among the six passengers.

The plane, which carried a crew of four, was due to arrive yesterday after taking off from North America on Monday.

Fourth Crash

This is the fourth Atlantic ferry-plane to crash, and the third in Britain. Two came down within five days last month after taking off for Canada.

Sir Frederick Banting, co-discoverer of insulin, was killed in another which crashed near Newfoundland on its way to Britain.

Among the victims in the latest disaster were Prof. E. B. Mowat, of the Bristol University, who had been lecturing in the United States for the Carnegie Trust, and Count de Baillet-Latour, economic counsellor to London to the Belgian Ministry for the Colonies.

In the past year Prof. Mowat has travelled all over America, visiting about 50 universities and speaking for the British cause.

Mr. J. D. Mowat, one of the Professor's five sons, told The Daily Mail last night: "He told up he would be home about the middle of this month. It would be just like him to fly if he had the chance."

Intelligence Work

Prof. Mowat, who was 54, served in the Naval Intelligence and on the secretariat of the War Cabinet in the last war. He has written about 60 books on European diplomacy, American history, and Anglo-American relations.

Count de Baillet-Latour went to America on a mission for the Belgian Government. He was an Old Etonian and a friend of Mr. Oliver Lyttelton.

The other passengers were: Mr. H. Taylor, of Farnborough, Hants, principal technical officer of the Air Ministry, London; Capt. S. Picking, of the United States Navy; Colonel L. H. Wranghan, of the Royal Marines; and Dr. Mark Benjamin, of the Central Scientific Office, Washington.

The crew were: Captain Kenneth Garden, of Coogie, Sydney, Australia; First Officer Geoffrey Panes, of Tunbridge, Kent; Radio Officer Samuel Walter Sydenham, of Edmonton, Alberta; and Flight-Engineer Charles Alvan Spence, of Little Neck, New York.

Berlin Off the Air at 8.15

Daily Mail Radio Station

Berlin radio went off the air at 8.15 last night, the earliest for weeks.

Before the end of the news programme the announcer broke in with an appeal to all listeners that the usual programme would be broadcast from the Breslau network.

It may have been a move to outwit the Voice That Will Butt In. Another possible explanation is R.A.F. or Soviet air activity.

U.S. Forces Issue

OIL-SHIP CRISIS FOR JAPAN

By FROOM TYLER, Daily Mail Foreign Editor.

TENSION has increased in Tokio as the first United States vessel laden with high-octane spirit for the Soviet Air Force approaches Japanese territorial waters.

To reach Russia's Far Eastern port of Vladivostok, American tankers must pass through the Tsugaru Strait, a channel linking the Sea of Japan with the Pacific, no more than ten miles wide at its narrowest point.

The Soviet Government recently warned Japan that any attempt to hinder the passage of petrol for Vladivostok would be regarded as "an unfriendly act."

This warning was a rejoinder to a Japanese protest made simultaneously to Moscow and Washington against the shipment of aviation fuel to Vladivostok.

That protest was renewed yesterday as the first United States Vladivostok-bound tanker entered Japanese waters.

While the vessel was approaching the Tsugaru Strait the following happenings were increasing tension in Tokio:

Omnibuses and taxis were ordered to run on "natural" gas and charcoal, petrol having been forbidden them by State ordinance.

Ex-Premier General Hayashi, as president of the Axis Development Association, a private organisation concerned with developing East Asia—was addressing a series of "admonitions" to the Premier, Prince Konoye, one of which invoked the "rights of self-defence of waters near Japan."

Formation of an "ocean safety zone" around Japan, presumably similar to the Western Hemisphere defence zone, was reported to be under consideration.

Japan's official spokesman was refusing all comment on Japanese-American relations, dismissing inquiries with: "The less said the better."

A dramatic situation has arisen this evening to reinforce the garrison in the Azores.
BACK PAGE—Col. FIVE

MINISTER IS ACCUSED BY T.U.C. MEMBER

CHARGES against a Cabinet Minister about his views on Russia, made by Mr. Jack Tanner at the Trades Union Congress at Edinburgh yesterday, were dealt with last night in a statement by the Ministry of Aircraft Production.

Mr. Tanner accused Col. Moore-Brabazon of having expressed the hope that the Russian and German armies would exterminate each other while we sat back and built up a dominating position in Europe.

"The allegations," says the Ministry, "are thought to arise from a passage in a recent extempore speech which was open to misinterpretation.

"Colonel Moore-Brabazon's views on Russia are those recently announced by him in public at Chertsey, when he said that everyone fighting there was fighting Britain's battle, and for that reason they should give all the help they could."

"By helping them they were helping themselves, for every title sacrificed against the Nazis was helping in our fight."
Report of the T.U.C. debate—Page THREE.

Poland Honours War Chiefs

Britain's Army and Air Chief—General Sir John Dill and Air Chief Marshal Sir Charles Portal—were decorated with the Grand Cross of Polonia Restituta (Poland Restored), by the Polish President, M. Rackiewicz last night. The decorations, said M. Rackiewicz, were symbols of our continued struggle for freedom.

Other British officers were made commanders and officers of the Order. Two Britons awarded the Polish Cross for Gallantry were missing from the birthday ceremony. Fl. Lt. W. H. Riddell, who rescued General Sikorski from France, was in London. The other, Cpl. G.M.S. W. A. Green, was "on active service."

Police May Stop Dances in Raids

If British towns suffer air raids this winter as heavy as those of last a dance curfew is likely to be imposed in local areas—by the police.

A Ministry of Home Security official said yesterday: "The police will decide whether the full cabaret, or dance floor must be cleared. The intensity of the raid, number of dancers, and size of the building will decide them."

3,853 Germans Die in RAF Raids

German radio declared in the foreign service last night, says A.P., that R.A.F. raids on Germany caused 3,853 deaths from the beginning of the war to August 20.

The number of injured was 9,445, the announcer added.

This Week for 19's

Reminder to the "nineteens." Men born between July 1 and December 31, 1922, both dates inclusive, must register for service next Saturday at their local labour exchange.

Those not yet 19 will not be called up before their birthday.

REPORT PROFITEERS

People who have been asked exorbitant prices for spare parts are invited by the Minister of War Transport to send him particulars.

RED TAPE IN COLD WATER

To Save Fuel

By Daily Mail Reporter

WHITEHALL — whose Civil Servants who have cheerfully protested workers in Britain —will not even be able to get into hot water this winter. The edict has gone out—everybody must wash their hands and faces in cold, to save fuel.

That nice warm wash before luncheon will become a memory. The other nice warm wash before going home will, in many cases, be postponed till the journey is over.

Night workers were exempt from the Spartan order. Stokers have been instructed by the Office of Works to supply warm water—if a strictly limited temperature—from 7 p.m. to 9 a.m.

The new rule applies to 400,000 Civil Servants in 16,000 Government buildings throughout the country.

Last winter each used up a ton of fuel. This consumption of 600,000 tons will be cut, not only by the hot water ban, but by limiting the temperature of the rooms to 60deg.

"Each degree above this heat puts up fuel consumption by 5 per cent.," an official said yesterday.

Experts claim that the best temperature of a living room is just over 60deg.

LATEST

RUSSIANS FLY ON TO WASHINGTON

Nome, Alaska, Tuesday.—The Russian Technical Mission to the United States, which arrived here yesterday, have left by flying boat for an average 500 miles to the south-east, on their way to Washington.—Reuter.

MORE TROOPS FOR AZORES

Lisbon, Tuesday. — Another contingent of troops left here this evening to reinforce the garrison in the Azores.—Exchange.

"You've made a V-man of me Mr. Barratt!"

"But you don't look as if you needed any V Campaign to make you believe in victory," I said, glancing at the fine physique and cheerful face of the man at my side as we walked homeward.

"No—not really," he replied, "but when you're having trouble with your feet, as I was about the time of Greece and Crete, every bit of bad news seems to get you down."

"That's true enough," I said.

"Well," he continued, "I was going to tell you—I walked into Barratts one day a pessimist, and walked out again—an optimist! You

simply don't know what the comfort of your shoes means to a man who lives on his feet all day!"

Don't I! For years I've been insisting on the importance of trouble-free feet. Now, I'd go as far as to say that no one has the right to be a "walking casualty." Anyway, there's no need. We mastered the art of easy, natural fit long ago at Barratts. And we're putting the same first-class materials and craftsmanship into our shoes as we've always done.

I'd welcome a line to Headquarters, if the war has put you out of touch with a Barratt branch.

Walk the **Barratt** way

Barratts, Northampton—and branches all over the country.

Britain's Harvest is in Danger

By PERCY W. D. IZZARD, Daily Mail Agricultural Correspondent

UNLESS there is more labour in the fields we shall lose a valuable percentage of our fine corn harvest, climax of the greatest production effort in our history.

The Ministry of Agriculture know this. They send out this week the message: "All hands to the harvest. Not an acre or a day must be wasted." I would have said, "Not an hour."

They are putting the case for Sunday work in the vital emergency of a ripe war-time harvest.

"Factory people are working double days a week to turn out the weapons of destruction that will enable us to win this war. Those whose calling lies more in the ways of peace will surely be doing no wrong if they also work on Sunday to secure the harvest under present conditions."

The War Office have agreed to lend military transport to help farmers in gathering the corn, when no other transport is available.

And the Board of Education are urging local authorities and school governors to keep schoolboy harvest camps open for an additional week or two.

IF a tragedy should happen the weather will be blamed. But it is by no means entirely the weather. It has already been announced, that one requirement is a plentiful supply of skilled labour at quick call. This harvest lacks that.

It is true there is a large amount of laid and twisted corn throughout the country, increasing and lengthening the work of saving it.

Skill and muscle are needed here. It is no task for jaded workers on holiday. It is beyond the power of the majority of land girls, valuable to work as they are, to set schoolboys to it would be farcical.

Thus weather and labour are involved together. The Women's Land Army are doing grand work, and many useful jobs are being done by voluntary effort in which all sections of the community are represented. But the crying need is for skilled men, and hundreds of farmers are in sore trouble because they have none.

WITHIN the last fortnight the National Farmers' Union have approached the Government on this matter.

They are thinking not only of the corn harvest, but also of the heavy winter's work before them and potatoes to follow it, and the plough is to be taken for 1942. The outlook alarms them.

This labour problem touches all Britain, and I hear that some Scottish farmers have been astonished to have unskilled men come to them offering their services for harvest at £5 and £6 a week.

That such a thing can happen is a telling commentary on the labour situation.

THE arrangement to give soldiers agricultural leave has not yet solved the problem. There is too much red tape in it, with the consequence that soldiers are not readily available.

Labour for this harvest must be at call to seize the odd hours if all the corn is to be got into stack.

Farmers are asking: "If skilled men can be obtained from the Forces to get coal, why can't farmers get skilled men to save their crops?"

The farmer's skilled men left him before the tie to the industry operated) to go to higher-paid work, or were taken into the Services. Thousands of them are in the Home Forces now.

It is in these men who are urgently needed as well.

The harvest is their food as well as that of civilians, and it is a moral obligation on the Government not to waste it. With these skilled men available to use the harvest through it can be saved.

CALM IN STRAIT

Fine weather continued in the Strait of Dover last night. The sea was calm under a blue sky. There was a light south-westerly breeze. Visibility was restricted by haze at mid-Channel.

RAF DESTROY 7,500 ENEMY PLANES

FIGHTERS of the R.A.F. have in the two years of the war destroyed 3,900 enemy aircraft for a loss of 1,400 fighters, the pilots of 450 being saved.

Anti-aircraft defences under the control of Fighter Command, including guns have destroyed 500 more.

These figures do not include the 3,000 enemy planes destroyed in the Middle East, on the Western Front up to Dunkirk, and in Norway and the theatres of war.

Together they represent a total of 7,500 enemy aircraft destroyed, in addition to the thousands destroyed

on the ground or so damaged that they were of no further use.

This year, says an Air Ministry review of the air war, the fighters and guns have accounted for over 1,600 German machines, 380 of them at night.

Since the large-scale daylight offensive against the Germans in Northern France began on June 14 the day fighters have shot down 446 of the enemy for the loss of 168 fighters.

There are now 15 fighter squadrons which have each shot down more than 100 enemy machines.

The leading pilot has destroyed

20 of the enemy, while four other pilots have brought down more than 15.

The leading pilot is believed to be Wing Commander A. G. Malan. The four "over 20's" are probably Squadron Leader J. Mungo Park (missing), Squadron Leader M. J. N. P. Pattle (missing), Squadron Leader Roland Tuck ; and Fit. Lt. E. S. Lock (missing).

One squadron of night Beaufighters has passed the 50 mark of enemy bombers destroyed.

Two Years' War at Sea—BACK Page.

Wheat Lost in Big U.S. Fire

SAN FRANCISCO, Tuesday.—One million pounds' worth of United States Government wheat awaiting shipment to China was burned out in a mysterious fire which destroyed the San Francisco granary export stores at Port Costa.—Exchange Telegraph.

Last month a big fire in New York harbour wiped out a pier where war supplies for Britain were loaded, and a big lumber yard in Philadelphia was burned out. In June a Jersey City river front fire did about £6,000,000 worth of damage.

Things to Come —by Berlin

Berlin radio last night broadcast a talk by a military commentator, in which he said :

"In widespread reconnaissance flights the German Air Force is now laying the groundwork for coming raids on England."

And Göring has taken over the preparations of plans for the invasion of England—according to a Tokio broadcast to-day, quoting a Berlin report.—B.U.P.

Ship Had Six Escorts But RAF Got Her

By Daily Mail Reporter

A FORCE of Blenheim bombers and Hurricane fighters yesterday found a German supply ship off Dunkirk. The weight of its escort was a tribute to the punishment the R.A.F. has inflicted on German shipping.

This one vessel was protected by fewer than six A.A. gun ships and four E-boats.

They and the shore batteries put up a tremendous fire, but the bombers drove through the barrage shells and hit the ship twice, leaving it enveloped in smoke.

A Hurricane squadron also dived and set one of the A.A. ships on fire. Other Hurricanes silenced the guns.

Not a German plane came out to join the fight, but on the way home an Australian Hurricane squadron found two Messerschmitts escorting E-boats.

The Australians set one of the E-boats on fire and shot down the two Me's.

A Flying Fortress of Bomber Command on reconnaissance bombed the German port of Bremen in the afternoon. Only two days before the port had been bombed by another Fortress on reconnaissance.

Beaufort planes of Coastal Command attacked an enemy convoy off the Norwegian coast yesterday at noon, and an Air Ministry communiqué. The largest vessel was hit by two torpedoes and probably destroyed. An escort vessel was also hit.

From all operations one Beaufort is missing.

'BRAZIL TO GET THE AZORES'

From Daily Mail Correspondent

NEW YORK, Tuesday.—Despatches from Brazil to-day hinted that the Portuguese Government may let left Rio de Janeiro is carrying with it Lisbon Brazil's reply to the reported suggestion that, backed by the United States, Brazil should take over the Azores and Cape Verde islands.

It is believed that the reply is favourable, but that no specific answer was given. Rio despatch to the New York Times said : "Of great significance may be the statement of Jose de Amaral, member of the Portuguese faction, who declared that the United States, Brazil, and Portugal were three Atlantic nations that must ensure their security."

St. Swithin's Total

Rain — 85in. of it — poured in London between St. Swithin's Day, July 15, and August 23. Forty days, and only 14 were rainless in London.

◀ NEWS CHRONICLE, LONDON, THURSDAY OCTOBER 23, 1941
More news from the Eastern Front, this time with Operation Typhoon, the German assault on Moscow. In fact, the Russian capital would be saved by a combination of Soviet reinforcements and fall rains that turned the ground to a sea of mud. Elsewhere, the *Chronicle* reflects growing pressures and discontent on the home front, with a Gallup poll critical of the British government's conduct of the war and an account of black-market racketeering. A small story also notes the death of England test cricketer Kenneth Farnes, killed during a night-flying exercise on duty with the R.A.F.

NEWS CHRONICLE, Thursday, October 23, 1941

STOMACH TROUBLE

LATE LONDON EDITION
News ☙ Chronicle

No. 29,785   THURSDAY, OCTOBER 23, 1941   RADIO PAGE 2   ONE PENNY

Best for Cooking — SIFTA SALT

Gallup Poll Sounds Britain on the Conduct of the War

ONLY 44% ARE SATISFIED: THE LOWEST YET

PUBLIC dissatisfaction with the conduct of events in this country since the German attack on Russia is reflected in the results of a Gallup poll taken within the last few days.

Two questions were asked. The first was:

DO YOU FEEL THAT BRITAIN HAS, OR HAS NOT, TAKEN FULL ADVANTAGE OF THE OPPORTUNITIES OFFERED BY THE GERMAN ATTACK ON RUSSIA?

The answers were:

	Per cent.
Has	29
Has not	49
Don't know	22

Less than a third of the public is thus of the opinion that all has been done that might have been done.

The second question was:

ARE YOU SATISFIED OR DISSATISFIED WITH THE GOVERNMENT'S CONDUCT OF THE WAR?

Here the answers were:

	Per cent.
Satisfied	44
Dissatisfied	38
Don't know	18

This result shows a remarkable drop in public satisfaction with the Government within the past four months, and since the German-Russian war has been in progress.

Last June, soon after Crete and before Hitler's attack on Stalin, this same question was asked, and the figures then showed that 58 per cent. were satisfied.

There has thus been a drop of 14 per cent. in the four months.

Altogether this question has been asked four times since the war began. The two other occasions were in November, 1939, when the results showed 61 per cent. satisfied, and in February, 1940, when the "satisfied" figure had fallen to 59 per cent.

The present figure of 44 per cent, thus registers both the lowest figure and the lowest "satisfied" percentage yet recorded.

M.P. CRITICS OF HOME SECRETARY

M.P.s are not satisfied with the attitude of Mr. Herbert Morrison towards a constitutional issue involving their rights and privileges, writes the Political Correspondent.

Unless plans are taken by the Home Secretary to clarify the position of members wishing to travel to any part of the British Isles in fulfilment of their duties a motion of censure against the Home Secretary will shortly be tabled.

No fresh application for a permit to travel to Ireland to investigate the reasons for the arrest of Mr. Cahir Healy, the Ulster M.P. detained under Regulation 18b, is to be made by Mr. J. McGovern, I.L.P. member for Shettleston.

Mr. McGovern was the centre of a stormy debate in the Commons on Tuesday, when Mr. Morrison was criticised by members of all parties for not granting him facilities to travel to Ulster and Eire.

PRISON VISIT

Mr. McGovern yesterday visited Mr. Healy in Brixton Prison and gave him an account of the debate.

Mr. McGovern told me afterwards:

"Mr. Healey emphasised that as an Ulster M.P. he refuses to recognise the authority of Mr. Morrison or his Advisory Council, and saw no reason for writing a letter—as suggested by the Home Secretary—in support of my application.

"I quite agree with his decision."

Ghost Voice Butts In Again

Listeners to the B.B.C. nine o'clock news heard, after an absence of two nights, the Ghost Voice interrupting again with its usual lack of originality.

When Bruce Belfrage, the announcer, said "Here is the news," the voice could think of nothing better than "The usual lies."

A Moscow claim that German attacks were repelled was met by a "variation on the same theme, "Moscow is wrong."

Other comments included "The Russians are losing," and "Too much talk."

The interjections were louder than previously, while the announcer seemed to be reading more deliberately than usual.

PUT OUT THAT WASTE PAPER

The drive for waste paper has started. Every scrap is needed, as was explained in Lord Beaverbrook's appeal yesterday.

Today, now, turn out your waste paper. Leave it for collection by the dustman.

If any reader sees that it is not being collected at once he should write to the News Chronicle, Bouverie Street, London, E.C.4, marking the letter "Waste Paper," and the proper authorities will be told.

KENNETH FARNES KILLED

Kenneth Farnes, the England, Cambridge and Essex fast bowler, was killed on Monday in a flying accident.

A pilot officer in the R.A.F., he went to Canada for training under the Empire scheme, was a given his wings, and returned to this country only a fortnight ago.

Farnes, who was on his birthday at University from 1931 to 1933, after going to the Royal Liberty School, Romford. A year after leaving Cambridge Farnes appeared in his first Test match against Australia.

NAZIS HALTED BEFORE FORTS OF MOSCOW
Battle For Don Basin Reaches Critical Stage

From DENIS WEAVER
News Chronicle Special Correspondent

STOCKHOLM, Wednesday.

BERLIN statements today that "the occupation of the Ukraine and the Donetz Basin is more important than Moscow" are interpreted by neutral observers here as an admission that Hitler's vast assault on the Russian capital—now three weeks old—has failed for the time being.

While there has now been 24 hours' silence concerning Moscow front progress on the part of Hitler's usually-voluble G.H.Q., Russian reports today announce local gains in the direction of Kalinen and state that the Nazi attack on Orel has been definitely broken.

Since these two points represent the extreme northern and southern claws of the enveloping movement, it appears certain that the Germans must rush up further reinforcements before hoping to achieve headway east of Mojaisk, their nearest approach to the capital yet and the point which marks the beginning of Moscow's outer defences.

While little is known of the strength of these defences, I understand they are at least as strong as Leningrad's and consist of a formidable chain of forts connected by intercommunicating trenches and including numerous large underground forts, whose construction was begun by Marshal Tukhashevsky in 1932 and developed and strengthened by Voroshilov.

The Hardest Nut For Panzers

They are likely to prove the hardest nut even the panzers have been called upon to try to crack, especially in forest country and with the thermometer dropping daily.

Reports reaching here suggest that the present lull on the central sector after three weeks of fantastic activity is due, quite simply, to "mutual exhaustion" since, while the German calap of incredible reserves of men, tanks, planes and supplies for what was to be—and was even claimed weeks ago to have been—the "final destruction of Russian military power," must be borne in mind, the Russian defence force also expended men and machines on a colossal scale.

It is equally clear to neutrals here, however, that a fresh assault on Moscow must be looked for, and soon—or the German army faces the winter without quarters.

New Assault on Moscow Likely

Noteworthy in this connection is the fact that Swedish newspaper comment, hitherto noncommittal, today speculates on Hitler's chances of seizing the Moscow stronghold before winter sets in, even suggesting that the possibility of failure would mean eventual retreat to German territory until the spring.

News from Russian sources today suggest that the Germans have failed to find the weak spot they sought in the Moscow front, since Orel—claimed by Berlin more than a week ago—has not fallen yet, while Russian counter-attacks around Mojaisk have set the ground strewn with dead and wounded Germans and blazing tanks.

Steel and snow have made the roads in this sector almost unusable, a foretaste of the immense help the winter weather may afford to hard-pressed Timoshenko.

Meanwhile the most critical battle is in progress for the Donetz Basin, where the Germans claim the capture of the town of Stalino, and both town and isthmus of Perekop, the last after being driven out by the Russians following its first "capture."

These claims are unsupported in reliable sources and appear improbable.

Even more doubtful is the further Berlin claim this afternoon that German troops have taken the town of Astrakhan, south of Perekop and the second isthmus leading to the Crimea.

Berlin messages contain assurances, probably for internal consumption mainly, that the Urals will be reached, and with this "the definite end of the war."

Turn to Back Page: Col. Six

MIDNIGHT SOVIET COMMUNIQUE SAID:—
Taganrog Falls, 35,000 German Casualties

The Russian communique issued at midnight read: "During October 22, our troops fought the enemy along the whole front.

"After many days of stubborn fighting, in the course of which the enemy lost about 35,000 men in killed and wounded, our troops evacuated Taganrog.

"On October 21 (Tuesday), 34 German planes were destroyed. Our losses were eight planes. Seventeen enemy planes were brought down near Moscow on October 21, and another 14 planes on October 22.

"Our squadrons on the Western front have dealt a number of heavy blows at enemy aerodromes during the past few days. Between October 11 and 18 alone, according to incomplete figures, about 500 German planes were destroyed on enemy aerodromes.

"On October 21, one of our air units on the Western front destroyed 80 German tanks, 180 lorries and two battalions of enemy infantry."

Eastern Campaign Has Made Hitler's Army in France Lose Heart

BY A SPECIAL CORRESPONDENT

Astonishing evidence, printed below, of the decline in the spirit of the German occupation troops in France was given to me yesterday by a neutral business man of high standing. He has spent half his life in France, has travelled recently in the occupied zone, and left Paris a few weeks ago, coming to England via Vichy.

SINCE Hitler's invasion of Russia conditions among German troops in occupied France appear to have changed entirely.

The rank and file continue to be more and more "fed up" and worried, but what is more serious for Hitler is that depression and discouragement has spread to the officers, and to many of them Hitler is no longer the "infallible" war lord.

As weeks and months passed the Nazi officers have been getting more and more critical and more worried.

WORM OF DEPRESSION

When I left Paris all I saw and heard, all the reliable reports I had, led me to the absolute conclusion that the German army of occupation is losing heart—I might say the officers more rapidly than the men.

One can see that the worm of depression has got into the fruit of the German military caste and is beginning to cause havoc.

Here are a few instances:

A few weeks ago a very high German officer who had just returned from the Russian front, chatted with two Frenchmen in Northern France, where he held an important command. One of the two Frenchmen was a senior officer whom he knew well.

WORSE THAN VERDUN

Asked for his impressions of the battles for Leningrad and Moscow, "the German officer said: "You were at Verdun like me... You know what a dreadful slaughter it was.... Well, the Russian front is a huge, immense Verdun, a hundred times worse.... Multiply Verdun a hundredfold and you will have an idea of the butchery."

---

100 FRENCH HOSTAGES FOR MURDERED NAZI

Petain and Darlan made urgent radio appeals to all French yesterday following the news that another German officer—a major at Bordeaux—had been shot dead in the street.

The Germans immediately seized 100 hostages. Earlier messages said 50 hostages seized would be shot today unless the major's murderers were found.

At the same time a curfew from 7 p.m. to 8 a.m. was clamped down on Bordeaux, and all cinemas and theatres were closed.

Fifty hostages were shot in Nantes yesterday for the assassination on Monday of the Nazi military commander of Nantes, and threat of death hangs over another 50 unless the two men who shot him are produced.

The 50 executed included 14 followers of General de Gaulle, recently arrested in Brittany and never tried.

Evidence that the Germans themselves lack faith in their terrible revenge was Darlan's dash to Paris to broadcast to the occupied zone.

"RANSOM IS HORRIBLE"

Petain, broadcasting in Vichy to unoccupied France, in voice trembling with emotion, declared: "Fifty Frenchmen this morning paid with their lives for those crimes without a name. Fifty more will be shot tomorrow if the culprits are not discovered.

"A stream of blood flows anew in France.

"Such ransom is horrible and does not bring the true culprits to light. Frenchmen, your task is clear. Help stop this killing.

"If one guilty man is found 100 French lives will be saved.

"I cry out to you about this in a broken voice. Don't let any more harm befall France."

PLOT, SAYS DARLAN

Darlan declared: "We believe these abominable acts are committed by agents of a foreign Power seeking to aggravate relations between the troops of occupation and the French population."

Four men who took part in the Bordeaux killing used the same tactics as the men who assassinated Colonel Holtz in Nantes on Monday.

Two held bicycles and followed their comrades as they stalked their major along the crowded Boulevard St. Georges and shot him in the back.

Then on their bicycles all four made their escape.

Italian Army Revolt Plot

From Our Own Correspondent

NEW YORK, Wednesday.—Reports that officers in the Italian Army are assuming the leadership of a movement aiming at eventual revolution to drive the Nazis and their Fascist servants from Italy have reached Washington.

It is stated that the army is sabotaging Mussolini's orders that troops should be dispatched to help Hitler.

Mussolini is said to have caused the arrest within the last ten days of most of the higher officials in the Sicilian administration.

An Old Horse is Bought for £4 And Sold for £22
BLACK MARKETEERS' NEW RACKET
By the Political Correspondent

FRUIT and vegetable racketeers, tracked down by the Ministry of Food, have rushed into a new line of business—the sale of horseflesh for human consumption at enormous profits.

Complaints about the racket are pouring into food offices, and the Ministry of Food is considering how to bring the ramp to an end. A new order may shortly be issued to curb the activities of this new black market.

Investigation has shown that horses of great use and value are being slaughtered to swell profits.

200 PER CENT. PROFIT

An example of dealings of this black market organisation was given to me yesterday. A horse, old and broken down, was bought for £4 before the war. It recently passed to the black market for £22, and when killed and distributed to the retailers the racketeers netted a profit of over 200 per cent.

Mr. Evelyn Walkden, M.P., yesterday asked the Ministry of Food to issue an order preventing the price and sale of horseflesh for human consumption.

In a Parliamentary question he asked if the Ministry was aware that since an order fixing the price of raw meat for dogs, cats and other domestic animals at 6d. per lb. became effective such meat was almost unobtainable.

PROFITS ARE THERE

He added that a number of retail shops known as "Pussy Butchers or Bonzo Butchers," had stopped dealing in meat or food for animals, and had transferred their businesses to sell only horseflesh for human consumption at prices up to 1s. 6d. per lb.

LONDON BLACK-OUT
6.21 p.m.—7.8 a.m.
Moon sets, 8.14 p.m.
Full Moon, November 4

Night Raider Down in Flames

An enemy raider was brought down in flames near a West Midland town last night.

H.E.s and incendiaries were dropped over wide areas, but the raid up to a late hour had nowhere developed on a large scale.

Heavy gunfire was heard on the outskirts of an East Midland town, where a few incendiaries fell. A stick of bombs fell near an East Anglian town.

R.A.F. bombers crossed the coast after dark, and within five minutes appeared to be bombing Calais and Dunkirk and objectives farther inland.

Two vivid flashes suggesting big explosions at Boulogne were noticed by a heavy anti-aircraft barrage.

Day fighters patrolling Northern France and the Channel attacked a German aerodrome and two small vessels. None of our aircraft is missing.

One Firm Makes Tank Every 45 Minutes

One 12-ton tank is now being produced every 45 minutes by the American Car and Foundry Company.

The company has now produced 2,000 tanks, 1,000 of them since August 1.

NATIONAL SAVINGS GROUP

Did you MACLEAN your teeth to-day?

Map of the Don Basin area. The Germans, Denis Weaver points out, have already complained of "the pitiless cold."

▶ THE FINAL GERMAN PUSH for Moscow began on November 15–19, when sub-zero temperatures had firmed up the ground, but the condition of the attacking units was poor. Some panzer divisions were down to 17 operational tanks each.

Chicago Daily Tribune
THE WORLD'S GREATEST NEWSPAPER

VOLUME C.—NO. 263   MONDAY, NOVEMBER 3, 1941.—32 PAGES   PRICE TWO CENTS

NAZIS TAKE CRIMEAN CAPITAL

Bears' Rally Fails; Packers Win, 16 to 14

WPA RELIEFERS GET 59 CENTS OF EACH $1 SPENT

Administration Eats Rest, Study Shows.

BY JOHN FISHER.

GREEN BAY GOES INTO 1ST PLACE; 46,484 AT GAME

F.D.R. ASSIGNS COAST GUARD TO NAVAL SERVICE

Transfer Effected by Executive Order.

NEWS SUMMARY of The Tribune

THEIR REAL WAR AIMS

NOW I CAN REBUILD AMERICA THE WAY I WANT IT!

WAR PARTY RIDES U. S. TO BRINK OF UNDECLARED WAR

BY ARTHUR SEARS HENNING.

AIM NEW DRIVE AT SEVASTOPOL, BIG NAVAL BASE

Air Bombs Set Fires in Black Sea Port.

BERLIN, Nov. 2.

Battle to Save 2 Policemen Shot in Tavern

CIO LAUNCHES DRIVE TO ENROLL MILLION ON FEDERAL PAY ROLL

Traps 5 Police in Flat; Law Gets Last Say

$10,000 IN CASH PRIZES!
For Naming the STATE CAPITALS!
FREE to Everyone!
SEE PAGE 14

▲ CHICAGO DAILY TRIBUNE, MONDAY NOVEMBER 3, 1941

The self-proclaimed World's Greatest Newspaper had a reputation for journalistic scoops— and for errors. After the presidential election of 1948, the *Tribune* famously declared "Dewey Defeats Truman." The announcement of the fall of Sevastopol turned out to be premature: the Crimean city withstood a siege of 250 days before it fell in July 1942. The city's fate, however, only just trumps what turned out to be the season's only defeat for the Chicago Bears, on track for their second National Football League (NFL) championship in a row.

Daily Express

No. 12,947   Saturday, November 22, 1941   One Penny

Libya battle goes 'extremely well': Enemy tank losses
(130 German, 50 Italian) are treble ours: deep advances

ROMMEL SURROUNDED

Germans must fight way out or surrender to British

R.A.F. DESTROYS SUPPLY PLANES

EXPRESS SPECIAL CORRESPONDENT   CAIRO, SATURDAY MORNING.

EARLY TODAY A CAIRO MILITARY SPOKESMAN GAVE OUT THE TREMENDOUS NEWS THAT GENERAL ROMMEL'S TANK FORCES IN LIBYA ARE SURROUNDED. BROKEN INTO TWO GROUPS, THEY ARE TRYING DESPERATELY TO BREAK OUT OF THE BRITISH RINGS, BUT ALL THE TIME THEIR POSITION IS BECOMING "MORE UNFAVOURABLE."

The larger group is in the Gambut-Fort Capuzzo area near the Egyptian frontier. The smaller one is south of Tobruk.

Three separate attacks were made by the Germans about 45 miles west of Fort Capuzzo in an effort to smash through. Each time they were beaten back with substantially heavier tank losses than those of the British.

The greatest desert battle ever fought is at its height. It is going "extremely well for General Cunningham and the initiative remains with the British."

Tank casualties generally are three to one in our favour. On the vast battlefield between the Egyptian frontier and Tobruk Rommel has lost 50 per cent. of his strength.

In Cairo, it is pointed out that the German forces east of Tobruk must either attempt to fight through the British lines and join the Axis troops west of Tobruk — or surrender.

It would be most difficult for them to smash through on the south and east, while Tobruk is still the formidable barrier which the Axis has been trying to break down for seven months.

POUNDED BY NAVY

The Germans, who have few ways of receiving supplies, are meanwhile being pounded by the Navy. Transport planes try to take up material which cannot be got over the bombed and shot away German land lines, but the R.A.F. is taking heavy toll of them. Some planes with trains of loaded gliders set out from Crete, flying only 500 feet above the sea. They met a similar end.

Co-operation between our air and ground forces is particularly close. The Army speaks in the highest terms of the very active assistance of the R.A.F. during the tank battles. Performance of American tanks has proved first-class.

Earlier, the communiqué from General Auchinleck's headquarters announced the destruction of 130 German tanks.

It said: The battle in Cyrenaica was joined in earnest yesterday (Thursday) afternoon. Following their rapid advance on the two previous days, our armoured forces on November 20 engaged German tanks in strength in the vicinity of Sidi Rezegh (16 miles from Tobruk's outer defence lines).

After losing 70 tanks and 33 armoured cars the German forces withdrew, leaving several hundred prisoners in our hands.

FINALLY DRIVEN OFF

Between this area and Sidi Omar (on the frontier) a further British armoured formation came into action against yet another concentration of German tanks which had advanced southwards from the Bardia-Gambut area.

During the first action on November 19 the enemy sustained 26 tank casualties against 20 of our own.

Yesterday morning the action was resumed, as the result of which the enemy was finally driven off in a north-easterly direction, losing a further 34 tanks.

In the Bir el Gobi area (40 miles south of Tobruk) the situation is less clear, except for the fact that an Italian armoured division originally deployed in this area has apparently exerted no influence on the battle now proceeding.

It will be remembered that this Italian armoured division was attacked and severely handled by British armoured forces on November 18, during their initial advance towards Sidi Rezegh.

Heavy pressure continues to be exerted upon the enemy holding defences between Halfaya (Hellfire Pass) and Sidi Omar.

"MAIN LINE" THREAT

Meanwhile, Imperial forces supported by further British tank formations are steadily making ground northward in a movement west of the latter locality.

In other parts of this huge battle arena, strong British armoured and mechanised columns have made deep penetrations in a number of directions all threatening the enemy's main line of communications.

Throughout yesterday our air forces were active over the whole battle area. Fighter sweeps engaged enemy formations attempting to bomb our armoured forces, and intercepted enemy reconnaissance aircraft.

Our fighters also attacked enemy dive-bombers at their base with great success.

Our bombers carried out repeated attacks upon the two main enemy armoured concentrations.

Their support of our own armoured forces about Sidi Rezegh was particularly effective. At least 24 enemy aircraft were destroyed and many severely damaged.

Drizzle

Dover Straits last night : Drizzle.

GAINS ALL ALONG

Airfield pilots captured

Express War Reporter ALAN MOOREHEAD

With the British Army, Thursday (delayed).

BRITISH and Axis armies are locked together now at three main points. One is at Bir el Gobi, the second is at Sidi Rezegh, the third is in the direction of Fort Capuzzo.

At noon today the position was this—

GOBI: A division of Italian tanks gave battle to one arm of our armoured forces.

Fifty Italian tanks — one brigade—were wiped out. Their crews were killed. Burned-out steel carcases are lying out there in the sand for any one to see.

This happened yesterday. The Germans rushed down armoured reinforcements overnight and with them now our tanks are in battle.

REZEGH: The second branch of the British armoured force arose upon an airfield in murky, rainy weather yesterday and captured 19 German aircraft, mostly Stukas, which were caught unawares.

FLUNG BACK

Fifty Germans—pilots and ground crews—were taken prisoner.

The enemy this morning made an infantry attack in an attempt to regain the airfield. They were flung back, and fighting now rages in the direction of Tobruk.

CAPUZZO: About 100 German tanks stole south from the coast. Their object being to damage our flank and force an unexpected battle.

The third branch of our armoured force went out to meet them.

These were American tanks and here for the miles away I watched them go into battle for the first time.

They have emerged this morning in command of the battle-field with 15 enemy tanks destroyed for certain and the rest in retreat.

That, briefly, was the situation two days after we had made contact with the enemy.

The essential point is that Rommel has decided to stand and fight it out.

We are now only on the offensive, gaining ground all the time.

Our aim is to wipe out the German armoured formations, and our

▶ BACK PAGE, COL. SIX

PETAIN TO MEET HITLER

Express Staff Reporter

NEW YORK, Friday.

INFORMATION in Washington today is that Marshal Petain and Admiral Darlan are to meet Goering in Occupied France next week, and then go on to meet Hitler.

Object of these conferences is believed to be a German demand for further Axis "protection" of French North Africa, in return for concessions to Petain in Occupied France.

Reports from France following the dismissal of General Weygand as Vichy Delegate-General in Africa, indicate that Petain will be unable to count on the support of Weygand's army in any deal Petain may conclude with Hitler.

A German radio message picked up in New York refers to "anxiety over the arrival of British reinforcements at Sierra Leone." The German message adds: "According to latest reports six more British warships have anchored at Freetown, and 26 British troop-transports, complete with ground personnel, are said to have been landed."

▶ BACK PAGE, COL. FOUR

Convoy reaches Archangel

From 'WALTER KERR'
(Express and N.Y. Herald-Tribune Reporter)

ARCHANGEL, Friday

A LONG line of heavily escorted merchant ships pulled alongside the docks of Archangel recently after a trip through Arctic waters.

4 A.M. LATEST

NAZIS ON DEFENSIVE IN KARELIA

MOSCOW, Friday.—On certain sections of Karelian front Germans and Finns have been forced on defensive, but they are fighting fiercely to capture one important position, says Moscow newspaper Red Star. A battalion of Finnish troops launched against the objective yesterday were forced to retreat to their original positions after heavy fighting, leaving many killed and wounded.—B.U.P.

bearing munitions of war from Great Britain to the Soviet Union.

On the snow-covered wharves were Russian troops ready to help in the unloading of airplanes, tanks and ammunition. They stared at the ships, pointed to the huge crates lashed to the decks and then went on with their jobs.

Our last day at sea was passed in a channel of thin ice that moved sluggishly with the tide and the current of the North Dvina River, where it empties into the White Sea between solid masses of ice on the banks.

Skies were overcast, and the thermometer registered ten degrees of frost.

Behind us were days of steady sailing from England. During those days no one German submarine, surface ship or bomber challenged the convoy.

24-HOUR GUNS

It probably would have been suicide to have tried. The escort vessels and the merchantmen were well armed, and their guns were manned 24 hours a day by crew and "passengers."

The passengers included several Russian officers, two members of the R.A.F. British tank experts, a few Polish officers and five newspapermen, three of them Americans.

The important fact is that the convoy got through, and the munitions it brought are significant. In Russia now will be Hurricane fighter planes equipped with their own guns and their own ammunition.

There are British-made tanks—enough of them to be of great value for a time in some sector of the front. There are sub-machine-guns from the U.S.A., tons of warm clothing and tons of food.

(World Copyright)

'Relief of Tobruk any minute'

A ADMIRAL OF THE FLEET SIR DUDLEY POUND, First Sea Lord, speaking at Bath last night, said:—

"Just before I came to this meeting I was told it was expected that Tobruk would be relieved almost immediately."

He added that the word "relieve" was entirely wrong.

"It is," he said, "a case of Tobruk bursting forth at a very inconvenient moment for the Germans."

Enemy admits 'Extremely strong attack'

Express Radio Station

BOTH Berlin and Rome last night paid tribute to Britain's great push in Libya.

Said a military spokesman in Berlin : "An extremely strong offensive; it cannot be regarded purely as a propaganda affair." Asserted Bremen Radio : "Britain appears to be charging up a blind alley."

MOODY MARIUS

Said the Italian News Agency Stefani : "Britain is employing superior forces."

Moody Marius—Marius Appellius, Italy's Radio Talker No. 1—did most of the talking from Rome. It began as a gay talk, but developed into an uneasy and cautious warning in mournful tones. Said Marius :

"It is a long war and a very hard war, and what is more, we are all in it this time. Either we all win or we lose, and lose everything."

"It is quite possible that the enemy will make progress in such and such a sector."

"KNOWS ALL"

"But don't draw any conclusions from the initial stages of the Libyan campaign. You can have complete confidence in the Axis troops in Africa, whose command has foreseen everything and has left nothing to chance."

"Victory is certain. One day—one fine day—the streets of London will yet hear the rhythm of marching Axis troops."

The Italian communiqué said : There were further developments on the Libyan front on Thursday.

"After having tenaciously held the enemy attack, our troops counter-attacked and repulsed the enemy armoured units, destroying numerous tanks and capturing prisoners.

"On the Tobruk front, there were violent artillery duels."

AXIS LOSE ONE TANK IN SEVEN

Express Military Reporter MORLEY RICHARDS

THE tank test has begun. British tanks v. German tanks.

There can be no doubt at all from last night's communiqué that thus far the Imperial panzers have come off best.

Destruction of 130 German tanks and approximately 50 Italian, means that General Rommel has lost practically one - seventh of his total strength.

It includes some 400 Italian tanks.

"There are roughly 400 tanks in a division, and Rommel possesses three—two Nazi and one Italian.

---

2 A.M. COMMENTARY

ing from Bardia was wheeling around to the south-west with the intention of joining the main force when the Imperial columns caught them.

This is the proof that our attack did achieve complete surprise. The enemy could not get out of the way in time and are being struck before the two divisions could unite.

Having gone round the rear of Sidi Omar it now becomes plain that General Cunningham's columns are driving towards the road that will cut the 17-mile gap between Tobruk and Bardia. The effect of this would be to bar isolating both enemy garrisons.

The communiqué does not say where the other Axis main communications have been threatened, but British tanks, keeping up their 80-mile-a-day dash, were

▶ BACK PAGE, COL. FOUR

The Italians were south of Tobruk and have obviously gone off westwards with the probable hope of linking up with Rommel's 15th Division in the vicinity.

Evidently the 21st Division mov-

---

69 to 14 is R.A.F.'s score in battle

Express Air Reporter BASIL CARDEW

THE Imperial air forces, in their third night and day of battle in Cyrenaica, established nearly a three to one superiority in planes destroyed, according to the R.A.F. official Middle East communiqué last night.

Twenty-four enemy machines were shot down or smashed up against the loss of nine of ours. Our score to date is 69 to 14.

The communiqué names Me. 110 fighters and Ju. 88 bombers, and large formations of Stuka dive-bombers escorted by Me. 109s. Against all these our fighters were particularly successful, making the kind of sweeps the Germans know so well in Northern France.

In the late afternoon of Thursday day, Royal Australian Air Force planes combined with Fleet Air Arm machines in tackling the big formation of Me. 109 fighters sky-diving down, sunning the Ju. 87 bombers. The fighters were severely mauled, many severely damaged, and were unable to keep the attackers off the Junkers. So two dived down.

One bomber party found numbers of dispersed 20-seater Ju. 52 troop-carriers standing on the ground. Two were left blazing and many others damaged.

Another group of our air attack went to Derna, Bardia, Benghazi, and Tripoli, North African ports.

Long-range bombers formed the third air raid, attacking Messina, the air and sea port in Sicily, and Naples, and Brindisi, convoy despatch centres.

Blenheims attacked shipping in the Gulf of Sirte, flying down through intense fire. Bombs dropped from mast height left a 3,000-ton vessel listing heavily, and a schooner low in the water.

OPINION

By the First Lord

Mr. A. V. Alexander, First Lord of the Admiralty, praised yesterday's Daily Express Opinion column when he spoke at a luncheon of the City Livery Club.

Given the use of sea power, he said, we could choose a theatre of war in which we could strike best, and through sea power we should bring this tremendous struggle to the end we all desired.

Mr. Alexander added that his listeners would no doubt have seen the remarkable article in the Daily Express, which put the case extremely well and which was sound, thoughtful, and constructive.

Report on Back Page.

Malta scatters them

MALTA, Friday.—A communiqué issued today said : In the last 24 hours the alert sounded six times when enemy aircraft crossed the coast. The bombs dropped caused no damage, but one serious casualty. One plane is believed to have been shot down, three were damaged.—A.P.

(Map caption labels:)
DERNA · BOMBED BY R.A.F. · OUR FIGHTERS DESTROY 15 PLANES · BENGHAZI AND TRIPOLI ALSO BOMBED · Martuba · Bomba · Timimi · AUSTRALIAN AND NAVAL AIRMEN STRAFE ALONG COAST · MEKILI · Gazala · TOBRUK · BOMBED BY R.A.F. · Gud el Ahmar · Acroma · Rezegh · Gambut · El Adem · S Ayes · BARDIA · 70 GERMAN TANKS WIPED OUT · Ft Capuzzo · SOLLUM · Tengeder · 24 GERMAN PLANES SHOT DOWN · Bir el Gobi · 60 NAZI TANKS DESTROYED · SIDI OMAR · Gobi Saleh · Ft Sheferzen · Ft Maddalena · CYRENAICA · EGYPT · Burfares · 0 10 20 · 50 · Miles

GERMANS BREAK RUSSIAN LINE AT TULA IN NEW MOSCOW THRUST: PAGE 4

▲ DAILY EXPRESS, LONDON, SATURDAY NOVEMBER 22, 1941

The *Express* reports the initial successes of Operation Crusader in Libya, but despite its suggestion that the Germans might surrender, General Erwin Rommel managed to escape, albeit with heavy casualties. As the front-page map underlined, however, the Allied advance had relieved the besieged port of Tobruk.

Crusader
NOVEMBER 1941

ROMMEL'S FIRST OFFENSIVE IN NORTH AFRICA IN SPRING 1941 TOOK HIM TO THE FRONTIER OF EGYPT. ATTEMPTS TO DISLODGE HIM EARLY IN THE SUMMER (OPERATION BATTLEAXE) failed, but there was a thorn in Rommel's side—the port of Tobruk with its garrison of mainly Australian troops lay behind his front line. The siege of Tobruk became of absorbing interest to the British public.

COUNTERATTACK

The British Eighth Army in Egypt launched Operation Crusader on November 18 to relieve Tobruk by striking into Cyrenaica. British light tanks suffered serious losses in various engagements with the Germans near Sidi Rezegh, southeast of Tobruk, from November 19 to 23. On November 22, the Tobruk garrison attacked besieging Italian units in order to link up with the Eighth Army advancing to relieve it. General Erwin Rommel then struck at the Allied flank, but sustained heavy losses. By November 26, 13th Corps' New Zealand Division had cleared a corridor between Tobruk and 30th Corps. Rommel's Axis forces eventually fell back west, thus relieving the immediate pressure on Tobruk, although fighting between the two sides continued. However, the British had saved the strategically vital Suez Canal from falling into German hands.

GOOD TIDINGS

At a time of darkening news, with German forces seemingly poised to take the Soviet capital city of Moscow, and news of the Japanese attack on Pearl Harbor coming through, the relief of Tobruk came as a great morale-booster.

 SOUTH AFRICAN TROOPS about to clear German troops from a building during Operation Crusader, the British attempt to relieve Tobruk.

Pearl Harbor

DECEMBER 7, 1941

MANY AMERICANS WERE WARY ABOUT THE GROWING TENSION BETWEEN JAPAN AND THE UNITED STATES. STILL, IT CAME AS A SHOCK TO MOST TO LEARN OF the Japanese attack on the U.S. Navy base at Pearl Harbor on Oahu in Hawaii early on the morning of Sunday December 7, 1941. Two waves of fighters and bombers launched from aircraft carriers attacked the U.S. Pacific Fleet at its moorings. The raid sank or damaged eight battleships, three cruisers, three destroyers, and a minelayer. Some 188 aircraft were destroyed, most on the ground, and nearly 2,500 people died.

DATE OF INFAMY

Next day, President Roosevelt addressed the U.S. Congress and called December 7 "a date which will live in infamy." Within an hour, Congress declared war on Japan. When Hitler declared war a few days later, the United States was also dragged into the war in Europe.

Many Europeans and Americans had long hoped for direct U.S. involvement in combat. Indeed, theories still exist that Roosevelt was aware of the impending attack at Pearl Harbor but did nothing to prevent it in order to have an excuse to join the war. Most commentators discount such a theory. The attack left the United States facing long years of war. Three days later, British prime minister Winston Churchill reacted to news of the Japanese sinking of the British battleships *Repulse* and *Prince of Wales* by saying "In all the war I never received a more direct shock." The Japanese would soon become supreme over the Pacific.

STRATEGIC DEFEAT

For the Japanese, the Pearl Harbor raid was a tactical victory—but it would prove to be a strategic defeat. The attack had damaged the Pacific Fleet, but had not destroyed it. All three fleet carriers were at sea on exercises and therefore survived to form the heart of a new fleet. More significantly, the United States had entered the war and would turn into a military and economic giant in the next four years.

▲ U.S NAVY SHIPS BURN AT PEARL HARBOR. The damage inflicted on the U.S Pacific Fleet was not fatal (all three fleet carriers were absent from Pearl Harbor on the day of the attack).

The Honolulu Advertiser   December 7, 1941 - 1

The Honolulu Advertiser

SOUVENIR EDITION

SPECIAL EXTRA

Hawaii's Territorial Newspaper

HONOLULU, HAWAII U.S.A.   SUNDAY, DECEMBER 7, 1941

JAPANESE BOMB PEARL HARBOR!

Hickam, Wheeler, Kaneohe Hit

The USS Arizona, burning after her forward magazines exploded, sank with nearly 1,200 hands lost.

'When I Came to, the Ship Was a Mass of Flames...'

Eyewitness Accounts of Brutal Bombing From Around Oahu

Officers were eating breakfast aboard the USS Arizona when a short signal on the ship's air raid alarm sounded.

"As I was running forward on the starboard side of the quarterdeck . . . I was apparently knocked out by the blast of a bomb," said Lt. Cmdr. S.G. Fuqua, the senior surviving officer.

The bomb was one of eight that hit the 26-year-old battleship.

"When I came to, and got up off the deck, the ship was a mass of flames amidships on the boat deck," he said.

Fuqua said he tried to extinguish flames in the gun turrets, but found the water mains had no water. Seventy wounded men were taken from the ruptured decks and sent to hospitals before Fuqua ordered all hands to abandon ship at 9 a.m.

Horrendous injuries

Wounded victims poured into the Army's Tripler General Hospital. Corridors were soon jammed with the wounded and dying, many left on the floor.

The injuries came from shrapnel wounds suffered as bombs fell; direct hits from machine-gun strafing by enemy planes; and our own anti-aircraft fire. Chunks of metal were lodged in necks, in chests, through legs.

Because of a severe shortage of gowns, bandages, anesthesia and other medical supplies like amputating saws, surgeons made do with what they could for the first part of the day. They lifted stretchers themselves when orderlies weren't available, held broken bones together on the way to surgery when there were no splints, and, in one instance, held open a vessel being catheterized, with a finger.

Abandon ship

Aboard the USS Utah, the

Blood Donors Are Urgently Needed

An urgent call for blood to be used in transfusions has been made by Queen's Hospital.

Any person willing to donate blood is asked to make his way to the hospital and go to the fourth floor.

flag was being raised as the first planes were spotted.

"Immediately thereafter, the air was filled with planes . . . clearly distinguished with Rising Sun insignia on the fuselage and red wingtips . . . flying low . . . and dropping aerial torpedoes and bombs," said S.S. Isquith, lieutenant commander of the Utah.

Isquith said the battleship was hit underwater and began to list. After a second underwater hit, he realized the ship would capsize and ordered all hands to abandon ship.

Fire all too real

Francis Ordenstein was playing football outside his family's (See Back Page, Col. 1.)

Martial Law Is Declared for Territory

Civilians Arrested

Faced with the prospect of invasion and sabotage, Gov. Joseph B. Poindexter today declared the Territory of Hawaii to be under martial law.

Censorship is in place, a blackout and curfew have been imposed and all citizens are commanded to obey orders of military officials.

Some suspected enemy agents or sympathizers have already been arrested and detained under martial law rules.

Lt. Gen Walter C. Short, commanding general of the Hawaiian Department, urged Poindexter to declare the state of emergency during a meeting in the governor's office at Iolani Palace shortly after noon.

The governor, after a radio telephone consultation with President Roosevelt, agreed.

Short becomes military gov- (See Back Page, Col. 6)

MORE THAN 2,000 DIE IN SNEAK AIR ATTACK

Scores of low-flying Japanese planes swooped down on Oahu from the north 90 minutes after dawn today in a surprise attack, raining bombs and terror on Pearl Harbor and other military installations.

When it was over, the huge U.S. Pacific Fleet lay crippled at' anchor and military air fields were heavily damaged.

The air raid by planes with the Rising Sun emblem of Japan clearly visible on their wingtips left more than 2,000 American soldiers, sailors and Marines dead or missing and more than 1,000 grievously injured.

The attackers poured their fury of bombs and torpedoes primarily on military facilities.

In Honolulu, bomb or artillery fragments rained down on civilian populations, leveling two housing areas more than two miles apart, and blowing up bits of houses far from the military bases. A bomb or errant shell fell near Iolani Palace, creating a crater on the Palace grounds.

Dozens of civilians are believed dead due to enemy action, explosions, fires and mishaps in the wake of the attack.

President Roosevelt announced the attack to the nation, and is expected to ask for a declaration of war on Japan tomorrow in an address to a joint session of Congress. Earlier today, the Territory of Hawaii was put under martial law.

Tonight, a tense, blacked-out Hawaii braces' for further attack or even an invasion of the Islands. The whereabouts of the Japanese fleet that is believed to have launched this morning's raids remain unknown, officials said.

Battleships ravaged

The Japanese warplanes spent their greatest fury on the big ships berthed around Ford Island.

A huge armor-piercing bomb blew up the USS Arizona, enveloping its bow in oil-fed flames. The battleship sank in less than nine minutes, entombing nearly 1,000 sailors and Marines in a watery grave. Another 200 were lost on deck.

Torpedoes ripped through the USS Oklahoma, rolling her over and imprisoning more men within.

The battleships California and West Virginia, wrapped in flames, sank at their moorings. The target ship Utah capsized with many of its crewmen still aboard.

Harbor horror chamber

Within minutes, the fiery, oil-laden harbor was turned into a watery horror chamber of broken and burned bodies. Men in varying states of shock and injury jumped from their ships and swam to boats or nearby shores to cheat death.

Navy boat crews searched the waters around the burning ships and made countless trips

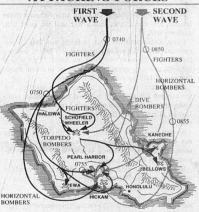

ROUTE OF ATTACKING FORCES

FIRST WAVE

SECOND WAVE

0740

0850

FIGHTERS

FIGHTERS

HORIZONTAL BOMBERS

0750

HALEIWA

FIGHTERS

SCHOFIELD WHEELER

DIVE BOMBERS

KANEOHE

0855

TORPEDO BOMBERS

PEARL HARBOR

0755

BELLOWS

EWA

HONOLULU

HORIZONTAL BOMBERS

HICKAM

FLASH BULLETIN

Japan declares a state of war

United Press reported that Tokyo radio has declared that a state of war exists between Japan and British and United States Forces in the Pacific. Japanese forces also attacked in Malaya, the Philippines, Hong Kong, Midway, Wake and Guam, according to news service reports.

Five U.S. Navy planes shot down

HONOLULU — Anti-aircraft batteries opened fire on a squadron of six U.S. Navy planes approaching Ford Island just before 9 p.m., shooting down five of them. At least three of the six Navy pilots are dead. The planes, launched off the carrier USS Enterprise, were landing after searching in vain for the Japanese fleet.

Stimson orders Army into uniform

WASHINGTON — Secretary of War Henry L. Stimson tonight ordered the entire U.S. Army into uniform — 1,600,000 men, including thousands of officers and men on duty in administrative posts who have been allowed civilian clothes.

(See Back Page, Col.1)

◀ THE HONOLULU ADVERTISER, HAWAII, SUNDAY DECEMBER 7, 1941
Within hours of the attack at Pearl Harbor on the island of Oahu, Hawaii's local newspaper had rushed out a special souvenir edition with accurate details of the attacks and eyewitness accounts of the bombing. The aftermath of the attack was still unfolding: the front page contains an urgent call for blood donors to help the wounded. There is also a first reference to the arrest of civilians: Japanese immigrants or Americans of Japanese ancestry were treated with great suspicion. In Hawaii, many Nisei, or second-generation Japanese Americans, volunteered for the U.S. armed forces in a remarkable display of loyalty.

▲ TOKYO NICHINICHI, TOKYO, MONDAY DECEMBER 8, 1941

The Japanese public learn of the attack on Pearl Harbor in reports that faithfully repeat the patriotic line of the militaristic government: "East Asian Troubles: UK–U.S. Hostilities Reach Peak. Firm Strike the Only Course. Natural Culmination of Nation's Fury. Giant Step toward Sacred Mission. It is clear that despite some advances in Japan–U.S. negotiations, major progress toward the sacred mission to win the war in China and establish the Greater East Asian Co-Prosperity Sphere, part of the great national plan for an impregnable empire, can only be achieved by sweeping the hostile maneuverings of Britain and the USA from the East Asian region, and this is the sentiment of all in our united nation."

▲ THE SUN, NEW YORK, WEDNESDAY DECEMBER 10, 1941

The news from the Pacific was stark, with Japanese victories over Britain's Royal Navy, traditionally the world's strongest maritime power. *The Sun* also covers U.S. preparations for war on the home front, with reports of an air-raid scare in New York, and details of a state-wide blackout rehearsal organized by Governor Herbert H. Lehman.

Defeat at Moscow

DECEMBER 1941

OPERATION TYPHOON, THE GERMAN OFFENSIVE TO CAPTURE MOSCOW, HAD BEGUN ON SEPTEMBER 30. ALTHOUGH DELAYED BY AUTUMN RAINS AND RED ARMY RESISTANCE, the Germans had got to within 20 miles (32 km) of Moscow on November 27. Now, however, unusually early winter weather (for which the Wehrmacht was ill equipped) proved too much and the panzer divisions ground to a halt.

RED ARMY ASSAULT

Then, on December 5, Marshal Zhukov led a counterattack around Moscow, using fresh troops partly brought in from the Soviet Far East, with reserves of new tanks (including the T-34, superior to any German machines) and with much better winter clothing.

German commanders on the ground immediately realized the danger of the position that they now found themselves in. They quickly requested permission to withdraw, which was denied

them by Adolf Hitler. On December 17, 1941, Hitler issued an order to all German soldiers on the Eastern Front: "Major withdrawal movements cannot be made. They will result in the complete loss of heavy weapons and equipment. Under the personal leadership of commanders and officers alike, the troops are to be forced to put up a fanatical resistance in their lines, regardless of any enemy breakthrough in their flanks and rear. Only this kind of fighting will win the time we need to move up the reinforcements I have ordered from the home country and the west." As the Soviet counter-offensive gathered momentum, German forces suffered horrendous equipment losses. Still Hitler forbade any withdrawals, believing, probably correctly, that any strategic retreat would spark a general collapse along the front.

BALANCE SHEET

By late 1941, the German Army had lost 302,000 troops killed on the Eastern Front. Soviet losses in Typhoon alone were colossal. From October 1941, the Soviet army and navy combined had lost a staggering 1,007,996 killed and missing.

▲ THE FATE OF THOUSANDS of German troops during Operation Typhoon: Death in the snow. Most German troops had no winter clothing on the Eastern Front in 1941.

Daily Express

YEAST-VITE
TONIC TABLETS
The Lightning Pick-Me-Up

Cadbury MEANS QUALITY

No. 12,972 — Monday, December 22, 1941 — One Penny

Fuehrer sacks von Brauchitsch, takes over command of the German Army, then makes sensational backs-to-the-wall appeal to soldiers in Russia

HITLER SOS TO ARMY

"Stop the retreat and hold on until the spring"

AFRAID OF INVASION, CALLS ON HOME FRONT TO 'BRACE ITSELF'

HITLER, after announcing last night that he has sacked his supreme army commander, Field-Marshal von Brauchitsch, and taken over the job himself, issued to his army and his Nazi formations in Russia a sensational appeal to hold fast in Russia and stop the rout.

Yesterday was Stalin's 62nd birthday. Yesterday marked the end of six months of war in Russia.

Hitler indicated that the German Army must withdraw still further when he begged the troops to stand fast on "the New Eastern Front."

"I know what you are suffering," he told them in effect, "but I am asking no more of you than was asked of the men who 25 years ago fought four winter campaigns in the East."

There was a note of fear—of a possible Russian offensive developing into an invasion of Germany—when he told the men they would have to fight for "the liberty of our people and the future security of its existence."

'OUR EXISTENCE'

Fear, too, of invasion from the west when he assured them that the defences of Europe from Arctic Norway to the borders of Spain were to be strengthened.

For the spring offensive which he hopes to launch he declared that new and better weapons would be provided.

The appeal (as quoted by Reuter) was issued from "the Fuehrer's Headquarters" and was dated Friday.

Here is the text of the appeal:—

"Soldiers of the Army and S.S. formations.—"The battle for the liberty of our people and for the security of its future existence—the battle which is to make it impossible for us to be threatened every 20 to 25 years with a war under a fresh pretext, but in reality for the same Jewish capitalist interests—is now approaching its culminating and turning point.

"The German Reich, Italy, and the nations allied with

'I follow my intuition'

Why Hitler took command

Here is the text of the Proclamation in which Hitler last night announced that he has sacked von Brauchitsch:—

WHEN the Fuehrer on February 4, 1938, assumed command over all the armed forces, this was done out of concern for the already threatening military struggle for the freedom of the German people.

The situation imperatively demanded that all powers should be concentrated in one hand.

'Inward call'

Only thus could the preparations for resistance succeed, a resistance which it was known would lead to a "total war" even more than did the World War of 1914-18—forced upon the German people by the same enemy.

In addition, the realisation of an inward call and his own will to take upon himself the responsibility weighed with the statesman Adolf Hitler when he resolved to be his own general-issimo.

The course of this war has more and more confirmed the recognition of this fact, but it was fully shown only when the campaign in the East assumed proportions that exceeded all past notions.

All decisions

The vastness of the theatre of war, the close connection of the conduct of land operations with the political and economic war aims, and also the numerical size of the armed forces compared with other parts of the armed forces have induced the Fuehrer to follow his intuitions and to influence in the strongest possible manner the operations and the equipment of the army, and to reserve to himself personally all essential decisions in this sphere.

Following up his decision of February 4, 1938, the Fuehrer therefore resolved on December 19 to assume personally the merits of the present Supreme Commander of the Army, General Field-Marshal von Brauchitsch, to combine in his own hands the leadership of the whole armed forces with the supreme command of the army.

FANATICISM

"It is their task, up to the coming of spring, to hold and defend with like fanaticism what they have hitherto conquered with immeasurable heroism and heavy sacrifices.

"From the new Eastern Front nothing else is today expected than what the German soldiers achieved in four Russian winter campaigns 25 years ago.

"Every German soldier must set an example to our loyal allies.

"Apart from this, however, fresh units will be formed, and above all newer and better weapons will be issued, as they were last winter.

"The defence of the front in the west will be strengthened from Kirkenaes (Norway) to the Spanish frontier.

"The difficulties of organising communications on this front today extending over a whole continent and stretching as far as North Africa, must be overcome. But this task will be successfully accomplished.

Preparations for an immediate resumption of offensive operations in the spring, and the enemy, in the east is finally destroyed, must be taken at once. Other defensive war measures are about to be taken.

"These tasks demand that the armed forces and the home front

▶ BACK PAGE, COL. THREE.

Was it prophetic? A picture taken of the five-day Hitler-Mussolini meeting on the Eastern Front. Studying war maps at headquarters; Italy's General Ugo Cavaliero, Mussolini, Hitler, General Keitel (behind him), General Alfred Jodl (Hitler's private adviser on strategy), and Major Christian. Brauchitsch was not there.

KAISER HITLER

Sacks 13 Generals, Makes Himself Supreme War Lord

Banner headlines, February 5, 1938 . . . Hitler had become "in fact as well as in theory Supreme War Lord, with even more power than the Kaiser had." Keitel at the same time became Chief of the High Command, and Brauchitsch—now sacked—Commander-in-Chief of the Army.

16—18 CALL UP:

Boys will register next month

DETAILS are issued this morning of the Call-up of Youth. Registration of boys between 16 and 18 begins in January. Girls will follow. There will be no compulsion.

Boys will be given a voluntary selection of pre-service organisations to join. Technical and educational courses are also to be expanded. Girls are to be offered training in nursing, cookery and preliminary technical courses.

FULL STORY ON PAGE THREE.

Misty again
Straits May, light north westerly breeze.

Crash kills 25
Twenty-five people were killed in a Naples train crash yesterday.

'Merits recognised' —but OUT HE GOES

WALTHER VON BRAUCHITSCH.
"He was a time-server."

Morley Richards in a 2 a.m. commentary says:—

It may mean this

ONE of three reasons must be the explanation of Hitler's extraordinary proclamation:—

(1) Germany may be on the verge of still another aggression directed either against Spain or Turkey, most probably Spain.

Defeat of Rommel's army in Libya has made it imperative for Hitler to secure the French and Spanish ports in North Africa if he intends to maintain a hold over the Western Mediterranean.

He may have planned to bypass Gibraltar and land in Morocco before General Auchinleck's Eighth Army can reach Tripoli.

Blaming generals

(2) He is seeking to hide the appalling casualties and extent of the German defeat in Russia by giving all his personal influence on the German people.

In other words, he is saving to them. It is true that many hundreds or thousands of German soldiers will never come home again. But that was the fault of over Brauchitsch and the other generals. Now I will see to it that the victory shall be ours.

It is reasonable to infer that Hitler foresees a sweeping onrush of the Russian armies that made Hayashi, former Japanese Premier, lead to the invasion of Germany itself.

As evident, too, that he fears for the morale of his soldiers when he compares them with their fathers twenty-odd years ago.

This may be the most damaging part of the Fuehrer's appeal.

He must know that wherever the German line eventually reaches in the Russian winter communism, many thousands of soldiers are doomed to die from the cold.

Desperate steps

That being so, it may be masterly on his part to try so adroitly to shift the blame to his generals.

But it is also clear-cut evidence that Hitler himself fears for the future of the war machine, as he has built up, and is taking dramatically desperate steps to keep it going.

(3) He has moved first to forestall the German High Command, with whom there is little doubt he was at variance over the conduct of the Russian campaign.

There has been a struggle between the old Prussianised army command and the political S.S. divisions—Hitler's personal army—ever since war began. While things went well it never came to a head.

By dismissing von Brauchitsch and asking the German people to pin their trust in him he may have forestalled a move by the German High Command to take complete charge of the future military conduct of the war.

NO HEIL

Germans not yet told

FOR the first time since Hitler took over Germany, Berlin radio closed its programme last night without the words "Heil, Hitler!"

Instead the announcer "bid a cordial good night to all listeners who now want to enjoy a well-deserved night's rest."

Up to midnight no mention of Hitler's proclamation had been broadcast to German home listeners. The announcement was only made to foreign broadcasts.

Jap general tells 'Axis—

'Must strike in Africa'

NEW YORK, Sunday.—General Hayashi, former Japanese Premier, in a broadcast today, said:—

"The Axis nations must open simultaneous offensives against British and American forces in Africa and the Far East. Failure to do so will enable the ABCD Powers to make dangerous concentrations in any sector they choose."—B.U.P.

Battle fierce in Philippines

New York radio said last night that fierce fighting is going on near Davao on the Philippine island of Mindanao where the Japanese landed considerable forces on Saturday.

Fighting has also increased around Vigan, on the north-west coast of the main Luzon Island. The Japanese landed more troops but so far they have been held.

Plane workers will double production

MELBOURNE Sunday.—A pledge to double production in the next three months was given today by Commonwealth Aircraft Corporation employees—Reuter.

Italians ordered: 'Behave like British'

CAIRO, Sunday.—A document captured from the headquarters of the Italian General Navarrini appeals to Italian troops "to behave like British."

GERMANS CUT OFF

Russians smash Leningrad ring

RUSSIA'S northern army yesterday broke the ring round Leningrad and cut off half the besieging force along the River Neva by encircling Shlisselburg, 25 miles east of the city.

More towns south-east of Leningrad and south of Moscow were officially announced to be taken and a special communiqué reported vast captures of German war material in three days' fighting, including 360 tanks and 3,059 lorries.—See Back Page.

We're beyond Benghazi

and take 10,000 prisoners

Express Military Reporter

GENERAL ROMMEL'S broken panzer forces, deserting their Italian infantry support, were last night running as hard as severe dust storms would allow them towards Tripoli. Second occupation of Benghazi by the British is due to be announced shortly.

The extent of our successes can be gauged from a Cairo statement last night, that 10,000 more Axis prisoners—4,000 Germans, 6,000 Italians—have arrived at prison bases.

Behind the Germans beyond Benghazi pounded our mechanised columns in unceasing pursuit. Overhead the enemy were being incessantly bombed and machine-gunned by British planes, which blew up many lorries packed with German soldiers.

Ragged columns

Last reported, the German forces were in ragged columns south of Benghazi, between that port and Solluk, which has a junction road connecting it to the 450-mile coastal road to Tripoli.

The Italians, in utter disorder, will attempt to fight abandoned, were north-east of Benghazi holding in the hill country.

News that a further 12 German tanks were destroyed and eight Italian tanks captured intact, reported from Cairo, brings to a almost a certainty that Rommel has not more than a score left.

It is just possible that there are a few in reserve in Benghazi, which he might be able to man in a last despairing stand to cover his headlong flight.

But it is not likely.

British columns are closing

▶ BACK PAGE, COL. THREE.

WE FALL BACK IN MALAYA

SINGAPORE, Sunday.

AN official statement issued in Singapore tonight said that the British forces in north-eastern Malaya have successfully withdrawn between Kota Bahru, where the

WORLD WAR NEWS
3 A.M. LATEST

WE HOLD HALF OF HONGKONG

OTTAWA, Sunday.—Colonel Ralston, Canadian Defence Minister, announced tonight delayed messages from Hongkong indicate garrison there is still stoutly holding large portion of the island, defending a line running north and south near its centre.—B.U.P.

Japanese made their initial landings, and Kuala Krai, 45 miles south.

Kuala Krai is on the central Malayan railway, 300 miles north of Singapore.

The statement added: "The loss of airfield facilities in northern Kelantan (the Japanese captured Kota Bahru and the vulnerability of communications prompted the decision to withdraw some days ago.

"This involved a series of co-ordinated night movements, which resulted in the bringing out of the greater part of the British force and the majority of stores and equipment, despite attempted enemy interference on land and in the air."

The first real pitched battle in Malaya, in which the Japanese are likely to encounter for the first time a solid Imperial front, is expected to begin soon in the Taiping area, south of Wellesley Province on the west coast.

A Japanese spearhead has reached Lenggong, on the main inland road through the valley of the River Perak, at the point where the river flows into Lake Shenderoh.

Lenggong is 30 miles south of Grit. Today's communiqué says he successfully countered a Japanese attack in this area.

SHIFTING GREAT GUNS IS MARGARET'S WAR WORK
... but she still keeps house for Dad

Tankers attacked off U.S. coast

NEW YORK, Sunday—Enemy submarines have opened up an offensive against American shipping along both coasts. Submarines off California yesterday sank the 6,912-ton United States tanker Emidio, and forced a second tanker to turn back to port.

The captain and 21 other survivors from the Emidio were picked up by a British tug today. Three lifeboats were destroyed by shellfire, and two missing. Twenty-two seamen are missing.

Battle raging for Hongkong racecourse

Express Correspondent PETER BURCHETT
CHUNGKING, Sunday.

BRITISH forces were still holding out at several points near Hongkong Island at 10.30 tonight (B.S.T.), according to enemy radio reports.

The Japanese said their troops were attacking British positions on the racecourse in Happy Valley, east of Jardine's Hill. Warships were said to be helping the land forces with bombardment of British forts and gun positions.

"YOUR DUTY"

The Colonial Office last night issued the text of a communiqué from Hongkong, saying that the Japanese first landed on the island by night, at North Point and Taikoo. The communiqué added:—

"The Governor sent the following message to all H.M. forces in Hongkong: 'The eyes of the Empire are on you. Be strong, be resolute, and do your duty.'"

Thames gunfire

German raiders were driven off by anti-aircraft fire in the Thames estuary area last night. No bombs were reported. Bombs in the north-east did no damage.

Call-me-Mr. is a lord

MR. REGINALD T. H. FLETCHER, Socialist M.P. for Nuneaton, who announced during the week-end that he wished to be called "plain Mr." instead of lieutenant-commander, is now one of four new Socialist peers—See BACK PAGE.

20-YEAR-OLD Margaret Stephenson's war job is picking up bare gun barrels with her crane and placing them just where they are wanted. "It's grand work and I enjoy it," she says. She makes up the rest of the year does the washing after work. "It's easy if you use the washing method. Just soak the clothes for 15 minutes in hot soap water—you don't have to boil them at all. Extra-dirty places are damped and a little dry Rinso smoothed in." Many women in Margaret's factory combine warwork with housework and say they enjoy life more because of it.

R. S. Hudson Limited.

▲ DAILY EXPRESS, LONDON, MONDAY DECEMBER 22, 1941

The *Express* speculates about Hitler's decision to take charge of the German Army and his call on forces outside Moscow for fanatical resistance. Whatever the precise significance, the *Express* was right to recognize a turning point on the Eastern Front, which for now more than balanced bad news about British forces in Malaya and Hong Kong.

THE DAILY MAIL, Tuesday, December 23, 1941.

Daily Mail

NO. 14,246   ONE PENNY   ★★   FOR KING AND EMPIRE   TUESDAY, DECEMBER 23, 1941

LATE WAR NEWS SPECIAL

"Their Effect is Practically Instantaneous"

BLITZKRIEG ON PHILIPPINES

Tanks, Planes, Guns in Jap 'Armada'

DUCE'S MEN COVERING ROMMEL'S RETREAT

Tripoli Road Pursuit

From ALEXANDER CLIFFORD, Daily Mail Correspondent

GIOVANNI BERTA, Monday.

TO-DAY the Battle of Cyrenaica is drawing to a close and the Battle of Tripolitania has begun. Somewhere near the border of the two provinces of Libya Rommel's Africa Corps are still heading westward, with the Eighth Army in pursuit.

Two delaying actions have failed to keep the Imperial Forces far from the Germans' heels.

Both were fought by Italians, one on the coast road and the other at El Abiar, 25 miles east of Benghazi.

The first we broke when our troops entered Cyrene and Apollonia yesterday. At El Abiar the enemy have been pressed back.

General Ritchie did not wait for the result of these engagements in his pursuit of the main quarry—Rommel and his Germans.

RINGSIDE SEAT

Our troops were yesterday approaching Agedabia, 120 miles south of Benghazi. From Agedabia to the Tripolitania border is only about 90 miles.

From a ringside seat I watched the Italians' last stand in the north, broken here as the sun set yesterday.

For two days they had been holding out keeping the British at bay while their infantry columns raced through green mountains towards Benghazi.

With intense fire from anti-tank guns, mortars, and field artillery they had defended their rock-built positions in the hills around Giovanni Berta while more troops came up to reinforce the Indian patrols who were investing them.

All day yesterday I drove across country with these reinforcements up rubble roads. We climbed from arid desert to a country of redbrown earth and low, green hills and stone walls which might have been in the Cotswolds or Yorkshire dales.

Stinging streams of rain sleet and hail beat into the cabs of our trucks, making it almost impossible to see the road.

STACK OF MINES

Once a big German plane came bombing and machine-gunning, and I decided to risk being hit rather than lie down in a muddy, waterlogged ditch in that weather.

Only when I saw the bomb actually leave the plane did I feel it time to move.

Towards evening we ran into sunny weather. All along the road the Italians had stacked thousands of land-mines, but they had not dug in one. They had been moving too fast.

We ran on ahead of the column and approached Berta by a road which seemed uncannily deserted. All round, standing a burnt-out and old-fashioned long-barrelled guns were littered about. But there was utter silence.

Suddenly a gun fired with startling loudness nearby. We looked through our glasses and saw men moving stealthily round the castle which crowns Berta's citadel-like hill. We drove on hurriedly into the shelter of some buildings.

An Italian Army officer came greeted us with: " Yours are the first cars to get along that road. The enemy is just over this ridge. Go up to the castle and watch."

We climbed up the rocky slope while a platoon of Sikhs with rifles at the trail moved off in the right wing to a fast crouching trot.

Guns were firing here and there but it was impossible to understand the lie of the land.

THE BARRAGE

We went to a corner of the castle and looked round. For half a mile the ground sloped down steeply to where Berta's modernistic white houses fringed the main road.

Then it rose again in a green hillside seamed with grey layers of rock. It was among these layers just 1,500 yards away, that the enemy were dug in.

Beside us, mortars were firing rapidly with a sharp hissing report. Their shells were landing down to the right of the slope in a sudden efflorescence of grey smoke, which blew away quickly.

Twenty-five-pounders firing from behind us were plastering a small track fringed with overturned lorries, playing death among these batteries.

Suddenly I saw a little man in

BACK PAGE—Col FOUR

GERMANS ENTER CAIRO UNDER GUARD

GERMAN troops enter Cairo—but as captives, not as conquerors. As they march through the centre of the city Scots troops and Egyptian mounted police, they provide a pleasant spectacle for the Egyptian civilians lining the streets. The Egyptians at one time had feared a different entry—a march in that would have meant their falling under the Axis yoke. Another picture in Page THREE.

AMERICANS FIGHT ON BEACHES

From Daily Mail Special Correspondent   MANILA, Monday.

AMERICAN and Filipino soldiers, blasted by bombs and raked by gunfire, are to-night holding fast in a solid wall of defence at Lingayen, against which 80,000 to 100,000 Japanese troops are throwing themselves in vain.

Lingayen is known as the gateway to Manila, capital of the Philippines, but so far it has been a dead end to the invader.

The Americans have closed the door tight and are administering 'tremendous losses on the enemy, who are now trying invasion on a huge scale.

Using 80 troopships and hundreds of self-propelled barges, the Japanese crept toward Lingayen protected by a large escort of warships under a ceiling of bombers.

American forces, though almost certainly outnumbered, were not caught by surprise.

Heavy guns drove off the destroyers and transports at one of the most important points, and although the enemy succeeded in landing at others, they were immediately engaged.

Fighting is furious and bloody along the sheltered coastline 100 miles north-west of Manila.

BOMBERS READY

The latest official statement of General MacArthur merely recorded that American forces are "behaving well."

MacArthur was smiling and confident and prefaced his tribute to the troops with, "I have some good news for you," which indicates that he is confident of smashing the latest invasion.

American bombers engaged in breaking up sections of the armada are believed to have sunk a number of transports. They were ready waiting and eager to meet the invaders.

Japanese attempts during the past week to confuse MacArthur with feints at various parts of Luzon Island have obviously failed dismally.

He shrewdly fought holding actions against minor beach landings and reserved his strength for the main attack, which came to-day in such fury.

FIVE BATTLES

The Japanese have succeeded in landing a number of tanks and heavy equipment, and small battles are in progress, though not on a great scale.

They are putting everything they have into this invasion attempt, using an enormous number of planes. But the latest report tonight is that the Americans are more than holding their own.

Fighting is also centred at Davao, on the southern island of Mindanao, and at three minor points on Luzon Island.

Manila was bombed twice to-day, but neither raid was heavy, and the raiders, numbering three in each case, did not linger.

To-night Japanese naval officials in Shanghai are boasting that the new landing heralds a big drive on Manila.

FROM HAINAN

The Japanese Fleet, it is believed here, came from Hainan, the big island 150 miles off the coast of Indo-China and 800 miles from the Manila.

An official Japanese version of the operations issued from Imperial headquarters said only that a large number of Japanese troops had landed at an undisclosed point on Luzon and were advancing to the south.

The official United States communiqué ran:

"Heavy fighting is in progress in Lingayen Gulf, 130 miles north of Manila, where the Japanese are attempting to make a landing in force.

"Under strong naval-air escort a fleet of 80 troopships appeared off the west coast of Luzon.

"Soon afterwards a large number of 150-man barges entered Lingayen Gulf, attempting landings in the vicinity of Agoo.

"Some of the Japanese force is estimated at from 80,000 to 100,000—from six to eight divisions.

"The attempted invasion is being met with fierce resistance by American and Filipino troops.

"Fighting is continuing near Davao, on the island of Mindanao."

Roosevelt Begins the Big Talks

From WALTER FARR   WASHINGTON, Monday.

MOMENTOUS Allied Supreme War Council consultations for shaping the whole future of the war have begun here to-day.

President Roosevelt announced this morning through his secretary, Mr. Stephen Early, that he had already held preliminary conferences for the joint planning of unity of action among the Allied forces opposing the Axis.

More important meetings had been arranged to take place later.

To prepare the way, the President saw M. Litvnov, representing Stalin, Dr Hu Shih, the Chinese Ambassador, and Dr Loudon, representing the Dutch Government.

There was an atmosphere of intense excitement as Mr. Stephen Early, grave of face, received the newspapermen in his study to make the announcement.

Grave News

The conversations have begun at a time when news from the Philippines is grave, and American and British circles here are beginning to talk more and more of concentrating on the defence of Singapore.

Apart from his diplomatic talks President Roosevelt has been in almost continuous conference with General Marshall, Chief of United States Army; Admiral Stark, Chief of Naval Operations; and Admiral King, Commander-in-Chief of the Pacific and Atlantic Fleets.

He has also received the British Military, Air and Navy representatives here, including Admiral Little, General Wemyss, and Air-Marshal Harris.

As far as Russia is concerned, it is significant that professors of New York University Law School, in an analysis of the situation published to-day, conclude that Russia is entitled to attack Japan without waiting until she is under threat from Japan's treacherous stab on the United States.

NEW DEFENCE LINE IN MALAYA

Hongkong's Secret Radio Link Keeps News Going

Hongkong was still fighting back last night against the Japanese invaders. A communiqué received in London said that on Friday the garrison, by a successful counter-attack, threw the Japs from the Wong Nei Chong Gap.

By Daily Mail reporter

HIDDEN deep in the rock, and ringed by protective guns, Hongkong's radio station still sends out messages. If the radio fails, all contact with the mainland and the rest of the world is at an end.

Yesterday as I sat in the quiet of the Chinese Embassy in London, a terse message came in from the defenders of the fortress.

It was one of the twice-daily bulletins transmitted to Chungking in code. The code was repeated to Britain.

The message cannot be printed. It gave the advancing Chinese commanders and our Military Mission in Chungking exact details of the military position.

Meanwhile the story of the unbroken endurance of the civilians on the island remains untold. The air is too heavily laden with vital military news to carry the tale of their heroism.

Rock Shelters

The chief secretary at the Embassy, M. Chai, filled in some gaps in the story last night. From news he had received he told me of the 3,000 white women and children who still remain.

He said: "Hongkong, like Chungking, has a wealth of caves in the rock which is Victoria Peak. There women and children take shelters.

"Strategically and in every other way these caves, 7,000ft. up, are a great vantage point.

"I understand that the civilians are living in the caves, with supplies of food and water. They could do much to hinder the enemy if he attempted to storm the Point."

Hongkong Fights On—BACK PAGE

UNSETTLED IN STRAIT

Weather was unsettled in the Strait of Dover last night, with showers of misty rain.

RAF Swoop in Thailand

From LAWRENCE IMPEY, Daily Mail Special Correspondent

SINGAPORE, Monday.

BRITISH forces, now rested and reorganised, are preparing to meet the Japanese in force on a new line running roughly north-west from Ipoh—the big tin-mining centre—along the Perak River.

This is a natural line, with the deep, swampy, banked river running through a narrow stretch of valley between a series of hills and mountains, some as high as 5,400ft.

The line pivots round Kuala Kangsar, about 15 miles northwest of Ipoh, but actually 50 miles away by the only road and rail route.

It is here that, according to today's communiqué, our troops "continue to hold their position" after inflicting heavy casualties on the Japanese, now advancing from the Grik road.

Airfields Attacked

With the Japanese advance from Grik, the first British position after withdrawal from Province Wellesley along the Krian River was obviously dangerous, exposing the men there to a danger of being cut off in the rear by troops descending this road.

The British accordingly withdrew in plenty of time and are now awaiting the Japanese along the Perak River.

To-day it is announced that the R.A.F. have been in action against Japanese airfields both in Thailand and in Northern Malaya.

The raid on the Thai bases took place on Sunday.

A number of enemy planes on the ground were machine-gunned from tree-top height and all were destroyed.

Six Jap planes were put out of commission in the raid on the northern Malayan airfield, the position of which is not given in the communiqué.

Our fighting took place yesterday near Kuala Lumpur. Three Japanese raiders were destroyed and we lost three fighters.

Praise for Dutch

In Singapore, despite the more favourable news to-day, it is at last admitted that we are really threatened here. The city is digging in, and should the Japanese ever arrive they will find the island strongly defended.

The most encouraging factor, so far as the public are concerned, has been the brilliant conduct of the Dutch, who, although operating cold minor naval and air forces, have nevertheless stayed rolling slowly against the Japanese in many war theatres.

It is with great appreciation that Singapore residents have seen Dutch bombers and fighters overhead.

The majority of people still maintain that Britain should reconstitute the position immediately with a political and military shake-up and the drafting in of Indian reinforcements.

NAZI ROUT BEGUN—KLIN VICTOR

WITH THE RED ARMY, WEST OF KLIN, Sunday (delayed).

GENERAL Vasily Kuznetsov, whose troops threw the Germans out of Klin, said to-day that the beginning of the rout of the entire German Army had begun.

He added: "There are, of course, still serious battles ahead, but our troops have begun to pursue the enemy decisively."

General Kuznetsov was speaking

Greatest Air Picture of the War
See BACK Page.

Brest: The Bombs Fell True

By NOEL MONKS, Daily Mail Air Correspondent

PHOTOGRAPHS taken of the big R.A.F. daylight raid on the German battle - cruisers Scharnhorst and Gneisenau at Brest last Thursday show that heavy armour-piercing bombs fell so close to the ships as they lay in two docks side by side that it is almost certain, they were badly damaged.

In announcing this yesterday the Air Ministry said that there is reason to believe that at least one bomb fell amidships and penetrated the deck of the Scharnhorst.

The picture showing this is obscured by the smoke of the bursting bomb.

Here is the Air Ministry report on attack: "It is quite certain that a heavy armour-piercing bomb fell between the starboard side of the Gneisenau's stern and the side of the dock in which she lay.

"The distance between the ship and the side of the dock is only 20 or 30ft, and the effect of an explosion in this confined area would be appreciable.

Submarine Pens

"Similarly, another bomb fell between the port side of the Scharnhorst's stern and the side of the other dock. The pictures reveal that a great number of bombs fell very close to the battle-cruisers.

"One of the two docks containing the battle-cruisers were closed at the time, and the chances into which they slide when open received a direct hit.

It is reasonable to assume, therefore, that the mechanism of the gates has been damaged and that the ships cannot be moved until the gates are repaired.

According to the Air Ministry not a single bomb fell in the civil town or the commercial sort of Brest.

The bombing was done from a great height in order to enable the bombs to penetrate the ships' armour, and it was therefore necessary for every bomber to make a very steady bombing run in the face of the fiercest barrage.

A tribute is paid by the Air Ministry to the magnificent work of the fighter escort, which kept the main body of enemy fighters away from our bombers.

Penang Wreckers

The "scorched earth" policy was carried out at Penang before evacuation, it was stated authoritatively in London last night. Prai power station and Penang tin smelting works were completely destroyed.

VON BOCK SACKED —'ILL'

VON BOCK, German Commander-in-Chief on the Moscow front, has now been sacked. The news comes from Berlin yesterday within 24 hours of the announcement of Von Brauchitsch's dismissal.

The explanation for Von Bock's dismissal is "ill health."

Kuibishev reported last week that Von Bock had been sacked but this command because of his failure to take Moscow.

Stock Follows Brauchitsch —BACK Page.

Rubber Control Board Formed

A Rubber Control Board has been appointed by the Ministry of Supply. It was announced last night.

Sir George Beharrell is chairman, and the members are Sir Walrond Sinclair, who will be concerned particularly with the United States, Mr. W. G. Essex, and Mr. J. R. B. Thompson. An additional member will be appointed later.

Sir George Beharrell is chairman of Dunlop Rubber Co., Sir Walrond Sinclair has been Rubber Controller since last April; and is chairman of the British Tyre and Rubber Co.

U-boats Attack U.S. Ships

From Daily Mail Correspondent

WASHINGTON, Monday. — Two United States merchant ships have been attacked by submarines in the Eastern Pacific, the Navy Department announced to-day.

One, attacked off the Californian coast on Saturday night, was undamaged. The other, the Lahaina, was shelled and sunk.

British Hold Out

New York, Monday. — British troops are still holding out in Sarawak, and are inflicting heavy losses on the Japanese, who landed last week, according to a broadcast from Batavia, capital of the Dutch East Indies, picked up in New York to-day.—B.U.P.

▲ DAILY MAIL, LONDON, TUESDAY DECEMBER 23, 1941

The *Mail* falls back on the by-now familiar German term Blitzkrieg—"Lightning War"— to describe the Japanese assault on the Philippines. There is better news from Libya and the Eastern Front. The "greatest air picture of the war" on the back page featured Halifax bombers on a daylight raid on the German battleships *Gneisenau* and *Scharnhorst*, trapped by the Allies in harbor in Brest, Normandy—and for now out of the vital Battle of the Atlantic.

Japan's Blitzkrieg

DECEMBER 1941

THE STUNNING EFFECTS OF THE JAPANESE ATTACK ON PEARL HARBOR ON DECEMBER 7 AND THE DISASTER THAT BEFELL THE BRITISH "FORCE H" ON DECEMBER 10 GAVE the Japanese a free hand to attack where they chose. They quickly took over isolated sectors, such as Hong Kong, Guam, and Wake Island. Major Japanese offensives were aimed at European colonies. Over 100,000 Japanese troops landed in Malaya on December 8. In January, there were amphibious landings in the oil-rich Dutch East Indies.

A Japanese offensive was now launched against the Philippines on December 8, when Japanese aircraft destroyed 100 U.S. planes at Clark Field, crippling the defense of the islands, which General Douglas MacArthur had hoped to base on air power.

JAPANESE ATTACK

On December 10, the main island of Luzon was invaded, and then there were landings on the southern islands of Mindanao and Jolo. The islands offered Japan the chance to gain naval and air bases. General MacArthur decided not to defend Manila, the capital, but declared it an open city in order to withdraw his forces westward to the Bataan Peninsula. MacArthur realized that Japan had air and sea superiority. He also knew that no reinforcements would be sent. His troops began a desperate resistance against Japanese attacks across the mountainous peninsula, which began on January 9, 1942. For several months the 80,000 troops resisted the Japanese, despite suffering from disease and supply shortages.

A LONG BATTLE

On April 3, the Japanese launched their final offensive on Bataan. The U.S. defensive line was penetrated on the 4th. Major General Jonathan Wainwright, commanding the U.S. and Filipino forces, could not mount an effective counter-attack, and the majority of his forces surrendered on the 9th. Remaining forces on Corregidor surrendered on May 5.

▲ HONG KONG UNDER ATTACK. This British colony was attacked by the Japanese 38th Division on December 8, 1941. After an amphibious assault, the garrison surrendered on December 25.

Malaya

DECEMBER 1941

A JAPANESE FORCE OF 100,000 TROOPS (THE 5TH AND 18TH DIVISIONS), UNDER GENERAL TOMOYUKI YAMASHITA, BEGAN LANDING ON THE NORTHEAST coast of Malaya and in Thailand after initial air attacks on December 8. Japanese units quickly moved southward down both sides of the Malayan Peninsula. British forces were mainly stationed in the south, having anticipated an attack nearer Singapore. Japanese aircraft soon destroyed most of the British aircraft. British reluctance to move into neutral Thailand before a Japanese attack enabled General Yamashita to complete his landings. British forces finally advanced into Thailand on the 10th, but could not halt the Japanese invasion. Well-equipped and experienced Japanese troops continued pushing southward, many by bicycle.

JAPANESE SUPERIORITY

British troops had not been trained for jungle warfare, whereas the Japanese had been. This meant that the Japanese continually outflanked and infiltrated British positions. In addition, the Japanese made a number of amphibious landings from the sea and behind British lines. The British were not inferior in numbers, with Malaya Command (Lieutenant General Percival) having 100,000 troops and 158 aircraft. However, few British troops had combat experience and many had had only minimal training. Worse, the British had no tanks. The army had the comfort of RAF support, though many aircraft were old and slow (when the Japanese attacked, many were destroyed on the ground).

RETREAT TO SINGAPORE

As 1941 drew to a close, the British in Malaya had been pushed back to the naval base of Singapore. By this time they were demoralized, whereas Japanese morale was high. The chances of holding Singapore diminished by the day.

▲ SINGAPORE SOON CAME UNDER JAPANESE attack as Yamashita's troops neared the city. Artillery and aerial bombardments killed thousands of the port's one million citizens.

VICTORY
MUST BE OURS

Jersey Observer

VICTORY
MUST BE OURS

COMPLETE WEATHER REPORT—Fair and continued cold tonight.

VOL. L.—No. 275. | THERMOMETER RECORD—6 A. M., 18; 8 A. M., 20; 10 A. M., 22 | TUESDAY, DECEMBER 30, 1941 | JERSEY CITY OFFICE 2606 Hudson Boulevard | UNION CITY OFFICE 417 36th Street | HOBOKEN 111 Newark Street | PRICE, 3 CENTS

Japs Attack Singapore; Philippine Army Holds

Malay Base Bombed

Claim Ipoh Has Fallen

By HAROLD GUARD

Singapore, Dec. 30—(UP)—Japanese planes opened a furious assault on Singapore and key points of the Malay Peninsula today as Japanese ground forces attacked heavily, and at heavy cost, on the Perak River line 300 miles north of this island.

Singapore, raid free since the first days of the Pacific war, was attacked four times by Japanese planes during the night.

A communique of the Malay command said some damage was done to thatched buildings, and fires in these buildings ignited a small gasoline store. Only four casualties were reported.

It was asserted that the Japanese had suffered enormous casualties in an attack on the Perak River line and elsewhere, it was added, the situation unchanged.

"The Japanese claimed the fall of Ipoh, the tin centre on the Perak River front, and the Malaya command had admitted Japanese penetration south of Ipoh. London, reporting that outnumbered British Empire troops were fighting doggedly against odds, suggested that the Japanese had almost surrounded, but might not have taken Ipoh.

(London reported also that two officers of the Chinese army were in Singapore, discussing joint Allied strategy and tactics. There have been suggestions that China might send troops to Burma.)

Singapore's first air raid alert in days was sounded at 8:20 last night. There was a second alert at 8:30 and then Japanese planes roared over the island.

Anti-aircraft guns went into action and searchlights beams darted over the sky. Soon the crash of bombs was heard.

Two waves of planes attacked in the bright moonlight, before the "all clear" was sounded at 10:40. Among targets of the aerial offensive timed with that on the ground, were Kluantan and Kluang on the Malaya coast.

It was asserted that the raids on Kuantan yesterday the Japanese failed to inflict casualties or damage, and there were few casualties in the Kluang raid. It was said also that there was no damage to Kuala-ampore aerodrome.

The Malaya Command communique said that when Japanese planes raided a railroad station yesterday a large Jater force which happened to be there "behaved with great calmness."

Allied planes which had heavily attacked Japanese positions in the Peninsula Sunday, were active yesterday in a number of successful reconnaissance the communique said.

Nazis Forced Back by Reds

Foiled in Attempt to Dig in—Russia Uses Parachutists with Good Effect—Germans Fire on Own Men

Moscow, Dec. 30—(INS)—Smashing the efforts of retreating Germans to dig in along new lines, Soviet forces kept pushing relentlessly forward today and recaptured still more towns and villages on the Russo-German front.

The Red Army newspaper Red Star gave a graphic account of the "havoc" caused by Soviet parachutists behind the German lines and told how, in the darkness, they managed to set the Germans to "exterminating their own men."

This report said that in nine days the parachutists blew up 29 bridges, burned 48 tanks, destroyed large quantities of weapons and wiped out 600 German officers and men.

"One night," Red Star related, "the parachutists encountered a long column of German motorized infantry, supported by tanks and armored cars.

"They opened fire on the centre and both ends. Confused by the darkness, both ends of the column started blazing away at each other, and the parachutists watched the Germans exterminating their own men."

The Russian High Command's midnight war bulletin said:

"In a number of sectors Soviet troops overcame attempts by the German forces to entrench themselves in new defensive positions. Soviet troops continued their advance and took a number of inhabited localities."

DRIVE DEEP WEDGES INTO LINES

The communique added that the enemy suffered "considerable losses in manpower and materials."

The government newspaper Izvestia said Russian troops in six days had "cleared the Germans from 193 towns and villages."

Soviet advices said the Russians had driven deep wedges north and south of German positions at Mosaisk and Malyaroaroslavis, west of the capital, and that the Nazis were beginning to withdraw from these areas to avoid encirclement.

The communique indicated that German plans to straighten their lines for the winter had been defeated.

(See REDS Page 13)

AIR RAID PRECAUTION DEMONSTRATION—Scenes at instruction meeting of air raid wardens held at School No. 37, First street and Pavonia avenue, Jersey City, last night, at which Mayor Hague was a speaker. At top, Captain Joseph Foley is shown speaking at left as Lieutenant Joseph Lynch (right) shows a homemade blackout for window. Lower left, Defense Council Chairman Frank J. Reardon pins warden's badge on James F. McGovern Jr., clerk of Hudson County Traffic Court. Lower right, Lieut. Lynch shows a method of taping window to prevent shattering.

Dangerous Fire Soon Checked

Rock Salt Causes Dense Pall of Smoke in Upper Hoboken Industrial Section—Second Alarm Is Sounded

Volumes of smoke shrouded the upper industrial section of Hoboken when a two-alarm blaze occurred on the top floor of the two-story brick building at 1610 Bloomfield street shortly after 10 o'clock this morning.

Rock salt stored in the second floor quarters of the Lehigh Salt Company, cast off the dense smoke. The fire occurred in the firm's storage rooms. About a dozen persons are employed by the company. On the first floor, the Brookhattan Hoboken Terminal is located.

Naval Threat To Manila Is Reported

Hopes of Aid From United States Rise

By FRANK HEWLETT

Manila, Dec. 30—(UP)—A Japanese naval threat to Manila was reported today while United States and Philippines forces made a stone-wall stand against vastly stronger Japanese invasion armies on the northern and southern Luzon fronts.

The Philippines Herald quoted reliable sources that during a heavy Japanese airplane raid yesterday on the Corregidor Island fortress at the entrance to Manila Bay, Japanese warships attempted to approach but were driven off by coast defense guns.

It was believed the Japanese ships were making a test of the island's strength with a view to a possible big scale attack from sea as well as land out an-

At headquarters of Gen. Douglas MacArthur, commander in chief, said at 1:30 a. m.:

"Everything is quiet."

There was a sudden surge of optimism in Manila, and hope rose that help was coming from the United States.

Completely unconfirmed reports of the arrival, or imminent arrival, of reinforcements swept the city. Regardless of these, such statements as the one that the Navy was mobile, and the assurance of President Roosevelt, caused a general public feeling that the effort of United States strength would be felt soon in the rice fields of Pagsalion, in the north, and the coconut groves of Tayabas in the south.

QUEZON, OSMENA INAUGURATED

President Manuel L. Quezon and Vice President Sergio Osmena were inaugurated at an informal ceremony at their secret headquarters in the interior today for a second term.

United States High Commissioner Francis B. Sayre, speaking at the ceremony, read a congratulatory message from President Roosevelt and said, in his own behalf, that the United States and the Philippines had become brothers in bloodshed for the defense of their common-

(See PHILIPPINES Page 13)

Fire Delays Traffic During Morning Rush

Fire gutted the second floor of the two-story brick building at 66 Montivello avenue, Jersey City—

trolley for some time, making family homeless and damaging the stock of the A & P. market on the ground floor this morning.

Occurring at the pre-work rush hour, the stoppage of the Jackson cars began shortly after the alarm was sounded at 7:38 o'clock and at one time about 16 trolleys were lined up on Montivello avenue. There bound toward Hoboken were permitted through before the trolleys routed to Greenville, as the usual track was freed of fire fighting apparatus.

A defect in a portable oil burner in the apartment occupied by the family of Mrs. Mary K—p caused the fire. The flames spread rapidly from the burner, which was thrown into the street, and reached the hanging ceiling of the building.

FIREMEN FIND ASSISTANCE NEEDED

A still alarm was received at 7:38 o'clock and when members of Engine Company 30 and Truck Company 2 arrived, assistance was needed and an alarm was sent from the box at Communipaw and Jackson avenues at 7:54 o'clock. Deputy Chief Richard Cullen, Battalion Chief Otto Wagner and Engine Company 8, 8 and 27 and Truck Company 12 responded and the still worked until 9:23 o'clock when the return tap was sounded.

Considerable over-hauling was needed on the upper floor of the building and smoke and water damaged the stock of the market below. Louis Goldberg, 114 Montivello avenue, owns the building.

Policemen, directed by Deputy Chief John Underwood and Captain Edward Gordon re-routed bus and automobile traffic. The emergency squad, commanded by Sergeant James Murray, also responded to the alarm.

Local Man Fined on Policy Slip Charge

(Special to Jersey Observer)

New York, Dec. 30—With the alternative of a ten days jail sentence or a fifty dollar fine was levied in Manhattan Special Sessions Court yesterday, on Charles Emanuel, of 339 Grove street, Jersey City, who pleaded guilty December 23, to a charge of possessing policy slips. Described as a collector by Patrolman Andrew Arlington who arrested him December 8, in the Jersey City man, who operates a grocery store at 334 Lenox avenue, Manhattan, had eighty-one slips with 2,110 numbers, the proceeds of one day's collection.

Hague Guards City Against Blast Danger

That he had taken steps to safeguard Jersey City from a repetition of the Black Tom disaster, even in the event of an air raid, by a regulation of ammunition in transit, was revealed by Mayor Frank Hague last night.

The meeting was called by the Mayor and Commissioner Frank Reardon, chairman of the Jersey City Defense Council, to instruct the wardens regarding the duties they will be expected to perform in case of an air attack.

More than 1,000 men and women who have enrolled for the home defense service fit the work in the downtown section were gathered in the auditorium of School No. 37, Pavonia avenue and Erie street, when the meeting opened.

MAYOR HAGUE'S ADDRESS

In opening the meeting, Mayor Hague said:

"My purpose in appearing before you tonight is to impress upon you the fact that you are now about to begin the serious stage of your work as air raid wardens in Jersey City. You have volunteered your services to the Jersey City Defense Council for the protection of your city in the event of an air raid, and, having volunteered for this work, you must accept your assignment and the responsibility that goes with it.

"As Mayor of Jersey City, I have spent a great deal of time and thought on matters concerning the protection of Jersey City, and I feel that everything that can humanly be done to assure maximum protection to the residents of our city has been done. This matter of affording protection and assuring proper precautions to the city by seeing that we have exercised every step to prevent a repetition of it.

"Following the conferences with the State Defense Council in

(See HAGUE Page 13)

STOCK PRICES

The following prices are furnished through the courtesy of Courtney & Co., 921 Bergen avenue, Jersey City.

	Prev. Close	11:30 Floor
Air Reduction	37½	38½
American Can	55½	55½
American Radiator	4	4
American Smelting	38½	N.S.
Amer. Telephone	121½	123
Amer. Tobacco B	47	46
Anaconda	27	27½
Bethlehem Steel	65	64½
Cerro DePas Corp.	31½	31½
Chrysler	44½	44½
Cities Service	2½	2½
Columbia Gas	1½	1½
Consolidated Ed.	11½	11½
El. Bond & S	1½	1½
Electric Auto Lite	18	18½
Engineer Pub. Ser	2½	N.S.
General Electric	25	24½
General Foods	36	36½
General Motors	29¾	29¾
Intern'l Nickel	25½	25½
Keenecott	37¼	36½
Montgomery Ward	24½	24½
N. Y. Central	7½	7½
Pennsylvania R.R.	17½	17½
Pepsi-Cola	19	19
Public Service	11½	11½
Radio	2½	2½
Socony-Vacuum	7½	7½
Sperry	27½	27½
Standard Brands	4	4
Stand. Oil of N. J.	33½	33½
United Carbide	63½	70
United Aircraft	35	34½
U. S. Rubber	14½	14½
U. S. Steel	52	52½
Western Union	23¼	N.S.
Westinghouse	74½	74½
Woolworth	25½	25½

*Ex.D.

Johnson Is Named Rationing Agent

(Special to Jersey Observer)

Trenton, Dec. 30—Under the special emergency powers granted to him by the Legislature, Governor Edison has appointed Robert W. Johnson, president of the Johnson and Johnson Company, of New Brunswick, to be Rationing Administrator for the state.

The naming of Johnson to this post was made at the request of the Federal Government that the state create an organization to carry out federal rationing regulations, such as the present time pertain to the purchase of new tires and tubes.

According to the understanding had by the governor yesterday, it was intimated that Johnson, will also be concerned with the rationing of other necessities which are becoming scarcer every day.

Edison and that local rationing boards, appointed by municipal executives, will soon be set up to complete the regulation network that will be needed to make the federal rationing orders effective.

Air Cadet Killed

Sykeston, Mo., Dec.—(INS)—Army authorities today reported the death of Richard A. Reid, 24-year-old cadet from White Plains, N. Y., killed in the crash of his plane while on a routine training flight. The crash occurred at the Missouri Institute of Aeronautics field.

Two in Lead for State Appointment

Trenton, Dec. 30—Sallie D. Dixon, 746 Harrison avenue, Harrison, and Marjorie H. Brawn, 280 Harrison avenue, Jersey City, took first and second place, respectively, in the state-wide examination for referee in the Workmen's Compensation Bureau, it was announced by the State Civil Service Commission.

The salary is $3,500 a year.

Aged Man, Hit By Auto, Dies In Hospital

Post traumatic shock caused the death of Peter Farley, 62, of 451 Pavonia avenue, Jersey City, in the Medical Center at 5:45 o'clock this morning, a few hours after he had been felled by an automobile while crossing the intersection of Newark avenue and Chestnut street.

Thomas Berry, 35, of 5 Claremont avenue, driver of the car, rushed the man to the hospital after the accident, which occurred at 3:40 o'clock, and he was attended by Dr. Norton the shock abrasions of the right leg and a possible fracture of the left hip.

Berry told police he left the Armour & Company plant, where he is employed, at 3:30 o'clock, and was driving west in Newark avenue and was making a turn into Chestnut street, when Farley stepped from behind a truck going east on Newark avenue.

ALONE ON MACHINE AT THE TIME

The car struck the man before Berry could swerve or halt it. Berry was alone in the machine at the time.

No complaint was made against him at the time of the accident, but later today he was arrested at his home by Lieutenant Leo Schrieber and Detective Philip Caulfield on a charge of manslaughter by automobile.

"As far back as last July 1 had several conferences with government and railroad officials with reference to the storing and transportation of ammunition in Jersey City. I was Director of Public Safety at the time of the Black Tom explosion in Jersey City in 1916 and have a vivid recollection of the havoc which that explosion caused; and with such resolution in mind, I determined to take every necessary step to prevent the recurrence of such a tragic thing in Jersey City."

To Test Sirens In Jersey City At 3 o'Clock

Through the office of Commissioner Frank J. Reardon, chairman of the Jersey City Civilian Defense Council, Mayor Frank Hague has issued a warning to all citizens that an experimental test of air raid alarm will be conducted by the Jersey City police and fire departments at 3 p. m. today.

The test is being made to evaluate the efficiency of the warning devices to provide adequate air raid warning coverage for Jersey City. The public is asked not to become alarmed. The test warning will consist of three short blasts of approximately 30 seconds each, repeated at frequent intervals. Patrol cars with parcel outlying sections of the city in order to report on the sound of the sirens.

In the event of an actual air raid alarm being received during the period of test, the sirens will sound continuously for a two-minute period, repeated several times with fluctuating notes. However, an actual air raid alarm is considered very unlikely in this territory during daylight hours, according to Civilian Defense officials.

During the test a siren citizens are requested not to phone to police and fire stations or municipal or Civilian Defense officials with inquiries concerning the authenticity of the air

(See SIRENS Page 13)

October Bar Test Passed By 21 Here

Trenton, Dec. 30—Twelve Jersey City residents were among the 101 candidates who qualified in the October bar examinations for attorney-at-law, it was announced today by the State Board of Bar Examiners.

They are Robert Oberndorf, Louis J. Messner, Gerold Kesseniger, Harold J. Brotiski, Daniel F. De Leur, Edward E. Corrigan, Jessie Murphy, Anna V. Wisnosky, Robert J. Mahlon, Arthur Mazid, and Harold B. Weil and Nicholas Zaggle.

The latter two were drafted into military service before they had completed their clerkships, but they were permitted to take the October examinations nevertheless. However, they will be required to serve the balance of their clerkships before being sworn in as practicing lawyers.

The swearing-in ceremonies will take place on March 2, 1942, with Supreme Court Justice Joseph L. Bodine administering the oath.

A total of 31 lawyers from Hudson County municipalities qualified as numerous spectators were attracted by the heavy smoke.

At 10:40 o'clock, Chief Gildoy ordered some of the fire companies to return to quarters. He said the fire began in a gasoline stove in a small office partition which adjoins the storage space on the second floor. Damage, Chief Gildoy said, will not be large because if the salt was moistened by the hose lines it can be dried out.

Treasury Balance

Washington, Dec. 30—(INS)—Treasury balance December 27—$3,456,454,158.82.

Internal revenue, $4,105,554.62. Customs receipts, $39,722,629.69. Receipts, $4,527,840,543.

Mayor Hague Adds to New Year's Warning

Mayor Frank Hague today asked Jersey City residents to cooperate with the State Defense Council in omitting the use of sirens and whistles in welcoming the New Year.

Have a good time, the mayor urged, but asked that no noise-maker similar to that used to warn of an air raid be employed.

Clearing House Report

Northern New Jersey Clearing House: Clearings, $11,400,000; balances, $8,900,000.

▲ JERSEY OBSERVER, JERSEY CITY, TUESDAY DECEMBER 30, 1941

Readers in New Jersey are updated on the rapidly developing situation in Southeast Asia, but the news does not yet reflect the rapid progress of the Japanese forces on all fronts. Meanwhile, photographs of air-raid precautions and siren tests in Jersey City—and the defiant "ears" beside the nameplate—remind readers that the war has come close to home.

1942

THE YEAR 1942 OPENED WITH VICTORIES FOR GERMAN AND JAPANESE FORCES. FROM JUNE TO DECEMBER, HOWEVER, ALLIED VICTORIES TURNED THE TIDE, AND IN WINSTON CHURCHILL'S WORDS THE YEAR MARKED "THE END OF THE BEGINNING."

IN THE FAR EAST, THE YEAR OPENED WITH A JAPANESE TRIUMPH: THE SURRENDER OF THE BRITISH AT SINGAPORE. THIS WAS FOLLOWED BY THE CONQUEST OF THE DUTCH EAST IN-DIES (NOW INDONESIA) AND THE PHILIPPINES. Japanese forces landed on New Guinea and in the Solomon Islands, threatening Australia, and moved up through Burma.

In May, however, the U.S. Navy halted the Japanese advance southeastward at the Battle of the Coral Sea and then in June inflicted a major defeat at the Battle of Midway in the central Pacific. U.S. Marines then landed on Guadalcanal in the Solomons and there and also in New Guinea the Allies inflicted severe defeats on the Japanese.

NORTH AFRICA

In the desert war in North Africa, Rommel's Afrika Korps won great victories in May and June, taking the crucial port of Tobruk, but was then halted on the Egyptian frontier in desperate defensive battles. A further German offensive was stopped in September, and then in November, Rommel was thrown back at the Battle of El Alamein.

THE "TORCH" LANDINGS

As the Battle of El Alamein was being decided, a vast Allied armada landed troops in northwest Africa in the "Torch" landings, demonstrating what could be achieved with sea power, and sealing the fate of Axis forces in North Africa. Early in 1942, German U-boats had enjoyed what they called the "happy time" against Allied shipping, but by the end of the year, new technology and new tactics had turned the tide against these submarine raiders.

▲ THE JAPANESE BATTLECRUISER *HIEI* took part in many naval actions of the Pacific War, including Midway. The *Hiei* was sunk in action off Savo Island on November 13, 1942.

The final turning point in 1942 was the battle of Stalingrad in the Soviet Union. Victories for the Germans in the spring, and a big German offensive in southern Russia seemed to be tipping the balance Germany's way on the Eastern Front. However, the Germans were held in the city of Stalingrad, and on November 19 a gigantic pincer movement cut them off.

▲ NEW YORK POST, MONDAY JANUARY 26, 1942

The *Post* sends birthday greetings to 62-year-old General Douglas MacArthur, then commanding the defense of the Philippines, and reports the enthusiastic welcome for the first detachment of some 4,000 U.S. troops to arrive in Northern Ireland. Readers could also catch up on the latest installment of an exciting anti-German serial, "Above Suspicion," by Scottish–U.S. thriller writer Helen Clark MacInnes.

Paris-Midi

LE BON TON DE PARIS
L'article de H.-R. Lenormand
LETTRES ET THÉÂTRE

DERNIÈRE 32ᵉ ANNÉE. — N° 4981 MARDI 10 FÉVRIER 1942 37, rue du Louvre, Paris ÉDITION
LE NUMÉRO : UN FRANC. — Abonnem.: 1 mois, 24 fr.; 3 mois, 70 fr.; 6 mois, 130 fr.; 1 an, 250 fr.

10 h. 30

De WASHINGTON :
L'incendie de Normandie aurait fait 200 morts. On annonce officiellement que 100 ouvriers gravement brûlés ont été hospitalisés. 120 autres, après avoir été pansés sur place, ont regagné leur domicile.

De MADRID :
On annonce d'Algésiras qu'un grand transport britannique, chargé de troupes et de matériel de guerre, a été attaqué, hier, dans l'Atlantique, par un sous-marin et que, portant de graves avaries, il a été remorqué dans le port de Gibraltar.

LES JAPONAIS
à quinze kilomètres
DE SINGAPOUR
Les Anglais évacuent Rangoon

CAPITALE DE LA BIRMANIE

TOKIO, 10 FÉVRIER.

LES UNITÉS JAPONAISES QUI AVAIENT DÉBARQUÉ A SINGAPOUR, DANS LA NUIT DE LUNDI A MARDI, ÉLARGISSENT RAPIDEMENT LEURS OPÉRATIONS ET ONT OCCUPÉ, AU DÉBUT DE L'APRÈS-MIDI D'HIER, L'AÉRODROME DE TENGAH. D'AUTRE PART, LE CORRESPONDANT DE L'AGENCE DOMEI ANNONCE QUE LA COLONNE QUI AVAIT ATTEINT L'AÉRODROME DE TENGAH, HIER, A 13 H. 30, A POURSUIVI SON AVANCE ET EST ARRIVÉE SUR LES BORDS DU TENGAH, RIVIÈRE SITUÉE A 15 KILOMÈTRES A L'OUEST DE SINGAPOUR.

TOUTE LA PORTION OCCIDENTALE DE L'ÎLE EST DONC AUX MAINS DES JAPONAIS.

« L'OCCUPATION DE CETTE VILLE NE SAURAIT TARDER », CONCLUT LE CORRESPONDANT.

Rangoon est évacuée

CHANGHAI, 10 Février.

Le gouverneur britannique Dorman Smith vient de donner à la population de Rangoon l'ordre de quitter la ville.

L'amiral William H. Standley est nommé ambassadeur des États-Unis à Moscou

WASHINGTON, 10 Février.

L'amiral William H. Standley vient d'être nommé au poste d'ambassadeur à Moscou.

La réélection du président Carmona vue par Berlin

BERLIN, 10 Février.

RAPIDE AVANCE DES UNITÉS DE L'AXE
et retraite épuisante des Anglais en Afrique du Nord

BERLIN, 10 Février.

COMMUNIQUÉ ITALIEN

ROME, 9 Février.

"Normandie"
EN FLAMMES
dans le port de New-York

« Normandie » (Photo archives Paris-Midi.)

NEW-YORK, 10 Février.

Un grave incendie s'est déclaré lundi, à 14 h. 30 (GMT), à bord du transatlantique français « Normandie », amarré au quai 57 sur l'Hudson.

Les victimes

(LIRE LA SUITE EN TROISIÈME PAGE.)

Les bolcheviks subissent de lourdes pertes sur le Donetz

GRAND QUARTIER GÉNÉRAL DU FUEHRER, 9 Février.

Le Fuehrer désigne le professeur Albert Speer comme successeur du Dr. Todt

BERLIN, 10 Février.

"Un fiacre allait trottinant..."

(Photo Paris-Midi.)

Les cantines
SCOLAIRES
de la Seine
pourraient nourrir
500.000 gosses

120.000 DE CEUX-CI SEULEMENT EN BÉNÉFICIENT POURQUOI ?

René PERNOUD.

LA LIGNE DROITE...
OÙ EST LE DEVOIR ?

Le retour à Paris des archives nationales

MÉRIDIEN DE PARIS
Volonté des familles

FERNAND DUVOIRE.

Cyclistes marchez à la file à un mètre du trottoir !

Jean-Pierre MAXENCE.

DE PRÉFÉRENCE

VOYAGE DANS L'IONOSPHÈRE
Pendant qu'il gèle sur la terre, à 150 kilomètres au-dessus de nos têtes, la température atteint 300 degrés

Un vice-régent serait bientôt nommé en Hongrie

BUDAPEST, 10 Février.

Une lettre d'un blessé de la L.V.P.

LA NUIT PROCHAINE
camoufles vos lumières
de 19 h. 31 à 8 h. 38

Afin de valoriser l'émission de timbres qu'elle mettra bientôt en circulation, la Légion des volontaires français a fait brûler, dans ses locaux de la rue Auber, une grande quantité de vignettes « Aviation » représentant une somme de 3 millions de francs. Voici des jeunes gens mettant les timbres à la chaudière. (Photo Lapi.)

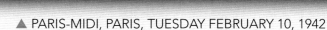

▲ PARIS-MIDI, PARIS, TUESDAY FEBRUARY 10, 1942

In occupied France, the pro-German newspaper reports the Japanese to within 9 miles (15 km) of Singapore. Alongside an assurance that schools in the Seine département have enough food to feed 500,000 students, the paper reports the destruction of the iconic French liner *Normandie*. Seized by U.S. authorities, *Normandie* was being converted to a troopship in New York when it was accidentally destroyed by fire.

◀ TOKYO NICHINICHI, (TOKYO DAILY NEWS), THURSDAY FEBRUARY 26, 1942.

The Japanese press is quick to celebrate the British Army's worst ever defeat: "Singapore Falls. British Army Fly White Flag: Unconditional Surrender. Empire Prepares for Decisive Battle. Official Announcement (15th, 22:10): Imperial Japanese Army forces based in Malaya took on enemy troops on the stronghold of Singapore Island, winning their unconditional surrender at 19:50 on February 15th. Battle of the Century!! The Singapore stronghold of British Imperial Forces, who for many years have been aggressors in East Asia, has fallen. Merely 70 days since the outbreak of the greater East Asian war, and after only seven days facing staunch fighting in a decisive and bloody battle on the fortress of Singapore Island, the enemy crumbled and evacuated the region." The cartoon shows a rampant lion on the Japanese flag.

▶ VICTORIOUS JAPANESE soldiers celebrate their victory at Singapore. British commander Lieutenant General Percival had been forced to surrender on February 14 as the water supply for Singapore's residents and the 85,000-strong garrison was cut. Japan had fewer than 10,000 casualties in Malaya. British and Commonwealth forces had lost 138,000 men, and thousands more would die in captivity. The campaign was one of Britain's greatest military defeats.

Channel Dash
FEBRUARY 12, 1942

IN FEBRUARY 1942, THREE OF THE HEAVY WARSHIPS OF THE GERMAN KRIEGSMARINE, THE BATTLECRUISERS *SCHARNHORST* AND *GNEISENAU* AND THE HEAVY CRUISER *PRINZ EUGEN*, BROKE OUT FROM BREST HARBOR IN France and returned to German waters after a daring voyage through the Straits of Dover in daylight. The RAF and Royal Navy attacks against the German ships were totally ineffective.

BREAKOUT

On February 12 the German ships were in the English Channel and heading north. By the time RAF aircraft had spotted them at 11:09 hours, the ships had gained a 300-mile (480-km) start. The German ships reduced speed at 11:20 hours to pass a British minefield and at 12:18 hours were attacked by Dover-based motor torpedo boats, though the boats launched their torpedoes at long range and failed to score any hits. At 12:30 hours the ships were attacked by six Swordfish torpedo-bombers,

who were all shot down. *Scharnhorst* struck a mine at 14:31 hours but suffered only minor damage. The last British attempt to stop the ships occurred at 15:30 hours, when destroyers and Beaufort bombers launched a series of attacks. Despite a hail of shells and bombs the ships survived. The British *Times* newspaper reported shortly after the so-called "Channel Dash": "Nothing more mortifying to the pride of sea power has happened in Home Waters since the seventeenth century." Ironically, the dash from Brest aided the war effort in the Atlantic for the Allies. From Brest they had threatened all eastbound Atlantic convoys. Now their position astride the vital British sea communications had been abandoned.

▲ THE GERMAN HEAVY CRUISER *PRINZ EUGEN*, one of the Kriegsmarine commerce raiders that made the dash through the English Channel in February 1942.

SEQUEL

There was a tragic sequel for the German ships that made the dash. The *Prinz Eugen* was torpedoes and put out of action 10 days later by a British submarine. The *Gneisenau* was hit two weeks later in Kiel by RAF Bomber Command aircraft and never went to sea again. The *Scharnhorst* was sunk by a naval force in northern waters in December 1943.

DAILY SKETCH, FRIDAY, FEBRUARY 13, 1942.

Daily Sketch

No. 10,222   (E**)   FRIDAY, FEBRUARY 13, 1942   ONE PENNY

GREAT SEA-AIR BATTLE IN STRAITS OF DOVER

SCHARNHORST, GNEISENAU OUT

ENEMY DASH TO HELIGOLAND

SCHARNHORST and Gneisenau, the German battle-cruisers, and the cruiser Prinz Eugen—survivor of the Bismarck encounter—which have been bombed more than 100 times in their hiding place at Brest, escaped yesterday in misty weather and a fierce naval battle raged in the Channel.

British long-range guns fired at extreme range. German big guns replied.

British destroyers, torpedo-boats, Fleet Air Arm and R.A.F. planes attacked the big enemy flotilla, which was heavily escorted by fighters.

Gneisenau and Prinz Eugen are believed to have escaped to Heligoland Bight.

This is the official communiqué:
"About 11 a.m. yesterday R.A.F. aircraft reported an enemy squadron consisting of the Scharnhorst, Gneisenau and Prinz Eugen, accompanied by destroyers, torpedo boats, E-boats and minesweepers, was approaching the Dover Straits.
"The enemy squadron was also heavily escorted by fighter aircraft.
"Visibility varied from three to five miles with low clouds and the enemy ships were never visible from the English coast.
"On receipt of the report coastal craft of the Dover Naval Command were immediately sent out to the attack, together with Swordfish aircraft of the Fleet Air Arm, strongly escorted by R.A.F. fighters.
"The attacks both by Swordfish and by the coastal craft were pressed close home in face of intense fire from all enemy surface vessels and opposition by the enemy.
"Reports indicate that the Swordfish scored at least one hit on one of the enemy heavy ships, and one of the motor torpedo boats also claims a possible hit, but owing to the intense barrage and a heavy smoke screen put up by the enemy it was impossible to see the results of the attacks.
"Six Swordfish aircraft are missing, but some of the crews have been saved. There were no casualties in the Coastal craft.
"During this time the Dover defences opened fire at extreme range, which was replied to by the enemy's shore batteries in the French coast.
"The enemy force was repeatedly attacked by aircraft of the R.A.F. strongly escorted by fighters.
"The attacks were pressed home with the greatest determination in the face of heavy anti-aircraft fire and strong fighter opposition, which resulted in the loss of 20 of our bombers (including five aircraft of Coastal Command) and 16 fighters.
"Fifteen enemy fighters were destroyed by our fighter escort and at least three more by the bombers themselves.

Continued on Back Page, Col. 4

MRS. F.D.R. WILL RESIGN A.R.P. JOB

Mrs. Roosevelt, wife of the president, announced yesterday that she would resign "very soon" as assistant director of the Office of Civilian Defence, because she had "always intended to resign when the organisation was completed."

She has been accused in Congress and in the U.S. Press of granting appointments in the O.C.D. to Hollywood and stage friends—an accusation she denied.—A.P.

THERE WERE THREE GERMANS—and radio pictures from Moscow show them (above) before being sent to the Eastern Front and (below) what happened to them there.

They've lost their martial bearing, these three Germans—Alfred Franke, Herbert Blum and Rudolf Pankratz by name. Ragged, footsore and frost-bitten, they are prisoners, captured by the Russians in the Donetz Basin.

MYSTERY DEATH OF JAP ENVOY

THERE are two versions of the mysterious death in Paris yesterday of Kato, Japanese Ambassador to Vichy.

First report said that he became giddy and fell from the balcony of the Embassy into the street.

The other version, given later by the Japanese Embassy, said that Kato died of a heart attack. He was Counsellor to the Embassy in London from 1932 to 1935.

CHINESE TAKE 3 KEY TOWNS

CHINESE forces have recaptured three key towns, it was announced in Chungking yesterday.

They are Nanchang, important road junction and capital of Kiangsi Province; Mengcheng, in the Ko river valley of Anhwei Province; and Koyang, 60 miles north-west of Mengcheng.

The Chinese, said the communiqué, drove back three Japanese columns which launched an offensive in North Anhwei Province last week.

SINGAPORE STILL FIGHTING ON

SINGAPORE is holding on. Singapore is fighting back. Counter-attacks on the Japanese left flank have been successful.

The Singapore radio station which yesterday radioed to the world: "We are not only going to fight . . . we are going to win," and then faded out, broadcast this official communiqué early this morning after a silence of some hours:

"Counter-attacks by our troops have been successful on the left flank of the Japanese.

"At 7.30 this morning Japanese military bombers with fighter escort fought an unsuccessful engagement against our air force over Malaya.

"Heavy fighting continues in the western and northern sectors. In the north of the island enemy activity has been intensified.

"Enemy air activity ceased during the night but was resumed early this morning. The enemy attack was supported by dive-bombing and machine-gunning as well as by medium tanks.

"The British line extends from the Naval Base in the north through the centre of the island to Tanglin in the south. From Sungei Sunya the line runs north."

Tanglin is the district to the north-west of Singapore City near the racecourse.

Tokyo, through the official Domei Agency, admits the ferocity of the British resistance in these words:

"British forces are still offering fierce resistance in the neighbourhood of Singapore Racecourse, some two miles north-west of the town, and in the region of the reservoirs, which lie more than four miles north of the town.

[In the reservoir region British artillery is powerful, and is fighting bitter big gun duels with the attackers.]

"Heavy fighting has been going on since yesterday around the city of Singapore.

"Two fortresses have turned their guns towards the interior of the island and have replied to the fire of Japanese artillery.

"Aerial reconnaissance shows Singapore is completely covered by clouds of black smoke from burning oil tanks. It is therefore impossible to reconnoitre the position in Singapore city."

Yet Berlin radio last night claimed that street fighting in Singapore City had ended and that the defenders had been overcome.

'Warships in Action'

Before that Tokyo claimed that the racecourse was used by their troops as a rest base the previous night, while advanced Japanese forces had penetrated into Singapore itself and were engaged in hand-to-hand fighting in the streets.

Not a single British defender could be seen in the north-west suburbs, it was said.

British naval guns are in action shelling Japs in the northern area —say British reports.

Continued on Back Page, Col. 3

'Daily Sketch' Man With U.S. Army

WILLIAM (BILL) COURTENAY, "Daily Sketch" Air correspondent, is now our accredited war correspondent with the American forces.

He is already with American forces on active service.

When the success of his lectures in America became known, the proprietors of the "Daily Sketch" readily agreed that his tour be extended from the original three months to six. He travelled 30,000 miles and spoke to 171 audiences in Canada and the United States.

Mr. William Courtenay

NAZIS SAY 45 DIE UNLESS—

THE Germans have ordered the execution of 45 Frenchmen held as hostages unless the authors of two recent attacks against Germans in Occupied France are discovered within a few days, said an A.P. message last night.

Twenty of the men are to be executed at Tours unless the person who attacked a German sentry is found by to-morrow. The 25 others will be executed at Rouen unless the people who threw bombs at Germans there are arrested before Sunday.

The Germans last year shot several Frenchmen held as hostages for the killing of two German officers at Bordeaux and Nantes.

TIMELY WORDS OF FAITH AND WISDOM

Specially selected daily from the Bible for readers of the DAILY SKETCH by Lord Caldecote.

FEAR NOT: FOR THEY THAT BE WITH US ARE MORE THAN THEY THAT BE WITH THEM. II Kings vi, 16.

▲ DAILY SKETCH, MANCHESTER, FRIDAY FEBRUARY 13, 1942

Bad news for British readers: the *Sketch* reports the successful dash of the German warships through the English Channel. Meanwhile, the good news from Singapore would prove to be largely wishful thinking: the British garrison surrendered two days later. The page is dominated by two contrasting photographs of three German soldiers before heading to war and after months on the Eastern Front. The *Sketch* observes (gloats?), "They've lost their martial bearing." At bottom right, politician Lord Chaldecote offers the latest in a series of daily thoughts from the Bible that suggest unmistakably that the Allies still had the backing of the Almighty.

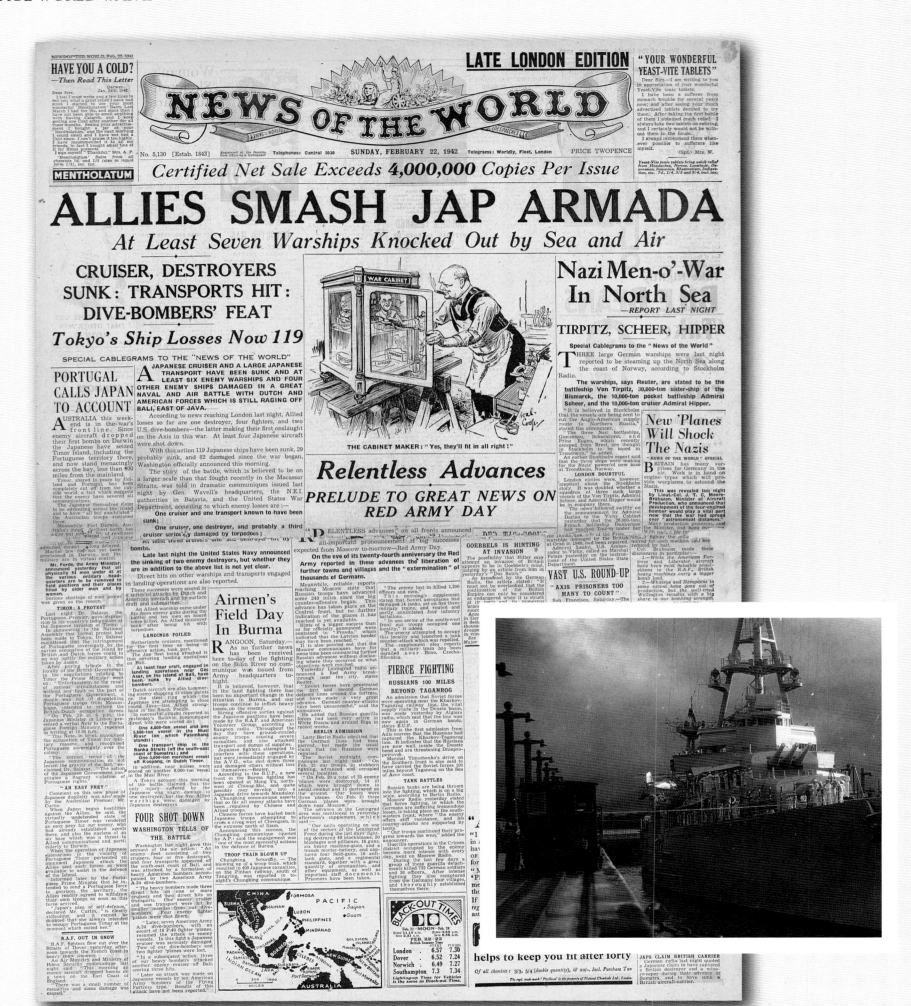

▲ NEWS OF THE WORLD, LONDON, SUNDAY FEBRUARY 22, 1942
Boasting sales that any modern newspaper would envy, Britain's populist
Sunday paper has positive tidings from all fronts, underlined by a cartoon
showing Winston Churchill collecting politicians for his "war cabinet."

▲ THE HEAVY CRUISER USS *HOUSTON* was part of the Allied naval
force operating off the Dutch East Indies in February 1942. Early in the
month, the ship had a gun turret blown off in an attack by Japanese bombers.
The *Houston* was later sunk at the Battle of the Java Sea.

EXTRA!

9 A.M. FINAL

Los Angeles Times

EQUAL RIGHTS
LIBERTY UNDER THE LAW · TRUE INDUSTRIAL FREEDOM

9 A.M. FINAL

VOL. LXI   WEDNESDAY MORNING, FEBRUARY 25, 1942.   DAILY, FIVE CENTS

L.A. AREA RAIDED!

Enemy Girds for Knockout Burma Blow

Reinforcements Moved Up as Defenders Fear Fall of Vital City Ne—

BY THE ASSOCIATED PRESS

Japan moved up reinforcements for the Battle of Burma and dispatched a strong naval force toward Dili, capital of Portuguese Timor, in widely separated theaters of the Pacific war today.

Australians announced a Japanese war fleet had been sighted off Dili and that invasion parachute troops had landed near Koepang, capital of the Dutch half of the island.

SHIPS REPORTED FIRED

Japanese transports in Dili Harbor, however, were reported afire and presumably this was a result of blows struck by the Dutch-Australian garrison of the Portuguese area or United Nations warplanes based on Australia or Java. The Japanese gained a foothold in both the Dutch and Portuguese sections of Timor last week.

Japanese raiders who flew at 20,000 feet killed one person and injured five yesterday in dropping 70 bombs on Port Moresby, Southern New Guinea island outpost less than 400 miles off the north tip of Australia, but were said to have caused no important damage to service buildings. The port was attacked again this afternoon.

Domei, Japanese news agency, said warships operating against Koepang had captured a Dutch freighter and a tanker.

The battle crisis heightened in

Turn to Page 2, Column 5

Today's Latest War Bulletins

BANDOENG, Feb. 25. (AP) — Allied aircraft sank two large Japanese transport ships in a raid on a concentration near Macassar, in the Southern Celebes, and a third elsewhere, a Netherlands Indies communique said today. Allied planes also raided an airdrome near Palembang, Japanese-occupied city in Southern Sumatra, and set three enemy planes afire, it was announced.

LONDON, Feb. 25. (AP)—An official spokesman said today the Consul General at Batavia, capital of the Netherlands East Indies, had been arranging since last December for evacuation to Australia of British subjects in the East Indies, "particularly women and children."

TOKYO, Feb. 25. (From Japanese Broadcasts) (AP) — Japa—

Turn to Page A, Column 6

In Colorado-- 56 Below Zero

KREMMLING (Colo.) Feb. 25. (AP) — The temperature in this Central Colorado mountain town —hot today but a week ago— was 56 degrees below zero.

The report is unofficial, from a railroad station agent's thermometer, but the weather bureau permits its publication now —for whatever aid and comfort it may give the enemy to know that Colorado can match Russian temperatures.

Fifth-Column Acts Reported During Raids

Three Japanese Seized; Mystery Movements and Lights Stir Residents

Mysterious lights, suspicious Japanese, robbery attempts marked the city's first air raid.

In the Tarzana Hills Burbank police saw a string of lights in V-form pointing toward the Lockheed aircraft plant.

Other lights were seen off Point Fermin.

Still others were reported at Redondo and in the hills back of Hermosa Beach.

Air Raid Warden Leo Schukin of Beverly Hills saw winking green and white flashes in the Windsor Hills.

Three suspicious Japanese, two men and a woman, were taken into custody on the Venice pier.

Police were called to stop prowlers who were trying to break in a bank at Laurel Canyon Drive and Ventura Blvd.

A garbage can was thrown through a jewelry store window at First and Broadway.

Home Damaged by Metal From Sky During Raid

Fragments of metal early today hailed from the sky to damage the home of Mrs. H. G. Landis, 1738 W. 43rd St., as Army searchlights and anti-aircraft fire probed the heavens for foreign planes menacing Los Angeles.

Mrs. Landis reported to author-

Turn to Page A, Column 6

Jap Planes Peril Santa Monica, Seal Beach, El Segundo, Redondo Long Beach, Hermosa, Signal Hill

Roaring out of a brilliant moonlit western sky, foreign aircraft flying both in large formation and singly, flew over Southern California early today and drew heavy barrages of anti-aircraft fire—the first ever to sound over United States continental soil against an enemy invader.

No bombs were reported dropped.

At 5 a.m. the police reported that an airplane had been shot down near 185th St. and Vermont Ave. Details were not available. Earlier, the Fourth Air Force in San Francisco said that at least one plane had been downed in the raid.

Sirens shrieked throughout the Southland at 2:23 a.m., and an immediate blackout was enforced.

Almost instantly the great fingers of light from the giant Army searchlights shot into the sky, clustering first in an area appearing above the vast El Segundo oil refineries.

Simultaneously the anti-aircraft defenses of the city roared into action and soon the entire southwestern skies of the city were ablaze with orange bursts.

The planes, flying in number variously estimated at from 8 to 20, flew at an altitude of

Turn to Page A, Column 1

▲ LOS ANGELES TIMES, WEDNESDAY FEBRUARY 25, 1942

A special edition reports a Japanese air-raid on southern California, along with fifth-column sabotage on the ground. The report proved false—only a handful of Japanese balloon bombs fell largely harmlessly on U.S. soil during the war—but its tone reflects the genuine fear that gripped many Americans about hostile attack.

THE DAILY MAIL, Tuesday, March 10, 1942

Make SOUP more nourishing by thickening with
BROWN & POLSON
CORNFLOUR
Best for 100 years

Daily Mail

LATE WAR NEWS SPECIAL

ROLLS RAZORS
now *unobtainable*

NO. 14,310 — ONE PENNY — ★ ★ ★ — FOR KING AND EMPIRE — TUESDAY, MARCH 10, 1942

RANGOON FALLS: JAPS PRESS ON

India Speeds Her Defences : Java Battle Ends

MR. KNICKERBOCKER, eye-witness of every major campaign of the last ten years, reports here the last days of the Java battle and warns of Japan's strength.

Lesson of Java for Australia

'Fight and Work —or Die'

From H. R. KNICKERBOCKER, Daily Mail Special Correspondent

AT AN AUSTRALIAN PORT, Monday.

THE last foreign fugitives have escaped from Java. From now on, this vast continent of Australia is a front-line fortress which must be held if the furious Japanese are to be stopped from over-running the world.

It was that under-valuation, plus Allied procrastination, which led to the loss of that opulent island of Java, which to-day, invaded and surrounded, has become a vast prison-cell for those brave Dutchmen who refused to join the "retreat from Asia."

We took part in that retreat and with 1,300 other refugees went out from Java in the last ship known to have successfully penetrated the Japanese-screen flung around the island by the Japs.

Three ships ahead of us were not so successful, and we picked up survivors from two of them ming our five-days voyage to the southern safety of an Australian port.

"Comparatively" is accurate. It is just three weeks since my last flying trip through Australia, and the sense of urgent danger has grown to such a degree that already the anticipation of bombing has become part of the mental background of inhabitant even the remotest part of this continent.

Now, posters here bring the terrifying figure of the Japanese intelligent-tryman with his tommy-gun just about to put one foot on Australia under a banner reading: "He is Coming South."

THE Japanese would find granaries and wool-barns and refrigerators bursting with food and materials for clothing here.

After acquiring the mineral and agricultural riches of Indo-China, Malaya, and the Dutch East Indies, the Japanese staff would require nothing but the immense cattle, sheep, and grain resources of Australia and New Zealand to complete one of the most economically impregnable empires in history.

It is now dawning on some of the hitherto complacent observers that if the Japanese are permitted to take New Zealand and Australia they will never be driven out

Indeed, after considering these naval position and organising the 300,000,000 to 300,000,000 Asiatics who have come under their control, or are about to do so, they may set forth again to war against the rest of the world on a basis of irresistible superiority of force.

MOST important of all is the fact that Australia is literally the last jumping-off place from which a counter-attack could be launched upon Japan from this part of the world.

The Australians know this, and they know that the Japanese know it.

Hence the Australians are convinced that they had better prepare for a life-and-death battle. This is simply a recapitulation of the thoughts of the hundreds among the pitiable population of our refugee ship who could still think.

In my judgment there is more sound thinking among Australians who sleep or lie unmoved on the bare deck of a vessel speeding away from the enemy than among many an economic military, or naval staff situated comfortably far from those hard-pressed folk who teach the reality of that war.

Scarcely one of us on this gallant vessel of ours could think back on Java without remorse and considerable bitterness, for all of us realised that just a few hundred more planes could have saved us.

WE Americans wondered constantly and vocally what we do with all our airplanes.

Sometimes it is difficult, even for an American who has spent years warning of the dangers of Nazi Germany, to remember that Hitler must be smashed first.

The little Japanese have grown fast to get him into perspective.

We are taking too long in smashing Hitler, and if the little Japanese has the time he needs to digest the enormous meal he is now preparing he may be too tough to handle.

So the people here want to handle him while he is still a man-size job.

On that point of the Japanese about to bestride Australia are the bitter words to all Australians: "Fight and Work or Die!"

AUSTRALIA TOLD 'DARKEST HOUR'

From Daily Mail Special Correspondent

MELBOURNE, Monday.

RANGOON, it was officially announced to-day, has fallen. In the Dutch stronghold of Java all organised resistance has now ceased. A general attack against Eastern New Guinea is expected to develop within a few days from the Japanese landings there yesterday.

This summarises the Far East news to-night.

To-day all Asia and Australasia are tense with the expectation of even greater events to come. The Battle of India and the Battle of Australia loom closer.

Already the Japanese claim to be pushing northwards from Rangoon towards the frontiers of India. Preparations to resist invasion are being speeded up from Calcutta to Madras and from Madras to Ceylon.

In Australia the Government is working all out to brace the people against the danger to come. There is full realisation in the Dominion that the ten or eleven divisions which overwhelmed the Dutch in Java in nine days are now free for new tasks—and are less than 800 miles from the shores of Western Australia.

Some of these divisions are likely to be used to reinforce the Japs now massing on the north-east coast of New Guinea. These troops are expected to attack Port Moresby at any hour. Every effort must be made to save that town from falling into their hands.

Port Moresby, with its fine, capacious harbour, is little more than 300 miles from north-eastern Australia. It would make an ideal invasion base from which to strike either at the north or the wealthy east coast of the Dominion.

Australia is fully alive to her peril.

Flaring placards of a grinning Japanese, with tommy-gun at the ready, setting foot on Australian soil stare out from every hoarding.

'RISE IN WRATH'

Mr. Heffron, Minister of National Emergency Services, gave this blunt warning to the people in a broadcast to-night:

"This is the darkest hour in our history. I solemnly call upon the people of Australia to rise in their wrath against the greedy devil who seeks our land and our wealth, who would despoil our manhood and womanhood.

"We are the sons and daughters of hard-fighting adventurers, and soon we must prove our right to the land won for us against the tempest, tears, sweat, and suffering."

The general awareness of the danger is reinforced by the presence of a handful of Dutch leaders from Java, preparing to collect the few fighting men who have been able to escape with them to continue the fight.

"At their head is Dr. Van Mook, Lieutenant Governor-General of the Netherlands East Indies, who arrived in Australia yesterday by plane with his Chief of Air Staff, 14 members of the Netherlands East Indies Governing Council, and other high Service officers.

"The party took off from the 'last strip of runway available' in Java, but the plane made two trips to the Australian mainland without incident.

"We are here to collect all the forces we can get together to continue the struggle," said Dr. Van Mook.

"A fair number of naval personnel have escaped. They want someone to rally them. I am sure that we can carry on the fight. Bandoeng has fallen, but our people are battling on with the resources they have left."

Rangoon A City of Flame

Fire-Raisers Busy as End Game

From DANIEL BERRIGAN, B.U.P. Correspondent

MANDALAY, Sunday (delayed).

RANGOON was to-day a dead city lying under a pall of smoke from fires, many of them started by saboteurs.

Arrivals from Rangoon to-day told of their last glimpse of the city—the great modern capital of Burma.

There were fires all over this city that once housed 400,000 people. Two districts, inhabited mostly by people of the poorer class, had been completely destroyed.

Debris littered the streets.

Shortage of equipment had forced the fire brigade to concentrate on the more important buildings, some of which were untouched by the fires, and to abandon fighting the flames which swept the poorer areas.

The city's radio and telephone and power systems operated until the very last, kept going by skeleton staffs working in a deserted city.

'Act!'

From Bombay Reuter reports that Sir Reginald Dorman-Smith, Governor of Burma, has broadcast this message to the officials of Burma:

"At this hour there is only one thing. It is courage and conviction to take a decision.

"You may be doubtful about your decisions and wish to refer them to your higher authority. Do not worry about referring to superiors. Act, provided your decision is calculated to embarrass the enemy and contribute to our war effort.

"I will back you, right or wrong."

New Guinea Expecting Major Invasion Soon

From CHRISTIAN FOLKARD, Daily Mail Special Correspondent

PORT MORESBY, Monday.

A MAJOR Japanese attack on New Guinea from their new bases at Salamaua and Lae may be launched within a few days. Their main objective will be Port Moresby, which is destined to play a vital part in the defence of Australia.

A simultaneous assault by air and sea is expected.

At present, the biggest job of defending this vast area falls on the shoulders of young Australian pilots who take off daily to raid enemy-occupied areas.

A low-flying attack on shipping at Salamaua yesterday scored several direct hits. All our aircraft returned.

Australian planes also reconnoitred the main enemy bases on New Britain Island.

Port Moresby was attacked by ten Japanese heavy bombers at noon to-day. There were no casualties.

Four hundred men, 1,800 women, and a number of children have been evacuated from New Guinea to Australia mainland. All the men are unfit or elderly.

JAPS TO STAY IN TIMOR

A report that Japanese troops will remain in Portuguese Timor was broadcast by Saigon radio last night. The announcement said:

"It is reported from Timor that the Portuguese reinforcements came after British and Australians occupied Portuguese Timor have arrived at Dilli, the capital.

"It is also reported that a Japanese-Portuguese agreement will be signed soon. According to a previous agreement between the Portuguese and British Governments the British troops were to have been withdrawn as soon as the Portuguese troops arrived.

"The people of Timor therefore expected the Japanese troops to leave, but it is officially announced that the Japanese troops have been authorised to remain on the island."

MERCY SHIP SAILS

The Swedish steamer Helleren has left the Baltic carrying 9,000 tons of wheat and other food for Greece. The vessel was chartered by Britain, and the Greek Government has paid for the food.

McNaughton Sees Roosevelt

From Daily Mail Correspondent

WASHINGTON, Monday. — Lieut.-General McNaughton, Commander-in-Chief of the Canadian Overseas Army, conferred for nearly an hour with President Roosevelt at the White House to-day.

Earlier in the day he had seen General George C. Marshall, United States Army Chief of Staff, and other American military men. He said he would return to Britain "in a matter of days."

Petain Takes a Rest

Marshal Pétain left Vichy yesterday for several days' rest in his country home at Villeneuve Loubon, says Swiss radio.

COMMANDER ATTACKS AN ADMIRAL

COMMANDER Edgar P. Young, R.N., speaking at East Sheen, S.W., last night referred to a speech made by Admiral of the Fleet Sir Roger Keyes as "reckless, foolish, and unworthy of a responsible public speaker."

Sir Roger Keyes, he said, had advocated an offensive spirit, but "the escape of the warships must be ascribed to other causes.

"If we had had, say, a dozen destroyers at our disposal, but had sent them out too late to overtake the enemy and to deliver their torpedo attack from an unfavourable position, the chances of success would have been insignificant—but in an infinitesimal degree—far less degree than work in our dockyards."

"Sir Roger Keyes must know."

Stalin Forestalls Hitler

BIG ATTACK ON OIL ARMY

Daily Mail Radio Station

THE Russians have launched two big attacks in the south in an effort to prise Hitler from his spring-boards for a thrust on the Caucasus oil districts.

The main attack, according to the German radio last night, is being delivered by a force of four to six divisions, probably totalling 90,000 men, somewhere along the 50-mile front between Taganrog and Stalino.

The Germans admitted that their positions had been breached at several points.

Heavy counter-attacks had been launched—but the Germans did not give their usual claim, that these actions had thrown back the Russians.

The second Russian attack, also according to Berlin, is around Kharkov, where heavy fighting is in progress.

Hitler's "Zero Hour": BACK

Late News Flash
U.S. 'SUBS' STRIKE AT JAP NAVY

Washington, Monday.

THE Navy Department announced to - night that United States submarines have sunk a Japanese destroyer and a naval tanker. Others have damaged a Japanese aircraft-carrier and three cruisers.—Reuter.

A. V. Roe's Son Killed

Squadron Leader E. A. Verdon-Roe, eldest son of Sir Alliott Verdon-Roe, the aircraft designer who gave his name to the Avro machine, is reported "presumed killed" in an Air Ministry casualty list published to-day.

RAF Bombs France By Day and Night

ANOTHER terrific attack was made on the invasion coast in the region of Calais and Cap Gris Nez shortly before 8.30 last night. Explosions shook the south-east coast towns, and from the cliffs the A.A. bursts could be seen above a bank of haze. The flashes illuminated the Channel.

Masses of ourselves threw their beams towards the English coast, which they almost reached. It seemed clear that very heavy bombs were being dropped.

This night assault followed a raid by a small force of our bombers escorted by fighters, yesterday afternoon on the power and industrial plant at Mazingarbe, near Bethune.

Three enemy fighters were destroyed by the fighter escort. Four of our fighters are missing, the Air Ministry stated.

RUMANIA BREAKS WITH BRAZIL

Rio de Janeiro, Monday.—An official source said to-day that Rumania had informed Brazil that relations between the two countries had been ruptured.—A.P.

U.S. MISSION CHIEF

Washington, Monday. — Mr. Louis Johnson, an ex-Assistant Secretary of War, is to be head of the United States Mission to India. K is announced in Washington.—B.U.P.

BASES: U.S. SAYS 'LEASE STANDS'

From Daily Mail Correspondent

WASHINGTON, Monday.—President Roosevelt to-day denied reports that the United States was seeking indefinite prolongation of the 99-years lease granted to America for bases in British colonies in the Western Hemisphere.

The United States Government, he said, did not seek sovereignty over the islands and colonies where the bases were located, nor was it asking for modification of the agreements.

The President's statement was made at the same time as the announcement that the British and United States Governments had set up a joint commission in the Caribbean to strengthen economic co-operation there.

Milk for Schools is Doubled

Double the quantity of milk for schoolchildren is to be released after next Sunday. Instead of one-third of a pint, each child will be able to have two-thirds of a pint per day.

When the restriction of a third of a pint was imposed towards the end of last year 775,000 children in England and Wales were affected.

King Gustav: An Operation

From Daily Mail Correspondent

STOCKHOLM, Monday. — King Gustav of Sweden, who is 83, to-day underwent an operation, performed by Professor John Hellstroom, a leading specialist in the Red Cross nursing home here.

A bulletin issued later said that his condition after the operation was wholly satisfactory.

Faulty Masks: 22 Sent Home

Twenty-two children were suspended from school at Leiston, Suffolk, yesterday until their parents have bought new parts for their gas-masks and made them gas-proof.

Miss P. T. Allan, the head-mistress, said the parents had received a fortnight's warning and been told they could buy parts from the police.

Output for Nazis

Eighty-five per cent of the total output of France's motor industry is being exported to Germany, says a Geneva dispatch to the official Soviet News Agency quoted by Reuter.

Some 3,500 aircraft, produced by French factories in 1941 were turned over to the Germans.

At one military parade in Paris the German troops were equipped exclusively with French arms. Not a single German-made lorry was to be seen.

The Germans are requisitioning all gas generator plants in France, the correspondent adds.

American Planes Bombed Poissy

THE R.A.F. raid on the Matford Works at Poissy, near Paris, was carried out by American-built Douglas Bostons, it was revealed yesterday. This is the first time it has been announced that Bomber Command has used Bostons.

Photographs taken during the raid have shown that it was highly successful. Vichy news agency said yesterday that there were no victims.

Leahy Tells Vichy 'Raids Justified'

From Daily Mail Correspondent

MADRID, Monday. — Admiral Leahy, United States Ambassador at Vichy, is stated to have turned down a suggestion that the United States should pass on to Britain a protest against the R.A.F. raids on Paris industrial areas.

The admiral is understood to have told the Vichy authorities bluntly that America was no longer willing to act as a channel for many reasons." Also that he thought the raids amply justified.

'Was I Quixotic?' Asks Dr. Lang

Dr. Lang, the retiring Archbishop of Canterbury, speaking in London yesterday, said sometimes he wondered whether he had been a little quixotic in giving up his great post. He added:

"There is no necessity, so far as I can see, certainly not of health, nor so far as I know of talking mental powers. When I read the letters of expostulation which I have received, I begin to wonder whether my step was really called for."

Briton Caught in Java

Mr. Kenneth Selby-Walker, Reuter's special correspondent in Java, is still in the island. At the end of his last cable sent from Bandoeng last Friday, he said: "I am afraid it is too late to leave Java. I have only myself to blame. Good luck. Hope to see you all sooner than you expect."

▲ DAILY MAIL, LONDON, TUESDAY MARCH 10, 1942

The British had ruled Burma since 1824 until the capital, Rangoon, fell to the Japanese in 1942. The shock was profound and, as the *Mail* points out, the implications for Britain's Australian colony were grim. The tooth-paste advertisement injects a little levity with a pun aimed at women involved in war work, who were often now the breadwinners as well as the shoppers in a family.

The fall of Burma

MARCH 1942

THE JAPANESE FORCES THAT HAD MOVED INTO SOUTHEAST ASIA IN DECEMBER 1941 SOON TURNED THEIR ATTENTION TO BURMA, A BRITISH COLONY AND THE SITE OF THE ONLY land route through which the western Allies could supply China, which was itself engaged in a war with Japan. The geography of the region meant that Thailand was critical to any Japanese attacks on Burma. In December the Thai government was forced to sign an alliance that allowed Japanese forces to pass through the country, and committed Thai troops to help the Japanese.

FIRST ATTACKS ON BURMA

The first Japanese attacks were very successful, taking the town of Moulmein, and British forces could do little to stem the tide and were forced to withdraw. In particular, the retreat across the Sittang river late in February was a disaster, with a great deal of equipment being abandoned when the bridge was blown early.

In spite of attempts to form a defensive line covering the capital Rangoon, the British forces under General Harold Alexander had to abandon the city on March 7. News of the fall of Rangoon was a further bitter pill for the British public. It came soon after the fall of Hong Kong and Singapore and coincided with Japanese naval success at the battle of the Java Sea.

JAPANESE VICTORY IN BURMA

Alexander next marshalled his forces to try to hold northern Burma. Chinese forces came down to help him, but Japanese forces proved too effective. Some Chinese forces were forced back into China, while others retreated back to India with the British.

The defeat in Burma in spring 1942 was just one of the string of Allied failures that marked this period. In spite of trying to maintain an upbeat tone, many newspapers in Allied countries found it hard to spot a silver lining in the woeful litany of defeat after defeat, seemingly on all fronts.

▲ RANGOON IN FLAMES. The British destroyed anything that might have been of use to the Japanese before they left the city, to begin the longest retreat in British military history.

THE DAILY MAIL, Monday, April 6, 1942.

THOUSANDS PRAISE THIS NAME
MACLEAN BRAND

LATE WAR NEWS SPECIAL

THICKER, RICHER GRAVY... USE BROWN & POLSON CORNFLOUR — BEST FOR 100 YEARS

Daily Mail

NO. 14,332   ONE PENNY   ★ ★ ★   FOR KING AND EMPIRE   MONDAY, APRIL 6, 1942

FIRST GREAT JAP AIR DEFEAT

Colombo Armada Intercepted Far Out at Sea

No 'Second Pearl Harbour'

Secret 'Dromes Beat Jap Plans

By COLIN BEDNALL, Daily Mail Air Correspondent

SUFFICIENT details of the Colombo air battle reached London last night to make it clear that the shooting down of 27 planes was only part of the great victory.

Well and ambitiously planned, with some at least of the raiders operating from dispersed aircraft-carriers, the Japanese, I believe, attempted another "Pearl Harbour." And they failed ignominiously.

To this extent, Ceylon's defences have given the Japanese their worst shaking yet, and one that may mean much to the future course of the war.

The Japs hoped to smash harbour installations and sink ships in one devastating raid. After Pearl Harbour, they did it at various other places.

At Colombo, however, they had a surprise which they will not quickly forget.

★

THEY were caught napping by a system of air defence which has been crashed into being in the past few months—perhaps weeks.

British fighters which met and decimated the raiders operated from a chain of secret aerodromes, of which even now nobody outside Ceylon has heard many details.

Several of these aerodromes have sprung up all over the country.

Berlin 'Finds' Lost Ship

New York, Sunday.—Berlin radio, heard here to-day, said that the Nazi auxiliary cruiser Kormoran, which some time ago sank the Australian cruiser Sydney, was itself sunk in the Atlantic and had an unexpected meeting with a German submarine.

57 SMASHED OUT OF 75 PLANES

From ALFRED PIERES, Daily Mail Correspondent   COLOMBO, Sunday.

JAPANESE air squadrons were sent reeling back from Colombo when they made their first attempt to raid this island key to the Indian Ocean in the early hours of this morning. Colombo has won the first round.

Fifty-seven raiders plunged flaming into the ocean, crashed into the paddy fields, or went staggering away riddled with bullets.

Official figures are that 27 were destroyed, five probably destroyed, and 25 more damaged.

Admiral Sir Geoffrey Layton, the Commander-in-Chief, in a broadcast to-night, said about 75 Japanese aircraft came over and bombed the harbour area, the Ratmalana railway works, and the aerodrome.

It was doubtful if damaged enemy planes could have reached their aircraft-carrier.

"I am sorry to say," he added, "that over half of those killed were patients of one of our medical establishments."

The island had ample warning of the attack. Fighters first intercepted the raiders over the sea. Twenty-five enemy planes were shot to pieces.

Those which got through swept down on the harbour and southern suburbs through low clouds, dive-bombing and machine-gunning.

PLANES ON WAY TO BURMA

From CEDRIC SALTER, Daily Mail Special Correspondent   CALCUTTA, Sunday.

THE British withdrawal from Prome means that the Imperial defences are now forced back on the outskirts of the Burmese oilfields at Yenanma, which are now only 60 miles north of the Japanese lines.

PEOPLE CALM

Fifth Columnists

SOME BALED OUT

Norwegian Ships Get to Britain
—But Not All

SOME of the 11 Norwegian ships that defied German air and naval forces in a dash from Gothenburg have reached Britain.

Order Lifted

IRA Gunmen Kill PC

A policeman, Constable Patrick Murphy, was shot dead during a gun battle between six I.R.A. men and a police patrol in Cawnpore-street, Belfast, yesterday afternoon.

South Coast Town Bombed

'Second Front': by War Minister

Roosevelt Has A Cold: Stays In

WASHINGTON, Sunday.—President Roosevelt had planned to attend an Easter Sunday service to-day, but had to stay indoors because of a slight cold.

Spain Releases Navy Men

R.A.F.-EYE VIEW OF MATFORD WORKS

Cabinet Decision on India To-day

From Daily Mail Special Correspondent   NEW DELHI, Sunday.

INDIA'S position in the war will now almost certainly emerge within 48 hours. By then it will probably be known whether nearly four hundred million people are to range themselves alongside the Allies or remain passive spectators as the war draws nearer to their homeland.

Sir Stafford Cripps to-day told Dr. Azad, president of the Congress Party, that Britain's reply to the party's note demanding a greater share in responsibility for the nation's defence will be delivered on Tuesday.

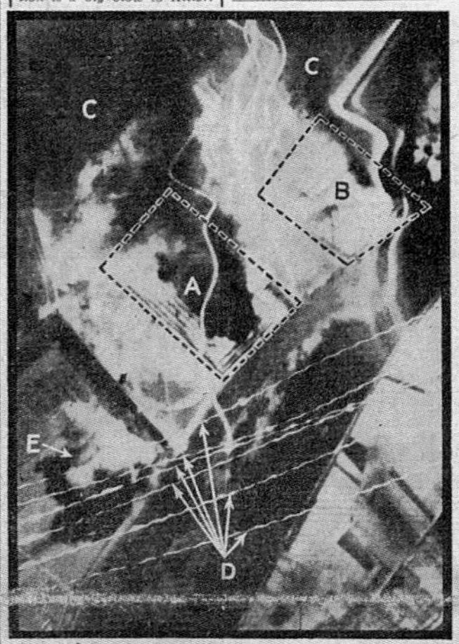

TO-NIGHT the British War Cabinet, New Delhi believes, will discuss the Indian Congress Party's demand for a bigger share in responsibility for India's defence. On the Cabinet's decision, it is thought, rests all hope of a favourable outcome of Britain's proposals.

U.S. MOVE AGAINST 40-HOUR WEEK

U.S. FREIGHTER TORPEDOED

'Fiercest' Land–Sea Attack On Bataan

From Daily Mail Correspondent   NEW YORK, Sunday.

GENERAL YAMASHITA, commanding the Japanese forces in the Philippines, yesterday launched his fifth major attack in a fortnight on the American and Filipino troops holding out in the Bataan Peninsula.

Shock Troops

Tea Control Tightened from To-day

Pensioners

CLEAR IN STRAIT

Fewer Train Meals

PART-TIME WORK—NO INSURANCE

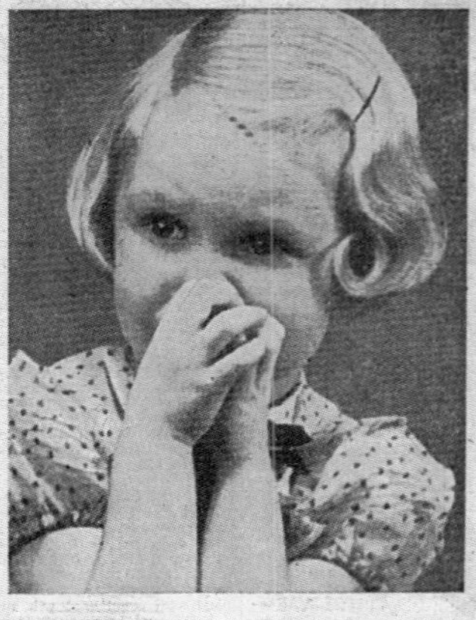

... Oh, what are they doing to daddy?

It's only twenty-one miles across the Channel — to the lands where the Nazis 'discipline' people with long whips, quick bayonets and starvation.

Don't fool yourself into thinking it can't happen here. It can—unless we fight back not only with every ounce of work and service, but with every ounce of personal sacrifice as well.

Are you really saving all you can?

... Let the cry be "less spending — more saving"

Issued by the National Savings Committee

RATNAPURA and Colombo, attacked from the air by the Japs, are shown in this map. In-[set] map indicates the distances from the Andaman Islands to Ceylon and Calcutta.—A.P.

▲ DAILY MAIL, LONDON, MONDAY APRIL 6, 1942

On Easter Sunday 1942, Japanese bombers attacked targets in Ceylon (now Sri Lanka), with little success. The Japanese claimed to have lost only five aircraft. Elsewhere, Britain waits to hear if it has the backing of India in the war, while despite all the military action there is still room on the front page for news that the U.S. president has a slight cold.

THE BOSTON HERALD

LATE CITY EDITION

Slightly Warmer
BOSTON AND VICINITY—Not quite so cold today with drizzle or light rain this morning. High tides—8:47 A. M., 9:21 P. M. Low tides—2:39 A. M., 3:04 P. M. Full report on page 2.

VOL. CLXXXII., NO. 101 — Boston Herald-Traveler Corporation — BOSTON, SATURDAY, APRIL 11, 1942—EIGHTEEN PAGES — ★★★★ — THREE CENTS

NURSES, TROOPS ESCAPE BATAAN, JAPS BOMB, STRAFE SWIMMERS

Anglo-Indian Negotiations in Collapse

Exclusive
MARSHALL TO TEST BRITISH ON INVASION

Lack of Ships Seen Bar to AEF Attempt At European Thrust

By JOHN MacCORMAC
[Boston Herald-N. Y. Times Dispatch]

WASHINGTON, April 10—The main and virtually the sole mission of Gen. George C. Marshall and Harry Hopkins in London, it has been learned in diplomatic circles here, is to ascertain whether the British government is justified in the stand it has taken against invading Europe this summer.

The arguments the British government has advanced against such an enterprise have been exclusively military. The question is whether they are completely valid and whether they have been colored by political thinking.

Information drawn by some newspapers and their readers here and in London, that the United States itself has in mind the sending of an American Expeditionary Force for this purpose in the near future are unjustified.

Those who know the shipping situation say that it puts any venture of this kind absolutely out of the question. So true is this that the chief argument advanced by the British government against a British attempt to open up a western front in Europe is that there are not available even enough ships for the transport and maintenance of an expeditionary force across the Channel or the North Sea. The argument is based on the estimate that it needs eight tons of shipping per head to transport a British soldier, his food and equipment, that a great deal of this shipping would be sunk in the effort and that neither Britain nor the whole allied shipping pool has the tonnage to spare.

A British Expeditionary Force in France, it is estimated, would have to contend with at least 30 complete equipped German divisions, something like 600,000 troops if all auxiliaries are counted.

(Continued on Page Three)

Today's Herald

	Page		Page
Amusem't Ads	12	Drama	8
Books		Editorials	12-13
Bridge	17	Financial	13-18
Churn. N.	11	For Parents	7
Class. Ads	13,16	George Ryan	4
Comics	17	Mail Bag	4
Com. Markets	15	Nation's Politics	3
Courts	16	Obituaries	4
Crossword	17	Orphan Annie	16
Cunningham	5	Radio	7,9
Dahl Cartoon	17	Sports	5, 6
Design for Youth	7	Patri.	
		Recipes	7
Garden	7	Society	7
Needlework	7		

WavellLooksto U.S. Planes After Naval Losses Peril Coast

By CRAIG THOMPSON
[Boston Herald-N. Y. Times Cable]

LONDON, April 10—Indian negotiations, which have seemed several times on the verge of a complete breakdown, only to have hopes revived on the basis that was reported to be a new formula, are now reported to be shattered.

The Congress party, which has been in almost continuous session, tonight told Sir Stafford Cripps, emissary of the British war cabinet, that the new defense formula was unacceptable. The decision is understood to have been unanimous.

The impasse was reached as the admiralty disclosed a new British disaster, the sinking of the aircraft carrier Hermes, which was added today to the toll of two heavy cruisers sent to the bottom by Japanese bombers in a four-day battle in the Bay of Bengal.

These sinkings seriously exposed the Ganges basin of India to direct assault, and Gen. Archibald Wavell was reported to be marshaling all available strength for its defense.

Failure May Not Hurt Cripps' Career

Though it appears that he failed, Cripps seems likely to come home as a man no less in stature than when he went out. He is regarded by officials and the public as having been the best man to make the effort to get an Indian agreement and one who would fail only if failure was inescapable.

Announcement was made at New Delhi that he would hold a press conference tomorrow in which he would tell the outcome of his mission, to be followed by a broadcast to India, probably telling the same story. There is much public interest.

U. S. CRITICS RESENTED

The blast at United States criticism followed by a strong call today for all Indians to rally behind the fire off the Atlantic coast, abandoned their vessels, but later reboarded their craft and now them brought safely to port, the navy disclosed tonight.

(Continued on Page Three)

DRIVE URGED BY LITVINOFF

Makes Third Plea for Russo-British Unity

By RUSSELL PORTER
[Boston Herald-N. Y. Times Dispatch]

PHILADELPHIA, April 10—For the third time in recent weeks Maxim Litvinoff, Russian Ambassador to the United States, called tonight for united efforts—"really united—by Great Britain and Russia, "with some supplementary aid from the United States," to smash Hitler into "complete destruction and final defeat" on the Russian front.

He also asked again for simultaneous offensives on other fronts to worry Hitler about the direction

(Continued on Page Four)

FORE RIVER WINS NAVY 'E' FOR SHIP OUTPUT SPEED

The Fore River yard of the shipbuilding division of the Bethlehem Steel Company, where 22,000 workers are employed on three eight-hour shifts, has constructed more than 760,000 tons of ships months ahead of schedule. It was disclosed last night when Secretary of the Navy Knox awarded it the navy's coveted E for excellence in production achievement.

During 1941, Fore River launched 16 ships, including the mammoth battleship Massachusetts, two cruisers, eight tankers, four trawlers and a destroyer.

During the same year it delivered six tankers and four trawlers from

(Continued on Page Four)

BREAD FOR JAP PRISONERS—Although their own rations were short, American and Filipino defenders of Bataan shared bread with captured Japanese soldiers. (foreground) deep in jungle behind defense line. (AP Wirephoto)

Crews Quit Torpedoed Ships, Then Man Them Into Haven

Find One Still Afloat, Board Her, Await Tow

NORFOLK, Va., April 10 (AP)—Crewmen of two American merchant ships, one torpedoed and the other attacked by submarine shellboarded their craft and now them brought safely to port, the navy disclosed tonight.

The crew of one vessel, a United Nations cargo ship, abandoned her under shell fire from a submarine the night of April 2, but reboarded the vessel several hours later and manned her until she was towed safely to an undisclosed east coast port the following day.

TWO KILLED, 7 MISSING

Two members of the ship's 34-man crew were killed by the raider's shells, seven were missing and four of the 24 survivors were hospitalized for treatment of nervous wounds, the fifth naval district said in announcing the attack today.

The torpedoed ship, of medium size, was attacked early Monday morning. She made an east coast port under her own power and with only one member of her 33-man

(Continued on Page Five)

SNOWDROPS MIXED IN SPRING BOUQUET

With the trees budding, crocuses just showing and the warm season about to start, Boston was swept by a belated spring snowstorm yesterday. The weather bureau said the April shower of snow, sleet and rain measured 0.46 inches precipitation, and left three-tenths of an inch of snow on the ground. The storm was believed to be about over at midnight.

25 IN CITY 'BEE' FINAL

Champion of 4 Grades To Be Crowned Today

By PAUL WAITT

This afternoon at 3 o'clock, 15 boys and 10 girls who have outspelled 40,000 of their mates in the Boston public schools Boston Herald Spelling Bee will march to the stage of Faneuil Hall to participate in the grand final event of this City group. Late this afternoon, the city's best 9th, 10th, 11th and 12th Grade speller will have been chosen —each with a gold medal for himself and a 15-inch silver cup for his school. Out of the 25 that started, four will remain, to cast aside classifications and fight it out for the crown as the superspeller of the Boston school system.

Clement A. Norton, chairman of the Boston school committee, will preside, and the South Boston High School Orchestra under the direction of Miss Margaret Virgin, will furnish the musical program. The event will be broadcast over Station WNAC.

(Continued on Page Four)

USO REFUTES VFW CHARGES

But Admits $5,000,000 Paid in Salaries

While denying 49,797,750 out of a total budget of $13,084,703 goes for salaries, national officers of the United Service Organizations, Inc., formed to assist and entertain men in the armed forces, admitted in an explanation of expenditures yesterday that approximately $5,900,000 of that amount is spent to pay administrative help and social workers at various camps and recreational spots.

John F. Hickey, assistant to Walter J. Cummings, treasurer of the national USO, and F. C. LeMocker of the administrative staff, came to Boston yesterday to answer charges made by the Suffolk county council of the Veterans of Foreign Wars. In addition to denying that only

(Continued on Page Two)

Weary Women, Men Defy Sharks, Guns, Reach Corregidor

By DEAN SCHEDLER

CORREGIDOR FORTRESS, April 9 (AP) (Delayed)— All night long last night, nurses dazed with fatigue and war-weary fighters braved Japanese bombers and shark-infested waters to escape stricken Bataan for the comparative safety of Corregidor fortress in Manila bay.

(This is the first cabled news dispatch to reach the Associated Press directly from Corregidor since the fall of Bataan.)

Across the narrow channel which separates Bataan peninsula from Corregidor came civilians, as well, all who could or dared make the trip to the fortress.

They came across in row boats, mostly. Some of them swam and were picked up in mid-channel by other small craft.

All the while, Japanese bombers dropped their bombs or viciously machine-gunned the channels.

I talked with soldiers who had gone many nights without sleep or had little to eat during the final days while they fought so valiantly against overwhelming odds.

Too Exhausted to Describe Flight

They tried to oblige by relating little bits of information concerning those awful last hours in which they stood, and retreated bit by bit in the face of terrific machine gun fire, cannon and aerial bomb fire.

But they were interested in only one thing—sleep.

The nurses arrived in small boats, stumbling ashore with weariness after days and long nights of work in hospitals under constant fire.

STILL CONFUSED

The soldiers, safe at last from sharks and aerial machine gun fire, could hardly impart their thoughts to me. Their experiences of the last few days and their situation still were unclear to them. It was as though they were groping for consciousness in a maelstrom.

They only knew that they were hungry and tired—and sleepy.

Meanwhile, during the night we could look across the water toward Bataan and hear tremendous explosions and see myriad-color fires as munition dumps were exploded. Men carried out the last defiant orders of the scorched earth policy.

SORROWFUL NEWS

The drama of the arrival of these refugees from the hell-fire of Bataan surpassed only the aching scene on Corregidor itself when soldiers and officers bent over the radios from the United States the story of the last of Bataan.

Seasoned soldiers, veterans of many a heavy bombing attack on this staunch island fortress, wept

(Continued on Page Four)

U. S. TO DRIVE ON INFLATION

5 Leaders Plan Broad Excess Billions Curb

By W. H. LAWRENCE
[Boston Herald-N. Y. Times Dispatch]

WASHINGTON, April 10—President Roosevelt today confirmed reports that top-ranking administration officials are drafting a new and more vigorous anti-inflation campaign, which reportedly includes still higher taxes, wage controls, profit restrictions, additional credit controls and a more general exercise of federal price fixing powers.

The goal of the program, it was stated authoritatively, is to absorb the $12,000,000,000 to $15,000,000,000 excess purchasing power which government economists estimate will remain from a national income of $110,000,000,000 in 1942, even if the treasury's pending $7,610,000,000 general tax bill and still $2,000,000,000 additional social security are adopted without reduction by the Congress.

OPA WARNING

A note of urgency was sounded by the Office of Price Administration's frank statement that "we are in the early stages of a serious inflationary spiral" which can be stopped in

(Continued on Page Fifteen)

Exclusive
U. S. Bomber Crews in Orient 'Sock Japs' on Business Basis

$70 Bomb in Right Place, They Say, Pays off Their High Training Cost
[Boston Herald-N. Y. Times Wireless]

AN ADVANCED ALLIED AIR BASE IN THE SOUTHWEST PACIFIC, April 10—We stood on the edge of a long runway and watched American bombers roar past on their take off. They were headed on a new mission. There was no waving goodbye to the Americans who manned them—young fellows with whom we had been talking of home and the Japs a short time before.

Helmeted heads flashing by to Jap" with regularity and effect.

When news of that particular mission is released, these dispatches will report it. Until then, it is worthwhile covering something about the kids as a whole on the job at this base. They talk frankly and without boasting and without false modesty.

For instance, this from a bombardier: "It cost the government $500 every time I went up to practice bombing back in the States. A

(Continued on Page Four)

BEATRICE LILLIE'S SON DIES IN ACTION

LONDON, April 10 (AP)—Sir Robert Peel, son of the actress Beatrice Lillie, was reported to have been killed in action with the British Navy in Asiatic waters. He was 21.

His mother, Lady Peel in private life, received the news at Manchester, where she was touring in a new musical.

lot of money has been spent on us to teach us our business. They have given us good training, good ships and good equipment generally. It is up to us to use what we have got. If we put one $70 bomb in the right place, we can discharge our debt."

The foregoing is the eminently practical viewpoint expressed by Lt. E. H. Hansen of Chicago, who was

(Continued on Page Four)

All Records Smashed!

Sunday, The Herald will publish the largest social and community news section in its history, with ten solid pages of social news and almost 100 pictures.

For several months now, The Herald's enlarged social section has attracted wide public attention. Featuring more news and pictures than any other paper in New England, it has drawn many new readers to The Sunday Herald.

Don't miss this Sunday's record breaker! It's the BIGGEST ever!

'Gansett Opens Today

Featuring THE SPRING HANDICAP
For $5000 Added

8 RACES DAILY

GRANDSTAND 50c — CLUBHOUSE $1
Phone PERRY 1440 for Reserved Seats, Grandstand and Clubhouse Boxes

Special Trains, Buses Direct to Track
SERVICE MEN IN UNIFORM ADMITTED FREE

DAILY DOUBLE - 1st and 2nd Races
Box Office Station 2 minutes later

POST TIME 2:30

NARRAGANSETT PARK
ROUTE 1A — PAWTUCKET, R.I.

Order Your Classified Ads

For Sunday's Herald Before 3 P. M.
TODAY

For your wedding reception call KIRkland 4800
HOTEL COMMANDER
16 Garden St., Cambridge

▲ THE BOSTON HERALD, SATURDAY APRIL 11, 1942

The *Herald*'s headline manages to suggest the desperation of the U.S. retreat on the Philippines to the Bataan peninsula and then the fortified island of Corregidor. The photograph shows Japanese captives being fed—but does not actually show U.S. prisoners, who were a rare sight in Allied media. Next to an advertisement for a horse racing meeting, the *Herald* reports its own record-breaking sales: a reflection of Americans' hunger for information.

Salute to Malta

APRIL 1942

FROM THE BEGINNING OF THE WAR IN THE MEDITERRANEAN, MALTA PLAYED A CRUCIAL ROLE. INDEED, ONE OF ITALY'S FIRST ACTS WHEN ENTERING THE WAR IN JUNE 1940 WAS TO BOMB THE BRITISH naval base on the island. Malta was 60 miles (96 km) south of Sicily and it lay directly across Italy's supply lines to North Africa.

A deadly game ensued. While Malta could be used as a base for submarines and aircraft, Axis supplies to North Africa were severely affected. For example, in September 1941, 25 percent of supplies destined for Africa were lost, mainly to Malta-based submarines.

MALTA'S COURAGE

However, keeping Malta operating and defending it from air attack was a strain on Royal Navy resources. Getting convoys through—either from Gibraltar in the west or from Alexandria in the eastern Mediterranean—was difficult and very costly. In March 1942, for example, one convoy delivered only 20 percent of its original cargo to Malta after attacks by surface vessels, aircraft and submarines.

The civilian population of Malta suffered almost daily air raids, and as a token of Britain's appreciation of the fortitude of its people, Malta was awarded the George Cross by King George VI on April 15, 1942.

AXIS RELUCTANCE TO INVADE

So why did Axis forces not invade Malta? The answer is twofold. Firstly, the Italian Navy could not guarantee safe passage for its troops and landing craft while the Royal Navy was dominant in the Mediterranean. Secondly, Hitler could have sent aircraft to support an invasion, but he was undecided about such an operation, especially after the invasion of Crete in 1941 almost ended in disaster.

So Malta remained a symbol of defiance against the Axis, even amid the bleak news of spring 1942.

▲ A BRITISH ANTIAIRCRAFT GUN stands ready to defend Malta against Axis air attack. The biggest threat to the island was being starved into submission due to U-boats sinking supply convoys.

The Daily Telegraph
and Morning Post

LONDON LATE EDTN.

No. 27,099   LONDON, FRIDAY, APRIL 17, 1942   Printed in LONDON and MANCHESTER   PRICE 1½d.

LAVAL PRESENTS NEW CABINET TO PETAIN

DISORDERS REPORTED IN OCCUPIED FRANCE

VICHY ENVOY TO U.S. SEES MR. WELLES

RUNDSTEDT IN PARIS: NAZI FEAR OF SECOND FRONT

Laval, Vichy's Chief of the Government, yesterday presented the names of his new Cabinet to Marshal Pétain, the Vichy Chief of State. Later it was officially stated that they would be announced after the last meeting of the old Cabinet to-day.

At the same time, reports from France declared that, with Laval's return to power, there had been a recrudescence of anti-German disorders in Paris and in Northern France.

Field-Marshal von Rundstedt has arrived in Paris to take command of the German Forces in the occupied zone. According to E. B. Wareing, the former Chief of our Paris Staff, in a report published below, the Germans are believed to be afraid of a second front being opened in France.

In Washington M. Henry-Haye, the Vichy envoy in Washington, last night visited Mr. Sumner Welles, Acting Secretary of State.

LAVAL'S TALKS IN VICHY

By E. B. WAREING, former Chief of our Paris Staff

Laval, France's new Chief of the Government, returned to Vichy yesterday with the list of his Cabinet Ministers in his pocket. He arrived shortly after midday, the time reported to have been fixed by the Germans for the formation of a French Government prepared to "collaborate" completely with Hitler.

Accompanied by de Brinon, the Vichy envoy in Paris, Laval at once went to Marshal Pétain's villa and started discussions with him. At one p.m. he motored to his country house at Châteldon, returning to Vichy to resume his talks with Pétain and Darlan at three p.m.

A Vichy communiqué last night stated that announcement of the composition of the new Government was being delayed till after the final meeting to-day of the retiring Council of Ministers.

It is understood that Laval has himself taken over the Ministry of the Interior, which has control of the French police.

According to the German radio, both Pétain and Laval will broadcast to the French nation when the new Cabinet is announced.

DARLAN'S POSITION
Hold On Fleet Precarious

Earlier it had been announced that a Government decree has provided that Darlan should be kept on the active list of the French Navy, without reference to the age limit rule.

This was probably due to the personal intervention of Pétain, in view of his assurances to the United States that the French Navy should not be allowed to pass under German control.

ANTI-GERMAN WAVE
Attacks Reported

Laval's life may be considered to be in danger. He was protected by bodyguards and a strong force of police in Vichy yesterday.

Indications at his return is already reported to have taken a violent form in the occupied zone.

According to agency messages from Vichy, a German troop train was wrecked at Caen, in Normandy, 35 Germans being killed.

A Lens, in Northern France's industrial region, civilians attacked a German sentry, taking his rifle, while a bomb was thrown at Illers, near Bethune.

French cyclists shot a German soldier who tried to stop them at Mercourt, near Vimy, and in Paris two hand-grenades, wrapped in newspaper, were thrown into a German headquarters, although no deaths resulted.

People were also reported to be marching the streets of Paris in protest against "collaboration" with Germany.

Other reports from Vichy stated that three forest fires had broken out near Paris and in Southern France "in circumstances which remain unknown."

One of the most spectacular was still burning in the Fontainebleau Forest, where more than 600 acres of woodland are said to have been destroyed. Another was at Collobrieres, near Toulon, where 1,000 acres of forest have been ruined.

When a similar anti-German outbreak took place a few months ago, it was followed by the execution of "hostages" by the Germans. One report last night declared that 20 Parisians had been executed in recent days.

Vichy radio last night reported the arrest of 300 persons in a Bordeaux police raid.

Coinciding with these reports was a German suggestion that a purge was now being carried out by French police of a mysterious "police force" engaged in "carrying out an illegal activity by making false rumours about various personalities." The Paris police force has already been reinforced by nearly 4,000 officers and men.

Laval also talked to Marquet, Mayor of Bordeaux, an ambitious and unscrupulous man who played a leading part in the Pétain-Laval armistice in 1940. He was a political rival of M. Mandel, former Minister of the Interior, now in British custody in Morocco.

Marquet, a man of wealth who has important relations with the Press, was rewarded for his share in bringing Laval to power by being given the Ministry of the Interior in the first Vichy Cabinet, but was displaced later.

Among others consulted by Laval are General de Brinon and concentration camp—Jean Scapini, the blind chief of the French ex-Servicemen, who has played a prominent part in negotiations regarding prisoners, and Alexis Carrel, the scientist who is a close personal friend of Lindbergh.

Laval is almost certain to announce concessions in the matter of prisoners to coincide with the formation of his new Government.

PETAIN SEES ADVISERS
Axis Use of Marseilles

Pétain, for his part, saw his advisers, Lucien Romier and Moyest, the new Naval Minister, with whom the decree maintaining Darlan beyond the age limit was doubtless discussed. Romier is a trusted counsellor whose post does not attribute to him any specific duties.

As already reported, Pétain, as soon as the crisis seemed to be impending, designated a third adviser—General Gillouin, to North Africa. Gillouin was one of the people who were instrumental in the dismissal of Laval (described by Jay Allen in THE DAILY TELEGRAPH yesterday), and the Marshal may have wished to remove him from Pétain's way.

On the other hand, he may have been given a mission in preparation for certain contingencies.

That the Germans propose to intensify their use of the port of Marseilles is shown by a reliable report that the Marseilles Chamber of Commerce has been authorised by special decree to take up a loan of over £750,000 to finance the extension of the docks and other port facilities.

Since the normal trade of the port has greatly shrunk, these extensions will be of use only to the Axis.

There are sound reasons for believing that the Germans are seriously afraid of the opening up of a second front in France. The arrival of Field-Marshal von Rundstedt to take over from Gen. Witzleben the command of the German army group in France is evidence of this.

Rundstedt, who commanded the German army in the Ukraine, was dismissed by Hitler, but subsequently recalled. He is 66, energetic and ruthless. He led the German advance guard against Poland.

Rundstedt's command in France is, however, a small one, probably between 20 and 25 divisions, supported by one or possibly more armoured divisions—about 450,000 men. Both the quantity and quality of these divisions have been reduced. They can be classified as second-line troops.

NAZI PROPAGANDA
Exaggerated Claims

German propaganda has made much of alleged concrete defensive works flanking the coast, and has even suggested that there is something like a continuous wall of defence.

This suggestion appears to be made mainly for propaganda purposes. Frenchmen from the coast who have recently arrived in Britain join Gen. de Gaulle assure report that they have seen nothing of such defences in their own particular area.

There is evidence that German nerves have been shaken by recent commando and air raids. The German man Press has also made little secret of the growth of French hostility towards the German army and the wish for a British invasion.

In the absence of any indications that German reinforcements have recently arrived in France, it appears that Field-Marshal von Rundstedt's transfer represents an attempt to substitute brains for attrition. He is engaged in working out defensive rather than offensive plans.

BRITISH IN NEW POSITIONS IN BURMA

ENEMY 25 MILES FROM MAIN OILFIELDS

NEW DELHI, Thursday.

Fighting back hard against the Japanese pressing up the River Irrawaddy towards the Burmese oilfields, the British forces which withdrew some days ago from the Mingaung area have established new positions near Yenchaung, north of Minhla. Minhla is less than 20 miles from Magwe. To-day's communiqué indicates that the Japanese are still about 25 miles from the main oilfields.

For days a magnificent cover-action was fought by men of the King's Own Yorkshire Light Infantry at Myingun, says a communiqué issued here, to make up the new line.

MAIN DEFENCES

The Japanese are only now nearing the main British defences. These are firmly held.

Facing the Japanese central thrust between the Irrawaddy and Sittang rivers are the British forces in the Taungdwingyi area, about 30 miles east of Minhla. They are still holding the strong bank of the Chinese expeditionary force.

The Chinese military spokesman said to-day, according to a message from Chungking, that the Chinese right flank in Burma is dangerously exposed.

HEAVY FIGHTING

Heavy fighting was continuous through the day on the whole front, with the Japanese incessantly throwing in men and aircraft.

Further east still the Chinese expeditionary force was forced slowly back on the Myohla front. The position here, said the spokesman, would be precarious if the Japanese turned east and cut the Chinese rear between Myohla and Mandalay.

Five and a half divisions of Japanese reinforcements are reported to be on their way to Burma. Two of them have already arrived at Rangoon, where, said the Chungking spokesman, the R.A.F. had sighted 40 transports.

He said that a Japanese column was advancing northward along the Salween River towards Loiwa, the capital of Karenni province, adjoining north-eastward from Toungoo.

The Chinese lines north of Thazyan, about 160 miles south of Mandalay, are stated to have been attacked.

Air Chief Recalled

"Col. Claire Chennault, commander of the American Volunteer Group of airmen, who have been fighting in Burma and China, has been recalled to active duty in the United States Army.

He has been nominated a brigadier-general, says A.P. He had been on the Air Force retired list while commanding the A.V.G.—Reuter, A.P. and B.U.P.

THE KING HONOURS MALTA

GEORGE CROSS AWARDED TO FORTRESS OF MALTA

DAILY TELEGRAPH REPORTER

The King, it was announced early to-day, has awarded the George Cross, the civilian V.C., to the scarred but defiant island fortress of Malta, most bombed part of the whole British Empire.

I learn that the King himself suggested making the award, which is the first time a decoration has been conferred by a sovereign on a part of the British Commonwealth.

The award was announced in the following cable sent by the King to the Governor of Malta, Lt.-Gen. Sir William Dobbie:

"To honour her brave people I award the George Cross to the island fortress of Malta to bear witness to a heroism and devotion that will long be famous in history."

Sir William sent the following reply to the King:

"The people and garrison of Malta are deeply touched by your Majesty's kind thought for them in conferring on the fortress this signal honour. It has greatly encouraged everyone, and all are determined that, by God's help, Malta will not weaken, but will endure until victory is won. All in Malta desire to express once again their loyal devotion to your Majesty, and their resolve to prove worthy of the high honour conferred."

THE ENEMY'S WORST

Sir William also received a cable from Viscount Cranborne, Secretary for the Colonies. This read:

"The people of this country can at the admire the blow you and the people of Malta are putting up against the very worst the enemy can do to you with all their massed bombers and fighters across the water.

You are setting us an example of courage which I believe cannot be surpassed. Good luck to you all."

A cable from Sir William himself said:

"The people have been wonderful, and we are confident that, by God's help, we are weathering the storm."

ARMS TO BE ALTERED

A George Cross is to be embodied at once in the Maltese arms.

The institution of the George Cross and George Medal was announced by the King in a broadcast on Sept. 23, 1940.

The Cross is intended to reward acts of performance by civilians of great valour and is the second award of the series to a member of the Services would have the V.C. The V.C. itself is moulded in the form of the Maltese Cross.

SOON ON MY FEET AGAIN

R.A.F. ONSLAUGHT SHAKES RUHR MORALE

SEVENTH HEAVY RAID IN ELEVEN NIGHTS

400 SPITFIRES IN THREE BIG DAY SWEEPS

BY OUR AIR CORRESPONDENT

Night operations had hardly ceased yesterday when R.A.F. day raiders crossed the Channel to launch a fresh attack.

This was the first of three big daylight sweeps in which more than 400 Spitfire fighters, besides Hurricane and Boston bombers, took part.

It was the fifth successive day on which Fighter Command had carried out almost continuous sweeps. Five enemy fighters were shot down, a sixth probably destroyed, and others damaged. Two of our fighters are missing.

Once again the Ruhr was the main target for Bomber Command on Wednesday night. They were over in force and left many fires burning.

BLOW FOR BLOW BY CORREGIDOR

GUNS REPEL RAIDS, BOMBARD ENEMY

FROM OUR OWN CORRESPONDENT

NEW YORK, Thursday.

Corregidor is still taking it, but it is also handing it out, the War Department reported to-day. The fort's guns yesterday scored hits on Japanese troop concentrations and columns of lorries on Bataan.

THE DAILY TELEGRAPH, LONDON, FRIDAY APRIL 17, 1942

The *Telegraph* seizes on reported disorder in occupied France as Pierre Laval is called back to political office as prime minister of Vichy. Meanwhile, Malta's resistance to air attack and naval blockade was rewarded by the award of the George Cross, Britain's second-highest award for valor, usually awarded only to individuals.

▲ THE SUN, SYDNEY, SUNDAY APRIL 19, 1942

For Australian readers, nervous at Japanese advances in the Pacific, *The Sun* has good news at last:
the Doolittle Raid, the first U.S. bombing attack on Japan. The raid did little effective damage, but
its demonstration that the Japanese Home Islands were not invulnerable shocked the Japanese and
was a cause of great celebration in the United States—and the Allied nations generally.

Chicago Daily Tribune

THE WORLD'S GREATEST NEWSPAPER

2 CENTS PAY NO MORE!

FINAL

VOLUME CI.—NO. 111 C   SATURDAY, MAY 9, 1942.—30 PAGES   PRICE TWO CENTS

REPULSE JAP FLEET!

SIX FLYERS DIE AS FOUR ARMY PLANES CRASH

Bomber with Ten on Board Missing.

(Pictures on page 6.)

Six army flyers were killed, 10 are missing and one escaped by a parachute jump in a series of air accidents yesterday. The accidents included a collision between two planes, plunge into the ocean by a bomber, and a crash of a training plane, while another bomber was reported missing since Wednesday. Details follow:

Bomber Falls Into Sea.

TACOMA, WASH.—An army bomber from McChord field fell into Puget sound and sank with its crew of three, the army air corps reported. The following were reported aboard plane:

Lieut. Col. Perry O. Hoff, 41, of Silver Spring, Md.

Capt. R. C. Alexander, 45, Seattle.

Capt. Angus C. B. MacPhee, 39, Tacoma.

The plane fell about a half mile from the mainland near Ketron island in Puget sound, about 30 miles south of Tacoma. Witnesses said the plane fell from considerable altitude and disappeared almost immediately. The water is deep near Ketron island.

It was the second bomber tragedy in this vicinity and the fourth in the nwide northwest within a week.

Planes Collide Above City.

PHOENIX, ARIZ.—A collision of two airplanes 5,000 feet above a residential district in the northwest section of Phoenix killed an army air corps pilot and a flyer for the air force ferrying command. A second flyer and a third parachuted to safety.

At Luke field the dead were identified as Second Lieut. John K. Austin of Chicago and Wray B. Smith of Atlanta, Ga.

Second Lieut. Jack O. Scott of Phoenix was saved by his parachute. He was injured when his head hit a concrete sidewalk.

Austin Instructor Student.

Austin was a student in the instructors' school at Luke field. He was engaged in instrument flying with Scott as a safety observer.

Scott reported that all but one Smith's plane as it approached from beneath until just before the collision.

Austin was a son of Mr. and Mrs. J. H. Austin, 7631 Cregier avenue. He was 21 years old and was educated at Hirsch high school and the 'niversity of Illinois. He entered the army air force last October and was commissioned on April 24. On the same day he married Miss Ruth Deswarte of Chicago. He topped his cadet training class of 400 and was assigned as a pilot instructor.

Ten Missing on Bomber.

TAMPA, FLA.—A MacDill field heavy bombing plane with 10 army men aboard was listed as missing by MacDill field officials. The plane left MacDill field Wednesday morning on a training flight and was due back Wednesday night.

The crew was identified as Second Lieut. Hugh W. Millit, 23 years old, the pilot, Houston, Tex.; Second Lieut. Charles E. Thomas III, 22, co-pilot, Macon, Ga.; Staff Sergt. Wilbert M. George, 21, Tampa; Pvt. Robert R. Pigman, 22, Berea, Ky.; Pvt. Raymond S. Lynch, 20, Lumpkin, Ga.; Pvt. Nelson L. Teal, 20, Bunkie, La.; Pvt. Elmer E. Mathauser, 23, Burwell, Neb., and Pvt. Charles R. Phillips of Waukesha, Wis.

Chicagoan Is Passenger.

Two passengers were identified as Pvt. Gordon J. Howard 23, son of Bert Howard, 729 Deyo street, Green Bay, Wis., and Sergt. Eugene L. Kastner, 23, son of Frank Kastner, 4411 South Troy street, Chicago.

Phillips, 19 years old, is the son of Mr. and Mrs. Eugene C Phillips of Waukesha. He enlisted in the air corps on Nov. 26, 1941. Phillips completed his training at Scott field 19 days ago. He became engaged last summer to Bette Chapman, Waukesha. He was a youth leader at the Baptist church there.

Hawaiian Veteran Killed.

SANTA MARIA, CAL.—Gordon M. Short, aviation cadet in the army air force from Taunton, Mass., was killed in the crash of his primary training plane. A private in the army air force in Hawaii when the Japanese attacked last December, Short was sent to Hancock College of Aeronautics here last March 7.

ROUNDUP OF WAR NEWS FROM MAIN FRONTS OF WORLD

Latest war developments:

American and South African troops were reported in London to be pouring into Diego Suarez, captured French naval base on the tip of Madagascar. Vichy said French troops still were fighting on the strategic Indian ocean island.

The British announced their fifth night air raid on the devastated area of Rostock, German city on the Baltic sea. This time RAF bombers said to have concentrated on the city's port, a military center and home of the Heinkel aircraft works.

Rush Aid to Ceylon.

New British reinforcements were rushed to Ceylon, off India's southeast tip, it was announced. There were reports that Japanese invasion forces were aboard ships off Rangoon ready to attack India. United States bombers raided Rangoon for the third time in four days. The Chinese said two Japanese columns driving along the Burma road into China were wiped out by counterattacking forces.

Defeat of the Japanese in the biggest naval battle of the war off Australia was announced by Gen. Douglas MacArthur. The navy department earlier said that 11 enemy ships had been sunk and six damaged by United States warships and planes in the Coral sea. American losses, it said, are not fully known at present.

Reds Stop Nazi Drive.

Russian war dispatches said that the Red army and air force had wrecked a three way German offensive aimed at soviet Karelia from Finland. They also reported that German air forces had been driven out of forward bases in the Arctic area.

[Details on pages 1, 5, and 6.]

THE PUBLIC ENEMY AND HIS SMOKE SCREEN

CAMPAIGN TO SQUELCH ALL CRITICISM

Female Army Approved by Senate Group

BY WILLIAM STRAND

[Chicago Tribune Press Service.]

Washington, D. C., May 8.—The senate military affairs committee today approved legislation creating a women's army auxiliary corps to assume behind the lines duties and release approximately 150,000 soldiers for fighting service. A similar bill which would establish a women's auxiliary corps for the navy is also pending before the senate. Both have been passed by the house.

Under the women's army bill, scheduled for senate action next week, volunteers will serve in a separate unit under supervision of the war department rather than as an integral part of the army. Women between the ages of 21 and 45 are eligible and they will receive the same pay as soldiers of comparable rank.

Excitement Promised.

Sen. Robert R. Reynolds (D., N. C.), military affairs committee chairman, said that those who enlist in search of excitement will not be disappointed. They can expect service "right up to the front lines," he said, and will be expected to do everything except shoulder arms.

The senator said the army plans to use some of the volunteers for such tasks as servicing fighter planes on foreign battlefields. Others will be assigned to jobs as telephone operators or to do confidential clerical and office work now being done by men physically fit to fight. The secret nature of this work precludes the employment of civilians.

Members of the corps would live in special barracks on military posts or immediately adjacent to the posts, chaperoned by officers of their sex, in addition to their salaries, they will receive subsistence and uniforms just as do members of the regular army.

Married Women Eligible.

Married women as well as single women would be eligible for enlistment and would be expected to serve abroad, if so assigned. They would be eligible for hospitalization and sick benefits but not for war risk insurance. Nor would they be subject to regular court martial, it was explained, but under the terms of the legislation it would be possible for the war department to mete out dishonorable discharges for infraction of regulations.

The war department has estimated that it would cost 16 million dollars to get the program under way. This

BEAUTIFUL CHILDREN.

On the back page of today's issue appears the regular Saturday feature, "Beautiful Children in Color." The pictures of the children shown are reproductions of photographs taken with The Tribune's famous color camera.

money, which includes salary, expenses and the cost of construction of housing facilities, would have to come from funds already appropriated or be asked in a separate bill as the pending measure merely authorizes creation of the corps.

The bill was approved by the committee in its present form several weeks ago but was recommitted when the war department made a last minute attempt to secure passage of a substitute measure providing that the women would not serve merely in an auxiliary corps "with" the army but actually "in" the army proper. The senate committee turned thumbs down on the "in" bill.

Mother Slain, Child Missing; Hunt Son, 16

Corpus Christi, Tex., May 8 [Special]—A 16 year old boy was being widely hunted tonight following the discovery that his mother had been shot to death in their fashionable Ocean drive home and his 3 year old sister apparently had been kidnaped. The boy is George Clude Hengy Jr., son of an electrical superintendent at the naval air station here. The boy was said to have undergone a period of hospital treatment last summer for "serious fevers" but was believed to have recovered.

Young George had not been reported seen since his mother's slaying last night. Also missing were a 22 caliber rifle, 500 rounds of ammunition, and the family sedan.

Left Alone in Next Room.

Left alone in the family home was the slain woman's baby, 10 weeks old, who lay in her crib in a room adjoining that where the mother was killed. Apparently the infant had been without care for about 12 hours before she was found.

The slaying was discovered by the elder Hengy today after arriving by plane from Austin where he had been on business. He asked he telephoned home but did not receive an answer.

Hurrying home, he questioned an elderly Mexican woman servant about the whereabouts of the family. The woman said she had left for her home only shortly before Hengy and that she believed Mrs. Hengy had gone shopping.

Discovers the Body.

On a divan in the living room Henry found the body of his wife. She had been shot above the right eye with a shotgun charge and in the heart with a .22 bullet.

A search of the house revealed that young George and his 3 year old sister, Zina, were missing and that the baby, Julia Ann, apparently was unharmed from her lack of care.

The Mexican woman said she had left the home about 6 o'clock last night, at which time young George was tinkering with fishing tackle. Authorities said Mrs. Hengy, who was 39, was shot about 10 p. m. last night.

PANDA MEI-MEI REPORTED DYING AT BROOKFIELD

(Picture on page 8.)

Mei-mei, the panda that took Sulin's place in the hearts of Brookfield zoo goers, is dying.

Veterinarians and zoological scientists who had spent experts in the country, have despaired of her life. It was learned last night. They gave up nearly two weeks ago. Only the care and desperate efforts of Edward H. Bean, the director, his son Robert, and Keeper Sam Parrett have kept her alive since.

Whether Mei-mei's dying of the same malady that took Sulin who the experts can't tell. They disagreed on what killed Sulin. Sulin was in Chicago only a little more than a year. Mei-mei has been here more than four.

Mei-mei's death will leave Brookfield here to be the mate of the older panda, the only one of his species here. If Mei-mei actually turns out a female until the postmortem proved otherwise. All the experts believe Mei-mei is a female, but only the postmortem when Mei-mei died will prove them right or wrong.

"It was a coolly executed killing," said Police Capt. Earl C. Dunn. "Mrs. Hengy apparently was shot as she lay asleep, the killer standing only about 5 feet away. She looked as if she had been taking a nap at the time."

GREATEST AIR AND SEA BATTLE 'CEASES TEMPORARILY,' MacARTHUR DECLARES

Allies Vow to Continue Attack After Blasting 17 Enemy Ships; U. S. Losses Undisclosed.

(Map on page 4.)

ALLIED HEADQUARTERS, Australia, May 9 (Saturday)—(AP)—Allied naval and air forces fighting with "marked skill, courage, and tenacity" have repulsed a Japanese invasion fleet off northeastern Australia in one of history's most fateful struggles, Gen. MacArthur's headquarters announced today.

With 11 or more of its warships sunk and 6 or more damaged—and presumably thousands of its finest warriors at the bottom of the Coral sea—the battered Japanese enemy was reported limping northward with United States and British imperial units in hot pursuit on the sixth day of the epic engagement.

"Our attacks will continue," the allied communique said in reporting that the battle had ceased "temporarily."

Tell How Japs Dived Off Two Fiery Carriers

ADMIRAL TO TALK ON W.G.N.

Rear Adm. Edward A. Evers, veteran of both the Spanish-American and World wars, will be interviewed on W-G-N at noon today on the strategy of a modern naval battle such as was fought in the Coral sea north of Australia.

AN ADVANCED ALLIED BASE, Australia, May 9 (Saturday)—(P).—Desperate efforts by Japanese destroyers failed to save the two aircraft carriers blasted by United States air and naval attack at New Guinea, and the crews had to dive overboard amid smoke and flames from the ships, authorities disclosed today. One carrier was reported sunk, the other damaged.

Japanese personnel losses in the battle may run into the thousands, they asserted.

Carriers Feel Brunt of Blow.

The large Japanese naval concentration was sighted several days ago heading in a southward direction. The United States forces fought them with bombers which pressed home the attack in the face of terrific anti-aircraft fire and the defense of Japanese Zero [naval] fighters.

The carriers were the main object of the initial assault.

The two carriers were attacked by American dive bombers and one was reported ripped asunder when two planes dived directly onto the flight deck with full bomb loads.

Toll of Australia's "Escape."

The second carrier was reported to have sunk after being set afire from stem to stern by torpedo hits.

After the sinking of the two carriers it was reported that the Japanese fleet scattered.

An American naval spokesman, talking of the great sea battle, said "there was a good chance that we might have been blasted out of our beds last night, if this had not happened, but we got in there and did the job."

One Japanese aircraft carrier was seen sinking, he said, and another was hit "from stem to stern."

HOME BUYING MADE EASY!

You can save time, money and tires if you let the real estate want ad columns in the Tribune be your home buying guide. Furthermore, you will be far more certain of finding what you want, because the selection in the Tribune is larger. The Tribune prints more real estate want advertising than any two other Chicago newspapers combined. See the offerings of choice homes in today's Tribune want ad section.

'SCORE OF SEA BATTLE'

U. S. Navy Count
JAP SHIPS SUNK
1 aircraft carrier.
1 heavy cruiser.
1 light cruiser.
2 destroyers.
4 gunboats.
2 transports or cargo vessels.
JAP SHIPS HEAVILY DAMAGED
1 aircraft carrier.
1 heavy cruiser.
1 light cruiser.
1 seaplane tender.
1 transport or cargo vessels.
[Total estimated tonnage of Japanese ships, 145,000.]

Jap Claims
ALLIED SHIPS SUNK
1 U. S. battleship.
2 U. S. aircraft carriers.
1 allied destroyer.
ALLIED SHIPS DAMAGED
1 British battleship.

Too Early to Predict.

The attitude at Gen. MacArthur's headquarters was that it was too early to say whether the result of the huge naval-air engagement was conclusive, and it was not yet clear whether the Japanese could reform and reinforce their units for another southward thrust.

The repulse of the Japanese occurred after allied air units discovered the enemy fleet streaming southward six or more days ago, and the communique concluded with these words:

"Our naval forces then attacked in interceptions. They were handled with marked skill, fought with admirable courage and tenacity, and the enemy has been repulsed."

Because of the lack of news

YANKS IN BRITAIN SEND MOTHER'S DAY NOTE TO U. S.

[Chicago Tribune Press Service.]

LONDON, May 8.—American army forces in the British isles thru their commander, Maj. Gen. James E. Chaney, have sent a Mother's day message to the United States.

"Members of the United States army forces in the British isles have only one message for Mothers' day," it said. "They want their mothers and relatives at home to know they will be ready to play whatever part is allotted to them in this great joint fight we are waging to see that American mothers of the future have a free, happy world in which to bring up their children."

THE WEATHER

SATURDAY, MAY 9, 1942

Sunrise, 5:36. Sunset, 7:57. Moonrise, 2:25 a. m. tomorrow. Venus is the morning star. Mercury, Saturn, Jupiter, and Mars are the evening stars.

CHICAGO AND VICINITY: Continued rather warm today with an occasional shower and cooler tonight; gentle to moderate winds.

TEMPERATURES IN CHICAGO

Official weather report on page 14.]

Total average net paid circulation

APRIL, 1942

DAILY in excess of

1,000,000

THE CHICAGO TRIBUNE

U. S. Envoy to India Told to Recover from Strain

NEW DELHI, India, May 8 (P)—Louis Johnson, President Roosevelt's envoy to India, has been advised to rest for two or three days to recover from strain resulting from overwork.

toward the south and southeast. First efforts were aimed at expanding his air bases, but our air force has consistently and effectively attacked his fields during

But the Daily Mail editorially noted that for months the world had been asking, "Where is the American fleet?" The answer is, that at least part of it is, and in preliminary action, the Mail said, the United States ships were "brilliantly successful."

[Continued on page 4, column 1.]

◄ CHICAGO DAILY TRIBUNE, CHICAGO, SATURDAY MAY 9, 1942

The *Tribune* leads with a report on the Battle of the Coral Sea, which had just taken place off the northeastern coast of Australia, between the Japanese Imperial Navy and the combined forces of the United States Navy and the Royal Australian Navy. The Allied naval force successfully prevented the Japanese from capturing Port Moresby on New Guinea and so protected Australia from invasion, but the triumph came at a significant cost, which included the loss of the carrier USS *Lexington*. The sea battle was the first to be fought entirely by carrier-borne aircraft—the opposing ships neither sighted each other nor fired directly upon one another.

▼ A JAPANESE AIRCRAFT in flames at the Battle of the Coral Sea. In the engagement, the Japanese lost 77 carrier aircraft.

EGYPTIAN MAIL

No. 8753 CAIRO. — SATURDAY, MAY 16, 1942. — ALEXANDRIA. 10 MILLIEMES

RUSSIANS CROSS DONETZ IN DRIVE ON KHARKOV

GERMANS RUSH UP RESERVES BUT FAIL TO STEM ADVANCE

Although Field Marshal Von Bock is throwing in his reserves, using them straight from their march up to the lines, they have been unable to halt Marshal Timoshenko's irresistible drive in the Kharkov Area, powerful Russian formations having yesterday smashed their way across the Donetz River on a 35-mile front between Volchansk, about 30 miles north-east of Kharkov, and Chuguyev, which lies about 20 miles to the south-west.

The latest reports reaching Moscow state that the Russians, after crossing the Donetz, have continued their advance and are now at point seven miles westwards of the river.

Soviet troops are also advancing on the Leningrad front, where the enemy is trying to hold on his second line of defence and is sustaining heavy losses, says Moscow radio.

In the Kerch Peninsula, the Russians seem to be retiring in good order, inflicting all the time heavy casualties on the Germans, who do not seem to have won the great victory they have claimed, and Kerch is still in Russian hands.

Germans Admit Retreat

Axis despatches from the Ukraine admit that the Russians have crossed the Donetz and that the Germans are «retreating slowly while awaiting reinforcements,» the arrival of which is said to be imminent.

Official details of the offensive reveal that the Russians in their drive are inflicting heavy losses on the Germans, taking many prisoners and capturing large numbers of guns, tanks and other war material, which may be taken as a further indication of the speed of the Russian advance.

Roads Littered With Corpses

According to the War Correspondent of the «Izvestia,» the road of the German retreat is littered with corpses and with all sorts of war material and equipment.

Describing the Soviet advance across the Donetz the «Red Star» says: «Red Army tanks started out against this water obstacle which they crossed to assault the main German concentrations. After the tanks had driven a wedge into the German line, Soviet infantry followed into the breach.

"The Germans," adds the paper, «attempted to recover lost ground and hurled in a group of tanks supported by aircraft. As the result of a fierce battle, the Germans retreated leaving over twenty tanks on the battlefield. The Red Air Force gave valuable assistance. The Luftwaffe was unable to wrest the initiative from our airmen and give sufficient protection to their men.»

Nazis Outwitted

In his account of the battle, the «Izvestia's» War Correspondent says: «The Nazis attemped to nip off the Soviet wedge in their lines by flank attacks, but this had been foreseen by the Soviet Staff, and they disposed their forces so that they, in their turn, would come upon the enemy's flanks, and they threw back the Germans, taking many prisoners.

«A large tank battle in another sectors,» adds the correspondent, "ended with the flight of the German tanks. The weather tends to hamper land operations, but in air battles during the first two days of the offensive, 28 enemy planes were brought down or the loss of three Soviet planes.»

Stalin Chose First Opportunity

Commenting on the offensive, Maurice Lovell, Reuter's Special Correspondent, after referring to Marshal Timoshenko's pressure on the deepening and ever-widening gap in the German defences, continues:

«M. Stalin chose the first opportunity of reasonable ground and weather conditions to order Marshal Timoshenko's offensive against Kharkov. Unlike the German offensive on the Kerch Peninsula, which is on a front of only twenty miles at the most, the Kharkov attack has been launched on a number of sectors, with correspondingly greater chances of manoeuvre and strategic development.

«The first Russian successes there are far greater than those on the Germans on the Kerch Front. All evidence shows that the Soviet offensive was quietly and well prepared. The blow was struck suddenly and skilfully with armoured forces as a Battering ram. Soviet tanks smashed in from two sides, then moved on immediately in the manner of the German technique last summer.

Germans Panic-Stricken

«The German troops, which had been driven back by the weight of the Soviet blow, panicked as the spearhead was followed up and fell back.

«Part of the preparation for Marshal Timoshenko's offensive was a sudden blow a few days ago, when bombers and fighters from two Soviet air units raided a large German base near the front and set fire to thirty twin-engined machines and brought down five of fifteen fighters which tried to intercept them.

"The latest reports from Kerch show that a desperate battle of tanks, planes and artillery is still going on. There are heavy German losses.»— Reuter and B.O.P.

Timoshenko Massed Tanks And Planes

IT IS now revealed that Marshal Timoshenko's offensive was prepared with extreme secrecy—division after division of fresh Russian reserves had been massing behind the front for weeks, while batteries of artillery and many Russian, British and American tank formations had already been assembled.

In making this revelation, the Stockholm correspondent of the «Daily Mail» adds that British Hurricanes, American Aerocobras and Tomahawks and Russian Stormovicks were brought up in strength to key points.

«As the Tomahawks struck,» he writes, "the Germans realised the danger and rushed up reserves, but the defences gave way with the Russians breaking through to a considerable depth.»

The impression is expressed by some military correspondents that by his rapid and important stroke Marshal Timoshenko has forestalled Hitler's offensive much as General Wavell upset Graziani's preparations for the invasion of Egypt in 1940.

In fact, that Germans had assembled at Kharkov large quantities of guns, tanks and supplies, which are now threatened by the Russian thrust. Already the Russians are reported to have captured great quantities of arms and equipment.

Hitler Has No Choice

«Frivolous self-confidence,» is how the 'New York Times' describes Hitler's embarkation upon the greatest of his aggressions, adding that he now moves at last in the direction in which he is forced to move.

«The consequences of his foolish underestimate of Russian fighting power,» says the paper, «deprive him of any choice but to return to the attack.

«The Battle in the Crimea is the first action in the long-awaited spring offensive, and the end of suspense and speculation brings a sense of relief, not merely because we know what to expect but because this move shows that the enemy was not waiting to decide where to strike. He may still have the power to strike hard, but he has lost the power to aim the blow in any direction he chooses.

"The enormous irony of Hitler's situation is that he has manoeuvred himself into a position where his fate depends on beating a land army bigger than that of all his other enemies combined and better organised for total war.

«There can be no question that the United Nations must strain themselves to the limit —and beyond—to help the Russians to hold this year. We are on the eve of the greatest battles of the war, and it is vital that we throw everything we can into the scales.» — Reuter and A.N.A.

Martinique Talks Making Progress

Washington, Friday.

IT is understood that the Martinique conversations are proceeding in a friendly atmosphere, and that there is no reason to doubt that the United States will receive satisfaction on the main points.

These are believed to be:—

1. **«Leases of 140,000 tons of French shipping, including seven tankers.**
2. **«Lease» of strategic points.**
3. **Control of foreign communications, including the radio at Martinique.**

Complete agreement, it is hoped here, will be reached through these friendly talks.

Laval Fails

At any rate it can safely be stated that M. Laval has failed completely in his attempt to take a hand in the negotiations, which were initiated in the best interests of France.

Contrary to inspired press reports from Vichy, there is no «note» from M. Laval to the United States Government.

This explains the insistence of Mr. Cordell Hull in emphasising that the State Department is dealing with Admiral Robert only.

The impression prevails in diplomatic circles that in accepting the «immobilisation» of the three French warships at Martinique, M. Laval showed his anxiety not to break with the United States. — Reuter.

Palestine Receives Australian Butter

Jerusalem, Friday.

A large contingent of Australian butter has arrived in Palestine. The Controller General of Supplies is expected to issue an order organising its distribution by the ration-card system. — A.N.A.

German Torpedo Boat Sunk: Two Trawlers Disabled

London, Friday.

An Admiralty Communiqué states, «British light Naval forces continue to harass enemy patrols and shipping which, from time to time, endeavour to creep along the Flemish and French coasts.

«Last night our light forces encountered two enemy armed trawlers off the French channel coast. They were at once engaged, and both trawlers were left disabled and sinking. No casualties or damage were suffered by our forces in this brief engagement.

«Early on Wednesday morning a patrol of our light forces encountered an enemy convoy close to the French coast. The weather conditions were very unfavourable for attack; as there was continuous rain and a rough sea, but our forces succeeded in penetrating the enemy's screen of escort vessels. A running fight followed, in which an enemy ship was hit by a torpedo. The Germans have admitted that one of their torpedo-boats was sunk in this engagement. Considerable other damage and casualties were undoubtedly inflicted on the enemy, but the weather conditions made it impossible to assess these with accuracy.

«A reconnaissance next morning showed that the enemy was still searching for survivors.—Reuter.

Col. Louis Johnson Undergoes Operation

New Delhi, Friday.

While in hospital recently in New Delhi, President Roosevelt's personal representative in India, Colonel Louis Johnson, underwent a minor operation for nasal obstruction. A second operation is necessary and it is understood that this is to be performed after Mr. Johnson's return to the United States.——Reuter.

Serious Earthquake In Ecuador

Quito (Ecuador), Friday.

A disastrous earthquake lasting two minutes has devastated part of the city of Guayaquil. Casualties, according to the first reports are estimated at several hundred killed and injured. Amongst the many buildings destroyed are the United States consulate, hotels, banks etc. The town of Milahro near Guayaquil was also partially wiped out, but details are lacking. The town of Esmeraldas was also partly destroyed, according to news brought to Quito by a Panagra pilot. Communications with Guayaquil and surrounding districts has been interrupted. The earthquake occurred at 02.15 GMT on Thursday.—Reuter.

High Mass For Malta At Westminster

London, Friday.

The Maltese flag will be flown over Westminster Cathedral on Sunday when a High Mass for Malta will be sung at 08.30 G.M.T. The mass is being said for the repose of the souls of those who have died in Malta and the address is to be given by the Archbishop of Westminster, Cardinal Hinsley. The whole of the service, including the Archbishop's address, is to be broadcast to the people of Malta together with a running commentary in Maltese. Accommodation is being reserved to members of the Maltese community in Britain and the Knights of the Sovereign Order of Saint John and Jerusalem will be represented as well as the Allied Forces. The Archbishop has invited General Sir William Dobbie, former Governor-General of Malta, to attend the service.—Reuter.

Air Marshal Sir Arthur Tedder, K.C.B., Air Officer Commanding in Chief, Royal Air Force, Middle East, and Air Commodore L.O. Brown, M.C., D.F.C., A.F.C., Air Officer Commanding, Royal Air Force, Levant, in specting Greek airmen at a training centre in Palestine.

DETAILED ACCOUNT OF MADAGASCAR OPERATIONS

London, Friday.

A detailed account of the Madagascar operations is given in a joint War Office and Admiralty communiqué following the receipt of reports from Rear-Admiral Syfret, Commander of the expedition, and Major-General R. G. Sturges, Commanding the land troops.

The communique says that the British Force arrived off Courrier Bay at dawn on May 5th, having been safely conveyed over a very long distance round the approaches to the bay which was heavily mined.

During mine-sweeping operations, the corvette "Auricula" struck a mine and sank. It is expected that the casualties are light. Troops, vehicles and stores were speedily disembarked despite the deteriorating weather. The first objective of the troops landed was a coastal battery overlooking Courrier Bay. This battery, taken by surprise, was soon captured, and the troops advancing eastwards by 16.00 hours that day captured the town of Diego Suarez on the north side of the harbour.

Another force which had been landed simultaneously at Ambararata was advancing eastwards supported by tanks. A French officer captured soon after the landing consented to carry to the District Commander a statement of the British intentions and the terms of surrender. At 11.00 o'clock the British advance troops were helped up by a defence on high ground about five miles south-west of Antsirana. An attack was launched shortly afterwards, but the position was not finally cleared up until that evening.

Destroyers Support Land Action

A strongly defended position across the isthmus, about two miles south of Antsirana which was contacted at 18.00 hours on May 5th, was attacked without initial success at 05.30 the following morning. Our Naval forces, notably two destroyers, supported the land actions by bombarding strong points when requested.

After dark on May 6th, the final assault on Antsirana was carried with the help of reinforcements. Simultaneously with the attack at 20.00, a force of Royal Marines was landed in the rear of the defenders, creating a valuable diversion and playing an important part in securing the speedy surrender of Antsirana. The destroyer which landed the marines negotiated minefields, passed between shore batteries on either side of the narrow Oranjia Pass and put alongside the quay of the port in darkness. This was successfully carried out without casualties or damage.

The Main Assault

The main assault, which met with strong initial opposition, in the early stages relieved several pockets of British resistance which had been formed inside enemy lines by the rapid infiltration of our advance troops that morning. As a result, it was found that casualties were far lighter than was at first feared.

Carrier-borne Naval aircraft played a conspicuously successful part in the operations, depriving the defence of air power by an attack on an aerodrome and subsequently rendering support and co-operation to both Naval and Military forces.

The following day, the coastal defence batteries on Oranjia Peninsula surrendered and on the afternoon of May 7th, ships of Admiral Syfret's force, preceded by mine-sweepers, entered Diego Suarez harbour. — Reuter.

ROMMEL NOT FOR RUSSIA

Berne, Friday.

Military quarters in Berlin deny that the Commander-in-Chief of the Axis forces in Libya, General Rommel, has been recalled to Germany, says the Berlin correspondent of the 'Basler Nachrichten'.

(Reports from Stockholm and other neutral sources stated that General Rommel had been recalled and might be transferred to the Russian front). — Reuter.

Jap Transport Hit In Raid On Rabaul

A communiqué issued by Allied Headquarters in Australia states that our Air Force attacked shipping at Rabaul, damaging a transport.

Our planes were intercepted by seventeen enemy fighters, seven of which were shot down. All our planes returned safely.»

Big Raid On Port Moresby

A later communiqué states «Port Moresby.— Port Moresby was attacked twice by enemy planes. Thirteen fighters strafed the aerodrome in the first attack, and 26 heavy bombers escorted by nine fighters attacked shipping in the harbour in the second raid. No damage is reported from either raid. We shot down two enemy fighters.

Deboyne Island.— The seaplane base was attacked by our air force. One seaplane was sunk and fires were started on ground installations.»

Emergency Regulations In Northern Territory

A message from Canberra announced that regulations were issued last night applying an emergency control to the Northern Territory and certain districts of Queensland. — Reuter.

R.A.F., M.E. Awards

Cairo, Friday.

The following awards are announced from Headquarters, Royal Air Force, Middle East:

BAR TO D.F.C.

Flying Officer James Robert Anderson, D.F.C.

D.F.C.

Acting Squadron Leaders Freeman Jesse Steel and John Roby Bloxham.

Flight Lieutenants John Phillip Gilliard, Ian Neil MacDougall, and Douglas Rivers Bagnall; Acting Flight Lieutenants Archibald Robert Hall and John Samuel Reeves.

Lieutenant Henry Hugh Smithers, S.A.A.F.

Flying Officers Brian Arthur Blake Attwood, John Gower Martin Hooper and John Thomas Dick.

Pilot Officers Edwin Charles Leonard Cordy, Charles Sydney Montagu and Frederick John Edward Ison; and Warrant Officer John Conleth Grehan.

D.F.M.

Flight Sergeants John Desmond Bingham, Arthur Moses, Grentfell Stephen William Challen, Christopher Walter Chalmers, Owen Leonard Hawes and Stephen Tebett Geary.

Sergeants K.K.J. Coleman, Charles Anthony Armstrong, Michael Collenette, George Williams, Graham Calderwood Tweedie, and Athol James.

Mexico Warns Axis

Mexico City, Friday.

It is officially stated that the Mexican Government has protested to Germany, Italy and Japan against the sinking of the Mexican tanker "Potrero del Llano» by a submarine off Miami on Wednesday.

If by May 28 Mexico has not received from the country responsible complete satisfaction and guarantees of compensation, she will «forthwith take measures which the national honour dictates.»

The «Potrero del Lalno» is the first Mexican ship sunk by a submarine since the war started. The news of the sinking of the vessel, which was Government owned, was released by the U.S. Navy Department yesterday.

According to the announcement, thirteen members of the crew, including the captain and all deck officers, lost their lives.

Vessels Brightly Lighted

The survivors stated that the vessel was brightly lighted with spotlights playing on the Mexican Flags painted on either side of the bridge.

Many people ashore heard the explosion and thousands at one of the United States most famous beach resorts watched the flaming vessel float past from the shore. — Reuter.

U.S. Commandos In Training

Washington, Friday.

The training of special task forces, similar to the British Commandos, will be one of the main objectives at the United States Army manoeuvres this summer.

Each man and each unit will be drilled for the particular parts they will have to play when actual operations are launched.

Smoke-screen and aircraft of all types, including parachute troop-carriers and transport planes for the armoured forces, will be utilised in these manoeuvres—Reuter.

British In Burma Extricated From Dangerous Situation

London, Friday.

It is officially revealed that the British forces retreating up the Chindwin Valley, in Burma, have extricated themselves from a dangerous situation.

The only other news from Burma available is that the Chinese are still fighting in the Mandalay area, near Maymyo and to the northwest of it. North eastwards the Japanese are advancing in two columns one going towards Paoshan over the Chinese frontier and the other towards Myitkyina.

R.A.F. Bomb River Transport

Royal Air Force bombers yesterday continued their attacks on enemy river transport, says a New Delhi communiqué. Barges on the Chindwin River were successfully bombed and machine-gunned. Two barges received hits and were left in flames and several others were damaged.— Reuter.

WAR COMMUNIQUE

«On the Northern sector our patrols engaged an enemy post, inflicting casualties. Brisk patrol activity on the rest of the front.».

8 Raiders Down Over Malta

Cairo, Friday.

It was announced from Headquarters, Royal Air Force, Middle East, to-day, that objectives in Libya were raided by our bomber aircraft during the night of 14/15th May.

Operations in Cyrenaica during the 14th May were curtailed by sandstorms.

In the course of enemy raids on Malta on the morning of the same day our fighters shot down four JU. 88's and three ME. 109's. A further JU. 88 was destroyed by anti-aircraft artillery.

From all operations one of our aircraft is missing.

▲ EGYPTIAN MAIL, CAIRO, SATURDAY MAY 16, 1942

The *Egyptian Mail*, one of two English-language papers that served the Middle East and Allied troops based there, reports on the Soviet drive on Kharkov even as the advance itself was running out of steam in the face of German counteroffensives. The paper also includes details of a less familiar part of the war: the British campaign to win Madagascar from Vichy France, which began in May 1942 and ended successfully in November.

KHARKOV

MAY 1942

IN MAY 1942, WHEN AXIS FORCES SEEMED TO BE ADVANCING ON ALL FRONTS, ONE FRONT AT FIRST SEEMED TO BE GOING THE ALLIES' WAY. THIS WAS IN THE UKRAINE, IN THE USSR, WHERE MARSHAL TIMOSHENKO BEGAN an offensive against the Germans near the city of Kharkov.

A close associate of Stalin, and one of the few Red Army commanders that the Soviet dictator really trusted, Timoshenko had fought alongside Stalin during the Russian Civil War. The Soviets had assembled large forces during the period beginning in February when spring rains had restricted movement. Timoshenko had at his disposal 765,00 men, 1,200 tanks, 13,000 artillery pieces and 900 aircraft. His offensive got off to reasonable start, but in the mobile warfare that ensued, with tank units able to motor freely across the Ukrainian plains, German superiority in tank tactics and expertise in combining tanks with infantry and anti-tank units led to Soviet defeat. Most Soviet tanks were destroyed, and 170,000 Red Army soldiers were killed or captured.

DISASTER AT KHARKOV

The scale of the disaster took some time to come out in the Western press, which was desperate for good news from the Eastern Front. The defeat was grim enough in itself, but it also badly weakened the Red Army in southern Russia just when the Germans were about to open their big summer offensive. Operation Blau (Blue) eventually became a plan to take over the southern Soviet Union. It consisted of two big drives, one toward the city of Stalingrad on the Volga and one toward the Caucasus.

ALLIED SUCCESS IN MADAGASCAR

Elsewhere, however, the Allies did enjoy one success in spring 1942 in the conquest of Madagascar. Controlled by Vichy France, Madagascar, an island in the Indian Ocean off the coast of Africa, had not seemed strategically important, but in April Japanese naval units had entered the Indian Ocean. Had they been able to cross the ocean and set up bases in Madagascar, then links between Britain and the Far East would have been threatened.

▲ RED ARMY TROOPS attack during the Kharkov Offensive in May 1942. Designed to weaken the German Army Group South, the Soviet offensive was a total disaster.

SPORTING FINAL
★★★★★★
BID AND ASKED PRICES

The Sun

Copyright, 1942, by The New York Sun, Inc.

SPORTING FINAL
Sport Results on Page 22
RACING CHARTS
This afternoon and tonight warm and humid with scattered thundershowers; gentle winds. Temperatures—Minimum, 71; Maximum, 78. (Detailed weather report on page 30.)

VOL. CIX—NO. 240—DAILY. Entered as Second Class Matter Post Office, New York, N. Y. NEW YORK, FRIDAY, JUNE 12, 1942. THREE CENTS

15 JAP SHIPS SUNK, LEXINGTON IS LOST IN CORAL SEA FIGHT

BASEBALL—RACING RESULTS on Page 22

BENNETT FAILS TO WIN BACKING OF LABORITES

A. L. P. Turns Thumbs Down on Attorney-General's Gubernatorial Plans.

HIGHERUPS' HANDS SEEN

Attitudes of Roosevelt and Lehman May Be Linked to Group's Action.

By GEORGE VAN SLYKE.

The American Labor party, acting through its State committee, announced today at the conclusion of a two-hour session that "not in any circumstances" would that party support John J. Bennett Jr. for Governor and by its action gave the candidacy of the Attorney-General at least a temporary setback.

Coming on the heels of Gov. Lehman's visit to the White House and an announcement that President Roosevelt had not given the indorsement of Mr. Bennett, that had been intimated by James A. Farley, State chairman, this action today by the Laborites was accepted as reflecting the view of both the White House and the Governor.

A Real Fight Ahead Now.

Democratic leaders who felt confident that they had the nomination tied up for Mr. Bennett, with his indorsement by forty-three counties with a majority of the votes in the State convention, were upset by this unexpected development. The campaign is thrown up in the air and every indication points to a real battle

Continued on Page 9.

PRESIDENT SETS SCRAP RUBBER PICKUP PERIOD

Roosevelt Orders Nation-wide Collection From June 15 to 30.

'GAS' STATIONS AS RECEIVERS

Offices, Factories and Farms Are Asked to Co-operate—1 Cent a Pound to Be Paid.

Washington, June 12 (A. P.).—President Roosevelt announced today that an intensive campaign for collection of the nation's scrap rubber supply would start on June 15 and last through June 30.

Individuals were urged by the President to search their basements, attics and back yards for all items of rubber that have been discarded or can be discarded. Offices, factories and farms also are being asked to co-operate.

Through arrangements with the oil industry 400,000 filling stations will serve as collection depots. They will pay 1 cent a pound for the rubber brought in, and the Government will reimburse them for that sum.

President Roosevelt, declaring that the rubber situation was extremely serious, again urged the people to cut down on pleasure driving and reduce both automobile speed and mileage.

He told a press conference he had no idea when a person with four tires might be able to get new ones. It may be a long, long time, he said. So, he added, it is a matter of common sense to make existing tires wear as long as possible.

As to Owners of Five Tires.

Reporters noted that he had mentioned persons with four

Continued on Page 7.

SUNK BY JAPS IN CORAL SEA

The United States aircraft carrier Lexington. Associated Press Photo.

WEEKLY FEATURES: Hobbies, Antiques, Pets and Other Popular Interests in This Issue.

MOUNTBATTEN VISITS

Commando Chief Confers With Canadians.

Ottawa, June 12 (A. P.).—Lord Louis Mountbatten, commanding officer of the British Commandos, was in Ottawa today for consultations with chiefs of staff of Canada's armed forces. He left during the afternoon by air for an undisclosed destination.

It has been known for some time that Canadian Navy and Army men overseas have been taking training in Commando tactics and airmen from Canada have taken part in Commando operations. On that basis it was considered likely in some quarters that the part to be played by Canadians in future Commando work might have been under discussion.

Lord Mountbatten, a cousin of the King, has been in Washington recently.

Torpedo Bombers Paced Coral Sea Battle; Avengers Shouted 'Remember Pearl Harbor'

Enemy Invading Squadron Battered From Skies by Americans With Loss of Only One Plane.

[By the commander of an American torpedo plane squadron in the Coral Sea battle, as told to Clark Lee.]

Somewhere in the Southwestern Pacific (A. P.).—At 8 A. M. our scout planes loom out of an overcast sky and come aboard. The word quickly spreads through the ship that they have sighted an enemy aircraft carrier and that we are to attack. The date is May 7—five months after Pearl Harbor.

In the room where the pilots of my squadron are seated with me around a large table, there is an atmosphere of tension. It eases as we set to work plotting our courses and planning our method of attack.

The pilot's flying gear—gloves, lifejackets, helmets—is beside their chairs. There is little conversation and I don't give any fight talk. Everybody knows what we are up against. We hear the fighters taking off above us. Then our turn comes and we walk up to the flight deck, where our planes are waiting, already warmed up and with crews aboard.

Young and clear-eyed, the pilots are obviously excited, but no more than if they were going out to play a tough game of football. They dig elbows into each others' ribs, slap shoulders and trade quick, comradely grins. One youngster boots another in the pants when he is slow going through the door.

I check them over: Young flyers not long out of Annapolis, warrant officers who recently made their ranks, enlisted pilots, boys who were in college only three years ago. Each knows his job as well as it can be taught by hundreds of hours' practice and training.

Nervousness Soon Vanishes.

They are a little nervous as we take off, but once in the air they steady up quickly. We don't waste any time getting into formation, for the enemy is nearly at the maximum range and gasoline may be precious. One circle and we are in line.

I take the squadron up through thick weather and we beeline for

Continued on Page 2.

U. S. PLANES LAND AT ANKARA FIELD

Three Crews Reported Put 'Under Observation.'

London, June 12 (A. P.).—The radio in neutral Turkey announced tonight that three American airplanes had made forced landings on an air field at Ankara, the capital, this morning and that the crews had been put under observation. The announcer gave no inkling of the flyers' destination or base.

This seemed to be another version of an earlier report broadcast by the German radio stating that British pilots, air mechanics and engineers had arrived at Ankara. Authoritative quarters in London refused to comment.

One unofficial source said that the Nazi broadcast may have been designed as part of a propaganda buildup to justify a German attack on Turkey.

The German announcer said that an "increase in the number of British has been observed in recent weeks" in Ankara's hotels and restaurants.

Sanity Tests Begun In Australian Stranglings

Allied Headquarters, Australia, June 12 (A. P.).—The first of a series of medical examinations to test the sanity of Private Edward Leonski of New York, accused of strangling three women, was conducted at the United States Army Hospital here today.

Naval Flight Commanders Tell How Diving Planes Hit Japs at Tulagi.

9 OR 11 WARSHIPS DESTROYED

Enemy Attacked Right in Harbor of Solomon Islands Base by U. S. Flyers.

Pearl Harbor, June 12 (A. P.).—American flyers, many yelling "Remember Pearl Harbor!" as they pushed their bombers into screaming dives, sank nine and possibly eleven Japanese warships and transports at Tulagi Harbor, Solomon Islands, on May 4, as a prelude to the battle of the Coral Sea. Participants in the battle said here today that they were certain that two heavy cruisers, three light cruisers, two destroyers and two large transports were sunk.

A seaplane tender and a third transport also possibly were sunk, as well as numerous small boats. Aircraft carrier squadrons delivered the furious assault and all returned without a scratch to their personnel.

Prelude to Destruction.

Devastating as the blow was to the enemy, it was but a sample of what was to come, for one of the officers in the engagement said: "We gave them a larger dose of the same stuff" in the ensuing battle of the Coral Sea, which lasted a week.

Lieut.-Commanders Joseph Taylor of Danville, Ill., and William Burch of Paducah, Ky., vividly described the blistering attack on the enemy base 1,000 miles northeast of Australia on little Florida Island in the center of the Solomon group.

Commander Burch said: "Aboard the carrier we had not heard anything about the little harbor of Tulagi until late one night when word was passed over the loud speaker: 'Prepare all squadrons for attack on ships in

Continued on Page 2.

92 P. C. OF CARRIER'S COMPLEMENT SAVED

At Least 20 Nipponese Vessels Damaged in Fight—One of Tokio's Newest Carriers Sunk and Another Hit.

By GLEN PERRY.
Special to THE NEW YORK SUN.
The New York Sun Bureau, Washington, June 12.

The Navy Department today announced the results of the battle of the Coral Sea in which, at the cost of the 33,000-ton aircraft carrier Lexington, a tanker and a destroyer, American sea and air forces utterly smashed a major Japanese attempt to take Port Moresby, New Guinea, to occupy the Solomon and Louisade Islands, and perhaps to attack directly the northern coast of Australia.

The Japanese paid a heavy price for their attack, losing—exclusive of ships damaged and possibly lost—fifteen vessels, including a new aircraft carrier, the Ryukaku; three heavy cruisers, a light cruiser and two destroyers. In addition it is probable that another cruiser, of a type unspecified, and a destroyer were sunk, while heavy damage was done to a second carrier, three cruisers, two aircraft tenders, three destroyers.

The navy explained that the delay in announcing the results of the battle of the Coral Sea had given the American Navy the security which was a corner stone in building up for the victory that came subsequently in the battle of Midway Island. The Coral Sea fight came to an end on May 8, with the sinking of the Lexington.

While it will probably not be known until the war is over, it is quite possible that some of the Japanese vessels reported as damaged never got safely to port. Their cases might easily parallel that of the Lexington, which was not lost until some time after the actual fighting had ended, and after a heroic fight to save her.

Lost Tanker and Destroyer.

In addition to the Lexington, the American Navy lost the tanker Neosho and the destroyer Sims. The navy communique does not state the number of American carrier-based and land-based and Australian land-based planes lost in the fighting. The Japanese are reported to have lost more than a hundred planes.

It is apparent from the navy communique that the battle of the Coral Sea, while reaching a crescendo at the end, actually lasted for something like two months. It began in early March, when the Japanese were seen to be concentrating transports and combatant ships at Salamaua and Lae, on the island of New Guinea. The objective was presumed to be Port Moresby, which would have made and ideal jumping off place for an invasion attempt on northern Australia.

One of Biggest in the World.

Thus the Japanese were turned by the battle of the Coral Sea from the offensive to action that was, however much it partook of the color of attack, essentially defensive in nature. This change was exploited by the American armed forces in the battle of Midway. As the result of the two battles the Japanese are worse off than they were before them, and the Allied position is correspondingly improved.

The Lexington was one of the two largest carriers in the world, the other being its sister ship, the Saratoga. She was originally designed as a battle cruiser but was converted to a carrier. She was also an old ship, having been launched in 1925 and commissioned in 1927. She was not as efficient a ship as the newer navy carrier.

Continued on Page 2.

In The Sun Today

Advertising News....Page 28
Amusements....Page 16
Antiques....Pages 14 & 15
Art....Page 15
Boats....Page 24
Books....Page 18
Cafe Life in New York....Page 11
Comics-Puzzles....Page 20
Contract Bridge....Page 11
Editorial....Page 18
Financial....Pages 25 to 28
Food-Nutrition....Page 8
Garden....Page 15
Home Service....Page 13
Let's Make Pictures....Page 28
New Records....Page 11
Obituary....Page 30
Pets....Page 13
Radio....Page 20
Real Estate....Pages 28 & 29
Retailing News....Page 28
Schools....Page 24
Society....Page 19
Sports....Pages 21 to 24
Stamp Collector....Page 12
Stars of the Week....Page 28
The Sun Dial....Page 17
These Days by Sokolsky....Page 17
Today in Washington....Page 17
Who's News Today....Page 17
Woman's....Page 8

School News Appears in the Night Edition.

Dave Boone Says:

There's been quite a spell of pact signing going on. Russia wanted that second front in 1942 pledge in writing, and she practically got it.

Any agreement between Moscow and London for twenty years takes in a lot of time, but both figured they might as well try for distance as well as direction, I suppose. What we see now is a sort of all-around promise to co-operate, with no more mutual distrust than will keep us all happy.

Molotov, Hull, Stalin, Eden, Kalinin and Roosevelt look strange in one group photo, but they've got the Nazis asking one question today. And that question is: "What's cookin'?"

Well, we're going to get gasoline rationing in colors now. It won't be any more comfortable, but it will be prettier.

But rationing, no matter what shade it's in, and no matter how severe it may get, seems almost a privilege when you realize it will help defeat war lords who could do what the Nazis did to that one Czech town of Lidice. They murdered every man, deported every woman and wiped out the town on a charge that somebody there harbored the killers of a Nazi hangman. There's the new order for you, stripped of all trimmings.

The Nazis are proving all-time specialists in stupid barbarism. If you studied Adolf's head carefully you'd find he had a special call for hatching that sort of stuff.

▲ THE SUN, NEW YORK, FRIDAY JUNE 12, 1942

The need to keep information from the enemy made it difficult at times to report engagements accurately or promptly. The *Lexington* was sunk in the Coral Sea on May 8, five weeks before *The Sun* ran the story. Meanwhile, the Battle of Midway had given the U.S. a victory that would prove the turning point of the Pacific War. Pundit Dave Boone mentions one of the great atrocities of the war, the Nazi massacre of 172 men and boys at Lidice, in Czechoslovakia, in reprisal for the murder of Nazi leader Reinhard Heydrich.

Battle of Midway

JUNE 4–6, 1942

TWO NAVAL BATTLES IN THE PACIFIC THEATER WERE OF CRUCIAL IMPORTANCE DURING MAY AND JUNE 1942. THE FIRST WAS THE BATTLE OF THE CORAL SEA. A JAPANESE INVASION force, heading for Port Moresby in New Guinea as part of a plan to establish bases that would threaten Australia's communications with the U.S., was intercepted by an Allied fleet. The fighting was confused, and took place over the three days, May 6–8.

AIRCRAFT BATTLE

The surface vessels never actually sighted each other; the action was fought by aircraft from the carriers on either side. The U.S. Navy lost one major vessel, the aircraft carrier *Lexington*, while the Japanese lost one smaller carrier, and had two others badly damaged. Critically, the Japanese called off their attempt to land at Port Moresby.

The Battle of Midway was fought early in June. The Japanese aimed to lure the U.S. carriers into a battle to defend Midway Island near Hawaii, and to confuse U.S. intelligence by wide-ranging operations, including an attack on the Aleutian Islands near Alaska. U.S. code breakers had cracked the Japanese naval codes, however, and the U.S. commander, Chester Nimitz, knew the Japanese plan. He also had more aircraft carriers than the Japanese had estimated: USS *Yorktown*, badly damaged in the battle of the Coral Sea, had been returned to service.

▲ AN AERIAL PHOTOGRAPH of the Japanese aircraft carrier *Hiryu* during the Battle of Midway. The ship was later set ablaze by a U.S. air attack.

JAPAN DEFEATED

During confused fighting, with naval aircraft again being the sole weapon, three Japanese carriers were sunk for the loss of the *Yorktown*. This heavy loss blunted any remaining Japanese ambitions in the central Pacific, and handed the strategic initiative in the Pacific Ocean firmly to the U.S.

BLACK-OUT ZERO HOUR TO-NIGHT UNTIL 4.57 A.M.
MOON 2.42 RISES P.M. MOON 2.18 SETS A.M.

Daily Express

No. 13,125 Monday, June 22, 1942 One Penny

"Rommel massed all his six divisions and fell on Tobruk . . ." Alan Moorehead, in Cairo despatch this morning, tells first full story of the last stand

WHY TOBRUK FELL: OUTGUNNED AND OUTNUMBERED 3 TO 1

THEY HAD NO AIR COVER

Fighter bases 100 miles off

Express Military Reporter MORLEY RICHARDS

ROMMEL, personally leading the attack on Tobruk, threw every available tank against the garrison.

The assault began early on Saturday morning, after heavy artillery pounding from the long-range German guns, Rommel followed General Wavell's plan of 18 months ago, when Wavell captured Tobruk.

Italian troops "contained" the perimeter from the north, down to a point eight miles above El Adem.

The German panzers which had gone most of the way to the Egyptian frontier to make sure that there was no danger to their flank—General Ritchie could produce no mobile striking force to challenge them—turned back on Friday.

Mass of planes

They re-formed at Sidi Rezegh and El Duda, on the ridge to the south-east above the beleaguered fortress.

A mass of German aircraft supported the first wave of tanks that swept forward to the 27-mile-long perimeter's outer defences.

The main force of the blow, on the usual German method, was directed in the smallest possible area with the greatest available weight. It came in on the south-eastern sector of the perimeter.

All day the battle raged, the British "defending bitterly"—to quote the Italian communiqué—but when nightfall came the enemy had reached the inner defences.

Their first tank attack was followed by wave after wave of motorised infantry drawn from the 90th Light Division. Those massed attacks were followed by more tanks, then another infantry assault to consolidate the positions gained.

Bombed all night

Throughout the night the bombing of the endangered British defences went on, and with the first daylight the ground attacks were renewed with increased violence.

It was seen by Saturday night that the defences to the north-west of the perimeter were only precariously held because of the collapse of our positions further east.

One important fact cannot be over-emphasised: the British garrison was without air cover.

IT was confirmed officially in London seven minutes after midnight that Tobruk has fallen.

Rome and Berlin had claimed earlier that after bitter fighting the British surrendered in the morning.

Berlin, in a midnight commentary, said that "the British, with strong tank support, tried to break out of the Axis ring, but they were repelled, and then offered to give up."

Alan Moorehead, describing the fighting in a despatch sent early yesterday and received last night, told how the British garrison was outnumbered by three to one in men and arms.

Blitzed, then attacked by masses of tanks

Express War Reporter ALAN MOOREHEAD

CAIRO, Sunday.

MASSING nearly the whole of their six divisions, the Germans and Italians fell on Tobruk yesterday, and early today a great part of the stronghold was in their hands.

The main attack began with a fierce air bombardment soon after dawn yesterday.

Then shortly before 9 a.m. two German panzer divisions and the Italian Ariete charged straight at the perimeter from El Duda to the south-east.

This was the point from which General Rommel prepared to attack Tobruk last November, and the point from which the British garrison eventually broke out in the last campaign. The defences were weakest there.

By nine o'clock the battle was locked on the shallow valleys of the escarpment that leads down to the harbour from El Duda.

When the defenders saw the massed tank formation coming in a huge sweeping cloud of dust, they stood briefly.

RUSHED THE GAP

Then, hopelessly outgunned, they fell back towards the interior British positions, about five miles north-east.

Immediately elements of the German 90th Light Infantry, who had been brought up in the night, rushed the gap.

They ran ahead of the tanks and dug in, using small arms fire, and protected by heavy guns established on a rise further back.

Then when the infantry was fully established, the German guns came on again.

Meanwhile other enemy forces and guns were engaging the British line for miles around the perimeter, and all Tobruk was under heavy fire.

By nightfall the two armies were at tight grips right inside the eastern perimeter, and the Germans had occu-

—HOW— according to the enemy IT ENDED

THE story of Tobruk as told in British and Axis communiqués yesterday:—

CAIRO, 12.27 p.m. Yesterday the enemy attacked the perimeter of Tobruk in great strength.

In spite of most determined resistance by our forces, the enemy succeeded in penetrating the defences and occupying a considerable area inside them.

Fighting continues.

ROME, 1.06 *(the regular Italian communiqué).*

Our motorised units, continuing their advance eastwards, have occupied Bardia.

Since yesterday an attack against Tobruk has been going on, supported by mass formations of Italo-German planes.

In spite of bitter enemy resistance operations are proceeding favourably. Last

CRIMEA DEFENCE PIERCED

MOSCOW'S midnight communiqué announced that the Germans at Sebastopol succeeded in driving a wedge into the Soviet defences yesterday at the cost of enormous losses, after repeated attacks had been repelled.

"In other sectors of the front no material changes took place," it said.

"During the week ending Saturday, 264 German aircraft were destroyed in air combat, on airfields and by A.A. fire. Our losses during the period were 103."

German regiment routed.—Page Three.

Sub. shells Vancouver Island

Express Staff Reporter

NEW YORK, Sunday.

CANADIAN territory was attacked for the first time in this war last night, when a submarine shelled the naval station at Estevan Point, Vancouver Island, off Canada's Pacific coast.

Colonel Ralston, Defence Minister, announced today: "The Commander-in-Chief, West Coast defences, has reported to the Dominion Government that the telegraph station at Estevan Point, Vancouver Island, was shelled by a submarine at 10.35 on Saturday night. No damage resulted."

Vancouver Island lies off Canada's coast close to the U.S. border, and on it, facing the mainland, is the important naval base, Esquimault. Estevan Point faces the open sea.

SOMETHING BIG OVER CHANNEL

Something big took place in the Channel and on the French and Belgian coasts on Saturday night.

For several hours up to early morning there was continuous heavy gunfire, punctuated by bomb explosions. Great flashes lit the High-powered surface craft and planes crossing and re-crossing the Channel were heard.

Comment last night on New York radio: "Another commando raid may have taken place at Dunkirk."

Bostons attack Dunkirk

DUNKIRK docks were attacked by Boston bombers late yesterday afternoon. One of the escorting fighters is missing. A German raider was shot down off England's south-west coast, and it is now known that a fifth German fighter was shot down on Saturday.

MALTA had a quiet day yesterday after shooting down five bombers on Saturday.

Train ban ends secrets leak

Railway employees are prohibited from posting uncensored letters for soldiers, under an order made over the week-end.

The ban results from leakages about troop movements contained in farewell letters given to railwaymen to post by soldiers going overseas.

Laval today

VICHY, Sunday.—Laval will make "an important speech" tomorrow night.—Reuter.

Beaverbrook, at great Birmingham Anglo-Soviet rally, declares:

"The need is—Second Front with no delay"

By WILLIAM BARKLEY

BIRMINGHAM, Sunday.

LORD BEAVERBROOK came to Birmingham today and saw the citizens of this vast munition factory parading their will to win with the vim, virility and patriotic fervour which he has seen displayed in Moscow.

Too long the fighting spirit of what he called us—"the warriors of the Old World"—has been hushed up and muted. But here we had martial music in every street, banners flying, men and women striding in processions to meet in immense concourse in the heart of the city.

Ten thousand marched in the processions, forming up under the walls of the town hall beneath a rostrum, from which he addressed them.

Half of them were uniformed men and women and boys and girls of the Air Training Corps, and the other half were men and women straight from the factory benches where they make the weapons to equip the Second Front.

Massing behind them were the public, estimated by the police to be between 20,000 and 30,000 more.

It was all in celebration of the Russian Alliance, and marked almost to the hour twelve months since the Germans assaulted Russia.

Russia's flag

Birmingham's Lord Mayor, Councillor Norman Tiptaft, standing beside Lord Beaverbrook, raised his robed arm and pointed to the flagstaff above the Council House. There for the first time in this city, he said, flies the Red Flag of Russia with the hammer and sickle.

All eyes turned towards it and a great cheer went up at this symbol of understanding.

The Red Flag and the Union Jack were sewn up together to drape the rostrum where for an hour Lord Beaverbrook discoursed to the men and women of Birmingham.

"We have been promised a Second Front," Lord Beaverbrook said. "We have been promised it by the Government. Now the need is for urgency. No unnecessary delay in sending forth our second expeditionary force to fight on the Second Front.

"We must work together in the war and for the peace," he said. "What we have got Russia is entitled to share. There may be hunger in Russia. We may have to share our bread with the Russians. Men we must give too, equipped with tanks and airplanes. That is the pledge of the Second Front."

False prophets

The prophets were false who said that first the blockade would win the war. Then the story was that bombers would win the war. The bombers had done wonderfully well, but you will not beat Germany by destroying the Ruhr.

"You will drive German industry elsewhere by bombing. You will damage the morale of a people already shaken. You will inflict a just revenge on the wicked scoundrels who made the war. But you have no right to believe that the bomber will bring the war to an end.

"Back to the British Army. It won the last war, and it will win this war if properly supported by bombers and fighting aircraft, and if driven with urgency, speed and with courage.

"The British Army is equipped and ready for the job and wanting to do it. The British Army wants the Second Front to show that Britain can fight in Europe, and to avenge Dunkirk."

Hatred

Hatred, stern and righteous, must be cultivated against all our enemies, but chief hatred for the chief villain, Germany. It was nonsense to say that the Germans are good and that only Hitler and his accomplices are bad.

Hatred through the fight, hatred to harden our hearts and sharpen our swords, hatred until victory comes—such was his call.

After victory, pity for the vanquished, but no pity for the leaders in Germany's career of crime. Then a peace upheld by the guns of the conquerors.

The square before the Town Hall resounded to three cheers for Soviet Russia.

Then these walls of ancient but progressive Toryism reechoed to a tune unheard here before—the Internationale.

LORD BEAVERBROOK'S SPEECH IS REPORTED ON PAGE TWO. PICTURES ON PAGE THREE

Faster corvettes

Canada is building bigger and faster corvettes to join the hundreds already protecting convoys against U-boats.

'TOBRUK BRINGS IT NEARER'

WASHINGTON, Sunday.

TOBRUK will bring the Second Front nearer. This is the opinion of Congress members in Washington to-night.

Andrew May, chairman of the House of Representatives Military Affairs Committee said: "A bad situation always provokes a new effort to meet it. This makes it imperative that we open a Second Front—and soon."

Mr. Harry Schwartz, a member of the committee, said: "I believe we are now ready to launch a campaign to relieve pressure against the Russians and the British in Libya. The sooner we get at it the better."—B.U.P.

2 JAP SHIPS HIT

Forces landed on Aleutian isle

Express Staff Reporter

NEW YORK, Sunday.

AMERICAN pilots report that Jap landings have now been made on Kiska Island—589 miles west of Dutch Harbour, U.S. base—where Jap ships were raided in the first days of the Aleutians attack.

The U.S. fliers sighted tents and huts on Kiska, where apparently the Japs are seeking to get up a base.

The pilots went on to attack a small force of ships in the harbour, sank a transport and scored hits on a cruiser.

A Navy Department communiqué issued today says:—

"Within the last few days the weather has been sufficiently clear to permit restricted air operations against Kiska, where tents and other minor temporary structures were observed to have been set up were observed.

"A small force of Japanese ships in the harbour were bombed by U.S. Army aircraft. Hits were reported on one cruiser and a transport has been sunk."

Previous Aleutians communiqués have reported three Japanese cruisers, one destroyer, one gunboat and one transport damaged in air attacks against the Kiska forces and those occupying Attu, furthest west of the Aleutians.

3 A.M. LATEST

SOUTH COAST RAID THIS MORNING

Enemy raiders bombed a south coast town early today.

AUSTRIAN TROOPS MUTINY

MOSCOW, Monday.—Austrian units quartered near Vienna mutinied and refused to go to the front, says supplement to Soviet communiqué. Mutiny was quelled by S.S. men.—Reuter.

The list grows

STOCKHOLM, Sunday.—Germany now reports 411 dead, 560 seriously injured, and 4,500 slightly injured in the 1,000-plane raid on Cologne. First figure was 166 dead.—B.U.P.

CHURCHILL–F.D.R. NEWS TODAY?

Express Staff Reporter NEWELL ROGERS

NEW YORK, Sunday.

MR. WINSTON CHURCHILL and President Roosevelt today carried their conference at a secret place into its fourth day, while Washington waited anxiously for news. It was said that there might be an announcement tomorrow; but nothing more.

The original plan is said to have been for an unannounced visit by the Prime Minister, to be made public only after he was back at No. 10, Downing-street.

Mr. Churchill decided some time ago to make the visit, according to competent quarters, and this fact disposes of a report that he brought "an urgent appeal" for help to defend Egypt.

Washington remains convinced that a decision about the Second Front will be taken, subject to three ualifying factors, which may affect the where and when:—

1—Egypt's safety; 2—Russia's situation; 3—Shipping to nourish the Secon Front.

There are reports that in field warfare the two leaders have reache the point of iscussing possible Commaners-in-Chief for the Anglo-American Expeitionary Force against Europe.

Lieut.General A. G. L. McNaughton, Canaian Chief in Britain, and General George C. Marshall, U.S. Chief of Staff, are mentioned as possibilities.

The New York Times says that Mr. Churchill wants to await the reduction of shipping losses before opening a Second Front, to rule out all possibility of failure.

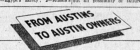

▲ BRITISH TROOPS SURRENDER to the Afrika Korps following the fall of Tobruk to Rommel's forces on June 21. Winston Churchill called the port's loss "a disgrace."

▲ DAILY EXPRESS, LONDON, MONDAY JUNE 22, 1942
Rommel's victory at the Battle of Gazala (May 28–June 13, 1942) resulted in the British retreating to Egypt, followed by the Afrika Korps. This made Tobruk's position hopeless.

Münchener Ausgabe

177. Ausg. 55. Jahrg. Einzelpreis für München 15 Rpf., für auswärts 20 Rpf. .·.

"Freiheit und Brot!"

Münchener Ausgabe

München, Freitag, 26. Juni 1942

VÖLKISCHER BEOBACHTER

Verlag: Frz. Eher Nachf., G. m. b. H., München 22, Thierschstraße 11—17. Sammelruf 2 21 31, nach 17 Uhr 2 21 24. Drahtanschrift: Eherverlag — Postscheck: München 113 46, Prag 723 03, Preßburg 58 40, Bern III 72 65, Budapest 135 32, Belgrad 602 37, Bukarest 249 68, Brüssel 200 797, den Haag 211 bek. Bayerische Hypotheken- und Wechselbank, München, Filiale Kaufingerstraße, Bayerische Gemeindebank, Girozentrale München, Brienner Straße 49, Bank der Deutschen Arbeit AG., München, Deutsche Bank, Filiale München, Depositenkasse Maximilianstraße, Reichsbankgirokonto, Kreditanstalt der Deutschen, Prag, Kommerzialbank Krakau, Slovenska Banka, Bratislava

Kampfblatt der nationalsozialistischen Bewegung Großdeutschlands

Schriftltg.: München 13, Schellingstr. 39, Sammelruf 2 08 01 - Briefanschrift: München 2 BS. Schließfach 294 - Drahtanschrift: Beobachter München - Berliner Schriftleitung Berlin SW 68, Zimmerstraße 88, Ruf 11 00 22 - Wiener Schriftleitung: Wien VII, Seidengasse 3—11, Ruf B 35 40 - Erscheinungsweise wöchentlich 7 mal - Bezugspreis in München durch Träger RM. 2.00 einschl. Zustellgeld, in Orten mit Agenturen RM. 2.— einschl. Zustellgeld, durch die Post RM. 2.90 einschl. 43 Pf. Postgebühr, ausschl. 42 Pf. Zustellgebühr - Anzeigen: München 22, Thierschstr. 11—17. Ruf 2 21 31, Anzeigenschluß 16 Uhr, 1 Tag vor Erscheinen - Gewünschte Einzelnummern sind nur gegen vorher. Einsendung v. 30 Pf. lieferbar

Capuzzo, Sollum und Halfaya genommen

Rommel überrannte die ägyptischen Grenzforts

Göring an den Vater des Oberfeldwebels Steinbatz

Berlin, 25. Juni

Wie im Bericht des Oberkommandos der Wehrmacht gemeldet, hat der Führer dem von einem Flug gegen den Feind nicht zurückgekehrten Oberfeldwebel Steinbatz als 14. Soldaten der Deutschen Wehrmacht das Eichenlaub mit Schwertern zum Ritterkreuz des Eisernen Kreuzes verliehen.

Reichsmarschall Göring richtete an den Vater des Oberfeldwebels folgendes Schreiben:

„Lieber Herr Steinbatz! Der Führer hat Ihren todesmutigen Sohn durch die Verleihung des Eichenlaubes mit Schwertern zum Ritterkreuz des Eisernen Kreuzes geehrt. Stolz und bewegt bringe ich Ihnen das mit der Versicherung zur Kenntnis, daß meine Luftwaffe den jungen Helden, der in den Reihen unserer kühnsten Jagdflieger 99 Luftsiege errungen hat, niemals vergessen wird.

gez. Göring, Reichsmarschall des Großdeutschen Reiches und Oberbefehlshaber der Luftwaffe."

(Siehe auch Seite 2)

Tagesbefehl an das NSKK.

Berlin, 25. Juni

Der neue Korpsführer des NSKK. hat folgenden Tagesbefehl an das NSKK. erlassen:

NSKK.-Männer!

Der Führer hat die Führung des Korps in meine Hände gelegt.

Ich habe das Werk Adolf Hühnleins als verpflichtendes Vermächtnis übernommen.

Es in seinem Geist fortzuführen, zu wahren und zu mehren, ist die Richtschnur meines Handelns.

Daß ihr mir hierbei vertrauensvoll zur Seite steht und mir auch in allem als sie — mit ganzer Hingabe in alter Bewährung erfüllt, ist die Bitte und Erwartung, die ich in dieser Stunde an euch richte.

Berlin, am 25. Juni 1942.

Kraus, Korpsführer.

In scharfer Verfolgung über Sidi el Barani hinaus vorgestoßen

vb. Berlin, 25. Juni

Fast jedermann, auch der Feind, hatte erwartet, daß die deutschen und italienischen Divisionen nach dem Sturm auf Tobruk eine Kampfpause einlegen würden. Denn diese glänzende Waffentat war nicht von einer ausgeruhten Truppe aus einer wohlvorbereiteten Ausgangsstellung heraus vollbracht worden, sondern von Männern und Maschinen, die drei Wochen lang unter der glühenden Sommerhitze der Wüste mit einem sehr starken und stark befestigten, wehrenden Gegner gekämpft hatten. Rommel aber hat wieder einmal das Unerwartete getan: Er ist unverzüglich zur Verfolgung der auf die ägyptische Grenze zurückweichenden 8. britischen Armee aufgebrochen, hat die Sollum—Halfaya—Capuzzo-Linie überrannt und steht heute — vier Tage nach der Eroberung Tobruks — 100 Kilometer jenseits der Grenze bei Sidi el Barani. Eine Leistung, die sowohl der Kühnheit der Führung wie dem Draufgängertum und der Ausdauer der verbündeten Afrikakämpfer das glänzendste Zeugnis ausstellt! Wie der neuen Erfolg hat auch die Luftwaffe hervorragenden Anteil.

Wir können uns lebhaft die Gefühle ausmalen, mit denen Rommels und Basticos Soldaten jene alten Kampfstätten des Nordafrikakrieges — Sollum, den Halfaya-Paß und Capuzzo — wieder betraten, die sie im vergangenen Sommer so zäh verteidigt haben und in denen im November und Dezember kleine, tapfere Besatzungen wochenlang buchstäblich bis zur letzten Granate und Gewehrpatrone und bis zum letzten Tropfen Wasser ausharrten, nachdem Auchinlecks Offensive über diese alte Verteidigungslinie hinweggerollt war.

Die Reichweite der Verfolgungsoperation ist aber auch ein zusätzlicher Beweis dafür, wie schwer die englische Nordafrikaarmee in den Kämpfen der letzten Wochen geschlagen worden ist und welche bitteren Verluste sie erlitten hat, denn andernfalls hätte sie in der Lage sein müssen, einem Angreifer, der sich so weit von seinen Ausgangsstellungen entfernt hatte, in den stark befestigten Grenzforts nachhaltigen Widerstand zu leisten. Damit hatte man in London augenscheinlich auch gerechnet; noch gestern versicherten englische und nordamerikanische Nachrichtenagenturen, daß die Sollum—Halfaya-Linie viele Vorteile habe und ihre Stellungen „so gut sind, daß die kommenden Schläge abgewehrt werden können". Reuters Luftfahrtkorrespondent fügte diesen optimistischen Erwartungen noch die Bemerkung hinzu, daß nach maßgeblicher Londoner Ansicht Großbritannien immer noch die Luftüberlegenheit auf dem westlichen Wüste besitze und diese in starkem Maße ausgenutzt habe.

Also wieder einmal britische Illusionen, die unverzüglich zerschlagen worden sind! Heute ist infolgedessen die anglo-amerikanische Presse wieder ganz auf Moll gestimmt, ohne jedoch die neuen Hiobsbotschaften vom afrikanischen Kriegsschauplatz im einzelnen schon zu verraten.

Ein Nachfolger für General Ritchie gesucht

Drahtbericht unseres Stockholmer Berichterstatters

dr. th. b. Stockholm, 25. Juni

Eine ganze Reihe von englischen Korrespondenten im Hauptquartier Auchinlecks erklärt, daß die Stellungen, die die 8. Armee jetzt eingenommen habe, schwer zu verteidigen seien. Es sei deshalb möglich, daß die Engländer sich weiter zurückzögen und sich auf eine bewegliche Verteidigung beschränkten, bis neue Verstärkungen eingetroffen seien.

Unter dem Eindruck der neuen Frontmeldungen ist auch der gestrige Londoner Versuch, den Verlust Tobruks und die Niederlage der 8. Armee zu bagatellisieren, rasch wieder aufgegeben worden. Der Berichterstatter des „Daily Expreß" in Kairo zum Beispiel erklärt; „Um sich weitere Schocks zu ersparen, muß man reinlarmachen, daß unsere Verteidigungskräfte ein großes Stück zurückgehen müssen. Ritchies Armee ist der zwei Divisionen beraubt, die er in Tobruk verloren hat, und außerdem eines Teils der Kampfwagen zweier Panzerdivisionen." Das ist nicht richtig, zu behaupten, daß die 8. Armee noch intakt sei, oder irgend etwas Ähnliches. Diese Behauptung machte kein Geringerer, als der stellvertretende Premierminister Attlee im Unterhaus! Vermutlich muß die 8. Armee jetzt mit Truppen aus General Stones" ägyptischer Armee verstärkt werden. Wenn sich die Grenzfestungen nicht halten lassen, so muß die 8. Armee um Aufschub kämpfen, bis genügend Zeit für die Zuführung von Verstärkung durch moderne Waffen gewonnen ist."

Es scheint sich zu bestätigen, daß der bisherige Befehlshaber der 8. Armee, General Ritchie, tatsächlich abgesetzt worden ist. Die englische Presse sucht jedenfalls eifrig nach einem Nachfolger. Sie nennen den Bedrücker Ägyptens, General Stones, wahrscheinlich nur deshalb, weil dieser gestern erklärte, daß das Kriegsglück wechsle und sie Vertrauen in die Zukunft habe. Wieso wechseln! Wo halten

Bescheidener Vorstoß gegen die Churchill-Diktatur

Sondersitzung des Pazifischen Kriegsrates

Drahtbericht unseres Stockholmer Berichterstatters

dr. th. b. Stockholm, 25. Juni

Churchill wird über das Wochenende in London zurückerwartet. Er nahm am Donnerstag in einer Sondersitzung des Pazifischen Kriegsrates teil, trat dann mit mehreren führenden Mitgliedern des Kongresses zusammen und hatte anschließend Unterredungen mit Lord Halifax und Staatssekretär Cordell Hull. An der Sitzung des Pazifischen Kriegsrates, der vor allem deshalb einberufen wurde, um Australien, Neuseeland und Tschungking-China zu beruhigen, nahmen neben dem kanadischen Ministerpräsident Mackenzie King und dem früheren holländische Ministerium van Kleffens teil.

Es könne kein Zweifel darüber herrschen, meint der Londoner Korrespondent des „Socialdemokraten", daß England in diesen Tagen die schwerste Krise des Krieges durchmacht und daß Churchills Kabinett der ernstesten Debatte im Unterhaus entgegengehe. Diese Debatte soll am kommenden Dienstag beginnen und zwei Tage dauern. Derjenige, den diese Debatte gilt und der von recht geringer Teil der englischen Öffentlichkeit als der Hauptschuldige an der vernichtenden Niederlage in Libyen betrachtet wird, aber immer noch in Washington und verfolgt offensichtlich die neueste Taktik, den Sturm des allgemeinen Unmuts und der Veränderung sich austoben zu lassen, ehe er vor das Unterhaus tritt.

Daß sich England in einer der schwersten Krisen dieses Krieges befindet, läßt sich sicherlich nicht bestreiten. Ob sich diese Krise aber zu einer Krise für Churchill selbst verdichten wird, ist noch sehr die Frage. Wir haben solche parlamentarischen Stürme schon zu oft erlebt, um zu glauben, daß der Sturm, der jetzt durch England geht, die Grundlagen der Churchill-Diktatur erschüttern könnte.

Ein Teil der Abgeordneten ist schließlich noch kritischer und angriffslustiger gestimmt als in früheren Fällen. Der auf dem rechten Flügel der konservativen Partei stehende Abgeordnete Sir Wardlow Milne, der gleichzeitig Vorsitzender der einflußreichen parlamentarischen Kontrollkommission für die Staatsausgaben ist, hat für ein Mißtrauensvotum die Unterschriften von ungefähr zwanzig Abgeordneten gefunden. Ein weiteres Mißtrauensvotum planen der erst kürzlich gewählte unabhängige Abgeordnete Brown und der konservative Abgeordnete Cunningham Reid.

Kein Zweifel, bei beiden die Vorstöße aus den Reihen der Unterhausmitglieder gehen diesmal weiter als sonst. Mit einem solchen Mißtrauensvotum ist man Churchill bisher nicht gekommen. Erschüttern aber können diese Anträge Churchills Stellung nicht, auch wenn hundert Abgeordnete gegen ihn stimmen sollten. Und schon liegt von seiten der Labour-Party der übliche Kompromißvorschlag vor: Eine besondere Kommission soll zusammentreten und die Ursachen des „Rückschlags" von Tobruk untersuchen. Der „Evening Standard" nennt diese Kommission ein Tribunal. Damit will man ihr einen revolutionären Anstrich geben und das Täuschungsmanöver gegenüber der Öffentlichkeit nur steigern.

Südafrika trauert um Tobruk

Lissabon, 25. Juni

In Südafrika herrscht nach einem Reuterbericht tiefe Trauer über den Fall von Tobruk, weil in der Festung ein großer Teil der unter Ritchies Befehl kämpfenden südafrikanischen Truppenverbände in Gefangenschaft geraten ist. Das Telegramm, in dem der stellvertretende britische Premierminister Attlee dem südafrikanischen Premierminister Smuts mitteilte, daß es zu einer verschwindend geringen Zahl der südafrikanischen Truppen gelungen sei, aus Tobruk herauszukommen, bildete die Sensation des Tages. Soweit bisher bekannt wurde, ist fast die gesamte südafrikanische Division vernichtet worden oder in Gefangenschaft geraten, ein beträchtlicher Prozentsatz der Südafrika zur Verfügung stehenden Truppen. Es handelt sich dabei um ausgesprochene Eliteeinheiten, die in absehbarer Zeit überhaupt nicht zu ersetzen sind.

„In fast allen südafrikanischen Städten gibt es jetzt zahlreiche Familien, die einen Toten beklagen oder von denen ein Mitglied in die Kriegsgefangenschaft geraten ist", meldet in einem amerikanischen Bericht. Die britische Führung wird im Lande der schärfsten Kritik unterzogen, und die Regierung erwartet schwere peinliche Stunden im Parlament, da ein großer Teil des Volkes der Auffassung ist, daß General Ritchie südafrikanische Truppen mit hoffnungsloser Posten stelle und ihnen den schwierigsten Teil der Kämpfe zuschob, während er die Regimenter des britischen Mutterlandes schone.

Außerordentliche Materialverluste der flüchtenden Briten

Berlin, 25. Juni

Wie das Oberkommando der Wehrmacht zu den jüngsten Erfolgen im Afrikastreitkräfte in Nordafrika mitteilt, hatten die Briten vergeblich versucht, sich in vorbereiteten Stellungen an der libysch-ägyptischen Grenze noch einmal zum Kampf zu stellen. Der Widerstand der sich hier verblutenden indischen Truppenteile wurde gebrochen und in unaufhaltsamen Vordringen die Grenze überschritten.

In rascher Folge fielen das Fort Capuzzo, Halfaya und Sollum durch die heldischen Kämpfe deutscher Truppen berndt geworden. Paß und der ägyptische Küstenort Sollum. Der Weg der vorwärtsstürmenden Achsentruppen führte an zahllosen Trümmerfeldern, brennenden Panzern und vernichteten Kolonnen vorbei. Die Materialverluste des flüchtenden Feindes sind außerordentlich hoch.

Nach der Einnahme von Sollum, dem für die Briten wegen der dortigen Hafenanlagen einen empfindlichen Verlust bedeutet, stießen die Achsentruppen in den Raum von Haggage el Aqaba, südostwärts Sollum, vor und warfen die stark angeschlagenen feindlichen Verbände unter Bagbag und bei Serawil weiter zurück. Als Folge dieser Operationen wurde der wichtige britische Versorgungshafen Sidi el Barani von den Achsentruppen genommen, die mit ihren Spitzen bereits südostwärts dieser Stadt weiter vordringen.

Auch im Laufe der letzten Nacht setzten die deutschen Kampfflugzeuge in mehreren Wellen ihre Angriffe fort. Zahlreiche Feldjäger wurden durch Bombentreffer zerstört und in Tiefangriffen den feindlichen Kolonnen, die auf der Küstenstraße nach Osten zu entkommen versuchten, schwere Verluste zugefügt. In wiederholten Angriffen wurden zahlreiche Kolonnen zersprengt und mehrere mit Munition und Truppen beladene Eisenbahnzüge in Brand geschossen.

Durch diese heftigen, bei Tag und Nacht geflogenen Angriffe haben die deutschen Luftwaffenverbände zu den schnellen und erfolgreichen Vorstößen der deutschen und italienischen Truppen bis zu dem Raum von Sidi el Barani wirkungsvoll beigetragen.

Zweifrontenkampf im Wolchow-Abschnitt

Berlin, 25. Juni

Wie das Oberkommando der Wehrmacht mitteilt, hatten die deutschen Truppen am 23. Juni nicht nur im Kampf um Sewastopol, sondern auch im nördlichen Abschnitt der Ostfront in den harten Kämpfen an der Wolchowfront weitere Erfolge. Angesichts der Kampfleiste ist dem deutschen Soldaten als besondere Aufgabe das Kämpfen gegen zwei Fronten gestellt, da eingesickerte feindliche Kräfte nicht hinter der eigentlichen Frontstellungen eingeschlossen sind. Bei den Abschnürung eines Widerstandsnestes bildenden deutschen Truppen kämpfen einerseits nach Osten gegen die Entsetzungsversuche des Feindes und andererseits nach Westen gegen die Ausbruchsversuche der eingekesselten Bolschewisten. Der Kampf wird weiter erschwert durch die völlige Wegloskeit und durch anhaltende Regenfälle moralistisch, nur schwer passierbaren Geländes.

In heftigen Gefechten haben die deutschen Truppen des Abschnürungsriegels den Versuchen des Feindes, den stählernen Ring zu sprengen, abgewiesen. Im Innern des Kessels entwickelte sich dagegen bereits das typische Bild der Vernichtung. Nach Abwehr von feindlichen Erkundungsvorstößen gegen den Riegelstellung drängen die deutschen Truppen in heftigen Kämpfen weiter gegen die eingekesselten Bolschewisten vor.

Auch die Luftwaffe richtete am 24. Juni starke Angriffe gegen die eingekesselten Bolschewisten. Schwere Bomben zerstörten die in Walddickicht angelegten Versorgungslager des Feindes sowie stark ausgebaute Waldstellungen. Dadurch gelang der deutschen Infanterie zur Verengung des Wolchowkessels wirksam zu unterstützen. Weitere Luftangriffe richteten sich gegen feindliche Bereitstellungen ostwärts der deutschen Riegelstellung. Mehrere durch belegte Ortsunterkünfte und Panzeransammlungen sowie die unter Schutz der Panzer aufgestellten Flakbatterien wurden von den Bomben deutscher Kampfflugzeuge erfaßt. Sechs feindliche schwere Panzer blieben nach Treffern brennend in ihren Ausgangsstellungen liegen, und drei Flakbatterien wurden zum Schweigen gebracht.

Seekrieg gegen die Sowjets

Von unserem Marinemitarbeiter Erich Glodschey

Der Entscheidungskampf gegen den Bolschewismus, der im weiten osteuropäischen Raum seine zerstörenden Kräfte zum Angriff auf die europäische Kultur gesammelt hatte, schien auf den ersten Blick ein reiner Landkrieg zu sein. Doch die nähere Betrachtung der Sowjetunion beim Kampfbeginn im einen Jahr erwies, daß Stalin auch zur See erhebliche Kampfmittel aufgehäuft hatte. Die Sowjetmarine war insbesondere mit Unterseebooten und Schnellbooten reichlich versehen. Sie hatte auch moderne Kreuzer und Zerstörer in ansehnlicher Zahl gebaut, während die neuen Schlachtschiffe noch in Nikolajew und Leningrad im Bau waren. Jedoch auch die drei modernisierten Schlachtschiffe aus der Zarenflotte — zwei in der Ostsee und eines im Schwarzen Meer — bildeten Kampfmittel, die man gerade in diesen Anfangskrieg verfügt. Uns ist Maitland-Wilson nur als Führer des britischen Expeditionsheeres in Griechenland bekannt, wo er so kräftig hinaus geschlagen wurde. Zu guter Letzt taucht in der Kandidatenliste für die 8. Armee auch wieder der unvermeidliche Wavell auf, der nach Aussage einer englischen Zeitung „der einzige englische General ist, dessen Name und Leistungen das öffentliche Interesse an sich ziehen könnten".

Andere empfehlen General Maitland-Wilson, der jetzt den Befehl über die 9. Armee in Syrien-Palästina führt und angeblich über große Erfahrungen im Wüstenkrieg verfügt.

die Briten in diesem Krieg etwa schon einmal einwandfrei gesiegt!

In der Ostsee waren am 22. Juni 1941 mindestens 70 Sowjet-U-Boote vorhanden, für die zwei Schlachtschiffe, vier Kreuzer, zwei Torpedokreuzer, mehrere Flottillen von Zerstörern und Torpedobooten und zahlreiche Fahrzeuge der Minensuchflotte und des Minensuchdienstes den Rückhalt bildeten. Die deutsche Kriegsmarine konnte angesichts ihrer Aufgabe, die atlantischen Seekriegführung gegen England, nur begrenzte Kräfte für die Ostsee abgeben. In erster Linie hatte sie die Aufgabe, die Sicherungsstreitkräfte für die Last des Kampfes zu tragen. Die Sperrwaffe legte durch Minenbarrieren vor allem dem deutschen Kriegsschiffe überwacht wurden. In wiederholten Angriffen hatte man die Flankensicherung an der Küste der Ostsee und des Schwarzen Meeres sowie des Nördlichen Eismeeres gleich wert erstrebten, wie auf den äußeren Meere Boote in Europa und Ostasien angewachsen war.

Im ganzen war es deutlich, daß die Bolschewisten ihre Flotte nicht nur zur Flankensicherung an der Küste der Ostsee und des Schwarzen Meeres sowie des Nördlichen Eismeeres gleich wert erstrebten, wie auf den äußeren Meere vor allem mit ihrer Unterseebootwaffe erstrebten, die auf oder mehr Boote in Europa und Ostasien angewachsen war.

In der Ostsee waren am 22. Juni 1941 mindestens 70 Sowjet-U-Boote vorhanden, für die zwei Schlachtschiffe, vier Kreuzer, zwei Torpedokreuzer, mehrere Flottillen von Zerstörern und Torpedobooten und zahlreiche Fahrzeuge der Minensuchflotte und des Minensuchdienstes den Rückhalt bildeten. Die deutsche Kriegsmarine konnte angesichts ihrer Aufgabe, die atlantischen Seekriegführung gegen England, nur begrenzte Kräfte für die Ostsee abgeben. In erster Linie hatte sie die Aufgabe, die Sicherungsstreitkräfte für die Last des Kampfes zu tragen. Die Sperrwaffe legte durch Minenbarrieren vor den Finnischen Meerbusen, um die Hauptmacht der Sowjetflotte am Ausbruch aus ihren damaligen Hauptstützpunkten Reval und Kronstadt in die übrige Ostsee zu hindern. Dabei half die kleine, aber tüchtige finnische Kriegsmarine wesentlich mit. Den leichten deutschen Sicherungsstreitkräften aber oblag die Aufgabe, den umfangreichen Ostseehandel zu sichern und den militärischen Nachschub über See durchzuführen und zu schützen, der zunächst für die Truppen in Finnland und dann auch für die an der Ostseeküste vorstoßenden deutschen Armeen bestimmt werden mußte. Dabei wurde die sowjetische Unterseebootflottille, die in erster Linie Libau als Stützpunkt benutzte, in den Krieg verwickelt, zumal sie nach wenigen Tagen ihren Stützpunkt verloren. Auch in der Folgezeit sind deutsche U-Boote von den deutschen Geleitzügen nicht gefährlich geworden. Die Stärke der deutschen Abwehr veranlaßte die Bolschewisten zu ihrer Hauptaktion gegen die deutschen Verkehrswege. In Minen bewegten sich viele ihrer U-Boote in Kronstadt festlegen und die Besatzungen an Land einzusetzen. Ein sowjetischer Seeverkehr außerhalb des Finnischen Meerbusens wurde von der deutschen Kriegsmarine vollständig verhindert. Sie konnte außer der bedeutende Anzahl sowjetischer Handelsschiffe an ersten Kriegstagen aufbringen oder sicherstellen und damit die deutsche Transporttonnage vermehren.

Marineeinheitabteilungen nahmen am Vormarsch des Heeres an der Küste teil, wo außer Libau bald Windau, Riga und Pernau erobert und im August ein weiter Ring um Reval geschlossen werden konnte. Bei den Kämpfen um Reval fand die größte Minenschlacht der bisherigen Seekriegsgeschichte statt. Auch das deutsche Heer August 1941 Reval stürmte, versuchten die Bolschewisten Truppen und Kriegsmaterial über See nach Kronstadt abzubefördern. Ihnen feindliche Kriegsfahrzeuge und 25 Transporter gerieten auf die Minensperre von Juminda. Auf ihr sanken 60 000 BRT., während die Luftwaffe diesen Erfolg verdoppelte, indem sie die in der Sperre festgehaltenen Handelsschiffe mit Bombentreffer versenkte.

Im Anschluß an die Einnahme von Reval war es als notwendig, die baltischen Inseln zu erobern. Die Kriegsmarine stellte dafür die notwendigen Transporte sicher. Minensuchboote und kleine Fahrzeuge den Übergang auf die Inseln Ösel und Dagoe mit, während die Kreuzer „Leipzig", „Emden" und „Köln" den feindlichen Inselbatterien wirkungsvoll beschossen. Als das Heer bis zum Ladogasee durchgestoßen war, rückte Marineartillerie bis an die Einschließungsfront vor Leningrad. Die sowjetische Ostseeflotte wurde in den Dreieck zwischen Leningrad, Kronstadt und Oranienbaum zusammengedrängt, verlor ihren Außenstützpunkt Hangoe und wurde seitdem durch die deutsche Artillerie von der Küste her...

▲ VÖLKISCHER BEOBACHTER, MUNICH, FRIDAY JUNE 26, 1942

The main story deals with events in North Africa: "Rommel overruns Egyptian border strongholds. Further advances following straight on from Sidi el Barani. Almost everyone, even the enemy, had expected the German and Italian divisions to pause after the assault."

121

Sevastopol falls

JULY 4, 1942

A T THE START OF JUNE 1942, ERICH VON MANSTEIN'S ELEVENTH ARMY BEGAN THE BOMBARDMENT OF THE HEAVILY DEFENDED FORTRESS OF SEVASTOPOL IN THE CRIMEA.

This was no easy task as some of the fortress's defenses dated back to before the Crimean War, and had been reinforced with modern, concrete strongpoints. It also had numerous defense lines belted around the city, heavily entrenched in favorable moun-

tainous terrain. Finally, there were heavy coastal artillery batteries on the shores. The fighting was heavy from the start, but by June 26 the Eleventh Army was grinding its way into the city. The last Soviet supply ships left the port loaded with wounded troops the same day. There would be no reinforcement—the Stavka had written off the garrison. Sevastopol finally fell to the Eleventh Army on July 4. In an epic battle, the Red Army had lost 156,880 killed and missing and 43,601 wounded around the port since October 1941. Manstein took 90,000 prisoners, as well as 460 artillery pieces, 760 mortars, and 155 antitank guns.

▲ TROOPS OF THE GERMAN Eleventh Army attacking at Sevastopol. Fortunately for the
Germans, the Red Army withdrew from the port rather than fight to the last man.

▲ GENERAL ANZEIGER (UNIVERSAL GAZETTE), FRANKFURT, THURSDAY JULY 2, 1942

This local German daily does not pay much attention to the niceties of layout, but there is no mistaking the celebratory tone of its announcement of the capture of the capital of the Crimea: "Sevastopol in German hands. Major Allied naval forces captured as German and Romanian troops take the world's strongest fortress."

▲ DAILY MAIL, LONDON, FRIDAY JULY 3, 1942

These were dark days for the British, after the fall of Tobruk and Rommel's long advance into Egypt, halted only at El Alamein. Churchill believed he may not have survived the vote of censure the *Mail* reports had he not led a National Coalition rather than a party government. Although no-one could know at the time, the First Battle of El Alamein was the Axis high tide in North Africa.

First Alamein

JULY 1942

ON JUNE 24, 1942, ROMMEL WAS GIVEN PERMISSION TO CONTINUE HIS ADVANCE INTO EGYPT. HE WAS DETERMINED TO ATTACK THE BRITISH EIGHTH ARMY, RECENTLY defeated at Gazala, before it had time to recover. At this time, it had lost 50,000 troops (half its strength) and its morale was at rock bottom. Rommel had 30,000 men and 200 tanks—not many, but German troops were flushed with victory and believed they could now take Egypt and the Suez Canal with ease.

MERSA MATRUH

On June 28, the Germans advanced and captured Mersa Matruh. Rommel believed he had trapped the Eighth Army, but he was wrong—the British had fallen back to positions further east. Nevertheless, the Desert Fox was now only 125 miles (201 km) from Alexandria. Auchinleck, commander of the Eighth Army, was determined to stand and fight at El Alamein. He had the 1st South African Division, 1st Armoured Division, and two infantry divisions. Erwin Rommel, confident of victory, attacked on July 1 when the

90th Light Division advanced, only to be halted by heavy British fire. Thus began the First Battle of El Alamein.

THE FIRST BATTLE OF EL ALAMEIN

Rommel believed his Afrika Korps was strong enough to punch through the British lines at El Alamein. He was wrong. Far from remaining on the defensive, British units launched devastating counterattacks that stopped the Afrika Korps in its tracks. The British had a large number of artillery pieces and used them to devastating effect during the battle. As well as inflicting heavy losses on the Afrika Korps, they had a demoralizing effect on many of Rommel's infantry units, especially the Italians.

By the middle of July, the British had seriously degraded the best German unit, the 21st Panzer Division, and had also destroyed two Italian infantry divisions. By July 27, Axis forces were on the defensive, having suffered 13,000 casualties and lost 7000 men captured. Egypt had been saved. The stage was all set for the British Eighth Army to build up its strength for a large-scale counteroffensive against Rommel's now greatly weakened army.

▲ A GERMAN PANZER III in Egypt in June 1942 during Rommel's attempt to finish the North African war in 1942.

3 Full Pages of Solomon Island Pictures in Today's Pictorial Review

13 Die as India Riots Grow

Read the New York Journal-American for complete, accurate war coverage. It is the only New York evening newspaper possessing the three great wire services—ASSOCIATED PRESS, INTERNATIONAL NEWS SERVICE, UNITED PRESS.

Journal NEW YORK American

AN AMERICAN PAPER FOR THE AMERICAN PEOPLE

In Two Sections—Section One

No. 19,949—DAILY TUESDAY, AUGUST 11, 1942 DAILY 3 Cents | SATURDAY 5 Cents | SUNDAY 10 Cents

7TH SPORTS RACING ☆☆☆☆☆☆☆ SPORTS EXTRA

REPORT VICTORY NEAR FOR U. S. IN SOLOMONS

LONDON, Aug. 11--(INS)--Allied attacks upon Japanese bases in the Solomon Islands "appear to have carried to a point where victory is possible if early successes can be exploited," the London Evening Star reported in a special Sydney dispatch tonight.

(According to United Press, the British Broadcasting Company reported the Allies are having "some successes" in the Solomons, and New Zealand sources called latest delayed reports from the Tulagi area "favorable."]

MELBOURNE, Aug. 11 (INS).—"Although the Japanese are counter-attacking strongly in the Solomons, we are holding our ground," Prime Minister John Curtin of Australia declared today.

Curtin's statement was the first official word in Australia on the progress of the Allied offensive, conducted in the main by American forces, against the Japs in the Solomon Islands.

"Communications are overtaxed and there is a delay in receiving news . . . . Considerable losses must be expected," he added.

Marines Smashing at Foes

By LEE VAN ATTA,
International News Service Staff Correspondent.

UNITED NATIONS HEADQUARTERS IN AUTRALIA, Aug. 11. — The fury of battle in the waters of the Southwest Pacific was extended today over a 2,500-mile arc north of Australia as Allied ships, planes and ground forces struck heavily at the Japanese from the Solomon Islands in the east to Timor in the west.

Marines and other ground forces under command of American Vice-admiral Robert L. Ghormley swarmed ashore under protection of naval guns and an air armada and gave battle to the Japs in the Tulagi area of the Solomons in an attempt to oust them from their footholds in the former British protectorate.

Japs Driven from Kokoda

Allied troops under direction of Gen. MacArthur, bolstered by reinforcements, opened an assault in the Papua area of New Guinea and forced Jap land units to retire from prepared positions at

Continued on Page 2, Column 1.

Pick Lehman as Convention Chairman

Highlights of the political picture today were:

GUBERNATORIAL — Governor Lehman was designated temporary chairman of the Democratic State Convention in a move to restore unity.

PRIMARIES—Light voting marks the primaries, although vital national issues are at stake. (Story on Page 3).

Gov. Lehman, regarded as in the camp of Senator Mead in the Democratic Gubernatorial battle, today was designated by Kings County Leader Frank V. Kelly as temporary chairman of the Democratic State Convention.

Lehman's selection, putting him automatically in the position of keynote speaker at the convention to be held in Brooklyn Aug. 19 and 20, demonstrated the control State Chairman Farley holds over convention machinery.

Designation of Lehman as temporary convention chairman was made under Kelly's powers as chairman of the committee empowered to recommend to the State Convention the names of its temporary officers.

LEHMAN ACCEPTS POST.

Announcement that the Governor had accepted the post was made at Democratic State Headquarters in the Biltmore Hotel.

Kelly's announcement followed reports that Lehman would make

Continued on Page 7, Column 6.

DeGaulle Visits Beirut

BEIRUT, Lebanon, Aug. 11 (AP).—General Charles de Gaulle, leader of the Fighting French, arrived from Cairo today in this area where some of his forces are garrisoned.

13 Die in New India Rioting: 200 Injured

By C. S. DE ANDRADE,
International News Service Staff Correspondent.

BOMBAY, Aug. 11. — With 28 dead and more than 200 injured since Sunday, violent new demonstrations flared again in Bombay today as the Indian National Congress Party's nation-wide struggle against British rule entered its third day.

Thirteen persons were killed and more than 30 wounded in ten separate incidents today.

A state of virtual martial law—while not officially imposed—was in effect. Regulations usually associated with martial law were promulgated in an effort to quell the disturbances.

At New Delhi, British troops patrolled the area surrounding the capital's Municipal Hall, following an attempt by rioters to set fire to the clock tower.

The incident left one dead, one wounded.

U. S. ENVOY IN PARLEY.

[Associated Press reported that Lauchlin Currie, President Roosevelt's Special Envoy to China who recently came to India, conferred today with the Viceroy, Lord Linlithgow, at New Delhi.

[A British deputy commissioner and several policemen were injured in a "violent clash" in the province of North India before police opened fire and dispersed a crowd of demonstrators, the All-India Radio reported, according to United Press.]

Monday night's demonstrations against the curfew order were

Continued on Page 5, Column 1.

N. Y. Raid Plotted by Germans

LONDON, Aug. 11 (INS).—The London Daily Telegraph reported from "somewhere in Europe" today that German industrialists and high party leaders are discussing the possibility of an air raid against New York shortly, to raise German morale.

Competent sources in London were not impressed, pointing out it would be necessary for the Germans to work an aircraft carrier close to the American coast, where it would be easy prey for United States bombers.

"The Germans would be well-received by New Yorkers, who wouldn't pull their punches," one commentator said.

General belief in London is that New York is too well defended and that raiders would be shot down before they could return to their carrier.

British Bombers Hit Axis Vessels

CAIRO, Aug. 11—(UP)—British light bombing planes have sunk an enemy reinforcement lighter and damaged another off the north African Coast, a communique said today, and fighter and fighter-bomber planes have attacked transport vehicles and encampments behind the Axis lines west of El Alamein.

British Empire patrols continued activities, it was said.

Leningrad Downed 2,190 Reich Planes

MOSCOW, Aug 11 (AP).—Leningrad front headquarters reported today that in one year on that front Soviet fliers destroyed 2,190 German planes, 1,750 tanks, 1,000 cannon and 4,500 trucks.

Nazis Start Forming Dutch 'Home Guard'

LONDON, Aug. 11 (AP).—The Netherlands News Agency reported that Nazi authorities have started organization of a Dutch Home Guard because of the threat of an Allied invasion.

Anton Mussert, head of the Dutch Nazi party, was quoted as having appealed to the Dutch for "a strong, trusted auxiliary police force."

San Francisco Bay Under Air Raid Alert

SAN FRANCISCO, Aug. 11 (INS).—The San Francisco Bay area was under a 33-minute air raid alert this morning, ordered when unidentified aircraft were reported approaching offshore.

The all-clear was issued at 8:43 a. m., when the aircraft were reported as friendly.

Nazis Thrown Back Near Stalingrad

LONDON, Aug. 11 — (INS) — Soviet artillery, air force and tanks have stemmed a main German drive northeast of Kotelnikov in the Stalingrad area and German paratroops dropped in the rear have been exterminated, Exchange Telegraph reported from Moscow today.

By JAMES E. BROWN,
International News Service Staff Correspondent

MOSCOW, Aug. 11.—German armies under Field Marshal Fedor von Bock opened a new drive against Stalingrad today as other mechanized forces plunged into the foothills of the Caucasian mountains near the rich Maikop oil wells.

A Soviet High Command communique admitted new Russian withdrawals in the Armavir area near Maikop and said the Germans were forced on the defensive near Kotelnikovo on the Stalingrad front.

Later, however, it was established that the Nazis had started moving toward Stalingrad again in the face of stubborn Red Army resistance.

NAZI BREAK-THROUGH.

[A Berlin announcement claimed that Soviet resistance had broken down completely on the north Caucasian front, that German troops are approaching the Terek River, which empties into the Caspian Sea, and that Russian formations southwest of Maikop are attempting to flee by boat from Black Sea ports.

[On the Stalingrad front Russian troops have been encircled and the way cleared for a German advance to the Volga, it was claimed.]

Front-line military information in Moscow admitted that German troops had broken through in the area of Krasnodar and Maikop and were smashing ahead despite strong Soviet resistance.

FIERCE BATTLES RAGING.

Waves of enemy attacks were launched without cessation and fierce battles were raging. Soviet tanks and aviation made superhuman efforts to slow down the enemy advance, but German motorized units, including tanks, motorcycles and mounted machine-guns, moved ahead.

The Russians put up a strong defense in the district of Maikop, apparently inflicting great losses upon the enemy before falling back, still intact and in good order.

(Other details on Page 2)

U.S. Air Drive Opens in China

By KARL ESKELUND,
United Press Staff Correspondent.

U. S. ARMY AIR FORCE HEADQUARTERS, Hengyang, Aug. 11. — Army bombers and fighters, striking in support of the new American offensive in the Southwest Pacific, blasted Japanese bases today along a 600-mile front in China from Hankow to Canton at the Pearl River estuary.

The attacks, in which tons of bombs were dropped upon Japanese air bases and supply centers, undoubtedly were designed in part as a diversion to prevent the Japanese from rushing aerial reinforcements to the defense of the Solomon Islands off northeast Australia.

HITS ON AIRDROME.

Chief targets of the attack were:

CANTON—Where heavy bombers led personally by Col. Caleb V. Haynes blasted docks and warehouses along the Pearl River for the second straight day, scoring direct hits on the Canton airdrome, setting large fires and probably destroying 15 twin-engine Japanese bombers on the ground.

NANCHANG — Where "Flying Dragons" of the 23rd American Pursuit Group led by Col. Robert L. Scott raided the Japanese base about 190 miles north of Canton, dumped 500-pound bombs on their objectives and shot down three Jap Zero fighters, one of which was bagged by Scott.

YOCHOW — Where American airmen bombed the Japanese railroad station between Changsha and Wuchang, as well as barracks and warehouses without encountering opposition. Five tons of bombs were dropped on the base of at least 2,000 Japanese troops.

HANKOW — Where a United States communique reported, two large fires were started in a low-level bombing attack on Japan's main Yangtze River base, wrecking newly-built warehouses.

Meanwhile, Col. Haynes, who led Sunday's American bombing attack on the Japanese invasion port of Haiphong in Indo-China, described the bombing as "the best raid I ever made." Large fires were started along a mile-long waterfront area by direct hits on ammunition dumps, warehouses and a large freighter.

JAPS DISLODGED.

CHUNGKING, Aug. 11 (INS).—Japanese troops entrenched in the western suburbs of Linchwan have been dislodged by Chinese attacking the city, it was announced today.

Laval Pins Freedom Hope to Nazi Victory

VICHY, Aug. 11 (INS).—Chief of Government Laval declared today at Compiegne, where he had gone to meet a train load of French war prisoners returning from the Reich, that "the hour of France's liberation will come in the hour when Germany wins the war."

The pro-Nazi Laval, chief proponent of French collaboration with Germany, disclosed 1,200,000 captured French soldiers still remain in German hands.

Meeting a train loaded with 1,000 returning prisoners, Laval admitted the Nazis would get far the better of the bargain in the plan to exchange war prisoners for able-bodied Frenchmen to work in German war factories.

Hitler, he said, had agreed to release 50,000 prisoners for every 150,000 French skilled craftsmen and workmen sent to Germany.

LONDON, Aug. 11 (AP).—A Reuter's dispatch from Stockholm today quoted the Vichy correspondent of the newspaper Svenska Dagbladet as saying Pierre Laval had called up police and troop reinforcements to protect the Vichy Government against a rumored coup d'etat.

THE WEATHER

Showers and slightly warmer.

Sun rises, 6:01 a. m.; sun sets, 8:01 p. m. High tide Governors Island, 8:57 a. m. and 9:00 p. m.

HOURLY TEMPERATURES

5 a. m.	69	10 a. m.	73
6 a. m.	69	11 a. m.	76
7 a. m.	69	12 Noon	80
8 a. m.	69	1 p. m.	80
9 a. m.	70	2 p. m.	82

Cpmplete Weather Table on Page 7

TODAY'S INDEX

Auctions	23	Lost and Found	2
Best Places to Dine	9	Obituaries	7
Comics	24, 25	Radio	24
Editorial Page	14	Real Estate	24
Financial	16	Society	6
Food, Cooking	26	Sports	17 to 20
Horoscope	24	Theatres	8, 9
		Want Ads	20 to 23

The New York Journal-American has the largest circulation of any evening newspaper in America. 230

▲ NEW YORK JOURNAL AMERICAN, NEW YORK, TUESDAY AUGUST 11 1942

Created in 1937 by the merger of two papers founded by William Randolph Hearst, the *Journal American* reflects Hearst's philosophy that headlines should bite the reader "like a bulldog." The victory in Guadalcanal in the Solomon Islands was the first defeat of the Japanese on land. The red-print headline reports riots that broke out in India, meanwhile, after Gandhi and other leaders of the Congress Party were arrested for calling for Britain to quit the country immediately.

Guadalcanal
AUGUST 1942

JAPANESE ATTEMPTS TO CUT OFF AUSTRALIA IN MAY AND THEN TO DESTROY THE U.S. PACIFIC FLEET IN JUNE HAD BEEN STOPPED AT THE BATTLES OF THE CORAL SEA AND MIDWAY. BY LATE SUMMER, THE U.S. WAS READY TO TAKE THE OFFENSIVE, AND CHOSE TO DO so in the Solomon Islands.

The 1st Marine Division went ashore on Guadalcanal on August 7, and initiated a long and punishing battle on land, sea and air. Fighting on Guadalcanal was intense, concentrating around the possession of an airfield known as "Henderson Field" (named after a U.S. pilot). Japanese night attacks and the problems of fighting in tropical conditions made things very difficult for the Marines, but they toughed it out as the autumn went on. Even when vastly outnumbered toward the end of the campaign, however, the Japanese troops put up enormous resistance.

FIERCE FIGHTING

Just as fierce was the fighting at sea and in the air. Henderson Field was crucial to the U.S. plan, because its capture would enable Marine aviators to attack Japanese transports and to provide air support for the ground troops. Meanwhile, naval battles were fought in a long stretch of water running through the central part of the Solomon Islands known as "the slot." Although the Japanese naval forces did well in these battles, partly due to the superior performance of their torpedoes during night fighting, the U.S. Navy gradually gained the upper hand.

Between February 1 and 9, the Japanese Navy evacuated the remaining 13,000 troops from the island. Japan's commanders had finally accepted defeat.

▲ U.S. MARINES COME ASHORE ON GUADALCANAL. The American landing on the island in August was spectacularly successful, but it took months of hard fighting to finally defeat the Japanese.

Sunday Pictorial

September 6
TWOPENCE
No. 1,434

DRASTIC BUS AND
RAIL CUTS—Official
See Page 3

EGYPT VITAL MOVES

British Win First Round: Back Page

DIEPPE: We Get All the Pictures

Once again the "Sunday Pictorial" has secured the pictures the world has been waiting for.

The pictures which show what happened inside Dieppe when our combined forces smashed through the strongest Nazi defences.

Here is a Canadian tank which fought its way into the heart of Dieppe. Behind it rises a pall of smoke from a burning building.

2 More Pages of Dieppe Pictures Inside

▲ SUNDAY PICTORIAL, LONDON, SUNDAY SEPTEMBER 6, 1942

Lord Rothermere's *Sunday Pictorial* was one of the first British papers to specialize in short articles, exciting language, and many dramatic photographs. Even a month after the disastrous Allied raid on Dieppe—presented here in highly positive terms—a gripping image from that battle is still worth virtually the whole front page, relegating British defiance in North Africa to the back of the paper.

Raid on Dieppe

AUGUST 19, 1942

THE DIEPPE RAID OF AUGUST 19 WAS THE LARGEST ALLIED COMBINED OPERATION THAT HAD TAKEN PLACE UP TO THAT POINT IN THE WAR. IT WAS INTENDED TO TEST WHETHER the techniques and tactics that the Allies had in place at the time were effective by attacking a small stretch of French coastline and then withdrawing after a few hours.

In the event, the raid was a disaster, and the Canadian troops, who provided the bulk of the Allied troops, suffered 4,000 casualties. The raid showed that meticulous preparation was needed and that new methods for delivering troops and their supporting equipment were needed.

NEW APPROACH

The Dieppe raid may have been a failure, but it represented a new confidence and aggression within the Allied camp. In the same month, U.S.

Marines landed on Guadalcanal, and Rommel's final offensive in North Africa was defeated at the Alamein position in what is often called the Battle of Alam Halfa. At the end of October, a new British commander, General Bernard Montgomery, launched the final El Alamein offensive that decisively threw Rommel back. In November, Allied landings in French North Africa, the "Torch" landings, opened a new front against the Axis powers. Also in November, Soviet forces under General Zhukov launched Operation Uranus, a pincer movement that cut off the German Sixth Army fighting in the city of Stalingrad.

▲ STANDING ON A KNOCKED-OUT Churchill tank, German soldiers watch a group of British prisoners being escorted to the rear after being captured during the abortive Dieppe raid.

ALLIED TRIUMPHS

Allied newspapers that had been desperate for any good news during the first six months of 1942 now found that they could legitimately report the triumphs of British, American, and Soviet forces against their foes. It would soon be the turn of German and Japanese newspapers to grasp at straws and to try to disguise the worst of the bad news from their readers.

DAILY MIRROR

Member of The   Associated Press

WEATHER RAIN, WARMER (Details on Page 2)   (Copyright, 1942, Daily Mirror, Inc.)   3 Cents Outside City Limits

Vol. 19. No. 111 C   New York,   MEN OF ACTION JOIN THE NAVY   Friday, October 30, 1942   FINAL 6 A.M. ★★★★

GUADALCANAL HURLS BACK 3 JAP RAIDS

— Story on Page 3 —

Allied Forces Advance Against Foe in Egypt

In this official British radiophoto received yesterday from Cairo, Allied infantrymen are shown advancing through gaps in enemy minefields just cleared by sapper units. Ammunition trucks may be seen moving up in the background. Necessity for removing minefield obstacles is reason for present slow pace of campaign. Yesterday, Allies beat back an Axis tank attack and downed 10 planes.   (Story on Page 2)

(AP Radiophoto)

▲ DAILY MIRROR, NEW YORK, FRIDAY OCTOBER 30, 1942

The *Daily Mirror* was one of the Hearst stable of tabloids that served up dramatic headlines and striking images. Here, news of the U.S. Marines' defense on Guadalcanal takes pride of place above a photograph of some of the 195,000 Allied troops who would take part in the Battle of El Alamein in Egypt. The newspaper's banner has been adapted to include a graphic urging recruits to join the Navy.

Sunday Pictorial

November 1
TWOPENCE
No. 1,442

'MONTY' ATTACKS IN EGYPT ONCE MORE
Last Night's Latest: Back Page

THIS latest battle-line picture—sent by radio last night from Cairo—brings to the people of Britain a vivid glimpse of the Eighth Army's ferocious battle to destroy Rommel.

It shows, dimly silhouetted in the swirl of battle smoke and desert san... with bayonets fixed, dashin... crew of a disabled enemy ta...

It shows, too, more grap... could, what war in the des... Rommel has lost many ta... in scenes like this in the la...

▲ SUNDAY PICTORIAL, LONDON, SUNDAY NOVEMBER 1, 1942
By the time British armored divisions broke through the last Axis defensive line at El Alamein in November, battlefield photography was becoming increasingly capable of capturing dramatic action, as in this image of advancing Desert Rats.

▲ SOUTH AFRICAN TROOPS use the cover of smoke to advance on enemy positions during the Battle of El Alamein. Axis losses were 59,000 killed, wounded, and captured. The British lost 13,000 killed and wounded.

The New York Times.

"All the News That's Fit to Print."

NEWS INDEX, PAGE 65, THIS SECTION

VOL. XCII...No. 30,969.

LATE CITY EDITION

Section 1

Copyright, 1942, by The New York Times Company.

NEW YORK, SUNDAY, NOVEMBER 8, 1942.

TEN CENTS

AMERICAN FORCES LAND IN FRENCH AFRICA; BRITISH NAVAL, AIR UNITS ASSISTING THEM; EFFECTIVE SECOND FRONT, ROOSEVELT SAYS

MARTIN RESIGNING PARTY RULE TO AID HOUSE WAR EFFORT

Republican National Chairman Will Quit Dec. 7 to Center on His Job as Minority Leader

DEMANDS 'BUNGLING' END

He Warns 'Those in Power' to Get Busy, Urging Committee in Congress to Help Them

By C. P. TRUSSELL

LEADS IN AFRICA

Lieut. Gen. Dwight Eisenhower
The New York Times (U. S. A. Air Force)

R.A.F. ROCKS GENOA; U.S. RAID ON BREST

Bombers From Britain Pound North Italy and Nazi Bases on European Coast

U.S. DRIVES ON BUNA

American Troops Flown to Area Closing In on Big Japanese Base

PAPUA IS OVERRUN

All Except Beachhead of Buna-Gona Seized in New Guinea Push

NAZIS NEAR LIBYA

British Drive Out to Bar New Stand by Enemy or Reinforcements

FOE BOMBED ALL NIGHT

Pursuers Reported to Be Within 40 Miles of Halfaya Pass

THE UNITED STATES LAUNCHES A GREAT OFFENSIVE

U.S. MEETS 'THREAT'

Big Expeditions Invade North and West Africa to Forestall Axis

EISENHOWER AT HEAD

President Urges French to Help, Calls Move Aid to Russia

By C. P. TRUSSELL

LANDING PLAN KEPT SECRET BY WRITERS

Americans Selected for Duty, Bureaus Sworn to Silence— News Electrifies London

By RAYMOND DANIELL

President's Statement

WASHINGTON, Nov. 7—President Roosevelt's statement announcing the opening of a second front in French North and West Africa follows:

War News Summarized

SUNDAY, NOVEMBER 8, 1942

Major Sports Yesterday

FOOTBALL

HORSE RACING

HOCKEY

◀ THE NEW YORK TIMES, SUNDAY NOVEMBER 8, 1942
Even readers eager to check the sports results that still appear on the front page could hardly have failed to take in news of Operation Torch, the Allied amphibious landings at Casablanca, Oran, and Algiers in North Africa. The first major Anglo-American operation of the war was in part an Allied response to Stalin's urging to open a second front to divert Hitler's forces. Under the headline, Americans who were not yet familiar with the general placed in charge of Allied operations in North Africa got their first glimpse of a man with whom they would later become highly familiar, postwar President Dwight D. Eisenhower.

▶ AN AMERICAN TANK CREW of the 1st Armored Regiment services their M3 Lee Grant tank after the Torch landings. Crews complained that the M3 "looked like a damned cathedral coming down the road."

"Daily Herald," Tuesday, Nov. 17, 1942.

LONDON BLACKOUT
5.39 p.m. to 7.52 a.m.
Moon Rises 3.18 p.m.
Moon Sets 1.53 a.m.
Lighting-up Time 5.39 p.m.

Daily Herald

No. 8346 — TUESDAY, NOVEMBER 17, 1942 — ONE PENNY

STOP PRESS

VICHY SHIPS AT ORAN

French steamers Diridon and Jamaique, which left Dakar and Marseilles at time of North African landings, have arrived safely at Oran, according to Vichy reports.—Reuter.

11 JAP WARSHIPS, 12 TRANSPORTS, SUNK IN BATTLE OF SOLOMONS

The desert skyline is broken by the smoke of burning lorries as the Eighth Army sweeps forward.

FIGHTING FRENCH ARE ALARMED AT RECOGNITION OF VICHY MEN IN NORTH AFRICA

DARLAN IS REPUDIATED BY GENERAL DE GAULLE

By W. N. EWER

STEPS are being taken to unravel the political tangle which Admiral Darlan's activities have created in North Africa.

Yesterday General de Gaulle saw Mr. Churchill.

Action will need to be rapid. For, whatever the immediate consequences of the Admiral's decision to change sides, the apparent recognition of him as a sort of Governor-General of North Africa has staggered and dismayed the Fighting French all over the world.

Their uneasiness has been further increased by reports that M. Flandin, the notoriously pro-German ex-Premier of France, is also in Algeria.

No Responsibility

Last night General de Gaulle's headquarters in London issued this statement:

General de Gaulle and the French National Committee announce that they are taking no part whatsoever in and assuming no responsibility for the negotiations in progress in North Africa with the representatives of Vichy.

Should these negotiations result in arrangements which would in effect confirm the Vichy regime in North Africa, such decisions could obviously not be accepted by Fighting France.

Impenitent

That is plain enough. It means that the Fighting French, who are delighted to co-operate with General Giraud, refuse flatly to co-operate with Admiral Darlan.

It is not just a question of Admiral Darlan's political past. That might, if he showed any sign of contrition, be forgiven.

More important is the Admiral's present conduct.

Caught in Algiers, he decided to join up: but in his own way and on his own terms.

He seems to have persuaded our soldiers that he and he alone could ensure quiet and order in North Africa, and enable them to give their whole attention to the task of fighting the enemy.

They gave him access to the radio, and he has used it to boost his own claims to authority.

Fiction

He has told the world that he has appointed General Giraud commander-in-chief of the French forces in North Africa.

But Giraud—as everyone remembers—had already spoken as commander-in-chief on the morning of the landing, "long before Darlan had even decided to change sides.

He has told the world that it is he who ordered and secured the cessation of hostilities—which is a distortion of the facts.

How far Darlan is an asset in establishing a quiet and orderly administration in North Africa is doubtful.

Liability

Equally certainly he is a heavy liability in other ways. The belief that he is our preferred and favoured collaborator will have the most demoralising effect on the Fighting French outside and the resistance movement inside France.

The situation, if it develops further, may become not merely embarrassing, but very dangerous.

French Guards Beat Nazis Back In Tunis Clash

FRENCH TROOPS HAVE BEATEN BACK A GERMAN FORCE IN TUNISIA.

Allied headquarters in North Africa describing the clash in a communiqué last night said that on Sunday afternoon a German reconnaissance unit composed of motor-cyclists and armoured vehicles, proceeding from Tunis to Djedeida (a railway junction half way to Bizerta), met a French battalion of Guards.

The French troops opened fire on the Germans, who were forced to retreat.

A later communiqué announced:—

"Small French military units have begun to co-operate with the Eastern and Central Task forces.

"At Oran a French force has joined United States troops at their stations. The clearance and maintenance of ports and harbours proceeds.

Small Naval Losses

"On the east, the British First Army has been reinforced by mobile United States units.

"The Royal Navy maintains control of the Western Mediterranean and its approaches.

"This naval force has sustained losses, but they have been small in proportion to the size of the operations, and the casualties on the whole have been light.

"To-day we took into custody the officer and crew of a U-boat which had been sunk off the North African coast."

German claims to have sunk 89 Allied ships around the North African coast were authoritatively described as "vastly exaggerated—even beyond the usual German naval claims."

Allied headquarters admitted that the concentration of vast numbers of Axis submarines in the Mediterranean and off the entrance of Gibraltar was a major hazard.

"But," it added, "such concentration is resulting in a great number of kills by the British and American navies."

More Air Raids

British and American troops were reported yesterday to be fighting Germans near Tunis and other points in the Protectorate.

General Nehring, a former chief of Rommel's Afrika Korps, is commanding the Axis forces in Tunisia, it was revealed last night.

He has appealed to French troops to fight side by side with Germans as comrades defending the cause of France.

Maintaining its attacks on the important aerodrome of El Aquina, Tunis, the R.A.F made three separate raids on Saturday night, adding considerably to the heavy damage and confusion already caused.

The first attack was carried out (CONTINUED BACK PAGE)

THE man behind the German descent on Tunisia

is 50-year-old General Wilhelm Student, chief of Hitler's paratroop and airborne forces.

He is a go-ahead officer of the Nazi school—in fact, a Rommel of the air.

He organised and directed the Nazi forces which turned us out of Crete.

In the paratroop attack on Holland—the first campaign of its kind the world had ever seen—he himself descended on Rotterdam aerodrome with a red parachute.

There has been no indication yet that he has actually landed in Tunisia, but there is no doubt his brain is behind this latest effort.

Early this year he was in Libya helping Rommel with supplies and reinforcements.

He returned to Germany with Rommel after the drive which took the Axis forces to Alamein.

Both men met Hitler and were feted. Then Rommel returned to Africa—and defeat. Now Student has been called on again to make a desperate effort to get Rommel out of his difficulties.

DARLAN SETS UP NEW COUNCIL

Admiral Darlan, "In the name of Marshal Petain," last night instituted a legislative council to assist him as High Commissioner for French North Africa.

Members of the council will be required to give their views on "general questions of the legislative, administrative or legal kind on which they are consulted by the High Commissioner."—Reuter.

Petain Picks Successor

PETAIN has already appointed a new successor to himself in place of Darlan, according to German sources last night.

They said the decision was made at the Vichy Cabinet meeting on Sunday, but gave no name.

Earlier yesterday Petain issued a message in which he declared Darlan "bereft of all public office and military command." It said:

Darlan desires to affirm that I am not able to make my thoughts known to the French people, and claims to be acting on my behalf.

Several times I have confirmed my order to him to defend North Africa.

He disregarded it under the pretext of preventing the chief rebel and felon, General Giraud, from usurping command of the troops.

Now he endorses his appointment.

The Admiral has put himself outside the national community.—Reuter.

GERMANS STILL KEPT IN DARK

GERMANS are still being kept in ignorance of the full extent of the Axis defeat in Egypt and Libya.

It does not seem to matter which, or how many routes, the fleeing enemy uses. It is impossible for him to escape the attention of the Allied Air Force.

They were told yesterday that Rommel's forces had reached the limit of their retirement, and were taking up long-prepared defensive positions on what might become a fixed line of resistance.

Considerable reinforcements, said a Berlin spokesman, had reached North Africa, in addition to large forces landed in Tunisia.

All the time it is occupying aerodromes deserted by the Luftwaffe only a day or two previously.

HE LEFT OUT AFRICA

Lieut.-General Dietmar completely ignored Libya and North Africa when he gave his weekly review over the German radio last night.

"The battle for Stalingrad," he said, "continues with undiminished violence, but our strategic aim has been reached."

COLD IN STRAITS

Straits: Moonlit, cold; sea choppy off French coast.

G.C.B. FOR GEN. BROOKE

The King has approved the promotion of General Sir Alan F. Brooke, Chief of the Imperial General Staff, to be Knight Grand Cross, Order of the Bath.

General Brooke, who is 59, accompanied Mr. Churchill on his visit to the Eighth Army—following which changes were made in the commands—and to Moscow. He also went to America with the Premier in June.

8th ARMY RACING TO BENGHAZI

From CLIFFORD WEBB — CAIRO, Monday.

NEWS travels fast—but not so fast as the Eighth Army in its pursuit of the Afrika Korps. That is why there is little news from G.H.Q. to-day.

The communiqué says that we have occupied the landing grounds at Martuba, 75 miles beyond Tobruk, and 20 miles south-east of Derna. That was yesterday.

As I write the Eighth Army is bowling merrily along towards Tripoli. It has probably reached and passed Derna, and may be on the Jebel Akdar region.

There are as yet no recorded signs of the enemy pulling his battered runaways together and trying to make some sort of stand.

Tripoli Last Hope

Rommel can only show fight if reserves of armour and weapons are available from Tripoli.

The speed of our pursuit and the pressure of our air attack have been such that it has been impossible for him to rush supplies through Benghazi by sea.

Allied pilots and observers already report that enemy traffic is beating it as hard as possible west of Benghazi right up to El Agheila.

There is much talk here about the eventual meeting of the Eighth Army with the First Army and the American Expeditionary Force in North Africa.

It is well to remember that apart altogether from other considerations, there are still well over 1,000 miles between the two forces.

One of yesterday's most successful air attacks was a surprise swoop on enemy transport 60 miles south of the Jalo Oasis.

Cannot Escape

Jalo is the junction of several inland tracks, the majority of which lead up to the coast between Benghazi and Tripoli.

It does not seem to matter which, or how many routes, the fleeing enemy uses. It is impossible for him to escape the attention of the Allied Air Force.

"TRUCKS WERE AIRBORNE"

"TRUCKS airborne and goods locomotives thoroughly machine-gunned," was the report of one Hurricane bomber pilot who took part yesterday in a goods train wrecking attack near Le Treport.

"Bombs hurled 15 wagons into the air.

"The formation skimmed the harbour and machine-gunned barges before heading for home."

Both United States and British fighters carried out other small raids over Europe.

A low level attack by American fighter planes was made on trucks loaded with German soldiers.

Two Hurricanes bombed barges which were being loaded on the Bruges-Ostend canal.

A German transport aircraft was intercepted and destroyed.

Mosquitos of Bomber Command attacked objectives in Western Germany.

None of our aircraft is missing from these operations.

TOWNS SEIZED BY GUERILLAS

Resistance to the Nazis is spreading in the Balkans, says a Reuter message from the German frontier.

In Western Croatia a big-scale revolt has broken out.

Between 10,000 and 15,000 guerillas, operating independently of General Mihailovitch's forces, have seized two towns.

Montenegrin irregulars which landed at the naval base of Tivat directed important harbour works and were back in their boats before they could be captured.

250 AIR CASUALTIES

Of a total of 250 names in an Air Ministry casualty list issued to-day 117 officers and other ranks have lost their lives and 109 are missing.

BATTLE OF SOLOMONS

From ARTHUR WEBB — WASHINGTON, Monday.

ELEVEN JAPANESE WARSHIPS, INCLUDING A BATTLESHIP, HAVE BEEN SUNK AND 12 TRANSPORTS DESTROYED IN A TERRIFIC THREE-DAY SEA AND AIR BATTLE OFF THE SOLOMONS.

Seven other enemy warships were damaged. American losses were two light cruisers and six destroyers.

Japanese losses, given in a Washington communiqué tonight were:

SUNK: One battleship, three heavy cruisers, two light cruisers, five destroyers, eight transports.

DAMAGED: One battleship, six destroyers.

DESTROYED: Four transports.

Washington naval circles said to-night that at least 24,000 Japanese must have died in the eight transports sunk.

And Admiral Nimitz, in a communiqué issued at Pearl Harbour, said this attempt to recapture Guadalcanal had been completely frustrated.

Moving On Guadalcanal

Air reconnaissance early this month, states the communiqué, revealed a heavy concentration of Japanese transports, cargo vessels and combatant units in the New Britain-N.W. Solomons region.

An attempt by the enemy to recapture our positions in the Guadalcanal-Tulagi area was indicated, and on November 10 it became evident that an expedition was being launched in force.

Japanese naval forces approached the S.E. Solomons from the north as other detachments, including many transports, moved south-eastward towards Guadalcanal from Rabaul and Buin, where the expeditionary forces had been assembling.

General MacArthur's aircraft were of great assistance to our naval forces both before and during the naval actions.

Jap Spearhead

Army bombers made repeated and successful attacks on units of the Japanese invasion fleet at Rabaul and Buin. [These attacks were announced by United Nations headquarters in Australia.]

The spearhead of the Japanese attack was a force composed of two battleships of the Kongo class and (CONTINUED BACK PAGE)

CLOSING IN ON BUNA

From RICHARD ODGERS — SYDNEY, Monday.

THE final Allied assault on the Jap beachhead at Buna, in New Guinea, is expected very soon.

Australian and American columns covering the enemy's southern and eastern flanks have now joined up and are advancing on a wide front.

The Japanese still have considerable forces in this area.

They are under the command of Lieut.-General Horii, a specialist in landing operations.

Enemy troops, gun positions, barges, supply dumps, and motor transport are being constantly blasted from the air.

The Australian advance has increased in speed now that the Wairopi bridge has been repaired.

Forward advanced elements which have crossed the Kumusi river and are scouting the trails and roads to Buna have been "absolutely unopposed," said a spokesman at General MacArthur's headquarters to-day.

The main body is now crossing the river with supplies and equipment on improvised bridges.

RUSSIANS ADVANCE AT STALINGRAD

From WALLACE KING — STOCKHOLM, Monday.

RUSSIAN troops have regained some more ground in the Nalchik sector in the Caucasus, while at Stalingrad Timoshenko has dislodged the Germans from positions they gained two days ago.

"In the course of the day," adds to-night's communiqué, "the enemy lost in killed and wounded up to 1,500 officers and men. Our troops destroyed two German tanks, six guns, 17 trench mortars, 11 machine-guns, and demolished ten pillboxes and firing points.

"Three German planes were brought down by A.A. fire.

"North-west of Stalingrad our troops strengthened their positions."

The advance made south-east of Nalchik is described as slight.

But it shows that the Reds are successfully staving off the Nazi attempt to break through to the Georgian military road.

Heavy Nazi Losses

During the last few hours the Russians have destroyed in this area another 26 tanks and wiped out 800 more Germans.

According to Axis-inspired reports a great battle is also going on in the Alagir sector 58 miles north of Mozdok, in the Terek bend.

Both in this area and in the Western Caucasus, north-east of the Black Sea port of Tuapse, the Russians seem to have brought in large reserves of men and planes.

In 21 days' fighting in the Tuapse sector, the Russians are reported to have killed about 15,000.

Berlin claims that German troops in the Caucasus have encircled and annihilated two groups and in another sector drove off Soviet attacks with heavy casualties.

It gives no indication, however, where these alleged successes occurred.

(Stalingrad fights on and Russians like us better—Page Two.)

U.S. TO FLOAT RECORD LOAN

The United States Treasury is about to float the biggest War Loan of all time.

It is hoped to raise between now and June 30 next £10,000,000,000 from the public.

The nearest approach to this is the British Government's 1914-18 5 per cent. War Loan (how 3½ per cent.), which totals something like £2,000,000,000.

SUBMARINE SINKS FOUR TRANSPORTS

Moscow Radio stated last night that a Soviet submarine of the Black Sea fleet, during a cruise of several days, penetrated an enemy minefield and sank four enemy transports.

An Istanbul cable says that the German tanker Ossag was struck by a torpedo in the Black Sea early yesterday morning while bound for Burgas, in Bulgaria, and had to return to Istanbul with a large hole in her stern.

It is believed the tanker was attacked by a Soviet submarine.

An 8,000-ton German tanker has been sunk in the Barents Sea.

▲ DAILY HERALD, LONDON, TUESDAY NOVEMBER 17, 1942
The *Daily Herald* has such a crowded front page that the weather forecast is relegated to only two lines.

▲ SOVIET TROOPS battle their way forward in the ruins of the city of Stalingrad at the end of 1942. There were 265,000 Germans and 11,000 Romanians trapped in the city, with little hope of relief.

"Daily Herald," Thursday, Nov. 26, 1942.

LONDON BLACKOUT
5.29 p.m. to 8.06 a.m.
Moon Rises 8.08 p.m.
Moon Sets 12.03 p.m.
Lighting-up Time 5.29 p.m.

Daily Herald

No. 8354 THURSDAY, NOVEMBER 26, 1942 ONE PENNY

STOP PRESS

NEW RUSSIAN GAIN

Moscow Radio said the new advance on one sector north-west of Stalingrad was made after two German infantry regiments, supported by 25 tanks, had failed to break up a Russian attack. Then Russians on next sector attacked and broke through.

2 a.m.: Moscow Reports New Three Mile Advance Against Gap

15,000 MORE PRISONERS TAKEN, ANOTHER PANZER DIVISION ROUTED

ANOTHER ADVANCE OF ABOUT THREE AND A HALF MILES BY THE RUSSIANS NORTH-WEST OF STALINGRAD WAS REPORTED AT TWO O'CLOCK THIS MORNING BY MOSCOW RADIO.

It followed hard on the good news given in a special communiqué issued in Moscow last night.

Yesterday, the sixth day of the great offensive, they increased their grip on the vital Stalingrad-Kharkov railway in the rear of the Germans.

This showed that despite increased opposition the Russians are gradually closing the gap west of Stalingrad, which forms the only way of escape for Hoth's forces.

Last night's special communiqué reported that the resistance had been overcome and new places occupied in the north-western section of the battle ground.

Three of these were stations in the area of the crossing of the railway over the Don west of Stalingrad, near the confluence of the River Chir.

They are Richkovsk and the twin towns of Novomaximovsk and Staromaximovsk.

Inhabited localities captured in addition were Malo-Nobatovsky, Biryuchkov, Rodionov, Bolshaya-Donchinka, and Malaya-Donchinka ...

... shadowed this move by General Zhukov.

They believe he will attack in strength when the Germans have sent large forces in an attempt to stem the Russians' Don-Volga threat.

Zhukov's aim, they say, is to drive towards Smolensk and roll up the Germans' "winter line."

The Germans last night admitted that they were taken completely by surprise by the Russian offensive.

ONE-GUN SHIPS GET JAP RAIDER

... by the stern. Her aircraft were seen to go down with her.

The Ondina's topmast and aerials were shot away.

She was still being engaged by the second raider when the Bengal closed with this vessel

Boats Gunned

The surviving raider then concentrated her whole armament on the tanker, which was hit repeatedly, and her master was killed.

When all the Ondina's ammunition had been expended the crew abandoned ship.

The enemy then closed and machine-gunned the boats, killing the chief engineer and three Chinese members of the crew, after which the abandoned ship was twice torpedoed.

After searching for survivors from her sunken consort the raider made off.

Then the Ondina's second officer, third engineer and the Australian gunlayer returned to the tanker with three others of the crew and the ship got under way.

WARSHIPS FOR INDIA

A number of small fast and well-equipped warships for the Royal Indian Navy have arrived in Indian waters from the United Kingdom.—Exchange.

TWO SOVIET ARMIES ARE RACING TO JOIN UP AND CLOSE POCKET TO TRAP HOTH

By Major E. W. SHEPPARD

MORE than a quarter of a million Germans of ...

U.S. DIVE-BOMBERS ATTACK ISLAND

AMERICAN dive-bombers and fighters from Guadalcanal have attacked Japanese installations at Munda, New Georgia Island, 180 miles away, in the Solomons.

This was announced by the Navy Department in Washington last night.

On Monday a United States Marine patrol on Guadalcanal killed 70 Japanese and captured five machine-guns in an enemy encampment on the north slope of Mambullo.

Patrol activity continues in the area.—Reuter.

NOW the men of Stalingrad go forward, too. Here are infantry attacking under shell fire in a suburb.
—British Newsreel Picture.

AIR MASTERY BATTLE RAGING IN TUNISIA

THE BATTLE FOR MASTERY IN THE TUNISIAN SKIES IS WORKING UP TO A TERRIFIC CLIMAX AS BOTH THE ALLIES AND THE AXIS POUR TROOPS AND SUPPLIES INTO THE PROTECTORATE.

Under constant air attack, reinforcements are being rushed by both sides to the narrow arena where the fate of Bizerta and Tunis must soon be decided.

Aircraft of the RAF and the United States Army Air Force have carried out extensive and successful operations against the enemy in Tunisia, stated an Allied H.Q. communiqué issued last night.

RAF bombers attacked the airfield at Bizerta on Monday night. One large explosion and more than 30 smaller ones were observed during the raid.

Other bombers attacked Bizerta again last night and concentrated on the docks and the shipping in the harbour.

Numerous bomb flashes were seen, and there was a big sheet of flame which appeared to have come from exploding petrol.

All the bombers returned safely.

14 Planes Down

Lockheed Lightning fighters of the Twelfth Air Force destroyed 14 aeroplanes in Tunisia yesterday.

These included seven Italian transport planes, which were shot down at Gabes, and two Junkers 88s, destroyed elsewhere in Southern Tunisia.

Four transport planes, one seaplane, and one tank were destroyed on the airfield at Gabes.

All of our planes returned safely. Four of them were damaged and one pilot was wounded.

"The British First Army," the communiqué ended, "is making satisfactory progress in operations against the enemy in eastern forward areas."

Movements of the British First Army and the American forces under General Anderson's command are going forward with the greatest secrecy.

With characteristic thoroughness General Eisenhower, the Allied Commander-in-Chief, is planning everything down to the last detail.

Nothing is being left to chance. The stakes are too great for that.

Many duels are taking place between German bombers and Allied fighters as the enemy tries to blast the Allied supply lines.

Well Equipped

Though the German ground troops so far landed in Tunisia are said to be relatively small numerically, they are very well equipped.

Allied naval forces and the RAF, often operating under the most difficult weather conditions, are trying to smash Axis supply lines to Tunisia.

While they are having their successes, it has been impossible to stop the Germans landing more men and supplies from the sea and from air transports, but by day and by night there is no "let-up" in the Allied efforts to harass the enemy.

The success of RAF long-range fighters from Malta in shooting down German air transports has been most valuable.

(Eden says Tunisia operations "extremely tense and serious": Page Three.)

Axis Sky Punch Is Harder

By EMERY PEARCE

GERMAN and Italian air resistance in the "Tunis Triangle" has greatly increased.

Many squadrons of Junkers dive-bombers and Messerschmitt fighters have been brought from the Russian front to Sicily and Sardinia, while the Italians have concentrated the bulk of their air force in the "toe" of Italy or the surrounding islands.

This is apparent from the fact that during the past few days intensified Axis dive-bombing and "strafing" attacks have considerably slowed down the advance of the British First Army.

Hitler has made up his mind to hold his bridgehead in Tunisia at any cost, so as to retain command of the vitally important Sicilian Narrows.

To do this he is prepared to weaken his already overtaxed Luftwaffe in the fierce Russian fighting and transfer squadrons of bombers and fighters to the Mediterranean.

Got Him Guessing

It is interesting to note that Hitler has not withdrawn any of his "static" fighter squadrons from North-West France. The Allied High Command has got him guessing.

The Axis appears to have temporarily achieved air superiority in Tunisia. But this should not be for long.

Spitfires, Lockheed Lightnings and Beaufighters in large numbers should soon reach our advanced airfields. When this happens it is certain that there will be terrific, concentrated air battles—for the prize of Tunisia and the Sicilian Narrows.

But do not expect speedy results. Once Hitler has decided to defend a place he goes about it very thoroughly. He will be prepared to lose many aircraft and men.

T.U.C. TO JOIN TALKS ON FUTURE OF INDUSTRY

Leaders of both sides of industry are to discuss post-war reconstruction with Sir William Jowitt, the Minister concerned.

This was revealed at yesterday's meeting of the General Council of the Trades Union Congress.

The Council agreed to be represented on a joint committee along with the British Employers' Confederation and the Federation of British Industries.

BIG GUNS MOVE UP TO EL AGHEILA

From GEORGE CRAWLEY *CAIRO, Wednesday.*

ADVANCED units of the Eighth Army are now close to Rommel's El Agheila line in Libya.

For tactical reasons their precise positions have not been revealed, but the official statement that they are keeping up their pressure on the retreating enemy between Jedabya and El Agheila shows clearly enough that the time has nearly arrived when Rommel must come to grips—or move westward.

General Montgomery is prepared for whatever fortifications the Germans may have manned along the El Agheila line, which stretches from the sea down to the salt marshes, providing the same kind of cover on his right flank as the Qattara Depression afforded the Eighth Army's left flank at El Alamein.

German accounts of bombardment by heavy British artillery at Jedabya indicate that the big guns are up and ready to deal with blockhouses and other strong points.

RAF Over Crete

The RAF has now turned its attention to one of the bases from which Rommel may be trying to draw airborne reinforcements.

On Monday night, in bright moonlight, heavy and medium bombers raided landing grounds in Crete, where a number of enemy aircraft were assembled.

A flight-lieutenant from Wiltshire described what happened at Kastelli Pediada.

"All our bombs fell in the target area," he said.

"Three healthy red glows were still visible 20 minutes after we had headed for our base, and just then the middle one exploded, sending flashes in all directions."

Axis air activity over the Cyrenaica battlefield continues to be negligible.—Reuter.

U.S. STAFF CHIEF LOST ON FLIGHT

BRIGADIER - GENERAL ASA DUNCAN, United States Army air commander in the European theatre, is missing.

His plane was forced down off the coast of Northern France while he was flying from England to North Africa on November 17.

Gen. Duncan

It is not known whether any of those in the plane survived, said the United States War Department last night.

General Duncan, who was 50, was a Command pilot and combat observer. He was made Chief of the Air Staff in the European Theatre in July.

He is the second general of the United States Army Air Force listed as missing.

Major-General Clarence Tinker was reported missing from the Battle of Midway Island in June.—Associated Press.

REYNAUD SENT TO BORDEAUX

PAUL REYNAUD, the former French Premier, and Georges Mandel, former Minister of the Colonies, two of the accused in the Riom war guilt trials, have been removed to Bordeaux.

They had been for some time at the Froma prison in the Pyrenees region.

This was disclosed in a British United Press message from the French frontier last night.

There has been no indication since the Nazis marched into Unoccupied France whether the war guilt trials would be resumed.

But it is expected that both Reynaud and Mandel will now be handed over to the Germans.

FRANCO NOT GOING TO LISBON

Reports of an impending visit to Lisbon by a Spanish delegation headed by General Franco were emphatically denied by the Spanish Embassy in Lisbon last night.

"No such delegation is here or expected," an Embassy spokesman stated.—Reuter.

RAF ATTACK ON TRAINS

British fighters yesterday attacked and damaged trains and other railway targets in Northern France and Brittany. One of our aircraft is missing.

TELL WAR AIMS SAYS WILLKIE

From ARTHUR WEBB *WASHINGTON, Wednesday.*

A RENEWED demand that there must be a definition of war aims by the peoples of the United Nations was made at Toronto to-night by Wendell Willkie.

He said that America must guard against moral force being used to continue "dollar diplomacy" and the maintenance of the old international order—the spawning ground of the present struggle.

Not only must we educate ourselves to accept the economic changes which must take place in the world, but we must convince the peoples to whom we had promised freedom that we really believe that "all men are created equal."

"The peoples of the world must win the war and they must win the peace," he declared.

Willkie said the war was either a grand coalition of peoples fighting for liberation or it was nothing.

There must be a great pooling of all our energies inspired by a united strategy, planned and fought on a global scale or it will be lost.

"We must declare the common purpose which drives us all, or we run the risk of having worked, sacrificed and suffered to win the war to no purpose."

Everywhere in his recent tour, said Willkie, he found encouragement on the fighting fronts and a resolution to win in the peoples behind the lines.

Willkie, who was speaking at a rally of the Canadian Aid to Russia fund, added: "You are here as citizens of the British Commonwealth of Free Nations—one of history's most exciting and magnificent achievements in self-government of the free peoples."

DANES JAILED

A Copenhagen report says two Danes have been sentenced by a German court-martial to ten and five years hard labour in a German prison for distributing leaflets urging German soldiers to turn their weapons against their superiors and refuse service.—Exchange.

RATION GIFTS MAY BE ALLOWED

You may soon be allowed to send your tea, sugar or butter ration to a relative. At present it is illegal to do so.

The Food Ministry is considering to what extent it can relax the rationing regulations to allow gifts or exchanges of rationed foods among families.

Mr. R. Purbrick, M.P., raised the question of exchanges in Parliament yesterday. Mr. W. Mabane, Parliamentary Secretary to the Ministry, asked him to renew the question in a week's time.

▲ DAILY HERALD, LONDON, THURSDAY NOVEMBER 26, 1942

On November 19, 1942, the Red Army had launched Operation Uranus to trap the German Sixth Army in Stalingrad. Soviet forces were huge: Southwestern Front—398,000 troops; Don Front—307,000 troops; and Stalingrad Front—429,000 troops. The Red Army also deployed 1,500 tanks for the attack. When the operation was launched, it brushed aside weak Axis resistance, as reported here.

▲ NEW YORK JOURNAL AMERICAN, NEW YORK, MONDAY DECEMBER 7, 1942

At the end of 1942, the United States had certainly struck back hard against the Empire of the Sun. On land, U.S. troops were poised to defeat Japanese forces on Guadalcanal, while at sea the U.S. Navy had dealt the Imperial Japanese Navy crushing blows at the Coral Sea and Midway. At the end of 1942, Japan was firmly on the defensive in the Pacific theater.

1943

THE PIVOTAL YEAR OF THE WAR, 1943 SAW THE ALLIES
CONSOLIDATE THE PROGRESS MADE IN 1942. HOWEVER, THE
FIGHTING IN 1943 WAS HEAVY, AND, WHILE THE ALLIES FINISHED
ON TOP, THEIR VICTORIES WERE BY NO MEANS INEVITABLE.

THE YEAR BEGAN WITH CLEARING UP AFTER THE ALLIED VICTORIES OF FALL 1942. THE RED ARMY WAS TRYING TO TRAP GERMAN FORCES IN SOUTHERN RUSSIA; THE U.S. MARINES COMPLETED the conquest of Guadalcanal; and Allied forces were advancing in North Africa. It was under these favorable circumstances that Roosevelt and Churchill had a meeting in Casablanca, Morocco, on January 14 to discuss future strategy. Roosevelt surprised the British by making unconditional surrender a war aim.

Although the Allies were on the offensive, their enemies were by no means defeated. At Kharkov in February, German forces launched a devastating counterattack that stopped the Red Army advance; in North Africa, Rommel's troops pushed the Allies back at the Kasserine Pass; and in Burma, British forces could make no headway. At sea, things were tough, too: in February, in the Atlantic, Convoy ON-166 lost 15 of 49 ships, while in March, Allied convoys to the Soviet Union were suspended.

Nevertheless, in North Africa the Allies ground on remorselessly, and on May 13 Axis forces in North Africa surrendered. British and American forces invaded Sicily in July and mainland Italy in September. Progress up the Italian peninsula was slow, but the Italian government had overthrown Mussolini and surrendered—only to be itself overthrown in a swift German operation.

HARD FIGHTING IN THE PACIFIC

In the Pacific, hard-won victories in New Guinea were followed by landings on the Gilbert Islands, which revealed how difficult it would be to shatter the Japanese defenses.

▲ THE ITALIAN ARMY on the retreat from the Don River on the Eastern Front. By the beginning of 1943, Axis forces in southern Russia were falling back and the front was in danger of collapsing.

Allied superiority at sea and in the air was manifest by the end of 1943. The battle of the Atlantic against the U-boats was being won, while Allied bombers were inflicting great damage on German cities.

However, the biggest Allied victory of 1943 came on the Eastern Front, where the Red Army defeated the final big German offensive at the Battle of Kursk in July, in the largest tank battle ever.

Rommel Fights Back In Libya

Weekdays Except Saturday,
3 Cents in City Limits
4 Cents Elsewhere
Saturday 5 Cents, Sunday 10 Cents

Journal NEW YORK American
AN AMERICAN PAPER FOR THE AMERICAN PEOPLE

No. 20,091—DAILY MONDAY, JANUARY, 4, 1943 In Two Sections —Section One

LATEST NEWS

REDS PURSUING NAZIS IN CAUCASUS

Judge Demands Data In Hoffman Release

He Wasn't Consulted By Poletti

Page of pictures and testimony in Hoffman case in today's Pictorial Review.

Queens County Judge Thomas E. Downs has demanded from the State Parole Board details of the recent commutation of Alexander Hoffman, Communist sympathizer, the New York Journal-American learned today.

Hoffman, CIO union official, and his secretary, Pearl Spivack, convicted of union terrorism and given long prison terms, had their sentences commuted by Charles Poletti after he had been in office only 17 days as Governor of the State of New York.

Judge Downs, in whose courtroom Hoffman, the Spivack woman and five co-defendants were found guilty of attempted arson, unlawful entry and conspiracy, called on Chairman Frederick A. Moran, of the Parole Board, to give details of Gov. Poletti's action with respect to parole.

NO CONSULTATION.

Gov. Poletti, who took office Dec. 2 after Gov. Lehman resigned to become Director of the Federal Foreign Relief Bureau, commuted the sentence of Hoffman on Dec. 19 without consulting either Judge Downs or District Attorney Charles P. Sullivan, prosecutor of Queens. Mrs. Spivack was freed the same day.

An attempt to unionize by terror the Kent Stores, Inc., a chain of 125 dry cleaning establishments in New York City, led to the conviction of Hoffman, general manager of the Cleaners, Dyers, Pressers, Drivers and Allied Trades Union,

Continued on Page 4, Column 2.

Queens County Judge Thomas E. Downs, who has demanded from the State Parole Board details of Poletti's release of Hoffman. The Judge, who sentenced Hoffman and six associates, was not consulted by Poletti. The Appellate Division and Court of Appeals had unanimously upheld Judge Downs in the convictions of Hoffman and the others.

Hirohito Leads Court New Year Festival

TOKIO, Jan. 4 (Japanese Radio recorded by AP).—Emperor Hirohito personally participated in the Genshi-Sai, age-old New Year's festival of the Japanese court, in the Imperial Palace today.

Bronx Girl Slain On Way to Work

A pretty young blonde, two stab wounds in her back, staggered up to two men at Wales ave. and 143d st., The Bronx, shortly after 7 a. m. today.

"I've been hurt," she gasped. "I'm very sick. Please take me to a hospital."

The two men summoned aid and rushed her to Lincoln Hospital. She died a few minutes after arriving there, before she could be questioned about the attack.

The young woman was identified as Dorothy Huber, 23, of 785 E. 149th st., The Bronx, who had been employed in the cake department of the Ward Baking Co., for the past year.

Police learned from her father, a baker at Ward's, and her brother John, also employed there, that she was home last night and left for work today as usual. The Ward plant, at 143rd st. and Wales ave., is about six blocks from the Huber home.

She left for work unaccompanied today, and so far as was learned there were no witnesses to the attack.

Indications of a struggle, however, were seen in the fact that her Rosary beads were found in front of one house on Wales ave., one of her shoes in front of another, blodstains n the sidewalk before a third, and her green hat in the gutter still a few feet further on.

The two men she stopped, Meyer Cohen, of 1051 Tiffany st., a Ward truck driver, and Vincent Tinney, of 551 Wales ave., carried her to the Ward plant, where they got someone to drive her to the hospital.

Flames Destroy Crosby Home

(Picture on Page 6)

HOLLYWOOD, Jan. 4 (UP).—The 20-room mansion of film crooner Bing Crosby was destroyed by fire last night with a loss of around $200,000.

Mrs. Crosby and their four children, Gary 9, Lindsay 4, and Phillip and Dennie, eight-year-old twins, escaped uninjured

Dies Report Hits Biddle for Failing To Act on Reds

Work of Group Baring Sabotage Sent to House

By DAVID SENTNER
New York Journal-American Washington Bureau.

WASHINGTON, Jan. 4. — The American people, as in no other war, must guard "that human liberty which is the essence of Americanism" and our internal safety against the machinations of fifth columns.

The Special Committee on Un-American Activities, headed by Representative Dies (D.-Texas), declared this today in a report to Speaker of the House Rayburn.

In addition to reviewing its work of checking Nazi, Communist, Fascist and Japanese subversive activities, the committee, which is expected to be continued by the new Congress, charged that hundreds of Communists still remained on the Government payroll.

The report charged Attorney General Biddle failed to deal with the 1,124 cases submitted by the Committee of Federal employes who were Communists or "fellow travelers."

"The Attorney General did not carry out the mandate of Congress, which was simply that an

Continued on Page 6, Column 1.

Hundreds Still On U. S. Payroll, Review Charges

From N. Y. Journal-American Washington Bureau.

WASHINGTON, Jan. 4.—Hundreds of alleged Communists, "Fellow Travelers" and members of suversive organizations are still on the Federal payroll.

No action has been taken against 19 officials of the Government allegedly belonging to organizations which the Attorney-General himself had found to be subversive.

Attorney-General Biddle has failed to follow the mandate of Congress to make a complete investigation of this situation despite the forwarding to him of the names of the 1,124 Federal Government employes who were allegedly members of subversive organizations.

So charged the Dies Special Committee on Un-American Activities today in its report to the House of Representatives.

In a section devoted to "Communists in Government" the report said:

"This committee's report is primarily concerned with the manner in which the Attorney-General dealt with, or rather failed to deal with, the 1,124 cases which were

Continued on Page 6, Column 2.

Stockholm Reports Dismissal of Keitel

LONDON, Jan. 4 (AP). — The London News Chronicle said today a Stockholm dispatch reported there that Field Marshal General Keitel "has followed his colleagues Col. Gen. Halder, Field Marshal Gen. Von Bock, Field Marshal Gen. Von Leeb, Field Marshal Gen. Von Kleist and Col. Gen. Guderian into oblivion.

Women Now Guards At Delaware Jail

GREENBANK, Del., Jan. 4 (AP).—Armed with machine gun and rifle, women are taking over operation of the main tower guard house at the New Castle county workhouse.

The women were selected after the prison lost many male guards to defense industries and the armed forces.

Jap Plot to 'Kidnap' Roosevelt Before Pearl Harbor Disclosed

WASHINGTON, Jan. 4 (AP).—How close Pearl Harbor came to being a much greater national humiliation than it actually was is disclosed in the White Book issued by Secretary of State Hull.

The final and most dramatic portion of the book reveals that the Japanese not only planned months in advance for "a surprise mass attack at Pearl Harbor," but did their diplomatic utmost to maneuver Japanese - American peace discussion in such a way that President Roosevelt would be in the hands of the Japanese Navy when its torpedo planes stabbed at the heart of American seapower in the Pacific.

Apparently unaware that Ambassador Joseph C. Grew informed the State Department on Jan. 27, 1941, of reports that Japan planned the surprise attack in case of "trouble," the Japanese Government a few months later began urging on the State Department a plan to bring President Roosevelt and Premier Prince Konoye together aboard a Japanese warship in the Pacific for a "frank exchange of views."

Japanese Ambassador Kichisabura Nomura broached the subject to Secretary Hull on Aug. 8. A few weeks later the subject was reopened by a message from Prince Konoye himself to President Roosevelt.

Nomura told Hull the same day (Aug. 28) that Konoye planned to meet the President "in a Japanese warship," and that his government was "very anxious that the meeting be held at the earliest possible moment."

On Sept. 6 Ambassador Grew informed Hull that Konoye assured him Japanese Army and Navy leaders were very favorable

Continued on Page 2, Column 4.

Rommel Puts Up Fight In Libya

LONDON, Jan. 4 (UP).—Field Marshal Rommel's Afrika Korps is making a determined and possibly a final stand in Libya, with the aid of important reinforcements including a force of Stuka dive bombing planes, advices from Africa disclosed today.

Rommel is making his stand on the Wadi Zem Zem, 230 miles from Tunisia and only 170 miles from Tripoli, capital of Libya.

His Stukas and other planes are offering a strong challenge to the Allied air force, which for weeks ruled the Libyan skies.

ITALIANS KNOCKED OUT.

United Press advices reported that an Italian rear guard, left to defend the Bu Ngem fort, on the eastern arm of the Wadi Bei El Chebir, had been knocked out. They set the place on fire and fled westward.

Stronger Axis rear guards were now holding the Wadi, or dried river bed, of Zem Zem, however, and the approaches to it and British mobile armored forces were hacking them all along their front.

The main eight army had now reached the Wadi Bei El Chebir,

Continued on Page 2, Column 5.

Hospital Closed In Oil Crisis

The city today closed its first hospital in a move to save 300,000 gallons of fuel oil during the next few months.

The institution, the Neponsit Beach Hospital for Children at Rockaway, will be closed until "warmer weather sets in" and its 104 children moved elsewhere today, according to Commissioner of Hospitals Bernecker.

They will be divided among other city institutions and the hospital's 119 staff members also will be shifted to other assignments, he added.

Dr. Bernecker said the closing of no other hospitals was contemplated at the moment.

In Washington a Senatorial committee called top-flight Government officials before it today for an inquiry into the entire gasoline and fuel oil rationing set-up.

Sen. Maloney (D.-Conn.), chairman, scotched any hope that the investigation might lead to increased allotments of the fuels.

Mayor LaGuardia, who revealed plans to close the institution on his weekly radio broadcast, blamed the decision on the new governmental order cutting fuel oil supplies another ten per cent.

Bearing out the Mayor's asser-

Continued on Page 5, Column 4.

Axis Generals Desert Men, Flee in Planes

By NATALIA RENE
International News Service Staff Correspondent

MOSCOW, Jan. 4.—Surging forward in a swift campaign to reconquer the Caucasus, Red Army troops today struck out in two directions from the captured rail town of Mozdok in a drive to trap Nazi armies around Nalchik to the south.

Soviet columns, pursuing the retreating Germans, forged ahead both northwest and west of Mozdok, 60 miles northwest of the Grozny oil fields, in twin drives on Kotiarevskaya and Prodhladnaya, important mid-Caucasus rail junctions.

Threaten to Split Nazi Armies

"After capturing Mozdok," the Soviet High Command said at noon, "out troops continued to advance northwest and west and occupied several inhabited localities. Fighting continues."

[UP said the Caucasus drive threatens to split the retreating Germans and that German generals were deserting their troops to flee by plane. Dispatches reported the flight of one high German general in the Velikie Luki sector and said that in the Don-Volga area, where 22 German divisions, or what is left of them, are trapped, a divisioned general had escaped. The plane carrying his staff crashed and three of the officers were killed.]

Capture of Prodhladnaya, 35 miles west of Mozdok, will place the Soviets in control of the railway which branches off from the Rostov-Baku line down to Nalchik where another Soviet army is pressing northward.

Two of Hitler's crack SS Elite Guard regiments were overwhelmed and forced to retreat in the steadily advancing Soviet push southwest and south of beleaguered Stalingrad. The SS troops at first attempted to resist, the High Command said, but withdrew hastily in the face of the Russian strength.

The Germans continued to lose heavily in manpower and equipment as Red Army troops smashed forward through Nazi defenses.

"On other sectors," the communique continued, "our troops continued their successful advance and occupied several inhabited localities."

NEAR RAIL JUNCTION.

Through this area southwest of Stalingrad one wing of the Russian army was pressing along the Stalingrad - Krasnodar Railway from captured Kotelnikovski toward the rail junction of Salsk.

Continued on Page 2, Column 4.

THE WEATHER

Occasional drizzle; somewhat warmer.

Sun rises, 8:20 a. m.; sun sets, 5:41 a. m. High tide at Governors Island, 7:06 a. m.; 7:29 p. m.

HOURLY TEMPERATURES

Midnight	33	5 a. m.	33
1 a. m.	33	6 a. m.	33
2 a. m.	31	7 a. m.	33
3 a. m.	37	8 a. m.	32
4 a. m.	38	9 a. m.	33

The New York Journal-American has the largest circulation of any evening newspaper in America. 230

It is the only New York evening newspaper possessing the three great wire services—ASSOCIATED PRESS—INTERNATIONAL NEWS SERVICE—UNITED PRESS.

▲ NEW YORK JOURNAL AMERICA, NEW YORK, MONDAY JANUARY 4, 1943

The catastrophe at Stalingrad placed Germany's Army Group A in the Caucasus in great peril. However, despite the headline, the Red Army was unable to trap German forces. The Wehrmacht retreat from the Caucasus never became a rout.

ARIZONA REPUBLIC

THE STATE'S GREATEST NEWSPAPER

Today **12** Pages

112 N. CENTRAL AVE.
TELEPHONE 3-1111

53rd Year, No. 259, Phoenix, Arizona

Monday Morning, February 1, 1943

STALINGRAD LOSS COSTS NAZIS ARMY OF 330,000

Heavy Bombs Smash Hamburg

Soviets Take 16 Generals, New Marshal

President Ends Long Journey

Trip's Last Leg Made By Train From Miami

Knox Finds Pacific Set For Offense

Jap Base Fired By Warships

Newly Arrived Stores Lost In Flames

Note Of Doom Found In Grim Nazi Talk

RAF Hits Port And Factories

Block-Busters, Incendiaries Are Used

Ground War Flares Anew In Tunisia

Germans Battle To Clear Way For Rommel

Worker Dies In Accident

Stars Of Honor Stress Design

Lost Seaplane Is Discovered

Cinch Yourself Right To Vote

Allies Attack Japanese Force

Submarine Lost

Chinese Recapture Kwangtung Villages

Army Plane Crashes In Utah, Kills Two

▲ FIELD MARSHAL FRIEDRICH PAULUS, the commander of the Sixth Army, was given his marshal's baton on January 30, 1943, in an attempt to stop him surrendering to the Soviets. The next day he capitulated.

▲ ARIZONA REPUBLIC, PHOENIX, MONDAY FEBRUARY 1, 1943
At Stalingrad, the German Sixth Army suffered 150,000 dead and 90,000 captured. The Luftwaffe, attempting to supply the army, lost 488 aircraft.

Münchener Ausgabe
35. Ausg. 56. Jahrg. Einzelpreis für München 15 Rpf., für auswärts 20 Rpf.

„Freiheit und Brot!"

Münchener Ausgabe
München, Donnerstag, 4. Februar 1943

VÖLKISCHER BEOBACHTER

Kampfblatt der nationalsozialistischen Bewegung
Großdeutschlands

Der Kampf der 6. Armee um Stalingrad zu Ende

Sie starben, damit Deutschland lebe

Getreu dem Fahneneid

Zweimal die Aufforderung zur Übergabe stolz abgelehnt

Aus dem Führerhauptquartier, 3. Februar

Das Oberkommando der Wehrmacht gibt bekannt:

Der Kampf um Stalingrad ist zu Ende. Ihrem Fahneneid bis zum letzten Atemzug getreu, ist die 6. Armee unter der vorbildlichen Führung des Generalfeldmarschalls Paulus der Übermacht des Feindes und der Ungunst der Verhältnisse erlegen.

Neben ihren Taten verblaßt alle menschliche Größe

Tokio, 3. Februar

Madrid, 3. Februar

Bukarest, 3. Februar

Zeichnung: Mjölnir

STALINGRAD RUFT ZUR TAT!

Die Helden der 6. Armee

Von
ALFRED ROSENBERG

▲ VÖLKISCHER BEOBACHTER, MUNICH, THURSDAY FEBRUARY 4, 1943

The front page puts the German defeat at Stalingrad in the best possible light: "They died so that Germany could live on. Faithful to their oath of allegiance.
Call to surrender twice proudly rejected. The fight for Stalingrad is over. The Sixth Army ... has been forced to bow to the superior numbers of the enemy."

▲ NEW YORK WORLD-TELEGRAM, TUESDAY FEBRUARY 9, 1943
At the beginning of February 1943, the Japanese Imperial Navy evacuated 13,000 troops in night operations from Guadalcanal. Their abandonment of the island marked the first land defeat for Japan in the Pacific war.

▲ U.S. TROOPS MOVE CAUTIOUSLY through an abandoned Japanese camp on Guadalcanal in early 1943. By this time, many Japanese troops still on the island were in a state of near starvation, and were suffering grave shortages of both weapons and ammunition.

"All the News That's Fit to Print."

NEWS INDEX, PAGE 27, THIS SECTION

The New York Times.

LATE CITY EDITION
Moderate temperatures and moderate winds today.

Temperatures Yesterday—Max., 44; Min., 32
Sunrise, 7:11 A. M.; Sunset, 7:01 P. M.

Section 1

Copyright, 1943, by The New York Times Company.

VOL. XCII..No. 31,095.

Entered as Second-Class Matter, Postoffice, New York, N. Y.

NEW YORK, SUNDAY, MARCH 14, 1943.

Including Magazine and Book Sections.

TEN CENTS
New York City and Vicinity

NEW CEILINGS SET FOR 7 VEGETABLES TO RESTORE SUPPLY

Mark-Ups Differ With Type of Wholesaler and Retailer in 14 Cities Affected

A WARNING ON MEAT RUSH

OPA Head Appeals to Public Not to Overbuy Before the Start of Rationing

12 Private Bus Lines Halt Tomorrow Under ODT Ban

Apartment Dwellers Must Walk to Subway or Rail Station—Areas in Manhattan, Brooklyn, Queens, Yonkers Affected

PRESIDENT ANXIOUS ON TAX SITUATION; OUTCOME IN DOUBT

House Leaders Studying Alternatives for 'Hodge-Podge' Ways and Means Plan

SURVIVAL SEEN UNLIKELY

Robertson Idea of Canceling Normal and First Surtax Liabilities for '42 Is Favored

By JOHN H. CRIDER

R. A. F. GIVES ESSEN WORST POUNDING; U. S. FLIERS SMASH FRENCH RAILWAYS; KHARKOV'S DEFENDERS PUSHED BACK

NAZIS STAB DEEPER

Red Army Yields Again West of City but Holds on North and South

GERMANS PAY HEAVY TOLL

Claim Towns West of Belgorod —Russians' Smolensk Drive Goes On Unchecked

Roosevelt-Eden Talks Begin; Briton Warns of a Long War

Visitor Says All Problems Will Be Discussed —Group of Senators Calls for Meetings of Allies to Form Permanent Organization

RAIDING STEPPED UP

British Drop 1,000 Tons of Bombs on Krupp's —Lose 23 Planes

FORTRESSES OVER AMIENS

Americans Blast More Nazi Supply Lines to Channel Amid Hard Fighter Action

MORGAN FUNERAL HERE ON TUESDAY

Body of Noted Banker Who Died in Florida at 75 is on Way to New York

RUSH OF TAXPAYERS INTENSIFIED IN CITY

4 Offices Crowded All Day—Downtown District Gets 22 Checks of Over $1,000,000

Fighting French Ask Control Over North and West Africa

By MILTON BRACKER

NEW ENEMY CONVOY HIT OFF NEW GUINEA

Allied Bombs Strike 2 of 5 Craft Guarded by 3 Warships —Other Vessels Sighted

Two Proposed Episcopal Canons Ease Remarriage, Stress Family

War News Summarized

SUNDAY, MARCH 14, 1943

Continued on Page Sixteen
Continued on Page Twelve
Continued on Page Twelve
Continued on Page Twenty-four
Continued on Page Eighteen
Continued on Page Eight
Continued on Page Five
Continued on Page Two
Continued on Page Fifteen
Continued on Page Twenty

▲ THE NEW YORK TIMES, SUNDAY MARCH 14, 1943

In March 1943, the Royal Air Force began a four-month bombing offensive against Germany's Ruhr industrial region. An air fleet of 367 bombers struck the Krupp Works at Essen, causing damage over a large area.

News Chronicle

No. 30,265   THURSDAY, MAY 13, 1943   ONE PENNY

IT'S ALL OVER: Von Arnim Captured, French Take Last Group of 25,000

IT is all over in North Africa. The enemy has ceased all organised resistance in all parts of Tunisia, it was announced last night at Allied H.Q.

In the final phases of the battle at least 150,000 German and Italian troops were captured—and among the captives is von Arnim, successor to Rommel, C.-in-C. of the Axis forces in North Africa.

Von Arnim was captured by the British yesterday at Cape Bon. The Allied blockade, by sea and air, had frustrated every plan for his escape. He is one of eight German generals who have fallen into Allied hands.

At almost the same moment as the news of von Arnim's capture was received in London there came the communique that announced the end of the campaign. It was a French communique, and this was what it said :

"Broken by the frontal push of our troops in the Zaghouan mountains, and outflanked and threatened with encirclement by our armoured elements, all German and Italian troops fighting between Zaghouan and Saouaf capitulated unconditionally.

"These troops consisted of the Italian Superbia division under General Geli and a German group under General Pfeiffer.

"They surrendered to the commander of the French armoured detachment and of the Moroccan division respectively.

"More than 25,000 prisoners have been taken, together with the whole of their war equipment and supplies."

This was the last organised resistance. There may still be small isolated units, but the battle is over.

With the end of the campaign the Allied air offensive has been switched to Sicily. Marsala and Catania have been heavily bombed.

GEN. VON ARNIM
will fight no more

AFRICA IS CLEAR OF THE ENEMY

From PHILIP JORDAN
News Chronicle War Correspondent

TUNIS, Wednesday.

THE great victory is won. Africa is virtually clear of enemy. British troops stand this morning on the extreme northern tip of Cape Bon.

The enemy is in the pocket to south of the peninsula.

ON PAGE TWO
Gateways Into Europe's Fortress ;
Von Arnim, Man Who Hates the British

now completely surrounded by forces infinitely heavier than their own.

This encirclement is formerly a matter of advanced reconnaissance elements, but of massed infantry and tanks prepared, if need be, to smash completely every man and gun contained within the hill area between Zaghouan and Bou Ficha. It will not be necessary.

For all practical purposes fighting has ceased. Thousands and thousands more German prisoners are now in our hands, and it will be some days before the total count is made and verified.

That last advance, it became clear two days ago, would meet with little or no opposition, for the sudden abandonment of the Hammam Lif gap by an enemy, still adequately supplied, showed once and for all that he is utterly demoralised.

STRAGGLING HORDES

Since then the enemy has been streaming down into willing captivity, straining resources for attending to them.

For the last three days one of the chief difficulties in speedily getting to and from Tunis along the coast road has been these straggling hordes of beaten men, few of whom have attempted to disguise their pleasure that, as one German said to me: "Now I shall live to see my son again."

Hundreds of lorries, most of them captured, have been standing by to carry prisoners back to tremendous cages prepared at the roadside to the rear area, whence the prisoners were distributed to prison camps.

Preparations were made to house and feed more than 100,000 men, and the margin, by the time all are trapped in, will be small.

These habilitated creatures, although they have delayed us, have been beaten not by overwhelming force but by good soldiers who knew their job.

FORCED IN BATTLE

Long and arduous though the campaign has been, history may well say that it paid us a hundred-fold to miss the prizes of Tunis and Bizerta in these first weeks when we so nearly took them.

Had we then captured what we came out to take we should not today be possessed of a new army of crack and veteran troops who have learned their job in a campaign infinitely more, than demanding infinitely more, than this campaign that the Eighth Army ever fought.

In these last six months an instrument of war has been forged in heat of battle.

When we came here we had an army of raw men. True, they were trained to that last item that "peace-time" training can make men. That, however, was not

Continued Back Page **B**

The Bey of Tunis Asked: 'How Is Your King George?'

From WILLIAM MUNDAY
News Chronicle War Correspondent

TUNIS, Wednesday.

HIS HIGHNESS SIDI AHMED, Bey of Tunis, asked "How is your King George ?" when the first British soldiers, chasing after the Germans, arrived at his sky-blue palace by the sea at Hammam Lif.

The Bey, temporal and spiritual head of 2,200,000 Tunisian Arabs, sat in his crimson-carpeted throne room surrounded by his court.

The representatives of the British Army were Lieut. John Henry and a battle-stained and slightly embarrassed sergeant with a tommy-gun tucked under one arm.

Since the Germans occupied Tunisia the 71-year-old Bey had stayed in his palace, maintaining his State without interference and being allowed to retain his personal army of 1,000 men and 50 officers.

On three occasions von Arnim himself called at the Palace to pay his respects to the Bey and members of the royal family in an endeavour to please the native population.

PALACE SHELLED

But when the Germans had to flee they did not hesitate to shell Hammam Lif, and the palace, in an attempt to hold the British Army's advance

Shells were still bursting around the palace late on Monday when a major-general arrived to receive the Bey's official welcome and congratulations.

Outside the palace, on the left of the main entrance, the Bey's Guards, in claret uniforms with bright blue facings and with thick dark stripes down the sides of their trousers, were lined up.

On the right was the guard of our troops, and nearby, in an ecstasy of excitement, was the Bey's royal band.

Our troops presented arms with clockwork precision and the British and ancient French muskets.

Enemy aircraft dropped bombs earlier in the day in the same area. Casualties included some deaths.

The band played the "Marseillaise" and "God Save the King."

Continued Back Page **A**

GERMANS MAY NOW END SHACKLING

By the Military Critic

With the exception of mopping up, the operations are over in Northern Tunisia.

The circuit of the peninsula has now been completed. The whole of the coastline is in our hands. The count of prisoners has not yet been completed.

The American Second Corps alone has taken 38,000 prisoners. The total is not likely to fall far short of 160,000.

The significance of these numbers affects issues other than strategy—issues constantly in the minds of people in this country.

NAZIS REPORT ATTACK

The barbarous shackling of British prisoners was an enemy measure he could never have contemplated had the prisoners on either side been numerically equal. Before this week the number of British prisoners in German hands was in round numbers 90,000. Germans in British hands numbered 36,000.

Today the position is reversed. The Allies will now add some 100,000 Germans to their original total.

This fact in itself should be sufficient to enable pressure to be brought with sufficient force to the enemy to abandon their monstrous disregard of the rules of warfare.

Soviet Air Raids as Prelude to Offensive

From Our Special Correspondent

MOSCOW, Wednesday.

NEWS of heavy fighting is expected here ; the intense Soviet air activity on many sectors of the front is the prelude to new offensives.

The Germans also started an air offensive, choosing as their principal objective the railways round Rostov, apparently trying to prevent Russian oil supplies reaching the front lines by the direct route.

The Luftwaffe attack against the station of Cheremnikovo, on the Kursk-Voronezh railway, was doubtless intended as a warning against concentrating troops which might threaten the flank of the Nazi wedge in the Mtsensk and Orel areas, which the invaders obviously consider to be rather vulnerable.

In the Kuban the Russians continue methodically to break up the second defence line round Novorossiisk.

Enough U.S. War Plant to Beat Axis

WASHINGTON, Wednesday.

A SWEEPING reduction in construction of new war plant and in machine tool output was ordered today by the War Production Board.

This was taken because, it was said, the United States now has the plants and tools needed to build production to beat the Axis.

It is estimated that £1,000,000,000 worth of approved Government-financed plants, projects, and machine tool contracts will be cancelled. This means that we can do the job needed to win the war on existing plant and plant-construction already stopped.

The announcement means that the machine tool bottleneck is finally broken, and a number of tool makers will now turn to direct production of munitions.

DAKAR CRUISER SINKS U-BOAT SUPPLY SHIP

Dakar, Wednesday.—The first major success of the Allied Dakar French fleet against the Germans was scored when the 7,800-ton French cruiser Georges Leygues sank a large German submarine supply ship on April 13 in the South Atlantic, and returned to port with 90 prisoners.

April Raid Casualties

Civilian casualties due to air raids in the United Kingdom during the month of April were : Killed (or missing believed killed) 172 ; injured and detained in hospital 265.

Rommel and Keitel Go To Salonika

ROMMEL and Keitel, German Chief-of-Staff, have arrived in Salonika for a military council on the defence of the Balkans.

German troops continue to arrive in Greece and Bulgaria.

In Bulgaria a man and a woman have been arrested for the attempted assassination of Jalieff, who was tracking down anti-Government radios, and the newspaper "Zora" now declares that "terrorist students" are the advance guard of the enemy.

A gun battle was fought in Sofia yesterday when police traced three wanted "Communists" to their hiding-place, according to the German radio, which said one of the men was killed and the other two were arrested.

Dimitrov, Bulgarian Communist, who lived in Moscow after being acquitted at the Reichstag fire trial in 1933, is now in Bulgaria, rousing Bulgarian opposition to the Nazis.—Reuter.

Berlin's order that all German civilians leave Bulgaria is being cemented, but, under Gestapo pressure, more than 800 have left already.

The Zagreb newspaper "Hrvatski Narod" reports heavy fighting in East Bosnia between German and patriot forces.—B.U.P.

Mosquitos Shoot Up Locomotives

Five locomotives were shot up by two Mosquitos of Fighter Command who went out over France yesterday afternoon.

Two were claimed by an Australian pilot, who damaged six trains in the space of six minutes recently. He dived on to a goods train and pulled it with cannon and machine-gun fire.

"Large pieces flew into the air," he said, "and the train stopped with smoke pouring from it. Half-way to Folligny I saw another train and gave it the same treatment. The first-box was hit and this train did not go any further."

Churchill Has Long Conference With Roosevelt: Wavell and India Service Chiefs are Also in U.S.

From ROBERT WAITHMAN, News Chronicle Correspondent

WASHINGTON, Wednesday.

MR. CHURCHILL, who had a long conference with President Roosevelt at the White House today, has come to Washington with a staff that includes Field-Marshal Sir Archibald Wavell, C.-in-C., India, Air Marshal Sir Richard Peirse, A.O.C., India, and Admiral Somerville, C.-in-C., Eastern Fleet (based on Ceylon).

The Prime Minister has come to map out with the President a plan which contemplates the junction of our forces and the pooling of our reserves for offensives on two sides of the world.

No other interpretation of the Washington meetings that have begun today is possible. Nor can it be doubted that the strategy which will now be worked out here is a direct outcome of the victory in North Africa.

A new route to the Middle East is open, and forces and supplies hitherto scattered can be unified and continuously reinforced along a broad lifeline reaching from the U.S. across the Atlantic to the Mediterranean and the Middle East to India.

Against this immensely improved background, the invasion of Europe, the greater reinforcement of Russia, reconquest of Burma, and the rescue of China can be co-ordinated ; and all indications are that the planning of the greatest global offensive in history is now under way.

ELECTRIFYING

The Prime Minister reached the White House in time for dinner last night.

The visit of Mr. Churchill to the White House retains its capacity for electrifying the U.S. capital, and for capturing the interest of Americans everywhere.

As the New York "Herald-Tribune" says today, the visit in itself can assure us that the new Allied gains will be "exploited with the same vigour, coherence and singleness of strategic purpose that made victory (in North Africa) possible."

Lord Beaverbrook has also arrived here, but he is not a member of the official party.

Casablanca Men In Washington

Besides the India Service chiefs, Mr. Churchill's team in Washington includes Lord Leathers, Minister of War Transport and Shipping ; Major-Gen. Sir Hastings Ismay, secretary, Committee of Imperial Defence ; Admiral of the Fleet Sir Dudley Pound, First Sea Lord and Chief of Naval Staff ; Lieut.-Gen. Sir Alan Brooke, C.I.G.S. (all of whom were at Casablanca) ; Air Chief Marshal Sir Charles Portal, Chief of Air Staff ; Lord Cherwell, statistical adviser ; and Brig. E. Jacob, assistant (military) secretary to the War Cabinet.

Premier to Broadcast

The Premier will broadcast from America at 9 p.m. on Friday.

ARNIM—AND 11 OTHER GENERALS

Allied H.Q., North Africa.—Maj.-General Count von Blomch, commanding the 90th Light Infantry Division, and Maj.-General Borch, commanding the 10th Panzer Division, are among the German generals now in our hands. With Arnim are 11 Axis generals who have been taken prisoner.

LONDON BLACK-OUT
10.25 p.m.—5.26 a.m.
Moon rises 2.5 a.m., sets 4.16 a.m. tomorrow. Full Moon May 19.

THE GREAT SURRENDER: SOME OF THE 25,000 GERMANS WHO YIELDED AT BIZERTA

ONLY once before has it been possible to take a picture like this—that was at Stalingrad. For the men you see here, packed almost shoulder-to-shoulder in a prisoners' cage, are Germans.

With a few Italians, they are some of the 25,000 who surrendered unconditionally to the United States Second Corps after the fall of Bizerta

Before they yielded the enemy tried to embark troops in barges and small coastal vessels. The R.A.F. soon put a stop to that. Then the white flag went up. More pictures on Back Page.

GERMAN MASS SURRENDERS ASTONISH THE BRITISH

With the First Army, Cape Bon, Tuesday night.

THE British major, who had been through Dunkirk, just stood by and watched — bewildered and astonished at the complete disintegration of the Axis forces on Cape Bon Peninsula even before they were hit.

"It's incredible," he kept saying. "They had plenty of guns, damn good positions and millions of mines. They could have put up a terrific fight, but they just packed up. Why?

"Our retreat in France was nothing like this. We fought back every yard, and with none of the things the enemy has here. The only difference is that the

From NED RUSSELL, B.U.P. War Correspondent

Luftwaffe's useless, but they had everything else to fight with."

All along the line our men—from privates up to leading officers—are also astonished. It has been a wild, fantastic day, like something out of "Alice in Wonderland."

It began at 3 a.m. with single reconnaissance cars taking prisoners in batches of hundreds at a time, and merely leading them to the camp.

DRIVING THEMSELVES

Driving across the peninsula, I saw more German vehicles than I have seen in the past six months. Every one was jammed with Axis prisoners.

The prisoners were driving themselves into captivity without guards in most cases. When the lorries were empty at the camp, the prisoners drove them back to get more prisoners.

I saw one batch of 500 prisoners who were indignant because we assigned four men to guard them. Even that four was mere formality.

It must have been the first time that any war correspondent has been free to drive anywhere he pleased into the German lines.

Dozens of them came up to me from the fields with their hands up when I stopped. They were surrendering to anyone in Allied uniform, holding up white flags and grinning thankfully when they were formally told they were captured. It was just as simple as that.

Occasionally I saw a guard, perhaps for a convoy of prisoners in lorries, but generally nothing more than one reconnaissance car. On the way we passed several German camps littered with abandoned equipment, rifles and cases

of ammunition. The troops had obviously died in panic.

The British forces simply drove into the German positions regardless of any danger. Sometimes a German picket in the hills would try to shell them, but the British Tommies went in and cleaned them up. The resistance was never more than half-hearted.

GOERING'S MEN GIVE UP

At one stage the remnants of the Hermann Goering Division unleashed a terrible barrage with all their guns to the hills on the western coast of the peninsula.

Then—crazy as it seems—they stopped for no reason, walked out on the road with their hands up and surrendered.

One German trooper I saw now knows what it was like on the other side in Greece and Yugo-Slavia. He was protesting bitterly as I went by but he had had to fight tanks with a rifle.

▲ NEWS CHRONICLE, LONDON, THURSDAY MAY 13, 1943

For the Wehrmacht, the collapse in North Africa was Germany's next great military defeat after Stalingrad. On Hitler's southern flank, the fighting would now move to the Mediterranean island of Sicily.

North Africa

MAY 1943

IN FEBRUARY 1943 ROMMEL HAD DEFEATED U.S. FORCES AT THE BATTLE OF THE KASSERINE PASS. HOWEVER, THIS GERMAN SUCCESS DID LITTLE MORE THAN DELAY THE INEVITABLE ALLIED VICTORY IN NORTH AFRICA. AFTER Kasserine, Rommel initiated an attack in March 1943, against Montgomery's forces at Medinine. The Germans assembled some 160 tanks, 200 artillery pieces, and 10,000 troops. However, Montgomery met the attack with 400 tanks, 350 artillery pieces, and 470 antitank guns. The weight of Allied numbers defeated Rommel's thrust and inflicted heavy casualties on Axis forces.

THE AXIS COLLAPSE

Medinine proved to be Rommel's last battle in North Africa, as Hitler recalled him back to Germany on sick leave. His attack, however, had weakened the Axis ability to withstand renewed British attacks in late March and early April 1943 that ruptured the Mareth Line defenses. By mid-April, the combined Anglo-American assaults from the west and Montgomery's advance from the south forced the Axis into a small perimeter around Tunis and Bizerte based on the last ring of hills before the open coastal plain. Axis soldiers continued to resist bravely, despite the obviously unfavorable circumstances. Hitler hoped that the resilient troops of Army Group Africa could hold their precarious bridgehead in Tunisia for a few more months to tie down Allied forces. The final battle for Tunisia took place in May when Allied forces pierced the Axis perimeter. The German commander, von

Arnim, had committed all his reserves, and the Luftwaffe was in the process of withdrawing to Sicily, so it was therefore unable to provide ground support. Allied units entered Tunis on May 7, and French and British forces surrounded the Italian First Army. This precipitated a mass surrender among Axis units. On May 12, the war in North Africa came to an end. Some 275,000 Germans and Italians entered captivity.

▲ FIELD GUNS AND VEHICLES of the British Royal Artillery Regiment on the road to Tunis in April 1943, during the last phase of the campaign in North Africa.

DAILY MIRROR, Tuesday, May 18, 1943.

Daily Mirror

MAY 18

No. 12,299
ONE PENNY

Registered at the G.P.O. as a Newspaper.

HUNS GET A FLOOD BLITZ

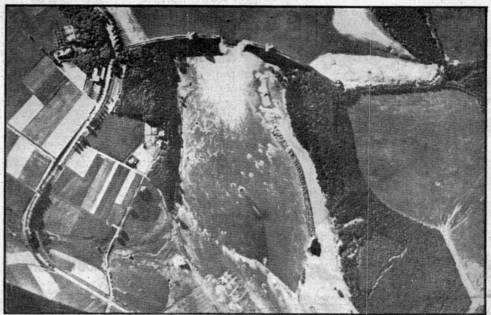

In this picture taken soon after the raid the great gap in the dam caused by mines can be seen. The valley below is inundated and the power house, seen in the other picture, is reduced to wreckage over which the torrent swirls.

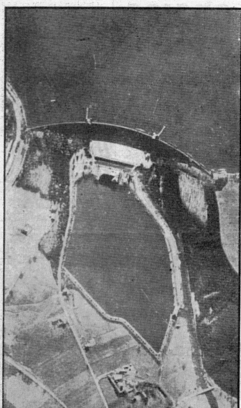

The Mohne Dam before the attack, showing the power house and the flood-free valley.

TORRENT RAGES ALONG RUHR

Factories smashed to pieces

HUNDREDS of square miles of devastation have spread through the Ruhr, Germany's most vital and most densely-populated industrial area, by the RAF's staggering attack on the Mohne and Eder dams, two of the biggest in the world.

Reconnaissance planes which dashed across Germany yesterday brought back an amazing record of the destruction which the force of Lancasters, led by Wing-Commander G. P. Gibson—who returned safely—unleashed when they shattered the dam walls with mines.

"The floods are spreading fast," reported the RAF.

"The waters are sweeping down the Ruhr valley. Railways and road bridges are broken down. Hydro-electrical power stations are destroyed or damaged. A railway marshalling yard is under water.

"The floods from the breached Eder dam are already as great as the floods in the Ruhr valley, but the country here is flatter and the water likely to spread over a greater area."

Swept Away

In the upper Ruhr the rush of the waters was so great from the Mohne reservoir, which contained 134,000,000 tons of water, that in the Dortmund area, twenty-five miles west of the reservoir, floods are rising steadily.

The Mohne dam, stretching across the western end of the reservoir which, in its fullest length, is about five miles, had been shattered for a length of one hundred yards.

The rush of waters was so great that the power station below the dam was swept away.

The Eder Dam was breached in two places. There was a hole

about 30 feet below the top of the wall, and another gap to the eastern side of the dam. Airmen say a torrent of water poured through and, below, a wave of some 30 feet high rushed through the valley.

It was in the early hours of yesterday morning, when the weather and light were exactly right, that the Lancasters roared in low through terrific fire.

Besides the Mohne and Eder dams, the Sorpe Dam, also on the River Mohne, was attacked.

Drew Enemy Fire

Wing-Commander Gibson, D.S.O. and Bar, D.F.C. and Bar, who was in charge of the whole operation, led the attack on the Mohne Dam. After he had dropped his mines he flew up and down alongside the dam to draw the fire of the light A.A. guns on it.

Guns were poking out of slots in the walls of the dam. The Lancaster's gunners fired back as Gibson repeatedly flew through the barrage, and this made some of the Germans' fire waver.

A flight-lieutenant, who dropped his mines later, said: "I was able to watch the whole process. The wing-commander's load was placed just right. A spout of water went up 300 feet into the air.

"A second Lancaster attacked

Continued on Back Page

LONDON ALERT

An Alert was sounded in the London area shortly before midnight. It was of short duration. Gunfire was heard and a bomb which fell damaged a house. The number of raiders is believed to have been very small.

NAZI BLOCKADE-RUNNER BAGGED BY COUSIN OF THE QUEEN

TWO more enemy blockade-runners have been scuttled after the Navy had intercepted them.

One of them was stopped by the Queen's first cousin, Captain R. G. Bowes-Lyon, M.V.O., who was in command of the cruiser Adventure.

Adventure sighted the German armed ship Silvaplana (4,793 tons) about 200 miles off Cape Finisterre, inward bound from the Far East with a valuable cargo of rubber and tin.

Within a few minutes, even before Silvaplana had lost way, the Germans proceeded to abandon ship.

The ship began to blaze and then sank.

The entire ship's company, including more than 100 Germans were rescued.

The other blockade-runner, the German motor vessel Regensburg (8,068 tons) was also heavily laden.

She was intercepted between Greenland and Iceland by the cruiser Glasgow (Captain E. M. Evans-Lombe).

Regensburg fired scuttling charges and her crew abandoned ship.

Every effort was made to rescue them but, owing to icy water and heavy weather, only six were saved.

Pyjama death riddle

A PYJAMA-CLAD woman, wife of a War Office official, was found dead with severe injuries at the back of her head in the gas-filled kitchen of her home at Barnet, Herts, yesterday.

Her neck was broken. She lay at the opposite side of the kitchen from the gas stove, the taps of which were turned full on.

She was Mrs. Elsie Roe, 33, of Greenhill Park, Barnet, whose 37-year-old husband, Mr. G. Roe, holds an important position in

the signals section in the War Office.

At first the tragedy—discovered by a milk woman who smelt gas fumes and phoned the police—had every appearance of suicide.

But detectives found head injuries and neighbours told of screams they had heard about 6.55 a.m.

Most had paid no attention as they had heard many disturbances during the night owing to the air raids.

Mrs. T. F. Morris, next-door neighbour, told the Daily Mirror

last night: "Mrs. Roe was an attractive woman and a devoted mother. She did war work in a St. Albans office."

Mr. Morris said: "We talked about the screams, but decided they were caused by a dog run over by a bus."

Mr. and Mrs. Roe spent several years in Nairobi, Kenya. They returned to England because of their two daughters, who were born there.

The girls, now aged 11 and 9, are at a convent boarding school at Hitchin, Herts.

A man was detained by the police last night.

▲ DAILY MIRROR, LONDON, TUESDAY MAY 18, 1943
The now legendary "Dambusters" Raid by RAF Lancaster bombers of 617 Squadron, led by Wing Commander Guy Gibson, was against the dams on the Möhne and Eder Rivers. The press exaggerated the amount of damage the raid inflicted on German industry.

New York World-Telegram

Copyright, 1943, by New York World-Telegram Corporation. All rights reserved.

Local Forecast: Cooler today, moderate to low humidity. Sunset, 8:31 p. m. Dimout, 9:31 p. m.

NIGHT
Latest Wall St. Prices

3 CENTS IN NEW YORK CITY
4c in Suburbs—5c Elsewhere

VOL. 75—NO. 307—IN TWO SECTIONS—SECTION ONE   NEW YORK, WEDNESDAY, JUNE 30, 1943.   Entered as second class matter Post Office, New York, N. Y.   'A'

U-BOATS' DEFEAT TOTAL THIS MONTH--CHURCHILL

U.S. LANDS ON JAP ISLE

'We'll Fight Until Japan Bites Dust'

War Work Seen Hit By Feuds in Capital

Also Are Expected to Affect Democratic Presidential Drive

By LYLE C. WILSON, United Press Staff Correspondent

EXTRA
By the United Press.

WASHINGTON, June 30.—Combined U. S. forces, striking the first blow in a new American offensive in the Pacific, have landed on Rendova Island in the Central Solomons, only five miles from the Jap base at Munda.

Riots Reported Sweeping Greece

Barrage Balloons Rise on L.I. To Protect Military Objective

Army and navy officers watch a demonstration of antiaircraft defenses on Long Island.

By HARRISON SALISBURY, United Press Staff Correspondent

LONDON, June 30.—Prime Minister Churchill said in a speech at Guild Hall today that the Allies had achieved a "total defeat" of the German U-boat attack in May and June—sinking more than 40 in May alone—and that Great Britain would fight on until Japan submits or "bites the dust."

Allied Raids on Reich Pay Off at $50 to $1

▲ NEW YORK WORLD-TELEGRAM, WEDNESDAY JUNE 30, 1943
U-boat losses in the Battle of the Atlantic were high in April and May 1943: 45 were destroyed. The U-boat threat diminished thereafter.

▲ A GERMAN U-BOAT IS DESTROYED by an Allied aircraft in the Battle of the Atlantic. Allied radar, longrange aircraft, and better weapons effectively ensured the defeat of the U-boats in 1943.

▲ DAILY MAIL, LONDON, FRIDAY JULY 2, 1943
The task of clearing Japanese forces from New Guinea and the Island of New
Britain was the responsibility of General Walter Krueger's U.S. Sixth Army,
under the supervision of Douglas MacArthur.

The Daily Telegraph
and Morning Post

No. 27,482   LONDON, MONDAY, JULY 12, 1943   Printed in LONDON and MANCHESTER   PRICE 1½d.

4 A.M.

ALL FIRST OBJECTIVES IN SICILY CAPTURED

LAND FORCES LINK UP WITH PARATROOPS

THREE AIRFIELDS NOW IN OUR HANDS

ALLIED ARMS & MEN STREAM INTO ISLAND

Continued progress in the Allied invasion of Sicily was reported in the following special communiqué from Gen. Eisenhower's headquarters received in London at 10.30 last night:

" Three Sicilian airfields are in our hands, and all first immediate objectives are believed to have been taken.

" American and British landing forces made contact with paratroops which had been dropped at selected points in Sicily on Friday night and Saturday.

" At the same time the main body of enemy forces has not yet been met.

" All reports of fighting say that contact has been made with Italian coastal defence units rather than with any mobile enemy forces."

An earlier communiqué [reported in Page 3] stated that casualties in the initial operations were believed to have been light.

The captured airfields are understood to consist of one at Pachino, a small town on the south-eastern tip of the island, three miles inland from Cape Passero, and two at Gela, a small port on the south coast, 20 miles west of the inland town of Ragusa.

Throughout yesterday streams of reinforcements—men, guns, ammunition and stores—were being landed under cover of the guns of the vast fleet of Allied warships and of our air forces.

2,000 SHIPS IN INVASION FLEET

Thus the second phase of the attack—the first was the initial landings—has been opened within 48 hours of the first glider troops descending on the island at 10.15 on Friday night. These were followed at 11.30 p.m. by parachute battalions.

By destroying enemy strongpoints and disrupting communications these airborne forces paved the way for the great invasion armada of 2,000 vessels, which began to land the main advanced forces at 2.45 a.m. on Saturday along 100 miles of the south and south-east coast of the island.

Guns of the warships pounded the enemy defence points; hundreds of aircraft swept the island, attacking airfields, road and rail communications, and enemy troop concentrations.

By six a.m. Admiral of the Fleet Sir Andrew Cunningham was able to wireless Gen. Eisenhower that the success of the operation was assured.

By 11 a.m. Air Chief Marshal Sir Arthur Tedder reported to the Supreme C.-in-C. that complete mastery of the Sicilian skies had been won.

As the advanced troops fought their way inland more troops with heavier weapons were being poured ashore.

The British forces appear to have formed the most easterly invading force with the Canadians in the centre and the Americans on the west in the Gela-Licata sector.

COASTLINE IN OUR HANDS

Last night it was reported that the whole of the 100 miles of coast-line which we had attacked was firmly in our hands and that Allied troops, having pierced the main coastal defences at many points, were advancing inland and joining up with the airborne troops.

Linking up behind Cape Passero, British and Canadian troops have captured the town Pachino, as well as the airfield outside it. A little to the west the Canadians have seized an enemy strong point in the hills one and a half miles from the coast, wiping out strong gun positions.

In the Gela area, where the Americans have captured two airfields, one on the coast and the other inland, Italian troops—only Italians have been encountered anywhere as yet—tried to repel them with a tank attack. But this attack was smashed before it could develop by salvoes from warships firing off the coast.

A Washington report last night said the Americans had reached the outskirts of the port of Gela. Other forces have cut the main coast railway further inland.

Despite Axis claims to have sunk many big ships, it is known that only a very small number were lost—all of them small ships. The Navy was able to report, " Casualties light."

Of the Italian Navy there has been no sign except for a small formation of E-boats seen at one point. These made off at high speed as soon as the spearhead of the invasion fleet was sighted.

Official Allied announcements so far contain little detailed information as to the actual progress made. The reason for this is that the inclusion of place names might give valuable information to the enemy, whose system of communication, for some time at least, was in danger of paralysis through the successful bombing of their headquarters at Taormina, on the east coast between Catania and Messina.

Berlin radio last night announced that the Axis forces, which are believed to total 400,000, including 100,000 veteran German troops, counter attacked at dawn yesterday. This presumably is the counter-attack—the only one reported in Allied communiqués—made by local Axis forces defending Gela.

According to Berlin military spokesmen yesterday one of the chief points of the Allied attack is round Syracuse. Should this fall, they said, Gen. Eisenhower would at once be able to land his main forces of armour.

Other Axis reports reaching Stockholm state that Licata and Canicatte, on the southern coast, are already in Allied hands, and that there is bitter fighting round Ragusa, only a few miles north-west of Pachino.

Early to-day it was reported by Gen. Eisenhower's headquarters that several thousand Canadian reinforcements were landed in North Africa within 24 ourhs of the Sicilian attack starting. Another big troop convoy from England arrived shortly afterwards.

Our Military Correspondent's Review—P2

THE CANADIANS "WALKED IN"

LARGE BRIDGEHEAD ESTABLISHED

From ROSS MUNRO,
Canadian Press War Correspondent
WITH THE CANADIANS IN SICILY,
Saturday (delayed).

Behind the enormous naval and air night bombardment the Canadians practically walked into Sicily. They met very little determined resistance on their beaches four miles south-west of Pachino on the south-east tip of the island.

They smashed through the beach defences as soon as they were set ashore and the infantry attacked inland, establishing an extensive bridgehead which was the Canadians' initial task in the invasion plan.

Some stubborn resistance has been put up by the Italians north and west of Pachino, and along other sectors of the front there have been heated engagements.

Big battles will probably come before long, but meanwhile numbers of prisoners are being captured. They have been coming from the front since dawn in batches of 50 or 100, guarded by one or two Canadians.

So far Canadian casualties appear to be very light. On one beach where two assault units landed, there were only had a dozen men wounded.

I landed at 5.15 this morning from a naval launch which guided assault infantry to the beach. There was scarcely a shot fired as I passed through the wire and penetrated into the countryside.

Two companies had got in shortly before us on our beach, and they, and some sappers, seemed to have a sharp engagement, but broke through the wire beach defences in about 15 minute.

(Continued on P. 4, Col. 6)

EISENHOWER THANKS NAVIES

'PERFECT TECHNIQUE'

From a Special Correspondent Representing the Combined British Press
ALLIED N. AFRICAN H.Q., Sunday.

Gen. Eisenhower to-day paid the following tribute to the work of the Allied navies in the Sicilian landings:

" In the Sicilian operation the United States and Royal Navies have again proved that even while engaged in operations covering the seven seas they can plan and successfully execute vast and intricate movements in support of land operations and ever in the remotest obstacles of distance, weather and enemy opposition.

" In this theatre the skill of the Allied naval commanders and staff under the leadership of Admiral of the Fleet Cunningham and his principal lieutenants—the American Vice-Admiral Hewitt and British Admiral Bertram Ramsay—are reflected in the precise timing and perfect technique displayed on the beaches of Sicily, where there were landed hundreds of ships and boats whose ports of origin were scattered over half a world.

" Their comrades of the air and ground forces unite in an enthusiastic and grateful 'well done.'

It can now be revealed that more than 2,000 vessels were involved in the landing operations.

The only enemy vessels seen by our ships were a small group of Italian E-boats, which made off at high speed when they saw the Allied navies.

CORSICA ALARM

AXIS SEND TROOPS FROM FRANCE
MADRID, Sunday.

The shifting of the Axis European forces as a result of the invasion of Sicily has led to the further strengthening of the Axis coastal garrisons from the Gulf of Lyons and the Pyrenees to Italy, according to frontier reports reaching here.

Coastal cargo boats of small French Mediterranean ports, with the Germans have been reconditioning as speedily as possible, are taking reinforcements to Corsica, the reports stated.

The island has been in a state of alarm, ever since the Sicily landing was announced, that the United Nations' strength in the Mediterranean will enable them to make other landings at the same time as the Sicilian operations.

Frontier reports indicated that even the Atlantic fortifications of Southern France have been called upon to provide troops for strengthening the Mediterranean defences of the Axis.—A.P.

FIRST PRISONERS AT DAWN

From Reuter's Special Correspondent
ON THE SICILIAN BEACHES,
Sunday Night.

The first Italian prisoners were made at dawn on the first day of the landing. They came down from the hills where they had been fighting and surrendered. Some waved the white flag.

A British naval officer commented: " The same as at Pantellaria."

At noon, barely nine hours after the initial attack went in, a seemingly endless chain of grey warships of the Royal Navy was streaming up and down while infantry and tank landing craft, arrived in succession.—Reuter.

This Morning's War News

Sicily
All first objectives captured. (P1)
First stage of attack successfully passed; airborne units paved way. (Pp 1 & 4)
Canadians walked in. (Pp 1 & 4)
Berlin admits "provisional success." (P1)
" Great risks must be taken."—Message to Navy. (P1)
Gliders made 200-mile trip. (P2)
Air, land and sea blows: communiqués. (P4)
Axis account. (P4)

Russia
Russians hold firm on both sectors of Kursk salient. Attack by 400 tanks north of salient repelled. (P1)

Air
Fortresses claim 1,100 German planes. (P2)

Solomons
Japanese convoy bombed. (P5)

FIRST STAGE OF ATTACK SUCCESSFULLY PASSED

AIRBORNE UNITS PAVED W

From RONALD LEGGE,
Daily Telegraph Special Correspondent
ALLIED H.Q., N. AFRICA, Sunday.

We have successfully passed the first stage of our assault on Sicily and are gradually amassing strength for the bigger clashes to come when we encounter the enemy's main strategic strength.

The completion of this opening stage has been marked by the linking up of our airborne troops with the main body of our invading forces.

It is now known that we have captured the airfield at Pachino, in the southern tip, where the British and Canadians form the attacking force. The Americans have captured two airfields in the Gela area.

Resistance so far has not been very strong or concentrated, and Italian troops only have been encountered. Considerably heavier fighting may be expected later, when the enemy counter-attacks develop and we make contact with the main body of resistance.

MOBILE DEFENCE PLAN

The Axis are obviously using mobile defence methods rather than the cordon system, in view of the long coast-line to be protected and Allied ability to strike suddenly in unexpected places.

The first indication of any exact locality where beach landings had been made came this afternoon, when a naval communiqué referred to the successful beating off of an enemy counter-attack at Gela, in south-eastern Sicily, midway along the coastline of the gulf of that name. American troops engaged in this sector repelled tank reinforcements coming from the interior.

Gela is situated on the main road running along the entire south coast as far as that point, where it sweeps inland slightly towards Ragusa. It is also at the junction with another main road running northwards, off which branch a number of bridging mountain highways giving access to Butera westwards and Nisceml eastwards. There are important airfields in both these localities.

(Continued on P. 4, Col. 3)

DUCE'S APPEAL TO KING OF ITALY
ZURICH, Sunday.

A Rome message reaching here states that Mussolini has asked the King to address the nation.

The message also states that the police have been ordered to take severe measures to prevent panic. A great number of arrests have been made at Naples.

Pavolini, Mussolini's former Propaganda Minister, will address the nation to-morrow and ask the people to maintain complete discipline. Scorza, the Fascist party chief, called an urgent meeting of the directorate to-night.—Exchange.

BERLIN ADMITS

"GREAT RISKS MUST BE TAKEN"
—Order to

*From EDWARD GILLINA
Representing the Combined*
ALLIED FORCE COMMAND,
Sunday

An inspiring message to all ships taking part in the invasion of Sicily was sent by Admiral of the Fleet Cunningham, C.-in-C., Mediterranean, the day night. It stated:

" We are about to embark on the most momentous enterprise of the war—striking for the first time at the enemy in his own land.

" Success means the opening of the Second Front, with all that it implies, and the first move towards the rapid and decisive defeat of our enemies.

" Our object is clear, our primary duty is to place our expeditionary forces in the enemy country and subsequently to maintain our military and air forces in the field.

" It is the fight of this duty which must be and are kept before us. The safety of our ships and all distracting considerations must be regarded as of second place or disregarded.

" In every commanding officer and rating rests the final and personal duty of seeing that flinching in determination or failure of effort on his part will hamper this great operation.

" I rest confident in the resolution, skill and endurance of you all to whom this momentous enterprise is entrusted."

LATE NEWS

GUERRILLA RAIDS 600 MILES IN NAZI REAR

Moscow radio reports guerrillas in Brest-Litovsk region, 600 miles behind German lines, wrecked 24 railway trains and raided German garrisons.

R.A.F. DAY RAIDS

R.A.F. Bostons yesterday bombed from tree-top level electrical power stations in Bethune area Northern France. Fighter Command Typhoons, Mustangs and Spitfires attacked locomotives, tugs, barges and lock gates in Belgium and France. Two planes missing.

MORE CANADIANS ARRIVE

Canadian reinforcements arrived North Africa, says A.P.

SIR HARRY OAKES'S NEW POLICE MOVE

Nassau, Bahamas.—Body of Sir Harry Oakes brought back here after plane had left with it for burial in U.S. and taken to mortuary from Nassau Hospital. Funeral had been arranged for to-day.—B.U.P.

LADY GOSCHEN DEAD

Viscountess Goschen died at her home, Seacox, Hawkhurst, Kent, yesterday, aged 81.
Obituary—P3

POPE SEES ENVOY

The Pope received Baron von Weizsacker, the German Ambassador to the Vatican, in a 20-minutes audience yesterday. German oversea radio announced.

RUSSIANS REPEL ATTACK BY 400 TANKS

GROUND GAINED NORTH OF KURSK

ENEMY HELD ON WHOLE FRONT

WEDGES BEING CUT OFF

FROM OUR OWN CORRESPONDENT
MOSCOW, Sunday.

The Russians are holding their own on both sectors—north and south—of the Kursk salient, despite seven days of terrific German pressure.

To-day the heaviest German attacks were switched from the Byelgorod area, in the south, to the northern part of the salient—but without success.

To-night's Soviet communiqué [received in London shortly before one o'clock this morning] stated:

" During to-day our troops in the Orel-Kursk direction [north of the Kursk salient] and the Byelgorod direction [south of the salient] continued to beat off attacks by enemy tanks and infantry.

" Our troops on both sectors during the day destroyed and disabled 162 German tanks. In air combat and by A.A. fire 31 enemy planes were shot down."

In the first week of the German offensive the Russians have knocked out 2,771 tanks and 1,068 planes.

A supplement to the communiqué said that the Germans, not having gained any successes during...

▲ THE DAILY TELEGRAPH, LONDON, MONDAY JULY 12, 1943
The invasion of Sicily was achieved by the U.S. Seventh Army and the British Eighth Army, using a total of 500,000 troops, airmen, and sailors.

▲ TROOPS OF THE BRITISH Eighth Army in Catania, Sicily. To capture the island cost U.S. forces 2,237 killed and 6,544 wounded. British losses were 12,843 dead and wounded.

Battle of Kursk

JULY 1943

J ULY 1943 WAS A KEY MONTH OF WORLD WAR II, WITH FIERCE FIGHTING EVERYWHERE. ON THE EASTERN FRONT, THE MAJOR GERMAN OFFENSIVE TO CRUSH SOVIET FORCES IN THE KURSK SALIENT (OPERATION CITADEL) LED TO A TITANIC BATTLE. GERMAN tactical skill proved very difficult for the Soviets to counter, but the Red Army stood firm, and its carefully-sited minefields and antitank guns took their toll. On July 12 a mass tank battle took place at Prokhorovka. Hundreds of tanks fought at close range, and, while the Soviet Fifth Guards Tank Army was almost destroyed, it succeeded in blunting the German offensive.

FAILURE AT KURSK

Hitler called off Citadel on July 13. This final major German offensive on the Eastern Front had been a costly failure, not least because Germany's carefully gathered strategic armored reserves had been lost. The Red Army now launched its own summer offensive. While the tank battle at Kursk in the Soviet Union was raging, German forces were also heavily engaged on the island of Sicily in the Mediterranean. The Hermann Göering Division had been shipped across to Sicily to bolster its defenders after the Allied landings. While the British forces under General Montgomery slugged it out with the German and Italian forces in the south of the island, General George Patton led U.S. units in a move round the north of Sicily that eventually forced the Axis defenders to withdraw to the Italian mainland. Patton proved himself to be an expert in mobile warfare, as well as demonstrating that he was a flamboyant and ruthless military commander.

THE PACIFIC WAR

Meanwhile, in the Pacific, there was also a great deal of tough combat action, where Australian troops were fighting hard in New Guinea, while U.S. forces were continuing to advance against the Japanese in the Solomon Islands.

▲ GERMAN INFANTRY HITCH A LIFT on a Panzer III tank during the Battle of Kursk. The Wehrmacht suffered 323 tanks destroyed during the confrontation with massive Red Army forces—losses that the Germans could ill afford.

The Daily Telegraph

and Morning Post

No. 27,492   LONDON, FRIDAY, JULY 23, 1943   Printed in LONDON and MANCHESTER   PRICE 1½d.

ALLIES ADVANCING ON NORTH SICILY COAST

CITIES AND TOWNS FALL AS TROOPS SWEEP ON

AXIS REINFORCEMENTS FLOWN TO ISLAND

HEAVY GERMAN LOSSES IN FRONT OF CATANIA

From RONALD LEGGE,
Daily Telegraph Special Correspondent
ALLIED H.Q., NORTH AFRICA, Thursday.

As the Americans and Canadians sweep through western and northern Sicily with little or no opposition, reinforcements of German troops are being flown to the island to man the defence line being hastily improvised across the north-eastern tip.

There is at present no indication of the precise point at which this line starts on the northern coast, but the southern end runs round the south-western slopes of Mount Etna to the Catania area.

In the west and north of the island towns are being occupied by Allied troops almost hourly. To-night they are only 15 miles from Palermo, capital of Sicily, and were reported to be occupying the ranges of hills dominating the northern coast.

In the extreme west they are reported to have occupied Marsala, which is stated to have been abandoned, and to be closing in on Trapani.

The Axis has evidently decided to abandon all its airfields, ports and naval bases in the island other than Messina, nearest point to the Italian mainland.

FRESH ALLIED FORCES LANDED

According to latest reports, fresh Allied troops with heavy equipment continue to land.

The Germans, who are using some of their reinforcements in an attempt to stem the tide of the Eighth Army's advance on Catania, are suffering an ever-mounting toll of casualties. But they are doing everything in the way of blowing up the bridges over roads and streams, to prevent a burst through in force.

The 15th Panzer Division which was operating north-east of Enna and was decisively defeated by the Canadians, is probably by now behind the "last ditch" defence line.

They appear, however, to have left rearguards to cover the road to Leonforte and Nicosia from Enna. Progress up this vital road is slow.

Once the battle of the Etna line begins Gen. Guzzone, the Axis C.-in-C., will find himself without local airfields and will have to depend on air support from the mainland.

AIR BASE TAKEN

First the Fascists Built

The latest list of captured towns includes Castelvetrano, Menfi, Sciacca, Caltabellotta, Bivona, San Stefano, Santa Caterina, Rammacca, Mussomeli, Campofranco, Marianopoli, Petroperzia, Mirabello and Mineo. Castelvetrano is the most important capture since the fall of Enna as it gives the Allies the use of one of the most modern airfields in Sicily.

Among the first built by the Fascist regime in the island it was used to accommodate and service planes patrolling the Sicilian Channel. It was from this airfield that came many of the bombers, torpedo-carrying aircraft and fighters that harried our Malta convoys in the dark days when the enemy won their short-lived ascendancy in the Mediterranean.

WHOLESALE SURRENDER

Bersaglieri's Record

All units of the Italian 26th (Assietta) Division which the Americans met in the west surrendered almost at the first shot. With Agrigento fell the reconstituted 10th Bersaglieri Regiment, famous and gloriously for the third time. Meanwhile the Italian-German "war" continues.

There have been further shootings by Italians of German officers who tried to prevent them surrendering.

On other occasions Germans have fired on Italians walking towards the American lines with white flags.

The chief concern of Italian prisoners seems to be that their families in Italy should be told that they are safe.

There may be some Italians still at liberty who ought to be in prison camps, for men taken around Gela complained that their officers had donned civilian clothing and went into hiding.

In the west the Americans have already destroyed 84 tanks and 160 aircraft and have seized 416 vehicles and vast quantities of ammunition, including 13,000,000 rounds of rifle ammunition.

Portrieres yesterday fought another round in the war for control of the air in the reconstituted Axis and struck further heavy blows in attacking the important Italian airfield at Grazanito, 80 miles north of Rome. Anti-aircraft fire was negligible and only one enemy fighter was sighted.

Hangars, administration buildings and parked aircraft were hit.

In addition to a sea-air bombardment of Crotone (described elsewhere on this page) Wellingtons made a direct hit on the important Italian airfield at the second night running. This time they raided the marshalling yards and dock installations.

Allied communiqués.—Ps.

Black-out (London) 10.48–5.24
Moon rises 1.17 a.m. to-morrow

U.S. AIRBORNE TROOPS ROUTED NAZI TANKS

VITAL PART IN SICILY LANDINGS

DAILY TELEGRAPH REPORTER
When American airborne troops landed in Sicily they drove back two waves of German tanks and knocked out 13 of them, some with bullets fired through the tank slits.

This was told us yesterday by Maj.-Gen. Joseph M. Swing, who was responsible under Gen. Eisenhower for co-ordinating the American plans. He has just arrived in London from Sicily on his way to the United States.

Gen. Swing said the Sicilian operation was the greatest airborne invasion yet made in one effort. He went on:

"When the Germans landed airborne troops on Crete they did so in a sort of shuttle service, without artillery. In Sicily we landed troops by air in one complete operation.

"The enemy armoured formations struck at our forces during the aerial landings near Gela. Fortunately one of our airborne combat teams, with light howitzers and other infantry weapons, was ready to deal with them.

"It took the whole brunt of the enemy attack at this point. These youngsters won the average age was just over 21, landed right between our line and that of the German 15th Panzer Division.

"They waited deliberately before firing and opened many hits—in some cases with rifle bullets aimed at the tank slits at 50 yards range. The tanks broke under the onslaught and retired twice.

"The airborne troops kept the German panzer division off all day Sunday and well into Monday. If that one lone combat team had not been on the spot the operation in the island area might well have ended in a serious débâcle."

GAINED ALLIES A WEEK IN SICILY

GLIDER SUCCESS

By Air Commodore Howard-Williams
Daily Telegraph Air Correspondent

Outstanding success attached to first use of glider-borne British troops in Sicily on the night of July 10. According to Gen. Montgomery, they made all the difference to the battle for Syracuse, and probably put us a week ahead in schedule.

Our parachute troops have also contributed materially to the success of the operations. Particularly was this so in the capture and denial to the enemy of the important bridge at Primosole, near Catania, on July 14. Troops which were dropped behind the Eighth Army and contributed so much to their early advances were British.

Two types of glider were used, most of them the American Waco, called the Hadrian, which carries about 11 tons or 15 troops, and the British Horsa.

The weapons carried by parachute troops include the Sten and Bren guns, the rifle and grenades.

To-day a British airborne division is stronger in fire-power than the German units landed in Crete.

This Morning's War News

Sicily
As Allies sweep on western and northern Sicily towards coast, German reinforcements are arriving by air to man "last ditch" defence line in north-east tip of island. (P1)
Italian port shelled. (P1)
Marsala's fall rumoured. (P1)
British infantry forced vital bridgehead. (P1)
"Montgomery massing artillery," says Bertorius. (P1)
U.S. airborne troops routed Nazi tanks. (P1)

Russia
Russians capture Bolkhov, 35 miles north-west of Orel. In 10 days 50,000 Germans killed. (P1)

Balkans
Invasion nerves and riots. (P1)

Parliament
Pensions Appeal Bill concession; reforms urged in Foreign Office; early war statement unlikely. (P3)

Mr. Churchill
Premier sees post-war task for Liberalism. (P3)

Midwives' Charter
National scales of pay and uniform for midwives. (P3)

New Constituencies
Scheme to redistribute Parliamentary seats in constituencies of 50,000 voters. (P3)

United States
Strike holds up plane production. (P5)
Mr. Patterson discloses Mussolini refused to declare Rome an open city. (P5)

Workmen's Compensation
Proposed workmen's compensation terms prematurely disclosed at Mineworkers' Conference. (P5)

Gen. Giraud
One aim, French Army to free France. (P5)

BRITISH INFANTRY FORCED VITAL BRIDGEHEAD

WAY TO CATANIA OPENED

Continuing his account of the Battle of the Simeto river, Our Special Correspondent, in the despatch below, describes how the Eighth Army overcame Nazi resistance.

From CHRISTOPHER BUCKLEY,
Daily Telegraph Special Correspondent
WITH THE EIGHTH ARMY, Sunday (delayed).

Under the light of a full moon last night, British infantry, supported by an artillery barrage, tanks and armoured cars, opened the road to Catania by breaking out forward from the bridge at Primosole over the Simeto river.

The enemy had already begun to withdraw their infantry and guns in the later part of yesterday afternoon and little opposition was encountered save on the left, or inland, flank from 88mm guns protecting the Gerbini airfields.

The battle of the bridgehead was really won in the course of yesterday, following the bitter fighting—much the hardest yet experienced in Sicily—of the previous three days.

I am now able to give the first connected account of the battle of the bridgehead from the time of the link-up on Wednesday of the British infantry with parachutists who had first seized the bridge the previous day.

The position at the end of Tuesday's fighting was that British parachutists had been driven from the north bank of the Simeto but maintained their position on the southern side.

Before dawn on Thursday reinforced British infantry went into action, recaptured the bridge and established a small infantry bridgehead on the northern bank.

All day on Thursday and Friday desperate fighting went on as the northern approaches to the bridge, our men seeking to extend their foothold and the enemy to wipe out troops who had crossed to re-establish themselves on the river line.

TANKS DRIVEN BACK

So pushed down were our infantry at this time that they were not able to extend their foothold to a greater depth than 100 yards beyond the bridge. They were precariously dug in one-man holes in the meadows and river bank, and that was all.

Friday was the critical day. The enemy were fully alive to the importance of the bridgehead and had concentrated very considerable fire-power—88mm field guns, mortars and tanks. A few of our tanks got across the bridge in the course of the day but were promptly driven back.

The difficulty was that the presence of the enemy's 88mm guns up Catania, Sicily's through. The railway embankment, running to the narrow defile of the bridge where they would be exposed to fire from every side without the ability easily to fan out to the sides.

Equally, small arms fire frustrated the efforts of our infantry to deal with attacks with its small-calibre guns at close quarters.

It looked momentarily like a deadlock and there was a real danger of our infantry beyond the river running out of ammunition and supplies.

This was averted by rushing across Bren carriers with heavy covering fire, and though we lost several in the process they were successful in carrying out their objective.

"MONTGOMERY MASSING HIS ARTILLERY"

BERLIN CONJECTURE

Capt. Sertorius, the German military commentator, last night said that "renewed attempts by the British Eighth Army to force the crossing of rivers south of Catania with strong tank and infantry forces have failed."

"The enemy have even failed to form a bridgehead on the northern bank of the rivers," he said. "The British on Wednesday suffered high losses in men and lost numerous prisoners and 13 more tanks. The day ended for them in marked failure.

"It appears as if Gen. Montgomery, following his practice in the North African campaign, intends now to create a strong artillery concentration to prepare his further attacks with his usual artillery barrage.

MARKING TIME

"Putting this into operation may however, be expected to give rise to some difficulty and to take a long time. It can be stated that the stiffening of the German-Italian defence on the eastern wing has made the position difficult and tense."

The Central and South-Western Sicily the classic, evasive movements of the Axis forces still continue occurring to plan. The pace of advance of the Seventh American Army has visibly slowed down.

"IN ITALY WITHIN 10 DAYS"

SENATOR'S FORECAST

SPRINGFIELD, ILL., Thursday.
Senator Scott W. Lucas, member of the United States Senate Naval Affairs Committee, said here to-day:

"We'll be in Italy within 10 days with a pretty fair-sized army.

"I don't think Italy will be in the war long. I think she will collapse.

"As soon as the Eighth Army pushes up Catania, Sicily's through. Then it will move into Italy through the mainland."—Reuter & A.P.

CHEAPER MILK IN THE PROVINCES

LONDON PRICE STAYS

Milk will be cheaper in the provinces from Sunday until Sept. 18. During this period, the Ministry of Food announced yesterday, the retail price in England and Wales outside the London area will be 2s 8d a gallon instead of 3s.

This reduces the curtings of retail dairymen outside the London area by 4d a gallon. In the London area the retail price of 3s a gallon remains unchanged.

"WOUNDED AT GIB."

—Five hospital ships are at present at Gibraltar," Vichy radio said last night. "Six four-engined transport planes landed there carrying wounded, who received medical attention before taking off for England.

"Repair yards are reconditioning two light cruisers, four destroyers, a submarine and several badly damaged merchant ships."

MR. SOONG'S VISIT

Mr. T. V. Soong, the Chinese Foreign Minister, is due to arrive in London shortly from the United States, where he has been staying for several months.

Mr. Soong is the brother of three famous sisters: Mme. Chiang Kai-shek, Mme. Sun Yat Sen, widow of the founder of the Chinese Republic, and Mme. Kung, wife of the Chinese Finance Minister.

LATE NEWS

GOEBBELS "NOT ALARMED"

Goebbels, in Das Reich, according to Vichy radio early to-day, wrote: "We are not alarmed by what happening on periphery Europe where decisive struggle begun. So far as is concerned we face events absolute calm. Success Allies in no way change position."

'RUMANIAN REVOLT DENIED'

Reports revolt broken out Bucharest categorically denied official Rumanian news agency, said Bratislava radio. (P1)

"AXIS PROPAGANDA"

Mgr. Micconi, auditor Papal Secretary, arrived at Lisbon, described as "Axis propaganda reports Pope planning five centre Rome if air-raids repeated, says Reuter.

As the Allies sweep through Western and Northern Sicily, the Axis is flying German reinforcements to hold the "last ditch" defence line in the north-east of the island. On the Italian mainland (inset) British naval and air forces have made a heavy attack on Crotone, 95 miles south of Taranto.

STRONG NAVAL FORCE SHELLS CROTONE

CHEMICAL WORKS HIT

From DESMOND TIGHE,
Reuter's Special Correspondent
WITH THE MEDITERRANEAN FLEET,
Wednesday (delayed).

A strong force of Allied warships this morning sailed to within 95 miles of Italy's great naval base of Taranto to pump broadsides into the harbour, at Crotone, in the toe of Italy, without any interference from enemy warships.

Six-inch guns of cruisers, escorted by destroyers, carried out the bombardment for five minutes. A big chemical works was among the targets hit.

It was the first time the Italian mainland had been shelled since 88mm gun's bombardment in 1940.

SAILED ON UNMOLESTED

An officer, describing the bombardment, said:

"As darkness fell the force turned for the Italian coast which, by then, could be clearly seen less than five miles away.

"The striking force formed line ahead and made a fine sight with the moon glinting on their huge bow waves as they ploughed through the sea at full speed. When midnight came all was quiet save for the roar of the engine-room fans and the swirl of the waters thrown high by the bows.

"Just after one o'clock in the morning we passed Cape Rizzuto and sighted the Gulf of Taranto. One of Italy's leading naval bases was now only eight miles away. We acted on unmolested.

"The target was on the beam at two o'clock as planned. The leading cruiser was to shell a chemical works, while others prepared to move into the harbour area. The destroyer escort was to look after any shore batteries.

FIRES IN HARBOUR

Then one by one the warships were brightly illuminated by the gun flashes. Fires started in the harbour area, but details of the damage were not observed.

Two shore batteries on either side of the town were now firing steadily but most inaccurately. It is doubtful if any ship in the force even saw a shell burst. In any case we steamed safely to base.

First Hit from Air

Before the naval bombardment R.A.F. Wellingtons had poured a heavy load of bombs on the airfield nearby and other objectives. Big fires were started and seven grounded aircraft destroyed.

LIFE IN SICILY NORMAL AGAIN

FISHING FLEET OUT

From Our Special Correspondent
GELA, Monday (delayed).
Fishing boats reappeared off the southern coast of Sicily to-day for the first time since before the invasion. Their catch will be sold through the official market.

In dozens of towns life is returning to normal. The mills are working; the bakers are baking. Hairdressers in barbers' shops are doing good business.

The ordinary Italian ration cards are still in force—they provide reasonable though not generous diet. Later, when war considerations are less immediate, it may be possible to increase them. There is food in the island, and in country districts there is little hardship, but feeding the big towns will be the problem.

In no single case has any municipal authority refused to co-operate with the military. Mayors and priests, and doctors and gendarmes are only too anxious to help.

SOVIET TROOPS TAKE BASTION TO OREL

50,000 GERMANS KILLED IN 10 DAYS' OFFENSIVE

From OSSIAN GOULDING,
Daily Telegraph Special Correspondent
STOCKHOLM, Thursday.

Beating off fierce counter-attacks, the Russians advanced to-day another four to five miles in the Orel area and captured a number of localities, including Bolkhov, the German "hedgehog" stronghold 35 miles north-north-west of Orel.

Announcing this, to-night's Soviet communiqué [received in London at 9.45 p.m.] says that with the capture of Bolkhov "our troops have liquidated a strongly fortified enemy area north of Orel."

The communiqué adds: "In 10 days of our offensive in the Orel direction more than 50,000 Germans have been killed and more than 6,000 taken prisoner.

"In the same period our troops captured:

"372 tanks; 720 guns; 300 mortars; 1,400 machine-guns and 128 dumps and stores;

"destroyed or damaged 776 tanks; and "destroyed more than 900 planes and 882 guns.

"In the Byelgorod direction (south of Kursk) our troops, overcoming enemy resistance and beating off his counter-attacks, advanced from three to four-and-half miles.

"In the south, in the Donetz Basin south of Izyum and south-west of Voroshilovgrad, local battles continued."

The supplement to the communiqué [received in London this morning at one o'clock] said that

LARGE-SCALE RIOTING IN SOFIA

MILITARY CALLED IN

Invasion nerves have gripped the Balkans, especially Bulgaria, from which reports have reached Switzerland, states Reuter, of rioting in the capital, Sofia.

The Sofia police were unable to deal with the large-scale rioting and demonstrations because they had been weakened by transfers to Macedonia, where there is unrest, and the military were called in.

Telephonic communication with the city was temporarily interrupted on Wednesday.

All military leave in Rumania has been cancelled and strong reinforcements of Axis troops have been sent to Macedonia, Thrace and Greece.

RAID WITH LEAFLETS

According to a B.U.P. message from Istanbul, bombs and leaflets were dropped by aircraft of unknown nationality on Bulgaria. The leaflets called on the Bulgarian people to overthrow the Filov Government, throw out the Germans and save the country from devastating bombing.

Over 40 deputies spoke in opposition to unlimited co-operation with the Axis when the Bulgarian Parliament met on Wednesday, said B.U.P.

Five persons, including a woman, were sentenced to death for espionage in Sofia yesterday, says the German News Agency.

MISSING ONE-ARMED PILOT

SQ. LDR. MacLACHLAN
Sqdn. Ldr. J. A. F. Maclachlan, D.S.O., D.F.C. and bar, the one-armed R.A.F. pilot, is reported missing. He is 24.

It was in 1941 that he lost his left arm. While helping to defend Malta he was wounded by a German cannon shell and had to bale out. A fortnight after his arm had been amputated he was flying again.

For a long time Sqdn. Ldr. Maclachlan specialised in night intruder flights. He commanded the squadron in which Flt. Lt. Kuttelwascher, the famous Czech flier, achieved many successes as an intruder pilot.

Three weeks ago it was disclosed that he was one of two officers who, flying Mustangs, penetrated to the Paris area and shot down six enemy aircraft in 15 minutes.

Sqdn. Ldr. Maclachlan was born at Styal, Cheshire. His mother lives at Haywards Heath. One brother is an R.A.F. pilot and another is in the Army.

▲ THE DAILY TELEGRAPH, LONDON, FRIDAY JULY 23, 1943

In the Western press, the Battle of Kursk barely got a mention, but it essentially decided the outcome of the war on the Eastern Front. The defeat meant that the German armies on the Eastern Front were now faced with a defensive war against an enemy who had far more troops, tanks, and aircraft.

HAMBURGER ZEITUNG

Kostenlos

Sonntag, 25. Juli 1943

23 Uhr

Der Terrorangriff auf Hamburg

17 Abschüsse — 125 Sowjetpanzer im Osten vernichtet

Berichte von unseren Soldaten

Erfolgreiche Flankenstöße

Großküchen eingesetzt

Obdachlosenzüge fahren ab Montag

Die ersten Bekanntmachungen

Fernverkehr der Reichsbahn

Die Straßen- und U-Bahn

Betreuung der Geschädigten

Die Kämpfe auf Sizilien

Feindkräfte zurückgenommen

Nachtgefechte im Kanal

Schwerter für Kampfflieger

Wer kann die Stadt verlassen?

Bekanntmachung der Polizei

Sonderzuteilung an die Bevölkerung

Lebensmittel und Kaffee

Zur Zeit kein Drahtfunk

▲ HAMBURGER ZEITUNG, HAMBURG, SUNDAY, 25 JULY 1943

The main headline reports the Allied air raids on Hamburg: "Terror unleashed on Hamburg. 17 planes shot down." The subheading underneath states: "125 Soviet tanks destroyed in the east."

Hamburg

JULY 1943

HAMBURG WAS A TEMPTING TARGET FOR RAF BOMBER COMMAND, AS IT WAS A KEY GERMAN SHIPYARD CITY WHERE THE *BISMARCK* AND 200 U-BOATS HAD ALREADY been built. Sir Arthur Harris, head of Bomber Command, ordered four major raids against Hamburg in the space of just 10 nights, known as Operation Gomorrah. The results were devastating for the city.

DESTRUCTION

A German report written after the RAF raid on July 24 stated: "Coal and coke supplies stored for the winter in many houses caught fire and could only be extinguished weeks later. Essential services were severely damaged and telephone services were cut early in the attack. Dockyards and industrial installations were severely hit. At mid-day next day there was still a gigantic, dense cloud of smoke and dust hovering over the city which, despite the clear sky, prevented the sun from penetrating through. Despite employment of all available force, big fires could not be prevented from flaring up again and again. Through the union of a number of fires, the air gets so hot that on account of its decreasing specific weight, it receives a terrific momentum, which in its turn causes other surrounding air to be sucked toward the center.

FIRESTORM

"By that suction, combined with the enormous difference in temperature (600–1000 degrees centigrade), tempests are caused which go beyond their meteorological counterparts (20–30 centigrade). In a built-up area the suction could not follow its shortest course, but the overheated air stormed through the street with immense force taking along not only sparks, but burning timber and roof beams, so spreading the fire farther and farther, developing in a short time into a fire typhoon such as was never before witnessed, against which every human resistance was quite useless." About 1,500 people were killed in this raid. The RAF lost only 12 aircraft. For the citizens of Hamburg, though, the nightmare was only just beginning.

▲ IN THE AFTERMATH of one of the RAF's raids on Hamburg, a firefighter battles the flames. Hamburg was heavily bombed over a 10-day period in July 1943.

Il Duce sacked

JULY 1943

AS GERMAN TROOPS WERE STRUGGLING TO ESCAPE FROM SICILY, THE ITALIAN MILITARY, GOVERNMENT LEADERS, AND THE COUNTRY'S MONARCH WERE STARTING to look for a way to end their alliance with Germany. It only seemed a matter of weeks before the conflict would spread to the Italian mainland, threatening to turn the country into a bloody battlefield. The first step that had to be taken was to depose the Italian fascist dictator, Benito Mussolini, and then negotiations had to be opened with the Allies for an armistice.

MUSSOLINI OUT

During the last week of July 1943, Italian military chiefs and cabinet ministers hatched a plot to force Benito Mussolini to stand down. This culminated in the Italian monarch, King Victor Emmanuel, relieving Mussolini of power on July 26. Humiliated, the former Italian dictator was arrested and led away by troops loyal to the new government. This heralded a tense six-week period of political maneuverings, as Italy's new

▲ ITALIAN DICTATOR Benito Mussolini in his glory days. After he had been deposed in July 1943, the Germans launched a daring raid to rescue him from captivity.

government tried to head off German intervention and negotiate an armistice with the Allies. Hitler was furious that his fellow dictator had been deposed and he remained suspicious that the Italians would soon change sides.

NEGOTIATIONS WITH THE ALLIES

Desperate to forestall German intervention, the Italians began negotiations with the Allies, which culminated in secret talks in neutral Portugal in the middle of August to broker an armistice. The Italians were very keen to make firm plans with General Eisenhower for Allied airborne and amphibious forces to land near Rome simultaneously with the signing of the armistice in order to preempt a German counterstroke. Eisenhower, however, did not have enough ships or planes to hand to launch such a coup de main operation, and so an amphibious operation into central Italy would probably not be possible until mid-September at the earliest. It was all in vain, though: German troops and tanks under the command Field Marshal Erwin Rommel quickly surged across the Alps to occupy northern Italy.

DAILY EXPRESS

No. 13,464 MONDAY JULY 26 1943 FOUNDED BY LORD BEAVERBROOK Black-out 11.2 p.m. to 5.29 a.m. One Penny

MUSSOLINI SACKED

King Victor of Italy takes over command of all the Forces

BADOGLIO IS NEW PREMIER

MUSSOLINI IS SACKED. ROME RADIO ANNOUNCED AT 10.55 LAST NIGHT THAT HE HAS BEEN DISMISSED BY KING VICTOR EMMANUEL.

King Victor, it added, had assumed the post of Commander-in-Chief of the armed forces. Marshal Badoglio has been appointed Prime Minister.

A message to the Italian people was signed by both the King and Badoglio.

The text of the King's message was: "Italians, in this solemn hour in the destiny of our country I assume the High Command of the entire armed forces.

"No consideration must stand in our way, and no recriminations must be made.

"We must stand against those who have wounded the sacred soil of Italy."

He called on every one: "To take his place of duty of responsibilty and his battle stations."

The dismissal follows with dramatic suddenness the meeting of Mussolini and Hitler at Verona last Monday.

Final Sicily battle near, Axis rush men

From HENRY BUCKLEY: AFRICAN H.Q., Sunday night

MORE German reinforcements were being rushed across the Straits of Messina today to reinforce the Etna Line as American and Canadian divisions swung into position beside the Eighth Army for the final battle of Sicily.

Axis paratroops have again been dropped behind our lines to attack transport as Allied troops probe the minefields and gun-nests prepared in the wild country north-west of Mount Etna.

The Canadians, fighting a heavy running battle against the 15th Panzer Division, have now joined hands with the Eighth Army to the north of the Catania Plain as the Germans withdraw into their new defences.

Further north, and for many miles along the road from Palermo eastward, the Americans are streaming down the coast to draw the bolt across the tip of the island.

It is revealed today that the 65-mile Axis line is manned along nearly half its length by Italians. They will face the American Seventh Army fresh from its victorious race to Palermo, Marsala, and Trapani.

Here is the approximate positions of the Etna Line: First it runs along the Dittaino river, central stream of the Catanian plain seven miles south of the city.

Here the Eighth Army, lying in sweltering heat, is holding exposed positions under incessant artillery fire, and occasionally improving them by night rushes.

Ten miles up to the river the line turns northward to Regalbuto, at the foot of Etna, and then north again through the mountains to the north coast.

For 35 miles it is manned by Germans and for 30 more in the northern sector by Italians.

ITALIANS HOLD HALF THE LINE

By MORLEY RICHARDS

DOMINANT news last night from Sicily was that the Canadians have fought their way north-east to re-establish a cohesive line with the Eighth Army.

The juncture was made probably somewhere between Leonforte and Regalbuto, which is one of the strongpoints along the base of the Axis defence triangle formed roughly by Messina-Catania-San Stefano.

Enemy dispositions for his final stand are now clear: the German 15th Panzer Division, the Hermann Goering Division, the Luftwaffe, and parachute troops are covering the Catania end of their base as far as Regalbuto. The Italians are holding the rest of the line for about 30 miles.

The German General Comrath's problem is whether or not to move Germans into the over-stretched Italian positions to stiffen their resistance at the risk of weakening his own sector to the point of collapse.

For some time past backward movements among his comparatively small force have been noted, but these were to organise the new line when the Catania-Enna position became untenable.

Now three threats to his triangle have developed:—

1—The Americans racing along the northern coastal road. They are now near San Stefano.

2—The Anglo-Canadian outflanking force tearing into the centre of his line.

3—The Eighth Army pounding Catania into ruins with its massed batteries.

Big exams may go

National Service at 18 after war

A PERIOD of six months on work of national importance for all boys and girls before passing from school to the University at the age of 18 or 19 is envisaged by the Norwood Committee on Secondary Education, whose report is issued today.

"Such a period so spent might do much to fuse the country into a single whole, with a common purpose and a common understanding," the report says.

The committee, under the chairmanship of Sir Cyril Norwood, president of St John's College, Oxford, and former headmaster of Harrow, was appointed in October 1941 by Mr R. A. Butler, President of the Board of Education, to advise on suggested changes in school curriculum and examinations.

In its report the committee suggests:—

1—Abolition of the School Certificate examination in its present form.

2—Abolition of the Higher Certificate examination.

3—A national scholarship contest for University careers.

SUBJECT CHOICE

In place of the present school certificate examination, the committee suggests that there should be freedom in the choice of subjects.

Each candidate would receive a certificate indicating his or her examination performance and school record, and would tell employers and university authorities much more about the pupil as an individual than the existing certificate.

Instead of the higher certificate examination there would be a twice-yearly test, without syllabus, for pupils of 18, with the limited purposes of clearing matriculation and the needs of professional bodies.

The existing machinery for awarding a limited number of State scholarships for the universities on the results of the higher certificate should be abolished.

Instead, awards up to the whole amount necessary for a university education should be made (after consideration of parents' income) to all recommended pupils.

The chosen pupils would be those of good intellectual attainment whose school records merit consideration.

William Barkley explains the report.—Page Three.

Jeff Dickson missing

Express Staff Reporter

NEW YORK, Sunday.—Captain Jeff Dickson, peace-time promoter of boxing matches and other big sporting events, is missing in action.

He is an intelligence officer in the American Air Force, and news that he is missing has been received by his wife, the former Miss Luise Mastbaum, Philadelphia society girl.

In the last war Dickson served as a N.C.O. with the American Expeditionary Force and was commissioned in the air force last year.

Frank Butler's story.—Page Three.

Axis air losses: 109 last week

In the week ending yesterday 109 Axis planes were destroyed over Europe, North Africa, and the Middle East.

R.A.F. and U.S. losses in these theatres during the same period were 72.

The figures are: Europe: Axis, 27; Allies, 24. North Africa: Axis, 79; Allies, 31. Middle East: Axis, 3; Allies, 17.

Guerrillas beat off large Axis forces

ISTANBUL, Sunday.—Yugoslav guerrillas are holding their own with three Bulgarian divisions and parts of three Italian and two German divisions sent to wipe them out before the Allies invade south-east Europe.—B.U.P.

Mihailovich: £8,500—alive or dead

The Germans have offered a reward of £8,500 for the capture, alive or dead, of General Mihailovich, the Yugoslav patriot leader.—Budapest radio.

A similar price was placed last week on Tito, the Yugoslav Communist partisan leader.

Stalin sees booty

Marshal Stalin spent nearly two hours at the Moscow exhibitions of German war material captured by the Red Army.

How the Germans fight on

Boys of 16 die like fanatics

From JAMES COOPER: MALTA, Saturday

BOYS of 16 are fighting in the crack Goering Division in Sicily—and are fighting hard. Slightly wounded Eighth Army officers, the first to return from Sicily, straight from the fighting south of Catania, revealed this fact to me this afternoon.

All said, too, how almost overnight German reinforcements turned weak Italian opposition into bitter fighting.

"Tell the people back home," said one, "that this is no vineyard picnic."

A Glasgow lieutenant gave this account of the fighting:—

"For the first week we were fed up. We would launch night attacks and walk miles without finding a single enemy soldier.

FOUGHT TO LAST

"Each day we dug in, and under the hot sun it was no joke, with little sleep. Then one night we were breezing along to the cross-roads near Gerbini when we ran into our first Germans.

"They had machine-guns and fought to the last man. We had quite a few casualties until we bayoneted the lot.

"I was amazed to find how young these Goering troops are now. One man's papers showed he was only 16, other not much more; but they all fought fanatically.

"We cut off 14 men lying in a field. Escape was impossible, but each man in turn got up and fired on us. They hadn't a chance, but even the fourteenth man, having seen all his mates killed one by one, still stood up fighting it out.

"We found another man who had buried himself in soil up to the chest to secure cover so that he could fire.

"The soil might protect him a little—but it was also plain that he had dug himself in so that he could not run away."

Though the Germans are fighting fanatically, they know they are fighting on the retreat. Recently they have refused to take any prisoners. Instead they march their captives at fast speed in the hot sun for a couple of hours, then release them, thinking them too exhausted to fight on for some time.

How the Italians give in

Surrendering, cheering too

From ALEXANDER CLIFFORD, Combined British Press Reporter

PALERMO, Saturday.—A U.S. artillery unit and two American and one British war correspondents took Castel Vetrano's great airport on the way to Palermo.

It was one of those almost comic opera days which you sometimes get against the Italians—days like we occasionally had in Libya and Abyssinia.

Italian resistance at Castel Vetrano consisted of a few rounds of gunfire and two or three bursts of machine-gun fire.

After that we got the biggest welcome we have yet had.

KISSES

It passed all reasonable bounds. The people threw themselves on to jeeps, clapping, laughing, and cheering.

They kissed the dusty, unshaven troops with rapture. Trucks were covered with flowers — mostly red geraniums which grow wild along the roadside. People came out with handfuls of almonds, tomatoes, or jugs of wine.

This ridiculous welcome set the note for the whole day. People

→ BACK PAGE, COL. THREE

U-BOATS' HOME

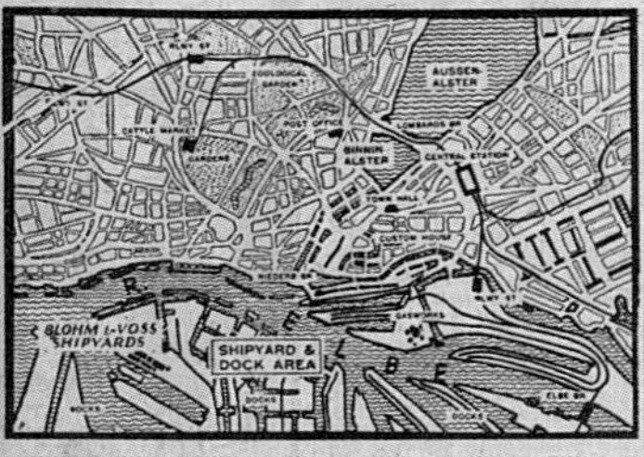

110,000 OTHERS DID THIS—

This man has only one urgent thing to say, and the white cloth and the high hands say it for him. An Italian soldier, defender of Sicily, surrenders, not unhappily, to the Canadians at Rosolini.

THE NOTICE

SICILIAN VILLAGERS gather round the local notice board. Latest news—General Alexander's proclamation to the occupied area.

'We can't beat Soviet in the field'

Express Staff Reporter

STOCKHOLM, Sunday.—For the first time the Germans stated that "it is impossible to beat the Soviet on the battlefield," and that "Germany is henceforth forced on the defensive."

This sensational statement has been made by Goering's Essener National Zeitung.

The paper analyses the situation on the Russian front and concludes that events there have taken a turn which "excludes for both sides the possibility of decisive offensive action, unless one or the other meets with insuperable difficulties in getting supplies.

"All that Germany now has to do is to keep her conquests and wait until Russia's resources in men and material are exhausted."

Ley, Labour Front chief, in an article today, says that the Allied air offensive against the Ruhr "found Germany unprepared, and was met only with improvised means."

He adds there were no plans, strategic or tactical, for facing the raids.

"The Allies have gained nothing by bombing the Ruhr, as their losses in men and material surpassed those which Germany suffered."

According to Ley, the Ruhr production of steel, iron, and coal did not stop—"not even for a second."

Blazing Hamburg raided again in day

U.S. HEAVY BOMBERS ALSO SMASH KIEL YARDS

United States Army 8th Air Force heavy bombers attacked Kiel and Hamburg yesterday, and medium bombers, escorted by R.A.F. Spitfires, attacked industrial targets near Ghent today, it was announced late last night.

Express Air Reporter

HAMBURG'S defences were swamped under a cascade of 2,300 tons of bombs on Saturday night when the R.A.F. carried out the greatest air attack of the war in 50 minutes.

This tremendous raid cost only 12 bombers, which compares with 43 lost in the June 11 raid on Dusseldorf, the previous record attack, when 2,000 tons were dropped.

The element of surprise was fully exploited, and two secondary forces carried out diversionary raids during the night.

Hamburg is an easier target to reach than the Ruhr, as practically all the route lies over the sea.

Germany's chief port—and greatest U-boat building centre—Hamburg houses 1,150,000 people. Vast fires were started, and dense smoke rose four miles high.

Explosion after explosion occurred in the bombed war plants.

The fires were seen 200 miles away by a light diversionary force attacking the Ruhr.

Besides creating a record for tonnage of bombs dropped, the raid beat all others for speed in delivery.

The unloading took ten minutes less than Dusseldorf's 2,000 tons, and represents 46 tons a minute—15cwt a second.

At the end of the attack the docks and U-yards were blotted out by smoke and fires.

Camouflage

The Germans have taken great trouble to camouflage Hamburg, and particularly the tell-tale lakes in its centre. Many searchlights were in action—one flier said he saw more than there were in the Ruhr.

He also reported a new kind of flak which burst like a rocket and scattered a spray of red fragments.

But there were few encounters with night fighters — though Flying-Officer G. Turner, of Winnipeg, piloting a Stirling, collided with one, saw it drop like a stone and then flew home to a safe landing with four feet of one wing missing.

The German News Agency put out this report on the raid—Hamburg's 99th:—

"Last night Hamburg was the target of a heavy enemy terror attack.

"A strong formation of enemy aircraft dropped high explosives and incendiaries, especially on residential quarters in the centre of the town. Several fires were caused.

"Thirteen of the attacking planes were shot down."

War reporter Dr Wieninger said on Berlin radio last night:—

"At 8 a.m., five hours after the

BACK PAGE, COL. ONE

TRAVEL PERMITS?

Government may take action

By GUY EDEN

ACTION by the Government to enforce its request to everybody not to travel during the holiday months is under consideration.

There are difficulties about imposing an actual travel ban as this would involve inquiry in every case about the purpose of the journey, and some official would have to decide whether or not it came within the "necessary" category.

Any action by the Government would not necessarily rule out all holiday journeys, because those of some classes of war workers are regarded as essential. So are those of Service men and women even on leave.

Ministers sympathise with those who are inevitably feeling the strain of nearly four years of hard war work.

But it is felt that nothing can be allowed to endanger military activities just now, and in spite of the difficulties some system of travel permits may be tried out.

This may limit travel to a certain distance, or put certain towns out of bounds.

Railways warn holidaymakers.—Page Three.

Secret radio: Three Bulgarians to die

Three Bulgarians have been sentenced to death in Sofia accused of sending military information from a secret radio station to a foreign power.—Axis radio.

World war news

BADOGLIO: "WE FIGHT ON"

Marshal Badoglio issued the following proclamation:

"Italians—on the orders of the King Emperor I am taking over military government of the country.

"The war continues.

"Italy, grievously stricken in her invaded provinces, in her ruined towns, maintains her faith in her given word.

RAIN SLOWS DOWN SOVIET ADVANCE

From ALARIC JACOB: MOSCOW, Sunday

MARSHAL STALIN'S clear intimation that the danger of a German summer offensive this year has been averted by a "successful completion of liquidation" of the German drive against the Kursk salient is giving great cheer to all Russians.

His order of the day would not have announced this good news in such positive terms unless the Soviet Command had ample reasons to believe that the Germans had shot their bolt for this summer — and missed their aim completely.

Counter-attacks by the Germans to the north of Orel were severe yesterday, and Soviet progress was not so rapid as heretofore. Bad weather must be having its effect at the front.

Moscow people tell me that never in their lifetime do they recall a high summer so bad as this one. Red Army men must often wonder whether this is not one of their own winter offensives after all.

Paved roads are few in the battle area, and on secondary roads the mud is as thick almost as when the snow is thawing.

Even so, tonight's Soviet communiqué reported more progress. It said:—

"Today our troops in the direction of Orel, overcoming enemy resistance and counter-attacks, continued their offensive and advanced from three to five miles, and occupied 30 inhabited localities.

"In the Byelgood direction there was reconnaissance activity and in some sections local fighting.

"In the south—in the Donbas area south of Izyum and south-west of Voroshilovgrad — there was strong reconnaissance activity.

64 tanks

"Yesterday our troops destroyed or disabled on all fronts 64 enemy tanks and shot down 56 enemy planes in air fighting or by anti-aircraft fire."

Harold King, Reuter's Moscow reporter, cabled last night:—

The situation around Orel is developing quickly towards a regular investiture of the city.

Von Kluge, the German commander, is playing a dangerous game. No considerable number of German troops have been withdrawn from the Orel cul-de-sac. In fact, fresh troops are being thrown in.

The Germans are now being hemmed in from three sides by the armies of Generals Rokossovsky, Vatutin, and Popov, who all took part in the German disaster at Stalingrad.

The thrust from the south is going particularly well. Soviet forces beyond Zmievka are now only 20 miles from Orel and are advancing directly on the city along the Kursk-Orel railway line.

This southern army has advanced nearly 20 miles in a week.

Latest dispatches from this southern region say that the Germans are everywhere retreating, in some sectors quicker than others, but still retreating.

Besides the thrust from the south, four or five other Russian columns are pressing in on Orel in an irregular arc from the north to the east of the city.

BACK FROM HAMBURG

"S for Sugar"—otherwise "Good health, then," bomber from the Rhodesian Squadron, with a dripping pint pot as its badge—has bomb No. 21 printed up to mark the Hamburg raid.

▲ DAILY EXPRESS, MONDAY JULY 26, 1943

Before he was sacked, Mussolini met Hitler on July 19 and told the German dictator that he endorsed the Führer's plan for the Nazi takeover of Italy.

Daily Mail

LATE WAR NEWS

NO. 14,747   ONE PENNY   ✶ ✶   FOR KING AND EMPIRE   FRIDAY, AUGUST 6, 1943

GERMANS PULLING OUT OF SICILY

Non-essential Men Escape in Gliders

'EIGHTH' CHEERED ALONG CATANIA STREETS

From Daily Mail Special Correspondent   ALLIED H.Q., N. Africa, Thursday.

THE Germans are preparing to get out of Sicily quickly, if they can. For days now they have been evacuating unessential troops by glider and small boats across the Straits of Messina, it is officially announced at Allied H.Q. to-night.

ITALY—THE TRUTH

THE DAILY MAIL to-day presents the first authentic account of present conditions in Italy. The story is told by a highly competent and reliable journalist who has important connections in Italy. He stayed five days in the north, gathering his impressions. His return to the Swiss frontier was made with great difficulty. Immediately the news of the Duce's fall reached London The Daily Mail commissioned its staff correspondent in Geneva to seek out this special envoy and facilitate his entry into Italy. He did so. And his story is told below.

Italy Knows She Has Been Duped

By Daily Mail Special Envoy Just Returned From Italy

THE Italian people want peace without delay. That is the outstanding fact I gathered during my stay in Northern Italy.

It is pretty plain that the Badoglio Government is only a temporary one. I found bitter disappointment — "bitterly deceived" was the remark of most people—that the anti-Fascist parties did not take over the Government immediately.

There is disappointment, too, because Badoglio has surrounded himself with soldiers and routined officials.

The Italians told me they did not like the setting-up of a veritable military dictatorship.

Undoubtedly the majority of the people, especially the workers, are overjoyed at the downfall of Mussolini and the end of the Fascist regime.

But to Milan I found the strong and resentment in the Government's action in banning all new political parties and the decision not to hold elections until four months after the end of the war.

When the newspapers of the Extremists, Il Mondo and La Riscossa, were suppressed, there was great indignation.

Here is a remarkable fact. I found that there is a "state of rebellion" against the radio commentators who have been broadcasting Axis propaganda.

The feeling is so strong that demands for the punishment of reprisals (alias Ansaldos), Salvatore Aponte, and the gloomy "War Woe" Ansaldo are being openly put forward.

I almost forgot that Mussolini and Ciano headed the list !

★

WHILE in Milan I gathered the first reliable information for the whereabouts of the deposed Duce. He is now interned in the luxurious villa of his mistress at Monte Mario, in Rome.

I found also that people were talking about the reported arrest of Alfieri, the Ambassador to Berlin. He had been visiting Rome and is said to have been stopped at Verona while trying to escape into Germany.

Why must the Italian Diplomatic Corps abroad been purged?

Rome Silent on Vital Cabinet

NO reference to the Allied demand for unconditional surrender was made by Rome after the meeting of the Italian Cabinet last evening.

In a German broadcast Rome radio said :

"The only way in which Italy could forfeit her place among the free nations would be by breaking her pledged word."

Half an hour later the Italian News Agency issued a communique saying that the meeting was under the presidency of Marshal Badoglio and outlining a series of domestic changes affecting finance, education, public works, agriculture, and food rationing.

All food is to be under military control and all employed in food distribution will be called up.

Berlin comment came from the Diplomatic Correspondent of the German Overseas News Agency, who said :

"It is stated in Berlin that London and Washington are mis-...

The evacuation yesterday speeded-up considerably when it was apparent that Catania was doomed.

Meanwhile, the main enemy forces thrown out of Catania have withdrawn 20 miles to the north, to the foothills of Mount Etna.

Their retreat was complicated by the Allied capture of Paterno, ten miles north-west of Catania, on the road to Adrana, round the west side of Etna.

The only way out left to them is the three-mile-wide corridor along the east coast between Etna and the sea.

Along it there are several points where stubborn rearguards could interfere badly with any advance. The corridor, however, would be under constant shellfire from warships off the coast, and it would be an admirable target for Allied planes.

Already the retreating Germans are being severely harassed from the air. Allied pilots returning yesterday from sorties freely reported the destruction of 3 lorries and the firing of 40 more.

U.S. PRESS ON

Allied pressure all along the front has stepped up.

Although there is no definite news from Sicily of the progress of the Americans along the north coast Mr. Stimson, United States Secretary of War, announced in Washington to-day that they have pressed on six miles from Carona.

They are within two miles of San Fratello, which stands on a promontory just beyond more than behind the enemy's Troina defence system.

The Germans are fighting a bitter delaying action against other American forces at Troina to cover the movement of their eastern and western flank.

When the Americans driving along the north coast reach San Fratello, Troina will be outflanked and the German position there will be desperate. They will be forced to pull back to Randazzo, on the north side of Etna.

One report says that an American force has already by-passed Troina on the south and is driving towards Nicosia, only seven miles south-west of Randazzo.

This new thrust to Randazzo has cause the collapse of the whole of the enemy's front in the centre of the Etna Line.

FEW CASUALTIES

The Eighth Army captured Catania with relatively few casualties.

Allied H.Q. announced that the Germans were forced out by superior numbers, the element of surprise and sudden pressure at a vital point.

The statement adds: "Thus important strategic results were obtained with a great economy of force, avoiding greater casualties on our side.

following the capture by Allied troops of Catania and Paterno. Inset map shows the small part of Sicily still in enemy hands.

BRITISH war correspondents entered Catania with the Eighth Army. Here is the story of the Daily Mail Special Correspondent, written in the ruins of a shop in the main street.

THIS CITY WEPT FOR HAPPINESS

Cheering Crowds Mob the 'Eighth'

Daily Mail Special Correspondent

CATANIA, Thursday.

WE have had a truly terrific reception in Catania. Our hands are sore from the multitude of handshakes, and our cheeks are wet with tears and kisses.

In 18 months of campaigning during which I have entered many towns and cities with the Allied Armies, there has never been anything to equal the welcome the Eighth Army received here this morning.

I entered Catania about half an hour ago with the advanced force. There the muscles have deeply touched the toughest of the soldiers.

The city is little more than a ruin. Every street, from the wide cross-lined main roads to the tiniest thoroughfare, has been blasted by bomb and shell. Hardly a house has escaped.

The people have lived through terrible hardships, yet there was no mistaking the enthusiasm with which they greeted us this morning.

They rushed out from cellars and dugouts; they were red-eyed, weary and hungry, but the ardour of their welcome to the British troops was amazing. We are their liberators.

Dramatic Fall

The fall of the city was dramatic. Night patrols discovered that the enemy had pulled out of Catania during the night. A company of mules in front of Catania and at dawn reconnaissance parties went out.

Lieut. Randall and his raised Pte. Grasher got within one yard of the first house and as they approached a road-block swung forward before flutter-flag waving white tablecloths.

There were still Germans about, but the infantry pushed forward during the day and at dawn the mommas pressed into Catania.

It was a cautious approach. The arsenal was firing furiously as we went past, emphasising the unmamy quiet everywhere.

Then an old woman came rushing out of the first house pointing to tell us that the Germans had cleared off in a hurry.

She burst into tears and kissed the grimy hands of the infantrymen in the carriers.

She and her children, she said, were very hungry. The Germans during the last days of their stay had stopped all distribution of food.

For four days the townspeople had been living on scraps and nuts of olive, oranges, lemons and tomatoes, which they had been able to gather.

Although they were hungry, the people, as we drove on, gave us food. They had, they had handfuls of nuts into the jeep and pressed forward fruit on us.

It was pathetic.

Some had had no water for 25 hours and they drank deeply from our water-bottles.

Why Rome Has Had a Respite

Weather Saved It —for One Night

ALLIED headquarters in North Africa disclosed last night that only unfavourable weather conditions prevented the bombing of Rome by Allied planes on Wednesday night.

The attack on Rome, it was added, will be renewed as soon as possible.

—The Daily Mail Air Correspondent writes :

—No Air Force could afford to give such specific advance warning of its intentions unless it were satisfied that there was no chance of meeting serious opposition.

With only 24 hours' preliminary warning of such an attack, the Germans, if they wished to, could bring up fighters from as far away as France to defend Rome.

But while they are successfully bullying Italy out of seeking peace terms they are apparently leaving the Italians virtually defenceless.

Berlin's Prospects

AN R.A.F. commentator in London yesterday, discussing the raids on Hamburg, said that if Berlin is attacked on the same scale up to 800 big bombers a night will be engaged.

"The commentator, while not committing himself to naming the zero hour for the opening of the Battle of Berlin, made this significant comment :

"Berliners must be watching the shrinkage of daylight with some concern. I would not like to give a hint when the dead-line will arrive."

Battle at Hamburg, by Colin Bednall—Page THREE, Picture—BACK Page.

The '50's' Will Register

But No Big 'Call'

Daily Mail Political Correspondent

Although there will be registration of women between 45 and 50, it does not appear to be the intention of the Government to call up many of them for war work.

The Ministry of Labour and National Service officials are being instructed to observe the greatest leniency in all cases. One of the principal objects of the Government is to find out how many women in these age-groups are working and whether they can be transferred to more useful war work.

But no general grounds there will be "hardship" exemptions on the grounds of health and some circumstances as well as any other factor.

The Labour Party are contemplating a drive to call the announcement should indicate an inquiry into the use of man-power in the Services.

Such an inquiry might include the investigation afresh of the position in the Civil Service, where it is claimed that many able women are not being fully employed.

Government Seaside Girls—Page THREE.

'CHURCHILL TO MEET FDR'

U.S. Forecast

From Daily Mail Correspondent

NEW YORK, Thursday.—President Roosevelt and Mr. Churchill may soon confer again to plan for the finishing touches on plans for new assaults on the European fortress, it is believed here.

The swift succession of Allied victories in Russia, Sicily, and in the air over Germany have created new opportunities, and it is thought the two statesmen will meet to give final shape to an all-out victory campaign.

Germans Seizing Italian Planes

CAIRO, Thursday.—It was authoritatively stated here to-day that Italian aircraft in some parts of the Balkans have been forcibly taken over by the Germans.

What is more, they have been painted with the German colours.—Reuter.

KING MICHAEL INJURED IN PLOESTI RAID

ISTANBUL, Wednesday. (delayed).

KING MICHAEL, who was making a visit to Campina, in the oil region, was injured in the Allied air raid on Ploesti on Sunday, Rumanian sources say here.

It was revealed that the raid covered a greater part of the oil region. At Campina 35 100 miles from Ploesti in the north oil district. Thousands of people are fleeing from the threatened areas, particularly Bucharest, Ploesti, and Constanza.—A.P.

Byelgorod Falls: Victory Order by Stalin

From Daily Mail Special Correspondent

Moscow, Thursday.

STALIN, in a special Order of the Day, to-night announced the capture of Byelgorod and confirmed the occupation of Orel—a double victory which comes one month to the day after the start of the German attempt to wipe out the Kursk salient.

The Order declares that these victories dispel the legend that "Soviet troops are unable to wage a summer offensive," and orders a midnight salute to the victorious troops to be fired by the guns of the Moscow garrison.

Here is the full victory order in which Stalin announced these successes of the Red Army : "To-day our forces on the Bryansk front, in co-operation on the flanks with the troops of the Western and Central fronts, as a result of fierce battles captured the town of Orel.

"Also to-day troops from the steppes and the Voronezh front broke the enemy resistance and occupied the town of Byelgorod.

"A month ago, on July 5, the Germans began their summer offensive from Orel and Byelgorod in order to encircle and wipe out our troops in the Kursk salient and to occupy Kursk.

"Having replied with the enemy attempts to break through to Kursk our troops then went over to the offensive, and on August 5 exactly a month later, occupied Orel and Byelgorod.

"They have dispelled the German legend that Soviet troops are unable to wage a summer offensive.

"To mark this victory the 129th, 380th Rifle Division, the first to crack into Orel and liberate the city shall be known as the 'Orel Divisions.'

"The 89th Guards and 305th Rifle Division, which were the first to break into Byelgorod shall henceforth be called the 'Byelgorod Division.'

"For the successful offensive operations I express my gratitude to all the troops which took part in the fight to liberate Orel and Byelgorod. Eternal glory to the heroes who fell in action for the freedom of our Fatherland and death to the German invaders."

THE victor of Orel, General Rokossovsky, pictured at his headquarters. He also played an outstanding rôle in the defence of Moscow in the autumn of 1941 and in the Soviet victories on the Don last year.

ETNA GERMANS FALLING BACK

Allied H.Q., N. Africa, Thursday Night.—The battered Germans, after abandoning their principal positions on each side of the Etna Line, are falling back in good order to a new defensive position.

The new position runs from the northern slopes of Etna across the narrowing peninsular formed by North-East Sicily. General Alexander's Allied armies are now streaming forward in pursuit of the retreating Germans.—Reuter.

Troops Thanked

Swedes Stop German Arms Trains

STOCKHOLM, Thursday.

THE agreement with Germany under which Axis troops and war material have been allowed to pass through Sweden has been cancelled by the Swedish Government, it is officially announced.

"Transit of war material will cease on August 15 and of soldiers by August 20.

The agreement, which allowed the passage of unarmed German soldiers across Sweden to and from Norway, has been justified on the grounds that it was only made after the collapse of Norway and would not therefore be considered an act of war.

The Swedes were compelled to enter into the agreement in June 1940, while the last Allied troops were being evacuated from Narvik.

It is estimated that between 12,000 and 15,000 Germans were carried across Sweden every week under the arrangement.—Reuter and B.U.P.

SICILY LOSSES 'MODERATE'

100,000 Prisoners

From Daily Mail Correspondent

NEW YORK, Thursday.—Mr. Henry Stimson, United States Secretary of War, announced to-day that American casualties in Sicily up to July 31, were 6,741, including 500 killed.

Of these, 3,571 were wounded and 2,370 were missing. He said these losses were considered moderate and added that British losses were not a great deal higher.

Mr. Stimson added that Axis losses were substantial. A hundred thousand enemy troops had been captured.

BIG SEAS IN STRAIT

Strait of Dover last night: Boisterous S.W. wind : heavy seas breaking over Dover Harbour walls.

Did you MACLEAN your teeth today?

Yes—keeps 'em healthy

Maclean's Teeth Paste—one size during war, 1/1 tube

▲ AS AXIS FORCES WITHDREW from Sicily, the Germans began moving more forces into the Italian mainland. These are Tiger I heavy tanks on their way to southern Italy.

▲ DAILY MAIL, FRIDAY AUGUST 6, 1943
One result of the loss of Sicily was Mussolini being toppled from power, leading to the dissolution of the Rome-Berlin Axis and Italy's surrender.

1D THE STARS AND STRIPES 1D

Daily Newspaper of U.S. Armed Forces in the European Theater of Operations

Vol. 3 No. 270 — New York, N.Y.—London, England — Wednesday, Sept. 15, 1943

'Fifth' Is Forced to Give Ground

Nazis Admit Pulling Out Of Bryansk

Lose Vital Base They Held Two Years; Red Drive Imperils Smolensk

Bryansk, main stronghold of the entire German defense system on the central Russian front, has been evacuated by the Germans and recaptured by the Russians after two years of Nazi occupation, Berlin radio admitted last night.

A few hours later, the Germans claimed two new Russian thrusts were endangering their positions at Smolensk, north of Bryansk, and at Novorossisk, last Nazi base in the Kuban.

In the recapture of Bryansk—which ranks with the victories at Kharkov, Kursk and Orel, in the great Russian summer offensive—Red Army forces smashed a head-on assault through a pill-box-studded forest defense zone, seized two main suburban railroad stations, and continued on over the bodies of 2,000 Nazi dead until they crossed to the west bank of the Desna River to reach the city.

On Railway to Smolensk

Supporting the Bryansk assault, other Russian forces battered three miles deeper into German defenses guarding Roslavl, midway station on the railroad between Bryansk and Smolensk.

Elsewhere along the vast front of the Russian onsurge between the Smolensk swamps and the Sea of Azov reports indicated that Nazi withdrawal was turning into a virtual rout—a flight for temporary safety behind the broad Dnieper River, with collapse most quickly before Kiev and Dnieperopetrovsk.

In a bee-line drive westward toward Kiev, the Russians announced encirclement and destruction of remnants of four German infantry divisions, while two Russian columns thrust ahead at a daily pace of six to nine miles toward the Ukraine capital. One column captured the railway station at Kruti, 10 miles east of Nezhin, on the main line to Kiev. It struck so swiftly that Nazi reinforcements were caught still on their trains, where they were wiped out or captured before they were able to put up a fight.

1,500 More Killed

Other Russian forces killed 1,500 more Germans in the southern Ukraine drive toward the Dnieperopetrovsk and Zaporozhe escape bridges on the Dnieper bend, and raced at the heels of Hitler's routed divisions with cavalry and mechanized troops.

The Germans were abandoning equipment in a desperate attempt to reach the bridges first. The speed of their pursuit indicated the Russians' determination to give the Nazis no time to organize a new defense at the mile-wide river barrier in the middle of the Ukraine.

Rokossovsky's mechanized forces pushed ten miles closer to Kiev from the Nezhin salient, and Vatutin's forces drove on seven more miles toward Kiev from the Priluki area. The Russians are already within artillery range of Nezhin and Priluki, some 80 miles from Kiev.

The Russian communique announced further gains of nine miles in the push beyond Chaplino.

Blitz at Peak 3 Years Ago

Germany lost the Battle of Britain—and very likely the war—just three years ago today.

On Sept. 15, 1940, in combats lasting from dawn until late at night, British airmen and anti-aircraft gunners destroyed 185 Nazi planes.

It was the largest number of enemy planes ever shot down over Britain, a destruction so costly that never thereafter did the Luftwaffe dare to strike in daylight against England in such strength. Day attacks gave way soon afterward to the long night fire raids of the late fall and winter.

Of the 185 planes brought down, seven were destroyed by ack-ack and the remainder by the overworked and outnumbered fighters of the RAF—the few to whom so many later came to owe so much. British losses were 25 fighters, but of these 12 pilots were saved.

Between 350 and 400 Nazi planes launched the principal attack against London and the southeast in two waves. Spitfires and Hurricanes met them over Maidstone and Canterbury, and above the Medway and Thames estuaries.

Where the Fortunes of Battle Sway

Fifth Army, locked in fierce battle with German panzers, give ground near Salerno. Eighth Army, on the south, captures Cosenza and moves north. Allied forces seize Bari, on the Adriatic, and are battling for Gioia airfield.

Violent Nazi Blows Unleashed on Yanks; Allies Gain in South

Americans Starting to Evacuate Salerno Bridgehead, Berlin Reports; Bari, In Italy's Heel, Falls to Allies

Powerful German counter-attacks forced Fifth Army troops to "give ground" yesterday on the 25-mile bridgehead along the coastal plain from Salerno to Agroploi in bloody fighting, with infantry, tanks, planes and even warships taking part in the battle, reports from Allied headquarters in Africa said last night.

As the fiercest struggle of the Mediterranean war entered its sixth day, Berlin and Stockholm reports said German panzer units had dented U.S. defenses on the outskirts of Salerno and that "the Allied evacuation of the area had begun under protection of strong naval forces."

Farther south, on the Calabrian peninsula, Eighth Army forces moved northward, capturing Cosenza, while Allied forces on the heel of Italy seized the Adriatic port of Bari and drove to Gioia, where a battle for the airfield is taking place.

German reports gave a picture of violent tank battles with heavy Allied casualties, and claimed that their reinforced army was smashing much of the Fifth Army, including some British divisions.

Gen. Eisenhower's headquarters said the Fifth Army, fighting under an intense artillery barrage from hidden enemy guns, is battling desperately to enlarge its Salerno bridgehead.

All along the front "bloody battles are raging and the Anglo-American forces are using infantry, tanks and planes against violent German counter-attacks. Although the Fifth Army has been forced back at a number of places, its troops have penetrated inland at other points.

"The Germans are counter-attacking desperately and, at certain points, have regained some of the ground previously taken by us," the communique from Eisenhower's headquarters said.

Three crack divisions of [illegible] the [illegible] Army which landed in the area six days ago. These are the 15th and 16th Panzer divisions and the Rerman Goering Division. The 15th and the Herman Goering divisions are veterans of the African campaign and there is no doubt they are tough fighters.

Allied troops, attempting to push their way inland from the coastal plains on which they are now located to the hills, are facing a terrific barrage from Nazi 88s, sweeping the coastal plain at many points.

Facing these guns and fighting hot artillery duels with them are units of Allied mobile self-propelled artillery which already have shown their superiority to the German weapons.

The Germans are doing everything possible to give their troops air cover and battles are taking place almost continuously over the battle area. The enemy have an advantage, however, because they control airfields within 50 miles of the battle zone while the nearest Allied field is some 130 miles away.

Throughout the day German radio claimed that the Allies have their backs to the sea and have begun to evacuate. There has been no official Allied confirmation of this, however, and even Sertorius, most reliable of all German commentators, said nothing to confirm these claims.

In Washington, Secretary of Navy Frank Knox said the landings at Salerno had been the "most hotly contested ever made by American troops" and that the surrender of the Italian fleet "practically clears the Mediterranean of enemy surface units." He emphasized that he meant only "surface units," and added the Germans can get submarines in there whenever they wish.

While the two forces advancing on Salerno from the south and east are only

(Continued on page 4)

Salamaua Falls; Allies Drive On To Get Lae Next

Sweep Through Wrecked Base Hot on Heels of Broken, Fleeing Japs

ALLIED HQ, Southwest Pacific, Sept. 14—Allied forces have captured Salamaua and are hot on the heels of the broken and disorganized remnants of the Jap garrison, fleeing northward along the New Guinea coast, the official communique announced today.

Hardly pausing in their victorious sweep into Salamaua, the Allied troops pressed forward in a drive to link up with Australian and American forces threatening the vital Japanese base at Lae, 30 miles north of Salamaua.

In addition to being cut off from all land assistance by two arms of a pincers squeezing ever tighter, plus being hopelessly isolated from the sea by constantly patrolling Allied warships, Lae is undergoing terrific aerial bombardments, and there was a possibility it might fall before the land attackers are joined by the Allied forces from the south.

More than 49 tons of bombs were rained on the base in the latest Allied blow, adding to the probability that Lae will look much the same as Salamaua, which was found to have been virtually wiped out by the weight of Allied bombing.

Five Ships Hit in Kuriles Raid

WASHINGTON, Sept. 14—The Navy Department announced today that five Japanese ships were damaged by American planes in the latest raid on the Kurile Islands, north of Japan. Liberators and medium Mitchells left one transport sinking, damaged a second and scored hits on three cargo vessels, in addition to pounding ground installations on Paramushiro Island.

RAF Harasses Shipping Off France, Holland

RAF Typhoons and Spitfires harassed enemy shipping off Cherbourg, Dunkirk and the Dutch islands yesterday, sinking one small vessel, leaving four on fire and damaging six others.

At the same time an enemy fighter was destroyed off the English south coast last night by two Typhoons flown by F/Sgt. R. L. Shelton, of Richmond, Va., and P/O W. Ahrens, of Rosewater, Sask.

7 Soldier Spouses, Yet Blond's No Divorcee

CINCINNATI, Sept. 14—Mrs. Vivian Eggers, blond and 34, was arrested here by FBI agents after she allegedly admitted having married seven soldiers "without bothering to divorce any of them."

Mrs. Eggers was quoted as having said she married five privates, a sergeant and a lieutenant between May of 1935, and June, 1943.

Soldiers Exempt On Tax Deadline

Members of the United States armed forces in the ETO need not worry about those income-tax declarations, due tomorrow.

Sept. 15 is the deadline when all U.S. taxpayers not in service must file declarations if the withholding tax clause under the new pay-as-you-go plan has not brought them up completely on their 1943 indebtedness. If not, they must file a declaration of estimated income-tax and Victory tax and pay half the amount due by Sept. 15, the other half by Dec. 15.

Exempted from this order are members of the Army, Navy, Marine Corps, Coast Guard and women's branches of the various services.

These may postpone the filing of their

(Continued on page 4)

Congress Back; Showdown Due On Father Draft

Big Issues Facing Session Are Manpower Needs, U.S. Post-War Role

WASHINGTON, Sept. 14—A showdown on Army manpower needs and clarification of what is to be the United States' position in the post-war world shaped up today as two of the most important issues facing the 78th Congress, reconvening after a summer recess.

The calling-up of pre-Pearl Harbor fathers was certain to precipitate a hot fight. Sen. Burton K. Wheeler, of Montana, who has served notice that he would press for action to postpone the drafting of fathers until Jan. 1, 1944, announced that he was amending his proposal to prohibit "indefinitely" the father draft.

"The Canadians are already disbanding some of their combat troops for civilian purposes," Wheeler said, referring to the just-announced plan to demobilize 20,000 Canadian troops to meet a manpower shortage in war plants, etc.

Sen. Alben W. Barkley, of Kentucky, Senate majority leader, said that he hoped to postpone consideration of legislation which would prohibit the drafting of fathers until Army and Navy chieftains could appear to explain the services' need for such men.

Sen. Guy M. Gillette, of Iowa, assert-

(Continued on page 4)

Award to French Reveals 6 Ships Lost in Russia Convoy

The sinking by enemy mines off Iceland on July 5, 1942, of six Allied vessels en route to Russia was revealed yesterday by the presentation of the Legion of Merit to Capitaine de Corvette Andre Bergeret, of the Fighting French, who rescued many of the survivors.

Capt. Bergeret was decorated on behalf of President Roosevelt by Adm. Harold R. Stark, commanding U.S. Naval Forces in Europe. At the same time Lt. Gen. Jacob L. Devers, ETO commander, presented another Legion of Merit to Fighting French Gen. Maurice Mathenet, who commanded the Moroccan division of the French forces in Tunisia.

The citation to Capt. Bergeret, signed by President Roosevelt and Secretary of the Navy Frank Knox, said he rescued 41 members of the U.S. armed guard and 121 members of the crews of the U.S. merchant vessels. In all 179 persons were taken aboard Bergeret's vessel.

"His prompt and efficient handling of rescue operations and his subsequent excellent care of survivors were valuable contributions to the successful escort of the convoy system in support of the Allied cause," the citation said.

The award to Gen. Mathenet, made by Gen. Devers on behalf of the President, cited the French commander's "exceptionally meritorious conduct of a high degree in the performance of outstanding services. . . . His untiring efforts and superb leadership contributed greatly to the successes achieved by forces under his command."

Expect Mussolini to Cancel Surrender, Reform Army

Berlin declared yesterday that Mussolini, as head of the new Italian Fascist government, would reorganize the Italian army, repudiate Italy's surrender and proclaim the end of the rule of the House of Savoy. Reports from Milan, Turin, Genoa and other cities controlled by the Germans told of Fascist reprisals against Allied sympathizers.

Mussolini's whereabouts was not known yesterday.

41 Italian Warships Safe With Allies; 26 at Malta

MALTA, Sept. 14—Forty-one Italian warships are now safe from Hitler's clutches in Allied ports. Here in Malta 26 ships alone have arrived since Saturday under the protection of Allied fleets and aircraft.

The total includes six battleships, nine cruisers, eight destroyers, six submarines and smaller units.

▲ THE STARS AND STRIPES, NEW YORK/LONDON, WEDNESDAY SEPTEMBER 15, 1943
On September 9, Lieutenant General Mark Clark's U.S. Fifth Army, plus the British X Corps, landed in the Gulf of Salerno, Italy. The Germans launched a fierce counterattack, and only massive aerial and artillery support saved the besieged Allies.

News Chronicle

NEWS CHRONICLE, Thursday, October 14, 1943
No. 30,397   THURSDAY, OCTOBER 14, 1943   ONE PENNY

ITALY DECLARES WAR ON GERMANY

Allies underline Badoglio's pledge of free elections

By VERNON BARTLETT

YESTERDAY afternoon Marshal Badoglio declared war on Germany. His own statement to the Italian people was broadcast by the weak wireless station at Bari and amplified by the more powerful station at Algiers.

At the same time the Italian Ambassador in Madrid was instructed to break the news to his German colleague that, "in the face of repeated and intensified acts of war committed against the Italians by the armed forces of Germany," the two countries were at war.

This declaration was immediately followed by identical declarations from the British, American and Soviet Governments confirming the obvious but bewildering fact that Italy had thereby achieved the status of "co-belligerent."

Thus Italy is at one and the same time a defeated enemy and a military ally. Each fact by itself is a welcome one. Combined they are, admittedly, bewildering, and it is necessary to remember certain basic considerations.

The first of these is that the Badoglio Government surrendered to the Allies without conditions.

Any subsequent discussion about the way in which the Italians can best co-operate to turn the Germans out of their country has taken place within the framework of the terms imposed at the time of that surrender.

GALLUP POLL ON "SHOULD BADOGLIO RULE?"

A STRONG majority of the British public dislike the idea that Italy may continue to be ruled by the present King and Marshal Badoglio after the Allies have liberated Italy from the Germans.

In the most recent Gallup Poll—which was, of course, compiled before yesterday's declaration of war by the Badoglio Government on Germany—a representative cross-section of the British public was asked:

"Do you think that the Italian King and Badoglio should be allowed to continue in office after the Germans are driven out of the country?"

32% said "Yes."
55% said "No."
13% said "Don't know."

(British Institute of Public Opinion : World Copyright Reserved.)

Serbs wreck a Krupps factory

FIGHTING their way into the little industrial town of Sarajevo, Yugo-Slav patriots wrecked an electric power station, all the blast furnaces and the mines and destroyed 27 railway engines and 150 waggons.

This was announced last night from headquarters of the Yugo-Slav National Army of Liberation. Fierce street fighting is still going on in the town.

Zenica, centre of the iron and steel industry in Bosnia, is on the railway which runs north from Sarajevo through Doboj to Brod on the Save.

The Germans are strengthening their forces at Doboj.

His Empire was a printer's error

By the Diplomatic Correspondent

ASKED in the House of Commons yesterday about the use of the titles "King of Albania" and "Emperor of Ethiopia" by King Victor Emmanuel in a proclamation broadcast from Bari on September 23, Mr. Richard Law, Minister of State, explained that the titleswere inserted in the decree through a mistake by a minor Italian official.

Mr. Law's tactful answer did not reveal that the "minor Italian official" is one of the better diplomatic jokes of the war.

What happened was that after the King and Marshal Badoglio had signed the proclamation, in which he was described simply and properly as "King of Italy," the draft document was sent to the local printer in Bari for printing.

He simply took out of the case the usual block of type which he kept ready set up for the printing of royal proclamations and decrees, in which of course the King was described in all the florid grandeur of his former titles, and set to work.

And the printed proclamations went forth to be posted and to be broadcast in that form.

CYCLONE

The result was a diplomatic cyclone. As soon as London and Washington heard of the broadcast, peremptory messages demanding to know "who?" and "why?" and "what the —?" hummed angrily along the wires to Italy, and, as Mr. Law revealed, the Allied liaison officer with the Badoglio Government was instructed to inform Marshal Badoglio that the use of these titles by the King was inadmissible.

East Coast raiders

Enemy aircraft which crossed the East Coast last night were met by anti-aircraft fire from coastal guns.

One plane which flew over an East Anglian town turned back without dropping bombs when attacked by a night fighter.

Continued Back Page (A)

EIGHTH ARMY DRIVE WITHIN TEN MILES OF KEY TOWN

From WILLIAM FORREST
News Chronicle War Correspondent

ALLIED FORCE H.Q., Wednesday.

ANOTHER big stride has been taken by the Eighth Army's left wing in its drive towards the Vinchiaturo Junction of the main roads from Foggia to Rome and from Termoli to Naples.

Pushing westwards into the Sannio Hills from Gambelusa, our fighting patrols reached Riccia, 12 miles from Vinchiaturo, while another force coming up from the south got even nearer the goal by capturing San Croce, only ten miles from Vinchiaturo.

But difficult hill country has still to be surmounted or circumvented before Vinchiaturo is reached.

The enemy, strong in artillery, has his guns sited in the hills round Cerve Maggiore. Bombing ahead of our troops, American Warhawks attacked these gun positions yesterday.

GUNS REINFORCED

To the north—on the Eighth Army's centre—heavy fighting is reported north-west of Colletorto. The capture of Bonefro, five miles from Colletorto, indicates that the battle is going in our favour.

Beyond the Volturno the Germans are bringing up more artillery to strengthen their defence of the river line, already formidable enough to give the Fifth Army pause.

The artillery duel across the swift-flowing flooded river is increasing in violence. Meanwhile, our patrols are still active on the farther bank.

8 miles apart

New York radio said last night: "Eighth Army, with forces now encircling Venafro, has flanked Volturno position. Some eight miles separate units of Eighth and Fifth Armies."

Overcast

Straits last night: Overcast and mild, with full moon shut out by fairly thick ceiling of light cloud; improved visibility; sea calm, with hardly a breath of wind.

U.S. move for post-war collaboration

From ROBERT WAITHMAN
News Chronicle Correspondent

WASHINGTON, Wednesday.

THE text was made public to-day of a resolution on American participation in post-war affairs which has been devised by a special sub-committee of the Senate Foreign Relations Committee and which is expected to be submitted to the Senate before long.

The resolution states: "It is resolved by the Senate of the United States that the war against all our enemies be waged until complete victory is achieved; that the United States co-operate with its comrades-in-arms in securing a just and honourable peace; that the United States, acting through its constitutional processes, join with free and sovereign nations in the establishment and maintenance of an international authority with power to prevent aggression and preserve the peace of the world."

Here is an air plan for victory

RONALD WALKER, News Chronicle Air Correspondent, has just returned from a three weeks' flying tour of the Mediterranean theatre of war. He has interviewed General Eisenhower, Air Chief Marshal Sir Arthur Tedder, Major-Gen. Carl Spaatz, Air Marshal Sir Arthur Coningham and Air Vice-Marshal Broadhurst, and talked with men of the squadrons in the field. The tour took him through Morocco, Algeria, Tunisia to Sicily and Italy and back to Malta and Gibraltar. Here is his first article.

Luftwaffe has "had it"

CONCEALED by the successes of the Allied Forces in the Mediterranean area during the past year is an event of far greater importance than any of the victories which have turned the tide of war in our favour.

High officers who served throughout the campaigns of the Middle East were as generous in their praise of Rommel.

They say he is the real Director of Training of the British Army. But if Rommel trained the British Army we have something more to thank the Germans for.

IDEAL TRAINING

In the long and arduous process of the ebb and flow of the desert campaigns, the advance from Alamein and the Allied invasions of North Africa, Sicily and Italy, we have evolved the pattern of modern warfare. It is a pattern which will shorten the duration of this present war and mould the development of air power in the future, the means of preserving peace. After a lot of muddled thinking and worse we have at last grasped the fact that air power cannot in the second world war has taken its proper place.

We have to thank the Germans for giving us an ideal training ground in which the elements of all three Services—sea, land and air —were vitally and directly employed.

In the campaigns of the Mediterranean where battles of the sea, land and air could never be separate events but part of the whole picture, the air has become the dominant factor.

Billy Brown of Berlin Town

"FRITZ FUERCHTENICHT" (Fritz Fear-Nothing), something of a Nazi counterpart of Billy Brown of London Town, was introduced on the German Home Service last night.

But instead of giving common-sense advice about travel, he deals with antidotes to R.A.F. letters in Germany.

Fritz figured in this chat at a club:

First Old Man : I wonder when they'll come over tonight?

Second Old Man: Well, we know that they can come over any time they like.

First Old Man: My wife shakes like a jelly. Every night she counts her buttons to make out whether the sirens will go.

After some more in this strain Fritz Fuerchtenicht broke in.

"If you followed the regulations there would be no need to be scared," he said. "I've lived with a suitcase in my hand for the past six months. That saves a lot of worry.

"You buy are responsible for panic and rumour. You're banking your whole war effort. You are ..."

A "Sorry Collection" on the Dnieper

On the Dnieper the Germans have pressed into service every possible type of plane, says Reuter's Moscow correspondent. They are using old Rumanian planes and all kinds of obsolete German types.

This "sorry collection" is being thrown into battle under the protection of groups of modern Messerschmitt fighters.

THEY SWAM THE VOLTURNO

From S. L. SOLON
News Chronicle War Correspondent

WITH THE FIFTH ARMY, Tuesday (delayed).

THE first Allied soldiers to cross the Volturno were two Spaniards now in the British Army—Private Joseph Villanova and Private Ferdinand Estero, who fought in the Spanish Civil War and one way or another.

"Ithought anyone who swam across was a hero," said Villanova, who is only 22, but had seven years of war.

They swam across at night and swam back after a successful reconnaissance.

They were over again last night in the drizzling rain and again they came back, but this time Villanova had two machine-gun bullets in him.

They were several hundred yards the other side of the river when they were challenged by a German sentry.

"Villanova replied, but then we heard the sharp pull back the bolt of his rifle," said Lieut. Kenneth Eve, of London, who led the patrol. "He never had a chance to fire Villanova opened up with his tommy-gun. Then the whole pack fashed up. The Germans must have loosed 25 machine-guns on us.

WOUNDED

The patrol scattered for cover, but Villanova was hit, and he was getting weaker.

"I put him on my shoulder and walked back to our boat, and then, swimming and pushing, we got back to our own side, though the current carried us a mile off our course."

In a trip from the Eighth Army front to the Fifth Army, I found what an obstacle the thick black mud can be.

We crawled down the mud gutted roads like those struggling on fly-paper. Across two swollen streams our car bogged above the wheels, and we could not continue our journey until it was winched to the opposite bank.

THE ORDERED PLAN

General Eisenhower talked to correspondents for an hour one morning in the historic room of the white villa on the Mediterranean shore where the invasion of Europe was planned. In the course of that talk he said:

"In the co-ordination of the three Services lies the most effective use of the air and the secret of modern war.

"But summing up can be added this: The offensive powers of the three Services do not add up. Working together they multiply."

BIG ALLIED FLEET ENTERS MEDITERRANEAN

Rabat, Wednesday.—A Allied Fleet, including the battleship King George V., the aircraft carriers Formidable and Illustrious and several destroyers, an American battleship and a cruiser, entered the Mediterranean recently, according to reports reaching Madrid from La Linea.

Senators' charges to be investigated

Washington, Wednesday.—President Roosevelt is understood to have asked the Administration to "trouble-shooter," Mr. James F. Byrnes, Director of War Mobilisation, to make an extensive investigation into all the matters arising from the charges against the allies of the United States here made by the five Senators their recent world tour.

Mr. Byrnes immediately got in Lend-Lease and Office of Information officials for consultation. He is also to discuss the charges with military and other officials.

President Roosevelt replied to certain specific criticisms at his Press conference yesterday. The production, control, and first result of this inquiry ...

Soviet diplomat's talks in Sofia

The Bulgarian Premier received the Soviet and Rumanian Ministers in Sofia on Tuesday, states Berlin radio.

Children so of ric...

From Our ...

CALCUTTA, Wednes...

"I WAS told stories of ... and daughters being by their parents for a ... ful of rice," said Mrs. Pau..., president of the All-In... Women's Conference, ... her tour of the famine a... of Bengal.

"I could never have imag... unless I had visited these part... she said, "that things could ... to such a miserable pass.

AID TOO LATE

The injury to the children would remain. It would require years to build up their bodies.

"A difficult problem for us will be the question of dealing with hopeless children," she added.

Mrs. Pandit regretted that Government help in granting transport and supplying controlled grain should have been so much delayed. The situation was deteriorating ...

Nazis face greatest crisis of war on Lower Dnieper

Red Army breaks through at four key towns

THE RED ARMY HAS BROKEN THROUGH THE NAZI DEFENCES SOUTH OF KIEV, AT ZAPOROZHE AND AT MELITOPOL. ON THE LOWER DNIEPER THE GERMANS (WRITES THE MILITARY CRITIC ON PAGE FOUR) ARE FACING THE GREATEST CRISIS OF THE WAR.

North of Kiev the Soviets have also pierced the German line and, forcing the River Sozh, are now fighting immediately before the road and rail centre of Gomel.

These sweeping successes were announced in Moscow's communique last night. An earlier report had stated that Soviet troops were fighting in the outskirts of Kiev.

The communique gave these details:

Melitopol.—Our troops, after three days' fighting, pierced the strongly fortified defence area north and south of Melitopol, forced the River Molochnaya and, having advanced between four and six miles, occupied more than 20 fortified points. Fighting is in progress in the centre of Melitopol. The Germans are suffering enormous losses in manpower and equipment.

TANKS, GUNS DESTROYED

Zaporozhe.—Our troops, after four days of stubborn fighting, pierced the defences, advanced between four and six miles, capturing more than 30 fortified points, and are fighting between five and three miles from Zaporozhe. Large numbers of Germans were destroyed, as well as many tanks and guns.

Dnieper (middle reaches).—On the west bank south of Kiev our troops pierced the defences and advanced four miles. Repeated counter-attacks were repelled with enormous losses.

Gomel.—South and north of Gomel our troops, having advanced three miles and crossed the River Sozh, forced several more miles and, having advanced several miles are fighting immediately in front of Gomel.

WITHDRAWALS

During the day 127 tanks were wrecked and 90 German aircraft shot down.

The Premier won over coal 'rebels'

THE intervention of the Prime Minister at the opening yesterday of the resumed coal debate in the House of Commons prevented what had threatened to be a Parliamentary revolt from developing any further.

The Labour attack (writes the Parliamentary Correspondent) died down, and the debate ended in an atmosphere, if not actual peace.

On nationalisation of the industry—the main demand of the miners' members—he was firm. It could be justified in war-time ere it it could be proved to be vital for the prosecution of the war, or was demanded by the majority of the country at a General Election. No case had been made out that it was a vital war measure, and a General Election would impede the war.

WANT REORGANISATION

Announcement of the breakthrough south of Kiev followed an earlier German admission that German defences on the west bank of the river had been withdrawn.

177 Jap planes wrecked

SOMEWHERE IN NEW GUINEA, Thursday.

IN the heaviest air blow yet struck in the South-West Pacific, Allied air forces attacked the enemy air base and stronghold of Rabaul, New Britain.

In the words of General MacArthur, the raiders "broke its back." These words appeared in a statement MacArthur issued from the Air Force "War Room."

This single midday assault, lasting more than two hours, achieved what MacArthur termed a crashing and decisive defeat.

3 DESTROYERS SUNK

At Rabaul 100 enemy aircraft were destroyed on the ground and 51 severely damaged, chiefly through strafing by Mitchells. Of the 40 fighters, which were all the Japanese could put in the air, 26 were shot down.

The total of 177 planes put out of action represents about 60 per ...

AIR MASTERY IN PACIFIC

Today's Australian communique (see this Col.) adds: "This operation, including the first phase at Wewak, gives us definite air mastery over the Solomons Sea and adjacent waters, and threatens the ...

—and this is the reality

Three men and a woman, from 64 to 41 have been in Berlin for working a political designed to shake belief in German victory, said the German News Agency yesterday.

DUKES OF GLOUCESTER'S RED CROSS & ST. JOHN FUND
Registered under the War Charities Act, 1940

Fund

▲ NEWS CHRONICLE, LONDON, THURSDAY OCTOBER 14, 1943
By late September, the Germans had retreated behind the Dnieper River, and the Red Army had inflicted losses of 230,000 on the Wehrmacht.

▲ GERMAN TROOPS RETREAT WEST in the fall of 1943. In September, Army Group South managed to evacuate 200,000 wounded soldiers west over the Dnieper River and then prepared to defend their position.

New York World-Telegram

2nd NIGHT
Latest Wall Street Prices

3 CENTS IN NEW YORK CITY
5 Cents Elsewhere

Local Forecast: This afternoon partly cloudy, colder, moderate winds.

SCRIPPS-HOWARD

VOL. 76—NO. 111—IN TWO SECTIONS—SECTION ONE.   NEW YORK, TUESDAY, NOVEMBER 9, 1943.   Entered as second class matter Post Office, New York, N.Y.

'44 VICTORY AT BIG COST FORESEEN BY CHURCHILL

500,000 Facing Red Trap

Reds Wreck Nazi Army, He Reveals

By the Associated Press.

LONDON, Nov. 9—Prime Minister Churchill gravely proclaimed the "impending ruin" of Germany today, but with all the force of his leadership and language warned that in his belief the Nazis' defeat could not come before 1944.

He asserted solemnly that the campaigns of next year might surpass the tragedies of Waterloo and Gettysburg, that "unless some happy event occurs, on which we have no right to count, 1944 will see the greatest sacrifice of the British and United States armies.

(Earlier news stories from London declared that the deadline date for the land invasion of the Continent has been set and has been communicated to the Russians.)

The valiant and brilliant Russian offensives have wrecked the German war machine and inflicted wounds "that may well prove fatal," Mr. Churchill declared.

The Prime Minister asserted that the back of the Nazi submarine warfare has been broken and that the devastating air war upon the Reich has "been one of the prime forces in the impending ruin of the Hitler regime."

In an address broadcast to the world, Mr. Churchill said: "I am myself proceeding on the assumption that the campaign of 1944 in Europe will be the most severe and most costly to the Allies yet fought.

"We must strain every nerve for its successful accomplishment. This is no time for relaxation."

Desperate Fight Ahead.

Hitler still has 400 divisions, promises a desperate struggle, and "we cannot exclude the possibility of new forms of attack upon this island," Mr. Churchill warned, his address being given at the inaugural luncheon of a new Lord Mayor of London.

He repeated later in his address that "the year 1944 will see the greatest sacrifice of life of the British and United States armies."

This year 1944 is also election year in the United States." Mr. Churchill said. "I am sure I speak for all those of both sides of the Atlantic when I say that I hope we can preserve that goodwill throughout the English-speaking world and all our armies."

His address was on the occasion of the induction of Sir Frank E. Newson-Smith, who succeeded Sir Samuel Joseph as Lord Mayor.

The traditional procession of the Lord Mayor through the streets preceded the luncheon.

Recalls 1940 Pledge.

On the same occasion last year Mr. Churchill disclosed that President Roosevelt was the author of the North African landing and that the landing was intended only to gain vantage ground for a new front against Hitler, a front which since has been opened, with more to follow.

Mr. Churchill recalled at the beginning of his address that in 1940 at the height of the blitz he pledged Great Britain never to give up the fight to liberate peoples from the Nazi yoke.

"There is nothing wrong with that," he said amid cheers.

Air Way May Signal Victory.

In the last year, he observed, there have been an unbroken series of Allied victories and "we have broken the back of the U-boat war, which at one time threatened our whole war effort."

He said the aerial campaign against Germany might well be

(Continued on Page Two.)

Wife Awaits Call to Defend De Marigny

Expected to Provide Climax Today at Oakes Murder Trial

By the Associated Press.

NASSAU, Bahamas, Nov. 9—Loyal Nancy Oakes de Marigny waited eagerly today to provide a spectacular ending to the defense of her husband, Alfred, accused of her father's murder, by asserting her complete faith in his innocence.

The 19-year-old daughter of Sir Harry Oakes will climax the defense by her final witness for de Marigny, just as her mother, Lady Eunice Oakes, was one of the most powerful factors in the case of the Crown.

Since the trial began the red-haired Nancy has maintained a lonely vigil in her cottage. She was in a Vermont college when her father was slain, but a few days after de Marigny was arrested flew to his side and marshalled attorneys and detectives to defend him.

Plans Fight to Finish.

Nancy has said she is positive he will be acquitted, but in event of his conviction she will continue the fight with all available means.

But before she testifies, Godfrey Higgs, chief defense counsel, planned to call Leonard Keeler, the criminologist who perfected a lie detector and is an authority on handwriting and fingerprints.

Dr. Keeler is expected to give further support to the defense contention that a fingerprint of-

Picture on Page 7.

fered by the Crown as one of de Marigny's taken from a bedscreen in the room where Sir Harry was slain, was faked. That theory received support from Capt. Maurice B. O'Neil of the New Orleans Identification Bureau, who stated positively that the print in evidence—Exhibit J—did not come from the screen.

Contradicts Miami Expert.

This was a direct contradiction of the testimony of Capt. James O. Barker of the Miami Identification Bureau, a Crown witness.

The defense called Charles Rolle, de Marigny's butler, who said he saw de Marigny return to his cottage about 1:30 a.m. on the night Sir Harry was slain after driving two women guests to their homes. De Marigny went to his bedroom, Mr. Rolle declared. The butler added that he locked the front door and left with the cook about 2:30 a.m.

(As the trial neared conclusion defense sources said they will petition and appeal to the Privy Council, the highest tribunal, if their client is found guilty, according to the United Press. A unanimous verdict of the jury is necessary for the death penalty.

(Power to commute a death sentence to life imprisonment rests with the Duke of Windsor, a friend of the slain baronet, who is in the United States.

(If eight or more jurors vote in de Marigny's favor, the verdict will be not guilty. Any other split vote is equivalent to a disagreement in which case the Crown has the privilege of retrying the case.)

H. M. S. Warspite Reported Damaged

From Axis Propaganda Sources.

By the Associated Press.

LONDON, Nov. 9—The famous British battleship Warspite was brought into Gibraltar yesterday in a damaged condition, the Berlin radio said today in a dispatch from La Linea, Spain. "No reasons for serious damage thus far have been stated," said the broadcast report, which had no con-

Guardsman, 16, Causes Blast Attempting to End Life by Gas

In what police described as "an apparent attempted suicide" by a 16-year-old New York Guardsman, the kitchen of a sixth-floor apartment at 120 Cabrini Blvd. in the Castle Village development was virtually wrecked by an explosion early today.

The youth, Phillip Arijewitach, son of Mrs. Yvette Arijewitach, suffered gas poisoning. After being dragged out of the apartment by neighbors was taken to

condition found to be not serious.

Police said the boy reportedly had been scolded by his mother some time yesterday for having stayed out too late.

The explosion occurred shortly before 3 a.m. and was followed by a small fire, which was quickly extinguished by firemen under the direction of Battalion Chief William Murphy. The concussion blew down a partitioning kitchen wall which crumbled over Mrs. Arijew-

---

Black Market Men Move in on Liquor

By MURRAY DAVIS,
World-Telegram Staff Writer.

The liquor industry, from top to bottom, is making "tremendous" profits, a distillery spokesman admitted today.

"Any crying that is going on now is of the future, not the present," he insisted.

Increased buying power, resulting from war work, has provided liquor stores with a "sellers' heaven," he said. Where the most expensive brands, usually the longest profit items, represented only from 10 to 15 per cent of the retail volume they now account for all but that percentage.

Can't Get Share.

"The price is of no consequence to a great majority of today's liquor customers," he added.

As a result a large percentage of the department and package stores are unable to get their fair share of merchandise and their regular customers must do without. Less scrupulous members of the industry, from distillers down through all branches to the bar keep, are busy in black market activities, it is admitted within the trade, and are resorting to numerous "stunts" to increase the size of each sales slip.

One of the most widely used "stunts," which now is being investigated by OPA, is the "gift" or "holiday package."

Retail package store proprietors defend this practice on the ground their suppliers use tie-ins on them and they must pass along the merchandise. These proprietors insist that salesmen representing many supply houses refuse to sell a case of whisky unless brandy, rum, cane gin and wine also is included in the order.

"There is a concerted attempt to push brandy, rum, cane gin and wine," a liquor buyer for a large department store said. "We have bought considerable quantities of these items, of course, for we have to supply our trade with something, but they don't dare put the pressure on us that is applied to smaller concerns."

Leads in Consumption.

Many of the "smaller concerns" will not sell a customer a bottle of whisky. They will sell, however, a "package" containing one bottle of whisky and from two to four other bottles of other wines and spirits at a total cost from $1 to $5 above the combined ceiling prices.

It is impossible to tell whether or not there is an actual liquor shortage here or to what extent if one really exists. There have been "official" estimates from the industry stating there is only a "two-year supply" and that there

(Continued on Page Seven.)

Christmas in Algiers

By JAMES E. ROPER,
United Press Staff Correspondent.

ALGIERS, Nov. 9—An American doughboy came to town because Santa Claus is here! Come get your mail.

And that was how Christmas came to North Africa in November—because the folks back home had remembered to mail those packages early.

The boys came tumbling out, eager to get their Yule gifts. And maybe the sun was hot overhead and the ground dusty underfoot, but the old-fashioned spirit of Christmas was there in the beaming faces as strings and wrappers flew off.

Yes, the wrappers flew off, even off the packages that some one had shouted "Santa Claus is here!" instead of "mail call," and the boys tumbled out, eager to get their Yule gifts.

Most of the gifts were something to eat, showing that folks back home—like the troops at the front—have learned a lot during the last year.

Colder Tonight

After first forecasting snow flurries for tonight, the Weather Bureau revised its prediction today and said it would be "much colder with increasing winds." The temperature dropped 14 degrees between 4 and 9 a.m., from 65 to 51.

Widener Riches Left To Son and Daughter

By the United Press.

PHILADELPHIA, Nov. 9—A son and a daughter of the late Joseph E. Widener, sportsman, financier and art collector, have been named principal beneficiaries of his estimated $25,000,000 estate, it was disclosed today.

Peter A. B. Widener 2nd and Mrs. Josef Winfield were named principal legatees in Widener's will. Probation of the document has been delayed because of the son's illness in Lexington, Ky. The heirs, it was estimated, would each receive between $625,000 and $1,250,000 a year income from the estates of Joseph Widener and his father, the late Peter A. B. Widener, who left between $50,000,000 and $100,000,000.

The trustees of the National Art Gallery, Washington, were given all books on art at Widener's Philadelphia suburban home.

Speeds Husband's Draft, Joins Wacs

By the Associated Press.

CLAYTON, Ala., Nov. 9—A woman approached Capt. George H. C. Stone, Gunter Field officer conducting an "air WAC" recruiting drive, and said:

"I am interested in joining the WAC but I don't want to leave until my husband is drafted. What can I do?"

"That is your problem, mam," the captain told her.

"Not any longer," she declared as she grasped a nearby telephone and called her husband's draft board.

"Put my husband in the next call," she told a Selective Service official. "I am joining the WAC."

What a Dividend! 27 Gallons Whisky

By the Associated Press.

BALTIMORE, Nov. 9—Stockholders in the Tom Moore Distillery Co. counted themselves pretty lucky people today—what with the whisky shortage—for the concern's directors declared a dividend of 27 gallons of bulk Kentucky bourbon whisky per share.

And—if stock is available some others may get in on the distribution. The directors made the dividend payable to stockholders of record Nov. 26.

The net value of the dividend for each $25 par value share was computed at $31.89. The whisky ranges in price, based on OPA ceilings from $1.07 to $1.51 a gal-

---

Huge Nazi Army Making Stand Near Rumania

Russians Hit Flank In Dnieper Pocket Trying to Cut Off Foe

By HENRY SHAPIRO,
United Press Staff Correspondent.

MOSCOW, Nov. 9—A Red army mobile column wheeled southward from the rapidly expanding Kiev bridgehead today and sliced into the flank of the lower Dnieper pocket in a bid to trap 500,000 Germans making a desperate rearguard stand before the approaches to Rumania.

Meanwhile Russian forces launched a powerful attack against the Crimea from the north, seeking down the Perekop isthmus to trap the tens of thousands on the peninsula.

(The Nazi-controlled Paris radio declared strong Red army forces were being hurled into the battle, according to the Associated Press.

Dent Nazi Flank.

(A Bern dispatch to the Swedish newspaper Svenska Dagbladet said that some contingents of German soldiers already had been evacuated by sea from the Crimea to Rumania, and that hundreds of Black Sea coastal ships and Danube River boats were assembled for a rescue. Red pressure on the Kerch Strait also was increasing, evacuated Germans said.)

Soviet field dispatches described a three-pronged Russian offensive spreading up to 45 miles beyond Kiev, threatening the last longitudinal railway east of pre-war Poland, and denting the flank of the German forces holding the Dnieper bend country.

Formidable Russian forces were reported sweeping southward against the Korsun-Dnepropetrovsk bulge, where the Nazis had staved off imminent disaster with a back-to-the-wall defense hinged on Krivoi Rog.

(A German communique said the fighting on the Kiev front had

(Continued on Page Two.)

[Map of Eastern Front with labels: LATVIA, Nevel, Velikie Luki, Rzhev, MOSCOW, LITHUANIA, Kaunas, Polotsk, Vitebsk, Vyazma, Tula, Vilna, Orsha, Smolensk, Grodno, Minsk, Mogilev, Bryansk, Orel, Pinsk, Gomel, Desna R., Kursk, POLAND, Korosten, Konotop, Lwow, Zhitomir, KIEV, Dnieper R., KHARKOV, Poltava, Rovno, Berdichev, Big R., Krivoi Rog, Dnepropetrovsk, RUMANIA, Balta, Nikolaev, HUNGARY, Odessa, Kherson, STATUTE MILES 0 100]

A. P. Map.

As 500,000 German troops sought to make a stand before the approaches to Rumania, Russian troops moved south from the Kiev bridgehead in an effort to strike the flank of the lower Dnieper pocket. Arrows show direction of attacks. Diagonally shaded area shows Nazi-held Russia.

The War Today

Tuesday, Nov. 9, 1943.

RUSSIA—Germans in disorderly retreat across western Ukraine abandoning planes and equipment; three Red Army columns racing toward pre-war Polish borders; Soviets tighten ring around trapped Nazis on Crimean Peninsula.

ITALY—Eighth Army advances four miles to capture strategic heights above Sangro River, 26 miles from Adriatic end of lateral road to Rome; Anglo-American Fifth Army beats off stiff German counterattacks; Flying Fortresses from Mediterranean bases knock out Fiat ball bearing plant in Turin.

PACIFIC—Allied fliers destroy 63 and probably 79 more Jap planes, sink or damage 8 ships and 34 barges in continuing attacks on enemy's southwest Pacific strongholds; Japs massing troopships for defense of northern Solomons; Marines consolidate position on Bougainville; American planes sink Jap destroyer and four other vessels off southeast China coast; Chinese column wins jungle line along upper Chindwin River in Burma.

(Continued on Page Ten.)

Knox Reports Japs Fighting for Survival

By the Associated Press.

WASHINGTON, Nov. 9—Secretary of the Navy Knox said today that the Japanese in the present South and Southwest Pacific battle area are now in a more "critical position" than they ever have been.

Mr. Knox told his news conference that "it is no longer a question of holding their outpost positions but one of actual survival."

Furthermore, Mr. Knox said, their casualties among cleaner cruisers, as the result of Allied air attacks in the Rabaul area, constitutes "nothing short of disaster to the Japanese.

"If they don't look out they'll be short of these very vital heavy craft when they want to go to sea with their fleet," Mr. Knox said.

During the last 10 days, Mr. Knox continued, the Japs have suffered a series of several important military defeats. He listed these as follows:

1. Landing of marines on Bougainville Island in the northwestern Solomons.

2. The night surface engagement in which Adm. William F. Halsey's force sank a Jap cruiser and a Jap destroyer.

Borrows Bus, Goes to Town

By the Associated Press.

SANTA MONICA, Cal., Nov. 9—To go into the bus business you need a bus.

Police said Edwin Kiedrowski, 17-year-old visitor from Milwaukee, managed it this way:

Observing that a large motor coach was parked nightly behind a bus station he instituted a midnight to dawn schedule between Santa Monica and Port Hueneme, 45 miles up the coast—without confiding in the bus company. He charged his passengers, chiefly sailors, 50 cents each, and business was brisk until bus officials began to wonder why the coach was almost out of gas every morning. They called the police.

Kiedrowski pleaded guilty yesterday on a charge of tampering with an automobile. A probation hearing was set for Friday.

Flying Forts Wreck Turin Bearing Works

By JAMES E. ROPER,
United Press Staff Correspondent.

ALLIED HQS., ALGIERS, Nov. 9—Flying Fortresses destroyed or damaged severely every building at the Fiat ball bearing works at Turin, third most important in enemy Europe, yesterday in photographs revealed that the plant was knocked "completely out of business for a considerable period," it was announced today.

(British Mosquito bombers hit western Germany again last night as a few German planes raided London for the seventh night in a row, it was announced in London today. The slight damage and casualties. Targets of the twin-engined British night raiders were not announced immediately, but presumably they lay in the industrial Ruhr and Rhineland. All returned safely.)

The Air Ministry announced in London that new reconnaissance photographs of the heavily bombed Ruhr industrial city of Kassel showed that the city had ceased to exist as part of the Nazi war industry "for some time at least." 50 factories having been destroyed or badly damaged, the Associated Press said.)

The Fiat aircraft engine works and motor car plant and railway repair shops adjacent to the ball bearing works were damaged.

Smoke mushrooming up from the

center could be seen for 80 miles, the U.S. Air Forces announced. All Fortresses and Lightnings returned safely from the raid, the first from Mediterranean bases on Turin.

The Berra radio, heard by CBS, said an official announcement issued in Rome acknowledged heavy material damage in Turin, and said there were a "considerable" number of casualties.

(Continued on Page Two.)

World-Telegram Index

	Page
Amusements	22 to 25
Books	20
Bridge	20
Camera News	20
Comics, Crossword Puzzle	20
Editorials, Talburt Cartoon	24
Eleanor Roosevelt	20
Ernie Pyle	3
Finance	28 and 29
Joe Williams	25
Metropolitan Movies	23
Movies, Alton Cook	23
Music	23
News Outside the Door	20
Obituaries	17
Radio	25
Ration Information	17
Raymond Clapper	24
Real Estate	27
Society	17
Sports	25 to 27
Theaters, Burton Rascoe	24
Tips on Tables, Paul Martin	25
Westbrook Pegler	24
William Philip Simms	24

The Weather

(Official United States Forecast.)
—This afternoon partly cloudy, New York and Metropolitan Area growing colder, with moderate winds.
New Jersey—Cloudy and colder with diminishing winds.

TODAY'S READINGS.

Chicago Daily Tribune

THE WORLD'S GREATEST NEWSPAPER

3 CENTS PAY NO MORE!   **FINAL**

VOLUME CII—NO. 279 C   MONDAY, NOVEMBER 22, 1943.—38 PAGES   PRICE THREE CENTS

NIMITZ STRIKES IN PACIFIC

TELL CHURCHILL NOT TO MEDDLE IN '44 ELECTION

Hint He Might Aid F.D.R. Assailed.

Farmers Rebel Against OPA Snoop Tricks

BY GAIL COMPTON

300,000 SLASH IN GOVERNMENT PAY ROLL ASKED

Byrd Group Makes Second Demand.

FOLLOWING THE FOREIGN POLICY,

BATTLE RAGES AS YANKS LAND ON MAKIN, TARAWA

Hold Beachheads After Shelling by Fleet.

War Summaries

Would Query High Staff on M'Arthur Aid

UNRRA STUDIES PLAN TO BAR COMPETITION FOR SCARCE SUPPLIES

Union Chiefs Score Tribune; Members Hail It for Expose

BY GEORGE HARTMANN

'A Typical Letter'

Rep. Ditter, Navy Man Die in Plane Crash

KENNEY KEEPS A PROMISE—WITH SLIGHT CHANGES

Leap Saves Policeman as Five Drive Car at Him

STALLING IN WAR TO AID F.D.R. IN '44 FEARED BY BABSON

THE WEATHER

MONDAY, NOVEMBER 22, 1943.

Tribune Features

Bags 17th Deer at 70; She Takes It in Stride

OCTOBER 1943 DAILY 930,000
THE CHICAGO TRIBUNE

LARGEST OF GILBERT ISLES

▲ CHICAGO DAILY TRIBUNE, MONDAY NOVEMBER 22, 1943

The heavy casualties suffered at Tarawa shocked the U.S. public, but it gave Nimitz a base for operations against the Marshall Islands. And for the first time in military history, a seaborne assault had been launched against a heavily defended coral atoll and had been successful.

Gilbert Islands

NOVEMBER 1943

THE U.S. OPERATION AGAINST TARAWA IN THE GILBERT ISLANDS, WHICH TOOK PLACE IN NOVEMBER 1943, WAS AMONG THE BLOODIEST ACTIONS OF THE WHOLE PACIFIC WAR. TARAWA Atoll was a little over 10 miles (16 km) long, but the bulk of Japanese defenses were concentrated on the islet of Betio, around 2 miles (3.2 km) long and 0.5 miles (0.8 km) wide. The 4,500 Japanese troops stationed on Betio, commanded by Rear Admiral Shibasaki, had created dense networks of fortified bunkers, trenches, and pillboxes, in which they sat out the U.S. Navy's heavy preliminary bombardment of 3,000 tons (3,048 tonnes) of shells in only two-and-a-half hours (bunkers constructed from sand-packed palm-tree logs proved especially durable).

BETIO

On November 20, the first troops of the U.S. 2nd Marine Division went ashore at Betio, straight into a hail of Japanese bullets and shells. Beach reconnaissance had

▲ U.S MARINES during the fighting at Tarawa Atoll. The Americans lost 3,407 dead and wounded on Betio and a further 118 on Makin.

been inaccurate, and many of the "Amtrac" amphibious vehicles grounded on a shallow reef, leaving the occupants to wade ashore under blistering small-arms and artillery fire. On the beach, soft sand made it difficult for the U.S. soldiers to dig in. In addition, radio communications between U.S. units broke down, resulting in 1,500 Marine casualties by the end of the day. In the evening, 75 percent of the island was still in Japanese hands. A Japanese counterattack would have driven most of the Marines into the sea, but the expected Japanese counterattack did not materialize because the preliminary bombardment had destroyed Japanese lines of communication.

TARAWA

However, a U.S. beachhead was eventually established, and over the next two days the Marines fought their way across Tarawa, with the defenders contesting every single yard of ground to the death. A final suicidal charge by the Japanese on the 22nd, however, signified that their resistance was crumbling, and on the 23rd the fighting finally stopped. It had been a bloody affair.

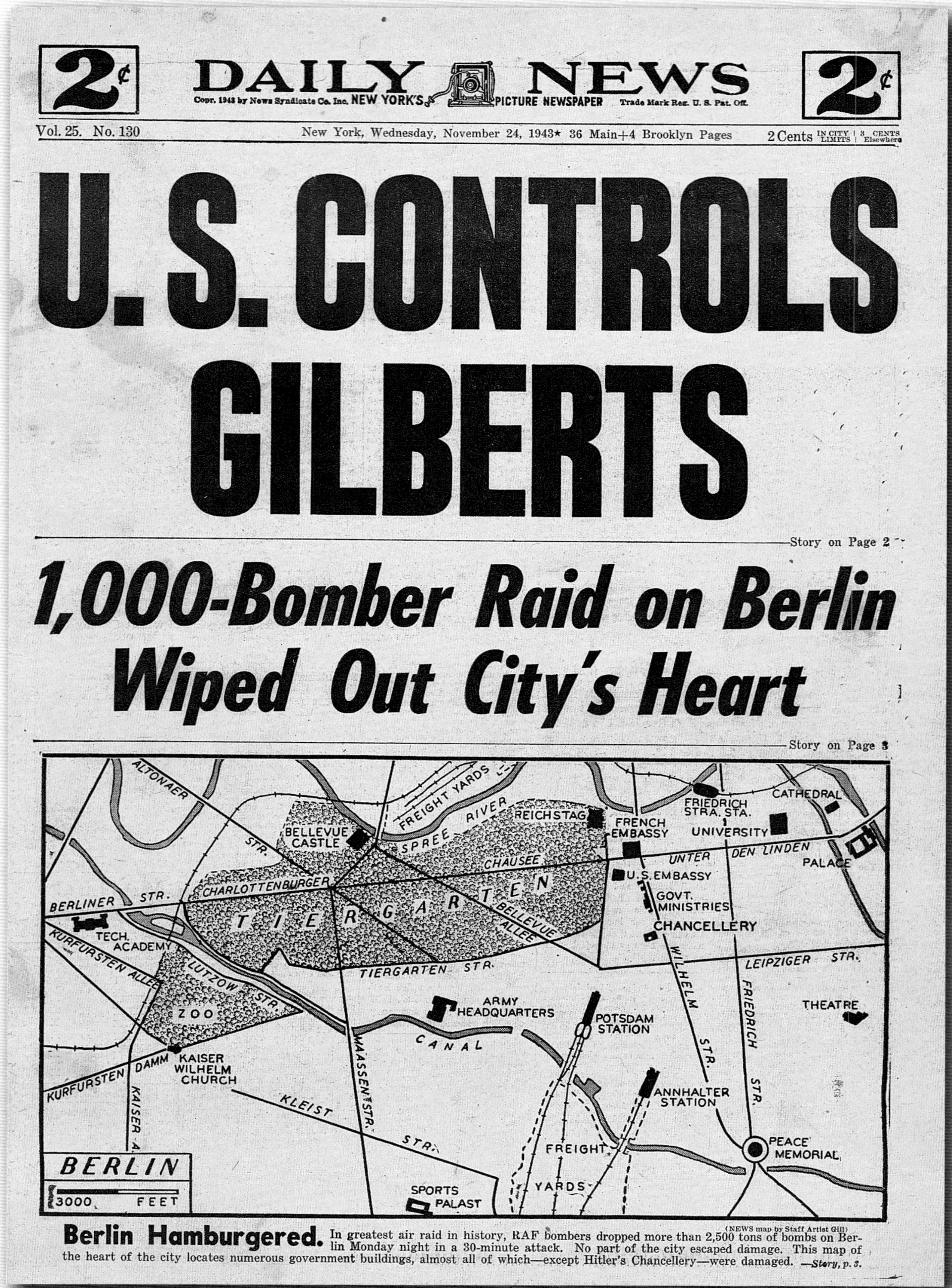

DAILY 📷 **NEWS**

2¢   2¢

Copr. 1943 by News Syndicate Co. Inc. **NEW YORK'S** PICTURE NEWSPAPER Trade Mark Reg. U. S. Pat. Off.

Vol. 25. No. 130   New York, Wednesday, November 24, 1943★ 36 Main+4 Brooklyn Pages   2 Cents IN CITY LIMITS | 3 CENTS Elsewhere

U.S. CONTROLS GILBERTS

—Story on Page 2

1,000-Bomber Raid on Berlin Wiped Out City's Heart

—Story on Page 3

Berlin Hamburgered. In greatest air raid in history, RAF bombers dropped more than 2,500 tons of bombs on Berlin Monday night in a 30-minute attack. No part of the city escaped damage. This map of the heart of the city locates numerous government buildings, almost all of which—except Hitler's Chancellery—were damaged. *—Story, p. 3.*

(NEWS map by Staff Artist Gill)

▲ DAILY NEWS, NEW YORK, WEDNESDAY NOVEMBER 24, 1943

On November 16, the RAF began a five-month bomber offensive against Berlin, Germany. During these attacks, 6,100 people were killed and 18,400 injured, and large parts of the city were destroyed, or "Hamburgered."

Daily Mirror

2¢
WEATHER
CLOUDY, RAIN.
(Details on Page 2)

3 Cents in Suburbs
4 Cents Elsewhere

2¢

Vol. 20. No. 160.   R   DAILY MIRROR, MONDAY, DECEMBER 27, 1943   COMPLETE SPORTS

BRITISH SINK NAZI POCKET BATTLESHIP SCHARNHORST

Trapped in Fight

LONDON, Dec. 26 (INS).—The Admiralty announced tonight that the 26,000-ton German battleship Scharnhorst has been sunk.

The Nazi "pocket" battleship was sunk off North Cape, the extreme northern tip of Norway, this evening when engaged by units of the British home fleet covering a Russian convoy, it was disclosed.

Text of a terse Admiralty communique read:

"This afternoon, Dec. 26, the German battleship Scharnhorst was brought to action by units of the Home Fleet under command of Admiral Sir Bruce Fraser, K. C. B., K. B. E., which were covering a Russian convoy. The

Scharnhor
Cape."

Laun
powerful
nine 11 in
Scharnhor
She norma

Often
with her s
last previo
out in a p
routes.

The S
inch guns,
smaller w

Complete details in later editions.

▲ DAILY MIRROR, MONDAY NOVEMBER 27, 1943
In the Battle of the North Cape, the *Scharnhorst* was sunk by vessels of the British Home Fleet. Only 36 of *Scharnhorst*'s 1,800-strong crew survived.

▲ THE BRITISH BATTLESHIP HMS *Duke of York* photographed after her naval gunfire had been instrumental in the sinking of the German battleship *Scharnhorst*. *Duke of York* survived the war.

1944

1943 HAD BEEN A YEAR OF HARD FIGHTING, WITH THE ALLIES MEETING BITTER RESISTANCE FROM THEIR ENEMIES. IN 1944, THE FIGHTING WAS JUST AS TOUGH, BUT THE RESULTS OF ALLIED SUCCESSES WERE SPECTACULAR.

ON THE EASTERN FRONT, THE YEAR OPENED WITH THE FINAL RELIEF OF LENINGRAD, BESIEGED FOR 900 DAYS. IN THE SUMMER, THE SOVIETS CLEARED GERMAN FORCES FROM Russian territory and then forced Germany's allies Romania and Bulgaria out of the war. The Red Army flooded into the Balkans, but further north stopped before Warsaw, allowing a revolt there to be crushed by the Wehrmacht.

In Italy, hard fighting in the spring eventually led to the capture of Monte Cassino, and then the fall of Rome on June 5—the day before the Allies launched the invasion of northwest Europe. D-Day was followed by the liberation of Paris in August. A sign of the increasing desperation in Germany was the attempt by

army officers to assassinate Hitler on July 20. The dictator survived, and condemned his people to almost another year of war. The final German offensive in the west, in December 1944, merely weakened the Wehrmacht defending the Rhine frontier.

THE WAR AT SEA AND IN THE AIR

In the Far East, there were two overwhelming naval victories for U.S. forces: at the Philippine Sea in June; and at Leyte Gulf in October. These were accompanied by advances across the central Pacific to the Marianas and landings on the Philippines.

Air attacks on the Japanese home islands became possible late in 1944, while the bombing raids on German cities increased in intensity. For a brief period in the fall, the Germans struck back, using V1 "doodlebugs" and V2 rockets, but the threat passed.

▲ IN THE FROZEN WASTES of northern Russia, Red Army troops and tanks advance during the offensive that finally liberated Leningrad. The city had been under siege for three years.

Daily Mail

NO. 14,890 — ONE PENNY — ✶✶ — FOR KING AND EMPIRE — SATURDAY, JANUARY 22, 1944

BERLIN'S WORST NIGHT OF TERROR

THE CZARS' SUMMER PALACES SACKED

THE Germans sacked Peterhof, the most brilliant and elaborate summer residence of the once Russian Court, where two centuries of architectural taste were reflected, Red Star revealed to-day. The Great Palace and Mon Plaisir Palace, where Peter the Great lived as he was building St. Petersburg, were burned. The Germans had made public rest rooms and a comfort station out of Peterhof Cathedral. Great damage is also reported from the ancient city of Novgorod, where not a building has been left intact.—A.P.

Fourth Offensive Opens Below Leningrad

BIG RAIL BASE OF MGA TAKEN

From Daily Mail Special Correspondent
Stockholm, Friday.

STALIN to-night announced the opening of the fourth offensive on the Northern Front in six days. It has been launched by the combined armies of the Leningrad and the Volkhov sectors and has captured the railway junction of Mga.

This new attack, announced in a Special Order of the Day, is clearly synchronised with the offensives already in progress south-west of Leningrad and west of Novgorod. It is aimed at driving the Germans from their great defences.

It is the beginning of the final phase of the Winter War and means that the 150 miles of the Northern Front from Lake Ilmen to the Gulf of Finland is ablaze.

Mga controls the railway south-east from Leningrad to the interior, and the advance westward will aid in freeing the close network of railways around Leningrad.

Its fall has also cut the main supply line to the garrisons of the German defences along the line to Kirishi and Chudovo, which lies north of Novgorod.

A hundred miles to the south of the new front the victors of Novgorod are now ten miles west of the city on the main road and railway through Batetskaya to Luga, less than 50 miles away.

The capture of Batetskaya, 20 miles west of the new Russian line, will cut the railway running north to Leningrad and complete the encirclement of all the Germans still manning the Volkhov River defences.

A considerable advance south-west of Leningrad was reported in the routine communique.

The town of Vitino, 36 miles from the city, has fallen. It cuts the main line to Leningrad along the Baltic coast.

Moscow added that the Germans encircled in this area have now been "liquidated." Remnants of the Novgorod garrison are being steadily chopped up in the woods west of the city.

Berlin to-night admitted a withdrawal "south of Ropsha," which agrees with the Russian report.

Many miles ahead of the troops advancing beyond Novgorod large numbers of ski battalions are carrying out their now classical tactics of harassing German supply lines and cutting up supply columns.

They are being actively assisted by thousands of Russian guerillas, who are also reported to have created very considerable confusion on the supply route from the west which runs to the Leningrad front along the Baltic coast line.

'DEFENSIVE BATTLE'

Heavy fighting is now spreading along the whole of the front north of the Pripet Marshes.

Reports from Moscow to-day said that battles are raging along the line south from Leningrad along the Moscow railway near Chudovo junction, and down the River Volkhov.

These attacks are obviously aimed at holding the Germans in their defences until the great pincer movement has been completed behind them.

Berlin reports from north of Nevel and the German communique to-day gave great prominence to what it described as the "Vitebsk defensive battle."

The battle, said the German, began on December 13 and by January 18 had cost the Russians 40,000 dead, 1,200 tanks, and 246 guns.

The Red Army had attacked with 50 rifle divisions and the Germans, under a major-general, had held their positions, added the High Command.

The reference to the commander suggests that the city is besieged A major-general would hardly direct a defensive battle against 40 enemy divisions (probably more than 500,000 men) unless his troops were surrounded.

NEW ADVANCE

A fresh series of attacks is also reported by Berlin from the Mozyr area where yesterday the withdrawal from a strongpoint was admitted.

The Moscow communique reported advances north-west of Kalinkovichi, with the capture of several places.

Although there is no news from Moscow about the progress of the great battle for the River Bug crossings near Vinnitsa on the Dnieper front, there is some indication that General Vatutin has begun to counter-attack.

Colonel Hammer said that a Russian tank attack north of Uman was repelled and ground gained.

In a further comment on the northern battle Hammer said :

"The enemy has not been able to make the break-through which he is striving to achieve, despite the constant arrival of fresh forces and an array of technical weapons remarkable even for the Eastern Front.

"No slackening of the fighting is, however, discernible. 18 pages day and night with extreme bitterness on both sides. Every inch of ground is hotly contested with its numerically superior attacker."

The Vichy radio also reported that the Germans "are now regrouping and carrying out a general shortening of their lines around Leningrad.

COLDER IN STRAIT

Strait of Dover last night: Fine Russian and cool; some low cloud banks; temperature nearing freezing point.

mail TRANSATLANTIC EDITION

U.S. PRESS QUOTE VOICE OF BRITAIN

On Germany's Fate

From DON IDDON
New York, Friday.

IT is becoming plain that extracts from the Transatlantic Daily Mail are to become a weekly feature of many American newspapers.

The Associated Press Agency sent out to-day to hundreds of newspapers throughout the country a 600-words story quoting passages from a special feature in the Transatlantic Daily Mail second issue on the future of Germany.

Extracts from the views of George Bernard Shaw, Mr. Shinwell, M.P., and Lord Vansittart were given great prominence.

Then came inquiries from editors from Cleveland, from Baltimore, and nearer at hand.

Cleveland asked permission to quote articles from the Transatlantic Daily Mail in full each week. Others wished for shorter extracts.

Letters Pour in

American newspapers gave the Transatlantic Daily Mail full credit. To-day's New York Post ran a front-page headline : "Shaw, Shinwell, and Vansittart on What to Do with Germany," while the New York Sun ran a similar story under the headline : "Three British Thinkers at Odds on Germany's Disarmament."

A number of radio commentators also quoted extracts from the second issue.

Meanwhile, letters continue to pour in. General of the Armies of the United States John J. Pershing, who rarely writes letters and never sees newspapermen, wrote to me:

"Thank you very much for the first issue of the Transatlantic edition of The Daily Mail, London, which I have found very interesting indeed.

"I appreciate your courtesy in introducing it to me, and am, of course, in entire sympathy with its one purpose—to contribute towards a closer understanding between the British and American people."

Federal Chief

Mr. J. Edgar Hoover, head of the Federal Bureau of Investigation, also also written. Lord Halifax has expressed his appreciation. So has British Minister Harold Butler.

Former head of the United States Supreme Court Justice Charles Evans Hughes sent a pleasant note. Presidential candidate Alf Landon has been in touch with us. And President Roosevelt's secretary, Stephen Early, writes :

"The President greatly appreciates your thoughtfulness in sending him a copy of this unique publication."

Governors of almost every State have written, together with mayors, business men, college professors, and leaders in every walk of American life. The Transatlantic Daily Mail strides forward in new triumph.

No Divorce Cases for the Magistrates

By WILSON BROADBENT, Political Correspondent

THE suggestion that divorce cases should be tried by magistrates has been rejected by the authorities. The highest legal opinion is opposed to the idea. The strongest reason advanced is that divorce is a serious social problem, and demands close scrutiny of individual cases. But three new judges are likely to be appointed immediately.

Divorce cannot be placed on the same level as the minor problems which are dealt with by local magistrates.

Nor are there sufficient stipendiary magistrates in the country to undertake the additional burden of divorce actions in their localities. They are already fully employed, as are county court judges.

It would mean appointing a large number of additional stipendiary magistrates or county court judges to deal with divorce actions—even undesirable cases—were allotted to them, instead of coming before High Court judges.

In the past it has been the custom to hear the majority of divorce actions in London because of the shortage of High Court judges, but there is no legal compulsion about this.

The Lord Chancellor has drafted a Bill, which will be debated in Parliament shortly for raising the maximum number of High Court judges in all the divisions from 35 to 42.

Under this Bill it will be left to the Lord Chancellor to determine when extra judges shall be appointed, up to the new maximum of 42, and also in which division they shall adjudicate.

It is understood that immediately the new Bill becomes law, the Lord Chancellor will appoint three new judges especially to deal with the arrears of divorce cases, and then two of these will go on circuit to try divorce actions in the provinces.

WE MAY HAVE LESS BUTTER

SOS for Supplies

The Ministry of Food has sent out an S O S to all butter-producing countries for more supplies, otherwise the ration of 2oz. a week may have to be cut.

Australia, where the ration of butter is half a pound weekly, has promised to do everything possible to increase her exports to this country. Everything depends on the available shipping.

The Hon. D. L. Campbell, Minister of Agriculture, Manitoba, said yesterday that the liberal allowance of bacon in Canada should be reduced so that more could be sent to Britain.

Air Command for U.S. General

ALLIED H.Q. North Africa, Friday.—General Eaker announced to-day the appointment of General John K. Cannon as commander of the Allied U.S. 15th Air Force.

General Cannon will also serve as commander of the Tactical Air Force, composed of British and American units, which acts in close support of the Fifth and Eighth Armies.—A.P.

India RAF Get 6

CALCUTTA, Friday.—R.A.F. Spitfires shot down six Japanese aircraft and damaged a number of others in a sharp air battle yesterday in Burma.—Reuter.

U.S. 'Subs' Sink 12

WASHINGTON, Friday.—American submarines have sunk 12 more Japanese vessels in the Pacific and Far East, according to a Navy communique issued here.—Reuter.

8 Down Last Night

London Barrage in Full Action

Eight German raiders were destroyed last night, it was officially announced early to-day.

By Daily Mail Raid Reporter

FIERCEST barrage for many months met German planes which last night penetrated the ring of defences.

The crash of shell fire increased as the raiders, coming in high from the South Coast, flew nearer, until at times the full force of the AA. guns appeared to be in action against the small number of planes which twisted and circled in the mesh of searchlight beams.

British and German planes were in the sky at the same time. The drone of the R.A.F. bombers was heard just before the general Alert.

The raiders dropped flares in great numbers. One group, which fell some distance away, silhouetted St. Paul's against their glare. Others were shot out by the ground gunners.

Shells Mark Course

From a point 20 miles out the crescent of bursting shells could be seen over London as planes were "handed" from one searchlight beam to another.

As the raiders sped away home bursting shells marked their course.

A big aerial battle was fought over a south-east town, when enemy planes were attacked by night fighters and ground defences.

A few bombs were dropped in the district causing some damage.

'NAZI FEELERS SPURNED'

U.S. on Peace Moves

NEW YORK, Friday.—The American Press to-day published reports from Washington that Germany has made several peace overtures to Britain in the past, but that all have been turned down.

"Parties representing Germany have been advised that the extremely terms on which Britain would make peace with Germany are unconditional surrender to the United Nations as a whole," said King's-bury Smith, International News Service correspondent, in a dispatch to the Journal-American.

John M. Hightower, Washington diplomatic correspondent of the Associated Press, said : "The British Government, in full agreement with the U.S., Russia, and the other United Nations, has taken, and will take, none of the proposals seriously until the Germans get ready for unconditional surrender."—Reuter.

'Conscription Will Stay after War'

Mr. A. T. Lennox Boyd, Parliamentary Secretary to the Ministry of Aircraft Production, said at Oxford last night : "I take it that universal military service as we have got it now would be accepted after the war by all political parties."

'Sixth Sense' Filled Shelters Before Raid

CITY 'DIVE-BOMBED' BY LANCASTERS

For the second time in 24 hours a great force of R.A.F. heavy bombers streamed out to the Continent last night over the east coast. Another force passed over the south-east coast. Shortly afterwards Berlin and Paris long-wave stations went off.

From WALTER FARR
Stockholm, Friday.

BERLINERS are to-day convinced that last night's 2,300-ton attack on the German capital was more terrifying than all the assaults that have gone before, Swedes who experienced the raid and who have reached Malmö, reported late to-night.

The raid, they say, was paralysing despite the fact that a "sixth sense" had warned many Berliners that it was "just the right night for an attack."

People queued at the entrances to the capital's deep shelters long before these were opened at five o'clock, and most of them stayed underground until the early hours of this morning—though Berlin's final "All clear" had sounded about midnight...

All eye-witnesses stress that the British squadrons bombed from a lower level than previously. One of them told me : "It seemed as if thousands and thousands of planes were diving straight for our shelters."

It is clear now that a great deal more than half Berlin has been laid waste. Casualties in last night's raid alone are believed to be in the region of 3,000 dead.

Here is the story of the "super attack" told to me by a Swede whose name I cannot give because he expects that in the future he will be compelled to return to Berlin.

"Last night seemed to come very near to the November vintage. Somehow Berliners sensed that there would be a raid.

"There was nothing really to go on. It was a night much like any of the other nights since January 2 the date of the previous big raid; but Berliners now claim they have a 'sixth sense' about raids.

"People rushed from theatres, which all finish about 5 o'clock, and there were very long queues outside the deep shelters all through Berlin."

'Oust Hitler' Army Plot

Gauleiter's Warning

From Daily Mail Correspondent
Geneva, Friday.

A WARNING to Nazi Party leaders that the German Army is planning a putsch to overthrow Hitler and make peace has been circulated by Gauleiter Erich Koch, one of the party's chiefs.

This is stated by the Gazetta de Lausanne, which quotes the circular letter sent out by Koch.

THE letter says : "The Führer is in danger. Parties of reaction are trying to displace him and establish a military dictatorship under which Germany would immediately start peace negotiations against the will of the people."

FEINTS

"No doing was to gain twelve sent five, but people were sure 'they were leaving and decided to make certain of a place down below.

"The R.A.F. tactical feints have played so on Berliners' nerves.

"When news comes out that a great fleet is heading for the capital and is then switched somewhere else in mankeeping ole

"In the shelters last night the people were saying 'Perhaps they won't come after all, but somehow it seems to be the right sort of night, and they have not been over now for nearly three weeks.'

"The rant must hitery o'clock.

"Some people brought tiny bottles of precious liquor down with them."

Pathfinders Work all through Raid

By Daily Mail Air Reporter

THE largest force of Lancasters and Halifaxes yet sent to the German capital by Bomber Command finished their task—from a comparatively low level—in half an hour, which means that the city was plastered at the rate of nearly 80 tons a minute.

The tonnage unloaded in the

GERMANS HELD IN ITALY

Haig Nicholson, Reuter Special Correspondent with the Fifth Army, cabled late last night : The critical stage of the Garigliano battle has safely passed. The Germans have thrown in every man they had, but have failed to push the British back across the river. Despite determined counter-attacks, British have held their positions and in some cases improved them. German casualties run into thousands.

latest attack was probably a good deal larger than in the previous heaviest raid—on the night of November 20.

At an one that occasion, our raiders bombed through cloud with the aid of sky markers—flares which hang in parachutes to mark the target.

Last night the Air Ministry let out another secret about the Pathfinders' work. They disclosed that their job is not completed, as is commonly supposed, by the time the bomb-shower of the main force start pressing their buttons.

A great cluster of sky markers, the Air Ministry said last night, "was continuously maintained over the target from 7.30 p.m. until 8 o'clock."

Fighters gathered over the target in large numbers as the attack developed, and the crews of one bomber group reported 40 sightings "all over the target area." Thirty-five aircraft are missing.

The Few Fund Has Passed the £20,000

By Daily Mail Air Reporter

ANNOUNCING last night that the Battle of Britain Memorial Fund has passed the £20,000 mark, the committee revealed that the heroes' shrine with which the memorial is to be commemorated in Westminster Abbey is to be known as "The Royal Air Force Chapel."

It was hoped that the fund would be largely subscribed in small sums by the many. That hope has been fully realised since The Daily Mail drew attention to the fact that donations were not coming in as quickly as was expected.

Many thousands of subscriptions of £1 or less have been sent from all parts of the country.

The King and Queen are among the subscribers. Queen Mary also sent a donation.

The fund will be closed on January 31, except for subscriptions from overseas. A new committee has been set up to administer the fund and pilot the memorial.

BACK PAGE—Col. FIVE

NAZIS ATTACK IN ITALY

Big Gains Claimed

The Germans have launched a full-scale counter-attack against the Fifth Army on the Garigliano.

Their attack appears to be concentrated along the line of our new advance and they claimed last night to have forced the British back to the "mountain fringe of the Garigliano plain."

Heavy fighting is reported from west of north of Minturno, and to have been "dislodged" from Castelforte, a town which has so far not been claimed by the Allies.

Gustav Line Threatened.—BACK PAGE.

Poland: No Soviet Reply to U.S.

From Daily Mail Correspondent
Washington, Friday.—Mr. Cordell Hull, Secretary of State, said to-day that the United States was keeping in close touch with the United States Ambassador in Moscow on the Polish situation, but that the Soviet Government had not yet accepted the American friendly offer of good offices.

Mr. Hull's phraseology "has not yet accepted" was regarded as an indication that he is still hopeful of Soviet acceptance.

So much hangs on Mr. Bevin's concession. It must be worded in such a way that no other workers in war industries can claim the same consideration.

Mr. Bevin himself was busy all day yesterday trying to find the correct form of words. He not discarded many formulae, but he has made up his mind that the problem of these boys must be settled before Sunday.

The whole scheme is in the melting pot, and if it is to be a success a quick decision must be made. Mr. Bevin knows that, and that is why he worried so hard yesterday to find a solution.

BEVIN'S PLEDGE ENDS PIT BOYS' STRIKE

By CHARLES SUTTON, Industrial Correspondent

THE 140 Bevin Boys who struck at Askern Colliery, near Doncaster, on Thursday for more money went back to their training centre yesterday after receiving a promise from a Ministry of Labour official that their claim would receive an answer to-day.

They wanted to know why they could not have an answer then and there, as they had been led to believe they would.

The official had to explain that there had begged a slight delay, but he gave them a promise that they would receive an advance on their first week's wages to-day, as well as a definite reply to their demands.

The hitch occurred when Mr. Bevin submitted his solution to the Treasury, which has to find the money. The Treasury was not satisfied that the wording of the solution was in the correct form.

3 BOMBS HIT DESTROYER

Enemy on Fire

Two enemy destroyers lying in the same Channel estuary were attacked by Coastal Command Albacores early yesterday morning.

Three bombs hit the stern of one destroyer, and large explosions were followed by a fierce fire. One Albacore is missing.

A pilot, Flying Officer D. C. Dawson, a Canadian, said : "The destroyer's gunners opened with everything they had, but I got away without being hit."

U.S. Strikers Go Back

DETROIT, Friday.—Some 3,100 foremen involved in a series of strikes at the eight Chrysler plants here returned to work to-day after voting to end the stoppage in compliance with the request of the War Labour Board.—Reuter.

All-day Blitz on France

Hundreds of Allied planes kept up a dawn-to-dusk battering of the Pas de Calais area yesterday. Eight types of bombers took a hand, from U.S. Forts to R.A.F. fighter-bombers.

Mosquitoes bombed at such low level that they were able to see the cannon, the enemy planes—including a flying-boat, the skeleton of a small Norwegian coaster—were destroyed during the day for the loss of two Mosquitoes.

▲ DAILY MAIL, LONDON, SATURDAY JANUARY 22, 1944

The Allies begin the year on the offensive, with advances at Leningrad and bombing raids on Berlin. There is even a heartening rumor from Germany that the army will try to oust Hitler. Domestic news also gets space, with butter shortages, a collection for a memorial in Westminster Abbey dedicated to the pilots of the Battle of Britain—and a discussion of Britain's divorce proceedings.

▲ THE DAILY TELEGRAPH, LONDON, MONDAY JANUARY 31, 1944

In a round-up of all theaters, the *Telegraph* prints a digest of "This Morning's War News." The news is positive for the Allies, with reports of an amphibious landing behind German lines at Anzio in Italy, and advances on the Eastern Front. While Germany continues to suffer bombing raids, Hitler's speech is taken as evidence of a decline in German morale.

EIGHTH ARMY NEWS

Dominion Premiers'
Declaration
(See Page Three)

No. 53. Vol. 4.   FRIDAY, 19th MAY, 1944.   ITALY

"The Enemy Has Been Completely Outmanoeuvred"

EIGHTH CAPTURE CASSINO

Battle For Hitler Line
Due To Start—*Communiqué*

A SPECIAL communique announced yesterday that Cassino and the monastery have been captured by the Eighth Army.

The official report says: "The final assault on the town was carried out by British troops while Polish troops took the monastery.

"The enemy have been completely outmanoeuvred by the Allied armies in Italy, following the original breach of the Gustav Line by the Fifth Army on May 14, and the subsequent rapid advance of French and American troops through the mountains.

"The troops of the Eighth Army have fought their way forward in the Liri Valley, and during the last 24 hours have developed the decisive pincer movement which cut Highway Six, and so prevented the withdrawal of the enemy.

"A substantial proportion of the First German Parachute division has been destroyed in its efforts to escape.

"Both armies have contributed to this victory.

"The Gustav Line south of the Apennines has now ceased to exist."

An earlier communiqué said that the "Battle for the Hitler Line is about to commence."

At Last They Saw The Sun

By FRED REDMAN

CASSINO, Thursday.

The whitest men in the Eighth Army saw the sun to-day for the first time for a fortnight.

I met them in the rubble heap that was Cassino—men who had lived and fought underground in a town where it was death to move by day.

This morning, while the Poles raised a triumphant flag over the Monastery, British forces wiped up the rearguard of the withdrawing Germans in Cassino with a Piat attack against a house where in the crumbling ruins a few Germans could be heard running about like rabbits.

I walked into Cassino along a narrow dirt track where none could walk in daylight during the long siege.

It was worn hard by the path of many beasts, for this was the route by which supplies were brought under cover of darkness to the British forces entrenched in cellars and caves in the town. It was lined with shell holes.

Lieut. C. P. Muir, pale from his 14 days underground, showed me a crypt which had been his headquarters. In its ancient passages they had cooked, eaten, slept and kept guard.

I looked for the Hotel des Roses and the Continental, remembered by tourists as

(Continued on Page 4, Col. 1.)

BOSTONS DROP FOOD TO ADVANCE TROOPS

WITH the heavy bombers out again against German supply ports on both sides of Italy the M.A.A.F. flew more than 2,000 sorties compared with the single enemy plane seen over the battle area. We lost 15 planes and shot down one.

Medium bombers blocked the main highway from Rome to the battlefront as fighter-bombers continued to pound objectives immediately behind the enemy line.

Mitchells and Marauders attacked the Frosinone road junction during the day, making the route impassable, and Wellingtons paid the same spot a night visit.

Mitchells also bombed one of the Viterbo landing grounds, potholing the runway. Thunderbolts added to the damage.

A bridge at Poggibonsi was attacked by Mitchells, while Marauders hit bridges at Ceprano, Cesano, Pesaro and Fabriano.

Bostons carried out a two-fold task. They dropped food to advanced Allied troops and bombed army targets near Valmontone.

Targets of Liberators were the causeway at Orbetello, and the docks at San Stefano, Piombino and Porto Ferrajo. Fortresses attacked Ancona on the east coast and troop concentrations in Yugoslavia.

Lightnings swept over northern Italy strafing airfields. They encountered about ten enemy planes and shot down one.

CARRIER PLANES BLITZ SHIPPING

LONDON, Thursday.

IN a daring sea-air operation, ships of the Royal Navy on Tuesday swept close in to the Norwegian coast to enable carrier-borne aircraft to make a sharp attack on shipping and shore installations, it was revealed here last night.

Taking the enemy by surprise Fleet Air Arm fighter-bombers swept in on a harbour, which in a moment was turned into a cauldron of smoke, escaping steam and flying wreckage.

Two medium-sized supply ships were left belching black smoke and three others were probably damaged.

Later German fighter-bombers attempted a retaliatory attack against our naval forces, but were forced to jettison their bombs before they could do any damage.

Striking again yesterday morning, this time 120 miles to the south, our bombers could only find armed trawlers as shipping targets.

In addition to shooting up two of these, our bombers flew as far as the enemy-held coast where they attacked a fish-oil factory working for the Germans.

BURMA TOWN BESIEGED BY ALLIED FORCE

A STRONG composite American-Chinese force captured the aerodrome at Myitkyina, largest city in Burma, which has been in Japanese hands for years and are directing fire into the city.

The strong Chinese advancing on the Siam border, have only 75 miles to go to meet up with the force of General Stilwell in Burma.

In New Guinea, Allies in pursuit of Japanese fleeing into the interior last made real contact with enemy 35 miles south of Aitape. Japanese troop concentrations are being attacked from the air.

Bevan Appeases

The clash between the parliamentary Labour Party and Aneurin Bevan, M.P. Member, over his "revolt" against Party, has been smoothed over by a letter from Bevan to the leaders undertaking to accept the standing of the Party.—Reuter.

REDS LEAVE HUGE FIRE

ATTACKS by Soviet bombers on German bases in White Russia are the main feature of the news from the Eastern front.

The Red Air Force has again raided Polotsk 50 miles south-west of Nevel.

Following a raid on the capital of White Russia, Minsk, seven large fires broke out at the railway junction, states the Russian communiqué.

These fires spread into one damaged a second.

Marshal Petain yesterday received Marshal von Rundstedt, German anti-invasion chief, says Vichy radio. German radio earlier quoted Rundstedt as having said "Invasion will begin any moment now."

Tanks line up in San Giorgio waiting to attack their next objective in the drive against the German southern line

GERMAN PRISONERS, dispirited and in many cases lousy, behind barbed wire in Eighth Army prisoner-of-war cages.

Limited Leave For Indian Ar[my]

MR. AMERY told Commons yesterday that arrangements on a limited scale had been made to grant home leave to certain officers and men in the Indian Army.

He had been asked by Viscount Suirdale "if in view of the fact that officers and men of the Indian Army are not covered by the scheme for repatriation of British Army personnel who have served continuously for long periods overseas, and in view of hardship imposed upon such officers and men who have served in the East for many years, he is making arrangements for granting leave at home for such personnel."

Amery replied: "Yes. Arrangements have already been made on a limited scale and I hope that in the year it will be possible to increase considerably the numbers of British officers of the Indian Army to whom home leave can be granted."

Viscount Suirdale: "Is he aware that many relatives of British people are unhappy about this?"

No answer was given.—Reuter.

◀ EIGHTH ARMY NEWS, ITALY, FRIDAY MAY 19, 1944

Eighth Army News was one of the many service newspapers issued to Allied troops, many of which were free. It had begun publishing three times a week in North Africa in 1943, but later became a daily, with editions published in Italy and Greece. Apart from such major national, theater, and service magazines and newspapers, there were also hundreds of individual ship, unit, and squadron newspapers, ranging down to handwritten wall newsheets. Here the news is of the Eighth Army's role in the victory at Monte Cassino, which guarded the route to Rome.

▼ SUPPLIES ARE OFFLOADED from ships at Anzio, Italy. In mid-February, 10 German divisions attacked the beachhead in an attempt to wipe it out. Only the intervention of Allied aircraft from the entire Italian Front saved the Allied troops at Anzio.

Daily Mail

NO. 14,994　ONE PENNY　★★　FOR KING AND EMPIRE　WEDNESDAY, MAY 24, 1944

LATE WAR NEWS

WHOLE GERMAN LINE IS CRUMPLING

Blows by Fifth, Eighth, and Beachhead Armies

ANZIO ATTACK LAUNCHED BY A THOUSAND GUNS

THE whole German line in Italy is crumpling under what now emerges as the greatest Allied offensive of the war. In the Liri Valley the Eighth Army is clean through the main defences. French troops have taken Pico and threaten the German flank and rear. The Beachhead Army, backed by 1,000 guns and the fire of the Fleet, is attacking in three directions. The battle goes well along the road to Rome: towards the big road junction of Cisterna, on the Appian Way; and towards the advancing Fifth Army. This last thrust appears to be the main attack. American troops, pushing rapidly through the mountains behind Terracina, are only 20 miles from the beachhead.

The Battle of the Poppies

General Clark Watches

Anzio Beachhead, Tuesday.
TANKS and infantry moved forward to the attack from the Anzio beachhead to-day through fields waist-high with red poppies.

The British had the honour of striking the first blow. They attacked last night. The American sector flamed into action this morning.

Picked units, specially trained for nearly a month behind the lines, rose up from the poppies and shallow ravines, where they had lain all night, and began to attack.

General Clark, Commander of the Fifth Army, watched the operation.—B.U.P.

Germans Threaten Allied Airmen

'TRIAL' BY NAZI COURTS

From Daily Mail Special Correspondent

STOCKHOLM, Tuesday.

BERLIN radio, following the issue of a series of charges against Allied airmen by the German Supreme Command, to-day announced that the German People's Courts will in future "try" shot-down pilots suspected of breaches of international law during the air offensive.

A barrage of propaganda against Allied flyers has been launched in the past 24 hours. Few here doubt that this is a counter-blast to the shooting of 47 R.A.F. officers in Stalag III.

The German High Command statement reads:

"The Supreme Command of the Wehrmacht deems it necessary, because of increasing attacks by Anglo-U.S. aircraft on German hospitals, to draw the world's attention to some of the most flagrant infringements of international law.

"In 50 detailed and fully proven instances violations are recorded in the period from January 24, 1944, to April 14, 1944.

"The Supreme Command of the Wehrmacht emphasises that since April 14, the British and Americans have renewed their raids on hospitals almost daily.

Red Cross Marking

"No dressing station, no hospital train, and no ambulance is any longer safe from attack.

"All the targets attacked were marked with the Red Cross so as to be visible from a distance. The pilots and machine-gunners were, therefore, in every instance able to recognise clearly the nature of the target attacked."

Other German propagandists are accusing Allied flyers of concentrating their railway attacks on "passenger trains filled with women and children, and even on farmers and labourers working in the fields.

Stalag III. Denial

The Air Ministry announced last night: "With regard to a report on the events at Stalag Luft III, which appeared in the Press this morning, while insufficient information is at present available to issue further statement of the circumstances in which 47 Air Force officers were killed, it can now be stated that nothing of the nature described in this report took place in the camp in question.

"The suggestion that the guards at Stalag Luft III ran riot and shot the prisoners is without foundation. As already promised, the Government will make a full statement as soon as a report is received from the Protecting Power."

[The story referred to by the Air Ministry did not appear in *The Daily Mail.*]

Germans Kill 50 More

MADRID, Tuesday.— Fifty men arrested on charges of being "suspects" or "terrorists" have been executed in the Paris and Versailles regions in the past week, states the Paris Prefecture of Police.

BIGGEST AIR WAR ESCORT

Attack Switched to Nazi Radar

WARPLANES striking from Britain's bases took the eve-of-invasion assault on Europe to new high levels yesterday.

The greatest fighter fleet ever sent on one offensive went out to escort big bombers in wide-ranging blows over Western Germany and France.

More than 1,000 Mustangs, Thunderbolts, and Lightnings supported about 750 Fortresses and Liberators.

And only one bomber formation saw anything of the Luftwaffe—a few F.W. 190's, driven off by the fighters.

Two railway yards and six German air bases in France, as well as military targets in Germany, were blasted. The cost: one bomber and three fighters.

In the meantime, medium and fighter-bombers and fighters of the Tactical Bases took on new anti-invasion objectives—coast and wireless centres.—"Against these "eyes" of the enemy attacks went on non-stop, hundreds of planes ranging back and forward over the sea.

All this followed one of the heaviest night assaults that Bomber Command has made for some time. More than 1,000 heavies plastered Dortmund and Brunswick, in Germany, as well as railway centres at Orleans and Le Mans, in France.

In the 24-hours up to last night more than 4,000 sorties must have been made on Western Europe.

Chief railway targets hit by the Fortresses and Liberators were at Epinal, the garrison town and railway centre in Eastern France, and Chaumont, but many miles to the north-west.

Airfields attacked were those in the German "second chain," well inland—from the coast—at Avord, Orleans-Brix, Bourges, Étampes-Mondésir, and Châteaudun were among them; and Caen, near the coast, was also attacked.

After the heavies, mediums of the R.A.F.

BRITISH P.O.W.s TAKE ITALIAN TOWN

Berne, Tuesday.—The underground newspaper "Ribbella" reports that 500 soldiers, mostly British who escaped from prisoner of war camps, have occupied the town of Meschio, near Vittorio Veneto.—B.U.P.

NIGHT R.A.F. OUT

Big formations of R.A.F. heavy bombers were crossing the east coast for more than an hour late last night, heading east and south-east.

FIRST DISPATCH FROM THE HITLER LINE

Infantry Stream Through, Riding on Tanks

From Daily Mail Special Correspondent

IN THE HITLER LINE, Tuesday.

THIS famous defence line, to which Hitler gave his name in the belief that it was impregnable, cracked like a rotten eggshell under the sledgehammer blows of our infantry and tanks in this morning's grey dawn light.

As I write, armour and infantry are streaming through the gap that has been ripped in the complicated and immensely strong chain of fortifications running across the Liri Valley from Piedimonte to Pontecorvo.

The Germans spent all the winter building these defences with characteristic Teutonic thoroughness. They consisted of hundreds of steel-and-concrete pillboxes, protected by wire and minefields, and an elaborate system of anti-tank and anti-personnel ditches.

But within 70 minutes of zero hour spearhead troops had smashed clean through the bewildered Germans and were astride the Pontecorvo-Aquino road behind the line.

The assault was prefaced by a typically pulverising Eighth Army counter-battery barrage. It must sound like the knell of doom to the enemy these days. For an hour 700 guns hurled shells on to the 2,000-yards front along which the attack was to be made.

CRASHED THROUGH THE WIRE

Then, as tanks and infantry began to move forward like ghosts in the early light of dawn, the guns began a creeping barrage which laid a curtain of fire in front of the advancing troops.

A wave of Shermans led the assault, crashing through wire and blasting forward machine-gun nests and pillboxes with their "75's."

Approaches to the line were thickly mined, and a number of tanks were stopped, but they continued firing while infantry cleared 15 anti-tank mines and opened up a path for the following armour.

We have massed a tremendous concentration of men and weapons on this comparatively narrow front, enough to deal a heavy blow. This does not mean that it is a rout, or that the assault is any kind of a picnic. On the contrary, the Germans are fighting with the same fanatical determination that they have displayed all along, and it has been bloody slogging every yard of the way.

Infantry are working so closely with the tanks that many come through the line clinging like limpets to the Shermans until they got among the Germans. Then they jumped off and engaged in fierce grenade and bayonet duels.

In the first hectic half-hour, when "all hell seemed to have broken loose in the Liri Valley," we lost some tanks—most of them to the formidable self-propelled 88's, of which the Germans have enormous numbers concealed in the woods, olive groves, and vineyards with which the countryside is patched.

On the northern flank the countryside is nondescript English, with gently rolling wooded slopes and narrow "shady" lanes that remind you of Surrey or Sussex.

But down towards Pontecorvo the terrain is east in typically Italian mould, slashed with rocky ravines and sparsely vegetated hills. This difficult tank country, and our armour has found the going tough.

It was around here that the Germans had constructed a formidable tank trap that came near to throwing the assault out of gear in the early stages.

ACROSS THE ROAD

The trap was a 20ft. wide and 8ft. deep, ditch, and according to one report there were more mines in it than currants in a Christmas pudding. Some of our tanks had their tracks blown off trying to cross it, and at this moment, in a drenching downpour that has surely abruptly followed the early morning's sunny promise, engineers are working feverishly to throw a bridge across it.

I spent part of the morning, while the first thrust was still in progress, at Advanced Headquarters, where I was able to listen-in to reports from the front line.

I heard that dramatic, "We have made our first objective" message received. The listening officer's quiet "Good show" seemed an understatement.

Other messages were flashed through in rapid succession. "Our boys are through the wire on the left." "Advance rather sticky."

THE GERMANS ARE GROWING JADED

Tanks Bite Deep into Hitler Line

From EDWIN TETLOW

EIGHTH ARMY FRONT, Tuesday.

KESSELRING'S jaded and desperate men barring our way to Rome—all 17 divisions of them—are to-night having to square up to heavy punches everywhere.

Our beachhead force at Anzio leaped suddenly to the attack a few hours before dawn this morning to stab at them in the flank.

Almost at the same moment Eighth Army tanks and men on the main front, under cover of a great barrage, mounted a new thrust against the shaky Hitler Line in the Liri Valley.

DEFENCE TANGLE

It is too early yet to tell how the battle is going on, but the most furious fighting of all is on the beachhead front and in the Rome yards stretch of valley between Aquino and Pontecorvo—the very core of the Hitler Line.

I have just come away from the battle here. Our tanks and infantry are deep into the innumerable fortified ditches, machine-gun posts, foxholes, and wired strong-points which the Germans have made.

Every yard and every position is being bitterly defended, but even more bitterly attacked.

There are heavy storm-clouds, low over the battlefield, promising more rain.

Our men have had all sorts of weather since they went in this morning—cold, heat, and rain, and the accompaniment of slithering cloggy mud.

Men and machines have crashed through masses of wire and a carpet of minefields guarding the Germans and as I write have hacked their way deep into the tangle of enemy defences.

Our first objectives were gained fairly early in the day. After a pause for regrouping and a short rest, we attacked again.

BIG BARRAGE

Meanwhile, south-east of the narrow battle-front, the French troops who had already got farther forward in the fighting yesterday were consolidating and holding the flank while new attackers made ground to-night against the word "Fire."

It was the cold, clear, dusty hour before dawn when hundreds of the Eighth Army gun crews got into their camouflaged pits and awaited the word "Fire."

Then they went into action to give the Germans another of their famous pre-attack barrages. Their targets for one hour precisely were enemy gun emplacements behind the Hitler Line.

Then the perspiring gunners had a breather while the range was changed.

Their next task for one hour and 40 minutes was to put in a painful creeping barrage on the main emplacements and positions of the Hitler Line.

They were covering a stealthy probe forward by tanks and infantry on the narrow front. Sappers were our spearhead. They went ahead of the fighting men, picking up mines and cutting wire in fields and copses on the right flank and rocky ground on the left.

They picked up more than mines. They drew the first blood of battle by collecting a number of prisoners who were occupying the most forward outposts and, numbed by the barrage, gave themselves up without a fight.

THE REAL CLASH

The real clash was not long in coming. The Germans had brought up big numbers of anti-tank guns and those which survived the barrage heavily engaged our advancing tanks.

They stopped some of them, but did not put them out of the fight. One of the first messages reaching headquarters from the front was from the commander of one squad-run whose radio said: "A Spitting thing I can do is to fire over the heads of our infantry, which I am doing."

The line is about 3,500 yards in depth, and its positions are so placed that they can enfilade any approaching enemy. So it was a slow and painful job for the infantrymen to push forward.

Some of them, however, were on their first offensive shortly after the start of the attack—magnificent.

Troops Said, 'We Shall Go Through'

From GRAHAM BEAMISH

BEFORE THE ADOLF HITLER LINE, Tuesday.

THROUGH the gloom and mist of the first light, infantry-men, with tommy guns and rifles, moved stealthily forward. The Eighth Army's major attack to smash the Hitler Line had started.

These troops, infantry and tank men, knew exactly what they were against. Tank crews knew that they had to negotiate at least one anti-tank ditch.

That was where those sometimes maligned, but ever efficient, engineers came into the picture. And what a job they did.

The infantry knew they were about to assault inevitable German minefields, acres of barbed wire, and then steel and concrete pillboxes.

Murderous Fire

But the paramount thought in their minds—and I talked to them not long before they went to the attack—was that they must smash Hitler's famed line, punch a hole so big that the Allied armies could first destroy his forces and then surge on to Rome.

They went in knowing full well that they were up against inflexible men who were wedged into one-man portable pillboxes sunk into the ground.

They knew that these men had astounding supplies of ammunition and food. They had seen them in Cassino, and seen the Gustav Line for a long time.

But they wanted forward instantly through a murderous curtain of cross machine-gun and anti-tank fire.

At one time Sir Sherman, ungainly, massive, efficient monsters, sat in the middle of the Hitler Line—thundering out defiance as the Germans poured through the defences before them.—Exchange.

NEW BULGAR PREMIER 'HITLER MAN'

Daily Mail Special Correspondent

ISTANBUL, Tuesday.

HITLER has had his way in Bulgaria.

Kristo Kalkov, described as Hitler's man, who is President (Speaker) of the Bulgarian National Assembly, is to form a Government in succession to that headed by Dobri Bojilov.

Reports reaching here giving this news said that the new Government will be as pliant a tool of the Germans as the enemy can wish.

It will accede to all demands from Berlin, and will try to keep Bulgaria in the war to the end.

As a consequence, it is expected that Russia will probably break off diplomatic relations with Sofia, and may even declare war on Bulgaria.

'ENEMY IS OUT FOR DECISION'

Germans Jumpy

ALL German reports of the Italy battle last night stressed its vast and critical nature.

Karl Praegner, German News Agency correspondent, said: "The Allied High Command is unless we are much mistaken, bent on scoring a victory in the course of to-day at any price.

"Since the early morning wide sectors of the front, both on the beachhead and in the south, have been resounding with an Allied drumfire such as has never been witnessed before.

"At first light exceptionally violent fighting developed both in the regions of Cisterna and Littoria and on the Southern Front at Terracina, Lenola, Pico, Pontecorvo, and Piedimonte.

"Mighty forces of battle planes and fighters supported Allied ground troops. No reports are yet to hand as to the issue of to-day's operations."

Praegner then admitted the loss of Pico in the previous day's fighting.

'Paratroops Used'

Reinhardt Albrecht, in a message from the Anzio beachhead, said: "A concentration of Allied warships is taking part in the coastal operation. Their barrage which is laying down an unbroken curtain of fire on our positions right up to the hills.

"American parachutists have also dropped on the Appian Way, where they are engaged in dogged fighting with German troops.

"The battle rages like hell under a scorching sun."

Captain Sertorius forecast the development of an American drive through Terracina along the Appian Way into the Pontine Plain, to join forces with the Anzio army.

Finally, in a sober summing-up of the Italian campaign against the background of the war, General Dietmar, spokesman of the German High Command, said:

"We go not underrate the moral strength of the enemy camp. It must therefore be our duty to be morally still stronger.

"The Anglo-Americans want to achieve a quick decision in Italy, It will require great efforts indeed to deny to the enemy a major success."

'What's It Like in the Strait?'

State of Sea.—Calm.
Weather.—A little warmer and more settled in the evening after slight rain and some cloud. Temperature at noon 10.30 p.m.—64deg. Visibility: Fair. Wind: Light, between north and east. Sky: Clear.
Barometer.— Very slight rise.

High Tide Across the Water To-day—1.39 p.m. and 2.20 p.m.

Ten Airmen Saved Off Nazis' Coast

150-miles Launch Rescue Trip

TEN airmen, the entire crew of a Flying Fortress which crashed in the sea, were taken on board a high-speed launch of the Air-Sea Rescue Service just off the coast of Occupied Europe.

The launch raced 150 miles from its base through heavy seas to reach them.

The Fortress, returning from Friday's mass raid on Berlin with two engines knocked out, "ditched" in the North Sea. The gunner was injured, but all the crew scrambled safely into their dinghies.

Staff-Sergt. Russel E. Gately, of Needham, Mass., said: "I shall never forget how glad I was. We could hear our rescuers searching—always in the distance. All through the night we sat waiting in the dinghy.

"On Saturday afternoon one of Coastal Command's lifeboat-carriers dropped us a lifeboat complete with motors. We soon had the motors going and a course set for England.

"During the night, however, we lost contact with the pilot overhead, and as dawn approached we lost only enough petrol to last us a few minutes. Luckily, at that moment the R.A.F. rescue launch came alongside."

TAX PAYER MAY HOPE—AFTER WAR

THE public, who have borne great hardships and privations in the war without complaint, are entitled to some little hope of relief from heavy taxation after the war, said Sir John Anderson, Chancellor of the Exchequer, said that to the House of Commons yesterday.

The gap between tax revenue and expenditure would still be considerable for some time after the war, he said, and they must aim to narrow the gap as speedily as possible.

The Treasury were making their plans for the post-war transition period.

Priorities, high and low, would have to be part of the Government's policy and administrative equipment for a time to absorb the same extent as during the war.

Speech in BACK Page.

MISSING HOARDS

More than 200,000,000 £1 notes were "missing," said Admiral E. Donaldson, chairman of the Southern Area Trustee Savings Bank, at Woking yesterday.

He knew, he said, that more than £1,000,000 was being hoarded in Portsmouth, and there were hoarders in Woking. Two dock workers in Portsmouth had £13,000 each when their houses were bombed.—A.P.

'RUSSIA GIVEN U.S. CRUISER'

Senator Asks Facts

WASHINGTON, Tuesday.— Senator Styles Bridges, a Republican, told the Senate to-day that he had been informed that an American cruiser had been transferred to Russia. He demanded to know the truth of the report.

Senator Bridges said the American people were entitled to know if naval transfers had been made.

He added that he had heard that more than one unit of the American Navy had been transferred to Russia.—A.P.

Helicopters Used on Burma Front

CALCUTTA, Tuesday.—Helicopters are being used in the airborne invasion of Burma by American units operating with the Third Tactical Air Force of the Eastern Air Command.

Pilots flying them, who undergot a special course of training, arrived in India by air in January. With them came their helicopters, ground crews, and technicians.—Reuter.

Chinese Drive Traps Japs

BACK Page.

Periscope Camera in U.S. Subs

NEW YORK, Tuesday.—The U.S. Navy revealed some details to-day of a hitherto secret camera with which accurate pictures are taken through the periscope of a submerged submarine.

The camera provides a complete photographic record of hits and sinkings in both still and moving pictures.

THE GERMANS HOARD DRUGS

'Shortage Likely'

Daily Mail Radio Station

The German people are hoarding drugs and medicines. A man described by the "Reich's Chief Apothecary" said this over German radio last night, and warned the people that if they continued to hoard there would be a serious shortage.

"There are unavoidable shortages—caused by the lack of chemicals—but the majority of drugs and medicines would suffice except for this unnatural consumption," he said.

He revealed that headaches are now a common illness" in Germany, and that people are trying to get rid of them by buying "valuable medicines."

Dr. Evatt was defending Australia's system of temporary economic and industrial controls.—Reuter.

Australians Told 'Don't Grumble'

SYDNEY, Tuesday.— Dr Evatt, Australian Minister for External Affairs, said here to-day: "We hear complaints from the Opposition parties and the newspapers about shortages of food, clothing, and housing. It is nothing but grumble, grumble, grumble. Compare what you have got in Australia with what they have in Britain."

Russia: No Change

Last night's Soviet communique again reported no changes on any of the fronts.

"I feel like another being"

TESTIMONY　Nov. 6, 1941

Mr.—wrote: "Being depressed, with dizziness and general weakness, I was advised to try Phyllosan, and after a month's trial found a vast improvement in my general health."

CONFIRMATION　Aug. 13, 1942

Mr.—wrote again: "I have taken Phyllosan ever since my attack over twelve months ago. The giddiness and depression have disappeared and altogether I feel like another being."

Start taking

PHYLLOSAN

to revitalise your Blood, improve your Circulation, strengthen your Nerves, increase your Stamina and Energy

Of all chemists: 3/3 and 5/4 (double quantity). Inc. Purchase Tax

The regd. trade mark 'Phyllosan' is the property of Natural Chemicals Ltd., London

▲ DAILY MAIL, LONDON, WEDNESDAY MAY 24, 1944

After months, Allied troops in Italy finally breached the Gustav Line in May 1944. The *Mail* also reports from the home front, where hoarding has led to a shortage of banknotes in circulation; at the conflict's end, it reports, the chancellor of the exchequer has promised there will be a decrease in income tax.

Monte Cassino

MAY 1944

THE GERMAN DEFENSIVE POSITIONS IN ITALY FROM LATE 1943 TO MID-1944 WERE BASED ALONG THE GUSTAV LINE. MAKING THE MAXIMUM USE OF THE MOUNTAINOUS TERRAIN, THE Gustav Line was centered on the town of Cassino, 1968 feet (600 m) above the Liri Valley, which overlooked the main route from Naples to Rome. To even get to the Gustav Line, the Allies had to cross two difficult rivers, the Garigliano and the Rapido.

Even when forces did move toward Cassino, they found the town impossible to take. German paratroopers created formidable defenses and could not be dislodged. When the town was bombed, the rubble merely made the defenders' task easier. Part of the problem was that the town was overlooked by mountains that gave German artillery spotters a clear view of Allied movements. Allied troops became convinced that a monastery at the top of the mountain above Cassino, Monte Cassino, was being used by the Germans, and this monastery was bombed in March 1944.

BREAKING THE STALEMATE

To break the stalemate at Cassino, the Allies landed behind German lines at Anzio, just south of Rome, on January 22. They got 50,000 men and their equipment ashore, but failed to move quickly, and were soon bottled up. At points it seemed that the Germans would drive them back into the sea, and the fighting was intense around the perimeter of the Anzio beachhead.

Stymied at both Cassino and Anzio, the Allies in Italy consequently found progress very difficult. Troops from many nations —including New Zealand, Poland, and India —were involved in trying to take Cassino. General Sir Harold Alexander, in charge of the British Eighth Army, eventually had to give up frontal assaults on the town. Instead, Alexander concentrated on moving forward in the surrounding mountains. In May, the monastery itself was finally occupied by French colonial troops from Morocco, and the road to Rome was opened.

▲ MONTE CASSINO after being bombed and shelled by Allied aircraft and artillery. Ironically, the rubble created ideal firing positions for German troops on and around the summit of the mountain.

Fall of Rome

JUNE 5, 1944

THE BATTLE TO DEFEND ROME WAS PERHAPS THE FINEST HOUR FOR THE GERMAN COMMANDER IN ITALY, ALBERT KESSELRING. THE ITALIAN CAPITAL WAS HELD FOR ANOTHER six months thanks to his prompt action to seal off the Allied bridgehead at Anzio. He mobilized the German Fourteenth Army, with eight infantry and five panzergrenadier divisions, to destroy the bridgehead within four days of the first landings on January 24, 1944. When Allied troops eventually advanced out of the bridgehead on January 29, they were met with a hail of artillery and machine-gun fire. Within a week, Kesselring's 125,000 troops were launching counterattacks. These were led by a number of panzer units, including a company of 11 Ferdinand super-heavy assault guns, a regiment of 76 Panther tanks, a battalion of 45 Tiger tanks, and 85 assault guns.

STALEMATE

Any idea that the Allies were going to be in Rome in a matter of days was now clearly out of the question. Nazi propaganda rejoiced in telling the world that the bridgehead was now a "death head." The German attack could not totally destroy the bridgehead, but a bloody stalemate ensued for months. Given the strategic situation, this was a major success for the outnumbered and outgunned German forces in Italy. Allied casualties were enormous: the U.S. Fifth Army lost 30,000 men, the British some 12,000. The Germans lost 25,000 men.

THE GERMANS RETREAT NORTH

In the end it was steady pressure on the Gustav Line at Monte Cassino that broke the German defense. With his troops about to be cut off in the area around Monte Cassino, Kesselring ordered another withdrawal. This time he paused at a series of delaying positions both south and north of Rome, until his troops were safe in the Gothic Line to the south of Bologna in mid-August 1944. Allied troops followed closely on the heels of Kesselring's forces, but he managed to evade every attempt to trap them. For the Allies, this meant another campaigning season in Italy, against well-led veteran troops.

▲ GERMAN PARATROOPERS in Rome on the eve of its capture by Allied troops. All German units made good their escape north toward what would become the Gothic Line.

"Daily Herald," Monday, June 5, 1944

BLACKOUT TIMES

Aberdeen .... 11.56 p.m. to 4.17 a.m.
Edinburgh .... 11.52 p.m. to 4.31 a.m.
Glasgow 11.55 p.m. to 4.35 a.m.
Moon Rises .... 8.53 p.m.
Moon Sets .... 5.54 a.m.

Daily Herald

No. 8825 * * * MONDAY, JUNE 5, 1944 ONE PENNY

STOP PRESS

TANKS IN ROME

Sherman tanks, decorated with poppies and daises, smashed into Rome, says a British United Press message.

Tanks, Guns Race Up Highway Six, Storm Into First Axis Capital

ALLIES IN ROME

Yard-By-Yard Battle Through Streets

BRITISH AND AMERICAN TROOPS ENTERED ROME LAST NIGHT. GENERAL ALEXANDER HAS ACHIEVED THE GREATEST VICTORY OF THE ALLIED WESTERN ARMIES EXACTLY 24 DAYS AFTER OPENING HIS MIGHTY OFFENSIVE FROM THE CASSINO LINE.

From his advanced headquarters he issued this special communique just before eight o'clock:—

"TROOPS OF THE FIFTH ARMY HAVE ENTERED THE LIMITS OF THE CITY OF ROME. SPORADIC RESISTANCE CONTINUES."

David Brown, Reuter's correspondent, wires that the Fifth Army is driving yard by yard into the populated areas of Rome.

Developed Into Race

The march on the capital developed suddenly into a race yesterday as all enemy resistance collapsed a few miles north of Valmontone, on Highway Six.

Fifth Army tanks and guns with lorry loads of infantry sped ahead.

An earlier announcement from General Alexander's headquarters gave news that the outskirts of the city had been reached early in the day.

BUT THERE OUR FORCES HAD BEEN HALTED IN HEAVY FIGHTING.

To the west of Highway Six another great battle raged all yesterday in the plain extending from the Colli Laziali—the northern rim of the Alban Hills—to the southern limits of the city.

This battlefield covered the last few miles of the Appian Way and a network of minor roads.

On the extreme right flank on the German line the position was confused.

The German High Command put out this statement:—

German troops fighting on the coastal sector of the Italian front have withdrawn to the Tiber river.

"The withdrawal was carried out according to plan and the German movements were not disturbed by Allied vanguards."

But the Allied headquarters statement reported that "the enemy continues to resist in the outskirts between the Colli Laziali and the Tiber."

War correspondents accompanied the Fifth Army in its drive up Highway Six.

As the first cars and jeeps appeared in Rome's outer suburbs, they said Italians emerged from their cellars, cautiously at first, then more boldly.

Soon their welcome was warm and genuine and they flung roses into the army vehicles.

They offered wine.

But the battle was not over and they were frequently sent scurrying back to the cellars by bursts of German fire from anti-tank guns and snipers.

Bridge Attack

Early yesterday R.A.F. heavy and medium bombers attacked a road-bridge across the Tiber. More than 100 vehicles were destroyed and 127 damaged.

East of Highway Six, Fifth Army tanks and troops, striking due north from Valmontone, captured Cave on Saturday and were storming Palestrina last night.

All resistance south of Valmontone collapsed on Saturday, when the French, advancing from Sgurgola, captured Colle Piso and Colle Ferro, and the final junction of the Fifth and Eighth Armies was effected.

The Eighth Army is continuing a full-scale advance in all sectors despite mines, demolitions and snipers.

It has captured Alatri, Fumone and Anagni.

"Shall Fight On," Said Rome Radio

JUST before the Allied troops reached Rome the city's German-controlled radio said:

"Anything may happen. Rome may fall. But we know that we shall fight on."

Another Rome broadcast said:—

"It is not yet known whether the United States Command will recognise Rome as an open city, although no German troops are left there.

"It is, however, the general impression that General Alexander wants to use Rome as a base for future operations.

"If so, the Allies would have to accept the entire responsibility for the ruin and the destruction which would inevitably befall the city."

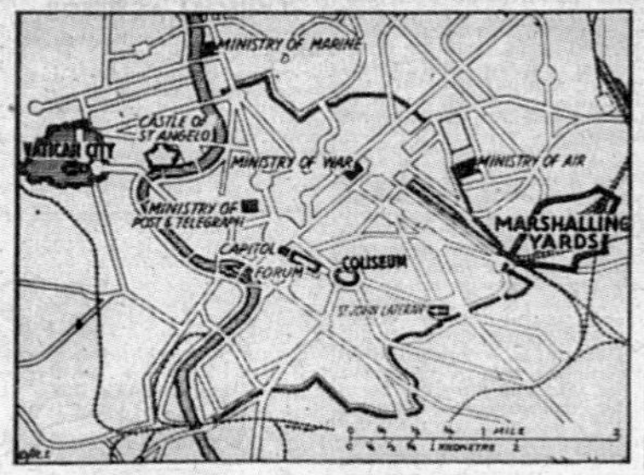

MINISTRY OF MARINE
CASTLE OF ST. ANGELO
VATICAN CITY
MINISTRY OF WAR
MINISTRY OF AIR
MINISTRY OF POST & TELEGRAPH
CAPITOL
FORUM
COLISEUM
MARSHALLING YARDS
ST. JOHN LATERAN
1 MILE
1 KILOMETRE

HORDES OF PRISONERS MARCH OUT

From EMERY PEARCE
"Herald" War Reporter

ROME SUBURBS,
Sunday morning.

IT is a fantastic sight. Hordes of German prisoners are coming down the road from Rome, guarded by one or two grinning Tommies.

The roads are chock-full of tanks and guns, all heading towards the city.

We drove here this morning along Highway Six and round the Colle Laziali, at the northern tip of the Alban Hills.

Spitfires kept constant watch over us, but on both sides of the road sniping, machine-gunning or small vicious mopping-up battles went on.

Often we drove through shell and mortar fire, which the enemy on either side was laying down on the road.

Like A Dagger

But Highway Six pointed like an Allied dagger at the heart of Rome.

Our armour crashed through, leaving American and British infantry to fan out and look after the Germans, cut off and isolated in many pockets.

As I write this, we are being held up by two 88mm. enemy guns, which are accurately hitting a cross-road a few hundred yards ahead.

It is a beautiful Sunday morning in this suburb, and a wedding party of about 15 people has just come out of a church behind us.

The bride and groom are a fine couple, and the bride, dressed in grey, has tears of joy in her eyes as we congratulate her.

They began the wedding service when the Germans held all Rome. They came out, married, with the British and Americans around them.

Now, very happy, the whole party is walking merrily along this road towards the shellfire. I wonder if they have a party.

THIS is Pontecorvo, a vital point in the Adolf Hitler line—battered and blasted as the Germans fought desperately there to stop the Canadians from breaking through.

The enemy left behind scores of booby traps, and as the Canadians entered the town put up a heavy mortar bombardment. Bulldozers were used to clear a track through the rubble.

All-Day Blows At Invasion Coast

THROUGHOUT yesterday large formations of Allied planes were crossing to and from the French and Belgian coasts in an unending stream.

Most of them went in the direction of Calais and Boulogne. Headquarters United States Strategic Air Forces announced:

"German military installations in the Boulogne area of France were attacked this morning by B17 Flying Fortresses and B24 Liberators of the 8th Air Force.

"P47 Thunderbolts and P51 Mustangs of the 8th Air Force provided escort.

"A similar force of bombers made a second attack in the same vicinity later in the day. They were escorted by P51 Mustangs of the 8th Air Force.

Bridges Bombed

"Thunderbolt fighter-bombers of the 9th Air Force this afternoon attacked bridges, railroad tracks and military rolling stock on the Oise River valley.

"Marauders and Havocs of the 9th Air Force this afternoon attacked military objectives along the coast of Northern France and a highway bridge at Courcelles-sur-Seine, 40 miles north-west of Paris.

"The bombers were escorted by Thunderbolts and Mustangs of the 9th Air Force."

The Oise runs south-west through Compiègne to join the Seine north-west of Paris.

PLANES DRIVEN FROM CONVOY

SEA Hurricane fighters from another new escort carrier, H.M.S. Nairana, have intercepted and driven off a number of Ju. 290s attempting to shadow a valuable convoy in the North Atlantic.

The existence of the Nairana is now disclosed for the first time.

In engagements a considerable distance from the convoy two enemy aircraft were destroyed.

Five survivors from one were picked up by the frigate H.M.S Inglis and made prisoners of war.

One of our aircraft was shot down.

The convoy suffered no damage and reached its destination without further incident.

Another Explosion In Arms Train

"Daily Herald" Reporter

A SURREY VILLAGE,
Sunday night.

IN a disused railway coach in a field here to-day in the countryside, railway experts have been holding a court of inquiry into the second ammunition train explosion in Britain in 48 hours.

This second explosion shook the area at 5 p.m. yesterday. It sent live shells whistling across the countryside. It lifted cases of live ammunition high into the air.

It littered the railway tracks with whizzing shrapnel and sent pieces of shell casing and railway truck thudding on to the platform of a near-by station.

While the blazing, bursting ammunition seared the fields and the hedges, firemen, hiding behind piled-up blocks of sleepers and a tiny platelayer's cabin, shot water on to a burning ammunition truck and risked death to get the fire under control.

Nobody was hurt and no civilian property was damaged in this explosion, which followed 37 hours after the Cambridgeshire explosion.

"Belching Smoke"

I was told the story of this spectacular Surrey incident by Peter Roy King, 19-years-old fireman-cleaner on the train, at his home to-night.

"There were 45 trucks on our train last night," he said. "My driver was Thomas Titchener, aged 45. Neither of us knew that any of the trucks contained ammunition.

"We were going pretty slowly up a hill, and Tommy Titchener saw that the ninth truck from the engine—a box truck with a metal roof—was belching out smoke.

"We went slow towards the next signal. It showed green, but we stopped there.

"Titchener got off the engine, telling me to stay at the controls. He dashed down the track, dived under the buffers and divided the rest of the train from our part.

"Then we drove off with the blazing truck on the end. We travelled 250 yards down track, then slipped the blazing van."

50 Yards, Then—

The engine, with Titchener and King aboard, travelled another 50 yards.

"There was a hell of a noise," King said. "The blazing van just started to shoot off bits and pieces all over the countryside. All the time there were explosions, and it went on like that for nearly an hour.

"From where I crouched on the footplate I could see shells whistling into the country. I saw whole shell cases and packets of ammunition and bits of truck showered into the air."

After a hard fight by the firemen, helped by Home Guards, the fire was finally put out. The van was a burnt-out ruin.

Titchener, King and the guard, Walter John Quinton, all gave evidence to-day at the inquiry.

SOLDIERS' PARENTS TO GET MORE

THOUSANDS of parents of serving men will receive a pleasant surprise from regimental paymasters this week in the form of a few shillings' increase in their dependants' allowances.

The conditions under which these allowances are being granted have been made more liberal and every case has recently been reviewed.

Where it has been found that the new conditions apply, the increases will automatically be sent out this week.

Parents of Servicemen, who have had their claim for a dependant's allowance rejected, and feel that they are entitled to one, should now write to their son's regimental paymaster, asking for the claim to be reopened.

Claims which have been rejected have not been subjected to the automatic review.

But don't write to the paymaster if you are receiving an allowance and it has not been increased. It means that your case does not come within the new limits.

AMGOT Has Already Fixed Rome H.Q.

From "Herald" Special War Reporter

ALGIERS, Sunday.

A "PHANTOM" city corporation is waiting near the battlefront to help in the administration of Rome directly the German forces have been driven out.

This elaborate organisation will carry out plans drawn up in minutest detail during the last few months by highly-trained committees of experts.

Far-sighted preparations have been made to deal with any of the great problems which may suddenly arise when we occupy this big overcrowded capital.

British and American authorities, in close co-operation with Italian officials of Badoglio's government, have tried to make provision for every urgent need of the population.

I understand that Allied policy in Rome will be for the existing Italian administration to continue, as far as possible, under Anglo-American guidance—as has been done elsewhere in liberated Italy.

Weeding Out Fascists

Most of the Fascist officials will probably have left with the retreating German army—or tried to leave.

Any remaining officials suspected of being unfriendly to the Allies will be weeded out though, as has happened before, they may continue to function for a little time till they can be substituted.

This phantom city corporation includes British and American officers of the Allied control commission, formerly known as A.M.G.O.T.

For months now they have been mentally living in Rome.

For instance, they have decided exactly which buildings they will commandeer for housing various Allied organisations and units.

That is only one of the minor details.

Far greater problems are provided by the question of feeding this huge new population which will suddenly become an Allied responsibility.

It is estimated that there are about 2,000,000 people now living in Rome, as the normal population has been swollen by 750,000 refugees from Naples and elsewhere, who are believed to be short of food.

Wheat And Milk

Enormous stocks including wheat, tinned milk and de-hydrated vegetables have been accumulated behind our front.

First supplies will be rushed into the city by road transport as soon as the city is liberated.

Rome has been carefully divided into districts for the distribution of food by Italian and Allied units under the direction of the Control Commission.

Precautions have been taken in advance to guard against black market racketeers trying to make underground sales of local produce which should go into the Allies' food pool.

Head of the racket-busters will be Correa, a former District Attorney, of New York, who has collected a staff of expert investigators.

The wheat harvest in liberated Italy this year is expected to yield 700,000 tons, and Correa and his men will work to prevent any of this stock falling clandestinely into the black market, where only well-to-do Italians could buy it.

Lessons learned in fighting the black market in Palermo and Naples will be used for tackling Rome racketeers.

One urgent problem will be the provision of badly-needed medicaments.

Clothing will probably be dealt with later as a less important matter.

Army engineers will be ready to set to work at once to restore any public services, such as water, gas or electricity, which may have been interrupted by enemy action.

Even should Germans have taken away fire-fighting equipment, the Army will be able to provide fire brigades for the city.

Vatican "Prisoner"

The liberation of Rome presents one very specialised problem—that of the Vatican City.

I understand that Lieutenant-Colonel Comte de Salis, a member of a very famous Roman Catholic family, will act as liaison officer with the Vatican if the Pope still remains.

The arrival of the Allies will be an almost overwhelming moment for our own "prisoner of the Vatican," the British Ambassador, Sir Francis D'A. G. Osborne, who has been for years now living in the heart of enemy-occupied territory.

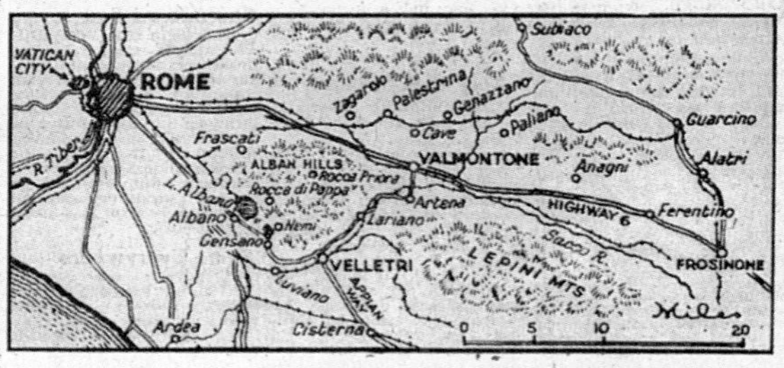

VATICAN CITY
ROME
R. Tiber
Subiaco
Zagarolo
Palestrina
Genazzano
Cave
Paliano
Frascati
ALBAN HILLS
VALMONTONE
Guarcino
Alatri
Anagni
HIGHWAY 6
Ferentino
Sacco R.
FROSINONE
LEPINI MTS
VELLETRI
Ardea
Cisterna
Miles
0 5 10 20

FREE GERMANS WRITE TO PREMIER

Free Germans in Great Britain yesterday sent a message to Mr. Churchill from their second delegate conference in London.

Expressing "gratitude toward our British hosts," the message went on to say:—

"Thousands of us have the honour of being soldiers in the British Forces, tens of thousands are working in war factories.

"But we want to do more than this. We want to accelerate Hitler's defeat. We want to call on the Germans to overthrow Hitler and thus lay the basis for a peaceful, democratic Germany."

"FIGHTERS ATTACK CHANNEL ISLES"

The German News Agency said yesterday that Allied fighter planes made repeated attempts to attack a German Channel Island base on Friday.

It claimed that five planes were shot down.

"TANK BATTLES AT JASSY"

THE Germans claimed yesterday that further heights had been won by the German and Rumanian troops north-west of Jassy, on the Rumanian front.

Strong Russian counter-attacks, supported by Stormovik planes and tanks, were reported in the German communiqué which said that they failed and that 25 Russian tanks were knocked out and 33 planes shot down.

The German news agency's commentator Von Hammer, claimed that the German artillery observers had captured posts from which they can observe all the Russian movements.

Reports from Moscow said that the Russians are still holding their positions both north-west and north of Jassy, despite repeated attacks by large tank and infantry forces.

Tank reinforcements have been rushed up to the assistance of the attacking Germans. Many of the tanks have been knocked out and the enemy is suffering heavy casualties.

GUSTY IN STRAIT

There was a gusty S.W. wind in the Strait of Dover yesterday and the sea was choppy.

The weather improved a good deal in the afternoon, there being much less cloud, with sunny intervals, but a strong wind was still blowing.

High tides at Dover and Calais to-day: 11.40 a.m. and 11.56 p.m.

NEW IRAQ PREMIER

General Nuries said Iraq Premier has resigned owing to ill-health. Hamdi Pachachi, 60-years-old President of the Chamber of Deputies, has formed a Cabinet.

NOEL COWARD TO SING IN BURMA

Noel Coward, who has arrived in Calcutta from Ceylon, is to fly up and down the Burma border singing in the monsoon rain to British troops.

He will give concerts twice a day, his equipment being an upright piano and a loud speaker.—"Herald" reporter.

▲ DAILY HERALD, LONDON, MONDAY JUNE 5, 1944

The fall of Rome was widely celebrated: the first Axis capital was in Allied hands, although the photograph of the ruins of Pontecorvo, on the road from Naples to Rome, suggests the heavy pounding it had taken. Meanwhile, the *Herald* reports increased air activity over Normandy's "invasion coast"—D-Day was only 24 hours away—and increased nerves at home, with a second suspicious explosion on an arms train.

▲ LOS ANGELES TIMES, TUESDAY JUNE 6, 1944

A special morning edition brought news to readers starting their day on the West Coast of the D-Day landing in France, by then about 12 hours old. At bottom right, the *Times* apologizes to advertisers that this edition carries no advertising, and explains that its duty to serve its readers means that it needs all available space to report "the greatest news story of all time."

Münchener Ausgabe
159. Ausg. 57. Jahrg. Einzelpreis für München 15 Rpf., für auswärts 20 Rpf.

Münchener Ausgabe
München, Mittwoch, 7. Juni 1944

VÖLKISCHER  BEOBACHTER

Kampfblatt der nationalsozialistischen Bewegung Großdeutschlands

Invasion setzte zwischen Cherbourg und Le Havre auf Moskaus Befehl ein

So begann die Schlacht im Westen

Der mit aller Energie sofort aufgenommene Kampf unserer Wehrmacht gegen die Aggressoren ist in vollem Gange

Die Sowjetoffensive am Kanal

Von Helmut Sündermann

Starke Teile der Luftlandedivisionen vernichtet

Berlin, 6. Juni

Um Leben und Freiheit Europas

V.B. München, 6. Juni

Der Schauplatz der Invasion

Von unserem Marinemitarbeiter Erich Glodschey

VB. Berlin, 6. Juni

▲ VÖLKISCHER BEOBACHTER (PEOPLE'S OBSERVER), MUNICH, WEDNESDAY JUNE 7, 1944
The official newspaper of the Nazi Party brings news of D-Day to its 1.7 million readers: "So begins the battle in the West." It also reminds Germans where it claims the impetus for the invasion comes from: "Invasion begins between Cherbourg and Le Havre on Moscow's orders." Another story underlines the invasion's links to the Soviet Union.

▲ SOLDIERS OF THE U.S. 4TH INFANTRY Division wade ashore under fire at Utah Beach in Normandy, France, on D-Day, June 6, 1944.

Daily Mail

LATE WAR NEWS

No. 15,015   ONE PENNY   FOR KING AND EMPIRE   SATURDAY, JUNE 17, 1944

BATTLE RAGES ROUND 'EMPTY' CAEN

German Troops Quit—Sluices Blown Up

Off to Normandy, with a laugh and the fighting spirit that will bring victory.

THE KING VISITS THE BEACHHEAD

The King visited the beaches in Normandy yesterday. He was accompanied by Sir Alan Lascelles and Captain Sir Harold Campbell, R.N.

GERMAN troops and all civilians have been evacuated from Caen, the German "hedgehog" in Normandy, according to unofficial reports from the front last night. Berlin admits that the sluices and dams in the city have been blown up and that the bridges in the area have been destroyed. German troops are still resisting stubbornly, and there has been little change in the fighting line.

Caen has been under constant fire from British warships for the last four days. A Paris report last night said the Caen civilians were being sent to the South of France.

American troops under General Omar Bradley have pushed forward another mile and a half in their drive from Pont l'Abbe across the Cherbourg Peninsula, and are now within two and a half miles of St. Sauveur.

A little farther south Allied troops are within five and a half miles of La Haye du Puits. North of St. Sauveur the Americans have reached a point four and a half miles from Valognes.

The American advance puts the German High Command in a quandary, for the more reinforcements they bring up the more troops there will be to be cut off if the Allies are able to sever these communications.

The Germans, however, have rushed up the 17th Panzer Grenadier Division between St. Sauveur and La Haye du Puits in a last-minute attempt to hold the key Cherbourg road, and General Bradley's troops are meeting stiffer resistance.

This road is now within range of all types of mortars as well as field artillery.

Guns 'Reap' Nazi Mass Infantry

400-yards Range

From NOEL MONKS

WITH BRITISH FORCES IN FRANCE Thursday (delayed).

GERMAN Panzer and infantry forces, which staged a strong attack against our forces near Villers-Bocage last night, were severely mauled by our tanks, artillery, and infantry.

They retreated in disorder leaving several hundred dead and wounded in a battle-scorched poppy field, and at least a dozen wrecked tanks. Our losses were Tanks, nil; infantry, slight.

[remaining column text continues]

500,000 MEN

'Write of the Major,' They Said

'Nameless' Hero of the Wounded

By Daily Mail Reporter

THIS is a story that the wounded want to be told about an "anonymous" young major of the R.A.M.C. who is working in a casualty clearing station somewhere between the beaches and the Orne bridges.

Went on Operating

Super Forts Smash at 'Sheffield' of Japan

One-fifth of Steel City Wrecked

Latest Allied raids in the Pacific have been on the Bonin Islands, about 500 miles from Japan, and Korea, on the Japanese mainland of Asia, the Japanese reported yesterday.

ONE-FIFTH of Japan's whole steel industry may have been wiped out as a result of Thursday's young raid by American Super-Fortresses (B 29's).

The main blow was at Yawata, "Sheffield" on the northern tip of Kyushu Island, most southerly of the main group.

The Weather Last Night

State of Sea.—Slight disturbance

Weather.—Cool, cloudy, but no rain. Little sun.

Temperature: Highest 66deg., 55deg later.

Visibility: deteriorating in evening.

Wind: West, slight.

Barometer.—Steady since noon.

High Tide: Across the Water. —10.17 p.m. and 10.36 a.m.

From China Bases

A 20th Air Force Bomber Command communique, reporting the raid, said: "Preliminary reports reveal that although enemy aircraft were encountered and anti-aircraft fire was moderate to intense, none of our planes was lost as the result of enemy action."

Pilotless Bomber
First Picture

THE 'SECRET WEAPON' ARRIVES

Robot May Be Fired By Parent Plane

OR CATAPULTED OVER

By Daily Mail Reporter

PILOTLESS planes said to travel at 500 miles an hour, which explode between five and 15 seconds after their engines have stopped, were launched against Southern England throughout Thursday night and at intervals yesterday.

It was the first large-scale try-out of the much-publicised new German "secret weapon." An earlier trial caused slight damage and casualties, but yesterday's was more serious.

Soon after Mr. Herbert Morrison had revealed to the House of Commons that the robot was being used, the Ministry of Home Security issued the following advice to the public:—

EXCLUSIVE "Daily Mail" picture of a pilotless plane over Southern England yesterday. It was travelling at great speed.

'IT CAN'T BEAT US!'

THE Home Secretary and Ministry of Home Security issued this statement last night:

OIL ENGINES

MAJOR ATTACK BY RED ARMY—FINNS

THE German radio last night reported that an Order of the Day issued by Marshal Mannerheim, the Finnish Commander-in-Chief, said the Russians have now started on a major attack in the Karelian Isthmus.

Stalag Luft 3: 50 Were Shot

Three New Names

THE Air Ministry deeply regrets to announce that information has now been received from the protecting Power that three more officers of the Royal Air Force and one Allied air forces were shot by the Germans in addition to the 47 previously reported after having escaped from Stalag Luft III, in March last.

7,000-TON COAL LOSS WEEKLY

In Pit Stoppage

Seven thousand tons of coal weekly is being lost by a strike at Upton Colliery, Yorkshire.

Transport Shortage

An unofficial report from the Helsinki correspondent of the Stockholm Aftonbladet said that the Russians are now only 33 miles from Viborg.

Navy Take Over in Dock Strike

Naval ratings were brought in at Aberdeen yesterday to do the work of 350 dockers who remained on strike.

The Queen Visits Wounded

The Queen visited one of the largest Canadian military hospitals in the Home Counties yesterday and chatted for nearly three hours with wounded just back from Normandy.

'Waves of Planes Over Hungary'

Strong Allied bomber formations flew over Hungary in several waves and from several directions early this morning, says an official announcement in Budapest, quoted by the German radio.

World Food Policy

It is expected that a permanent organisation to give effect to the food and agriculture policy approved by the Hot Springs conference will be set up early next year.

FIFTH CAPTURE GROSSETO

Fifth Army captured Grosseto and eliminated last important German strong-point before Pisa, it is announced in Rome.

PAS DE CALAIS RAIDED

Medium forces of Fortresses and Liberators attacked three German aerodromes near Paris and Lille and military installations in Pas de Calais region.

RUSSIANS CAPTURE 100 PLACES

Russian communique says Soviet troops captured more than 100 places in Karelian Isthmus drive.

U.S. CUT MAIN CHERBOURG ROAD

Americans have captured St. Lauteur, cutting the last main road from Cherbourg.

BACK PAGE—Col. THREE

S.S. General Killed

Major-General Fritz Witt, commander of the S.S. 10th Hitler Youth Division, has been killed in action in Normandy, states the German News Agency.—Reuter.

A great deal better since taking Phosferine

"I am employed in a factory and for many months I had been feeling very much run-down and in a rather highly strung nervous condition. This, I attributed to the indoor confinement, lack of fresh air and the long hours of work, but since commencing on Phosferine tablets I can truthfully say I am feeling a great deal better, and do not suffer from a loss of appetite or from sleeplessness." (Signed) P. B., Glasgow.

Phosferine, as thousands have freely testified, has relieved many depressing symptoms of weakness, removed many a risk of serious illness, saved many a worker from becoming laid up. Ask your chemist for this really good tonic today.

PHOSFERINE
THE GREATEST OF ALL TONICS
for Depression, Brain Fag, Influenza, Anaemia, Headache, Neuralgia, Debility, Indigestion, Sleeplessness.

BLACK-OUT TO-NIGHT

LONDON	11.04 to	4.37
BELFAST	11.48	5.01
BIRMINGHAM	11.40	5.04
EDINBURGH	12.00	4.45
LEEDS	11.33	4.50
LIVERPOOL	11.38	4.58
MANCHESTER	11.35	4.53
NEWCASTLE	11.45	4.56

▲ DAILY MAIL, LONDON, SATURDAY JUNE 17, 1944

As the *Mail* reports, Caen proved to be far from empty: The *Hitlerjugend* Division defended the town fiercely. The front page features a remarkable photograph of one of the first "doodle-bugs," the V1 flying bombs launched by the Germans from France. The King and Queen are both reported to be in action on morale-boosting duties, in France and the Home Counties, respectively. A short note refers to the mass escape from Stalag Luft 3—later filmed as *The Great Escape* (1963)—and the executions of many who took part.

Battle for Caen

JUNE–JULY 1944

FOLLOWING THE D-DAY LANDINGS ON JUNE 6, 1944, ALLIED ARMIES HAD MADE SLOW PROGRESS IN THEIR EFFORTS TO EXPAND THE NORMANDY BRIDGEHEAD. GERMAN DEFENSES AND THEIR FIGHTING tenacity had nullified Allied material superiority, and the lack of progress was deeply worrying to both the Allied Supreme Commander, General Eisenhower, and the British prime minister, Winston Churchill. Both feared that Allied forces would either be trapped inside the bridgehead indefinitely or would have to endure months of World War I-style fighting to break out.

CAULDRON AT CAEN

British and Canadian forces on the eastern flank of the Allied bridgehead were under the overall command of General Bernard Montgomery, who wanted to capture Caen swiftly and then thrust his armored divisions inland to rout the enemy. For the next six weeks, Montgomery launched his troops forward in a series of set-piece battles of growing intensity, as more forces poured into the bridgehead and became available to him. First he sent forward the British 7th Armoured Division, the famous Desert Rats, on a daring outflanking attack to the west of Caen. German Tiger tanks ambushed the force and sent it reeling back to the bridgehead. Next, the British XXX and VIII Corps began Operation Epsom to envelop Caen, but four Waffen-SS panzer divisions concentrated to hammer them hard and stop them in their tracks. Into July, Montgomery continued to chip away until

his infantry had reached the gates of Caen. He then launched Operation Goodwood to outflank the town from the east. Three British armored divisions, with almost 900 tanks, backed by 10,000 infantry, 700 guns, and 2,000 heavy bombers, were to smash through the now weak German lines and break into open country. The Germans weathered the massive bombardment, and an improvised line of Tiger tanks and 88mm Flak guns ripped the British attack force apart. Confusion reigned in the British ranks, and the attack stalled without breaching the German lines. In the aftermath, some 270 burning hulks of British tanks littered the battlefield.

▲ BRITISH TROOPS round a wall on the approach to Caen, France, in early June 1944. German booby traps and snipers were a constant threat for Allied soldiers.

Daily Mail

LATE WAR NEWS

NO. 15,026   ONE PENNY   **   FOR KING AND EMPIRE   FRIDAY, JUNE 30, 1944

RUSSIA: GERMANS FACING DISASTER

Main Front Now Torn Wide Open

43,000 PRISONERS TAKEN SO FAR

Front is Burst Wide Open

FRESH retreats and soaring losses announced by Moscow last night are turning the defeat of the Germans in White Russia into disaster as the Red Army advances at blitzkrieg speed on East Prussia, Northern Poland, and the Baltic States.

On the southern half of the front, Bobruisk, key defence bastion, has fallen. It cost the Germans 16,000 killed and 18,000 prisoners.

On the northern half, two of the four Soviet armies engaged have taken 25,000 captives and killed 52,000 of the enemy—making a total of 43,000 prisoners so far.

Berlin: The Outlook is Confusing

So Are Comments

Russia

France

Flying Bombs

Goebbels

NEW MARSHAL

'HITLER'S FINN C-in-C DIES'

PARIS CROWD RIOTS

As Prisoners Pass

'Beaus' Hit Two Convoys

U.S.-Finn Break

On Way to London

Rommel Hits Back: Mass Blow by Panzers

WE SEIZE BRIDGES INTACT

Infantry Widen the Corridor

From RONALD CLARK
WITH BRITISH FORCES, Thursday Afternoon.

SCOTTISH troops who were piped to battle through fields dotted with the vivid red of poppies are now fighting hand-to-hand with the Germans for the capture of the third bridge across the Odon river.

BIGGEST ASSAULT YET

ROMMEL yesterday launched the heaviest counter-attack yet made in Normandy, according to an American broadcast from the front shortly before midnight.

Tough Going

Taken by Surprise

Germans Using More

Eisenhower's Big Talks

From STANLEY BURCH

RAID ON AUSTRIA

MR. FRASER IN CANADA

FLYING-BOMB LAIRS HIT

Fighters' Good Day

10 Die as Planes Crash

New RAF Chief, Overseas Ops.

Weather in the Strait

SCHLIEBEN IS HERE, BOOTLESS

Lost in Accident

By Daily Mail Reporter

Dempsey is Knighted

Steak for Lunch

Lost His Boots

RE-REGISTRATION WITH RETAILERS

▼ SOME OF THE 2.5 million Red Army troops who took part in Operation Bagration. The Russians also deployed 5,200 tanks, 31,000 artillery pieces, 2,300 rocket launchers, 70,000 motor vehicles, and 5,300 aircraft.

▲ DAILY MAIL, LONDON, FRIDAY JUNE 30, 1944

The Allies face a familiar foe in Normandy—the legendary Erwin Rommel—but on the Soviet front, Operation Bagration has opened a wide gap in the German line. While Churchill and Eisenhower meet to discuss Allied strategy, the *Mail* also reports that Scottish troops marched into a recent battle in northern France accompanied by the sound of the bagpipes.

Daily Mail

LATE WAR NEWS

FIELD-DAY

NO. 15,029   ONE PENNY   **   FOR KING AND EMPIRE   TUESDAY, JULY 4, 1944

MINSK FALLS TO ENCIRCLING DRIVE

Red Army Storms White Russia Capital

STREET FIGHTING IN POLOTSK

MINSK has fallen. In 24 hours two Soviet armies, swinging in north and south, closed round the 12-miles deep concentration of German forces. In a co-ordinated lightning stroke they stormed this last enemy bastion on pre-war Russian soil that guarded the road to Königsberg, Warsaw, and Riga.

Marshal Stalin, announcing this victory in an Order of the Day last night, described the final onslaught by the forces of Marshal Rokossovsky and General Chernyakhovsky as "a deep outflanking manœuvre."

Success was achieved only one day after the battle had begun by a combination of terrific air power, tanks, and Kuban Cossacks.

Ten days after the start of the Red Army's summer offensive, the bulk of the 200,000 German troops in the Minsk area are now threatened with extinction.

Forward units of the twin Soviet armies, which have long by-passed Minsk itself, are now swinging together to complete the encirclement of Von Bosch's shattered forces.

The Red Army men are less than 140 miles from the East Prussian border. The trapped Germans have no escape railways left. To get away they must travel minor roads and cart tracks which one by one are being cut behind them.

Fourteen air generals joined in the last headlong assault on Minsk. Marshal Rotmistrov, Soviet tank genius, handled the armour. Three cavalry generals directed the Cossacks.

The routine Soviet communiqué reported that on July 1 and 2 Rokossovsky's First White Russian Army captured 3,858 prisoners, among them Major-General Konradi, commander of the 36th Infantry Division. This gives Rokossovsky a total haul of 39,338 captives.

General Chernyakhovsky's Third White Russian forces have taken another 13,536 Germans, including Major-General Michael's, of the 206th Infantry. The total capture of this Soviet force is now 33,256.

Altogether the four Russian armies have now taken 82,682 prisoners, including eight generals.

POLOTSK GONE

Moscow announced that General Bagramyan's men are fighting in the streets of Polotsk, northern hinge of the shattered enemy defence line across White Russia.

Berlin has tacitly admitted that this bastion of the Baltic has been abandoned, or is being abandoned, under pressure of "furious" Soviet attacks.

New defence line west of the city is being assailed in the Soviet drive for the Gulf of Riga.

Bagramyan's armoured spearheads are 60 miles beyond Polotsk, fanning out across the old Polish frontier, thrusting on towards Dvinsk and Riga, capital of Latvia.

They are attacking Molodechno, rail junction on the route into Poland, and the whole Polotsk garrison of Germans are caught in yet another trap at this end of the 200-mile bulge.

To the south, too, part of Rokossovsky's forces are spreading their front across the pre-1939 border of Poland in their thrust for Baranovici.

To commemorate the Minsk success a salvo of 24 salvos from 324 guns—the maximum number—was fired in Moscow last night.

In the afternoon, a few hours before the city was stormed Moscow reported that fresh units had been thrust into the fight, and that the final battle promised to be one of the fiercest and bloodiest in the Russian campaign.

The Germans threw crack S.S. units into action in a bid to hold the Russians outside the city.

BREAK-THROUGH

Masses of Russian self-propelled guns pounded the defences. Tanks, infantry, and cavalry were concentrated behind the gun positions waiting for the signal for the last assault.

When Marshal Rokossovsky's columns moved in they met German armour and infantry counter-attacking viciously in an attempt to hold their flank positions, to stop the Russians breaking through to complete the encirclement more.

The Russians and the Germans counter-attacks and then, smashing forward with enormous power, broke through the German lines.

On all sides round Minsk there was the same evidence of the disaster which has struck the Germans. Thousands of German dead line the highways. The Russians are advancing so fast they have no time to bury them.

The German defeat was hastened by the complete air mastery that the Russian Air Force has established. Their low-level fighter-bombers were out at dawn bombing and gunning the Germans retreating along the roads to the west.

The "cushion" of Russian marsh and steppeland which once stood between the German Army and the homeland has all but vanished.

From now on, the Germans cannot afford to yield any position as Russian advance at Minsk without bringing "the threat to Germany itself catastrophically nearer."

Neutrals Resume Italy Relations

Rome, Monday.—Seven neutral Powers to-day opened routine diplomatic business with the Italian Foreign Office, when their representatives officially visited the Italian Foreign Under-Secretary.

The diplomats represented the Vatican, Afghanistan, Eire, Sweden, Spain, Argentina, and Switzerland.—Reuter.

The Finest Soldiers on Earth

Make You Proud to be British

Daily Mail Special Correspondent
WITH THE EIGHT ARMY,
Fojano Della Chiana,
Monday.

GENERAL LEESE'S infantry proved themselves as tough as any of the footslogging old sweats of the last war when yesterday they left their lorries and chased crack German paratroops ten miles under a torrid sun.

Their swift advance, which took them well beyond the north shore of Lake Trasimeno, was one of the most sensational of this campaign and certainly set up a record for foot soldiers in Italy.

It was all the more astonishing since it followed hard fighting the previous day, when they had to battle their way from ridge to ridge towards the village of Gabro-Sanso across country which an officer described to me as "the perfect model for rearguard fighting."

THIS morning, for the third day in succession, they are pressing on again. I saw one column a couple of hours ago trudging along a winding, sun-baked road down which the Germans were retreating.

Swirling, choking dust-clouds which have returned to plague us on this front, had quitted them. In uniform greyish-white from head to head.

Only where little rivulets of sweat trickled down from under their camouflaged steel helmets could you detect the tan they had collected in the last few weeks of sunshine.

They were tired—they must have been after 36 hours' action—but you would never have guessed it if you had seen them slogging through the ankle-deep, powdery dust in the breathless heat of an almost tropical morning.

But it would have made you ashamed to be British to have seen them, not to spoke of all your super-tanks and guns and planes and secret weapons, the British infantryman is still the backbone of our Army and the finest soldier in the world.

★

"TELL 'em at home the P.B.I. can still blinking well march!" shouted one as he recognised my correspondent's flashes. "We don't need any blooming lorries. We can walk to Berlin," and another.

That's the spirit with which these are advancing, and their only regret is that they don't get closer to the enemy more often.

Most of yesterday they were shelled and sniped as they pushed forward but even Kesselring's tough para-boys are no match to this with our infantry at close quarters.

"They have done a magnificent job," an officer told me this morning. "After Saturday's battle they dug themselves in and snatched a few hours' sleep in slit trenches. Just there were loudspeaker shouts ready to move off, with their boots and weapons freshly polished as though they were going on parade by dawn."

A TEN-MILES march may not sound very impressive to veterans of the last war, but ten miles under this grilling sun is quite some walk.

And when you throw in the ever-present dust, full battle-kit, rifles and automatic weapons to be carried, and remember also that they were mopping up pockets of enemy resistance all day, it exceeds into the realm of the heroic.

The enemy is still going back fast to-day. There is no doubt that we have bustled him off his balance.

We had an instance of this yesterday, when two ambulances carrying British wounded took the wrong turning and drove into a German-occupied village.

They were captured, but an hour later, when the Germans heard this industry were marching down the road towards them, they piled into their vehicles and drove away, leaving not only the prisoners but a considerable quantity of equipment behind.

Flying Fort Had German Crew

BUENOS AIRES, Monday.—Nine Germans stepped out of a Flying Fortress which made a forced landing at Valencia, according to a report received here to-day from Spain. All were interned.

The plane, which was un-damaged, bore German markings. It had apparently been patched together from parts of Fortresses which had been shot down in Europe, it is being drawn up."

Moscow Gets Bananas

Moscow, Monday.—Bananas have appeared for sale in one of Moscow's leading stores.—Reuter.

MOVE TO KILL EIRE TRAVEL RAMP

By Daily Mail Reporter

WITH restoration of modified passenger and cargo services between Great Britain and Northern Ireland, regulations against further "racketeers" are likely to be enforced.

To prevent Black Market operations it is expected that passenger service will be restored on the same basis.

First people to benefit will be heavily cut from to-day, according to Paris Radio. Many stations will be closed, and few trains will operate after 30 p.m.

purchase of tickets considered on the production of travel permits. Several hundreds yesterday flew from Dublin to Bristol to attack targets in Rumania, and then on to land in Italy, and Algiers made last night.

It is expected that passenger service will be restored on the same basis.

First people to benefit will be hundreds of business men no doubt on both sides of the Irish Sea whose travel.

permits were cancelled when the ban was imposed.

Shipping services between Eire and Great Britain will also be restored next Monday

Travel between Britain and all Ireland was suspended on March 13—a first step, as Mr. Churchill put it, to "isolate Southern Ireland from the outer world during the critical period now approaching."

ATTACKS by R.A.F. and American heavy bombers on the flying-bomb bases in the Pas de Calais have been held up by appalling weather conditions.

Vast Cloud is Aiding Fly-Bombs

But the Fighters Still Get Them

By COLIN BEDNALL,
Air Correspondent

WITH THE U.S. 8TH AIR FORCE, Monday.—Remember that this is the week during which you must concentrate all your efforts on disrupting the enemy communication system.

The great thick cloudbank blocking off the Pas de Calais area reached even greater size and density yesterday.

The tops of the clouds rose to astronomical height, again making bombing operations a complete impossibility.

This freak weather, which would almost seem to have been produced to order to suit the enemy, must greatly reduce the part which the Air Forces can play in keeping the "secret" weapon in check.

From the results seen of the bomber operations which have been possible during the past fortnight the effect of our bombing might be very different if any sort of continuity could be achieved.

A high proportion of the flying bombs sent over yesterday were destroyed by our fighters.

R.A.F. planes swarmed over the sky and pounced on the bombs. Two pilots of Air Defence of Great Britain have each shot down three flying bombs in a single patrol during the past 24 hours.

The German radio last night said that the missile is being used "solely with the determination to put a stop to the terror tactics of the British leaders."

'THIS WEEK IS DECISIVE'

Italians Warned

Italian patriots were told that this week will be decisive in a broadcast from Algiers last night, giving instructions from Allied H.Q.

The broadcast was addressed particularly to the patriots operating in the Spezia area. It said:

"This is definitely the decisive week for you."

Italy Fighting—BACK Page.

'Finns a Tragedy' —Swede Premier

Per Albin Hansson, the Swedish Prime Minister, in a speech broadcast last night by Stockholm Radio, said:

"What has occurred during the past few days stands out as a tragedy.

"One had hoped that Finland would find a way out of what the Finns themselves regarded as a separate war, a way to peace which both the Finnish nation and the Finnish Government seemed to desire so earnestly."—Reuter.

Americans Strike South on 40-Mile Front

The West   'BRITISH POISED FOR ATTACK'

Progress is made in Normandy on both British and American sectors.

GENERAL MONTGOMERY'S campaign in Normandy entered a new phase yesterday when American divisions in the west went over to the attack on a front of 40 miles from the base of the Cherbourg Peninsula.

They struck southwards on a great arc running from a point south of Barneville-sur-Mer to the area of St. Lo.

The drive began in a blinding rainstorm after a furious bombardment by heavy artillery, reported Reuter's special correspondent in a cable last night. American infantry waded through water knee deep, and even chest deep in places.

In two and a half hours troops on the west coast advanced nearly three miles to seize a 400ft. hill north of La Haye du Puits and other important high ground.

Farther inland other units cut the Barneville-Carentan-Caen railway at St. Jores after an advance of five miles. St. Jores lies south-east of St. Sauveur le Vicomte, where the Americans first drove.

TITO DRIVES BACK BULGARS

Yugoslav Partisans have cleared the Bulgarian troops from the Jablanica area of Yugoslavia, states the night communiqué from Marshal Tito's N.Q.—Reuter.

LUFTWAFFE TRIES TO STEM SOVIETS

The Germans threw several hundred planes into the White Russian battle yesterday in a bid to check the Soviet advance, said the German Overseas News Agency.

BRITISH IN FRENCH MUD-BATH

Just Like Their Fathers Knew

From RONALD CLARK
WITH BRITISH FORCES IN NORMANDY, Monday.

THEIR fathers told them all about the mud in the last war. How they squelched and plopped down watery trenches, and how they charged knee-deep across seas of mud.

Now they know for themselves. For the first time since the invasion began, British troops on the Normandy front are wallowing in a mud-bath.

All night long the rain poured down, and as I write this despatch it has resolved itself into a grey, featureless drizzle. Vehicles bumping up to the front are squirting jets of water high into the air as they move through muddy grooves rent deep.

A rain must has dissolved the horizon into a grey composition of trees.

There is scarcely a plane in the air, and only the occasional whine of a stray shell from a solitary battery shows that the action—and the death for some of us—is lurking somewhere in that mist.

Amphibious

Life in the trenches is almost an amphibious operation. Damp and moisture comes from the walls and floors despite ground sheets, canvas floorings, and tents.

I waded troops on one sector where they were throwing lead tea in mass tins under the dripping branches of tree-tops.

Even the green grass is browning under the trample of many boots.

Traffic moving across the fields has stripped the outer covering of the earth, revealing great gashes of raw soil dozens of feet wide running for miles across crop fields.

At noon a slim shaft of sunlight tried to pierce the clouds, but it gave up the attempt, and the previous covering descended on the battle front until it looked more like one of Turner's landscapes.

Activity is almost at a standstill.

GermansSend 6 Divisions from Russia

Daily Mail Special Correspondent
MADRID, Monday.

AT least six German divisions from the Russian front have been moved to France, and three of them placed under Rommel's command, according to reports reaching Madrid from France to-night.

All-night fighting has been added to Rundstedt's general reserve.

Rundstedt has also been drawing divisions from Holland, Denmark, Belgium, and the southern sectors of the French coast.

This regrouping has been made necessary by heavy losses in the Cherbourg Peninsula.

Poles Defeating German Attack

The Germans have started an "all-out offensive" with three divisions against the Polish underground army in the Lublin area, according to a report received by the Polish Telegraph Agency.

A battle is reported to have been in progress since the middle of June, with the Poles constantly repelling the enemy.

across the peninsula to cut off strong German forces which have since been destroyed in the battle for Cherbourg.

Elsewhere smaller gains were reported as German machine-gun and mortar nests and concrete road blocks.

So far it is not known whether the American attack is designed to bring Montgomery's right wing into the rest of the front, or something bigger.

German reports last night forecast that the whole front of two miles from the west coast of the Cherbourg Peninsula to Caen will be aflame.

"General Montgomery is set on enlarging the Allied wedge into

BACK PAGE—Col. FIVE

Our Vigilance is 'Uncanny'

A German radio reporter last night paid the Allies' vigilance over the Channel coast area is enormous.

"The enemy's on the look-out everywhere," he said. "Whether it shines or rains he gives no respite to our columns. Once he recognises his target his destructive fire pours down from his planes and artillery."

Stimson on Visit to Italy

ALLIED H.Q., Italy, Monday.—Mr. Henry Stimson, United States Secretary for War, landed at an airfield in Italy late this afternoon.

He will hold war conferences with the Allied military leaders here and also inspect troops, hospitals, and front-line installations.—Reuter.

SHUTTLE RAID ON RUMANIA

Britain-Soviet-Italy

Strong forces of American heavy bombers yesterday flew from Russia to attack targets in Rumania, and then on to land in Italy, and Algiers made last night.

The planes, according to Algiers, originally flew from England to Russia and yesterday's flight completed the triangular shuttle service.

Other heavies—Italian-based attacked Hungarian and Yugoslav oil refineries and transport facilities.—B.U.P. and Reuter.

'NOT LONG NOW'

From Daily Mail Correspondent
DAR-ES-SALAAM, Monday.—The Aga Khan, in a message from Switzerland to his followers in Africa, says he thinks the war will soon end.

Russians Cut Doomed Armies in Two

THE Red Army has sprung a vast double trap east and west of Minsk in their drive to split and then annihilate the Germans in White Russia, declared Colonel von Hammer, ace enemy military commentator, last night.

In a succession of gloomy messages he explained that the inner jaws in this twin encircling movement were closing west of the Beresina across the main roads which lead back to the White Russian base.

The outer jaws were coming together behind Minsk, with strong mixed reinforcements supporting the Russian forces.

(They have closed since he made this comment.)

"Powerful," "determined," "fierce," and "furious" were the descriptions von Hammer gave to the Soviet attacks.

He admitted that, as announced from Moscow on Sunday night, the last two railways running behind and from Minsk to Brest-Litovsk and Vilna have been cut.

"Great battles," were fought for the Minsk-Vilna line, he said. "A heavy tank action opened with fresh Russian formations yesterday evening."

The Germans withdrew according to orders."

FOUR CAPTURE A THOUSAND

By Loud-speaker

SHAEF, Monday.—Four British N.C.O.s caused the surrender of the last 1,000 Germans holding out in Cherbourg by "loud-speaker," has been awarded the United States Bronze Star.

They were members of an amplifying unit lent to the U.S. Army. One of them, Sergeant Clinton, speaks German. They went forward from the American lines on their loud-speaker truck, and urged any moment by the German guns, had the desired effect, and the Germans came out of their powerful position waving a white flag.—Reuter.

This appeal, carried out with the truck liable to be blown to bits at any moment by the German guns, had the desired effect, and the Germans came out of their powerful position waving a white flag.—Reuter.

3 Generals Killed

In a later dispatch, he reported "Powerful Soviet tank formations and motorised infantry are to-night sweeping towards the north-west.

"Three assault forces are striking towards Dvinsk and Riga as their determined drive to reach the Baltic coast.

"But the main pre-occupation of the Soviet High Command is to reach Minsk and annihilate the Polotsk force German generals—Mart nek, Pfeffer, and Schünemann have been killed."

'Old Glory' to Fly over Rome

Rome, Monday.—On the suggestion of President Roosevelt the U.S. flag that flew over the Capitol in Washington when war was declared on Japan and on Germany will be raised in Rome on July 4.

American bands will play at réveillé and retreat ceremonies.—Exchange.

Maquis Cut Cable Lines to Lisbon

Lisbon, Monday.—All cable, radio, and possibly postal communications between Portugal and France have been cut from to-day, due to increased difficulties in reception and transmission.

This confirms reports that Maquis' action has almost entirely severed communication services via the Pyrenees.—A.P.

Japan Sees Danger

Daily Mail Radio Station

Erwin Wickert, German Far East reporter, broadcasting from Tokyo yesterday, said that since the American attack on the Marianas there is no village, and, indeed, no human soul in Japan, unaffected by the war. Everyone knows that the name Marianas means : Danger Near.

Weather in the Strait

State of the Sea.—Almost calm.

Weather.—Warm, but still overcast after half an inch of rain in four hours. Maximum temperature 60 deg., 64 deg. at 7.30. Visibility fair. Wind S.W., light. Barometer.—Steady.

Paris 'Tubes' Cut

Services on the Paris Metro will be heavily cut from to-day, according to Paris Radio. Many stations will be closed, and few trains will operate after 30 p.m.

'Pacific End Soon'

The German radio last night broadcast this cable from its Tokio correspondent : "The decisive battle in the Pacific will be fought this summer. People in Tokio are convinced of this fact. The curtain of the last act in the Pacific, as in Europe, is just being drawn up."

▲ DAILY MAIL, LONDON, TUESDAY JULY 4, 1944

Good news piles up for the Allies: the French Resistance has cut communications from Vichy France to Iberia, and Muscovites can once again enjoy bananas. The significant advances on the Eastern Front jostle for attention with reports from war correspondents with British infantry in Italy and Normandy: after heavy rains, the latter has come to resemble the trenches of World War I.

175

fortuna cloth

THE SUN

FOR AUSTRALIA

Sun, Moon, Tides
Sun.—Rose 6.55, sets 5.08.
Moon.— Rose 7.28 am, sets 6.01 pm.
High Water—Port Demond: Today, 9.14, 9.14; tomorrow, 9.50, 9.50.

PENFOLDS PORT

No. 10,776 — SYDNEY: FRIDAY, JULY 21, 1944 — PRICE 2d

GERMANY IN CHAOS, ALL FORCES CALLED TO STAND BY HITLER

Hitler—"Screams murder and gives order for purge."

LONDON, Friday.—*Germany has been thrown into violent confusion and probably civil war by announcement of a plot to kill Hitler.*

Hitler accused officers of trying to murder him, ordered a bloody purge and some officers have been shot, including Count Colonel von Stauffenberg.

Marshal Goering says that dismissed generals had formed a new Reich "Government of usurpers" and he called upon the Luftwaffe to obey no one but himself or his nominee.

Policeman Himmler now to rule the German Army.

Admiral Doenitz issued a similar call to the Navy and said that "mad generals" had plotted Hitler's death.

Hitler has given Gestapo Chief Himmler full power over the Army and decreed that no one is to take orders from the "usurpers" and it is everyone's duty to arrest or kill any person passing on such orders.

Navy and Air Force have sworn allegiance to Hitler, but the Army has not yet done so.

All telephone links with Germany have been cut since 7.40 last night.

"OBEY ME" THEY CRIED

Goering—"The Air Force must obey me only." Doenitz—"The navy must obey me only."

Reich Crisis May Bring Big War Change

LONDON, Friday. — Hitler's sensational midnight speech reveals a major internal crisis, if not a widespread revolt against his regime, declares Reuter's Continental observer.

Hitler's references to "senseless and criminally stupid officers" being responsible for the plot, and Admiral Doenitz's mention of "mad generals," leave no doubt that the revolt is led by part of the army leadership.

Hitler Issues Orders To Shoot On Sight

Hitler made a dramatic midnight broadcast accusing an officers' clique of trying to murder him and the entire German High Command in a bomb plot.

Wounded Men Hitler Spies

LONDON, Friday.—All the German officers wounded with Hitler had been used by him as personal spies to watch the German High Command, declares the London "Daily Express" military writer.

STOP-PRESS

Radio Appeal To German Officers

Editorial

MR. BEASLEY RETURNS

MR. BEASLEY found in the United States a "true appreciation of Australia's war effort."

▲ THE SUN, SYDNEY, FRIDAY JULY 21, 1944

Australia's *Sun* reports the sensational news from Germany of the failed assassination attempt on Adolf Hitler, and speculates that it might lead to civil war in the Nazi homeland. This never happened. Instead, the plotters were mercilessly hunted down.

Kill Hitler!

JULY 20, 1944

I N EARLY JULY 1944, THE ALLIES WERE WINNING VICTORIES ON ALL FRONTS. IN THE PACIFIC WAR, U.S. MARINES WERE TAKING GUAM IN THE MARIANAS CHAIN, WHILE IN EUROPE THE RED ARMY WAS STORMING WEST AND THE Allied landings in Normandy were threatening Paris. The sole ray of hope for the Germans seemed to be new weapons, among which were the V1 flying bombs, sometimes called "doodlebugs."

DEATH PLOT

The high command of the German army knew that resistance to the Allies was becoming impossible, but most German soldiers still obeyed their superiors. There were exceptions, however, and on July 20 some of these officers tried to assassinate Hitler.

Colonel Claus von Stauffenberg was a member of a group that had been plotting to kill Hitler for some time. He was chief of staff of the Replacement Army, which controlled German Army units in and around Berlin. At a meeting in Hitler's headquarters in East Prussia, von Stauffenberg placed a briefcase full of explosives near Hitler. Von Stauffenberg then left the meeting. The briefcase exploded when it was timed to, but a large table leg absorbed much of the blast. Four officers were killed, but Hitler himself escaped with minor injuries.

The conspirators expected Hitler to have been killed, and they quickly tried to take over in Berlin, but Hitler spoke to members of the Berlin garrison by telephone, reassuring them that he was still alive. The Nazi apparatus then hunted down most of those involved in the plot. Many senior officers had known of the conspiracy, including Field Marshal Erwin Rommel. He committed suicide, but the Nazis said he died of wounds sustained during an air attack. It was felt too dangerous to admit that he had been involved. Others were not so fortunate. They were tried and then hanged using piano wire.

▲ HITLER SHOWS MUSSOLINI his bomb-damaged conference room following the failed assassination attempt.

EXTRA

5¢

Journal NEW YORK American

AN AMERICAN PAPER FOR THE AMERICAN PEOPLE

R

Daily 3 Cents, Saturday 3 Cents in New York City
New York City; 18 Cents Elsewhere, 18 and 35-Mile Zone, 25 Cents Elsewhere

LATEST NEWS
LATEST SCRATCHES

No. 20,645—DAILY   FRIDAY, JULY 21, 1944   In Two Sections —Section One

GUAM INVADED!

Yanks Storm Ashore, Beachheads Captured

By JOSEPH A. BORS, International News Service Staff Correspondent

WASHINGTON, July 21.—The Navy announced today that U. S. Marines and assault troops have stormed the beaches of Guam; and that waves of supporting forces are pouring in behind them in the long awaited campaign to recapture that former American island from

Parley Split As V.P. Poll Nears

By SANFORD E. STANTON

CHICAGO, July 21.— The battle between Sidney Hillman's Communist dominated Political Action Committee and conservative New Dealers over selection of a Vice-Presidential candidate reaches its climax today on the floor of the Democratic National Convention.

It will be Vice-President Henry A. Wallace, backed by Hillman and the CIO, versus Sen. Harry Truman, of Missouri, the candidate of the big city leaders and the South, when the balloting begins this afternoon. There are 14 other candidates in the field, but an informal poll early today showed Wallace had 454 pledged votes to 295½ for Truman.

President Roosevelt, accepting the fourth term nomination in a radio address last night from a Pacific Coast naval station, gave
Continued on Page 4, Column 4.

See Texas Revolt Spread to South

By WILLIAM S. NEAL
Special to the N. Y. Journal-American.

CHICAGO, July 21.—Leaders of the "Dixie Revolt," rebuked by the Democratic National Convention, predicted today that the flames of the anti-New Deal rebellion will sweep over many Southern States and may decisively affect the Presidential election.

The convention refused to seat the full anti-New Deal Texas delegation. Instead, it voted to divide Texas' votes between the regular (anti-New Deal) and "rump" pro-Roosevelt delegations, with the result that most of the regular delegation walked out of the convention.

"I already have received many calls from Southern delegates from other States protesting

Huge Purge On to Crush Reich Revolt

LONDON, July 21 (UP).—Hitler appeared to have regained firm control of Germany today with loyal army, navy, Luftwaffe and Gestapo forces ruthlessly tracking down generals and other leaders of an abortive revolt that threatened to plunge the Reich into civil war.

Heinrich Himmler was given command of all armed forces within the Reich and ordered by Hitler to restore order at all cost.

The dreaded Gestapo chief embarked on an unprecedented reign of terror in an effort to wipe out all vestiges of the militarist coup designed to topple the Nazi hierarchy from power and take Germany out of the war.

Orders were issued to all armed forces, as well as to civilians to arrest or shoot on the spot all suspected of participating in the revolt.

DNB, the German agency, said "army battalions"—a bat
Continued on Page 2, Column 5.

Russians Reach Lwow Outskirts

LONDON, July 21 (INS).—German defenders of the Polish city of Lwow were reported today by Reuters in a dispatch from Moscow to be erecting barricades in the northern outskirts of the city to meet the threatened breakthrough of the Red Army.

Fierce fighting was said to be under way on the approaches to Lwow.

[UP reported two powerful Russian armies, outflanking the fortress city of Brest Litovsk, in a giant pincers on Warsaw, with one of the armies only 94 miles from the Polish capital.]

(Earlier Details on Page 2)

PURGES REBELS—Heinrich Himmler, chief of the Gestapo, has embarked on a ruthless reign of terror in an effort to wipe out all vestiges of the revolt against Hitler.

British Seize New Heights Below Caen

By KINGSBURY SMITH
International News Service Staff Correspondent

SUPREME HQ., Allied Expeditionary Force, July 21.—The British 2nd Army, hurling waves of infantry forces against Germans behind strong tank units, pressed their advance beyond the Normandy communications center of Caen today to seize additional strategic high ground.

Headquarters of Gen. Eisenhower announced that the British had extended their hold of high ground below Caen from the Orne River to the vicinity of Verrieres, about five miles south of Caen.

(The Nazi agency DNB admitted that the British continued to press ahead east of the Orne and succeeded in gaining some ground.

(Violent fighting was reported to have flared up between the Americans and Germans east of the Carentan-Periers road.

(DNB said that Nazi Field Marshal Rommel had brought up new troops getting their first
Continued on Page 2, Column 8.

the Japanese. "The landings on Guam are continuing against moderate ground opposition," the communique said.

[The invasion followed the most intensive bombardment in preparation for any amphibious operation in the Pacific war, according to UP. The bombardment covered a period of 17 consecutive days.]

[The steady, daily bombardment appar-

A large detailed map of Guam appears on Page 2.

ently knocked out many Japanese shore defenses and drove the enemy from the beaches, said AP.]

Thus American fighting men returned to the Far Pacific outpost approximately two and a half years after the Japanese seized that territory with little opposition from a small Marine garrison.

In an early morning communique Pacific Fleet headquarters said Marines and Army troops established beachheads on Guam July 20 with the support of carrier aircraft and surface units of the mighty 5th Fleet.

120 Miles from Saipan

The Navy said that the early waves of assault forces were being supported by planes and warships which were hammering enemy defenses on the island, approximately 120 miles southwest of recently-captured Saipan.

[Guam, said A.P., has nearly 625 square miles of tree-and-brush studded mountains, offers the Japanese a greater defense area with the prospect of more fighting as bitter as Saipan, and create the task of having to dig the enemy out of caves and crevices when fighting reaches the mountains.]

The amphibious operations are being directed by Rear Admiral Richard L. Conolly. The expeditionary troops are under the command of Marine Maj. Gen. Roy S.
Continued on Page 2, Column 1.

THE WEATHER
Partly cloudy, moderate winds.
Sun rises 5:42 a. m., sun sets, 8:22 p. m. High tide at Governors Island, 10:15 a. m. and 10:39 p. m.

HOURLY TEMPERATURES
(Complete Weather Report on Page 2)

TODAY'S INDEX
Auctions ......17 Lost and Found 2
Best Places to ...   Obituaries 20
Dice ....7 Radio 18
Comics ...18, 19 Society 4
Editorial .....18 Sports 9
Financial .....10 Theatres 6, 7
Food, Cooking .4 Want Ads..16, 17
Horoscope 18

The Journal-American has the largest circulation of any evening newspaper in New York City.

It is the only New York evening newspaper possessing the three great wire services—ASSOCIATED PRESS —INTERNATIONAL NEWS SERVICE—UNITED PRESS

(PHONE YOUR NEWS TIPS TO CORTLANDT 7-1212)

▲ NEW YORK JOURNAL AMERICAN, FRIDAY JULY 21, 1944

Politics continue as normal despite news of U.S. landings on Guam, a key "stepping stone" in the advance toward Japan. Franklin D. Roosevelt's New Deal came under attack from both conservatives and communists for over a decade. The Nazis are reasserting control in Germany, but losing ground in Normandy and Poland. The *Journal American* also reports a shortage close to its heart: newsprint.

Wiener Illustrierte

63. Jahrgang Nr. 33   Wien, 16. August 1944   Preis **20** Pf.
Zuzüglich 2 Pfennig
bei Hauszustellung

Die erste Waffe der Vergeltung „V 1"

Seit Wochen hämmert unsere erste Vergeltungswaffe auf London und Südengland. Die britischen Jäger, die in großer Zahl gegen die „Flügelbombe" angesetzt werden, sind nicht in der Lage, sie zu erreichen. Ein Antrieb gibt der „V 1" ihre hohe Geschwindigkeit

PK-Aufnahme: Kriegsberichter Lysiok (Transocean-Europapress)

◄ WIENER ILLUSTRIERTE (VIENNA ILLUSTRATED MAGAZINE), AUGUST 16, 1944. The weekly German-language magazine boasts the first image of a V1 flying bomb. In fact, the bomb had already been in use for two months. The appearance of the cover feature may have reflected a desire to promote positive news at a time when progress for the Axis was limited.

▶ THE V1 "FLYING BOMB" was designed to spread terror among the civil population of Britain and to help turn the tide of war in the West. It reality, the weapon had little real effect on the course of the conflict.

WARDONIA BLADES For Better Shaves

No. 15,069   ONE PENNY

Daily Mail

FOR KING AND EMPIRE

LATE WAR NEWS

SATURDAY, AUGUST 19, 1944

CODE IN DER NOSE
If you have a Head Cold or Catarrh insert "Mentholatum" into your nostrils. It clears away congestion, stops irritation, restores free breathing.
MENTHOLATUM

DECISIVE BATTLE OF FRANCE HAS NOW BEEN WON

Kluge's Beaten Army is Being Pursued—and Destroyed

From ALEXANDER CLIFFORD   NORMANDY, Friday

WE have won a decisive victory in Normandy. The German Seventh Army is now in full retreat. You can state this tremendous news as simply as that to-day. Overnight the situation has suddenly become sharp, clear, and overwhelmingly important. The Germans here are defeated. This is what has, in fact, happened.

Most of those German divisions are, after all, still trapped in the pocket. Only yesterday did the Germans themselves recognise the extent of their plight. The gap is now down to three or four doubtful miles. The panzer divisions are trying to fight their way through it in a tremendous running battle.

You can call the victory decisive without hesitation. It does not mean that the Germans will immediately cease fighting. It does not mean that this particular battle will not drag on for a few days yet. It does not even guarantee a big bag of prisoners in the end.

But it does mean that the best German divisions are irretrievably mauled and disorganised. It means that they can never again bring a really serious force against us in Western Europe. It means they will probably never again be able to organise any sort of a front in France.

Tanks Are Swinging North Again

THE DRIVE FOR PARIS—

3 Powers Agree on Germany

FDR and Premier to Meet Soon

WASHINGTON, Friday

PRESIDENT ROOSEVELT stated to-day that a general understanding had been reached between Russia, Britain, and the United States regarding the occupation of Germany.

'Must Be Occupied'

No Reasons

GAS MAY BE NAZIS' V3
Stockholm Report

F-Bomb Depot Bombed

Russians Storm Big Vistula Stronghold

WARSAW AID FROM R.A.F.
1,750-miles Flights

MAQUIS STORM A GARRISON
550 Germans Give In

Road to Koenigsberg

Liberator Sank 2 U's in 22 min.
Saved Normandy Convoys

Crew Awards
By COLIN BEDNALL, Air Correspondent

Straddled

Two-way Drive for Toulon
FALL 'EXPECTED SOON'

THE Riviera invasion continues to go well. Allied reports last night stated that advancing spearheads were closing in on Toulon.

LATEST

'FINAL NAZI CATASTROPHE' —EISENHOWER

RUSSIANS TRAP THREE DIVISIONS

RESISTANCE IS CRUMBLING
From EDWIN TETLOW, GENERAL WILSON'S H.Q.

'More Troops in Florence Area'

—And the Man Who Leads It

GENERAL "Blood and Guts" Patton, in command of the Third United States Army approaching Paris. In this picture he is talking to a French boy "somewhere in France."

Italians Here Can Go to the Pictures
But 'Pubs' Barred

LAVAL FLEES FROM PARIS
May Go to Germany

German Papers Late
From Daily Mail Correspondent

CANDIDATE WOUNDED

"Wonderful the way this pre-war overall has lasted!"

THANKS TO THE GENTLE BUT PENETRATING WAY Extra Soapiness DEALS WITH THE DIRT

SUNLIGHT SOAP

Teeth white back and front —no more "White Lies"

SOLIDOX TOOTHPASTE

▲ DAILY MAIL, LONDON, SATURDAY AUGUST 19, 1944

The game is up for occupied France: although the flight of Pierre Laval only makes the bottom of the *Mail*'s front page, it is the clearest confirmation of the optimistic headlines at the top. In a first reference to an issue that would dominate the postwar world, the *Mail* reports the Allied powers' agreement on the occupation and division of Germany, although details were not yet finalized.

Falaise Pocket

AUGUST 1944

BY THE END OF JULY, THE U.S. FIRST ARMY HAD BROKEN THROUGH THE GERMAN LINES THAT LAY TO THE SOUTH OF THE NORMANDY BEACHHEAD, IN AN OFFENSIVE CODENAMED OPERATION COBRA. German counterattacks were stopped with great loss by Allied fighter bombers. With the font line now fluid, General George Patton's Third Army began a drive to the east that surrounded 20 German divisions in the so-called Falaise Pocket. Ten thousand Germans died in the pocket, and a further 50,000 surrendered. As the pocket was being reduced in size, more Allied forces were coming into southern France, in landings known as Operation Anvil. They swiftly liberated the port city of Marseille and then moved up the Rhône valley.

THE GERMAN COLLAPSE

The German position in France had collapsed, and the capital, Paris, was liberated on August 25, with the honor of taking the surrender being given to the Free French 2nd Armored Division. In a fit of anger, Adolf Hitler had ordered that Paris be destroyed before German forces withdrew, but this order was never carried out, and the city was reclaimed by the Allies with relatively little damage to its historic buildings and bridges.

Success in the West was mirrored in the East. The Red Army forced Hitler's ally Romania to surrender and declare war on Germany, and by early September the Soviets had conquered Bulgaria. A tragic episode in this offensive on the Eastern Front was the Warsaw Rising. In early August, Polish resistance fighters, the Polish Home Army, rose up against the German forces occupying the city. The Red Army was close by, but chose not to intervene. RAF planes tried to drop supplies to the Poles, but they lacked any heavy support weapons. The revolt was crushed.

▶ SMASHED GERMAN VEHICLES in the Falaise Pocket in August 1944. Devoid of air cover, Wehrmacht columns were at the mercy of roving Allied ground-attack aircraft.

▼ U.S. FORCES PARADE through Paris, France, after its liberation in 1944. For political purposes, the city had officially been liberated by the French 2nd Armored Division and not by the Americans.

▲ NEW YORK WORLD-TELEGRAM, WEDNESDAY AUGUST 23, 1944

New Yorkers learn of the liberation of Paris in August 1944, against a backdrop of opinion polls about the approaching presidential election. The paper also features an eyewitness account from the Western Front by the legendary reporter Ernie Pyle, one of the few correspondents to have a picture byline. Pyle's empathic reporting earned him a reputation as the friend of the ordinary soldier.

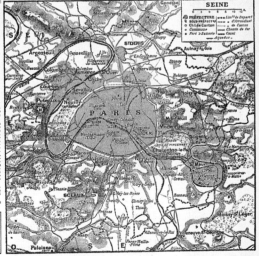

▲ L'ECHO D'ALGER (ALGERIAN ECHO), ALGIERS, THURSDAY AUGUST 24, 1944
Algeria's French-language daily, set up in 1915, celebrates the liberation of Paris with two contrasting photographs: "What we'll see tomorrow," with celebrating crowds at the Arc de Triomphe, and "What we won't see anymore," the Place de l'Opéra filled with German-language road signs.

▲ THE PHILADELPHIA INQUIRER, THURSDAY AUGUST 24, 1944

The surrender of Romania and its revolt against German rule is the latest good news for the Allies, while in France attention switches to the race for the German border. At home, John Foster Dulles criticizes the secrecy surrounding the Dumbarton Oaks talks, called to establish the postwar political order, but a poignant story of the death of a local hero is a reminder of the fighting still to come.

Signal
EXTRA

**Warsaw . . .
The truth about!**
Countess Tarnowska, President of the Polish Red Cross, arriving at the German outposts. She was sent by General Bor-Komorowski to parley on behalf of the insurgents

▲ MEMBERS OF THE POLISH HOME ARMY in Warsaw march to do battle against the Germans. Despite heroic Polish resistance, the uprising had been suppressed by October 2—150,000 Poles were killed.

▲ SIGNAL, AUGUST 1944
Signal was a German magazine, often printed in English and distributed around Europe. This edition shows a Red Cross representative arriving in Warsaw, evidence that the Germans were observing international conventions.

The Daily Sketch

NEWS AND PICTURES

No. 11,019 ★★   FRIDAY, SEPTEMBER 8, 1944   ONE PENNY

General Patton Crushes German Bid To Stem Advance

U.S. TANKS OVER MOSELLE

British Are Only 70 Miles From Cologne

IMPORTANT new gains by the Allied armies in the great two-way advance on Germany were reported in the battlefront messages early to-day.

1. General Patton, meeting his first real opposition since he smashed across from Normandy, last night stormed over the Moselle at two points in the Toul area.

2. Swinging north-east across Belgium, General Dempsey's British Second Army have reached the Albert Canal on a 10-mile front and are piling up huge quantities of armour before moving forward.

The Allied line now runs on a great arc 225 miles long between Antwerp and Toul, the fortress town due west of Nancy.

We control five main crossings over the Meuse and hold 50 miles of the west bank of the Moselle, a tributary of the Rhine.

Eighteen miles north-east of Namur, an American column has captured Huy. The advance here is already driving on Liege.

Further south, Sedan has been liberated and Bievres, 18 miles to the south-east, occupied.

The two new bridgeheads across the 80ft.-wide Moselle were built up by U.S. Third Army infantry who crossed the river under the covering fire of tanks and artillery.

C.S.M. P. H. Wright, V.C., being congratulated by fellow members of the sergeants' mess at a southern England camp where a "Daily Sketch" photographer found a celebration party in full swing. It was nearly eight o'clock last night when his commanding officer gave him the news.

ALL-OUT BALKAN DRIVE

WITH the Russians sweeping across the Balkans—Berlin reported them last night as having reached Greece—Allied land, sea and air forces have begun a combined all-out assault against the German lines of communication in Yugoslavia.

The offensive is designed to smash the German escape routes in the Balkans, it was stated at Allied Mediterranean H.Q.

British warships in the Adriatic, Marshal Tito's armies, the Balkan Air Force, and the 15th U.S. Air Force are taking part.

Allied H.Q. added that the battle began a week ago, with "Land Forces Adriatic"—the official title of the Allied units in Yugoslavia — and Slovene patriots participating.

The Allied land forces are Commandos who have been staging raids lasting between one and four days, says B.U.P.

'Russians In Greece'

German sources said that the Russians, advancing 160 miles in two days through Bulgaria, reached the Turkish border and entered the Demotica area of Greek Thrace.

In London and Moscow it is believed that only a strong junction of Tito's men with Malinovsky's troops is required to spring the trap on these divisions.

Malinovsky has crossed the Danube with his main forces at Ruschuk and is driving along the good highway to Sofia, while Tolbukhin's men are in Bulgaria on the eastern flank and are driving towards Salonika.

The Battle For Prussia

In the mighty battle raging north-east of Warsaw Russian forces are trying, for the fifth day, to dig a decisive hole in German defences guarding East Prussia.

Col. von Olberg, Berlin war commentator, last night admitted that the Germans had withdrawn a mile or more—the first time since the offensive started that the Germans have admitted retreat.

"It was to avoid the danger of a Russian breakthrough on the southern border of East Prussia," he said.

The Russian communiqué last night referred only briefly to this fighting. It said: "To-day, south-west of Lomza, our troops fought their way into several inhabited localities."

Nazi Counter-attack

First big counter-attack by the Germans was launched against the Americans in this sector.

They succeeded in throwing back across the river some troops in the Pont-à-Mousson area, half-way between Metz and Nancy.

The establishment of the new bridgehead is regarded as of the highest importance. It means that the outer defence of Germany is pierced. It was achieved in the teeth of bitter German resistance by near perfect ground and air co-operation between the army and the 19th Tactical Air Command.

General Dempsey is moving his tanks and guns on to the south side of the Albert Canal, said a cable from Doon Campbell, Reuter's correspondent.

Here, again, there was fierce resistance and shell fire. The *Turn To Back Page, Col. 1.*

They Beat The Fly-Bombs

LEFT: Prof. Sir Thomas Merton, named yesterday as the inventor of a 1s. range-finder which enabled night-fighter pilots to destroy many flying bombs.

"The idea for this little gadget came to me suddenly," said Sir Thomas yesterday, "and within a matter of hours I had made one up from odd scraps of material."

RIGHT: Squadron-Leader Joseph Berry, D.F.C. (won over Italy) and Bar, named as the R.A.F. Tempest pilot who has destroyed more than 60 flying bombs—all but three at night.

Berry is 24, married, and his home is at Sunnydale-road, Nottingham. He was an income-tax collector till he joined the R.A.F.

Full Story and Pictures—Pages 3, 4 and 5
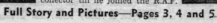

'Truly Great Victory—By Montgomery'

—U.S. TRIBUTE

A SPOKESMAN of the U.S. Third Army said in France yesterday that Field-Marshal Montgomery's victory was a truly great one which entirely upset the German plans for withdrawal and perhaps the course of the war.

"The two greatest events of the war to date," he went on, "were Gen. Omar Bradley's strike south of St. Lo and Montgomery's advance through Belgium, which was magnificent."

Montgomery drove into Brussels yesterday morning in pouring rain. The crowds in the cafés and restaurants did not recognise the grey-green touring car until it stopped in front of the town hall.

The Field-Marshal got a terrific reception, and people rushed up, cheering and shouting.

Later the Field-Marshal talked with Prince Bernhard of the Netherlands and the Commander of the armoured and infantry forces at the Albert Canal.

The King Decided D.C.M. Deserved The V.C.

'Daily Sketch' Correspondent

BEHIND the announcement this morning of the award of the V.C. to C.S.M. Peter Harold Wright, of the Coldstream Guards, lies a story of the personal intervention of the King, who, on his visit to the Italian battlefield, said to Gen. Alexander:

"If ever a man deserved the V.C. it is this man to whom I have awarded the D.C.M."

The King asked General Alexander to check all the facts of the story of the Sergeant-Major's gallantry and to report to him personally.

New Investiture

General Alexander did so. The sequel appeared in last night's *London Gazette* which stated briefly that the D.C.M. awarded to C.S.M. Wright and announced in the *Gazette* on January 27 had been cancelled.

Heading a special supplement to the *Gazette* was the announcement that the King had awarded the sergeant-major the Victoria Cross and giving the full story of the gallantry that had won the admiration of the King and led to his personal intervention.

Sergeant-Major Wright, whose home is Old Hall, Wenhaston, Suffolk, will return his Distinguished Conduct Medal and again attend an investiture to receive the V.C. from the King.

The King's personal intervention was thoroughly in accordance with military procedure, which covers such an eventuality.

When the King heard the full story of C.S.M. Wright's gallantry at Salerno he followed the full constitutional procedure which requires that the commander in the field shall be consulted.

The King visited his troops in Italy at the end of July and there, during his meeting with General Alexander, he had the opportunity of discussing the award, which he had waited for since he heard the full story.

General Alexander ordered a full investigation in the field. The reports from eye-witnesses he forwarded to Sir James Grigg, Secretary for War, who then made the recommendation to the King that the D.C.M. should be cancelled and the Victoria Cross awarded.

Immediate Award

It was pointed out in London last night that C.S.M. Wright was given the immediate award of the D.C.M., the highest award that a G.O.C. in the field could bestow on him on his own initiative.

It was in Italy, at Salerno, last September, that C.S.M. Wright, seeing his company held up, went forward and found there were no officers left.

He immediately took charge, crawled forward to see what the opposition was and returned with the information that three Spandau posts were holding them up.

Single-handed he attacked each post in turn with hand grenades and *Turn to Back Page, Col. 4.*

TIMELY WORDS OF FAITH

They had devised devices . . . saying, Let us destroy . . . Therefore thus saith the Lord of hosts, Behold, I will punish them.

Jeremiah 11, 19-22.

▲THE DAILY SKETCH, FRIDAY SEPTEMBER 8, 1944

American general George S. Patton was tailor-made to be a media star. Never mind that his army didn't have enough fuel to get into Germany, he was a winner, and the press and the public loved him. At the foot of the page, an altogether more modest hero is celebrated. Stories such as that of Thomas Merton, inventor of a diffraction rangefinder, began to emerge more toward the end of the war. Along the same lines, the words of faith have turned to the subject of vengeance.

Patton's tigers

SEPTEMBER 1944

IN AUGUST AND SEPTEMBER 1944, THE ALLIED SUPREME COMMANDER IN EUROPE, DWIGHT D. EISENHOWER, FACED A TRICKY DILEMMA. HE COULD SEE GREAT OPPORTUNITIES AS THE GERMAN ARMIES FELL BACK, BUT THE FUEL to keep his tanks running was in short supply, and, the further his forces advanced, the more severe the logistics problem became. Two of his subordinates, General George S. Patton of the U.S. Third Army and General Bernard Montgomery of the British 21st Army Group, each wanted to be given priority.

MONTY WINS

Eisenhower eventually decided that Montgomery should get the lion's share of resources, because his line of advance would open up Channel ports that would solve the logistics problem. Patton was a master of mobile warfare and although he was only given permission to conduct a "reconnaissance in force" across the Moselle River, he inflicted severe losses on the German forces he met, in a series of big tank battles. He

▲ GENERAL GEORGE S. PATTON, the charismatic commander of the U.S. Third Army, who wanted to strike at the Nazi heartland in September 1944.

believed he could have broken into Germany itself had he been given the support he had wanted from Eisenhower.

A BRIDGE TOO FAR

Meanwhile, Montgomery pressed on into Holland. He conceived an ambitious plan to drop airborne forces to secure bridges and then to drive north with armored units to link up with the paratroops. Unfortunately, the northernmost airborne landing at Arnhem was a total disaster. Two German panzer divisions were refitting near the town and when they swung into action, the paratroopers were unable to take and hold the bridge. For their part, Allied armored ground forces were unable to reach Arnhem. On exposed roads in flat countryside they were easy targets for antitank guns.

This setback meant that the Western Allies would have to pause before invading Germany. In the East, the Soviet Red Army entered Germany in September, with an advance into East Prussia from Lithuania and Poland. It also entered Hungary.

▼ PARATROOPERS of the British 1st Airborne Division in action at Arnhem, Holland. Operation Market Garden was supposed to end the war before the end of 1944. In reality, it failed and cost 8,000 Allied dead and captured.

▲ THE DAILY TELEGRAPH, LONDON, THURSDAY SEPTEMBER 28, 1944

Amid the growing prospect of Allied victory, the failure at Arnhem gave the British public pause for thought, although the bravery of the British airborne troops is celebrated as "one of the most glorious operations in history." Despite the setback, signs of victory are here in news that the Home Guard is preparing to disband and an advertisement urging savers not to take the war as won.

▲ THE DAILY TELEGRAPH, LONDON, TUESDAY OCTOBER 24, 1944

The *Telegraph* reports the flow of German refugees from East Prussia, but makes no mention of the rumored atrocities that accompanied the advance of the Red Army. In France, the first trials of collaborators in the Épuration légale, or "legal purge," reach the courts, with a death sentence for newspaper editor Georges Suarez.

The New York Times front page, October 26, 1944:

"All the News That's Fit to Print"

The New York Times.

LATE CITY EDITION
Sunny, cool and windy; fair and becoming cooler tonight.

VOL. XCIV..No. 31,687.

NEW YORK, THURSDAY, OCTOBER 26, 1944.

THREE CENTS NEW YORK CITY

U. S. DEFEATS JAPANESE NAVY; ALL FOE'S SHIPS IN ONE FLEET HIT; MANY SUNK; BATTLE CONTINUES

SPECIAL PRIVILEGE SOLD BY NEW DEAL, DEWEY CHARGES

Says Roosevelt Backs Plan for 1,000 to Put '$1,000 on the Line' to Aid Campaign

PARTY LETTER IS QUOTED

Governor Declares in Chicago Administration Lacks 'Honesty' to Solve Post-War Problems

By ALEXANDER FEINBERG

No Extra Gasoline For Trip to Polls

By The Associated Press

PRESIDENT ELATED

Gives News From Halsey That Foe Is 'Defeated, Damaged, Routed'

TEST IS ON, KING SAYS

Practically All Japanese Fleet in the Battle, Admiral Believes

By LEWIS WOOD

SEA POWER OF LAND OF THE RISING SUN SHATTERED IN BATTLE

BATTLESHIP IS SUNK

Seventh Fleet Smashes Two Japanese Forces Converging on Leyte

REMNANTS IN FLIGHT

They Are Hotly Pursued —Third Enemy Force Is Hit Off Formosa

WAGNER ACCLAIMS PARTY FARM POLICY

He Says That Dewey Is Vague on Agriculture—Calls His Platform 'Double Talk'

By CLAYTON P. KNOWLES

ALLIES CUT UP FOE IN WEST HOLLAND

British Hammer Germans in One Area of 's Hertogenbosch —Canadians Tighten Traps

By CLIFTON DANIEL

'17 Hours of Hell' Raised In Sea Battle Off Leyte

By RALPH TEATSORTH
United Press Correspondent

AMERICANS MAKE BIG LEYTE JUMPS

Troops Push Westward on Isle —Southern Coast of Samar to the North Now Held

AIR PLANT IN JAPAN SMASHED BY B-29'S

Omura Target Is 'Perfectly Patterned,' Pilots Say—Foe Lists 100 Planes in Attack

U. S. and Britain Recognize Italy; Action Is First With an Ex-Enemy

By BERTRAM D. HULEN

War News Summarized

THURSDAY, OCTOBER 26, 1944

Russians Invade North Norway; Take Kirkenes in Wide Advance

By W. H. LAWRENCE

▲ THE NEW YORK TIMES, THURSDAY OCTOBER 26, 1944

There is no mistaking the significance of the massive U.S. naval victory at Leyte Gulf, which left 10,000 Japanese sailors dead, 500 aircraft destroyed, and the Imperial Japanese Navy emasculated, particularly when accompanied by news of B-29 raids on Japan's Home Islands targets. Presidential hopeful Thomas Dewey has turned his criticism of Roosevelt to FDR's ability to handle the postwar country.

Leyte Gulf
OCTOBER 23–26, 1944

FOLLOWING THE U.S. LANDINGS ON LEYTE, THE JAPANESE PUT IN MOTION THEIR SHO PLAN, IN WHICH A PART OF THE COMBINED FLEET WAS USED TO DECOY THE U.S. CARRIER FORCE, WHILE the remainder concentrated against the American's landing area and attempted to destroy the amphibious armada. The resulting naval Battle of Leyte Gulf had four phases.

FOUR DEFEATS

At the Battle of the Sibuyan Sea (October 24) U.S. aircraft launched massive attacks on the ships of the Southern Force and Center Force. They immediately hit Japanese battleships *Yamato*, and *Musashi*, and also their heavy cruiser *Myoko*. *Myoko* was forced to head back to Brunei, and the *Musashi* was eventually sunk. The Center Force was forced to retreat west. During the Battle of Surigao Strait (October 24–25), Japan's Southern Force was engaged by ships of the U.S. Seventh Fleet. Two Japanese battleships, one cruiser, and three destroyers were sunk by American naval gunfire.

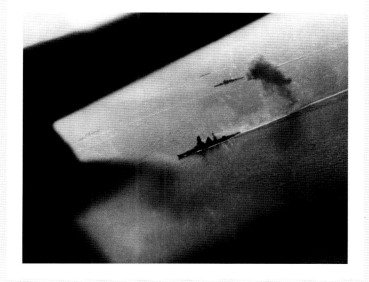

▲ THE JAPANESE BATTLESHIP *Nagato* (foreground) and a cruiser under air attack at Leyte Gulf. *Nagato* survived the battle, unlike 35 other Japanese ships.

The Japanese Second Striking Force, following on behind, retreated west. Further defeat followed at the Battle off Cape Engaño (October 25–26), when aircraft of the U.S. Third Fleet engaged the aircraft carriers of the Northern Force. The Japanese lost all four carriers, one cruiser, two of nine destroyers, and all 130 aircraft. Finally, at the Battle off Samar (October 25), the Japanese Center Force fought the ships of the Seventh Fleet and sank four U.S. ships. However, the Japanese lost three ships, broke off the battle, and headed north. The Battle of Leyte Gulf was over. The Americans had eliminated the threat of Japanese warships to amphibious operations in the Philippines.

IMPERIAL SUNSET

The result was that the Japanese Combined Fleet was finished as a fighting force, not least because its heavy losses in trained pilots were irreplaceable. Further, the Battle of Leyte Gulf marked the undeniable collapse of Japanese naval power in the Pacific. From then onward, suicide air strikes that had their inauguration at Leyte Gulf became an increasing tactic by a desperate Japanese military, that, in reality, was a broken force no longer able to oppose the mighty U.S. Navy.

SUNDAY EXPRESS

NOVEMBER 5 1944   BLACK-OUT (London) 5.57 p.m. to 7.31 a.m.   Founded by LORD BEAVERBROOK   Moon ◑ Rises 9.31 a.m., Sets 2.49 p.m. (Mon.).   TWOPENCE

BUDAPEST—THE LAST HOURS

Soviet hurls 90,000 tank-men into the battle, guns shell heart of capital

Troops and refugees panic inside city

BUDAPEST IS AS GOOD AS LOST TO THE GERMANS. "NOTHING CAN SAVE THE CITY," SAID MOSCOW RADIO LAST NIGHT, AS WITH SOVIET TANKS ALREADY FIGHTING IN THE OUTSKIRTS OF THE HUNGARIAN CAPITAL, ALL RUSSIA HOURLY AWAITED OFFICIAL NEWS OF ITS FALL.

Latest news of the position inside Budapest came from New York radio, which said a Russian column had reached the suburbs and that the defenders had been driven behind the city's inner defence line.

Budapest radio said last night that bombs were then being dropped on the city.

Messages reaching Stockholm reported that civil war is in full swing in some parts of the besieged city with armed patriots locked in battle with German and Hungarian stormtroops. In other areas the Nazis have already begun looting.

Although Berlin yesterday announced that the German High Command had decided to impose a security black-out on news of operations in the Budapest area, a German front-line correspondent was allowed to broadcast this message :—

"Salvos from the Red Army guns are bursting in the heart of Budapest as Soviet aircraft drone over the capital. A cavalcade of refugees in long columns of carts and cars is passing through the streets. Lorries of all kinds are ceaselessly rolling over the Danube bridges."

Szolnok is captured

And Colonel Ernst von Hammer, German High Command spokesman, admitted that the Red Army had made deep penetrations on the Budapest right flank where "a critical situation arose."

DR. MAX KEULL GERMAN NEWS AGENCY WAR CORRESPONDENT, ALSO HAD SOMETHING TO SAY : THE SOVIET HIGH COMMAND HE WROTE LAST NIGHT HAS THROWN NEARLY 90,000 TANK TROOPS INTO THE BATTLE FOR BUDAPEST, WHICH HAS NOW REACHED "A DRAMATIC CLIMAX." HE ADMITTED THAT THE FIRST PART OF THE SOVIET OPERATION PLAN HAD UNSUCCESSFULLY SUCCEEDED.

Despatches from the front to Moscow reported wild disorder in the Hungarian capital as panic-stricken German and Hungarian divisions fled into its even more panic-stricken streets.

Capture of Szolnok, Hungarian strongpoint on the Tisza river south-east of Budapest, was announced in an Order of the Day from Marshal Stalin last night.

And last night's Soviet communiqué reported that Red Army troops had also fought their way into Cegled and Abony, as well as more than 40 other places between the Rivers Danube and Tisza.

While the collapse of German resistance in Central Hungary drew near, Moscow yesterday heard that the big battles of East Prussia, which quietened down last week-end after the Germans had sacrificed thousands of lives in another "prestige" stand, were flaring up again.

Colonel Karpov, Stalin's star military analyst revealed in a broadcast that German counter-attacks in this area have been going on for several days north and south of Goldap.

The defenders, he said, concentrated large infantry and tank forces in a narrow stretch of terrain only a mile or two wide.

"Tense battles have been going on from the start he added "Many of the German forces have been made up from recently formed reserve detachments."

Nazis out of Greece, quitting Albania

A SPECIAL announcement issued at Allied H.Q. Mediterranean last night said patrols had reported that, apart from small individual parties, no German troops remained on the mainland of Greece.

The announcement added that British troops had landed in the vicinity of Salonika preparatory to entering the town.

The Greek campaign has lasted 34 days—one of the shortest in the war.

Retreating north from Salonika up the Vardar Valley towards Skopje the Germans have blown up road and rail bridges to delay the British patrols pursuing them over the Yugoslav border.

Some Germans are trying to escape through Albania where R.A.F. 'planes have seen small columns in the vicinity of Lake Prespansko at the junction of the Greek-Serbian-Albanian border.

March on Valona

A war reporter at German H.Q. in S.E Europe said yesterday that Communist elements had been penetrated into Tirana capital of Albania and that partisan pressure was growing throughout the country.

Partisan detachments in the van of a British battle group are marching on Valona, which has been evacuated by the Germans, it is added

Skopinka is almost entirely in the hands of the extreme left wing Elas who are well disciplined and armed, reported an A.P. cable from Athens

They are quitting the port in order under the direction of a party of British experts.

AMERICAN STATUES DEFACED
At Albert Memorial

TWO 8ft. marble figures representing America at the Albert Memorial were found early today smeared with red paint.

A large polished marble block underneath bore the word "Hideous" in red paint. The figures are inside a 6ft. iron railing.

One statue, which is of a woman holding a wreath of laurels and a nation, was completely smeared.

Soldiers who tried to take a photograph of the cleaners removing the stains were forbidden by the police.

Mussolini's broadcaster

Home police have rounded up Mario Appelius, Mussolini's broadcaster during the war. He had been hiding in a Rome nursing home under a false name.—Reuter

---

The great mystery may be solved on Wednesday

IS HITLER ALIVE?

THE question as Germany is asking—Is Hitler still alive?—may be answered on Wednesday, the anniversary of the 1923 Munich beer cellar putsch Hitler has never yet failed to speak to the old gang of the Nazi Party on November 8

Hitler's voice has not been heard since the night after the generals bomb plot, when he went to the microphone to prove he was alive and to countermand all orders of the rebels. Since then all major German declarations have been made by Himmler and Goebbels, now undisputed bosses in the Reich.

On Tuesday anniversary of the 1917 Soviet revolution Stalin is expected to speak as usual Last year the liberation of Kiev capital of the Ukraine, was announced This year is is likely Stalin will be able to announce that the German invader has been cleared from the last inch of Soviet soil

Record set up

During the operations yesterday was set up a record for this type of operation, with 1,500 flying hours. Strong U-boat forces made determined attempts to interfere with the convoy. They were prevented and no concentrated attack developed. The only loss was the sloop Kite

All the battles were fought inside the Arctic Circle.

Vice-Admiral F. H. G. Dalrymple-Hamilton flying his flag in the escort carrier. Vindex (Captain

'Human torpedo' factory bombed

Twenty RAF Typhoons yesterday attacked a "one-man human torpedo" factory at Utrecht. The raid was carried out in the afternoon, when it was known that the "fish workers would be off." Twelve direct hits were scored

Munich bombed

Italy-based heavies bombed targets at Regensburg, Munich and Linz yesterday Bochum bombed last night.—See Back Page

---

Navy planes got every ship through
3 U boats sunk in Arctic battles

NAVAL aircraft have scored their biggest triumph of the war in shepherding a large and important convoy to Russia and back without any of the merchant ships sustaining either loss or damage.

Of the three U boats sunk, one was destroyed entirely by Navy planes, and they played a major part in the destruction of the other two.

These planes, from the escort carriers Vindex and Striker, also shot down an enemy shadower and probably damaged several other U boats.

First port of call—Flushing . . .

BRITISH troops, mopping-up, keep a sharp look-out for snipers as they clatter through a street in Flushing—one of the two key points in the first phases of the Walcheren invasion. . . This street is dry. To capture the H.Q. of the city's German garrison, the Hotel Britannia, attackers had to wade waist high in water.

Allies storm to within three miles of Moerdijk bridge

ALLIED troops in Holland have stormed to within three miles of the German "escape hatch" towards Rotterdam—the Moerdijk bridge, longest on the Continent.

They have cut deep new wedges into the salient still held by the German rearguards below the Maas, says Associated Press correspondent Roger Greene.

The Germans are being hammered with anti-personnel bombs on the muddy beaches. They have no cover except dykes and slit trenches, says Reuter's correspondent Harold Mayne.

By the time a few attacks has been made they were in such a state of panic that they were running from one dyke to another in a hopeless attempt to escape.

Two more bridges

VINDEX

Dropped marker

Escorts including the destroyer Keppel, the frigate Loch Dunvegan and the sloops Peacock and Mermaid carried out depth charge attacks. Oil and much other evidence of destruction was later seen on the surface of the sea. It is considered that this U boat was sunk.

A third U boat was sunk by the concerted action of naval aircraft and H.M. ships.

A Swordfish sighted the enemy as it was submerging and attacked with rockets. The aircraft then dropped a marker on the position The Keppel by Rugge; the Peacock by Tadcaster; the Whitehall by Cheltenham; and the Kite by Braintree and Bocking

SCHMIDT HELD FOR 18 HOURS
Sunday Express Correspondent GORDON-YOUNG WITH THE FIRST ARMY, Saturday

THERE is a bitter contest going on for the little hilltop hamlet of Schmidt, 16 miles south of Aix-la-Chapelle (Aachen).

The Germans appear to have rushed better quality troops and a number of tanks to the area of the First Army's advance in an attempt to repair foot ground.

Tonight Schmidt is little more than a smoking ruin with mortars and small arms still blazing on the hillsides around it.

The first German counter-attacks came just after night o'clock this morning when the Americans had held the hamlet for about 18 hours.

This attack was repulsed but the Germans tried again half an hour later, throwing in infantry and tanks, and this drive forced the Americans back about one mile from the village.

Three assaults

There is bitter fighting still going on tonight as a result of the third wave of assault from the Germans, which ocean at four o'clock this afternoon, but the Americans are fighting stubbornly.

They want Schmidt, which stands at a useful cross-roads position, and they mean to have it.

American Army Air Force planes were able to help the infantry during a patch of clear weather this morning by bombing Schmidt and strafing the German troops trying a renewed attack.

The sloop Mermaid is steaming as it was submerging and attacked with rockets. Shortly afterwards a long oil-slick and much wreckage appeared The sloop Mermaid added her gunfire to break up and repulsed over counter-attack.

"Big air landings coming"

The German High Command reports airborne and landing sea landings to supplement the three-pronged all-out land offensive which they forecast General Eisenhower will launch shortly.

This statement was made last night by Ludwig Sertorius, German Overseas News Agency military correspondent and recognised spokesman of the German High Command.

Mr. Eden back

RADIO—PAGE 7

Sir J. Dill dies in Washington

FIELD - MARSHAL SIR JOHN DILL, head of the British Military Mission in Washington and former Chief of the Imperial General Staff, died last night in a military hospital in Washington.

Sir John had been ill for several months with anaemia. He was nearly 63.

The British Information Service in Washington last night issued a statement saying

The British Joint Staff Mission deeply regret to announce that Field-Marshal Sir John Dill, head of the British Joint Staff Mission in Washington and the senior member of the Combined Chiefs of Staff Committee in Washington, died yesterday.

The statement added : For some months the field-marshal had been suffering a refractory type of anaemia, for which no special treatment is yet known (a medical source).

Mr Roosevelt at Boston, Massachusetts, last night, said—"Never believe in my lifetime has a campaign been filled with so much misrepresentation, distortion and falsehood."

Referring to the war he said "Although victory over the Nazis and the Japanese a certain and inevitable, the war is still far from over. It is tough and hard and bloody fighting ahead of us."

(Labour favours Roosevelt.—Page 5)

DEWEY ACCUSES F.D.R.
Prolonging war

MR DEWEY, making his final main campaign speech last night, said the American people should be told what had happened since September to upset General Eisenhower's forecast that Germany would be defeated in 1944

He bitterly attacked the reported plan of Mr. Morgenthau, the U S Secretary of the Treasury, to reduce Germany to a nation of farmers, and declared that it had given Germany fresh heart

"It stiffened the will of the German nation to resist. Almost overnight the German retreat of the Germans stopped. They stood and fought frantically," Dewey said.

"In spite of repeated blood transfusions in the long run the strain

went on the docks industry can never again be allowed to return to the casual condition.

We are asking the industry to co-operate but if the news on a permanent scheme to take the place of, the war scheme

"A permanent scheme there must be and if the industry cannot provide us with one the Minister of Labour must provide one," he added.

"We are anxious to try at the earliest moment—in honour of the sacrifices you have made—to rehabilitate your social and domestic life."

'GAP' IN SWITCH OF MAN-POWER—BEVIN

THE assurance that, as war industries are cut down, there was going to be a build-up of civil industries was given by Mr Ernest Bevin, Minister of Labour and National Service, at Bootle last night.

But, said Mr. Bevin, there was going to be some gap in the transference.

He disclosed that 7,250,000 women had been called up for national service Of the single women between the ages of 18 and 41, 95 per cent, were working in either the Services or on national service of some kind.

Have patience

"It is had not seen for this marvellous army who have played so magnificent a part we could not have built up the great forces which are bringing victory to us," he said

Problems after the war would be very difficult and trying and we must have a little tolerance and patience.

Mr. Bevin gave this warning. "When you have to deal with a difficult job you pay a bit of people wanting to exploit it for their own purposes." he said

If you people along to you in some political parties and ask you to join in demonstrations, don't do it. Go to your trade-union branch and your troubles will be dealt with properly."

During the war we introduced the decasualisation scheme, he

Coast town shaken

Violent explosions were felt at Deal last night from across the water. Windows and doors rattled on the coast and well inland into Kent Some explosions seemed to come from Dunkirk and to last several seconds Others, less violent came from a more northerly direction. —(Our contributor, 37 miles due east of Deal.)

Smuts will be there

General Smuts would attend the Peace Conference, says Senator Conroy, South African Minister of Lands.—Reuter.

WALCHEREN (map)

War latest

MacARTHUR'S NEW ATTACK

General MacArthur's communique from Leyte, Philippines, says the 24th Division has begun a land and over-water assault on Pinamopoan, seven miles west of Carigara and the north end of the narrow Ormoc Corridor.—Reuter.

BOMBERS HIT JAP BASES

A communique from Admiral Chester Nimitz, C-in-C., Pacific, says that American planes have struck again at Japanese shipping and air bases in the Palau, Marshall, Marianas, Yap and Makru Islands.—Reuter.

Belisha's future
To support Premier
By MAURICE WEBB

MR. HORE - BELISHA made statements yesterday which confirm the forecast that he will join the Conservative Party before the next general election.

Questioned about his future by constituents at Devonport yesterday, he said he wanted to see a strong Britain with a two-party system, and if Mr. Churchill made an appeal on national grounds he would support him.

He said he did not want to see a Socialist Government, and thought the Liberals had lost their place in the game through internal quarrels.

No small parties

Unless the Liberal Party had a clear policy to put before the electorate he did not see much use in keeping alive something ineffective.

Mr. Hore-Belisha added that he thought numerous small parties were ineffective.

These statements in his constituency by the ex-War Minister will be regarded in political quarters as an indication of his intention to apply for membership of the Conservative Party.

It can be stated that he is unlikely to take this course until the election is more imminent, but it may be confidently assumed that he will contest Devonport next time as a Conservative.

LONDON'S ALERT AFTER A LULL

A brief alert was sounded in London last night, the first since early last Tuesday, the last evening alert was on October 31.

When fly bomb attacks were resumed over the East Coast people stood in the streets and cheered as gunners shot several into the sea.

One bomb which got through was held by searchlights until a fighter shot it down.

A flying bomb fell in open ground in Southern England Blast damaged several small houses and three people were cut by glass.

Gestapo killed

One hundred an ten Gestapo agents were killed and 40 wounded in the R.A.F. attack on their Jutland headquarters in Aarhus University, Danish Press Service said yesterday.

Franco asks for seat at Peace Table

GENERAL FRANCO, in an interview in Madrid yesterday, spoke of the part he wanted Spain to play in the establishment of peace.

He said : "All logic and welfare of humanity demands that those nations which have shown the desire for peace by remaining at peace must take part in the peace treaty.

"Neutral countries must be heard and listened to in the efforts to organise the future of the world."—B.U.P.

There's nothing like a Guinness after a hard day's work

GUINNESS IS GOOD FOR YOU

NOV. 11th—1918-1944
Please give generously this year

G.E. 1177. D

▲ SUNDAY EXPRESS, LONDON, NOVEMBER 5, 1944

As the Germans pull back in Greece and Albania, and face British advances in Holland and a Soviet onslaught in Budapest, the *Express* repeats the kind of rumor that suggests the full collapse of Germany: Is Hitler even still alive? Meanwhile, Thomas Dewey, probably resigned to losing the following month's presidential election, now accuses FDR of prolonging the war unnecessarily.

Fall of Budapest

NOVEMBER 1944–FEBRUARY 1945

HITLER DECLARED THAT BUDAPEST WOULD BE A "NATIONAL REDOUBT," AND THE HUNGARIAN CAPITAL CITY COULD BOAST AN IMPRESSIVE GARRISON OF SOME 180,000 TROOPS, including two SS divisions. However, Budapest suffered the fate of other cities that had come to be the focus of military activity in the final campaigns of World War II. Cassino, in Italy, and Caen, in France, were flattened by Allied air and artillery attack; similarly, Budapest was flattened by Soviet artillery. Rather than incur heavy infantry casualties in hand-to-hand fighting, the Red Army used massed artillery barrages.

BUDAPEST SURRENDERS
The Germans tried to relieve their forces in Budapest, but the relief forces ground to a halt some 20 miles (32 km) short of the city in January 1945. On February 13, the garrison surrendered; 50,000 of them had died in the fighting in the ruins of the city. The postwar

▲ A RED ARMY MORTAR TEAM in action in the suburbs of Budapest, Hungary, at the end of 1944.

shape of central and eastern Europe was beginning to emerge, especially indicated by the growing importance of communism, backed up by the presence of the Soviet Red Army. In Yugoslavia, Tito's communist partisans were taking over, while Soviet-dominated governments were being established in other states throughout the region. In Greece, communist guerrillas were fighting British Army units that had moved into the country as the Germans had moved out.

NEW WEAPONS
The only hope for German survival now was for a new range of powerful weapons to be deployed in an effort to turn the tide of the war. Most important was the V2 rocket, of which more than 1,000 were launched against Britain, but they had no significant effect. Allied air power was now overwhelming, and late in the year the RAF sank the last German capital ship, the battleship *Tirpitz*.

▲ DAILY MAIL, LONDON, SATURDAY NOVEMBER 11, 1944

The first V2 rocket killed three people on September 8, 1944, in west London. The blast was attributed to a gas explosion. The government's news blackout lasted for two months before the *Mail* introduced its readers to the full story, complete with diagrams and eyewitness reports. Meanwhile, the latest story about Adolf Hitler hints that the German dictator is losing his sanity.

▼ V2 WAS AN ABBREVIATION of *Vergeltungswaffe* 2 (retaliation weapon 2). The military and psychological impact of this *Wunderwaffe* (wonder weapon) was minor and did not fulfill any of the hopes of the Nazi regime. A total of 1,269 rockets were launched at Britain, with 1,225 V2s hitting London.

▲ DAILY EXPRESS, LONDON, TUESDAY NOVEMBER 14, 1944

Although the German battleship *Tirpitz* had spent the war largely confined to Norwegian waters and could no longer influence the course of the conflict, the loss of an enemy warship still had a huge symbolic importance for the British, particularly when illustrated with a dramatic sequence of images. More rumors abound about the Nazi leadership, particularly concerning Hitler's health and Goering's whereabouts.

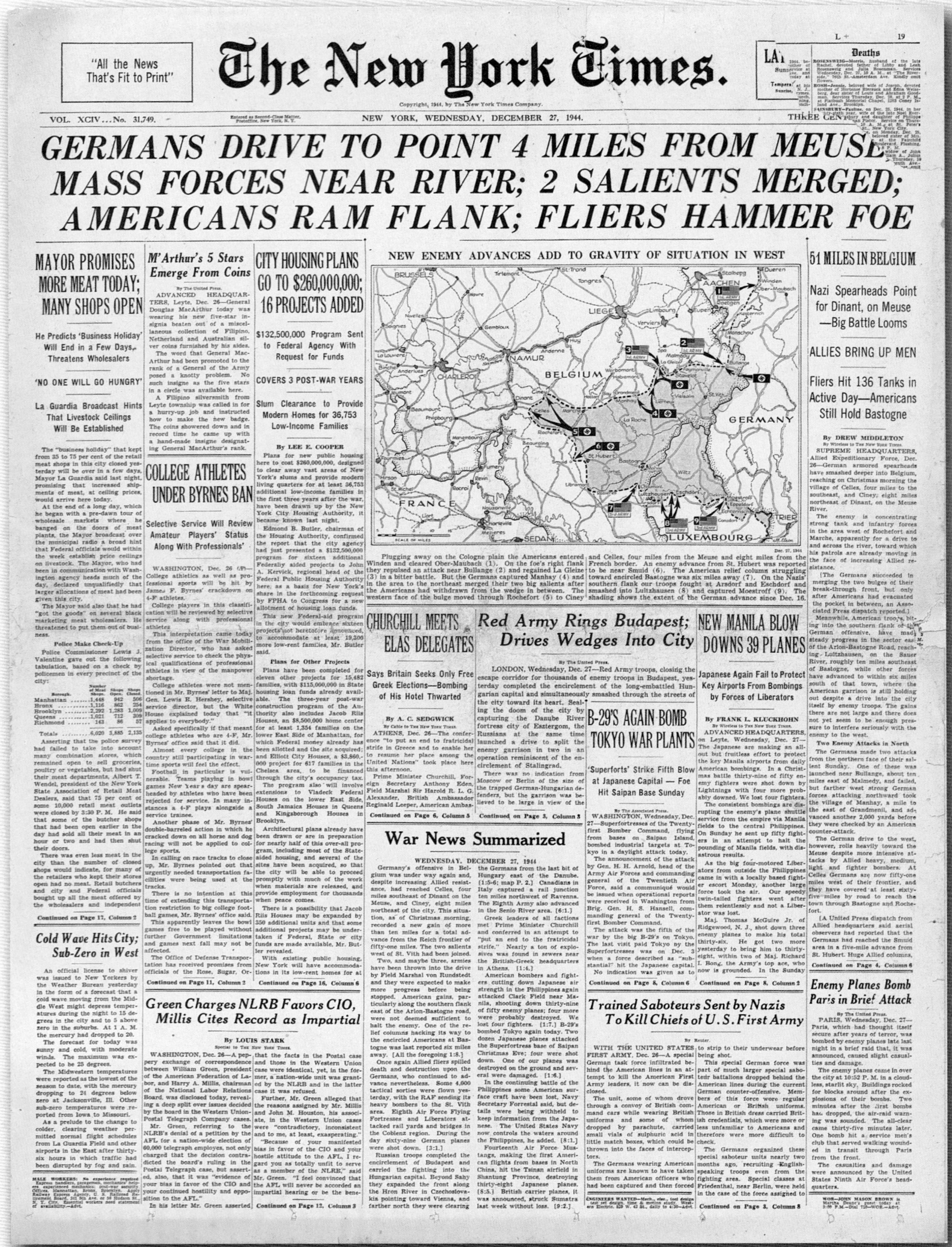

"All the News That's Fit to Print"

The New York Times.

VOL. XCIV...No. 31,749. NEW YORK, WEDNESDAY, DECEMBER 27, 1944. THREE CENTS

GERMANS DRIVE TO POINT 4 MILES FROM MEUSE; MASS FORCES NEAR RIVER; 2 SALIENTS MERGED; AMERICANS RAM FLANK; FLIERS HAMMER FOE

MAYOR PROMISES MORE MEAT TODAY; MANY SHOPS OPEN

He Predicts 'Business Holiday' Will End in a Few Days, Threatens Wholesalers

'NO ONE WILL GO HUNGRY'

La Guardia Broadcast Hints That Livestock Ceilings Will Be Established

The "business holiday" that kept from 35 to 75 per cent of the retail meat shops in this city closed yesterday will be over in a few days, Mayor La Guardia said last night, promising that increased shipments of meat, at ceiling prices, would arrive here today.

M'Arthur's 5 Stars Emerge From Coins

By The United Press.

ADVANCED HEADQUARTERS, Leyte, Dec. 26—General Douglas MacArthur today was wearing his new five-star insignia beaten out of a miscellaneous collection of Filipino, Netherland and Australian silver coins furnished by his aides.

The word that General MacArthur had been promoted to the rank of a General of the Army posed a knotty problem. No such insigne as the five stars in a circle was available here.

A Filipino silversmith from Leyte township was called in for a hurry-up job and instructed how to make the new badge. The coins showered down and in record time he came up with a hand-made insigne designating General MacArthur's rank.

CITY HOUSING PLANS GO TO $260,000,000; 16 PROJECTS ADDED

$132,500,000 Program Sent to Federal Agency With Request for Funds

COVERS 3 POST-WAR YEARS

Slum Clearance to Provide Modern Homes for 36,753 Low-Income Families

By LEE E. COOPER

Plans for new public housing here to cost $260,000,000, designed to clear away vast areas of New York's slums and provide modern living quarters for at least 36,753 additional low-income families in the first three years after the war, have been drawn up by the New York City Housing Authority, it became known last night.

COLLEGE ATHLETES UNDER BYRNES BAN

Selective Service Will Review Amateur Players' Status Along With Professionals'

NEW ENEMY ADVANCES ADD TO GRAVITY OF SITUATION IN WEST

Dec. 27, 1944

Plugging away on the Cologne plain the Americans entered Winden and cleared Ober-Maubach (1). On the foe's right flank they repulsed an attack near Bullange (2) and regained La Gleize (3) in a bitter battle. But the Germans captured Manhay (4) and in the area to the northeast merged their two big salients after the Americans had withdrawn from the wedge in between. The western face of the bulge moved through Rochefort (5) to Ciney and Celles, four miles from the Meuse and eight miles from the French border. An enemy advance from St. Hubert was reported to be near Smuid (6). The American relief column struggling toward encircled Bastogne was six miles away (7). On the Nazis' southern flank our troops fought at Arsdorf and Eschdorf and smashed into Lultzhausen (8) and captured Moestroff (9). The shading shows the extent of the German advance since Dec. 16.

51 MILES IN BELGIUM

Nazi Spearheads Point for Dinant, on Meuse—Big Battle Looms

ALLIES BRING UP MEN

Fliers Hit 136 Tanks in Active Day—Americans Still Hold Bastogne

By DREW MIDDLETON

By Wireless to The New York Times.

SUPREME HEADQUARTERS, Allied Expeditionary Force, Dec. 26—German armored spearheads have smashed deeper into Belgium, reaching on Christmas morning the village of Celles, four miles to the southeast, and Ciney, eight miles northeast of Dinant, on the Meuse River.

CHURCHILL MEETS ELAS DELEGATES

Says Britain Seeks Only Free Greek Elections—Bombing of His Hotel Thwarted

By A. C. SEDGWICK

By Cable to The New York Times.

ATHENS, Dec. 26—The conference "to put an end to fratricidal strife in Greece and to enable her to resume her place among the United Nations" took place here this afternoon.

Prime Minister Churchill, Foreign Secretary Anthony Eden, Field Marshal Sir Harold R. L. G. Alexander, British Ambassador Reginald Leeper, American Ambas-

Continued on Page 6, Column 5

Red Army Rings Budapest; Drives Wedges Into City

By The United Press.

LONDON, Wednesday, Dec. 27—Red Army troops, closing the escape corridor for thousands of enemy troops in Budapest, yesterday completed the encirclement of the long-embattled Hungarian capital and simultaneously smashed through the streets of the city toward its heart. Sealing the doom of the city by capturing the Danube River fortress city of Esztergom, the Russians at the same time launched a drive to split the enemy garrison in two in an operation reminiscent of the encirclement of Stalingrad.

There was no indication from Moscow or Berlin of the size of the trapped German-Hungarian defenders, but the garrison was believed to be large in view of the

Continued on Page 3, Column 3

B-29'S AGAIN BOMB TOKYO WAR PLANTS

'Superforts' Strike Fifth Blow at Japanese Capital — Foe Hit Saipan Base Sunday

By The Associated Press.

WASHINGTON, Wednesday, Dec. 27—Superfortresses of the Twenty-first Bomber Command, flying from bases on Saipan Island, bombed industrial targets at Tokyo in a daylight attack today.

NEW MANILA BLOW DOWNS 39 PLANES

Japanese Again Fail to Protect Key Airports From Bombings by Forces of Liberators

By FRANK L. KLUCKHOHN

By Wireless to The New York Times.

ADVANCED HEADQUARTERS, on Leyte, Wednesday, Dec. 27—The Japanese are making an all-out but fruitless effort to protect the key Manila airports from daily American bombings. In a Christmas battle thirty-nine of fifty enemy fighters were shot down by Lightnings with four more probably downed. We lost four fighters.

The consistent bombings are disrupting the enemy's plane shuttle service from the empire via Manila fields to the central Philippines. On Sunday he sent up fifty fighters in an attempt to halt the pounding of Manila fields, with disastrous results.

War News Summarized

WEDNESDAY, DECEMBER 27, 1944

Cold Wave Hits City; Sub-Zero in West

Green Charges NLRB Favors CIO, Millis Cites Record as Impartial

By LOUIS STARK

Trained Saboteurs Sent by Nazis To Kill Chiefs of U. S. First Army

Enemy Planes Bomb Paris in Brief Attack

▲ THE NEW YORK TIMES, WEDNESDAY DECEMBER 27, 1944

The initial success of the German Ardennes Offensive brings an unaccustomed note of panic to New Yorkers, alongside stories of a meat shortage, bitterly cold winter temperatures, and a clampdown on athletes' exemption from military service. There is better news from the Philippines and Japan, and also a promise of democracy for Greece from Winston Churchill, while New York plans a housing program to sweep away slums in the postwar period.

Battle of the Bulge

DECEMBER 1944

ADOLF HITLER LAUNCHED OPERATION WATCH ON THE RHINE, HIS ATTEMPT TO CAPTURE ANTWERP, THEREBY SPLITTING THE ALLIES IN TWO, ON DECEMBER 16, 1944. SURPRISE WAS total and there was dense cloud and fog, which negated Allied air superiority, but the Germans failed to take the towns of St. Vith and Bastogne immediately, which narrowed their attack front. By the 22nd, the Americans, having lost 8,000 of 22,000 men at St. Vith, pulled back from the town, but the men of the 28th Infantry, 10th, and 101st Airborne Divisions continued to hold out stubbornly in Bastogne against one infantry and two panzer divisions. On the same day the Germans mounted their last attempt to reach the Meuse.

ALLIED COUNTERATTACKS

On December 26, the U.S. First and Third Armies launched counterattacks against the north and south of the German "bulge" into the Ardennes. The U.S. Third Army's 4th Armored Division relieved Bastogne, as Hitler was informed by his generals that Antwerp could no longer be reached by his forces. The only hope of salvaging any sort of victory in the Ardennes was to swing the Fifth and Sixth Panzer Armies north to cross the Meuse west of Liège and come in behind Aachen. However, this presupposed the capture of Bastogne and an attack from the north to link with the panzers—both increasingly unlikely. At Bastogne at the end of December, General George S. Patton, his forces swollen to six divisions, resumed his attack northeast toward Houffalize. At the same time, General Hasso von Manteuffel, commander of the German Fifth Panzer Army, launched another major attempt to cut the corridor into Bastogne and take the town. The fighting was intense, but Patton's forces stood firm and defeated the German attack. The last German assault against Bastogne was defeated in early January 1945, and then the Allied counterattack began. On the northern flank, the U.S. First Army attacked the northern sector of the "bulge," while the southern sector was assaulted by the U.S. Third Army. The Battle of the Bulge was over. German forces had been repulsed.

▲ GERMAN PANZERGRENADIERS race forward during the early stages of Hitler's Ardennes Offensive.

1945

THIS YEAR SAW THE END OF THE MOST DESTRUCTIVE WAR IN HUMAN HISTORY WITH THE SURRENDER OF FIRST GERMANY AND THEN JAPAN. THE DEATH TOLL WAS A STAGGERING 50 MILLION.

IN JANUARY THE SOVIET RED ARMY LIBERATED AUSCHWITZ DEATH CAMP, BRINGING TO LIGHT THE SICKENING OBSCENITY OF THE HOLOCAUST, ITS SCALE BECOMING CLEARER AS MORE NAZI CONCENTRATION CAMPS WERE liberated in the following months. The Red Army continued its offensive from the east, while from the west the Allies established a bridge across the Rhine River at Remagen, in March 1945.

THE END OF THE WAR IN EUROPE

The Western Allies raced the Russians to be the first into Berlin. The Russians won, reaching the capital on April 21. Hitler killed himself on the 30th, two days after Benito Mussolini had been captured and hanged by Italian partisans. Germany surrendered unconditionally on May 7, and the following day was celebrated as VE (Victory in Europe) day. The war in Europe was over. In the Pacific, however, it had continued to rage throughout this time. The British advanced further in Burma, and in February the Americans had invaded Iwo Jima. The Philippines and Okinawa followed and Japanese forces began to withdraw from China. Plans were being prepared for an Allied invasion of Japan, but fears of fierce resistance and massive casualties prompted Harry S. Truman—the new American president following Roosevelt's death in April—to sanction the use of an atomic bomb against Japan. Such bombs had been in development since 1942, and on August 6 one of them was dropped on the Japanese city of Hiroshima. Three days later, another was dropped on Nagasaki.

No country could withstand such attacks, and the Japanese surrendered on August 14. The biggest conflict in history had lasted almost six years. Some 100 million people had been militarized, and 50 million had been killed. Of those who had died, 15 million were soldiers, 20 million were Russian civilians, six million were Jews and over four million were Poles.

▲ SHIPS OF THE U.S. FLEET assembled off the island of Luzon. Landing craft carrying troops and heading for shore can be seen in the bottom of the photograph.

FOLLOW THE WAR ON ALL FRONTS WITH THE 3 GREAT WIRE SERVICES---AP, INS and UP---DAILY IN THE NEW YORK JOURNAL-AMERICAN

YANK PLANES BATTLE JAPS IN CHINA SEA

5¢

NEW YORK Journal American

AN AMERICAN PAPER FOR THE AMERICAN PEOPLE

Daily 5 Cents, Saturday 5 Cents in New York City; 10 Cents Elsewhere | SUNDAY, 10 Cents in New York City and 50-Mile Zone, 15 Cents Elsewhere

No. 20,816—DAILY FRIDAY, JANUARY 12, 1945 In Two Sections—Section One

7 SPORTS COMPLETE

New Red Offensive

Nazi Escape Route Cut To 2 Mi.

By THURSTON MACAULEY,
International News Service Staff Correspondent

PARIS, Jan. 12.—The German escape route out of Field Marshal von Rundstedt's ill-starred salient in Belgium was cut to a width of less than two miles in the Bastogne area today by U. S. 3rd Army troops slashing out against disorganized resistance east of that city.

Forces of Field Marshal Montgomery and of Lt. Gen. Patton's 3rd Army advancing against the blunted tip of the once-menacing but now rapidly-closing bulge linked up at St. Hubert, last Nazi road hub in that area.

American troops, supported by the British 2nd Army, concentrated on a final assault to wipe out the salient, closing in steadily on the retreatin genemy units which have fallen half-way back to the German border from their farthest point of penetration into Belgium.

SEIZE 1,200 NAZIS.

Topping off 24 hours of steady gains around the German pocket southeast of Bastogne, the 3rd Army today herded more than 1,200 prisoners, most of them from a crack paratroop division, into prison pens.

Most of the Nazis were seized at night when Patton's forces advanced under the cover of fog and darkness and overran an encircled pocket of two Nazi battalions.

U. S. 1st Army captives in the last 24 hours totalled 103, to make a total of 18,348 taken since the

Continued on Page 4, Column 3.

Mutiny On Nazi Ship

LONDON, Jan. 12 (AP).—The Swedish radio reported today that at least 350 German sailors were killed when panic and mutiny broke out aboard a German cruiser after it struck a mine off the Swedish coast.

Civil Penalties Urged for War Job Slackers

By WILLIAM THEIS,
International News Service Staff Correspondent.

WASHINGTON, Jan. 12.—Lt.-Gen. William S. Knudsen, the Army's production trouble-shooter, told Congress today that pressure legislation is needed to provide war-workers immediately but that it would be "better to leave the Army out of it."

Testifying on the pending "work or fight" bill, Knudsen backed up mounting sentiment in the House Military Affairs Committee that anything short of a national service act should impose a civil rather than a military penalty against unwilling war workers.

Concerning the provision of the bill providing Army induction if an essential worker leaves his job or fails to heed a local draft board request to take essential work, Knudsen said:

"It would be bad if you put them in the Army. The Undersecretary (Patterson), testified here that the Army didn't want them. It would be better to leave the Army out of it. Army service battalions now being used are being trained to go overseas."

'CANNOT STRESS ENOUGH.'

The former auto industry leader declared he could not "stress enough the advantages we'll get from having these needed men as soon as possible."

He said, under questioning, that

Continued on Page 10, Column 1.

President's Son Takes Part in Luzon Landing

ABOARD VICE ADM. KINKAID'S FLAGSHIP, Lingayen Gul, Jan. 11 (Delayed), (AP).—Lt. Cmdr. Franklin D. Roosevelt, Jr., son of the President, and Lt. Cmdr. Charles Francis Adams, son of the former Secretary of the Navy, each has command of a swift little destroyer escort engaged in the Luzon landing operation, it was disclosed today.

Triple Air Output In Plant Speedup

WASHINGTON, Jan. 12 (AP).—Fifty per cent of all war production programs will rise at "a tremendous rate" under a new speed-up which includes a three-fold increase in critical aircraft in six months, WPB Chairman J. A. Krug revealed today.

Partly to equip new French army divisions for the fight against Germany, about $2,500,000,000 worth of new arms output is being added to the 1945 schedule, Krug said.

The expansion brings 1945 total output to some $64,500,000,000, slightly higher than 1944, and is "a more difficult program to meet," he added.

Krug revealed for the first time that B-29 Superfortress production exceeds 135 a month.

"There will be plenty of jobs for everybody in war industry and everybody who wants to get into war industry," he said.

"The feeling of the average worker last Fall, when he didn't know whether or not he would be laid off, can now be dispelled."

The Italians have wanted arms

Continued on Page 10, Column 2.

Germans See Big Push for Krakow

LONDON, Jan. 12 (AP).—The German radio said today the Russians had opened an offensive on a broad front in southern Poland, striking from the Vistula bridgehead west of Baranow toward Krakow.

The Russians established the Baranow bridgehead, 125 airline miles south of ruined Warsaw, during the Summer. In drives across the rolling Polish plain, they struck within 35 miles of Krakow, ancient capital of the Polish kings and a city of 254,000.

"The first attacking waves were completely wiped out," the Germans asserted.

"Succeeding columns which reached the main battle lines were forced back in extremely violent fighting. Bitter fighting is going on for some penetration areas."

Meanwhile, west of Budapest "a big new battle has flared up and the German relief forces have resumed their all-out attempts to break through the city," BBC said.

The last chapter of the siege of Budapest itself was being written in a narrow strip of Pest, on the east bank of the Danube, with the Nazis squeezed into an area approximately two miles long and one mile wide.

Greek Civil War Halted by Truce

ATHENS, Jan. 12 (INS).—Civil warfare in Greece was brought to a virtual end today by the signing of a truce between British forces, the Greek government and representatives of the EAM.

Establishment of the truce will enable Greek government and EAM representatives to discuss settlement of outstanding political questions blamed for the outbreak of the civil war.

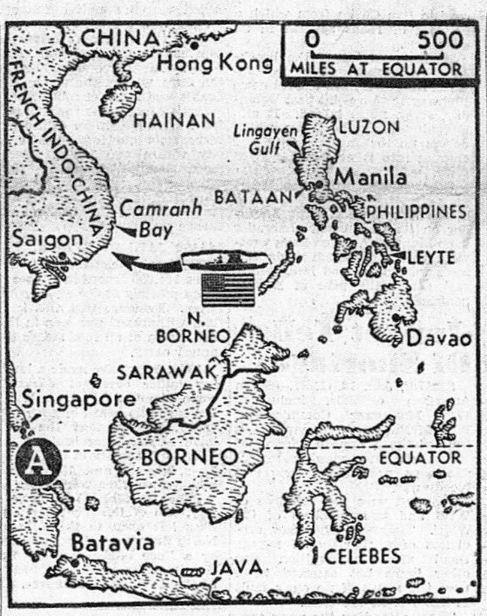
CHINA
Hong Kong
0 500
MILES AT EQUATOR
FRENCH INDO-CHINA
HAINAN
Lingayen Gulf
LUZON
Manila
BATAAN
PHILIPPINES
Camranh Bay
Saigon
LEYTE
N. BORNEO
SARAWAK
Davao
Singapore
A
BORNEO
EQUATOR
Batavia
JAVA
CELEBES

NEW BLOW . . . A giant air-naval battle was reported raging between Saigon and Camranh Bay, off the Indo-China coast, where hundreds of U. S. 3rd Fleet planes were attacking a huge Jap reinforcement convoy in what may be the biggest naval engagement since the battle of the Philippines last October. Earlier, Superforts attacked installations at Singapore (A). AP Map. Jan. 12, 1945.

Blaze Empties Beauty Shop

More than two score women, about half of them wearing sheets over their dresses, fled to the street today as flames threatened the Marion Beauty Shop, at 200 W. 49th st., at Seventh ave.

The ladies, who had been in various stages of being beautified, upset the Times Square neighborhood as they came down out of the beauty shop, on the second floor, and then dashed for cover from the chill winds.

The fire, which was confined to the Perfect Gift Shop, on the ground floor, did not reach the beauty shop, although flames leaped up high enough to burst a second floor window.

Soldier to Hang In Envoy Killing

ATTLEBRIDGE, Eng., Jan. 12 (AP).—A 12-man Army court martial today sentenced Pvt. George E. Smith, of Pittsburgh, to hang for murdering Sir Eric Teichman, British diplomat.

Smith, standing in front of the court, swayed as the sentence was read but recovered his composure and left the courtroom handcuffed to one of his escorts. He smiled faintly as he went out.

In a tense atmosphere the American colonel who served as president of the court martial read the verdict.

The verdict and sentence are subject to review by Smith's commanding officer and by the staff of Gen. Eisenhower. Smith also can make an application for pardon to President Roosevelt.

Teichman was shot when he accosted Smith and a companion, Pvt. Leonard Wojtacha, of Detroit, Mich., while they were hunting on his estate Dec. 3. Wojtacha faces a charge of being an accessory.

Smith's defense had contended he was a homicidal degenerate with the mental age of nine.

In a Canteen "foxhole" a girl has to know all the answers. Read "Hostesses, Heroes and Heels," one of many fascinating features in the Home Magazine with Saturday's Journal-American.

Agno Crossed In Stiffening Luzon Fight

Big Battle In Making

By CLARK LEE
International News Service Staff Correspondent

WITH MacARTHUR'S FORCES AT LINGAYEN, Jan. 12.—Stiffening, but still spotty and isolated, Jap resistance gave indications today that the real battle of Luzon may start in the near future.

[U. S. 6th Army forces, surging across the Central Luzon plains on a 20-mile front, expanded their invasion beachhead to at least 200 square miles and sent patrols probing across the Agno River only 90 miles from Manila, UP reported.]

While American patrols pushed far inland on the main roads from Lingayen City and Dagupan to Manila without encountering enemy forces, in other sectors our soldiers were beginning to meet the Japs.

[The 6th Army, which widened the Lingayen Gulf beachhead to 25 miles, has overrun 50 miles of road networks commanding the north ends of four main highways to Manila, AP reported.

[Gen. MacArthur is making preparations to launch a general offensive with strong tank support as the prelude to the decisive battle of Luzon, a Jap front line correspondent on Luzon reported today, adding: "Grim fighting has been raging this morning."]

One large group of the enemy was reported entrenched in the hills which rise out of the flat country southwest of San Vicente.

CLEAR PLAIN OF JAPS.

The rest of the central plain, however, seemed to be clear of Japs, who are apparently staying as much as possible outside the range of our battleship gun fire.

Tokyo Radio claimed Jap forces were counter-attacking the one

Continued on Page 2, Column 1.

Jap Convoy Seen Target

By RALPH B. JORDAN
International News Service Staff Correspondent

PEARL HARBOR, Jan. 12—Pacific Fleet carrier planes, making a bold penetration of South China Sea waters once firmly controlled by the Japanese, were "attacking the enemy" today off the coast of French Indo-China.

Scene of the attacks, according to a Pacific Fleet Headquarters communique, was between Saigon, 650 miles north of Singapore, and Camranh Bay, 800 miles southwest of embattled Luzon in the Philippines.

The brief communique announcing the historic naval-air battle follows:

"Carrier aircraft of the Pacific Fleet are now attacking the enemy off the coast of French Indo-China between Saigon and Camranh Bay."

About 90 U. S. carrier planes, Tokyo Radio said, raided the Saigon area for nine and a half hours today. Tokyo also said a major naval battle was "imminent" near the Philippines.

Exact targets of the naval airmen were not revealed, but it was believed Imperial Japanese Fleet units, or a Luzon-bound reinforcement convoy had been intercepted by carrier task forces on the alert for an offensive move by the enemy navy.

RICH TARGETS.

Since the communique stressed the scene of action was "off the coast," it was presumed that shore installation were not under attack, although Camranh Bay is one of the finest harbors on southern Asia capable of accommodating a fleet of capital ships.

Rich targets in the vicinity might have been discovered last week when Adm. Halsey's 3rd Fleet carrier planes probed along 500 miles of the South China coast, while others plastered

Continued on Page 2, Column 5.

The Journal-American, only New York afternoon newspaper to carry the three great wire services, presents a complete picture of the American invasion of Luzon and of the sea battle off Indo-China:

INS reports Yank air armada attack on Japs off French-Indo China. Targets are believed to be Jap fleet units or reinforcements bound for Luzon. On Luzon stiffened Jap resistance indicated real battle may start soon.

UP reports hundreds of carrier planes of Halsey's 3rd Fleet attack Japs off Indo-China, indicating big naval battle is under way or imminent. On Luzon 6th Army tanks surge across central plains.

AP says tremendous naval air-battle likely is raging. On Luzon swift advance is reported by 6th Army.

Put This in Your Pipe and Smoke It: Tobacco to Be Scarcer . . . and Butter, Too!

By ERWIN D. SIAS
International News Service Staff Correspondent.

WASHINGTON, Jan. 12.—An upward boost in ration point value of butter—from the present 24 to perhaps 28—was predicted today by a Government official in view of sharply increased military requirements for that food item.

The new butter ration may go into effect for February.

WFA recently announced that to meet urgent military demands, 20 per cent of the creamery butter produced in February and 25 per cent in March will be set aside for sale to the Government.

WASHINGTON, Jan. 12 (UP).—Pipe smokers, who so far have largely escaped the plight of cigaret smokers, may soon be joining them in line at tobacco store counters.

Tobacco industry spokesmen, here to seek price increases, said today the shortage of pipe tobacco will become severe by March.

John R. Murphy, general manager of Smaller Tobacco Manufacturers, said raw tobacco prices and other production costs had doubled since 1942, while price ceilings remained the same.

"The OPA," Murphy said, "insists on considering pipe tobacco production as a part of the cigaret industry, which is making money, and not as a separate business which is not."

16 Pages of your favorite Color Comics, plus the big, colorful Home Magazine section and other great features, with Saturday's Journal-American.

TONIGHT—10:05—WOV—dial 1280. Tom Morgan, famous correspondent, reports and analyzes the news Monday thru Friday.—Advt.

The screen unfolds a daring love drama, Hedy Lamarr, G. Brent, P. Lukas in 'EXPERIMENT PERILOUS,' tomorrow at RKO Albee, Fulton and DeKalb, B'klyn, plus 'Girl Rush.'—Advt.

THE WEATHER

Cloudy and warmer.

Sun rises, 8:20 a. m.; sun sets, 5:50 p. m. High tide at Governors Island, 7:51 a. m. and 8:12 p. m.

AVERAGE TEMPERATURES

7 a. m.	24	12 Noon	31
8 a. m.	24	1 p. m.	34
9 a. m.	27	2 p. m.	37
10 a. m.	28	3 p. m.	39
11 a. m.	28	4 p. m.	37

(Complete Weather Report on Page 17)

TODAY'S INDEX

Auctions	21	Lost and Found.	2
Best Places to Dine	7	Obituaries	18
Comics	22, 23	Radio	22
Editorial	14	Society	6
Financial	18	Sports	16, 17
Food, Cooking	6	Theatres	7 to 9
Horoscope	22	Want Ads	19 to 21

The Journal-American has the largest circulation of any evening newspaper in New York City 230

It is the only New York evening newspaper possessing the three great wire services—ASSOCIATED PRESS—INTERNATIONAL NEWS SERVICE—UNITED PRESS

—(PHONE YOUR NEWS TIPS TO CORTLANDT 7-1212)—

▲ NEW YORK JOURNAL AMERICAN, FRIDAY JANUARY 12, 1945

The Soviet Vistula–Oder Offensive merits its red headline because it helps relieve the pressure on the Allies in the Ardennes on the Western Front. As the reports from the Philippines show, and as the *Journal* boasts, access to the three wire services allows the paper broad coverage of international news.

The Daily Telegraph
and Morning Post

LONDON LATE EDTN.

No. 27,976   LONDON, TUESDAY, FEB. 13, 1945   Printed in LONDON and MANCHESTER   PRICE 1½d.

3 POWERS DECIDE ON GERMANY'S FUTURE

ZONES OF OCCUPATION: H.Q. IN BERLIN

8-DAY TALKS IN CRIMEA: POLAND AGREEMENT

UNITED NATIONS SECURITY CONFERENCE IN APRIL

Decisions of far-reaching importance to the future of the world were announced in a communiqué issued last night at the conclusion of eight days' conversations between Mr. Churchill, President Roosevelt and Marshal Stalin.

THREE-POWER CONFERENCE :- FIRST PICTURE

Mr. Churchill, President Roosevelt and Marshal Stalin in the grounds of the Livadia Palace, Yalta, Crimea, where the Three-Power talks have just been held. A picture of the conference in session on Page 5.

RUSSIANS 75 MILES FROM DRESDEN

BATTLE FOR NEW RIVER CROSSING

SECOND DRIVE ON BERLIN ROAD

CLEVE CAPTURED, BRITISH DRIVING ON TO GOCH

AMERICANS TAKE PRUM

"NAZI GERMANY DOOMED"

LATE NEWS

647,052 MOTOR VEHICLES IN FIVE WAR YEARS!

THE MOTOR INDUSTRY — PRODUCTION FOR VICTORY

DETTOL ANTISEPTIC

▲ THE DAILY TELEGRAPH, LONDON, TUESDAY FEBRUARY 13, 1945

The *Telegraph* carries the first picture of the three senior Allied leaders at the Yalta Conference in the Crimea. Despite Churchill and Roosevelt's suspicions of Stalin, they had little choice but to concede his demands that the Soviet Union dominate much of Eastern Europe after the war—the Red Army already effectively occupied much of the region.

Пролетарии всех стран, соединяйтесь!

Всесоюзная Коммунистическая Партия (больш.).

ПРАВДА

Орган Центрального Комитета и МК ВКП(б).

№ 38 (9809) | Вторник, 13 февраля 1945 г. | ЦЕНА 20 КОП.

«Нашей непреклонной целью является уничтожение германского милитаризма и нацизма и создание гарантии в том, что Германия никогда больше не будет в состоянии нарушить мир всего мира».

(Из заявления руководителей трёх союзных держав о результатах работы Крымской Конференции).

Конференция руководителей трёх союзных держав— Советского Союза, Соединённых Штатов Америки и Великобритании в Крыму

За последние 8 дней в Крыму состоялась конференция руководителей трех союзных держав — Премьер-Министра Великобритании г-на У. Черчилля, Президента Соединенных Штатов Америки г-на Ф. Д. Рузвельта и Председателя Совета Народных Комиссаров СССР И. В. Сталина при участии Министров Иностранных Дел, Начальников штабов и других советников.

Кроме Глав трех Правительств, следующие лица приняли участие в конференции:

от Советского Союза — Народный Комиссар Иностранных Дел СССР В. М. Молотов, Народный Комиссар Военно-Морского Флота Н. Г. Кузнецов, Заместитель Начальника Генерального Штаба Красной Армии генерал армии А. И. Антонов, Заместители Народного Комиссара Иностранных Дел СССР А. Я. Вышинский и И. М. Майский, Маршал Авиации С. А. Худяков, Посол в Великобритании Ф. Т. Гусев, Посол в США А. А. Громыко;

от Соединенных Штатов — Государственный Секретарь г-н Э. Стеттиниус, Начальник Штаба Президента адмирал флота В. Леги, Специальный Помощник Президента г-н Г. Гопкинс, Директор Департамента Военной Мобилизации судья Дж. Бирнс, Начальник Штаба Американской Армии генерал армии Дж. Маршалл, Главнокомандующий Военно-Морскими Силами США адмирал флота Э. Кинг, Начальник Снабжения Американской Армии генерал-лейтенант Б. Сомервелл, Администратор по военно-морским перевозкам вице-адмирал Е. Ланд, генерал-майор Л. Кутер, Посол в СССР г-н В. Гарриман, Директор Европейского Отдела Государственного Департамента г-н Ф. Маттьюс, Заместитель Директора Канцелярии по специальным политическим делам Государственного Департамента г-н А. Хисс Помощник Государственного Секретаря г-н Ч. Болен, вместе с политическими, военными и техническими советниками;

от Великобритании — Министр Иностранных Дел г-н А. Иден, Министр Военного Транспорта лорд Лезерс, Посол в СССР г-н А. Керр, Заместитель Министра Иностранных Дел г-н А. Кадоган, Секретарь Военного Кабинета г-н Э. Бриджес, Начальник Имперского Генерального Штаба фельдмаршал А. Брук, Начальник Штаба Воздушных Сил Маршал Авиации Ч. Портал, Первый Морской Лорд адмирал флота Э. Кеннингхэм, Начальник Штаба Министра Обороны генерал Г. Измей, Верховный Союзный Командующий на Средиземноморском театре фельдмаршал Александер, Начальник Британской Военной Миссии в Вашингтоне фельдмаршал Вильсон, член Британской Военной Миссии в Вашингтоне адмирал Сомервилл, вместе с военными и дипломатическими советниками.

О результатах работы Крымской Конференции Президент США, Председатель Совета Народных Комиссаров Союза Советских Социалистических Республик и Премьер-Министр Великобритании сделали следующее заявление:

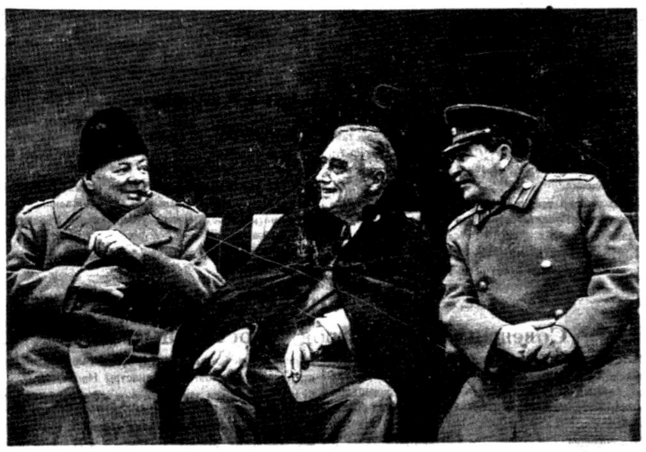

Конференция руководителей трёх союзных держав — СССР, США и Великобритании в Крыму. На снимке: г-н У. Черчилль, г-н Ф. Д. Рузвельт, тов. И. В. Сталин. Фото С. Гурарий.

I
Разгром Германии

Мы рассмотрели и определили военные планы трех союзных держав в целях окончательного разгрома общего врага. Военные штабы трех союзных наций в продолжение всей Конференции ежедневно встречались на совещаниях. Эти совещания были в высшей степени удовлетворительны со всех точек зрения и привели к более тесной координации военных усилий трех союзников, чем это было когда-либо раньше. Был произведен взаимный обмен самой полной информацией. Были полностью согласованы и детально спланированы сроки, размеры и координация новых и еще более мощных ударов, которые будут нанесены в сердце Германии нашими армиями и военно-воздушными силами с востока, запада, севера и юга.

Наши совместные военные планы станут известны только тогда, когда мы их осуществим, но мы уверены, что очень тесное рабочее сотрудничество между тремя нашими штабами, достигнутое на настоящей Конференции, поведет к ускорению конца войны. Совещания трех наших штабов будут продолжаться всякий раз, как в этом возникнет надобность.

Нацистская Германия обречена. Германский народ, пытаясь продолжать свое безнадежное сопротивление, лишь делает для себя тяжелее цену своего поражения.

II
Оккупация Германии и контроль над ней

Мы договорились об общей политике и планах принудительного осуществления условий безоговорочной капитуляции, которые мы совместно предпишем нацистской Германии после того, как германское вооруженное сопротивление будет окончательно сокрушено. Эти условия не будут опубликованы, пока не будет достигнут полный разгром Германии. В соответствии с согласованным планом вооруженные силы трех держав будут занимать в Германии особые зоны. Планом предусмотрены координированная администрация и контроль, осуществляемые через Центральную Контрольную Комиссию, состоящую из Главнокомандующих трех держав, с местом пребывания в Берлине. Было решено, что Франция будет приглашена тремя державами, если она этого пожелает, взять на себя зону оккупации и участвовать в качестве четвертого члена в Контрольной Комиссии. Размеры французской зоны будут согласованы между четырьмя заинтересованными Правительствами через их представителей в Европейской Консультативной Комиссии.

Нашей непреклонной целью является уничтожение германского милитаризма и нацизма и создание гарантии в том, что Германия никогда больше не будет в состоянии нарушить мир всего мира. Мы полны решимости разоружить и распустить все германские вооруженные силы, раз и навсегда уничтожить германский генеральный штаб, который неоднократно содействовал возрождению германского милитаризма, из'ять или уничтожить все германское военное оборудование, ликвидировать или взять под контроль всю германскую промышленность, которая могла бы быть использована для военного производства; подвергнуть всех преступников войны справедливому и быстрому наказанию и взыскать в натуре возмещение убытков за разрушения, причиненные немцами; стереть с лица земли нацистскую партию, нацистские законы, организации и учреждения; устранить всякое нацистское и милитаристское влияние из общественных учреждений, из культурной и экономической жизни германского народа и принять совместно такие другие меры к Германии, которые могут оказаться необходимыми для будущего мира и безопасности всего мира. В наши цели не входит уничтожение германского народа. Только тогда, когда нацизм и милитаризм будут искоренены, будет надежда на достойное существование для германского народа и место для него в сообществе наций.

III
Репарации с Германии

Мы обсудили вопрос об ущербе, причиненном в этой войне Германией союзным странам, и признали справедливым обязать Германию возместить этот ущерб в натуре в максимально возможной мере.

Будет создана Комиссия по возмещению убытков, которой поручается также рассмотреть вопрос о размерах и способах возмещения ущерба, причиненного Германией союзным странам. Комиссия будет работать в Москве.

IV
Конференция Об'единённых Наций

Мы решили в ближайшее время учредить совместно с нашими союзниками всеобщую международную организацию для поддержания мира и безопасности. Мы считаем, что это существенно как для предупреждения агрессии, так и для устранения политических, экономических и социальных причин войны путем тесного и постоянного сотрудничества всех миролюбивых народов.

Основы были заложены в Думбартон-Оксе. Однако, по важному вопросу о процедуре голосования там не было достигнуто соглашения. На настоящей Конференции удалось разрешить это затруднение. Мы согласились на том, что 25 апреля 1945 года в Сан-Франциско в Соединенных Штатах будет созвана Конференция Об'единенных Наций для того, чтобы подготовить Устав такой организации соответственно положениям, выработанным во время неофициальных переговоров в Думбартон-Оксе.

С Правительством Китая и Временным Правительством Франции будут немедленно проведены консультации и к ним будет направлено обращение принять участие совместно с правительствами Соединенных Штатов, Великобритании и Союза Советских Социалистических Республик в приглашении других стран на конференцию.

Как только консультации с Китаем и Францией будут закончены, текст предложений о процедуре голосования будет опубликован.

V
Декларация об освобождённой Европе

Мы составили и подписали Декларацию об освобожденной Европе. Эта Декларация предусматривает согласование политики трех держав и совместные их действия в разрешении политических и экономических проблем освобожденной Европы в соответствии с демократическими принципами. Ниже приводится текст Декларации:

«Премьер Союза Советских Социалистических Республик, Премьер-Министр Соединенного Королевства и Президент Соединенных Штатов Америки консультировались между собой в общих интересах народов своих стран и народов освобожденной Европы. Они совместно заявляют о том, что они договорились между собой согласовывать в течение периода временной неустойчивости в освобожденной Европе политику своих трех Правительств в деле помощи народам, освобожденным от господства нацистской Германии, и народам бывших государств — сателлитов оси в Европе при разрешении ими демократическими способами их насущных политических и экономических проблем.

Установление порядка в Европе и переустройство национально-экономической жизни должно быть достигнуто таким путем, который позволит освобожденным народам уничтожить последние следы нацизма и фашизма и создать демократические учреждения по их собственному выбору. В соответствии с принципом Атлантической хартии о праве всех народов избирать форму правительства, при котором они будут жить, должно быть обеспечено восстановление суверенных прав и самоуправления для тех народов, которые были лишены этого агрессивными нациями путем насилия.

Для улучшения условий, при которых освобожденные народы могли бы осуществлять эти права, три Правительства будут совместно помогать народам в любом освобожденном европейском государстве или в бывшем государстве — сателлите оси в Европе, где, по их мнению, обстоятельства этого потребуют: a) создавать условия внутреннего мира; b) проводить неотложные мероприятия по оказанию помощи нуждающимся народам; c) создавать временные правительственные власти, широко представляющие все демократические элементы населения и обязанные возможно скорее установить путем свободных выборов правительства, отвечающие воле народа, и d) способствовать, где это окажется необходимым, проведению таких выборов.

Три Правительства будут консультироваться с другими об'единенными нациями и с временными властями или с другими правительствами в Европе, когда будут рассматриваться вопросы, в которых они прямо заинтересованы.

Когда, по мнению трех Правительств, условия в любом европейском освобожденном государстве или в любом из бывших государств — сателлитов оси в Европе сделают такие действия необходимыми, они будут немедленно консультироваться между собой о необходимых мерах по осуществлению совместной ответственности, установленной в настоящей Декларации.

Этой Декларацией мы снова подтверждаем нашу веру в принципы Атлантической хартии, нашу верность Декларации Об'единенных Наций и нашу решимость создать, в сотрудничестве с другими миролюбивыми нациями, построенный на принципах права международный порядок, посвященный миру, безопасности, свободе и всеобщему благосостоянию человечества.

Издавая настоящую Декларацию, три державы выражают надежду, что Временное Правительство Французской Республики может присоединиться к ним в предложенной процедуре».

VI
О Польше

Мы собрались на Крымскую Конференцию разрешить наши разногласия по польскому вопросу. Мы полностью обсудили все аспекты польского вопроса. Мы вновь подтвердили наше общее желание видеть установленной сильную, свободную, независимую и демократическую Польшу, и в результате наших переговоров мы согласились об условиях, на которых новое Временное Польское Правительство Национального Единства будет сформировано таким путем, чтобы получить признание со стороны трех главных держав.

Достигнуто следующее соглашение:

«Новое положение создалось в Польше в результате полного освобождения ее Красной Армией. Это требует создания Временного Польского Правительства, которое имело бы более широкую базу, чем это было возможно раньше, до недавнего освобождения западной части Польши. Действующее ныне в Польше Временное Правительство должно быть поэтому реорганизовано на более широкой демократической базе с включением демократических деятелей из самой Польши и поляков из-за границы. Это новое Правительство должно затем называться Польским Временным Правительством Национального Единства.

В. М. Молотов, г-н В. А. Гарриман и сэр Арчибальд К. Керр уполномачиваются, как Комиссия, проконсультироваться в Москве в первую очередь с членами теперешнего Временного Правительства и с другими польскими демократическими лидерами как из самой Польши, так и из-за границы, имея в виду реорганизацию теперешнего Правительства на указанных выше основах. Это Польское Временное Правительство Национального Единства должно принять обязательство

(Окончание см. на 2-й стр.).

▲ PRAVDA, MOSCOW, TUESDAY FEBRUARY 13, 1945

"Over the last eight days, a conference has been held in the Crimea among the heads of the three Allied powers: British Prime Minister, Winston Churchill, President of the United States of America, Franklin D. Roosevelt, and the Chairman of the Council of People's Commissars of the USSR, Joseph Stalin."

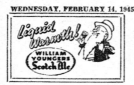

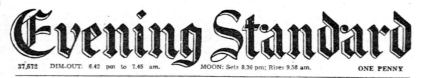

WEDNESDAY, FEBRUARY 14, 1945

FINAL NIGHT EXTRA●

Liquid Warmth! WILLIAM YOUNGERS Scotch Ale

Evening Standard

37,572 DIM-OUT: 6.42 pm to 7.45 am. MOON: Sets 8.36 pm; Rises 9.58 am. ONE PENNY

Maximum Price 25/3 per Bottle. Quality unrivalled since 1805 SEAGERS GIN

THE BLASTING OF DRESDEN

1350 Forts and Liberators Over Germany To-day After Night Attack by 1400 'Planes of R.A.F. Bomber Command

KONIEV INSIDE BERLIN PROVINCE

Marshal Koniev, crossing river barriers, to-day continued his advance towards Dresden and the heart of Germany as the gap between his forces and those of Marshal Zhukov narrowed to about 15 miles.

A link-up between the two forces for an outflanking drive south of Berlin is expected soon, says Reuter.

Koniev's men are to-day storming the Queis River, half-way between Breslau and Dresden, now less than 70 miles ahead.

The Germans are said to be showing increasing alarm over the possibility of a new Oder crossing by Zhukov's forces in the sector just beyond Koniev's right wing.

A Soviet blow here would split the remaining co-ordination between the German forces on the Berlin front and those in Silesia.

In Brandenburg

Berlin to-day named Cottbus and Guben, twin bastions guarding the south-eastern approaches to the capital, as the main objectives of Koniev's northern drive.

According to the German communiqué the Russians have reached Sorau, eight miles west of Sagan, and less than 30 miles from Guben.

This means that Marshal Koniev's forces have crossed the border into Brandenburg. Sorau is five miles inside the border and under 90 miles from the Reich capital.

To-day's German communiqué also admitted that the Russians have widened their penetration area north-west of Breslau.

"In the area south-west of Breslau," it stated, "the enemy hurled freshly brought up forces into the battle. Despite the stubborn resistance of our troops who were backed by Volkssturm and alarm units, the enemy in Lower Silesia was able to gain ground to the west and north-west.

"Bunzlau was lost during bitter fighting. Many enemy attacks against the fortress of Glogau were beaten back.

"In Southern Pomerania the Russians launched vain attacks. Fighting stubbornly the defenders of Arnswalde, Schneidemuhl and Poznan held out.

Stettin Hears Guns

"In the southern part of West Prussia, the Russians continued their breakthrough attempt in the area of Konitz and Tuchel. Heavy fighting is in progress.

"Enemy attempts to push in our front on both sides of the Elbing-Koenigsberg autobahn from the west, and at Zinten from the east, failed, as did pinning-down attacks between Wormditt and Landsberg."

Massed formations of Koniev's tanks are attacking west of Breslau in the direction of the town.

A Moscow military commentator broadcast this afternoon that Stettin can now hear the rumble of the Soviet guns.

German radio reported this afternoon that the Red Army had established another bridgehead across the Oder in the Frankfurt sector facing Berlin.

Martial Law Ends In Greece

Martial law ended in Greece to-day. The decree lifting it also annulled all sentences passed by the military courts in their trials of E.L.A.S. supporters.

To-day's Official Gazette promulgated the amnesty signed by the Government last night for all political offences committed during the events of December.

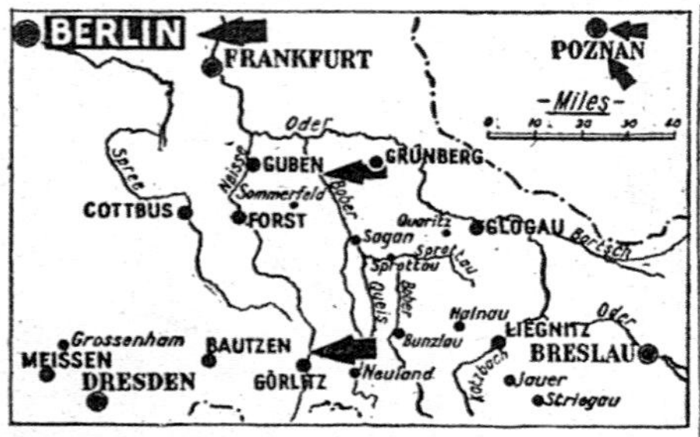
BERLIN
FRANKFURT
POZNAN
Miles
0 10 20 30 40
Oder
Spree
Neisse
GUBEN
GRÜNBERG
Sommerfeld
COTTBUS
FORST
Sagan
Sprottau
GLOGAU
Queis
Bober
Hainau
LIEGNITZ
Oder
Grossenham
MEISSEN
DRESDEN
BAUTZEN
GÖRLITZ
Bunzlau
Naumburg
BRESLAU
Jauer
Striegau

FIRES SEEN BY KONIEV'S MEN

More than 1350 Liberators and Fortresses of the U.S. Eighth Air Force to-day attacked transportation and industrial targets in Dresden, Chemnitz, and Magdeburg, and a road bridge across the Rhine at Wesel.

The bombers were escorted by more than 900 Mustangs and Thunderbolts of the same Command.

BURNING DRESDEN, POUNDED LAST NIGHT BY 800 BOMBERS OF R.A.F. BOMBER COMMAND, WAS AGAIN HIT TO-DAY BY AIRCRAFT OF THE U.S. EIGHTH AIR FORCE.

The raids were in support of Marshal Koniev's troops who are less than 70 miles away.

Russian troops may have seen the fires burning in the city last night after a double raid by our bombers. Crews of the bombers said that they could see the glow 200 miles away.

Two great blows were struck at Germany to-day. One 300-mile long stream of airplanes flew from the west, and other formations went from the south.

The Germans may be using Dresden—almost as large as Manchester—as their base against Koniev's left flank. Telephone services and other means of communication are almost as essential to the German Army as the railways and roads which meet in Dresden.

Its buildings are needed for troops and administrative services evacuated from other towns.

Dresden has large munition workshops in the old arsenal.

No major attack has been made before on the town.

Six hundred more bombers struck last night at the synthetic oil plant at Bohlen, south of Leipzig, and Magdeburg.

JAPS AND PEACE

Tokyo radio, which is rigidly controlled by the Government, broadcast to-day that the Japanese Foreign Minister's policy is "not to reject any hand which offers peace."

The spokesman of the Japanese Information Bureau, Iguchi, said: "The Yalta Conference was a masterpiece of power politics.

"The only way to re-establish peace in the world is by a just policy as outlined by Foreign Minister Shigemitsu, whose principle is not to reject any hand which offers peace."—Associated Press.

10,000 Tons of Bombs on Budapest

Allied and R.A.F. bombers of the Mediterranean Allied Air Force flew more than 4500 sorties over Budapest and dropped about 10,000 tons of bombs on it between April 1 and late in 1944, says Reuter.

SUNSHINE FOR SIX HOURS

By mid-afternoon the sun had been shining in the Straits for just on six hours. The temperature at 2 p.m. was 50, and the westerly breeze had backed a little to the south-south-west.

"Last Ditch Stand In Bavaria"

The Germans are hastily preparing Bavaria for a last ditch defence, said Moscow radio to-day.

Princess Elizabeth

Princess Elizabeth, who is suffering from mumps, is "progressing normally."

MONTGOMERY ADVANCING ON THIRD SIEGFRIED BELT

Hochwald Line Is 10 Miles Ahead

Montgomery's British and Canadian tank columns are now fighting their way forward towards Rundstedt's third and final Siegfried defence belt—the Hochwald Line—guarding the west bank of the Rhine and about ten miles beyond present Allied positions, said war reports reaching Reuter to-day.

Since the offensive began six days ago Allied troops of Montgomery's command have advanced up to 10 miles into the German lines along the front of 14 miles.

Canadian troops north-east of the Reichswald Forest are extending their six-mile hold on the west bank of the Rhine.

In the Prum sector General Patton's Third Army forces are flinging back all German attempts to recapture this communications centre for roads leading to Coblenz and Cologne.

Farther south, elements of three U.S. Third Army divisions are fighting through the Siegfried defences from the Our River bridgehead between Echternach and Wallendorf.

This is How Part of the "West Wall" Looked to the British

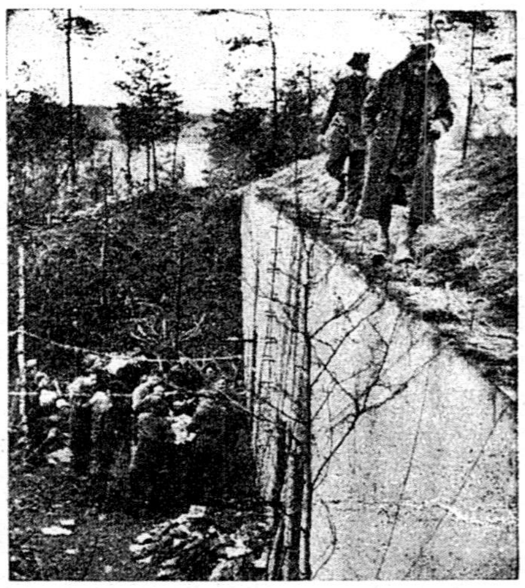

Sergeant-major Leonard Allington, of Birmingham, and Sergeant Gordon Dudgeon, of Glasgow, inspect a captured Siegfried Line strongpoint with ten-feet thick walls, while their comrades in a Scottish artillery regiment eat a quick meal before resuming the battle.

Double Onslaught Repulses Nazis

From RONALD MONSON

WITH THE FIRST CANADIAN ARMY, Wednesday.

Flame-throwers roaring on from the south-east fringe of the Reichswald Forest belched death into the ranks of the Germans trying to prevent the British advance beyond the forest late yesterday.

Behind them came men of the North Country regiment which had carried out the final clearing up of the forest.

The enemy who survived broke and fell back before the double onslaught.

Away on the north-east of this advance other troops, moving down after mopping up near Cleve, fought their way along roads leading south-east to Udem and to Calcar.

A British motor battalion after routing out Germans from the woods just south of Cleve, dashed on down the Udem road, 2000 yards beyond Bedburg.

Hasselt Captured

Reaching the Cleve State Forest, they found it full of Germans.

The Air Force and artillery were called in and the woods were plastered from end to end.

Few of the enemy were left in fighting condition when the guns ceased and the airplanes went home.

One pocket in a copse north-

(Continued on Back Page, Col. Two)

Spitfire Up With Waaf On its Tail

Evening Standard Reporter

A Waaf flight mechanic, 35-year-old Margaret Ida Horton, of Woodmansterne-lane, Banstead, Surrey, was working on the tail of a Spitfire when the aircraft suddenly took off.

She clung on for ten minutes until the extra weight on the tail was noticed by the pilot. By then the Spitfire had gained considerable height.

Throttling back carefully the pilot landed safely with Miss Horton still clinging on.

She was severely bruised and had to be taken to hospital suffering from shock. She is now recovering.

"The matter is now subject of an inquiry," an official of the Air Ministry told me.

Parachute Padre Is War Captive

News has been received at Beaumont College, Old Windsor, that the Rev. Bernard M. Egan, who was reported missing at Arnhem, is a prisoner of war in Germany.

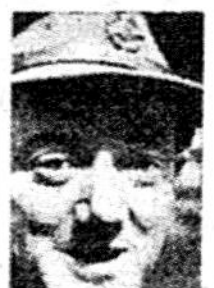

Rev. B. M. Egan

Fr. Egan, who was the first padre to make a parachute descent from a glider, was wounded, and is now in hospital suffering from severe injuries to his legs. He was a master at Beaumont College.

His mother, Mrs. S. A. Egan, who lives at Buntingford, Herts, told the Evening Standard to-day: "I have received five letters from my son, who is in hospital at Stalag 9. In his last letter, which I got yesterday, he told me he is now able to walk about again with the aid of two sticks

M.P. ON YALTA FLIGHT DISASTER

"Wrong Type Of 'Plane Alleged"

Mr. Granville (Ind., Eye) asked the Air Minister in Parliament to-day if he had any statement to make on the recent accident in which 15 British Service people and officials lost their lives on their way to the conference between the Prime Minister, President Roosevelt and Marshal Stalin.

Sir Archibald Sinclair replied: "I deeply regret the loss of life caused by this accident. The aircraft was a York belonging to the R.A.F. It was of standard design, and fitted with standard equipment. The R.A.F. pilot and crew were highly experienced. The aircraft was obliged to come down in the sea.

"A court of inquiry are now sitting.

Mr. Granville: "There is a good deal of serious concern in the public mind as to the repetition of these accidents.

"In view of the fact that this might have happened to any of the aircraft engaged on the flight, can you give an assurance that all machines engaged in the Prime Minister's flight were given adequate mechanical supervision and inspection right throughout the journey?"

Highly Efficient

Sir Archibald.—I cannot give an assurance about right throughout the journey, but I can give an assurance that the maintenance arrangements of Transport Command are highly efficient.

Earl Winterton (Con., Horsham and Worthing).—Will you look into the allegations that have been

(Continued on Back Page, Col. Five)

"Every German Will Kill, Murder, Poison"

"Every enemy, no matter when or how he penetrates into Germany, will be met by fanatical men, women and children, who know what treatment is in store for them and therefore wish to kill, murder and poison all who attempt to oppress them."

This extract from the broadcast by Paul Schmidt, the German Foreign Office spokesman, in which he declared that the Yalta declaration released Germany "from all moral scruples," was quoted by the Swedish paper Svenska Dagbladet to-day, says Reuter.

Large scale thefts of arms from Volkssturm barracks outside Berlin have sharpened German fears that a rising may be attempted once the military situation worsens, private Berlin reports to Stockholm said to-day, quoted by British United Press.

The main German long-wave radio station, Deutschlandsender, has apparently been moved from the Berlin region to a safer area.

Deutschlandsender has so far been broadcasting from Koenigswusterhausen, 15 miles south-east of Berlin. It went off the air after 1 a.m. because of approaching raiders; yet among the numerous warnings put out every few minutes by the German achtung stations there was none reporting raiders over the Berlin area.

▲ EVENING STANDARD, LONDON, WEDNESDAY FEBRUARY, 14, 1945

The bombing of Dresden, launched in support of Soviet advances into Germany, killed more than 100,000 people, but the civilian casualties are to some extent balanced by the avowed German intention to fight to the last against invasion. The *Standard* also finds room for a remarkable story of survival of a female mechanic carried into the air by a Spitfire.

DAILY EXPRESS

No. 13,948   Dim-out 6.44 pm to 7.43 am   THURSDAY FEBRUARY 15 1945   Moon rises 9.58 am sets 10 pm   One Penny

WHAT HAPPENED IN MANILA: Express reporter sends a story of mass murders of men, women and children by Japanese. 'At first it seemed beyond belief'

THE HORROR OF MANILA

Thousands of people locked in houses and then burned alive

Express Staff Reporter HENRY KEYS: Manila, Wednesday

AT last the Japanese have matched the rape of Nanking. In Manila they have piled outrage on outrage, infamy on infamy, until it has become a city of nightmarish horror.

I have spent two days tracking down the truth about Manila. At first it seemed beyond all belief.

Then gradually as I spoke to the stunned Filipinos, still trembling with the shock at what they had suffered, and as I saw the misery and the agony that has been endured, I realised its truth.

As we have advanced over ground fiercely contested by the Japanese, we have seen terrible exposures of murder.

Only today American soldiers found in one compound 30 bodies of Filipinos who had been bayoneted, shot or burned. The bodies of a woman and suckling child were among them. Both had been killed with the same shot.

But all is surpassed by the happenings in that part of Manila south of the Pasig river.

There, besides the destruction by fire and explosives of block after block of buildings, there has been wanton mass murder of men and women.

Civilians have been burned to death in their homes, or slaughtered by bayonets, spears and machine guns as they attempted to flee before the flames.

Children, beggars and other Filipinos who were reduced almost to starvation under Japanese rule have been employed to fire sections of the city at the rate of 300 worthless pesos a fire.

Masked women have betrayed Filipino patriots to the Japanese. Defenceless and alone, the former French Consul, M. Louis le Rock, was hacked to death by a sabre.

Crippled wrecks

I have known the Japanese many years. I knew they were bad, but not as bad as this. I have walked through hospitals so crowded that beds line the corridors.

I have seen the mutilated bodies of the dead and the burned and crippled wrecks who have survived the terror.

Americans infantrymen advancing about Marque de Camille-street found 30 Filipino women, their hands tied behind their backs, lying dead in the roadway. Their wounds showed that they had been bayoneted to death.

Further on they found two Chinese with sabre wounds in their necks.

Throughout the area were the ruthlessly butchered bodies of little children.

The Japanese herded a host of women and children in the old cathedral church in Intramuros.

Then they marched three or four thousand men captives to the dreaded Fort Santiago — the Gestapo-like headquarters of the Japanese military police just outside the wall of Intramuros.

By flare-light

That night at Fort Santiago, by the light of oil flares and flashlights, the men were lined up.

Then women wearing masks passed in front of them, accompanied by Japanese soldiers. Here and there the women would pause, and without speaking point out men to the Japanese.

The men were then informed that they were believed to be guerrillas or anti-Japanese.

This grim, ghostly betrayal continued for eight hours, the victims being taken aside and then bayoneted or shot with the pistols.

An eye-witness said he had no idea how many were selected in this way, but it was certainly a great number.

Those remaining when the ordeal was over were weak and trembling with fear. The Japanese told them that they would be released, but that they would be kept in Fort Santiago for three days.

The prisoners were given water and food, which a Japanese told them had been sent in by their families

The survivors

During these three days the surviving prisoners were kept in wooden garages and buildings, sometimes crowded as many as 100 and more to one compartment.

They were heavily guarded. About dusk on Friday, February 9, the Japanese closed and barricaded all the doors.

A little later the eye-witness, a man named Kasoin, smelled petrol. A few minutes later the wooden buildings were in flames.

The captives screamed in terror as they were caught in the flames.

Only one escaped.

A woman doctor, Josephina Vulalas, a resident physician in the Philippine General Hospital, told me of the things that happened to her and her family. They lived in the Paco district.

"The Japanese started shelling Paco on February 7," she said. "They kept shelling blocks of houses until they started a fire.

"We stayed in our house until we received a direct hit. We went outside but there were Japanese soldiers guarding each street. We stayed at our house all that night and the next day in which our house received two direct shell hits. My brother

BACK PAGE, COL. ONE

GOEBBELS SHUTS HIS PAPER

GOEBBELS' own newspaper, Der Angriff, will be published for the last time on Saturday.

This was announced last night by the German Overseas News Agency, which said that there will then be only one Berlin evening paper, the Nachtausgabe.

Newsprint restrictions were also announced for two big illustrated newspapers, the Berliner Illustrierte and the Illustrierte Beobachter.

The agency said : "Both papers will be published in very limited quantities, and the major portion will be sold abroad."

Goebbels founded Der Angriff, and for a time wrote its leader. When all other Berlin papers were Nazified, Goebbels remained undisputed master of Der Angriff, and used it to back him up in the Nazi Party internal crises before the war.

The sunniest day

Yesterday was the sunniest day of the year in the Straits of Dover with eight hours of sunshine and a temperature of 50 degrees.

EAST: One hedgehog is captured, Breslau siege begins

KONIEV THROUGH ON WIDE FRONT

ALARIC JACOB cabled from Moscow at midnight :—Koniev has broken through again tonight on a 50-mile front south-west of Liegnitz and his spearheads are aiming for Gorlitz, on the road to Dresden. His left flank is fighting in the Riesen mountain foothills on the borders of Czechoslovakia.

From E. D. MASTERMAN: Stockholm, Wednesday

MARSHAL KONIEV'S twin drives beyond the Oder towards Berlin and Dresden swept on irresistibly along a 65-mile battlefront today as a Stalin Order as "large communication centres and strong bastions of the German defences."

In Pomerania Zhukov has stormed Schneidemuhl, the attack on Dresden brought confusion to Southern Germany comparable only with that in the north after the last big raid on Berlin.

More than 7,000 Germans were killed and 3,000 captured there. A few hours after these announcements from Moscow, Berlin revealed:—

1.—That the ring of encirclement round Breslau was now closed nine miles west of the city after a big tank battle, and that another Russian encirclement was shaping further west.

2.—That the Russians had made numerous crossings of the River Queis which flows beyond the Bober and less than 70 miles from Dresden.

3.—That the situation on the Oder front had become more serious.

4.—That with the fall of Budapest a new and fierce battle had flared up only 77 miles from Vienna.

SEVEN TOWNS

The Silesian towns taken are:—
Newsalz, on the Oder. 75 miles north-west of Breslau.
Freistadt, six miles south-west of Neusalz.
Sprottau, on the Bober, 25 miles west of Glogau.
Neustadtl, 20 miles north-west of Glogau.
Goldberg, 17 miles south-west of Liegnitz.
Jauer, 35 miles west of Breslau.
Striegau, 30 miles south-west of Breslau.

Neusalz is the furthest point in the Berlin direction so far officially revealed on Koniev's front.

But German despatches say that Koniev is advancing now on a 30-mile front north-west towards Berlin, and is striking for the cities of Kottbus and Guben, both less than 70 miles from the capital.

Fighting street by street is reported by the enemy in Borna and Sommerfeld beyond the Bober River, and about 35 miles west of the Oder in this sector.

Koniev is only a few miles from a link-up with Marshal Zhukov's left wing, where the Oder bears to the west.

Neutrals breaking from Nazis

By GUY EDEN

GERMANY may shortly find herself without a friend in the world, or even a single nation which is on formal "speaking terms" with her.

There are indications that several nations at present neutral are considering breaking off diplomatic relations with Germany, if not actually declaring war.

The military situation is making it increasingly difficult for Germany to get supplies from any of the few remaining friendly nations. A formal breach would have an important psychological effect in Germany.

FRANCO

One reason for the change of attitude is that the neutrals "want to be on the peace conference band wagon" but, it is not certain that like arrivals will be given a place

Spain may be Germany's last friend, but it is thought possible that even Franco may recall his representative on the plea that it is physically impossible to maintain contact with the Nazi Government, as all foreign Embassies and Legations are now moving out of Berlin away from Allied bombing.

Evidence is mounting that civil government in Germany is breaking up in all parts of the country, and not merely in those under direct Allied attack. Central government is collapsing

FLEEING

Whole towns and wide areas are being left to govern themselves. Nazi officials are fleeing. Complete absence of communication between one area and another is causing chaos in housing refugees, food supplies and preserving order.

Last night came news from Washington that the Ambassadors of Chile, Peru, Ecuador and Paraguay, have signed the United Nations declaration after declaring a state of belligerency against Japan

The Pope has a cold

ROME, Wednesday.—The Pope has a slight cold and remained in his private rooms today.—Reuter.

GREAT RHINE-DRESDEN BLITZ

The war's greatest air offensive was being kept up this morning, according to enemy reports.

German radio indicated that most of the Reich was covered, and at one o'clock today the Dresden area was again mentioned.

The Berlin-Stockholm telephones were cut between £30 and 10.30 last night, when the capital had an alert.

More than 4,000 of these attacks were by the Tactical Air Forces based on the fronts from Holland to the Swiss border.

Including the night blitz on Dresden, about 9,000 sorties have been flown in 24 hours.

The total for today is not yet complete, but midnight reports show that 300 engines, 2,500 rail trucks and more than 700 motor vehicles were destroyed or damaged, and 250 rail cuts were made.

The Tactical Forces lost 22 planes, but three pilots are safe.

There were five signs of the Luftwaffe, but two jet planes were destroyed.

Among many bridges bombed was the Cronus Prinz Wilhelm bridge at Coblenz. Many enemy troop concentrations and fortified bridge are reported.

Typhoon rocket planes helped to break up German counterattacks in the Canadian Army sector.

DECIDED AT YALTA

The Daily Express Air Reporter writes:—

THE mighty Anglo-American air blows on Dresden are the first result, I learned last night, of the Chiefs of Staff conference between the Russians and the Western Allies at the Crimea Conference.

For the attacks now aimed at giving direct support to Marshal Koniev's advancing troops 70 miles to the east.

At the conference the Chiefs of Staff formulated detailed plans for this close support of each other's armies in the co-ordinated plan for victory.

Dresden, nearly the size of Manchester, was blasted and set ablaze by 800 R.A.F. heavy bombers at night—they dropped 650,000 incendiaries—and by about the same number of American Flying Fortresses and Liberators in daylight yesterday, only a few hours later.

Again, a vast bed of bombs was poured down.

ARTERY SEVERED

From the Daily Express Stockholm reporter:—

REPORTS reaching Stockholm are unanimous in saying that the attack on Dresden brought confusion to Southern Germany comparable only with that in the north after the last big raid on Berlin.

Dresden had become the chief supply base for the German defenders west of Silesia. Over the railway lines and highways running through the city the German High Command tried to pump men and material into the gravely menaced defences.

Now the Dresden artery is severed, temporarily at least. Railway stations and yards have been demolished, bridges and viaducts blown up, and factories laid in ruins.

'Vienna, beware!'

Moscow radio told the Viennese last night. "Your gates are wide open. The fate of Budapest—ruins and ashes—should be a warning to you."

Premier speaks in Athens

'LET HATREDS DIE'

From ERIC GREY

ATHENS, Wednesday.—Mr. Churchill set his seal on the Greek agreement today when he addressed 20,000 Athenians massed to greet him in the now famous Constitution-square.

"Let right prevail. Let party hatreds die. Let there be unity. Let there be resolute comradeship. Greece for ever. Greece for all."—these were the words with which Mr. Churchill ended his speech, amid the cheers of the citizens of Athens.

Mr. Churchill arrived in Athens by air straight from the Big Three conference at Yalta. He entered in an open car and drove to the ramp of the old palace overlooking the Unknown Soldier's Tomb and the square.

With him was Archbishop Damaskinos, the Regent, his black cassock fluttering in the wind.

'The dawn is bright'

The sun was about to set in a clear sky as Mr. Churchill, with the Regent at his side, addressed the crowd. He said—

"These are great days. These are days when the dawn is bright, when the darkness rolls away.

"A future lies before your country, a great future.

"There has been much misunderstanding and ignorance of our common cause in many parts of the world, and there has been misrepresentation of the issues fought out here in Athens.

"But now these matters are clearing, and there is understanding of the part Greece has played, and will play, in the world.

"Speaking as an Englishman, I am very proud of the part which the British Army has played in protecting this great, and immortal city from violence and anarchy.

"Our two countries have long marched along the dusty hard road, shoulder to shoulder in friendship and loyalty.

"The present and prosperity and happiness of the Greek people is dear to all the nations of the British Commonwealth and Empire.

'Let no one swerve'

"We who have been associated with you in every struggle for Greek liberty, we will march with you till we reach the broad highlands of justice.

"Let no one fail to do his country. Let no one swerve from the high road of truth and honour. Let no one fail to rise to the occasion of this great moment and of these splendid days.

"Let the Greek nation stand first in every heart. Let it stand first in every man and woman.

"Let the future of Greece shine brightly in their eyes.

Archbishop Damaskinos, who introduced Mr. Churchill to the crowd, said that nature had made this great festival for the presence among them of the glorious son of England—Winston Churchill.

Tonight Athens is celebrating for the first time since the revolution. The British official said that fires are attending a State banquet at the Regent's palace, the Parthenon is floodlit and singing and marching through the

---

£200,000 SWINDLE

Clubman, ex-staff officer, gets 12 years

Express Staff Reporter

JOHN PRESCOTT HALLETT, ex-R.A.F. wing commander, ex-London company director, a member of famous London clubs, has been brought back to England from India, to serve a sentence of 12 years' penal servitude, originally promulgated as for 15 years, for obtaining more than £200,000 unlawfully from a wealthy Indian.

He was court martialled on charges of forgery, larceny and embezzlement. He pleaded guilty. The allegations against him were that he approached a wealthy Indian with offers of concessions for properties in Burma.

He said that he was acting with the authority of Lord Louis Mountbatten, Allied command of the South-East Asia Command.

When "deals" had been negotiated, Hallett drew up agreements and forged signatures of highly placed officers. He received in rupees sums totalling more than £200,000.

The first hint that led to Hallett's downfall was when it was noticed that he was spending money lavishly. He was a member of the Intelligence Staff of S.E.A.C. and formerly lived with his R.A.F. pay.

THE TRAIL

Inquiries were made. The R.A.F. Special Investigation Branch discovered that Hallett had sent £60,000 to London banking accounts with instructions that certain debts should be discharged.

From that point a trail led to London back to India and then to London again.

Group-Captain Nicholas, who commands the Special Investigation Branch—he was with the Portsmouth police before the war—took over the inquiries.

Then Treasury solicitors were called in and later the help of Scotland Yard was sought.

Police took over and they took Lottis. On September 21 last year the R.A.F. detectives arrested Hallett in Eastern Bengal.

In a safe in his quarters more than £130,000 was found. More deposits in a Ceylon bank were recovered.

NO AUTHORITY

At Hallett's court martial, it was made clear that he was acting for Greek liberty, we will march with you till we reach the broad highlands of justice. No Allied officer is in a position to offer or make concessions in Burma or any other part of enemy-occupied British territory.

Hallett was described as a man of great personal charm and plausibility, and a skilled business negotiator.

In this case, Lady Astor told the Ministers, the father was earning £7 to £9 a week.

Hallett is serving his sentence in a civil prison in England.

Nelson weds

WASHINGTON, Wednesday.—Donald Nelson, President Roosevelt's personal

---

Child cruelty laws tighter

Express Political Correspondent

THE Home Secretary, Mr. Herbert Morrison, told an all-party deputation of M.P.s yesterday that the force of public opinion was strong enough to prevent any widespread cruelty to children.

But he added that he intended, by administrative action, to tighten up the law to ensure that every possible

4.30 a.m. LATEST

SWEDISH A.A. DOWNS TWO

STOCKHOLM, Wednesday.—Swedish A.A. fire sent two planes into the sea off Southern Sweden tonight.—A.P.

JAP ISLE GETS 69TH BLOW

Admiral Nimitz's communiqué reports that Iwojima, in the Volcano Islands, has been bombed for the 69th time.

step was taken to protect children.

He will not wait for the report of a committee which is to inquire into the law relating to children with foster parents or in institutions.

Nearly 50 M.P.s attended the meeting, and all urged—in an interview lasting 90 minutes—that the law should be made much more severe in all cases of cruelty to children.

The Ministers of Health and Education were also present.

Viscountess Astor described how once she saw two of the dirtiest children she had ever set eyes on being pushed along the road in a pram by a third equally grimy child.

She followed them all the way home to a squalid back street. When she got there she found a mother of low mentality in a house that was filthy beyond description.

Her intervention met with a rather hostile reception at first, but ultimately the children were sent to a better place.

Yet in that case, Lady Astor told the Ministers, the father was earning £7 to £9 a week.

She made a strong plea not to allow the wholesale indictments about when so many women were performing a Christian service to humanity by looking after unwanted children with motherly solicitude.

Britain, she said, had done

ANTI-FREEZE KILLS

NANCY, Wednesday.—Soldiers and a French civilian are among more Americans and Frenchmen who have died here in a bar in Nancy. They had all drunk a glass of anti-freeze mixture. Favouring and coloured, the anti-freeze contains 95 per cent. methyl-alcohol—

FAMILY '5/- PLAN' TODAY

Express Political Correspondent

THE Government's plans for family allowances will be made public today. Sir William Jowitt, Minister of National Insurance, presented a Bill to the House of Commons yesterday.

The plans closely follow the White-paper on insurance Allowances of 5s. a week will be made for all children under school-leaving age, except the first in any family. These allowances will go on until the child leaves school or until the July 31 after the 16th birthday if the child remains

'Japs may begin peace moves soon'

NEW YORK, Wednesday.—Japanese peace moves soon, were anticipated by Mr. Earl Dickover, chief of the Japanese Affairs Division, U.S. State Department, in a speech today.

"As the war in the Pacific progresses," he said, "certain elements in Japan may soon come forward with an offer of a negotiated peace to avert a crack-up with resultant chaos in Japan. This must not be accepted.

Stalin accepts voting p

NEW YORK, Wednesday.—A compromise suggested by the method of voting sanctions on proposed World Security Council was accepted by Americas and Russia at the Crimea Conference. America originally wanted the Council to have the right to accuse even a big Power of aggression and to enforce sanctions.

At Yalta Stalin agreed the Council should now be the powers of aggression by any as members.

Roosevelt agreed that should be imposed by agreement of the Powers — Britain, France and China.

HALLETT
Spent lavishly.

◀ DAILY EXPRESS, LONDON, THURSDAY FEBRUARY 15, 1945
Even after years of the war, the eyewitness account from Manila by *Express* reporter Henry Keys makes for upsetting reading. Trapped in the city, Japanese naval personnel turned on the civilian population: some 50,000 Filipinos died.

▼ SCENES OF DESTRUCTION in Manila after the fighting had finished on March 3. The Japanese lost 20,000 killed in a hopeless defense of the city.

A DRINK OF
QUALITY & CHOICE
Chamber's
DARJEELING TEA
Head Office & Factory
DARJEELING
Bombay—Sitaram Bldg.,
Crawford Market,
Nagpur—Gaya & Co., Itwari.

LARGEST NET SALES of any Daily Newspaper Printed in Northern, Southern, Central or Western India

REGD. No. B111

MAY 1945
Order Now

The Times of India

ESTABLISHED 1838.

HENNOL
CURES
GRAY HAIR
PERMANENTLY

PEARLINE, P. O. Box 421, BOMBAY.

NO. 48. VOL. CVII.   D.   BOMBAY: SATURDAY, FEBRUARY 24, 1945.   PRICE TWO ANNAS.   DO NOT PAY MORE

AMERICANS CROSS SAAR RIVER

Many More Towns Taken In Drive Forward

CANADIAN UNITS ENTER MOYLAND

LONDON, February 22.

THE U. S. Third Army, continuing its forward drive, has taken 24 more towns and crossed the Saar river in assault boats south of Saarburg.

This is the first Allied crossing of the Saar south of Saarburg, which has been entered by Gen. Patton's tanks. The town stands on the Saar river only eleven miles south of Trier.

The Third Army has also captured Vianden and Dasburg and cleared Saarburgon on the west bank of the river Saar. After clearing the town, the Allies advanced three miles and are now on the heights less than a mile from Konz, four miles from Trier, at the junction of the Moselle and the Saar rivers.

The whole of the triangle between the rivers Saar and Moselle has been cleared by the American Third Army after advances of up to two miles. American troops are now along the Saar river for 25 miles from its junction with the Moselle to Saarlautern.

American armour is attacking the Siegfried fortifications at Serrig, two and a half miles south of Saarburg where the crossing of the Saar river was made. Nearly 2,000 prisoners were taken yesterday.

It is reasonable to surmise that other great events will take shape if Fied Marshal Montgomery is able to break the determined German resistance to the British and Canadian advance in the northern sector. The Germans are not fighting merely to retain their hold on this dreary, flooded stretch of country. They hope have thrown in elements of at least three *Panzer* four parachute and three infantry divisions in a battle of great ferocity.

First Canadian Army troops have entered Moyland, the German strong point on the Cleve-Calcar road just north of Calcar. Goch has been finally cleared.

Scottish and other British troops, fanning out from Goch as the Canadians fight to clear Moyland are battling for every foot of the way. Among the elements of the 5th divisions opposing them is the wellknown *Panzer* Lehr Division, which fought skilfully to cover the Ardennes retreat.

With Goch virtually cleaned up, the Canadian First Army's attacks are again gaining momentum. At the same time the British are closing in along the Goch-Udem railway line.

SHAEF "COMMUNIQUE"

General Eisenhower's communique issued on Thursday said:

"Between the Rhine and the Maas Allied forces continued to make good progress, in the Moyland sector woods to the south of the town have now been cleared of the enemy. Our forces driving down from the north have reached the line of the Goch-Udem railway at a point about two and a quarter miles west of Udem. Goch is now clear of the enemy. South-east of Goch we made gains of up to 2,000 yards.

"Strong points and gun and mortar positions in the wooded country west of Calcar and near Goch were attacked by rocket-firing fighters and dipper bombers which went in just ahead of our ground forces. The fortified village of Calcar was subjected to repeated bombing and strong attacks by other fighter-bombers. Behind efforts of the communications targets in the enemy lines at Brakwede, Bunebeck, Cleves and Xanten were attacked by medium, light and fighter bombers.

"In the area south-west of Julich, our forces captured the town of Haur and are fighting in Garsdorf. Further south-west near the Luxembourg-German border, we captured Dahlem and entered Dasburg. In the Vianden area, our units reached the German border six and a half mile south-east of the town. Just south-east of Vianden, we have taken Roth. In the Metzendorf area east of Vianden our forces repulsed a heavy counter-attack. Our units now traversed the Prum river on a six-mile stretch in the area north of Reihersscheim.

"In the Saar-Moselle triangle, our forces cleared Temmels, just north-east of Grevenmacher, and our armour pushed beyond Onsdorf to a point three and a half miles north-west of Saarburg, which has been entered by other armoured elements. Our forces have reached the Saar river south of Saarburg and have taken Hamm and Taben. The towns of Freudenburg and Kastel..."

Thursday's German communique said: "Attacks of the First Canadian Army in the Cleve area have considerably slackened in force. The Third American Army on the upper Our penetrated German positions in some sectors, while east of Vianden the Germans held their ground against the bulk of enemy attacks. Between the Moselle and the lower Saar our troops are engaged in heavy defensive battles against strong enemy infantry and tank forces pressing on towards Saar fortifications. Street fighting has flared up in the suburbs of Forbach."

Shirtings

JUPITER MILLS
JAYABHARAT MILLS
AHMEDABAD

Heavy Raids From Italian Bases

ROME, February 23: The 15th Air Force, co-operating with the Allied air forces based in Britain and France, today attacked communication targets in Southern Germany, Austria, Northern Italy and Yugoslavia.

The heavies took off with 1,850 tons of bombs—the biggest load ever carried by the 15th Air Force in a single operation—to join in blanketing Germany and Central Europe.

Among the targets of the 15th Air Force were the Kempten railway yards on the line from Munich to Lake Constance, the Rosenheim yards, south-east of Munich, and Attermdorf on the bypass line from Salzburg to Munich.

The Austrian Alpine rail network in the rough triangle between Munich, the Brenner Pass and Klagenburg was also bombed. Nearly 1,000 bombers took part in this tenth consecutive day's attack.—*Reuter.*

A View Of Iwojima, Scene Of Fierce Fighting

Fiercest Fighting Here
Landing Beach
4,500 Yards
Main Airfield
Mt. Suribachi

This aerial view of Iwojima, in the Volcano islands, shows the beach where the U. S. Marines landed on February 20, later capturing the main airfield, Suribachi Field No. 1, near Mt. Suribachi.

Over 6,000 Aircraft Blast Reich

SMASHING BLOW AT COMMUNICATIONS

LONDON, February 23.

Over 6,000 aircraft based in Britain, the Low Countries, France and Italy—the maximum strength of the combined British and American Bomber and Fighter Commands—took part today in what were the greatest ever co-ordinated attacks on the German communications system.

"The Marines have apparently now taken nearly half of Iwojima from shore to shore; they are heading into the plateau on the northern end of Suribachi and meeting with bitter opposition", said an American broadcast from Guam, according to an earlier message.

German communications throughout Western and Central Germany may have been put out of action for some time as a result of the widespread air assault on roads and railways.

"The raids covered Germany's entire secondary system of communications after the virtual breakdown of the main road-rail traffic caused by the previous air attacks.

More than 1,400 American Liberators and Flying Fortresses, escorted by more than 800 fighters, on Thursday bombed more than 20 communications targets over a wide area in Central Germany, says an official announcement from the Headquarters of the U. S. Strategic Air Force in France.

The attack was aimed at disorganising and disrupting rail networks over an area of 38,000 square miles, through the very heart of the Reich.

Among the targets attacked were the marshalling yards at Luneberg, Stendal (west of Berlin), Halberstadt, Ludwigslust, Uelzen, Salzwedel, Wittenberg, Hildesheim, Kreiensen, Peine Northeim, Vienenburg, Bangernhausen and Gottingen. All are at the function of two or more main rail lines.

HUGE TONNAGE DROPPED

The raids were the biggest and most important of their kind of the war. The tonnage of bombs dropped is estimated to be 3,500. The record is over 4,000 tons.

The fighters which guarded the Flying Fortresses and Liberators along their routes fanned out to provide close support as the heavies smashed their many widespread objectives. After completing the escort, a number of fighter groups dropped down "on the deck" adding to the havoc by strafing the rail lines.

Nearly the whole of German industry hinges on the movement of numerous raw materials to factories, of components to assembly centres, and of finished products to their destinations. Because her oil production has dropped to a new and critical low level as a result of Allied strategic bombing, nearly the entire burden of this vital industrial transportation has fallen on the one-time efficient German rail system.

A stream of refugees, 60 miles long, travelling in every conveyance imaginable, was reported by the fighter pilots returning from Germany.

"There must have been 10,000 people strung out on the roads of North-western Germany, between Emden and Munster, moving northeast and east", said one pilot. At least three jet-propelled Messerschmitts were destroyed in the air by fighters during the day's operations.

The Americans lost eight bombers and 16 fighters in their raids yesterday on Germany, Austria and Northern Italy. It was officially announced. More than 3,000 American planes took part.

A store of explosives, probably V-2 warheads, blew up with a mighty explosion when R. A. F. Spitfire bombers pinpointed a rocket site in the Netherlands today, announces the Air Ministry. Hours later, as more Spitfires were on the way to attack other rocket targets, fierce fires were still blazing on the site and a ten-mile long streamer of smoke was pouring from the ruins. The explosion which followed the bombing was so violent that pilots, flying high and awaiting their turn to attack, felt it rock their machines.

MOUNT SURIBACHI CAPTURED

American Success On Iwojima

GUAM, February 23.

The American flag was raised on the summit of Mount Suribachi by Marines of the 28th Regiment at 10.30 a.m. (Philippines Time), on Friday, Admiral Nimitz announces.

The landing on Capul Island was made by units of the 10th Corps of the New American Eighth Army. The opposition to the landing was slight.

The 11th Airborne Division, advancing along the west coast of Laguna de Bay, south-east of Manila, reached the town of Muntinglupa. Seven hundred and twelve artillery pieces of all calibres and 705 machine-guns were seized or destroyed in the northern and central part of the Luzon plain.—*Reuter.*

ASSEMBLY PASSES CUT MOTION

Railwaymen's Allowances

NEW DELHI, February 22: A cut motion, moved by Mr. Jamnadas Mehta, asking for more dearness allowance to railway employees was passed in the Assembly today by 51 votes to 42. The House also discussed, on a cut motion moved by Mr. H. G. Stokes, on behalf of the European Group, the financial position of railways, with special reference to post-war development. After a debate the motion was withdrawn.

A resolution, moved by Mr. G. S. Motilal, seeking to raise the number of elected members of the Upper House to 40 and to broaden the franchise was rejected today by the Council of State by nine votes to three.

In reply to a question put by Mr. Manu Subedar, Sir Azizul Haque, Commerce Member, said that the premises occupied by the People's Free Reading Room and Library at Dhobi Talao, Bombay, had not been requisitioned by the Government.

(Details on page 7)

CIVILIANS LOCKED UP BY MILITARY

Assembly Explanation

NEW DELHI, February 22: Replying to a question in the Central Assembly today put by Mr. C. S. Gupta whether it was a fact that civilians were imprisoned in military detention camps or the Eastern Command without any trial or charges, Mr. C. M. Trivedi said that it had been necessary for operational, security reasons to detain powers under the Military Safety (Powers of Detention) Ordinance, 1944, to the General Officer Commanding-in-Chief, Eastern Command, to enable him to detain certain personnel who would enter India from, or after having been in, territory for the time being occupied by the enemy.

Asked for the number of civilians so imprisoned Mr. Trivedi stated that in the interest of security he was unable to give that information.
—*United Press.*

Russians Capture Town Near Guben

MARSHAL KONIEV'S SUCCESSES WEST OF SORAU

MOSCOW, February 23.

THE Russians have captured Schenkendorf, one and a half miles south of the important communications centre of Guben, according to the latest Soviet "communique." Other places captured include Gross-Saerchen (16 miles west southwest of Sorau), Teuplitz (14 miles west north-west of Sorau), and Triebel (14 miles west of Sorau).

In East Prussia, the Red Army has captured Zinten, 21 miles south of Konigsberg. This town was the central bastion of the main German pocket in the province.

Four thousand German officers and men were killed in the fighting at Zinten, says the Soviet "communique."

Marshal Koniev, it seems, has made a considerable break-through in his all-out attack on the Neisse Line, the main water barrier across the southeastern approaches to Berlin, cables *Reuter's* special correspondent.

The Marshal's drive is being directed principally in the direction of the important town and junction of Kottbus, which lies right in the path of any advance towards the Spree-Oder Canal and the region due south of Berlin.

Guben and Furst must first be reduced if either of these two thrusts is to be successful, and of the two the second is the more important.

Soviet troops are storming up to the Neisse at all sectors between Guben and Gorlitz, the two major river bastions.

Heavy pressure is being exerted against Guben, 65 miles from the capital, and Gorlitz, within 50 miles of Dresden. Fierce hand-to-hand clashes are taking place in the Oder valley, with Soviet tanks bodies rallies to the eastern outskirts of the town.

Far to the rear of the Berlin front, the correspondent adds, the battle of encircled Posen is now drawing to a close. Two thousand Germans are still fiercely resisting along the battlemented walls of the citadel, and the German commander has now issued an appeal to his guns and mortars for a last desperate stand.

In East Prussia, a violent armour and artillery struggle is going on between Konigsberg and the sea. By swinging their massive panzer batteries ram repeatedly, without the slightest regard for losses, the Germans have gained some ground, and the issue whether or not they will achieve a break-through to escape from the port of Pillau is still in the balance.

SOVIET "COMMUNIQUE"

Thursday night's Soviet communique says: "Our troops in the Samland peninsula west of Konigsberg were repelling strong enemy attacks launched with tanks and infantry. They were forced to yield some ground on the northern shore of the bay, after inflicting heavy losses on the enemy in manpower and equipment.

"South-west of Konigsberg, our troops continued to fight for the destruction of the encircled enemy grouping in East Prussia, and further tightening the encircling ring and captured the town of Zinten as well as other inhabited places.

"During offensive fighting, from February 19 to 22, west of Konigsberg, our troops destroyed 66 German tanks and self-propelled guns, 74 guns, 180 machine-guns and over 300 lorries. The enemy lost over 6,000 killed.

"South of Danzig, as a result of offensive fighting, our troops occupied several inhabited localities. Yesterday (Wednesday) our forces in this sector took over 500 prisoners and captured five self-propelled guns, 65 pieces of field artillery and 24 armoured transport cars.

"Fighting in Posen for the destruction of the German garrison holding out in the citadel continued.

"South of Guben, in Brandenburg Province, our troops reached the river Neisse and have occupied over 40 inhabited localities.

"In the forests south-east of Guben, our troops were engaged in destroying an enemy grouping and killed 2,000 of the enemy, among them two Colonels.

"Our troops in the area of Breslau were engaged in the liquidation of the encircled enemy group, and during fighting, occupied three suburbs of the city.

"On the north bank of the Laarube, east of Kosarein, our forces repelled heavy attacks. During yesterday (Wednesday's) attacks, 46 German tanks and self-propelled guns were destroyed.

"In other sectors of the front there was quiet activity and fighting of local importance at some points.

"On all fronts yesterday (Wednesday) 186 German tanks were destroyed or disabled and 80 planes were shot down."

"Last night our heavy bombers made a mass raid on war industrial objectives in Konigsberg. About 40 large conflagrations broke out, accompanied by heavy explosions. Particularly large fires were seen in the area of the machine building works and gas works.

"Our bombers, the same night, also raided similar objectives in the Czechoslovak town of Bratislava. Fires and heavy explosions were caused."

GERMAN REPORTS

Berlin: Thursday's German communique reports that the main fighting in Lower Silesia is between Zobten, south of Breslau, and in the Lauban-Goben area. On the Russian are continuing steady pushing moves to break through to Guttau and beyond the Neisse.

"Between Sommerda and Metze, on the Vistula, the Russians made slight initial gains, the communique adds. In East Prussia the Soviet onslaught has increased in force and the Russians made some slight breaches.

Lord Lloyd George

LONDON, February 22: Lord Lloyd George, who is ill at his Criccieth home, had a comfortable night on Wednesday, but there was no improvement in his condition.—*Reuter.*

Turkey May Declare War On Axis

SIMILAR ACTION BY SYRIA & EGYPT

CAIRO, February 22.

Turkey is likely to declare war against the Axis at a special session of the Turkish Parliament, according to usually well-informed political circles here, wires "Reuter's" special correspondent.

The same circles forecast that Syria and the Lebanon will quickly follow Turkey's example.

Istanbul: The Turkish National Assembly has been summoned to meet in a special session on Friday. An announcement on an important decision is expected.

London: Reports that the Egyptian Government would declare war on Germany as forecast in the press were not denied in London on Thursday, writes *Reuter's* diplomatic correspondent. British official quarters were not prepared to anticipate any way of comment on these reports, but any decision the Egyptian Government might take.—*Reuter.*

Alexandria Comedy

CAIRO, February 22—Alexandria celebrated the end of the war for a few hours yesterday—by mistake. A short circuit caused all air raid sirens in the town to sound, and since this has been suggested as the means of announcing the end of hostilities, there were scenes of great enthusiasm and rejoicing in streets and squares.—*Reuter.*

Americans Land On Capul

MANILA, February 23.

American forces landed on Capul Island, in the San Bernardino Straits, between Luzon and the northern Samar Island, announces Thursday night's communique.

The communique states: "The island is the key to the Straits through which passes the main navigation route to Manila Bay from the United States."

▲ THE TIMES OF INDIA, BOMBAY, SATURDAY FEBRUARY 24, 1945

Founded as *The Bombay Times* in 1838 to serve the British residents of western India, the *Times* uses an annotated photograph to explain the fighting on Iwo Jima. The story is flanked, appropriately, by details of Allied advances on Germany from the west and the east, respectively.

Iwo Jima
FEBRUARY 1945

IWO JIMA WAS A SMALL ISLAND BETWEEN THE MARIANAS AND JAPAN ITSELF, BUT IT HAD TWO AIRFIELDS AND WAS JUST THREE HOURS' FLYING TIME FROM TOKYO. THE AIRFIELDS THERE WOULD ENABLE FIGHTER escorts to protect U.S. B-29s attacking the Japanese home islands.

The preparations for the invasion of Iwo Jima were meticulous, and the landings were preceded by an enormous bombardment, but the fighting on the island was as tough as anything U.S. forces had encountered in the Pacific so far. It showed how Japanese forces were not giving up.

LANDINGS ON IWO JIMA
Under the command of Lieutenant General Holland M. Smith, the U.S. 4th and 5th Marine Divisions landed on February 19. Resistance was at first light, but then the attackers were hit by intense artillery and small-arms fire from the 21,000-man Japanese garrison. However, despite casualties, the Americans had 30,000 men on the island by the end of the day. Within days, U.S. Marines had raised the American flag on the summit of Mount Suribachi in the south of the island (February 23). Five days later they had captured two-thirds of the island. The U.S. Marines now had to turn north to clear the rest of the island. As the fighting on Iwo Jima became more intense, the U.S. 3rd Marine Division was committed to the battle. On March 5, the troops of the 5th Marine Division defeated a large-scale Japanese

counterattack. The island was declared secure by the Americans following 26 days of combat. The capture of Iwo Jima breached the Japanese inner defensive ring around their home islands. In order to keep up the momentum, the Americans next planned to move even closer to the Japanese home islands by capturing the Pacific island of Okinawa. Casualties in the fighting on Iwo Jima had been heavy. U.S. forces had suffered 6,821 killed and 19,217 wounded; Japanese losses were 20,867 killed and 1,083 taken prisoner.

▲ SOLDIERS OF THE U.S. 5TH MARINE Division on the black volcanic sands of Iwo Jima. In the background stands Mount Suribachi, which was captured by U.S. Marines within three days.

Across the Rhine

MARCH 1945

ALLIED TROOPS IN THE WEST WAITED UNTIL FEBRUARY 8 TO LAUNCH THEIR PUSH TO THE RHINE RIVER. SIX ARMIES ATTACKED ALONG THE ENTIRE LENGTH OF THE FRONT from Holland to Switzerland. German troops put up local resistance, but a coordinated defense was beyond the capabilities of the battered armies west of the Rhine. The truth was that the German Army was in ruins and Nazi war production was grinding to a halt under the weight of Allied bombing and a dire shortage of raw materials. Within a month, the Allies were at the river and preparing to strike into the heart of the Reich. In the northern sector of the front, 52,000 German troops were captured.

THE RHINE

The first Allied bridgehead was established over the Rhine River on March 7, and Allied troops began several major amphibious operations to breach the water obstacle on the 22nd. Field Marshal Walther Model's Army Group B was cut off in the Ruhr Pocket on April 1. Just over two weeks later, 370,000 German troops surrendered amid the ruins of the Third Reich's industrial heartland. Model decided he did not want to achieve the dubious distinction of being the second German field marshal to be captured (after Paulus at Stalingrad), and so committed suicide.

INTO THE HEART OF THE REICH

Allied troops now advanced across western Germany, with British troops heading for the Baltic coast in the north and the Americans driving southwest to deal with the so-called Nazi "National Redoubt" in the Alps, which proved to be another of Hitler's flights of fancy. Other U.S. troops headed into the heart of Germany itself and also into Czechoslovakia. By prior agreement, the Americans and the Soviets met up on the banks of the Elbe River. In Italy, Allied troops at last punched their way through to the Po Valley and then they began driving north toward the Austrian Alps and into Yugoslavia to link up with Marshal Tito's partisan forces. German resistance in the West was half hearted at best. The Nazi war effort was, effectively, now collapsing. The stage was set for the capture of Berlin.

▲ GERMAN PRISONERS TAKEN BY THE ALLIES in March 1945. By this time, Germans were surrendering to the British and Americans in droves.

The New York Times.

"All the News That's Fit to Print"

LATE CITY EDITION
Cloudy and continued mild today and tomorrow.
Temperatures Yesterday—Max., 55; Min., 38
Sunrise today, 7:59 A. M.; Sunset, 7:81 P. M.

Copyright, 1945, by The New York Times Company.

VOL. XCIV....No. 31,827.

Entered as Second-Class Matter, Postoffice, New York, N. Y.

NEW YORK, THURSDAY, MARCH 15, 1945.

THREE CENTS NEW YORK CITY

1ST ARMY FANS OUT IN THE RHINE BRIDGEHEAD; 7TH JOINS 3D IN SMASHING AT SAAR SALIENT; RAF USES 11-TON BOMBS; RUSSIANS CUT ODER LINE

$13,898,000 MORE AID TO STATE EDUCATION IS ASKED BY DEWEY

Changes Put to Legislators Also Top Friedsam Formula by $17,857,000

TECHNICAL COURSES URGED

Governor's Proposals, Framed by a Committee, Would Cut the Size of City's Classes

Text of Albany report on revision of State school aid, Page 38.

By LEO EGAN
Special to The New York Times.

ALBANY, March 14—Governor Dewey asked the Legislature today to enact a new formula for the distribution of State aid to education and to set up a special commission to establish and develop State-financed technical institutes at a sub-professional level for returning veterans and mature students not desiring academic college training. His recommendations were based on a report submitted by a special committee of five that he had appointed earlier this year to study the problem.

Laborite Retracts On Churchill 'Lie'

By The Associated Press.

LONDON, March 14—In an angry mood, Prime Minister Winston Churchill today forced caustic Laborite Richard Stokes to withdraw in the House of Commons a charge that the Prime Minister had "lied" during arguments over the merits of British tanks.

JOB CONTROL BILLS GO TO CONFERENCE

House, 211 to 177, Backs Its Measure—Navy to Let Army Take 18-20 Inductees

By C. P. TRUSSELL
Special to The New York Times.

WASHINGTON, March 14—The House stood by its May-Bailey bill for "limited national service" today and by a vote of 211 to 177 forced it to conference for a showdown with the Senate's "voluntary" manpower mobilization measure.

STATEN ISLAND ACTS TO END CRIME WAVE

Grand Jury Subpoenas Police and Army Officers—Indicts Two in March 7 Attack

Magistrate Jails 'Speak' Owner, Second Attacks Curfew 'Hysteria'

The Ludendorff railroad bridge, over which supplies and troops of the First Army are pouring, spans the river from the shattered buildings in the foreground to the smoking hills on the far side where our men are fighting. Yesterday the bridge was hit by attacking enemy airmen. *Associated Press Wirephoto*

Victory Flag Raised on Iwo; Airfield Is Used by Bombers

By ROBERT TRUMBULL
By Wireless to The New York Times.

GUAM, Thursday, March 15—The United States flag was formally raised on Iwo at 9:30 A. M. yesterday, although fighting continued unabated in the northern sector and in a small pocket in the northeastern part of the island, Pacific Fleet headquarters announced today. The communiqué gave 20,000 as a "very close approximation" of the Japanese dead in the twenty-three days of the Iwo battle through yesterday.

THRUST FOR BERLIN MADE BY RED ARMY

Pravda Says River Is Crossed at Kuestrin—Offensive in East Prussia Renewed

By The United Press.

LONDON, Thursday, March 15—The Moscow newspaper Pravda reported yesterday that the Red Army had crossed the Oder River opposite Kuestrin and was driving toward Berlin through powerful fortifications, but the Soviet communiqué told only of Russian advances on the East Prussian and Czechoslovak flanks of the long front.

Huge Bombs Hit Reich Rails In Vast Air Attacks by Allies

By SYDNEY GRUSON
By Wireless to The New York Times.

LONDON, March 14—Specially modified Lancasters of the Royal Air Force dropped some of the world's biggest bombs, eleven-ton missiles 25 feet 5 inches long, on the German main line rail viaduct at Bielefeld, north of the Ruhr, today if the first attack with this latest "secret weapon" from the Allied arsenal.

3 POWERS EXCHANGE NOTES ON RUMANIA

Eden Terms Radescu Ouster Purely Soviet Affair—Implies Defense of Ex-Premier

By CLIFTON DANIEL
By Wireless to The New York Times.

LONDON, March 14—Foreign Secretary Anthony Eden told the House of Commons today that the British, United States and Soviet Governments now are exchanging communications about the general situation in Rumania, where the Russians recently took heavy-handed action to re-form the Government.

OUR GRIP WIDENED

U. S. Troops Push Out in Three Directions on East Bank of Rhine

7TH REACHES SAAR

Nazis Fall Back Before It—Third Clears West Bank of the Moselle

By DREW MIDDLETON
By Wireless to The New York Times.

PARIS, March 14—Doughboys of Lieut. Gen. Courtney H. Hodges' First Army struck out to the north, east and south from the Remagen bridgehead today, while to the southeast the forces of the United States Third and Seventh Armies bit into the right flank and center of the German defenses of the Saar Basin.

War News Summarized

THURSDAY, MARCH 15, 1945

Gains north and east of the Remagen bridgehead brought the Ruhr superhighway completely under domination of United States First Army artillery. Troops driving from Honnef were a mile and a quarter from the road. Advances against heavy opposition were reported from the Linz and Kalenborn areas. The bridgehead had been expanded to a length of ten and a half miles and a depth of five and a half.

Osaka Arsenal Believed Razed; Japan Revamps B-29 Defenses

By The United Press.

GUAM, Thursday, March 15—The Osaka arsenal, one of the most important war plants in Japan, was believed to have been blown up in a huge explosion at the end of yesterday's incendiary raid by 300 giant Superfortresses, it was announced today.

▲ THE NEW YORK TIMES, THURSDAY MARCH 15, 1945

The *Times'* photograph shows the Ludendorff Bridge at Remagen—the last intact bridge over the Rhine—captured by the U.S. 9th Armored Division on March 7. Eisenhower called the bridge "worth its weight in gold," but its value proved to be more symbolic than practical. After German bombing, it collapsed on March 17, 1945.

Okinawa
APRIL 1945

OPERATION ICEBERG WAS THE CODE-NAME GIVEN TO THE AMERICAN INVASION OF OKINAWA. ADMIRAL CHESTER W. NIMITZ, COMMANDER-IN-CHIEF OF THE PACIFIC FLEET AND Pacific Ocean areas, had assigned Vice Admiral Richmond Turner as commander of the amphibious forces and Vice Admiral Marc Mitscher as commander of the fast carrier forces. The U.S. Tenth Army was led by Lieutenant General Simon B. Buckner, and comprised 183,000 men. The island, only 325 miles (520 km) from Japan, had two airfields on the western side and two partially-protected bays on the east coast—an excellent springboard for the proposed invasion of the Japanese mainland.

THE U.S. LANDINGS

The landing by the U.S. II Amphibious Corps and XXIV Corps was virtually unopposed. The Japanese commander, Major General Mitsuru Ushijima, had withdrawn his 80,000 men behind Shuri, where he had built a major defensive line. The battle for the island was split into four phases: first, the advance to the eastern coast (April 1–4); second, the clearing of the northern region of the island (April 5–18); third, the occupation of the outlying islands (April 10–June 26); and fourth, the main battle against the dug-in elements of the Thirty-Second Army

which began on April 6 and did not end until June 21. On April 7, the Japanese battleship *Yamato* was sunk on her way to Okinawa by U.S. aircraft. Ushijima committed suicide on June 16. The military value of Okinawa was great. The island was sufficiently large to house great numbers of troops; it provided numerous airfield sites close to the enemy's homeland; and it furnished fleet anchorage, helping the U.S. Navy to remain in action at Japan's doors. However, the scale of losses suffered on Iwo Jima and Okinawa convinced the U.S. president and his military chiefs that any invasion of Japan would result in unacceptably high losses. The decision was therefore taken to use atomic bombs on Japan to hasten the end of the war.

▲ THE *YAMATO* WAS THE WORLD'S largest battleship in 1945. Part of a Japanese battle group sent to attack U.S. shipping around Okinawa, the ship was sunk by U.S. aircraft before it reached the island.

The New York Times.

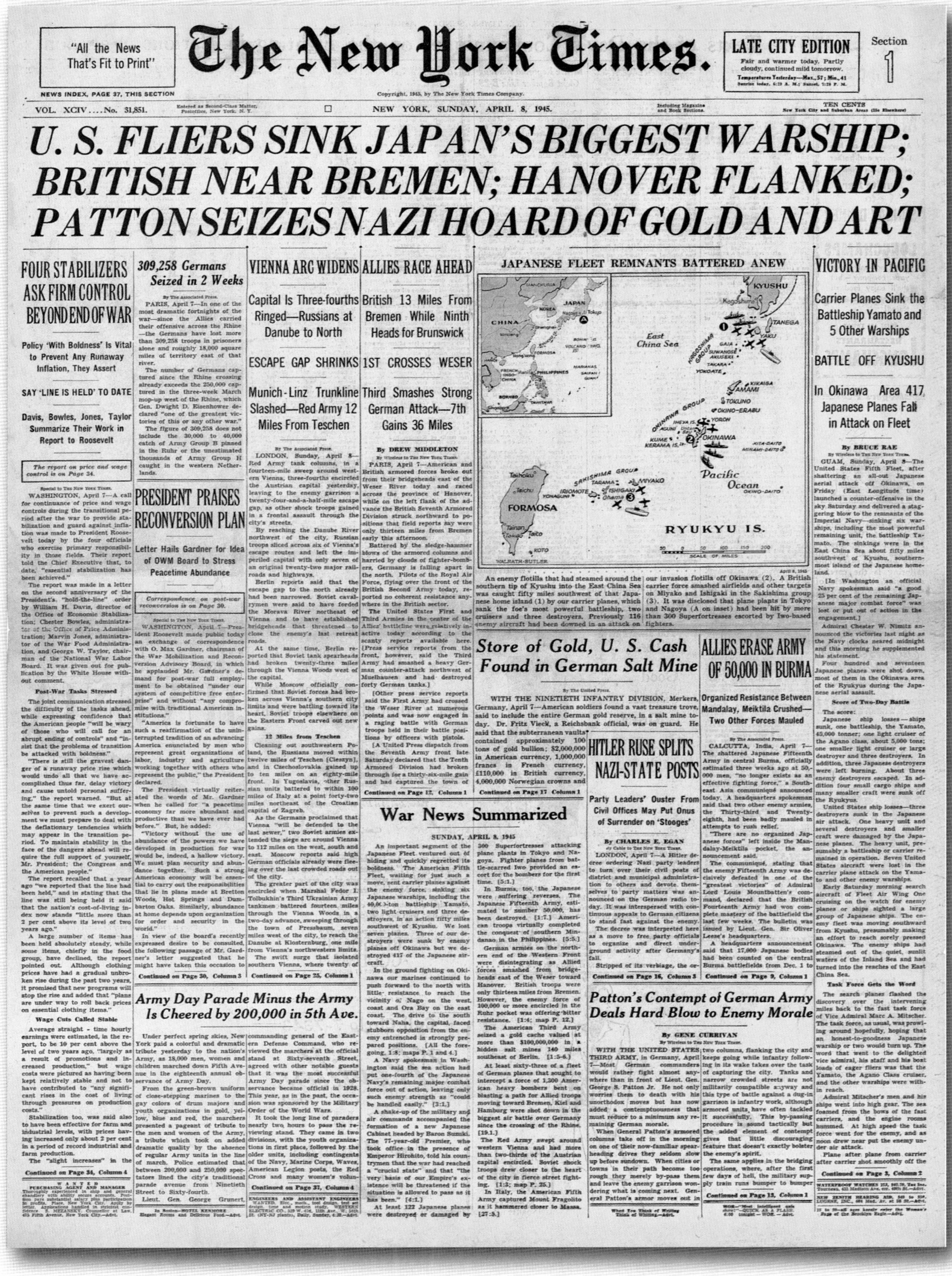

"All the News That's Fit to Print"

NEWS INDEX, PAGE 37, THIS SECTION

LATE CITY EDITION
Fair and warmer today. Partly cloudy, continued mild tomorrow.

Section 1

VOL. XCIV....No. 31,851.   NEW YORK, SUNDAY, APRIL 8, 1945.   TEN CENTS

Copyright, 1945, by The New York Times Company.

U. S. FLIERS SINK JAPAN'S BIGGEST WARSHIP; BRITISH NEAR BREMEN; HANOVER FLANKED; PATTON SEIZES NAZI HOARD OF GOLD AND ART

FOUR STABILIZERS ASK FIRM CONTROL BEYOND END OF WAR

Policy 'With Boldness' Is Vital to Prevent Any Runaway Inflation, They Assert

SAY 'LINE IS HELD' TO DATE

Davis, Bowles, Jones, Taylor Summarize Their Work in Report to Roosevelt

309,258 Germans Seized in 2 Weeks

PRESIDENT PRAISES RECONVERSION PLAN

Letter Hails Gardner for Idea of OWM Board to Stress Peacetime Abundance

VIENNA ARC WIDENS

Capital Is Three-fourths Ringed—Russians at Danube to North

ESCAPE GAP SHRINKS

Munich-Linz Trunkline Slashed—Red Army 12 Miles From Teschen

ALLIES RACE AHEAD

British 13 Miles From Bremen While Ninth Heads for Brunswick

1ST CROSSES WESER

Third Smashes Strong German Attack—7th Gains 36 Miles

By DREW MIDDLETON

JAPANESE FLEET REMNANTS BATTERED ANEW

VICTORY IN PACIFIC

Carrier Planes Sink the Battleship Yamato and 5 Other Warships

BATTLE OFF KYUSHU

In Okinawa Area 417 Japanese Planes Fall in Attack on Fleet

By BRUCE RAE

Store of Gold, U. S. Cash Found in German Salt Mine

ALLIES ERASE ARMY OF 50,000 IN BURMA

Organized Resistance Between Mandalay, Meiktila Crushed—Two Other Forces Mauled

HITLER RUSE SPLITS NAZI-STATE POSTS

Party Leaders' Ouster From Civil Offices May Put Onus of Surrender on 'Stooges'

By CHARLES E. EGAN

War News Summarized

SUNDAY, APRIL 8, 1945

Army Day Parade Minus the Army Is Cheered by 200,000 in 5th Ave.

Patton's Contempt of German Army Deals Hard Blow to Enemy Morale

By GENE CURRIVAN

▲ THE NEW YORK TIMES, SUNDAY APRIL 8, 1945

Although the fighting raging on Okinawa would be some of the fiercest and most costly of the war, the *Times* is focused firmly on the postwar recovery of the economy, reporting Roosevelt's reception of a "reconversion" plan from a government committee. The Japanese loss of *Yamato*, the world's largest battleship, came as part of Operation Ten-Go, a suicide attack by the last of the Imperial Japanese Navy on U.S. forces off Okinawa.

The New York Times.

NEWS INDEX, PAGE 15, THIS SECTION

LATE CITY EDITION
Partly cloudy and cooler today.
Cloudy and warmer tomorrow.
Temperatures Yesterday—Max., 61; Min., 59
Sunrise today, 5:18 A. M.; Sunset, 7:18 P. M.

Sections
1 AND 3 AND 5

VOL. XCIV..No. 31,858.   Entered as Second-Class Matter, Postoffice, New York, N. Y.   NEW YORK, SUNDAY, APRIL 15, 1945.   Copyright, 1945, by The New York Times Company.   Including Magazine and Book Sections   TEN CENTS   New York City and Suburban Areas (Else Elsewhere)

NATION PAYS FINAL TRIBUTE TO ROOSEVELT AS WORLD MOURNS; HYDE PARK RITES TODAY; AMERICANS CLOSE TO SPLITTING OF REICH

GERMAN LINES CUT

3d Army 78 Miles From Russians—9th Fights on Road to Berlin

RAF RIPS POTSDAM

Ruhr Pocket Is Nearly Bisected—Northern Holland Almost Won

By DREW MIDDLETON
By Wireless to The New York Times.

PARIS, April 15—Sweeping eastward on a scythe-shaped front, Gen. Dwight D. Eisenhower's armies drove closer to Berlin on the north, smashed into the rear areas of the German armies facing the Russian forces east of Dresden in the center and looked forward on a broad front toward Czechoslovakia today.

At last reports tanks of the Fourth Armored Division of Lieut. Gen. George S. Patton's United States Third Army were about seventy-eight miles from the nearest Russian positions near Goerlitz and Cottbus. Farther south the Eleventh Armored Division of the Third Army was last reported less than eighteen miles from Czechoslovakia.

[Press services pointed out that these advance elements were operating under a partial security blackout and a special dispatch from the Third Army front said that the Germans appeared to have nothing in the way of defenses to prevent an eventual link-up between the American and Soviet forces in southeastern Germany.]

Battle on Berlin Approaches

Meanwhile other columns of tanks and infantry, winding over the enemy's military roads, made gains of from five to thirty miles and closed to the Elbe River at points along a front of 150 miles. Resistance was stiffening in the north where the United States Ninth Army troops, fighting their way toward Berlin across the Brandenburg Plain, reported several counter-attacks.

[In a tactical air strike with heavy bombers—an operation of the type General Eisenhower has employed just ahead of other major advances since St. Lô and Caen—about 750 British Lancasters hit Potsdam, German Army center eighteen miles west of the Reich capital, Saturday night, and also bombed Berlin.]

Tanks and infantry of the United States Ninth and First Armies are now forty-five to sixty miles from Berlin on a front extending from the west bank of the Elbe east of Sachsen on the north to the area of Dessau, reached by First Army troops today. Dessau is sixty miles southwest of the outskirts of Berlin.

Elbe Crossings Increase

Several crossings on the Elbe now have been made, but Supreme Headquarters reported no deep penetration into Brandenburg from any of them. It is probable that Lieut. Gen. William H. Simpson is concentrating his Ninth Army armored forces beyond the river before his final bound for Berlin.

Rumors of deep advances on the road to Berlin abound here. One radio report puts the American troops nineteen miles from the German capital, but this is highly improbable.

At the same time American forces smashing into the Ruhr pocket have almost bisected that area. To the north British and Canadian troops, assaulting the Germans' Netherlands fortress, have virtually cleared Arnhem and almost all of the northern Netherlands.

Half way across Europe from Lieut. Gen. George S. Patton's Third Army came the Atlantic front flared into action. Eighth Air Force Flying Fortresses and Liberators hammered German fortifications at the mouth of the Gironde River and French troops launched a number of attacks in this area and around Bordeaux.

Positions of the Ninth and First

Continued on Page 8, Column 2

199,480 Casualties For Allies in Italy

By Wireless to The New York Times.

ROME, April 4 (Delayed)—Since last May 11, when the Allied push to Rome started, overall Allied losses have been 199,-480, as against the German total of 245,000, it was learned today.

Although the break-down into killed, wounded and missing is not available, it is an interesting testimonial to the shared burden of the campaign to record that United States losses were 82,599 and British—including Empire forces—81,707. Other nations contributed as follows: France, 23,334; Poland, 9,214; Brazil, 2,112, and Italy, 354, for the total of 199,480.

RED ARMY DRIVING ON BERLIN, FOE SAYS

Germans Report Giving Way Near Kuestrin — Russians Race On in Danube Valley

By The Associated Press.

LONDON, Sunday, April 15.—The Germans said last night that massed Russian Army forces yesterday had broken into powerful fortifications thirty miles east of Berlin in a "preparatory" offensive that already had developed into a big armored battle on the Imperiled German capital's approaches.

Scores of tanks, Berlin reported, were locked in preliminary sparring, indicating that the last grand-scale, long-planned Red Army offensive aimed at engulfing Berlin, linking with the Americans and ending the war in Europe, had opened.

There was no confirmation from Moscow, but dispatches reported a zero-hour atmosphere in the Soviet capital.

With captured Vienna behind them, Russian armies in the south wheeled toward Hitler's mountain lair at Berchtesgaden, drove within sixty-three miles of the Austrian city of Linz and in Czechoslovakia battered within twenty-nine miles southeast of the war production city of Brünn [Brno], Moscow disclosed.

Meanwhile, Marshal Tito's Yugoslav Army broke through German lines in northeastern Yugoslavia, forced three major rivers and in a thirty-two-mile sweep westward stormed six strong points and a dozen smaller places, the Yugoslav communiqué announced.

The action was fought in the plains of the Srem lowland between the confluence of the Drava and Danube Rivers and north of the Sava River, where the Germans held fortified positions northwest of Belgrade.

In their dash westward, the Yugoslavs captured Vukovar and Borovo on the Danube, Valpovo on the Drava, and the rail junctions of Osijek and Vukovci.

[A second communiqué, reported by the Federal Communications Commission, said that the island of Rab in the Adriatic was "rather the draft of an

Continued on Page 6, Column 4

TRUMAN SORROWS

He Attends Services at White House and Then Goes On to Hyde Park

HOLDS CONFERENCES

President Has Luncheon Talk With Hopkins and Meets Byrnes Again

By BERTRAM D. HULEN
Special to The New York Times.

WASHINGTON, April 14—President Truman was the chief official mourner at the funeral services for Franklin D. Roosevelt in the East Room of the White House today. The President remained quietly in his office in the executive wing of the White House during the afternoon, being joined there at 3:30 o'clock by Mrs. Truman and their daughter, Miss Mary Margaret Truman.

Shortly before 4 o'clock they went to the Executive Mansion for the services, accompanied by the President's military aide, Colonel Harry Vaughan, who was his aide when he was Vice President.

Mr. Truman returned to the executive offices for a short time after the funeral and then, with his wife and daughter, went to their apartment on Connecticut Avenue.

The President later went to the funeral train for the trip to Hyde Park and the burial tomorrow morning.

The Truman family will move on Monday into Blair House, the official Government residence near the White House and across Pennsylvania Avenue from the State Department, and reside there until Mrs. Roosevelt completes her personal arrangements and moves away from the mansion which has been her home for twelve years.

Wallace in Funeral Cortege

Although the day was officially set aside as one of mourning and Government departments and agencies were closed during the afternoon, the pressure of official duties was such that President Truman engaged in a series of conferences during the morning and then worked in the early afternoon on the address he will deliver before the joint session of Congress on Monday at 1 o'clock.

Going to the executive offices early this morning, the President was joined there by James F. Byrnes of South Carolina, the former Director of War Mobilization and Reconversion, and by Secretary of Commerce Henry A. Wallace. Both accompanied him to Union Station and in the funeral procession when the body of the President was borne on a caisson to the White House.

Later in the morning, Mr. Truman conferred alone with Mr. Byrnes, as he had yesterday. The former Senator and envoy to Turkey, the former official Justice of the United States Supreme

Continued on Page 2, Column 7

Yanks Seize von Papen in the Ruhr; Figured in Scheming of Two Wars

By The Associated Press.

PARIS, April 14—Franz von Papen, the gray fox of German diplomacy and a notorious international figure since he was expelled from the United States in 1915, was captured in the Ruhr pocket by the United States Ninth Army on April 10, Allied headquarters disclosed tonight.

The 65-year-old former Chancellor of the German Republic, Vice-Chancellor under Adolf Hitler and later Ambassador to Austria and Turkey was seized at a small hunting lodge near Stockhausen, twenty-five miles southeast of Hamm. Taken with him were his son, Capt. Friedrich Franz, and his son-in-law, Baron Max von Stockhausen.

The capture was made by Lieut. Thomas McKinley of Lexington, Ky., and seven soldiers. They were Sgt. Stephen A. Witchko of McKees Rocks, Pa.; Hugh G. Fred-

erick, Adamsville, Ala.; Herbert A. Stephen, Chicago, and Waldo L. Elder, Burlington, Iowa, and Pfc. Jesse H. Leonard, Lexington, N. C.; Denver M. Terrill, Bunker, Mo., and Anthony L. Giulisti, Chicago.

Von Papen, famed for landing on his feet in many a desperate situation, including the Nazi purge of 1934, in which he was marked for death, exclaimed on his capture:

"I wish this war were over."

"So do eleven million other guys," replied Sergeant Frederick as he led away the man who has been named in countless unconfirmed rumors as a "would-be peace negotiator.

Elements of the Ninty-fifth Division overran Stockhausen, and a battalion commanded by Lieut. Col. Robert L. A. Ashworth of Butte, Mont., took von Papen on his estate. Von Papen's son was

Continued on Page 8, Column 1

PRESIDENT ROOSEVELT'S BODY IN THE WHITE HOUSE

With representatives of the armed services standing guard, the flag-draped coffin lies in the East Room of the Executive Mansion
Associated Press Wirephoto

WORLD RIGHTS BILL URGED BY BISHOPS

Catholic Welfare Board Says Dumbarton Oaks Plan Is Draft of Alliance of Big Powers

The statement by Catholic Bishops is on Page 7.

WASHINGTON, April 14—The Archbishops and Bishops of the administrative board of the National Catholic Welfare Conference stress the obligation of this country "to safeguard the freedom of all peoples" in the framing of a world organization at the San Francisco Conference, their statement, adopted prior to President Roosevelt's death, being made public today.

The document describes the charter framed at Dumbarton Oaks as "rather the draft of an

Continued on Page 7, Column 4

Millions in City Ignore Rain To Pay Honor to Roosevelt

By ALEXANDER FEINBERG

Five minutes before 4 o'clock yesterday afternoon, the hour when funeral services for Franklin D. Roosevelt were begun in the White House, spattering raindrops slanted through the unwonted darkness in Times Square. They glistened like fresh tears on a woman's cheek. A small, elderly woman standing in a knot of people under the theatre marquee at Broadway and Forty-third Street turned to her woman companion.

"Isn't it ironical?" she said quietly. "It is the rain he liked so much."

Throughout the city millions of persons stood with bared head and many knelt in the rain in an outpouring of mass sorrow and reverence seldom witnessed in American life. They remembered him on his frequent trips to the city while he was their Governor and their President, riding in an open car, smiling in the rain, as so often happened.

By 4 o'clock a steady shower

Continued on Page 6, Column 4

NATIONS SET ASIDE DAYS OF MOURNING

Courts Don Crape in Memory of Roosevelt in a Tribute Without Precedent

One to three days of national mourning were decreed yesterday in a host of foreign countries while courts donned crape and ordinary citizens prayed in an unprecedented tribute to Franklin D. Roosevelt. American forces overseas also held special services everywhere.

Foreign newspapers and broadcasts were filled with tributes to the late President and descriptions introducing his successor, Harry S. Truman, to their countries.

In Britain, where many newspapers devoted approximately three pages of their four-page wartime editions to Roosevelt and Truman, the court went into mourning and the King and Queen called off a scheduled week-end trip to attend a Glasgow event.

The British public will honor

Continued on Page 2, Column 7

Molotoff Coming to Conference; Stalin Acts at Truman's Request

By JAMES B. RESTON
Special to The New York Times.

WASHINGTON, April 14—The be welcomed as an expression of White House announced tonight that, in response to a request by President Truman, Marshal Joseph V. Stalin, Premier of Soviet Russia, had agreed to send Vyacheslaff M. Molotoff, Foreign Commissar and Vice Premier, to the United Nations Security Conference in San Francisco.

As a direct and immediate result of this intervention by the President and despite the fact that the Russians had previously refused a similar request, the White House was able to announce that "today the President was advised by Marshal Stalin that Foreign Secretary Molotoff would attend the San Francisco conference."

It was clear from the announcement that the death of President Roosevelt and the natural desire of the Russian Government to explore the intentions of the new

Continued on Page 7, Column 6

RITES AT CAPITAL

War Leader's Fearless Faith Called by Bishop Dun a Bequest to All

TWO HYMNS SUNG

Voices of Notables Join in the Favorite Songs of the Late President

By FRANK KLUCKHOHN
Special to The New York Times.

WASHINGTON, April 14—In the flower-walled East Room of the White House simple funeral rites were held this afternoon for Franklin D. Roosevelt, thirty-first President of the United States and wartime leader.

President Truman, Anthony Eden, who flew here from London, and other distinguished officials of this and foreign Governments attended, with members of the family and friends, a service which was in marked contrast to the public demonstration that marked the arrival of the funeral train in Washington this morning.

The Rt. Rev. Angus Dun, Bishop of the Episcopal Diocese of Washington, officiated in a service before the flag-draped coffin which lasted only twenty-five minutes but which was impressive because of its lack of pomp and eulogies.

Roosevelt's Words Repeated

It consisted of two of the late President's favorite hymns, reading of psalms and lessons from the scriptures and a final statement by the Bishop that Mr. Roosevelt's first words on entering the White House, "the only thing we have to fear is fear itself," should lead the American people to go forward "without fear of the future, without fear of our own Allies or friends and without fear of our own insufficiencies."

A special train with President Truman and other dignitaries aboard left here at 11 o'clock tonight for Hyde Park, where a burial service will be held tomorrow morning at 10 o'clock on the Roosevelt estate.

Though the body of Mr. Roosevelt did not lie in state, as did that of Abraham Lincoln, who also met death at a critical moment of the nation's history, an estimated 500,-000 men, women and children turned out this morning to watch the coffin borne with military honors through the streets of the capital.

Solemn Passage of Cortege

As early as 8 o'clock spectators began taking up positions. By the time the cortège began moving down Pennsylvania Avenue from the Union Station, solemn throngs had gathered not only along the route but also deep into side streets. Many persons leaned out of windows and lined the roofs of buildings to pay a final tribute as the black, flag-draped caisson, drawn by six white horses, passed by in the midst of an impressive cavalcade.

As the procession, stretching for a mile, passed slowly along the route from the station, where members of the family and ranking officials and diplomats had met the train, two bands, one Marine and one naval, played solemn music.

First in line came armored troops in carriers, then trucks bearing infantry and a Marine band. A battalion of midshipmen from Annapolis came next, followed by the Navy band, a detachment of Marines, Wacs, Women Marines, Waves and Spars.

They moved in perfect unison before the caisson, while the huge crowds stood silent and immovable within the cordons of veteran Marines, soldiers and sailors who lined the entire route.

Behind the coffin came black limousines bearing the family, Cabinet officers, Army and Navy leaders and diplomats.

Overhead a group of Army Liberators, flying in formation, added to the impressiveness of the public demonstration.

The progress of the cortège was

Continued on Page 3, Column 2

500,000 IN CAPITAL VIEW FINAL MARCH

Processional From Union Station for White House Funeral Holds Throng Silent

By WILLIAM S. WHITE
Special to The New York Times.

WASHINGTON, April 14—Along the route that seemed heavy with a still and severely controlled grief, and which were silent but for the somber intermittent hymns of the military bands and the soft footfalls of marching service men and women, the body of Franklin D. Roosevelt was carried today upon a black caisson of honor back to the White House for the official farewell of the United States and of all the friendly world.

Among the most faithful of the many, many thousands who kept watch upon this last return of the late President to Washington were the thousands of men and women who had stood from early morning in Lafayette Park, just across the street from the old mansion, peering sadly at the doors behind which lay the nation's casualty.

And, at 4:25 o'clock, when the large, black limousines rolled away from the White House portico signal that the funeral services had ended, these thousands still were in their silent groups.

They had elected to stand all day at the point where the sad procession was ended, while many of these their number—500,000, by Secret Service estimate—were ranged in anxious sorrow from

Continued on Page 3, Column 5

War News Summarized

SUNDAY, APRIL 15, 1945

The grief-stricken nation's capital said farewell to Franklin Delano Roosevelt with solemn grandeur. A hushed throng of 500,000 paid its last tribute to the war President as the mile-long funeral cortege moved from Union Station, where the body of the nation's thirty-first Chief Executive arrived at 10 A. M. down Pennsylvania Avenue to the White House.

In the East Room of the White House a simple service was held at 4 P. M., while millions throughout the country and the world bowed in silence. President Truman and Britain's Foreign Secretary, Anthony Eden, headed the group of dignitaries and members of the family who witnessed the twenty-five-minute ceremony. Bishop Angus Dun, who officiated, held out as a guide to his fellow-countrymen Mr. Roosevelt's first statement on entering the White House: "The only thing we have to fear is fear itself." [1:8.]

Allied armies smashed ahead and the splitting of the Reich appeared near. American forces rolling across Germany's waist for a junction with the Red Army in the center of the German armies facing the Russians east of Dresden. At last reports they were about seventy-eight miles west of the Soviet lines at the closest point. To the north, tanks and infantry moved to the Elbe on a 150-mile

front after gains of five to thirty miles, while other troops, already across that last water barrier on the way to the German capital, punched closer to Berlin. [1:1; map:P. 8.]

The Red Army penetrated strong German fortifications thirty miles east of Berlin in a "preparatory" offensive directed at the Reich's capital, according to Nazi reports. [1:2.]

About 750 RAF heavy bombers hit Potsdam, German Army center west of Berlin, and the Reich capital itself in an evident softening-up attack ahead of the advancing Americans. Early in the day 1,150 unescorted United States "heavies" bombed the Nazis in the Gironde pocket of southwestern France, prior to a land attack by French troops against the foe barring our use of the port of Bordeaux. [8:1.]

Franz von Papen, former German Chancellor and envoy to Turkey, was captured by American troops in the Ruhr pocket. [1:2-3.]

In Italy, the Eighth Army stormed across the Sillaro River, the third water obstacle cleared in its five-day-old offensive. [9:8, with map.]

Tokyo's "arsenal area" was still ablaze hours after hundreds of American Superfortresses had dropped bombs on the Japanese capital. [10:8.] On Okinawa the marines moved to within twelve miles of the northern tip of the island. [10:1.]

▲ THE NEW YORK TIMES, SUNDAY APRIL 15, 1945

The paper is dominated by an image of the coffin of Franklin D. Roosevelt, who had died of a cerebral hemorrhage three days earlier, lying in state in the White House. Roosevelt, whose domestic policies had made him deeply divisive, had nevertheless steered his country to the verge of victory, as the news from Germany makes clear. He was deeply mourned by the U.S. public.

▲ NEWS CHRONICLE, THURSDAY APRIL 19, 1945

The *Chronicle* carries images from Belsen, a camp liberated by the British a few days earlier, that it says confirms rumors of Nazi atrocities. There is no reference to the Final Solution, however: the full scale of Nazi campaign against the Jews and others only became apparent after the defeat of Germany. Reporters Colin Wills and Richard Crossman also collaborated with Alfred Hitchcock to compile an official movie of the camp, to act as evidence of German atrocities, but the movie was never released due to delays in production and the appearance of movies from other camps..

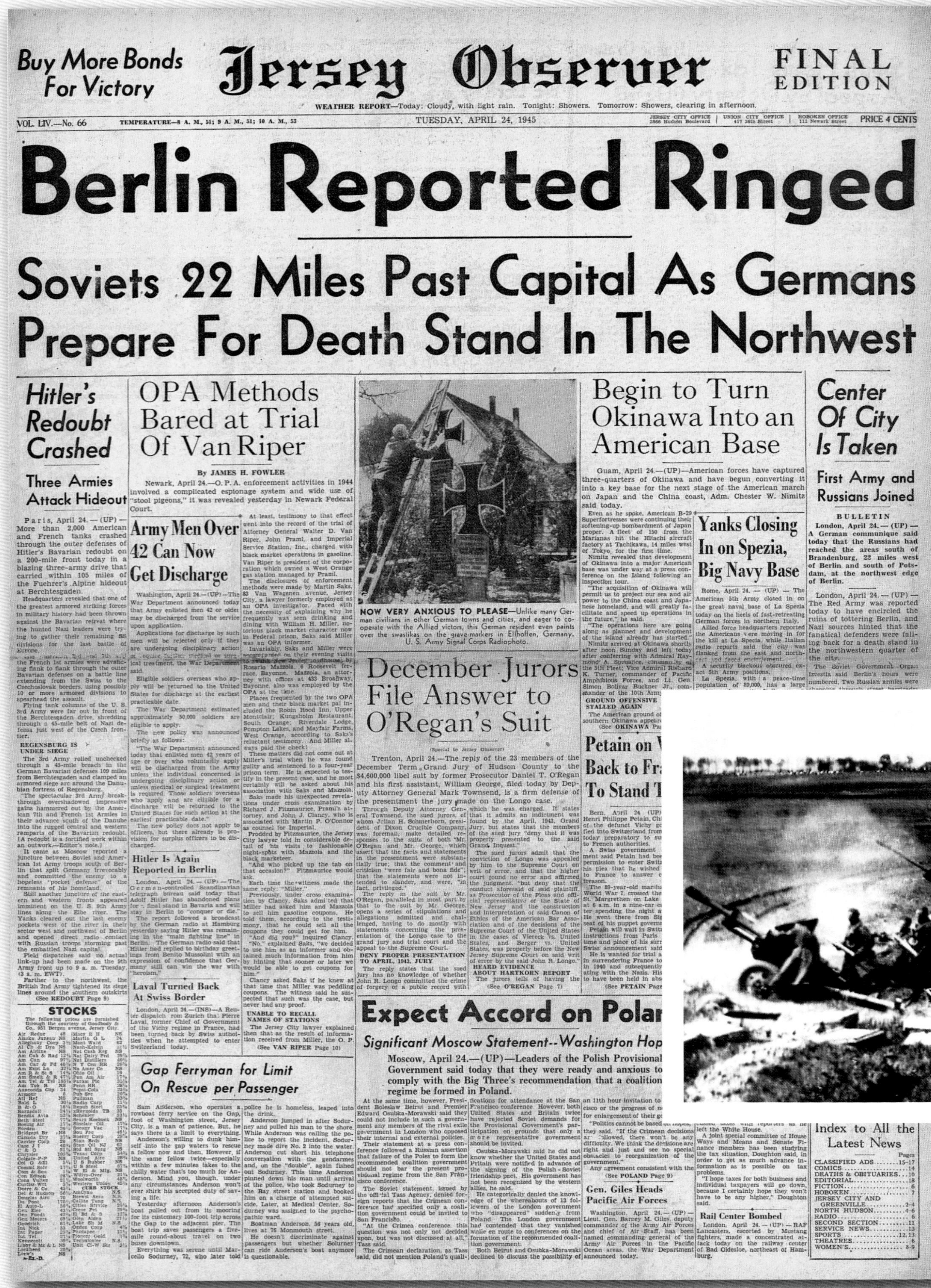

Buy More Bonds For Victory

Jersey Observer

FINAL EDITION

WEATHER REPORT—Today: Cloudy, with light rain. Tonight: Showers. Tomorrow: Showers, clearing in afternoon.

VOL. LIV—No. 66   TEMPERATURE—8 A. M., 51; 9 A. M., 51; 10 A. M., 53   TUESDAY, APRIL 24, 1945   JERSEY CITY OFFICE / UNION CITY OFFICE / HOBOKEN OFFICE   PRICE 4 CENTS

Berlin Reported Ringed

Soviets 22 Miles Past Capital As Germans Prepare For Death Stand In The Northwest

Hitler's Redoubt Crashed — Three Armies Attack Hideout

OPA Methods Bared at Trial Of Van Riper

NOW VERY ANXIOUS TO PLEASE—Unlike many German civilians in other German towns and cities, and eager to cooperate with the Allied victors, this German resident sets paint over the swastikas on the grave-markers in Ellhoffen, Germany. U. S. Army Signal Corps Radiophoto.

Begin to Turn Okinawa Into an American Base

Center Of City Is Taken — First Army and Russians Joined

Yanks Closing In on Spezia, Big Navy Base

December Jurors File Answer to O'Regan's Suit

Petain on Way Back to France To Stand Trial

Expect Accord on Poland

Significant Moscow Statement—Washington Hopeful

Gap Ferryman for Limit On Rescue per Passenger

Gen. Giles Heads Pacific Air Forces

Rail Center Bombed

▼ FOR THE BERLIN ASSAULT the Soviets concentrated a massive force of troops and equipment: 2.5 million soldiers, 41,000 artillery pieces (some of which are shown below), 6,200 tanks and assault guns, 100,000 motor vehicles, and 7,200 aircraft.

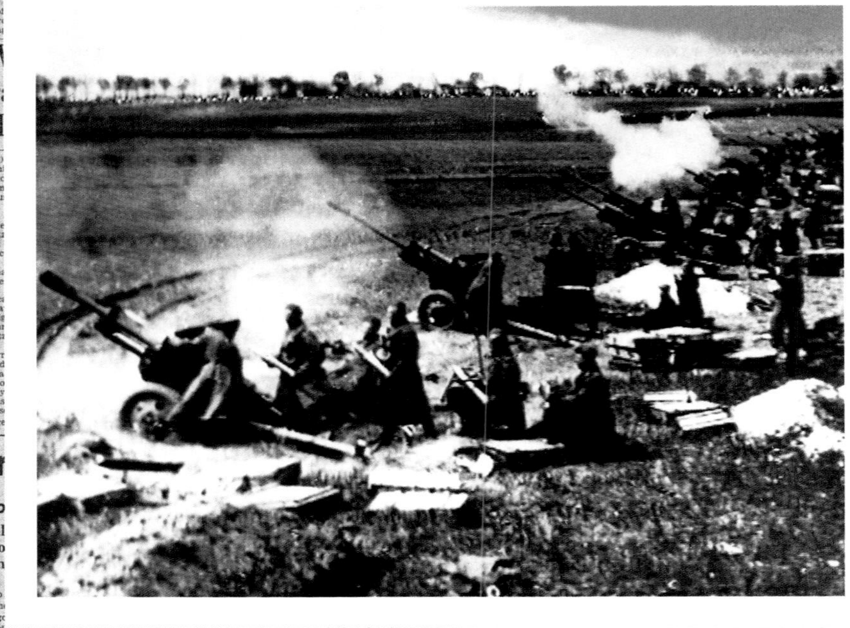

▲ JERSEY OBSERVER, JERSEY CITY, TUESDAY APRIL 24, 1945

The end is in sight as Soviet divisions lay siege to Berlin, and Jersey readers turn back to news from closer to home, including the story of a bizarre rescue on a local ferry. Hitler's decision to return to Berlin underlined the Germans' announced determination to fight to the last. The photograph shows a German civilian eager to paint out swastikas on graves in a cemetery of war dead.

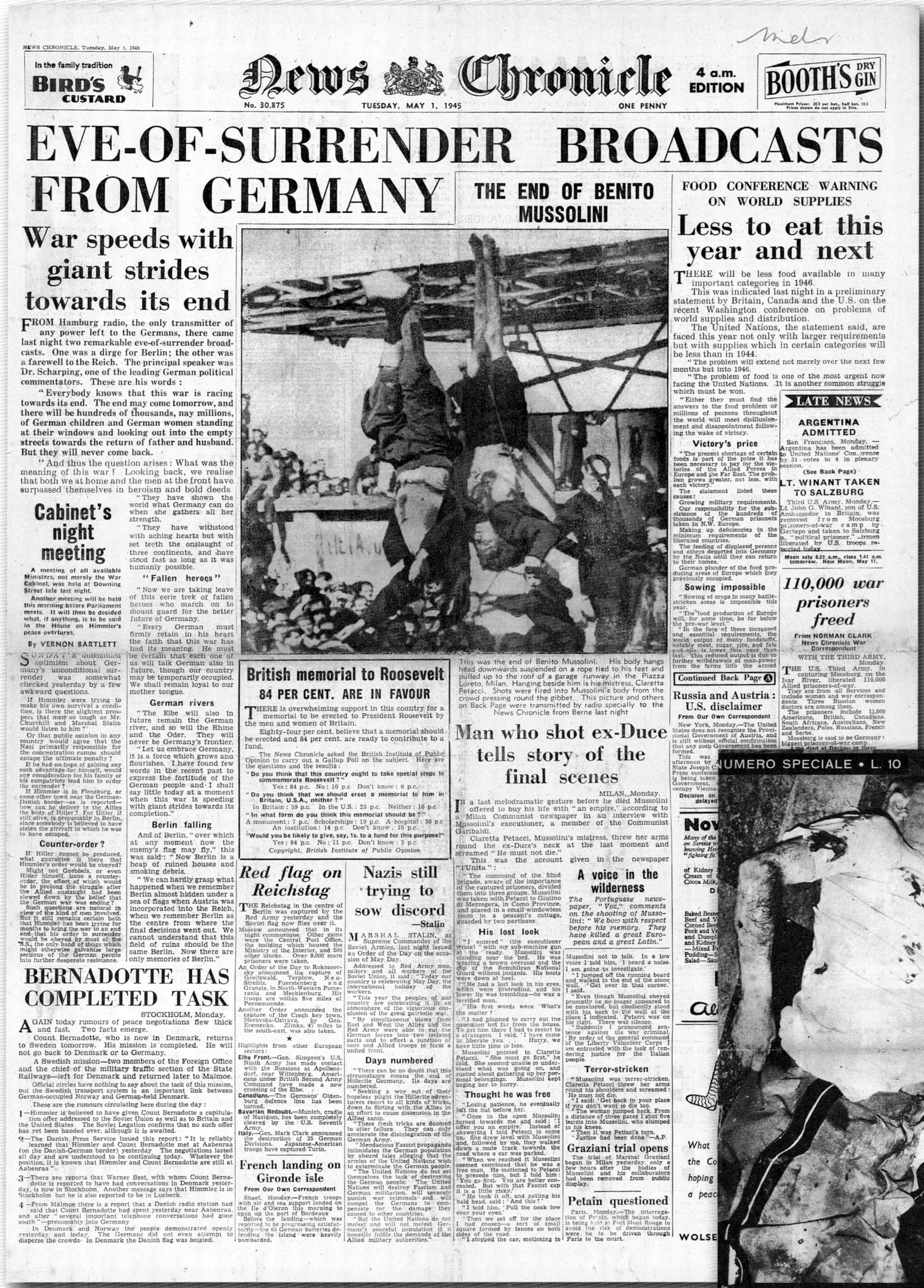

NEWS CHRONICLE, Tuesday, May 1, 1945

In the family tradition
BIRD'S CUSTARD

News Chronicle

4 a.m. EDITION

BOOTH'S DRY GIN

No. 30,875   TUESDAY, MAY 1, 1945   ONE PENNY

Maximum Prices: 25/3 per bot., half bot. 12/3
Prices shown do not apply in Eire.

EVE-OF-SURRENDER BROADCASTS FROM GERMANY

War speeds with giant strides towards its end

FROM Hamburg radio, the only transmitter of any power left to the Germans, there came last night two remarkable eve-of-surrender broadcasts. One was a dirge for Berlin; the other was a farewell to the Reich. The principal speaker was Dr. Scharping, one of the leading German political commentators. These are his words:

"Everybody knows that this war is racing towards its end. The end may come tomorrow, and there will be hundreds of thousands, nay, millions, of German children and German women standing at their windows and looking out into the empty streets towards the return of father and husband. But they will never come back.

"And thus the question arises: What was the meaning of this war! Looking back, we realise that both we at home and the men at the front have surpassed themselves in heroism and bold deeds.

Cabinet's night meeting

A meeting of all available Ministers, not merely the War Cabinet, was held at Downing Street late last night.

Another meeting will be held this morning before Parliament meets. It will then be decided what, if anything, is to be said in the House on Himmler's peace overtures.

By VERNON BARTLETT

SUNDAY'S unbounded optimism about Germany's unconditional surrender was somewhat checked yesterday by a few awkward questions.

If Himmler was trying to make his own survival a condition, is there the slightest prospect that even so tough as Mr. Churchill and Marshal Stalin would listen to him?

Or that public opinion in any country would agree that the Nazi primarily responsible for the concentration camps should escape the ultimate penalty?

If he had no hope of gaining any such advantage for himself, would any consideration for his family or his compatriots lead him to offer the surrender?

If Himmler is in Flensburg, or some other town near the German-Danish border—as is reported—how can he deliver to the Allies the body of Hitler? For Hitler, if still alive, is presumably in Berlin, since somebody is believed to have stolen the aircraft in which he was to have escaped.

Counter-order?

If Hitler cannot be produced, what guarantee is there that Himmler's offer would be obeyed?

Might not Goebbels, or even Hitler himself, issue a counter-order, the effect of which would be to prolong the struggle after the Allied onslaught had been slowed down by the belief that the German war was ending?

Such questions are natural in view of the kind of men involved. But it still remains certain both that Himmler has been trying for months to bring the war to an end and that his order to surrender would be obeyed by the S.S., the only body of thugs which might otherwise continue large sections of the German people into further desperate resistance.

BERNADOTTE HAS COMPLETED TASK

STOCKHOLM, Monday.

AGAIN today rumours of peace negotiations flew thick and fast. Two facts emerge.

Count Bernadotte, who is now in Denmark, returns to Sweden tomorrow. His mission is completed. He will not go back to Denmark or to Germany.

A Swedish mission—two members of the Foreign Office and the chief of the military traffic section of the State Railways—left for Denmark and returned later to Malmoe.

Official circles have nothing to say about the task of this mission, but the Swedish transport system is an important link between German-occupied Norway and German-held Denmark.

These are the rumours circulating here during the day:

1—Himmler is believed to have given Count Bernadotte a capitulation offer addressed to the Soviet Union as well as to Britain and the United States. The Soviet Legation confirms that no such offer has yet been handed over, although it is awaited.

2—The Danish Press Service issued this report: "It is reliably learned that Himmler and Count Bernadotte met at Aabenraa (on the Danish-German border) yesterday. The negotiations lasted all day and are understood to be continuing today. Whatever the position, it is known that Himmler and Count Bernadotte are still at Aabenraa."

3—There are reports that Werner Best, with whom Count Bernadotte is reported to have had conversations in Denmark yesterday, is now in Stockholm. Another message says that Himmler is in Stockholm but he is also reported to be in Luebeck.

4—From Malmoe there is a report that a Danish radio station has said that Count Bernadotte had spent yesterday near Aabenraa, and after "several important telephone conversations had drawn up—presumably his terms."

In Denmark and Norway the people demonstrated openly yesterday and today. The Germans did not even attempt to disperse the crowds. In Denmark the Danish flag was hoisted.

German rivers

"The Elbe will also in future remain the German river, and so will the Rhine and the Oder. They will never be Germany's frontier.

"Let us embrace Germany. It is a force which grows and flourishes. I have found few words in the recent past to express the fortitude of the German people and I shall say little today at a moment when this war is speeding with giant strides towards its completion."

Berlin falling

And of Berlin, "over which not a moment now the enemy's flag may fly," this was said: "Now Berlin is a heap of ruined houses and smoking debris.

"We can hardly grasp what happened when we remember Berlin almost hidden under a sea of flags when Austria was incorporated into the Reich, when we remember Berlin as the centre from where the final decisions went out. We cannot understand that this field of ruins should be the same Berlin. Now there are only memories of Berlin."

THE END OF BENITO MUSSOLINI

This was the end of Benito Mussolini. His body hangs head downwards suspended on a rope tied to his feet and pulled on to the roof of a garage runway in the Piazza Loreto, Milan. Hanging beside him is his mistress, Claretta Petacci. Shots were fired into Mussolini's body from the crowd pressing round the gibbet. This picture and others on Back Page were transmitted by radio specially to the News Chronicle from Berne last night.

British memorial to Roosevelt
84 PER CENT. ARE IN FAVOUR

THERE is overwhelming support in this country for a memorial to be erected to President Roosevelt by the men and women of Britain.

Eighty-four per cent. believe that a memorial should be erected and 84 per cent. are ready to contribute to a fund.

The News Chronicle asked the British Institute of Public Opinion to carry out a Gallup Poll on the subject. Here are the questions and the results:

"Do you think that this country ought to take special steps to commemorate Roosevelt?"
Yes: 84 p.c. No: 10 p.c. Don't know: 6 p.c.

"Do you think that we should erect a memorial to him in Britain, U.S.A., neither?"
In Britain: 50 p.c. In the U.S.: 25 p.c. Neither: 16 p.c.

"In what form do you think this memorial should be?"
A monument: 37 p.c. Scholarships: 19 p.c. A hospital: 50 p.c. An institution: 14 p.c. Don't know: 10 p.c.

"Would you be likely to give, say, 1s. to a fund for this purpose?"
Yes: 84 p.c. No: 11 p.c. Don't know: 5 p.c.

Copyright, British Institute of Public Opinion.

Man who shot ex-Duce tells story of the final scenes

MILAN, Monday.

IN a last melodramatic gesture before he died Mussolini offered to buy his life with "an empire," according to a Milan Communist newspaper last night in an interview with Mussolini's executioner, a member of the Communist Garibaldi.

Claretta Petacci, Mussolini's mistress, threw her arms round the ex-Duce's neck at the last moment and screamed "He must not die."

This was the account given in the newspaper "l'Unita":

"The command of the 52nd brigade, aware of the importance of the captured prisoners, divided them into three groups. Mussolini was taken with Petacci to Giulino di Mezzegara, in Como Province, and placed in a small windowless room in a peasant's cottage, guarded by two partisans.

His lost look

"I entered," the executioner wrote " with my sub-machine gun at the ready. Mussolini was standing near the bed. He was wearing a brown overcoat and the cap of the Republican National Guard without insignia. His boots were down at heel.

"He had a lost look in his eyes, which were stretching, and his lower lip was trembling—he was a terrified man.

"His first words were 'What's the matter?'

"'I had planned to carry out the execution but far from the house. To get him there I had to resort to a stratagem. I said, 'I have come to liberate you ... Hurry, we have little time to lose.

Mussolini pointed to Claretta Petacci. "She must go first," he said. She seemed unable to understand what was going on, and rushed about gathering up her personal belongings. I started urging her to hurry.

Thought he was free

"Losing patience, he eventually left the hut before her.

"Once in the open Mussolini turned towards me and said: 'I offer you an empire.' Instead of answering I told Petacci to come on. She drew level with Mussolini and, followed by me, they walked down a mule track towards the road where a car was parked.

"When we reached it Mussolini seemed convinced that he was a free man. He motioned to Petacci to precede him, but I told him: 'You go first. You are better protected.' But with that Fascist cap in his knees—

"He took it off, and putting his bald head, said: 'And this?'

"I told him, 'Pull the cap low over your eyes.'

"Then we set off for the place I had chosen—a sort of small square formed by fences on both sides of the road.

"I stopped the car, motioning to

Terror-stricken

"Mussolini was terror-stricken. Claretta Petacci threw her arms round his shoulders and screamed 'He must not die.'

"I said: 'Get back in your place if you don't want to die too.' The woman jumped back. From a distance of three paces I shot five bursts into Mussolini, who slumped to his knees.

"Then it was Petacci's turn.

"Justice had been done."

Graziani trial opens

The trial of Marshal Graziani began in Milan yesterday, only a few hours after the bodies of Mussolini and his collaborators had been removed from public display.

Petain questioned

PARIS, Monday.—The interrogation of Petain, which began today, is being held at Fort Mont Rouge to avoid the risk of demonstrations were he to be driven through Paris to the court.

Red flag on Reichstag

THE Reichstag in the centre of Berlin was captured by the Red Army yesterday and the Soviet flag now flies over it.

Moscow announced that in its night communique. Other gains were the Central Post Office, the building which housed the Ministry of the Interior, and 200 other blocks. Over 9,000 more prisoners were taken.

An Order of the Day to Rokossovsky announced the capture of Greifswald, Terplow, Reck-Stralin, Fuerstenberg and Granzie, in North-Western Pomerania and Mecklenburg. His troops are within five miles of Prenemuende.

Another Order announced the capture of the Czech key town, Moravska-Ostrava, by Gen. Eremenko, Zilinka, 47 miles to the south-east, was also taken.

Highlights from other European sectors:

Elbe Front—Gen. Simpson's Ninth Army has made contact with the Russians at Apollensdorf, near Wittenberg, Americans under British Second Army Command have made a new crossing of the Elbe.

Canadians—The Germans' Oldenburg defence line has been turned.

Bavarian Redoubt—Munich, cradle of Nazidom, has been completely cleared by the U.S. Seventh Army.

Italy—Gen. Mark Clark announced the destruction of 29 German Divisions. Japanese-American troops have captured Turin.

Nazis still trying to sow discord
—Stalin

MARSHAL STALIN, Supreme Commander of the Soviet Armies, last night issued an Order of the Day on the occasion of May Day.

Addressed to Red Army men, sailors and all workers of the Soviet Union, it said: "Today our country is celebrating May Day, the international holiday of the workers.

"This year the peoples of our country are celebrating it in an atmosphere of the victorious conclusion of the great patriotic war.

"By simultaneous blows from East and West the Allies and the Red Army smashed up the German forces into two isolated parts and to effect a junction of ours and Allied troops to form a united front.

Days numbered

"There can be no doubt that this circumstance means the end of Hitlerite Germany. Its days are numbered.

"Seeking a way out of their hopeless plight the Hitlerite adventurers resort to all kinds of tricks, down to flirting with the Allies in an effort to cause dissension in the Allied camp.

"These fresh tricks are doomed to utter failure. They can only accelerate the disintegration of the German Army.

"Mendacious Fascist propaganda intimidates the German population by absurd tales alleging that the armies of the United Nations wish to exterminate the German people.

"The United Nations do not set themselves the task of destroying the German people. The United Nations will destroy Fascism and German militarism, will severely punish war criminals and will compel the Germans to compensate for the damage they caused to other countries.

"But the United Nations do not molest and will not molest Germany's peaceful population if it honestly fulfils the demands of the Allied military authorities."

French landing on Gironde isle
From Our Own Correspondent

Sheaf, Monday.—French troops with air and sea support landed on the Ile d'Oleron this morning to open up the port of Bordeaux.

Before the landing—which was reported by the progressing satisfactorily—the 61 German batteries defending the island were heavily bombarded.

FOOD CONFERENCE WARNING ON WORLD SUPPLIES

Less to eat this year and next

THERE will be less food available in many important categories in 1946.

This was indicated last night in a preliminary statement by Britain, Canada and the U.S. on the recent Washington conference on problems of world supplies and distribution.

The United Nations, the statement said, are faced this year not only with larger requirements but with supplies which in certain categories will be less than in 1944.

"The problem will extend not merely over the next few months but into 1946.

"The problem of food is one of the most urgent now facing the United Nations. It is another common struggle which must be won.

"Either they must find the answers to the food problem or millions of persons throughout the world will meet disillusionment and disappointment following the wake of victory."

The statement listed these causes:

Victory's price

"The present shortage of certain foods is part of the price it has been necessary to pay for the victories of the Allied Forces in Europe and the Far East. The problem grows greater, not less, with each victory.

Growing military requirements.—Our responsibility for the subsistence of the hundreds of thousands of German prisoners taken in N.W. Europe.

Making up deficiencies in the minimum requirements of the liberated countries.

The feeding of displaced persons and others deported into Germany by the Nazis until they can return to their homes.

German plunder of the food produced during areas of Europe which they previously occupied.

Sowing impossible

"Sowing of crops in many battle-stricken areas is impossible this year.

"The food production of Europe will, for some time, be far below the pre-war level.

"In the face of these increased and essential requirements, the world output of many foodstuffs, notably meat, sugar, rice, and fats and oils, is lower this year than last. This reduced output is due to farming withdrawals of man-power from the farms into the armed

Continued Back Page

Russia and Austria: U.S. disclaimer
From Our Own Correspondent

New York, Monday.—The United States does not recognise the Provisional Government of Austria, and is still without official confirmation that any such Government has been formed.

This was the afternoon by the State Department. Press confirmation is being taken at its face value, but the Government, occupy Vienna.

Decision on delayed.

LATE NEWS

ARGENTINA ADMITTED

San Francisco, Monday.—Argentina has been admitted to United Nations' Con erence by 31 votes to 4 in plenary session.

(See Back Page)

LT. WINANT TAKEN TO SALZBURG

Third U.S. Army, Monday.—Lt. John G. Winant, son of the U.S. Ambassador to Britain, was removed from Moosburg prisoners-of-war camp to Gestapo and taken to Salzburg a "political prisoner," airmen reported by U.S. troops reported today.

Moon sets 4.57 a.m., rises 1.41 p.m. tomorrow. New Moon, May 11.

110,000 war prisoners freed

From NORMAN CLARK
News Chronicle War Correspondent

WITH THE THIRD ARMY, Monday.

THE U.S. Third Army, in capturing Moosburg, on the Isar River, liberated 110,000 Allied prisoners-of-war.

They are from all Services and include women and war correspondents. Three Russian women doctors are among them.

The prisoners include 11,000 Americans, British, Canadians, South Africans, Australians, New Zealanders, Poles, Russians, French and Serbs.

Moosburg is said to be Germany's biggest prisoner-of-war camp.

NUMERO SPECIALE • L. 10

CRIMEN

ANNO I - N. 9 - ROMA 4 MAGGIO 1945
SPEDIZIONE IN ABBONAMENTO POSTALE
ESCE IL VENERDÌ - QUATTRO PAGINE - L. 10
PREZZO DI VENDITA FUORI ROMA L. 10

"IL MALEDETTO SANGUE DEI TRADITORI" (Mussolini - discorso al "Lirico" di Milano, 16 dicembre 1944)

▼ ON APRIL 28, 1945, fascist dictator Benito Mussolini and his mistress Claretta Petacci were executed by communist partisans. Their bodies were then hung up in Milan's Piazzale Loreto. Below is how the episode was recorded in an Italian publication.

▲ NEWS CHRONICLE, NEW YORK, TUESDAY MAY 1, 1945

New York learns of the imminent end of the war in Europe, and prints a graphic photograph of the grisly fate that befell Italian dictator Benito Mussolini and his mistress, Claretta Petacci.

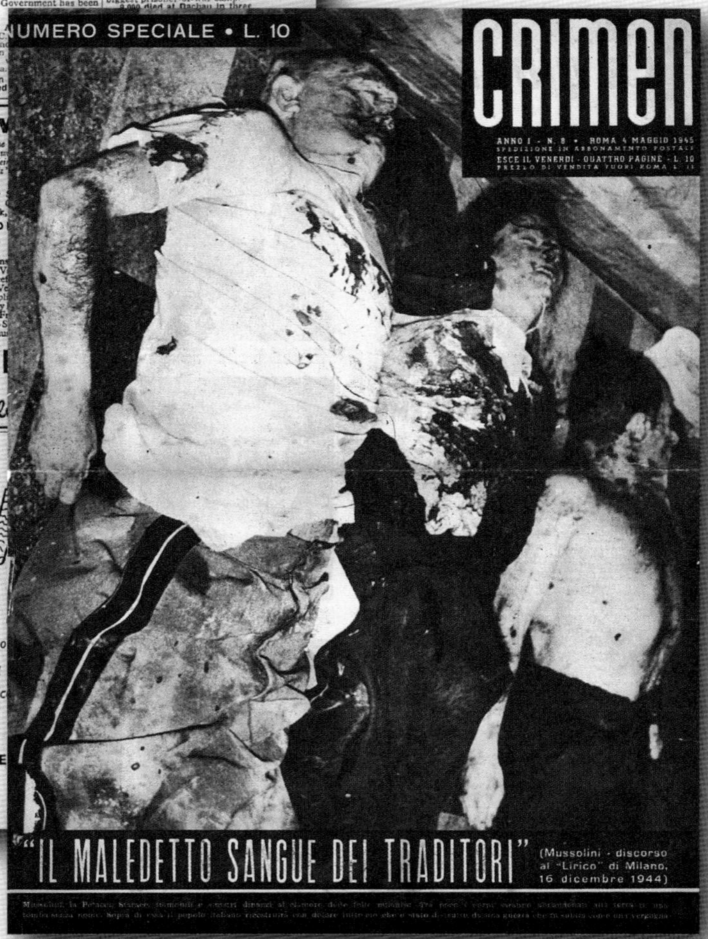

Death of Hitler

APRIL 29, 1945

O N APRIL 16, 1945, ADOLF HITLER IS-SUED HIS ORDER OF THE DAY TO THE GERMAN PEOPLE PRIOR TO THE BAT-TLE OF BERLIN: "FOR THE LAST TIME OUR DEADLY ENEMIES, THE JEWISH Bolsheviks, have launched their massive forces to the attack. Their aim is to reduce Germany to ruins and to exterminate our people. Many of you soldiers in the East already know the fate which threatens, above all, German women, girls, and children. While the old men and children will be murdered, the women and girls will be reduced to barrack-room whores. The remainder will be marched off to Siberia. Above all, be on your guard against the few treacherous officers and soldiers who, in order to preserve their piti-ful lives, fight against us in Russian pay, perhaps even wearing German uniform. Anyone ordering you to re-treat will, unless you know him well personally, be im-mediately arrested and, if necessary, killed on the spot, no matter what rank he may hold. If every soldier on the Eastern Front does his duty in the days and weeks which lie ahead, the last assault of Asia will crumple, just as the invasion by our ene-mies in the West will finally fail, in spite of everything."

THE RED ARMY CLOSES IN ON BERLIN

By the end of the month, the Soviets had fought their way into the city and were close to final victory. On April 29, Hitler or-dered his troops to fight to the last man and bullet. The Führer then dictated his last po-litical testament, in which he stated: "I die with a joy-ful heart in the awareness of the immeasurable deeds and achievements of our soldiers at the front, of our women at home, and achievements of our peas-ants and workers, and the contribution, unique in history, of our youth, which bears my name." Shortly afterward, he put a pistol to his head and pulled the trigger. His new wife, Eva Braun, also com-mitted suicide.

▲ ONE OF THE LAST PHOTOGRAPHS taken of Hitler (on the right) reveals a gaunt, broken figure amidst the ruins of the Reich that he promised would last a thousand years.

The Daily Telegraph
and Morning Post

LONDON LATE EDTN.

No. 28,042   LONDON, WEDNESDAY, MAY 2, 1945   Printed in LONDON and MANCHESTER   PRICE 1½d.

GERMANS ANNOUNCE HITLER'S DEATH

DOENITZ APPOINTED NEW FUEHRER

HIMMLER THROWN OVER: APPEAL TO FIGHT ON

ATTEMPT TO DIVIDE ALLIES: "BOLSHEVISM THE ENEMY"

THE DEATH OF HITLER WAS ANNOUNCED OVER THE GERMAN RADIO SHORTLY BEFORE 10.30 LAST NIGHT. IT SAID THAT IT TOOK PLACE AT HIS COMMAND POST IN BERLIN, NOW ALMOST COMPLETELY OCCUPIED BY RUSSIAN TROOPS.

The announcement said: "It is reported from the Fuehrer's H.Q. that our Fuehrer, Adolf Hitler, has fallen this afternoon at his command post in the Reich Chancellery fighting to the last breath against Bolshevism and for Germany. On Monday the Fuehrer appointed Grand Adml. Doenitz [C-in-C. of the German Navy] as his successor. Our new Fuehrer will speak to the German people."

Adml. Doenitz, in his radio statement, said: "German men and women, soldiers of the German Wehrmacht! Our Fuehrer, Adolph Hitler, has fallen. The German people bow in deepest mourning and veneration. He recognised beforehand the terrible danger of Bolshevism and devoted his life fighting it.

"At the end of this, his battle, and of his unswerving, straight path of life, stands his death, as a hero in the capital of the Reich.

"All his life meant service to the German people. His battle against the Bolshevik flood benefited not only Europe but the whole world."

"THIS FATEFUL HOUR"

"The Fuehrer has appointed me as his successor. Fully conscious of the responsibility, I take over the leadership of the German people at this fateful hour.

"It is my first task to save the German people from destruction by the Bolsheviks, and it is only to achieve this that the fight continues.

"As long as the British and Americans hamper us from reaching this end we shall fight and defend ourselves against them as well. The British and Americans do not fight for the interests of their own people, but for the spreading of Bolshevism.

"What the German people have achieved and suffered is unique in history. In the coming times of distress of our people I shall do my utmost to make life bearable for our brave women, men and children.

"To achieve all this I need your help. Trust me. Keep order and discipline in towns and the countryside. Everybody do his duty.

"Only thus shall we be able to alleviate the sufferings which the future will bring to each of us and avoid collapse. If we do all that is in our power to do the Lord will not abandon us."

DOENITZ'S ORDER OF THE DAY

As Supreme Commander, Doenitz issued following Order of the Day:—

"German Wehrmacht, my comrades. The Fuehrer has fallen. He fell faithful to his great idea to save the peoples of Europe from Bolshevism. He staked his life and died the death of a hero. With his passing one of the greatest heroes of German history has passed away.

"In proud reverence and sorrow we lower our flags before him. The Fuehrer has appointed me his successor as Head of the State and Supreme Commander of the German Wehrmacht.

"I assume supreme command of all units of the German Wehrmacht with the determination to continue the struggle against Bolshevism until the fighting troops and the hundreds of thousands of families of the German Eastern territories are rescued from enslavement or extermination.

"Against the British and Americans I shall continue the struggle so far and so long as they hinder me in carrying out the fight against Bolshevism.

"STRUGGLE WITHOUT QUESTION"

"The situation demands from you who have already accomplished such great historical feats and who are now longing for the end of the war further struggle without question.

"I demand discipline and obedience. Chaos and downfall can only be prevented by obedience without reserve to my orders. He who at this moment shirks his duty is a coward and traitor, for he brings death or slavery to the German women and children.

"The oath of allegiance you swore to the Fuehrer now applies to each one of you without further formality to myself, the successor appointed by the Fuehrer.

"German soldiers: do your duty. The life of our people is at stake."

"TWILIGHT OF THE GODS"

The announcement of Hitler's death was presaged by German radio from shortly before 9 p.m. onward.

First, the so-called "Bremen and Hamburg" radio, which transmits from Hamburg, interrupted its transmission shortly before 9 p.m. The announcer asked listeners to stand by for "a Government statement" to be broadcast at 9 p.m.

At 9 p.m. there was no announcement. The only change in the programme was that, at that hour, Hamburg linked up with other transmitters for a concert of Wagner and Weber works.

Then at 9.30, Hamburg interrupted its broadcast with the announcement: "Achtung, Achtung! In a short time the German Rundfunk will broadcast a grave and important announcement to the German people."

(Continued on Page 6, Column 6)

RUSSIANS REACH LAST BERLIN STRONGHOLD

While Moscow last night awaited news of the fall of Berlin Hamburg radio said that nothing had been heard from the Reich capital since the afternoon.

Russian troops had broken through to the vicinity of the Brandenburger Gate, at the western end of the Unter den Linden, said a message received in Moscow—now linked with Berlin by telephone.

This brings the Russians to the edge of the Tiergarten, Berlin's Hyde Park, where, according to German reports, the Nazi leaders, including Hitler, had been directing the last-ditch defence.

Fourteen thousand prisoners were taken in yesterday's fighting, announced last night's Moscow communiqué, and over 100 blocks of buildings captured in the centre of the city.

The district of Charlottenburg, north-west of the city's centre, and Schoeneberg, near the Templehof airfield, to the south, were cleared of the enemy.

South of the city battles continue to rout encircled enemy troops.

Thousands of Katiusha rocket guns are concentrating on the last pocket of resistance in the centre of the city. Night is turned into day by the glow from fires and rockets is reflected on to the streets from the shroud of smoke and dust.

Speaking to Moscow by telephone, Gen. Berzarin, Russian commandant in Berlin, said: "We have set up district commandants. Germans are clearing the streets, collecting abandoned arms and putting houses in order.

"We are using German officers and engineers to put factories into operation again. Several power stations will be started in two or three days. We have opened 20 hospitals for people who suffered from bombing and shelling.

People in some districts are starving. We have opened bakeries and food shops and we are taking steps to bring vegetables from the suburbs."

MUSSOLINI'S SECRET GRAVE
BRAIN TO SURGEONS

MILAN, Tuesday.

The bodies of Mussolini, Clara Petacci, his mistress, and Achille Starace, the Duce's chief lieutenant, were secretly buried in the Maggiore Cemetery in Milan at 6.15 last night. A Roman Catholic chaplain conducted a five-minute service for all three.

The graves are unmarked. Mussolini's body lies in an unpainted pine coffin bearing the number 187, and no other identification. The only witnesses of the burial were the 15 members of the cemetery staff. The position of the graves is being kept secret. Empty graves have been dug to lay a false scent.

The brain of the former Duce was removed for surgeons and criminologists to study.

KING LEOPOLD FREE ANY HOUR
BORDER REPORT

VADUZ, Liechtenstein, Tuesday.

King Leopold is expected to arrive in Liechtenstein hourly, according to officials in Vaduz, the capital.

Recent reports from Brussels have said that, following negotiations between the Germans and the International Red Cross, the Germans had decided to release the King. It has been said that his wife and his four children were with him in Germany.

LAVAL NOW NEAR CAPTURE
From Our Own Correspondent

ZURICH, Tuesday.

Laval, with the two former Vichy Ministers, Deat and Luchaire, are now at Hoechst, only a few yards from the Swiss frontier at St. Margrethen. It is expected that, unable to get away, they will be arrested by the advancing French troops.

ENVOY'S U.S. TALK

Mr. Bonnesen, the Swedish Minister, recently called on Mr. Grew, United States Acting Secretary of State, said Reuter. A Swedish Legation spokesman said the call was "purely routine business, and in no way connected with the negotiations for Germany's surrender."

Adolf Hitler, whose death was announced by German radio last night. House painter, corporal, demagogue, dictator. A typical pose. Other pictures on Page 5.

COUNT BERNADOTTE SAW HIMMLER 11 DAYS AGO
From W. E. MUNDY, Daily Telegraph Special Correspondent

STOCKHOLM, Tuesday.

Count Folke Bernadotte, who last week transmitted Himmler's offer to unconditional surrender to the Western Allies only, and who returned to Stockholm yesterday after a second visit to Denmark, said to-night:

"The last time I met Himmler was 10 days ago [April 21] in Luebeck [the German Baltic port now threatened by the British Second Army]. I have not seen Himmler during my last visit to Germany and Denmark."

A Swedish Foreign Office spokesman said late to-night the Count carried no reply from Himmler.

Two Swedish Foreign Office officials, M. Eric von Post and M. Sverker Astrom, accompanied by Maj. Carl von Horn, transport and communications expert of the Swedish General Staff, travelled to Copenhagen yesterday morning.

Swedish diplomats negotiated throughout yesterday in Copenhagen with Werner Best, Reich Commissar in Denmark, and other unnamed Nazi representatives, for a bloodless German capitulation in Denmark. Surrender in Norway was also discussed, according to authoritative Swedish circles here to-day.

Count Bernadotte paved the way for the arrival of the Swedish officials in Copenhagen by securing German authorisation for talks to begin. He then handed over the negotiations to the representatives of the Swedish Foreign Office.

It is stated here to-day that Count Bernadotte's task regarding a German capitulation had now been completed and the Swedish diplomats had taken over.

Count Bernadotte, after spending Sunday at a castle at Babernaa, 12 miles north of the German frontier, returned to Copenhagen late in the evening and stayed at the Hotel d'Angleterre.

Yesterday he visited the Swedish Legation in Copenhagen and the Danish Red Cross headquarters. He also called at the royal palace at Amalienborg, where he was the guest of King Christian of Denmark at dinner.

DANES EXPECTANT

Large crowds gathered in Copenhagen streets throughout yesterday. The atmosphere in the capital was tense as rumours spread through the city.

German cyclist units are patrolling the streets as usual, and German vigilance has not been relaxed.

Information from Danish underground sources is that the German forces in Denmark total about 110,000 men, of whom 17,000 are air force and 25,000 naval personnel. Both these groups had been drafted into the country to act as ground troops.

The German troops are stated to be second and third class. Included in the total are about 10,000 Hungarians, Austrians, and Ukrainians, the latter from the forces of the Russian renegade Gen. Vlassof.

It is computed that the Germans have about 100 aircraft left in Denmark, but many of them are training planes and stated to be museum pieces.

A Danish police force estimated at 5,000 men in the south of Sweden is ready to return.

BRITISH THREAT TO LUEBECK
ELBE BRIDGEHEADS LINKED UP
From DOUGLAS WILLIAMS, Daily Telegraph Special Correspondent

SHAEF, Tuesday.

The bridgeheads across the Elbe, formed by the American and British forces of the British Second Army, have linked up. The united forces are pushing on towards Hamburg and the Baltic port of Luebeck.

Between the British troops and Luebeck there is now a gap of only 18 miles. This means that the tanks of the 11th Armoured Division have covered nearly half the distance between the Elbe and the port.

The narrow gap represents the only remaining escape route for the Germans in all Denmark. Yet many of the enemy forces are moving towards Denmark rather than into it in retreat before the Russians.

R.A.F. fighters, attacking a German column 35 miles south-east of Luebeck, destroyed over 100 vehicles and damaged twice as many more.

Redoubt Front

In the south the United States Seventh Army cleared Munich, and south-west of the town are pushing beyond Fuessen into the valleys of the Austrian Alps. Other armoured units continue to move towards Innsbruck and the Brenner Pass.

Gen. Eisenhower has issued an Order of the Day congratulating the Seventh Army on the seizure of Munich, "the cradle of the Nazi beast."

The French Army now controls the northern shore of Lake Constance, while eastwards other French columns are thrusting eastwards through Immendstadt to Kempten.

The United States Third Army captured 17,000 prisoners yesterday. Gen. Patton has reached this Czechoslovakian frontier at a point 50 miles south of Pilsen. His tanks made a 25-mile advance to the south to-day to reach the River Inn on the Austria-German frontier in the vicinity of Braunau, Hitler's birthplace.

Atlantic Front

On the Atlantic, the French attack to clear the Ile Deleron in the mouth of the Gironde made good progress. A commando drove landed during the night behind the enemy's lines and seized four strongpoints. Naval operations against the fortress of La Rochelle started yesterday.

GLIDER MEN EAST OF ELBE REPORT
AHEAD OF BRITISH
BY OUR SPECIAL CORRESPONDENT

SHAEF, Tuesday.

An unconfirmed report last night from Hamburg radio said United States airborne troops and transport gliders were landed ahead of the British Second Army east of the Elbe at Bleckede, 27 miles south-east of Hamburg, and Boizenburg.

The Hamburg report said: "In North German Plain and in Mecklenburg the battle has reached a new climax only 40 hours before the British crossing of the Elbe. Yesterday afternoon American airborne troops were landed at Bleckede, east of the Elbe."

Transport gliders landed supplies. These airborne troops are now supporting the Second British Army.

British troops were reported to have cut the Berlin-Hamburg railroad at one point. Paris radio broadcast unconfirmed reports that British tanks had reached the Baltic.

ITALY ADVANCES

In Italy, the Fifth and Eighth Armies overran Asti and, although it is moving strong German resistance north of Lake Garda, pressing on in an attempt to protect the Brenner, the Fifth Army has made fresh gains.

New Zealand troops of the Eighth Army drove east. Last night reached Monfalcone and made contact with Marshal Tito's forces driving west from Trieste. They made a record advance of over 55 miles in 30 hours.

The British Sixth Armoured Division has entered Udine, north of the Gulf of Trieste. Fifth Army forces, advancing along the Gulf of Genoa, occupied Spotorno, Savona and Noli. During the 24 hours to yesterday evening, the Eighth Army was estimated to have taken 10,000 prisoners. North-west of Milan, a special communiqué announced last night.

"Lay Down Your Arms."

A proclamation from Marshal Graziani, Commander of the Ligurian Army, was broadcast from Rome last night, appealing to Germans and Italians of the Ligurian Army to lay down their arms.

PACIFIC NAVAL, AIR BASES
SAN FRANCISCO TALKS
From Our Own Correspondent

WASHINGTON, Tuesday.

A Sub-Committee on the Senate Naval Affairs Committee will go to San Francisco to-morrow. It will discuss post-war Pacific naval and air bases with members of the American delegation.

Announcing this to-day, the chairman of the committee, Senator Walsh, said: "I think members of our committee are generally opposed to the idea of international trusteeship for such bases. I anticipate that they will endeavour to impress this point of view upon the delegation."

Most of his colleagues, he explained, felt that the United States should take full possession of any islands won from Japan that were needed as bases.

The American Navy has opposed the trusteeship proposals, which have been supported by some members of the State Department.

R.A.F. FIGHTERS DESTROYED 6,977
LOST 2,998 PLANES

The Air Ministry last night issued the following statement on the number of enemy aircraft destroyed since the beginning of the war by home-based Commands and R.A.F. losses up to April 28:

Aircraft destroyed—
R.A.F. Bomber Command, 759.
By Fighter Command in defensive and offensive operations, 6,977.
By Coastal Command, 175.

R.A.F. losses—
Bomber Command, 7,597.
Fighter Command, 2,998 (in offensive and defensive operations).
Coastal Command, 434.

COLD MAY DAY

After a sunny start May Day was one of the coldest for years in the Straits of Dover. Showers of rain to-day there were between 45 and early in the afternoon the sky was overcast. The midday temperature was 42 and it was only little higher an hour later.

This Morning's War News

Germany
Germans announce Hitler's death: Doenitz appointed new Fuehrer; Himmler discarded; Appeal to fight on; Attempt to divide Allies; "Bolshevism the enemy." (P1)

VE-Day Plans
To broadcast; official arrangements for celebrations. (Pp 1 & 6)

Austria and Italy
Two armies converge on Brenner Pass; Eighth link with Tito. (P1)

Parliament
Germans know all about camps, says Lord Simon; Mr. Churchill may make statement this week. (P5)

San Francisco
Argentina admitted to talks. (P5)

KING TO BROADCAST ON VE-DAY

ALL CHURCHES TO BE OPEN, BELLS TO RING

FLOODLIGHTING, BONFIRES AND VICTORY PARADES

The cessation of hostilities in Europe will be announced by the Prime Minister over the wireless, the Home Office stated last night. At nine p.m. the same day the King will address his people throughout the world.

In a circular letter to local authorities issued last night the Home Office expressed the Government's views on the form that national celebrations should take.

The letter said that the arrangements might be subject to revision if the end of hostilities took the form of a declaration by the Allied Powers that organised resistance had ceased.

Among suggestions made by the Home Office were the following:—

CHURCHES of all denominations to be open for services and private prayer; church bells will ring throughout the country;

THANKSGIVING DAY will be celebrated on the Sunday following VE-Day. The King will attend a special service to be held in London and will be represented at similar services in Edinburgh, Cardiff and Belfast;

FLOOD LIGHTING may be used except on the coast. Bonfires will be allowed;

ENTERTAINMENTS—Music halls, cinemas and theatres should keep open to usual hours. Dance halls may remain open longer. Applications for extension of hours in licensed premises should be received sympathetically.

The text of the Home Office letter is as follows:

His Majesty's Government have had under consideration the way in which the defeat of the enemy in Europe should be celebrated. They think it would be helpful to local authorities in making local arrangements to have some indication of the Government's views as to the form which should be taken by any celebrations of the unconditional surrender of the enemy.

The end of warfare in Europe will not be the end of the struggle, and there should be no relaxation of the war effort until the war in the Far East has been won. It will, however, be the general desire of the nation to celebrate the victorious end of the European campaigns before turning with renewed energy to the conquest of the Japanese foe.

Accordingly, as already announced, the day on which the cessation of organised resistance is announced will be VE-Day, and the day following will be public holidays.

RADIO ANNOUNCEMENT
Church Services

The news that hostilities in Europe have ceased will be announced by the Prime Minister over the wireless. At time o'clock in the evening of the same day his Majesty the King will speak to his peoples throughout the world.

The general feeling of the nation will, no doubt, be one of thankfulness for victory, and it is expected that
(Continued on P. 6, Col. 2)

TWO ARMIES CONVERGE ON BRENNER

Two Allied forces are converging on the Brenner Pass, Germany's key link with Italy.

Striking south into Austria, Seventh Army troops are within 16 miles of the northern end. Driving north, Allied troops in Italy are less than 50 miles away from the actual Pass.

Control of the Pass will cut the Vorarlberg, the mountainous western tip of Austria, where the Swiss border runs east-west for a short way, from the Austria-German territory to the east.

S.S. LEADER ARRESTED

Gen. Besche, notorious S.S. leader who played a prominent part in the extermination of Russians and Poles in Poland, has been arrested at Buchaslavs, Moscow radio reported. He was recognised by a woman whose husband and children were killed by him before her eyes.

LATE NEWS

GERMANS PACKING IN COPENHAGEN
Copenhagen, Tuesday.—Germans to-night packing huge removal vans in front of Dagmarhus, S.S. headquarters. Documents being burned by the ton. Military trucks roaring along streets and many unarmed Germans to be seen. Throughout day shots and explosions heard in various parts of capital. German local authorities be intends evacuation of city.

GERMANS ALLOW FOOD INTO HOLLAND
Shaef announces agreement with the Germans to permit Allied food into Holland by sea, road and air for starving population.—A.P.

SAN FRANCISCO CHAIRMAN
Gen. Smuts has accepted chairmanship of General Assembly Commission of United Nations Conference.

"We're thanking those fighting lads of ours by keeping our weekly War Savings right up to scratch."

LET'S SAVE AS HARD AS THEY FIGHT

Issued by the National Savings Committee

AUSTRALIA CUTS MEAT RATION
HELPING BRITAIN
From Our Own Correspondent

SYDNEY, Tuesday.

Mr. Chifley, Acting Prime Minister of Australia, to-day announced a new cut in the meat ration, to begin next week. The adult civilian ration will be cut by 12½ per cent. and supplies to cafés by 25 per cent.

"The choice facing Australia is either to cut the present rate of consumption or cut down on exports to Britain. But to reduce supplies to Britain at present would be unthinkable, and every Australian will share that opinion. The Australian Cabinet had no hesitation in reaching its decision."

Mr. Chifley explained that the factors mainly responsible for the cuts were the severity of the drought, which was still causing meat supplies to diminish over a large part of Australia, and a world shortage of meat.

GERMAN-SWISS LINES CUT

All telegraph communications between Germany and Switzerland have been interrupted, an official statement by the Swiss postal authorities said last night.

PREMIER AT PALACE

Mr. Churchill was received in audience by the King at Buckingham Palace yesterday and remained to lunch.

5 Years Ago To-day

Mr. Chamberlain stated that Allied forces had been withdrawn from Southern Norway.

3 Years Ago

President Roosevelt announced Lend-Lease aid for Persia and Iraq.

▲ THE DAILY TELEGRAPH, LONDON, WEDNESDAY MAY 2, 1945

Hitler's death resulted in a wave of euphoria in Britain. At long last, the man who had heaped so much misery on the British people for five long years was no more.

Daily Mail

NO. 15,286   ONE PENNY   ✶✶   FOR KING AND EMPIRE   THURSDAY, MAY 3, 1945

'Only folly can delay general capitulation'—President Truman last night

COLLAPSE: BERLIN, ITALY, AUSTRIA FALL

Million Germans surrender to Alexander's armies

THE Wehrmacht in Europe has collapsed. Berlin has fallen. Nearly 1,000,000 Germans in Northern Italy and Western Austria have surrendered unconditionally to Field-Marshal Alexander. Germany's Southern Redoubt has been torn to ribbons. These were the highlights of the war news last night as Germany tottered to complete defeat.

Surrender of the shattered remnants of Berlin's garrison was announced in an Order of the Day by Marshal Stalin to Marshals Zhukov and Koniev. The end came at three o'clock yesterday afternoon. By nine o'clock 70,000 German prisoners had been counted.

It was left to General Webling, an obscure artillery commander, to give up the keys of Berlin to the Russians after 11 days' fighting. Stalin's Order described Hitler's former capital as "the centre of German aggression and cradle of German imperialism." There was no mention of Hitler, Göring, Goebbels, or any of the old Nazi gang.

Surrender of the German armies in Italy and Western Austria was announced by Mr. Churchill to a cheering House of Commons. President Truman, announcing the news in Washington, said: "Only folly and chaos can now delay the general capitulation of the everywhere-defeated German armies."

In Northern Germany the whole pocket covering the North Sea ports and Denmark is swiftly collapsing. Germans running blindly from the Russians are being swamped. Denmark is cut off. British troops have raced 50 miles across its southern approaches, captured Lübeck, and swept beyond to another Baltic port—Wismar.

Montgomery's British and American forces are storming forward on a 40-miles front to meet Rokossovsky's army. The Russians are less than 26 miles away after seizing Rostock, on the Baltic, and a number of other towns to the south.

'A gallant army'- by Premier

The MPs cheered

By PERCY CATER, Parliamentary Correspondent

NEWS that Mr. Churchill was to make an important announcement flashed round the House of Commons a few minutes before he entered the chamber at 7.21 last night to tell of the surrender of 1,000,000 enemy troops to the Mediterranean Command.

M.P.s hurried in. The public gallery was well filled, but the Premier had to wait six minutes until he could interrupt a debate.

Part of the ritual was that the Serjeant-at-Arms had to march to the table of the House and gave hon. to the Mace, which rests underneath when the House is in Committee.

At 7.22 Mr Churchill rose amid an expectant cheer.

He read the first few factual paragraphs in his statement. Then he folded up the typewritten document, put it away with his other rimmed spectacles, and without any further notes described what had happened.

'Record, I believe'

Terrific cheers greeted his statement of the unconditional surrender to Field-Marshal Alexander of the land, sea and air forces commanded by the German Commander-in-Chief of the South-Western Command and of Army Group C.

"A record, I believe, for the whole of this war," said the Premier.

With more cheers surging every few moments, he paid tribute to "as gallant an army as ever marched" to Field-Marshal Alexander "who had always enjoyed the fullest confidence of the House of Commons "; and to General Mark Clark, "one of the most efficient and daring of American soldiers."

The Prime Minister then paid his tribute to the courage and resolution of Field-Marshal Alexander's forces:

"What has made it particularly difficult and depressing for the army is the tremendous inroad that has been made on it to help forward the great operations elsewhere.

"Thus, in June and July last year, what very nearly amounted to an army was taken from this command in Italy, while only very small corresponding results took place on the enemy side.

"Moreover, this force which attacked was of so many different nations that only some personality of commanding qualities could have held them all woven together.

All nations

"Look over the whole list of these men who fought. Take our own contribution first, which was a much the largest:

" British and British-Indian divisions of the highest quality;

" Poles, who always fought with the greatest loyalty;

" New Zealanders, who have marched all the way from the beginning right up to the very spearpoint of the advance;

" South African Armoured Division.

" There has been a great force from the United States, second in numbers only to our own.

" There have been the Brazilian forces which have made very steady advances, and a Negro division of United States troops which also distinguished itself.

" A Jewish brigade, which we formed a year or so ago, has fought in the front line with courage.

" The Japanese of American birth who entered Turin, and finally the free Italians, who have played their part in clearing their country from the German Fascist yoke."

The Premier also paid a warm tribute to the British and American air forces and to the Royal Navy which supported the land forces.

The mourner

Mr. de Valera, Eire's Prime Minister, accompanied by Mr J. P. Walshe, Secretary to the Department of External Affairs, called on the German Minister in Dublin, Dr. Eduard Hempel, yesterday to express his condolence.

SLEET IN THE STRAIT

Strait of Dover yesterday: Slightly warmer, but sleet in the afternoon. Day temperature 55 degrees; at 10 p.m., 41. Barometer

CIVILIANS IN CHAOS

Roads leading from the Lübeck area towards Denmark are an inferno of destruction, British planes, swooping on the fleeing Germans, have smashed more than 1,000 lorries. For miles the highways are cluttered with burning German transport mingled with frantic civilian refugees.

An hour before announcing the fall of Rostock last night, Marshal Stalin reported that the big German pocket south-east of Berlin has crumbled. The Russians captured more than 120,000 Germans.

In Denmark and Norway collapse is near, although last night the German commanders are still in control of their forces and have declared that they will fight on. Control was apparently lost for a brief while in Denmark — the censorship collapsed, troops left their posts, evacuation began. But by last night the Army was back at its post and the censorship again in force.

In the doomed Southern Redoubt, Patton's tanks are closing on the ruins of Hitler's Berchtesgaden "fortress. Swarming into Austria, other Third Army forces are 16 miles from Linz — about 70 miles from the Russians beyond Vienna.

Many of the military position in Western Holland is obscure. But the Germans are now allowing the Allies to send food to the hungry Dutch by land as well as by air.

They quibble to the end

ITALY, Wednesday Night. SURRENDER of the German armies in Italy came after many secret comings and goings among German and Allied military emissaries. The documents were finally signed in the King's palace at Caserta, near Naples.

The surrender was negotiated on behalf of Field-Marshal Alexander by his Chief of Staff, Lieut.-General W. D. Morgan. It was signed in the presence of a group of Allied officers, including Russians and six members of the Allied Press and Radio, after negotiations lasting several days.

The surrender sets the seal on all the magnificent victories of Alexander's forces — North Africa, El Alamein, across North - Africa, Tunisia, Sicily, Cassino, Anzio, the Gothic Line, and the Po Valley.

It took place in a small room on the second floor of the gigantic Caserta Palace. The Germans entered, dressed in civilian clothes —smartly cut check sports coats, grey-flannels and brown shoes.

General Morgan, red-faced, white-haired, stood grimly at one end of the highly polished table, surrounded by other Allied representatives, glittering with gold braid, and high decorations.

The tall, fat, heavy-jawed German lieutenant-colonel, representing the surrendering Wehrmacht General von Vietinghoff, squinted his bloodshot, pale blue eyes in the glare of camera floodlights.

A little behind him stood a

RANGOON TRAP FOR JAPS

Air drop cuts escape

Japanese troops in Rangoon are caught between two Allied forces following the air and sea landings on Tuesday and early yesterday on both banks of the Rangoon river below the capital.

These forces are striking from the south as the 14th Army drives towards the north.—Reuter.

Gestapo killed Hitler

After War Council

OFFICIAL German circles in Berne say they are convinced Hitler met his death last Thursday during a German Headquarters secret war council between Army and party leaders, say the Daily Mail Zurich correspondent.

Himmler announced at the meeting that he had decided to capitulate and had begun negotiations with the Allies.

When Hitler, lying ill in an adjoining room, heard this he rushed into the meeting shouting he would never agree to surrender.

Himmler's friends took him back to his room. Shortly after Himmler announced the Führer had died from a heart attack, but he had been killed by Himmler's men, and with him, a number of the highest leaders of the Nazi Party.

Lost magic

"The spell is broken. While Hitler lived, most Germans thought, on hoped, that by some magic stroke he might yet save them.

"But now that hope is gone, and Admiral Doenitz will have to face the hard fact, as Himmler did more than ten days ago, when he told Count Bernadotte : ' Germany is finished. All I want to do now is to stop the killing.' "

Himmler prefaced his approach to Britain and the United States through Count Bernadotte in this way : He did not at any time try to make a bargain for his own life. He knew then that the game was up. How much more must he realise this now !

All the evidence reaching London last night indicated that Himmler still controls what is left of the Gestapo, the German Home Army, and the Nazi Party. He is a power still to be reckoned with.

To that extent, Admiral Doenitz is thought to have a free hand, to the title of Führer, or at least consented to his doing so. They also believe that Himmler and Doenitz are working hand-in-glove.

It is noticeable that Admiral Doenitz has reacted in precisely the same way as Himmler in his attitude towards Russia.

United

It can be said that both might be prepared to surrender to the Western Allies, but they do not want to humble themselves to Soviets Russia.

But there is no chance of them escaping this necessity. The three Powers are completely united in their approach to the problems of unconditional surrender.

The biggest surprise yesterday was the replacement by Admiral Doenitz of Joachim von Ribbentrop as Foreign Minister by Count Schwerin von Krosigk.

Nothing is known as to the whereabouts of Ribbentrop. He may be dead, but he is more likely to have fled.

The fact that he has been replaced indicates all too clearly that the Nazi Party is split from top to bottom for the others, the latest news as:

Hitler's death is accepted by the British Government, although the possibility that his end has been faked has not been lost sight of.

Goebbels might be dead, although the last news was that he intended to remain in Berlin to the very end.

Göring, if he is not in the last stages of madness, has been removed to some place in the hope of escaping the advancing armies.

Field-Marshal Keitel's whereabouts is not known, but as Admiral Doenitz has assumed leadership of the Reich, it is thought that he, too, must be dead or ill.

Count Schwerin von Krosigk is an Oxford-educated member of the Junker class who was politically active before Hitler came to power in 1933.

In the dark

"This is a hard life for an old soldier," he complained, but would not comment when told about German concentration camps.

He declined to speculate on when Germany began to lose the war, stating : " I have been too close to see."

Plenty of the good news still to come

By WILSON BROADBENT, Diplomatic Correspondent

IT is thought in London that it will be some days, in spite of yesterday's chaotic events in Germany, before there will be any political developments of first-class importance.

Hitler's death has added to the chaos which now governs Germany. For the time being, therefore, it is expected that Admiral Doenitz will endeavour to exercise some kind of authority in the hope that he can snatch something from the wreck.

It is a hopeless venture on his part, but he is described as a man of formidable character—and not necessarily a fervent Nazi.

"This is not all the good news — we have plenty more to come," said a member of the Government after Mr. Churchill had made his statement in the House of Commons last night.

Ultimately, it is thought that Admiral Doenitz will have to admit failure, for the death of Hitler is calculated to have a profound effect on Germans in all walks of life.

3 Wednesdays

Danes Protest to Britain

From Daily Mail Correspondent

COPENHAGEN, Tuesday. —Denmark yesterday sent to the Edited Kingdom British Government a note of protest against recent British air raids on Danish targets in Copenhagen.

Wednesday, April 3, 1940. The Daily Mail published its last dispatch from Copenhagen (above) on Wednesday, April 10, it recorded the fall of Denmark's capital. It received its first dispatch in five years from Copenhagen.

Nazis in Denmark: We fight on

RADIO CALL TO TROOPS

GENERAL LINDEMANN, German C.-in-C. in Denmark, last night issued a radio order that his troops will fight to the last.

Lindemann's statement, issued at a moment when the British advance to the Baltic has completely isolated his forces, followed widespread reports that the evacuation of Denmark had begun.

Some units apparently did begin to leave their posts, but the Germans regained control, got the soldiers back to battle stations, and re-established their censorship, which had temporarily broken down.

General Böhme, C.-in-C. in Norway, has also declared he will continue to fight. Böhme's naval commander, Admiral Ciliax, is reported to have been dismissed because he supported capitulation.

Before the Germans regained control in Denmark, a Daily Mail Special Correspondent managed to send out the first dispatch to England since April 1940. His cable, sent via Stockholm, is given below.

First Dispatch (In five years) from Copenhagen

From Daily Mail Special Danish Correspondent

COPENHAGEN, Wednesday.

DENMARK's new Prime Minister, Wilhelm Buhl, to-day defied the German troops and Gestapo men in Copenhagen, and went to the residence of King Christian, Amelienborg Castle, for the swearing-in of the new Government.

By this act he restored the functions of his post, in abeyance for three years under German occupation.

"It gesture was made under the very noses of the Germans, to whom he and the King have long seemed anathema.

I understand that King Christian accepted the appointment of a Cabinet of 17, with eight posts going to the old political parties, and eight to the Resistance Movement. Buhl holds the seventeenth

Both the King and the Government agreed not to begin functioning until SHAEF arrives and approves the new Government and its programme.

The important post of Minister of

SPANIARDS ARREST LAVAL

Refused to leave

BARCELONA, Wednesday. PIERRE LAVAL, arch-traitor of France, after fleeing from Germany by air, is under arrest here. He is detained incommunicado in the Montjuich Fortress, held at the disposition of Allies.

He arrived, with six other

HITLER, GOEBBELS, COMMITTED SUICIDE

Russian communiqué says : Dr. Fritsche, Goebbels' lieutenant, taken prisoner in Berlin, testifies Hitler, Goebbels, and Gen. Krebs committed suicide.

French people, at Barcelona's airport this afternoon in a 40 presumably from their part of Germany close to the Swiss frontier.

Immediately the U.S. Ambassador protested to France. France ordered them to leave. He offered them sufficient petrol to take them to the nearest frontier—France— with a further escort to see they did not land anywhere else in Spain.

But, fearing to go back to France, they refused. Thereupon they were arrested.

The Spanish Foreign Ministry announced to-night that will order, under the Laval, M. Bonnard, ex-Vichy Minister of Education, Eugene Bonnard, his son, Paul Marnud, and Maurice Gabolde.

Laval, the announcement said, declared that he would surrender only to a " commission representing the Allied Nations.— A.P.

Why I failed: By von Rundstedt

Allied air power upset plans

From JOHN HALL, Daily Mail Special Correspondent

NEAR INNSBRUCK, Wednesday. FIELD-MARSHAL von Rundstedt, who gave himself up to-day after an American soldier found him sitting by the fire in a cottage, blamed Allied air might for his failure to repel the Normandy invasion.

Allied bombers, he said, not only shattered German supply lines and upset all efforts to move defence forces, but they carried the war right home by hitting his headquarters at Bad-Nauheim.

He complained that this unceasing attack completely his heart trouble.

Rundstedt, after asking for coffee and cognac, said he would like to go back and see his Wife.

"This is a hard life for an old soldier," he complained, but would not comment when told about German concentration camps.

Rundstedt was found last night when Americans reached Bad Tolz. They were told that a high general was living in an annexe to the local hospital.

Lieut. Joseph Hall went to a cottage nearby and knocked. Frau Rundstedt opened the door.

The field-marshal was inside, sitting by the fire in the dark—the electricity supply had been cut off half an hour before.

He put on his best uniform, picked up his baton, and walked into town—to give himself up.

BACK PAGE—Col. EIGHT

Looking for the moon

Sir Edwin Appleton, F.R.S., after giving a scientific address in Manchester last night, said that scientists were trying to radiolocate the moon. When asked why they were doing that, he said that because of the secrecy over radiolocation he could not give a reason.

THE GERMAN SIGNS.—Here is one of the two German agents signing the unconditional surrender document that means the end of enemy resistance in Italy. The scene was Caserta.

Signing the surrender

THE BRITON SIGNS.—Lieut.- General W. D. Morgan, Chief of Staff, A.F.H.Q., is seen here signing the surrender document on behalf of the Allied Mediterranean Command.

BACK PAGE—Col. FIVE

▲ DAILY MAIL, LONDON, THURSDAY MAY 3, 1945

In the West, German soldiers readily gave up to the British and Americans, but on the Eastern Front fighting continued, as the Wehrmacht resisted the Soviets to allow as many civilians as possible to escape to Anglo-American-controlled areas of Germany and Austria.

End of the Reich

MAY 1945

DESPITE THE DEATH OF HITLER, MANY THOUSANDS WOULD DIE IN EUROPE BEFORE THE FIGHTING ENDED. ON MAY 1, 1945, THE SOVIET THIRD SHOCK ARMY CAPTURED THE REICHSTAG, the 5,000 defenders suffering 50 percent losses. In Berlin, General Krebs, Chief of the General Staff, asked the Soviets for surrender terms, but Stalin wanted unconditional surrender and so the fighting went on. However, the Germans were out of ammunition and they began surrendering anyway. Admiral Dönitz, following the death of Hitler, took over as the new German head of state. He ordered stiff resistance in the East, where tens of thousands of German civilians were still desperately trying to escape from the Red Army

BERLIN

On May 2, General Weidling, commander of the Berlin garrison, surrendered to the Soviets. The Battle of Berlin had cost Germany a total of 500,000 killed and captured; Soviet losses were 77,000 killed and 272,000 wounded. Josef Goebbels and his wife Magda committed suicide, but not before killing their six children. General Krebs also killed himself. Four days later, Breslau surrendered to the Soviet Sixth Army, the 40,000-strong garrison having suffered 30,000 killed.

THE FIGHTING GOES ON

Also on May 6, the Soviets launched the Prague Offensive with more than two million Soviet and Polish troops ranged against a weakened Army Group Center. On May 10, German troops in Prague began to surrender. The fighting in and around the city cost the Soviets 10,800 killed and 38,000 wounded. By this time the majority of German troops in Germany had now surrendered, with 150,000 laying down their arms in East Prussia. The Red Army annihilated the last pocket of German Army resistance in Bohemia on May 19.

The bitter war on the Eastern Front was over at last. The guns finally fell silent.

▲ THE SOVIET HAMMER AND SICKLE flies over the Reichstag in the middle of a shell-blasted Berlin in May 1945.

NIGHT EDITION
★★★★★
LATEST MARKET PRICES
SCHOOL NEWS ON PAGE 13

The Sun

LATE NEWS
SCHOOLS — PICTURES
Today partly cloudy; tonight clear; tomorrow
showers at night.
Temperatures—Minimum, 46; Maximum, 58.
Sun rises 5:48 A. M. Sun sets 7:58 P. M.
(Detailed weather report on page 24.)

Copyright, 1945, by The New York Sun, Inc.

VOL. 112—NO. 207.   Entered as Second Class Matter Post Office, New York, N. Y.   NEW YORK, MONDAY, MAY 7, 1945.   FIVE CENTS EVERYWHERE

GERMANY SURRENDERS

Some Sing, Some Pray, Some Weep

City's Reaction to Surrender News Mounts in Intensity as the Day Progresses.

At first New York city took the news of Germany's surrender today with a quiet satisfaction that the long-expected word was official, and then its long pent-up emotions let loose in force with paper, prayer, laughter and tears.

About 200 persons were gathered in Times Square when the official news of the surrender finally registered. Inside of an hour 20,000 celebrants had poured out from office buildings and factories to mill about in confetti, ticker tape and torn up telephone books which floated down in multicolored showers in the morning sunshine.

At 10:10 A. M. all traffic was cut off from the Times Square area and the crowds took over the streets for themselves. Trolley cars made an effort to continue for a while, the motormen clanging their bells fruitlessly against the surging tide, and finally gave up.

While some screamed and sang in uninhibited joy, others knelt quietly, in doorways, in front of the Father Duffy statue.

First Confetti Showers.

Obviously prepared for a long time for today's celebration, the garment district responded at the first announcement at 9:30 with showers of confetti and paper. The Times Square area soon followed suit and it spread throughout the city by 10 A. M., in the factories around Lafayette, down the Wall street canyons, up and down Broadway.

Thousands of office workers in the financial district deserted their desks and staged impromptu demonstrations around Broad and Wall streets. The chimes of Trinity Church, Broadway and Wall street, added their mellow notes to the din of horns and voices and the whistles from all the boats in the harbor float through the area.

The Police Department immedi-

In The Sun Today

School News Appears in the Night Edition.

MARKET IS CALM ON NEWS OF V-E

Business began as usual on the New York Stock Exchange this morning after the news of Germany's surrender. President Schram said the Exchange would have no statement to make in advance of President Truman's proclamation.

Prices generally were, unchanged to small fractions higher. United States Steel opened on 500 shares a quarter of a point higher at 68¾. Bethlehem was down an eighth. American Radiator began on 3,000 shares at an eighth advance. The turnover in shares was only moderate in the first half hour. Cotton opened virtually unchanged.

The Stock Exchange announced that after the presidential proclamation of V-E Day it would observe two minutes of silence. President Schram said:

"The announcement of the complete and final defeat of Germany is the best news that any one living ever heard. It marks the end of tyranny. Our people should kneel and pray in humble tribute to the millions of brave men and women who have given their lives to reach this objective.

"But we must not forget that our country is still at war. A hard task lies ahead. Let us all concentrate now upon consummating the defeat of Japan as thoroughly as our European enemies have been defeated."

Some Were Skeptical.

In Pennsylvania Station today several thousand servicemen and women were unaware for some time that the European war was ended. The radio in the USO lounge was out of order, and when attendants tried to tell them the news, most of them expressed disbelief and remarked: "We've heard that before."

Although the response today was forceful, none of the violence of spirit of the Armistice celebration in 1918 was shown. People seemed to feel in the mood to offer grateful thanks that this much had been accomplished, but that there is still so much to be achieved.

At 11 A. M. a thanksgiving service was held on the 158th street side of the Bronx County Building with pastors of the Catholic, Protestant and Jewish faiths participating. At 5 P. M. a prayer meeting will be held on the steps of Borough Hall in Brooklyn, Borough President John Cashmore has announced.

Dave Boone Says:

Well, the European war is ended. The surrender came in a little Red Schoolhouse with Superman wearing the superdunce cap.

And the three R's in that particular school so far as the Nazis were concerned stood for Regret, Repudiation and Ruin.

The school was full of books, but the Germans were in no mood to burn any.

The news of final victory came in slower than election returns, but when the triumph was finally announced there were no districts missing.

Watch out for moves to stir up trouble between the democracies and the communists in the thousand and one tasks of restoring order, establishing new governments, naming new leaders, and so on.

VICTORIOUS

Gen. Dwight D. Eisenhower.
Associated Press Photo.

VON BOCK SLAIN

With the British Second Army, May 7 (A. P.).—The bullet riddled body of German Field Marshal Fedor von Bock was discovered by British troops yesterday near a roadside north of Hamburg, where he apparently was slain in an Allied strafing raid.

The ex-commander of the Central Army group in the German invasion of Russia in June, 1941, had been dead for about a week.

London Crowds Cheer News Of Long European War's End

German Commander in Prague Declares He Won't Recognize Surrender—Churchill Goes to Buckingham Palace.

London, May 7 (A. P.).—The European war—considered alone, it was the greatest war in history—ended today with the unconditional surrender of Germany. The surrender to the Western Allies and Russia was made at Gen. Eisenhower's headquarters at Reims, France, by Col.-Gen. Gustaf Jodl, Chief of Staff for the German Army.

This was announced officially after German broadcasts had told the German people that their new Fuehrer, Grand Admiral Karl Doenitz, had ordered the capitulation of all fighting forces and called off the U-boat war.

In London joy was tempered only by the realization that the war against Japan remains to be fought out and that many casualties are still ahead.

Late in the day Prime Minister Churchill emerged from his residence at No. 10 Downing Street and drove to Buckingham Palace.

It previously had been an-

Nazis Yield to Allied Big Three At Eisenhower's Headquarters

Reims, France, May 7 (A. P.).—Germany surrendered unconditionally to the western Allies and Russia at 2:41 A. M. French time today. (This was at 8:41 P. M., Eastern war time Sunday.)

The surrender took place at a little red school house which is the headquarters of Gen. Eisenhower.

The surrender which brought the war in Europe to a formal end after five years, eight months and six days was signed for Germany by Col.-Gen. Gustav Jodl. Jodl is the new Chief of Staff of the German Army.

It was signed for the Supreme Allied Command by Lieut.-Gen. Walter Bedell Smith, chief of staff for Gen. Eisenhower. It was also signed by Gen. Ivan Susloparoff for Russia and by Gen. Francois Sevez for France.

Gen. Eisenhower was not present at the signing, but immediately afterward Jodl and his fellow delegate, Gen. Admiral Hans

Continued on Page 2.

▲ THE SUN, NEW YORK, MONDAY MAY 7, 1945
On May 4, 1945, the German delegation to Field Marshal Montgomery's HQ at Lüneberg signed the surrender, to come into effect at 08:00 hours on May 5.

▲ A GRIM-FACED Admiral Hans von Friedeburg (center) and Field Marshal Bernard Montgomery (third from right, seated) finalize the German surrender.

THE STARS AND STRIPES
MEDITERRANEAN

Vol. 2, No. 155, Wednesday, May 9, 1945   ITALY EDITION ✶ ✶ TWO LIRE

BIG 3 HAILS VE-DAY; JAPS NEXT-TRUMAN

N.Y.C. Goes Joy Crazy On Victory

By Sgt. MILTON LEHMAN
(Stars and Stripes Staff Writer)

NEW YORK, May 7 (Delayed) — The Big Town greeted the news of the wars' end in Europe today as was expected it would — it went crazy with joy.

Newstands were besieged from 9 AM and dealers were selling as fast as they could make change. Such headlines as "Nazis Quit," in white letters on black in the New York Post; "Nazis Give Up, Surrender to Allies and Russia announced" in the World Telegram; "It's VE-Day (in black), Last German Units Yield (in red letters), and "Remember Pearl Harbor," (white letters on black) in the New York Journal-American.

Over the radio, which supplied the best running account of news developments, commentators were on hand early to give the account of surrender from what news was available, minute by minute.

One New York radio spokesman observed that the world had been expecting this news. Another said, ad libbing when his prepared script ran out, "whenever big things happen, New Yorkers always want to throw things down from the window."

Toward Times Square, which always has been the reaction hub of America's biggest city, ripped-up phone boots, memo pads, old letters, newspapers, confetti, and all available paper in a paper-shortaged country poured from the windows onto the street. Persons sometimes stuck their heads out of windows as though expecting a procession to pass in the street but this day in New York was without processions.

Soldiers were most quiet of all

(Continued on Page 2)

PRESIDENT TRUMAN

GENERAL EISENHOWER

Big Four Attitude Assures Parley's Success -- Molotov

SAN FRANCISCO, May 8 (ANS) —Agreement among the Big Four on what amendments to the Dumbarton Oaks proposals shall be sponsored by the U. S., Britain, Russia and China is so complete, V. M. Molotov announced today, that success of the world security organization meetings here is virtually assured.

Big Four discussions on amendments are at an end, he said at a press conference yesterday, adding that he hopes the work of the United Nations conference will be finished in two or three weeks.

Unanimity on amendments concerns major changes, he made it clear, and does not imply that there will be no individually sponsored proposals to change certain provisions of the Dumbarton Oaks agreement.

Referring to editorials declaring that revision of treaties concluded during the war might be desirable, Molotov said: "It seems that treaties are implied which have been signed by the defeated Axis

(Continued on Page 2)

VE-Day Ceremony At Caserta Today

AFHQ, May 8 — A VE-Day ceremony will be held tomorrow for American and British servicemen at 10 AM in the Royal Palace Grounds at Caserta, it was announced today.

It was announced that hours for curfew and bars will not be extended.

Yanks Score Gains On Okinawa Island

GUAM, May 8—Advances were scored yesterday by the U. S. 10th Army along the entire front in southern Okinawa, Adm. Chester W. Nimitz announced today.

The 7th Infantry Division, paced by flame-throwing tanks, pushed forward for gains in the center, while the 1st Marine Division reached the village of Dakeshi, and the 7th Division swept ahead on the east flank on an undesignated point.

Admiral Nimitz disclosed that 36,535 Japanese have been killed thus far in the Okinawa campaign, which began April 1. American ground casualties have been 2,373 killed, 11,432 wounded and 514 missing.

Kyushu airfields, north of the Ryukyus, were raided again by Superforts, which bombed through an overcast with precision instruments. Fifty B-29s participated.

MANILA, May 8 — Allied warplanes were operating yesterday from the captured airfield on Tarakan Island, just off Borneo, Gen. Douglas MacArthur disclosed today. Australian troops were clearing the Panosian oil fields, while fighting continued in the northeast corner of Tarakan City.

War's Official End Today, 0001 Hours

The war against Germany ended officially at 0001 hours today under the surrender terms signed at 0241 hours Monday.

The victory in Europe was proclaimed yesterday in broadcasts to their peoples and their Allies of all the United Nations by President Harry S. Truman, Prime Minister Winston S. Churchill and Marshal Joseph V. Stalin.

The order to cease fire was given to German forces on land, sea and air on Monday, but resistance continued on a few scattered fronts of the European continent where the costliest war of all time had raged for more than five years and eight months.

Mr. Truman declared that this "is a solemn but glorious hour." He said that "his only wish is that Franklin D. Roosevelt had lived to witness this day."

"The flags of freedom fly all over Europe," the President said. But he told the country that the war was only half over. He warned the Japanese that they can expect nothing but complete destruction unless they, too, surrender unconditionally.

Mr. Truman asked Americans to stick to their jobs until complete victory over Japan is won. He proclaimed next Sunday a national day of prayer in memory of those who fell in the cause of freedom.

"Hostilities will end officially at one minute after midnight tonight, Tuesday, May 8," Mr. Churchill declared.

Mr. Churchill said that "the Germans are still, in places, resisting Russian troops, but should they continue to do so after midnight, they will, of course, deprive themselves of the protection of the laws of war and will be attacked from all quarters by Allied troops."

The Prime Minister went on:

"It is not surprising that on such long fronts and in the existing disorder of the enemy, the commands of the German High Command should not in every case be obeyed immediately.

"This does not, in our opinion, with the best military

(Continued on Page 2)

Doenitz Proclaims End Of Nazi Party In Reich

LONDON, May 8—In slow solemn words, Grand Admiral Karl Doenitz, designated chief of the beaten German Reich, today proclaimed the end of the Nazi party and announced that the guns would cease fire at midnight tonight.

In a broadcast to the nation over the Flensburg radio, Admiral Doenitz called on the German people to "walk, dignified and courageous, in the hope that our children may one day have a free, secure existence."

"The Nazi party has left the scene of its activity," the admiral declared, adding that all connection between the state and the party had been severed.

"The foundations upon which the German Reich was built have gone. With the occupation of Germany, power has passed to the hands of the occupying troops it depends upon them whether I and the Reich government which I appointed can stay in action or not."

Unit Censorship Lifted; GIs May Reveal Location

MTO HQ., May 8—GIs stationed in the Mediterranean Theater may, as of today, send letters home without submitting them for unit censorship, it was announced here today.

With the declaration of VE-Day, Americans in this theater may correspond with maximum freedom of expression, provided they observe basic military security requirements. This will still be observed through the base censor spot check system.

A circular issued today by MTOUSA Headquarters permits, in short, soldiers to elaborate to their heart's content regarding battles and experiences they underwent while overseas, provided they don't indulge in speculation or fact as to military plans or troop movements, which still come under the heading "information of value to the enemy."

Henceforth, locations of individuals and units in Italy, Sicily, Sardinia and Corsica only, may be stated in letters, unless they have been alerted for movement to another theater.

Despite the radical change in policy GIs must still send their letters and postcards through U. S. Army Postal channels only. And, all letters and cards must still carry the military return address of the

(Continued on Page 8)

▲ THE STARS AND STRIPES, ITALY EDITION, WEDNESDAY MAY 9, 1945

The Stars and Stripes served U.S. troops in the Civil War and World War I. It was revived in the European theater in April 1942. A Pacific theater edition followed in 1945.

COMPLETE NEWS—MAGAZINE SECTION—COMIC FEATURES

New York Post

5¢ IN NEW YORK CITY AND SUBURBS

10¢ ELSEWHERE IN THE UNITED STATES

FOUNDED 1801, VOLUME 144, NO. 219. COPYRIGHT, 1945, NEW YORK POST CORPORATION.

BLUE FINAL LATE SPORTS • BACK PAGE •

TWO SECTIONS

NEW YORK, MONDAY, AUGUST 6, 1945

36 PAGES

EXTRA

ATOM BOMB

(2,000 Times as Powerful As Any Ever Made Before)

DROPPED ON JAPS

Story on Page 3

IMPEACH BILBO, VETERANS DEMAND

Story on Page 5

▲ NEW YORK POST, MONDAY AUGUST 6, 1945

The first atomic bomb was dropped on the Japanese city of Hiroshima on August 6, 1945,
killing 100,000 people. Three days later, a second atomic bomb was dropped on Nagasaki,
killing 35,000 people and wounding 60,000 more.

The atomic bomb

AUGUST 1945

THE "MANHATTAN PROJECT" WAS THE CODENAME FOR THE U.S. ATOMIC WEAPONS PROGRAM. THE ORIGINS OF WHICH REACHED BACK TO 1939, WHEN TOP SCIENTISTS, INCLUDING Albert Einstein, persuaded President Roosevelt of the military possibilities for fission chain reactions of atomic elements. Official work began in February 1940 and the War Department took over control following the attack on Pearl Harbor by Japan. The program assumed the name Manhattan Project in 1942 after army engineers from Manhattan were assigned to the task.

RESEARCH

Eminent scientists such as Ernest Orlando Lawrence and Philip Hauge Alberson spent the next three years working on ways of producing usable amounts of the uranium-235 and plutonium-239 suitable for the fission process. The job of turning fissionable material into a nuclear weapon fell to Robert Oppenheimer at a laboratory established in 1943 in the desert at Los Alamos, New Mexico. Oppenheimer had to devise a weapon to create a supercritical mass of fissionable material to produce an explosion, and in the summer of 1945 the Hanford Works gave him enough plutonium-239 to conduct a test. On July 16, 1945, the first atomic bomb was test exploded at Alamogordo, New Mexico. The U.S. now had its atomic bomb.

The decision was taken to drop the atomic bomb because the estimates of casualties (both Japanese and American) in any ground invasion of Japan were enormously high. The question of whether Japan would have surrendered is still debated. Cut off from raw materials and having been utterly defeated in Manchuria by a Soviet invasion that began just after the first atomic bomb had been dropped on Hiroshima, Japan may well have seen sense and surrendered. In the event, the dropping of two atomic bombs meant there was no choice.

▲ THE DISTINCTIVE MUSHROOM CLOUD that was formed by the atomic explosion during an American test in 1945. The bomb was dropped on two Japanese cities in August to end the war.

Buy More Bonds For Victory

Jersey Observer

WEATHER REPORT—Today: Partly cloudy. Tonight: Clear and cool. Tomorrow; Clear and sunny.

VOL. LIV.—No. 156. TEMPERATURE—8 A. M., 68; 9 A. M., 71; 10 A. M., 75 THURSDAY, AUGUST 9, 1945 JERSEY CITY OFFICE / UNION CITY OFFICE / HOBOKEN OFFICE PRICE 4 CENTS

Reds Invading Manchuria

Jap Steel Center Is Shelled By U. S. Fleet

Drop Second Atom Bomb

1,500 Carrier Planes Assault Enemy Positions

Halsey's Fliers Hammer All Day At Heart of Nipponese Empire

Guam, Aug. 9.—(UP)—Admiral William F. Halsey's Third Fleet sailed into Japan's homeland waters today to spearhead a mighty air-sea assault on the heart of the empire in which some 1,500 planes lashed the dwindling strongholds of Japanese resistance.

Hoboken Files $4,120 Tax Rise Pleas

Treasury Balance

Clearing House Report

STOCKS

A Daily Report on Local Happenings

Nagasaki Blasted At Noon

Naval Base Wiped Out

Guam, Aug. 9.—(UP)—Preliminary reports indicated that the second atomic bomb to be dropped on Japan all but obliterated Nagasaki, a major naval base and Japan's 11th largest city, during the noon rush hour today.

RADIO TOKYO SILENT ON RAID

STATE COUNCIL MEETING CALLED

Crash Head-On With Japanese Kwantung Army

Russians Cross Border From East and West in Pincer Move

London, Aug. 9.—(UP)—A Red Army of 1,000,000 or more men crashed into Manchuria from the east and west at key points along a 2,000-mile front today and—Tokyo said—collided head-on in battle with Japan's crack Kwantung army.

Armour Is Given Divorce On 3 Counts

Newark Sailor Dies in Boston Fire

Russia "Too Busy"

RED ARMIES INVADING MANCHURIA have crossed the border of the Japanese puppet state from the East and West colliding head-on with the crack Kwantung Army. Above map shows how Japan is in the grip of a vast pincers drive.

Score Rescued at Fire

Two Hurt Fighting 3-Alarm Blaze in Greenville

Midnight rescues participated in by a Coast Guard fire fighter, civilians, firemen and police, marked a three-alarm blaze in a four-story, 24-apartment buff brick flat at 621-627 Ocean avenue, Jersey City, last night.

Fire Captain Malaria Victim; Was Bitten by Mosquito

Grimshaw Questions Bayonne Police Head

Index to All the Latest News

MALARIA VICTIM

Captain James Flynn

▲ JERSEY OBSERVER, NEW JERSEY, THURSDAY AUGUST 9, 1945

Despite the dropping of a second atomic bomb, the Japanese carried on fighting. As an incentive to get then to surrender, 1,000 U.S. aircraft bombed Tokyo on August 13–14. The next day Emperor Hirohito broadcast the Japanese surrender.

▲ LOS ANGELES TIMES, WEDNESDAY AUGUST 15, 1945
The American people were wildly happy when Japan finally
capitulated. Pearl Harbor had been avenged and U.S. forces
were about to occupy Japan itself.

▲ PRESIDENT TRUMAN ANNOUNCES Japan's surrender to members of the
press at the White House in Washington, D.C. Truman had taken over as president
following Roosevelt's death in April 1945.

INDEX